# Lessons From
# **OUR FIRST TWENTY YEARS**

## Laurence F. Rowston
MA (UTAS Hist), Dip. Theol. (M.C.D.)p

Published in July 2023.

Published by The Baptist Union of Tasmania,
159 Wellington St, Longford, Tasmania 7301.
Copyright, L.F. Rowston, 2023.

ISBN 978-0-9590122-5-5

Other titles by the L.F.Rowston:

> MA as book: *Spurgeon's Men: The Resurgence of Baptist Belief and Practice in Tasmania 1869-1884*
>
> *Baptists in Van Diemen's Land, the story of Tasmania's First Baptist Church, the Hobart Town Particular Baptist Chapel, Harrington Street, 1835-1886*
> ISBN 0-9590122-0-6
>
> *One Hundred Years of Witness,*
> *A History of the Hobart Baptist Church*
> ISBN 0 9590338 0 7
>
> *Yesterday, Today & Tomorrow,*
> *A History of the Burnie Baptist Church*
> ISBN 0 959012214
>
> *Possessing the Future,*
> *A History of the Ulverstone Baptist Church 1905-2005*
> ISBN 0 959012222
>
> *God's Country Training Ground,*
> *A History of the Yolla Baptist Church 1910-20105*
> ISBN 978-0-9590122-3-1
>
> *Baptists in Van Diemen's Land 2,*
> *the story of Launceston's First Baptist Church,*
> *the York Street Particular Baptist Chapel, 1840-1916*
> ISBN 978-0-9590122-4-8
>
> *75 Years of Christian Witness,*
> *A history of the Lenah Valley Baptist Church, Hobart, Tasmania.*
> (In conjunction with Maurice French)
> ISBN 978-0-9590122-6-2

Cover (1): The Yolla Baptist Church Opening Day August 1910.

Cover (2): The Blackwood Creek Baptist Church

# Contents

Forward .................................................................................................... 11
Introduction ............................................................................................. 13
Chapter 1 Perth Baptist Church ............................................................. 14
    Introduction ......................................................................................... 14
    The Rev William Clark ........................................................................ 16
    The Rev William George Gillings ...................................................... 17
    The Rev Robert Williamson ................................................................ 18
    The Rev Rides Cooper ......................................................................... 20
    The Rev John Edwin Walton .............................................................. 21
    The Rev Henry Clark ........................................................................... 24
    The Rev Stephen Howard ................................................................... 24
    The Rev Alfred Metters ....................................................................... 25
    Appendices ............................................................................................ 26
    Conclusion ............................................................................................ 46
Chapter 2 Blackwood Creek .................................................................... 48
    Introduction ......................................................................................... 48
    William Ross ......................................................................................... 48
    The Rev George Lake .......................................................................... 50
    William Kenner .................................................................................... 51
    Vincent George Britton ...................................................................... 52
    The Upper Liffey Baptist Chapel ....................................................... 53
    Appendices ............................................................................................ 54
    Conclusion ............................................................................................ 62
Chapter 3 Bracknell Baptist Church ...................................................... 63
    Introduction ......................................................................................... 63
    Baptist Beginnings .............................................................................. 63
    The Rev George Lake and Teacher William Kenner ...................... 64
    Home Missioner Vincent G. Britton ................................................. 64
    Robert Steel .......................................................................................... 66
    Appendix: Robert Steel ....................................................................... 70
    Conclusion ............................................................................................ 71
Chapter 4 The Christian Mission Church ............................................. 73
    Introduction ......................................................................................... 73
    The Rev John Henry Shallberg .......................................................... 74
    The Rev Daniel Walter Hiddlestone ................................................. 75
    The Rev George Soltau ....................................................................... 80
    The Rev Charles Mortimer Cherbury ............................................... 87
    The Rev Henry James Lambert ......................................................... 88
    The Rev Joseph Tanner Piercey ......................................................... 89

- Assistant Pastor George Craike ............ 92
- Appendices ............ 94
- Conclusion ............ 113

## Chapter 5 Deloraine Baptist Church ............ 116
- Introduction ............ 116
- The Rev James Samuel Harrison ............ 117
- Pastor Harry Wood ............ 120
- The Rev Edward Vaughan ............ 121
- The Rev Alfred Hyde ............ 124
- The Rev Herbert Davies Archer ............ 125
- Harry Wood's Return ............ 127
- The Rev Samuel Archer Harris ............ 128
- The Rev Howard Leslie Elliott ............ 128
- William Henry Short ............ 130
- The Rev Vincent George Britton ............ 131
- Appendices ............ 132
- Conclusion ............ 146

## Chapter 6 Longford Baptist Church ............ 148
- Introduction ............ 148
- The Rev Robert McCullough ............ 148
- Pastor Harry Wood ............ 150
- The Rev Alfred Hyde ............ 151
- The Rev Henry George Blackie ............ 152
- The Rev Herbert Davies Archer ............ 154
- The Rev John Macallister ............ 155
- The Rev A John Casley, ............ 156
- Pastor Harry Wood Returns ............ 158
- Appendices ............ 159
- Conclusion ............ 168

## Chapter 7 Launceston Baptist Church ............ 170
- Introduction ............ 170
- Launceston in the 1880s ............ 170
- The Rev Alfred Bird ............ 172
- Pastor Harry Wood ............ 175
- The Rev Alfred James Clark ............ 176
- The Rev Edward E Harris ............ 178
- The Rev George Wainwright ............ 180
- The Rev Walter J Eddy ............ 181
- Appendices ............ 182
- Conclusion ............ 204

## Chapter 8 Hobart Baptist Church ............ 205

- Introduction .................................................................................................... 205
- Hobart's Beginnings ...................................................................................... 205
- The Rev Robert McCullough ....................................................................... 216
- The Rev Morison Cumming ......................................................................... 219
- The Rev James Blaikie ................................................................................. 221
- Appendices ................................................................................................... 225
- Conclusion .................................................................................................... 236

## Chapter 9 Latrobe Baptist Church ................................................................. 239
- Introduction .................................................................................................... 239
- The First Baptist Presence in Latrobe ........................................................... 240
- The Rev Henry George Blackie ..................................................................... 242
- The Rev Alfred Hyde ..................................................................................... 243
- John Chamberlain .......................................................................................... 244
- Pastor Harry Wood ........................................................................................ 247
- William Henry Short ...................................................................................... 248
- Rev Albert Metters and a sermon on Hell .................................................... 250
- The Rev John Edwin Walton ......................................................................... 252
- The Rev Charles Palmer ................................................................................ 253
- Appendices ..................................................................................................... 255
- Conclusion ...................................................................................................... 261

## Chapter 10 Sheffield Baptist Church .............................................................. 263
- Introduction .................................................................................................... 263
- The Rev Henry George Blackie ..................................................................... 264
- Pastor Harry Wood ........................................................................................ 265
- The Rev Edward Vaughan ............................................................................. 267
- Pastor Albert E. Blackwell ............................................................................. 268
- The Rev John Casley ..................................................................................... 268
- The Rev Robert Williamson .......................................................................... 270
- The Rev Charles Henry James Warren ......................................................... 270
- The Rev Vincent G. Britton ........................................................................... 270
- Pastor William Llewellyn Heaven .................................................................. 272
- The Rev Henry Saunders ............................................................................... 274
- Appendices: .................................................................................................... 274
- Conclusion ...................................................................................................... 289

## Chapter 11 Devonport Baptist Church ........................................................... 290
- Introduction .................................................................................................... 290
- Baptist Beginnings with the Rev Albert Hyde .............................................. 291
- The Rev George James Mackay .................................................................... 295
- The Rev John Edwin Walton ......................................................................... 296
- The Rev George James Mackay's Second Devonport Pastorate ................. 298
- The Rev Albert Metters ................................................................................. 301

Appendixes: ........................................................................................................ 303
Conclusion ........................................................................................................ 310

## Chapter 12 Burnie Baptist Church ............................................................. 312
Introduction...................................................................................................... 312
Baptist Beginnings........................................................................................... 313
Pastor Harry Wood........................................................................................... 313
The Rev Thomas Vigis ..................................................................................... 315
The Rev Samuel Harrison ............................................................................... 316
The Rev Joseph Tanner Piercey ..................................................................... 317
The Rev Peter W. Cairns.................................................................................. 318
The Rev Oswald R. Linden.............................................................................. 320
The Rev Charles Palmer.................................................................................. 320
The Rev Robert McCullough........................................................................... 321
The Rev Frederick Augustus Leeder ............................................................. 322
The Rev Edward Burchell Woods .................................................................. 323
Appendices:...................................................................................................... 326
Conclusion ........................................................................................................ 351

## Chapter 13 Ulverstone & Penguin Baptist Churches............................... 353
Introduction...................................................................................................... 353
George Edgar Harrison ................................................................................... 355
Pastor John (Jack) William Fisher.................................................................. 356
The Rev John Robertson................................................................................. 357
Pastor Ernest Albert Salisbury....................................................................... 358
The Rev Charles Henry James Warren ......................................................... 360
Pastor William Llewellyn Heaven.................................................................. 360
Sterling George Clarke ................................................................................... 361
The Rev Albert Butler...................................................................................... 362
The Rev Vincent George Britton.................................................................... 362
The Rev F. J. (Jack) Fisher ............................................................................... 364
Appendices....................................................................................................... 366
Conclusion ........................................................................................................ 379

## Chapter 14 Wynyard Baptist Church ......................................................... 381
Introduction...................................................................................................... 381
Baptist Beginnings........................................................................................... 382
Pastor William Henry Short ........................................................................... 382
Pastor John W. (Jack) Fisher........................................................................... 384
Pastor Robert Steel and Albert Butler .......................................................... 385
Pastor Ernest Albert Salisbury....................................................................... 386
The Rev William Llewellyn Heaven .............................................................. 387
Ernest Charles Walsh...................................................................................... 387
The Revs Arthur Charles Jarvis and Wilfred Lemuel Jarvis ....................... 389

| | |
|---|---|
| The Rev Alan Paton Dawson | 392 |
| Appendices | 392 |
| Conclusion | 402 |

## Chapter 15 Yolla Baptist Church .................................................... 404

| | |
|---|---|
| Introduction | 404 |
| J. W. (Jack) Fisher | 404 |
| Albert Ernest Salisbury | 405 |
| Alfred Butler | 407 |
| Ernest Charles Walsh | 408 |
| Walter Stanley Simpson | 409 |
| Alfred Harrald James | 410 |
| The Rev Albert Edward Holloway | 411 |
| Alan Paton Dawson | 411 |
| Henry Roy Tunks | 411 |
| Ernest Eric Watson | 412 |
| Return of Alan Paton Dawson | 413 |
| Arthur T Jessop | 413 |
| Wesley J. Bligh | 414 |
| Edwin Charles Mcintosh Brown | 415 |
| E. D. Mackey | 415 |
| Cecil M. Jobling | 415 |
| Appendices | 416 |
| Conclusion | 435 |

## Chapter 16 Smithton Baptist Church ............................................. 437

| | |
|---|---|
| Introduction | 437 |
| Robert Steel | 438 |
| Albert Edward Holloway | 439 |
| Edward Robert Bampton | 440 |
| George Levison Dibden | 441 |
| George Philp | 441 |
| The Rev James Clemens Salter | 442 |
| The Rev Alfred Ernest Albury | 443 |
| The Rev Ernest Charles Walsh | 443 |
| Cecil M. Jobling | 444 |
| Charles Percy Gordon Nibbs | 445 |
| Appendices | 445 |
| Conclusion | 461 |

## Table of Images .................................................................................. 463

| | |
|---|---|
| BIOGRAPHIES | 467 |

# FOREWORD

This is an astonishing project that Laurence Rowston has completed. His research on Tasmanian Baptists is widely acknowledged. This latest book is essentially a history of the first forty years of the resurgence of Baptist belief and practice in Tasmania which commenced in the late 1870s with each church or outpost placed in its context. The detail is remarkable with no source in "Trove" or other printed manuscript ignored. Anyone wishing to understand the extraordinary faith and work of these pioneers, many of them memorable characters, must look here.

For the individual churches and indeed for local historians this is of course a rich source of historical awareness. But Laurence has also sought in a few brief but direct comments to prompt the contemporary church to reflect on what might be learnt from the dedication and vision of these pioneers who often worked in extraordinarily harsh conditions.

The historical survey as it relates to each congregation or mission is quite remarkable. But the wider value of this book is the comprehensive biography of any minister or other significant leader who served in Tasmania at that time. The comprehensive selection of photographs enhances the book. Many of those pastors who worked in that state also had extended and valued leadership throughout the nation or elsewhere. These biographies are perhaps the most valuable content of this remarkable book and extend its value beyond Tasmania.

Laurence acknowledges at various points the genealogical research of Canberra historian Barbara Coe and many families will be grateful for the family details. His bibliography will also be invaluable for future researchers.

The dangers in eliciting "lessons" from a historical survey are that they can all too easily degenerate into somewhat subjective critiques of the modern church. In general Laurence has managed to avoid this danger and his "lessons" are brief and suggestive. The extremely harsh and demanding problems posed by these pioneers are challenging.

I warmly commend this remarkable book by Laurence, whose status as the leading historian of Baptists in Tasmania is again confirmed.

Ken R. Manley

# Introduction

With the advent of the Covid virus, the closure of the Baptist Fellowship I was leading in Hobart and the publishing of "Baptists in Van Diemen's Land Part 2" in 2020, I had time on my hands so I envisaged another book which would make use of the unused material in my files on Tasmanian Baptists. This book is the result.

The official presence of Baptists in Tasmania began in December 1834 with the arrival of the Rev Henry Dowling, who had been pastor of the Colchester Particular Baptist Church. Based in the North of Van Diemen's Land, Dowling became pastor of the Launceston York Street chapel, which opened on 27 December 1840. A group of Hobart Town Baptists had previously constituted the first Baptist Church in the Australian colonies on 14 June 1835. Their Hobart chapel was officially opened on 21 March 1841. Baptist fortunes were never great. The Hobart cause never gained strength, suffering disorder and division. It closed in 1886. The York Street work struggled on until 1916.

It was at the beginning of the 1870s that Baptist work began a new chapter. The eminent London preacher, the Rev C.H. Spurgeon, had begun sending out young students from his Pastors' College. The active interest and generosity of Mary Ann and William Gibson, wealthy pastoralists of Native Point, Perth made this possible. The Gibsons paid for the passage of these men. They also built churches, chapels, halls and manses. On 27 May 1884 the Baptists formed the Baptist Union of Tasmania, a General Baptist work with a combined membership of 305.[1] This book, "Lessons from Our First 20 Years" considers the first twenty years of fifteen of these churches as well as the Reed Memorial Church in Launceston.

We must not think that this book is dealing with just the domestic and the insignificant; we are dealing with an important part of Tasmania's history (as well as Australia's history) as we consider the lives of many pastors both before and after they came to Tasmania. This was the time when the churches building spaces were scarcely enough for the churches' needs; the reverse applies today for those churches which still exist.

The twenty-year account of these churches begins for the most part by giving the town settings the Baptists found themselves in when they arrived.

The conclusion to each chapter speaks of different aspects of church life back then compared to what we find in our churches today. But this

---

[1] Laurence F Rowston's entry on Baptists in "The Companion to Tasmanian History" edited by Dr. Alison Alexander (2005).

aspect of the book is but a mere glance at what truly is an immense subject and the focus of countless books.2 But for many of our present churches to turn around, it will need more than "ten steps, seven lessons and three tricks".

We can rightly describe many pastors profiled in this book as our Pioneers. Living comfortably was never on their minds. They had a stalwart faith and gave robust endeavour to raise up an Association of Baptists following the demise of the earlier Calvinist Baptists. In this latter group were brave souls who never accepted resignation. In them we find real diversity when we look beyond those who came from the Pastors' College in London. It was a diversity which didn't apply just to theology or social engagement; some had their origins in other denominations. There are a number of mentions about the Primitive Methodists because this branch of Christianity supplied to us a number who certainly showed leadership in our midst.

The biographies in this book have been for a great part sourced from newspaper accounts written by journalists a step or two away from the churches, hence the end product is not of a triumphal or parochial nature as newspaper journalists rarely talk up the work of God's kingdom nor speak the language of Zion.

It is obvious that in these early years we had some formidable personalities in our ranks including the non-clergy who took the initiative when it came to church building and the care of those who were at a disadvantage. The building of God's kingdom filled both their imaginations and their minds. They were a succession of saintly men and women who gave Tasmanian Baptists their distinctiveness and justified our separate existence from other denominations.

We read of people and churches which as it were, dragged their feet, and of others who took a leap of faith. We will read of people who were "fired up", some of which in their zeal burned themselves out and died before they could enjoy a worthy retirement. Here I think of Albert Butler for one. Then we will read of those who would not retire and here I think of Robert Steel. Then there are those who made such a poor beginning but went on to most successful ministries and here I think of Albert Edward Blackwell. Then there were those who poured themselves into our Tasmanian Baptist work for decades and here I can think of Vincent George Britton, Edward Burchell Wood, John Edwin Walton and William Ross. Again, there are those who came from other Church communities to become leaders amongst us and here I think of Samuel Harrison, Frederick J. Dunkley and Joseph Tanner Piercey.

---

2 One such book being "Congregational Transformation in Australian Baptist Church Life, New Wineskins Volume 1" edited by Darren Cronshaw & Darrell Jackson. Quote of Katherine Willis Pershey, Christian Century 2022.

Finally, we will learn of those we lost from our Baptist ranks, much to our loss, and I think of Ernest Albert Salisbury and Henry Roy Tunks.

May their stories encourage us to see that such pioneer work belongs not just to the past but also is also possible today as we face different challenges. Their stories show us what God can do when he has all of a man or woman's life.

I have already mentioned that newspapers proved a major information source and without them the information available would have been considerably limited indeed, but that is not to say our own Tasmanian and Australian Baptist publications and that of the London Pastors' College have been of little use; far from it. We bless those who in those years devoted their time to record what we still have today. What is written allows us to look at the past and see how different things were, to appreciate people's attitudes and behaviour, their way of life and belief in times gone by.

This book purposely fails, except on a few occasions, to make an extended reference to the folk who made up the congregations and yet without such lay men and women there would have been no church. Another criticism of this book could be that the churches in these early days were male orientated because the contribution that women made was not celebrated as it should have been. But when the sources I had were not enough to unearth the personal details of the Pastors involved, namely who were their wives, I drew on the expertise of Family Historian Barbara Coe of Canberra who freely gave of her time in researching them. She supplied many of the names of those who stayed in the background.

As mentioned, the biographies contained in this book do not always represent the most important figures in churches, although they all were important. Other stories might also be told which were pivotal to the lives of the churches mentioned. Dozens of outstanding Baptist men and women were the main stay of the churches in question and of them I have spoken little. I will leave their stories to those who wish to undertake that work. Life is too short.

But, these stories of the Pastors do help us to grasp a feeling for those times. We can see something of the power and effectiveness in what they did, the way that God honoured their work, and we can grasp a little of the way that God was at work in the more private and inner parts of their lives.

It is obvious that a full account of the twenty years of each of the churches is impossible. To tell the complete story of any church would also entail a search of Church and Deacons' minute books.

There are two types of churches given. First there are the self-supporting churches which attracted leading pastors from the mainland (and sometimes further afield). For many of these pastors their biographies are usually restricted to the one church in question.

Then there are the Tasmanian Home Mission churches where pastors are often in training and move from church to church. Their biographies are for the most restricted to their first and final placements.

There have been times when dates found in our Baptist publications have differed from that which is to be found in the newspaper. In practically all cases I have accepted the newspaper dates as the correct ones because of their immediacy. I am indebted to Dr Marita Munro of the Victorian Baptist Archive for access to its collection. I am also indebted to the Dr David Parker and his archivist Rodney Kirkpatrick of the Queensland Baptist Historical Society for the giving of their time in searching out information on a number of Queensland Baptist pastors. In South Australia, my thanks to the Rev Gordon Crabb who surveyed a number of biographies of men who served in South Australian Baptist ranks. My thanks also go to Susan Patterson and Helen Kosmeyer for proofreading the manuscript and making important suggestions and also extends to Pastor Dan Evenhuis who undertook the extensive layout of this book. They each carried this out with utmost care. Helen is one who has spent most of her life in our Tasmanian Baptist Churches. Further my thanks go to Rev Dr. Ken Manley for his assistance with and endorsement of this work.

Even though I am writing about a Christian culture which is in many ways different from our own, taken as a whole, this is a stimulating story of sacrifice and service which makes a good read, especially the individual biographies. These life stories ought to be an encouragement and inspiration to us all whether we are Baptist or not. Our tomorrows grow out of our todays and yesterdays. To belittle our past and stand mournful of our present indicates a failure of faith in our God. We need to greet the future with optimism.

# Chapter 1 Perth Baptist Church

## Introduction

The Perth Baptist Church is rightly seen as the Mother Church of the Denomination.[3] It was the need to register the Perth chapel as a denominational place of worship in the early 1860s and find pastors that set off a chain of events which saw the revitalisation of the Baptist faith in Tasmania and led to the formation of an association of churches, the Baptist Union of Tasmania. The name Gibson was associated with the Perth Church for nearly half a century.

William Gibson Senior and his wife Mary Ann had had a long association with the York Street Particular Baptist chapel in Launceston, an association which continued even after they built their own chapel at Perth. It would be a number of years before William himself would submit to a Baptist baptism. It took place on 14 April 1867 in his Perth chapel with his son, William Gibson

---

REGISTRY OF BAPTIST CHAPEL, PERTH.

Longford, 11th June, 1863.

NOTICE is hereby given that the seperate building known as the Baptist Chapel, Perth, in the district of Longford, having been duly certified according to law as a place of religious worship, was registered for the solemnization of marriages therein, in pursuance of the Act of Council of the colony, 2nd Victoria, No. 7, intituled an Act for Regulating Marriages in Van Diemen's Land and its dependencies.

Witness my hand this 11th day of June, 1863.

P. JACOB,
Deputy-Registrar for the District
of Longford.

*1-1 Extract from 'The Examiner'*

---

Junior, and their chief shepherd, William Bye.

Following the transfer of the Anglican parson, the Rev Alfred Stackhouse, to Longford in 1860,[4] William and Mary Ann built this chapel so, according to the Rev John E Walton, "they could worship God in greater harmony more in keeping with Mary Ann's Baptist and William's Presbyterian views." It was at first a community church.[5] The foundation-

*1-2 The 1862 Perth Baptist Chapel*

---

[3] Day-Star May 1889 p66.

[4] LEx 27 May 1876 p5; 10 June 1876 p4. The present Perth Anglican Church building dates from 1878. In 1838 both the Wesleyan Methodists and the Anglicans were in the process of opening churches in the town. Cornwall Chronicle 18 August 1838 p2; Launceston Advertiser 14 January 1836 p2; SB 10 February 1903 p47.

[5] J E Walton, 'In Memory of William Gibson', Day-Star, August 1892 p114-116.

stone of a building was laid on 9 May 1862. As a Baptist Church it began as a Particular (Calvinistic) one.

The chapel was opened later that year, on 28 September 1862.[6] Then, a year later it would be called the Perth Baptist Church. This came about because a young couple wanted to be married there and thus it needed to be registered under a denominational banner. So it acquired the "not too popular title of Baptist".[7]

A Sunday school was formed in 1863. During the next seven years Gibson Senior struggled to obtain preachers so he made use of the colony's Congregationalists and fellow Baptists holidaying from Victoria, preachers such as the Rev S. Wilson from the Ebenezer Baptist Chapel, Tarnagulla, or the Rev Charles Mortimer Cherbury from Collingwood in Melbourne.[8] The Gibsons offered generous hospitality to these "many wearied workers in the Lord's vineyard" who wanted a low cost holiday.[9] They in turn kept the Gibsons informed on the availability of preachers.

Wilson was engaged at the Perth Baptist Church for twelve months.[10] On completion of his engagement, the Rev W. Tranter also from the Ebenezer Baptist Chapel, Tarnagulla, supplied for a year. Then a Tasmanian based Congregationalist, the Rev D. B. Tinning, officiated for a time. In 1868 Tinning began a twenty-two years' ministry based in Richmond.[11] Jesse Pullen who had been in charge of the Baptist chapel in Deloraine since 1859, also supplied for some months. Gibson Senior would plead with them to stay on. This need for a settled Pastor was met with the arrival of one of the Pastors' College graduates from London, the Rev Alfred William Grant, in July 1869.

*1-3 The Rev Alfred W Grant*

Six months later, on 2 January 1870, nineteen members formed the Perth Baptist Church.[12] For all Gibson's expense in bringing out Grant and his family, Grant departed in just one

---

[6] LEx 23 October 1862 p4.

[7] LEx 13 June 1863 p5 and advertisement p6, 23 June 1863 p3; Day-Star August 1892, pp114-116.

[8] For Cherbury's stay at Perth, see LEx 30 September 1862 p5 and 17 March 1863 p3; for a Cherbury biography see Ch4.

[9] Day-Star May 1890; LEx 22 July 1862, p2.

[10] LEx 23 October 1862 p44 and 20 November 1862 p5.

[11] LEx 2 April 1868 p44, 19 November 1870 p5; Congregationalism in Australia by G Lindsay Lockley p125.

[12] Perth Chapel Minutes.

year to the Ballarat Baptist Church.[13] The Rev Charles Cater who had been a Launceston City Missioner followed.

The Rev Thomas Crabtree from Monague Street Baptist Church, England, came for six months from 18 December 1872.[14] A month before his arrival, the chapel and school-room were placed in Trust by Gibson. By now the Perth church had a manse close by and yards and stables for horses and vehicles coming from a distance. Although it was never stated, these and subsequent years show that the Gibsons saw their immense wealth as a sacred trust to be used for more than their own benefit.

Our story for the purpose of Perth Baptist's first twenty years begins with the arrival of the Rev William Clark.

## The Rev William Clark

The Pastors' College trained man, the Rev William Clark from the Ashford Baptist Church, Kent, commenced at Perth on 17 December 1874. The Church had not had a settled Pastor for nearly three years.[15]

Clark had none of the flamboyance of Grant but proved a popular preacher, a friend of the poor and a visitor to the sick.[16] Scholarly, he could give insight into elementary Greek in a Greek class.[17] At a Bible Society meeting he advocated that people seek a practical religion, for religion, he said, was not more reading of God's Word, but the following in the path of truth that distinguishes the true Christian from the mere professor.[18] He commenced a Young Men's Mutual Improvement Society supported by numerous donations of books and finance.[19] He also had an earnest interest in home missionary work and gave Religious Instruction at the Perth Public School.[20]

In June 1876 Clark gave a lecture on his voyage to Tasmania. The Launceston Examiner reported, "The lecture was admirably got up, being amusing, interestingly enlivened by some fourteen pieces of music, including three solos and four or five quartettes given by the choir of the church." Clark spoke of a seaman falling from the yards and being swept away, of experiencing a cyclone before reaching the Cape, of the ship being driven for three weeks before furious gales; and having a mighty wave sweep away

---

[13] For Grant's story, see Spurgeon's Men thesis.

[14] LEx 10 June 1873 p3; Daily Telegraph (Launceston) 7 April 1886 p3.

[15] Weekly LEx 19 December 1874 p7; LEx 12 December 1874.

[16] LEx 25 May 1876 p3.

[17] SB 11 January 1912 p19.

[18] LEx 20 February 1875 p2.

[19] LEx 17 June 1876 p5.

[20] LEx 25 December 1875 p5, 20 January 1876 p3.

every fowl and nearly all the pigs on board.

As a Baptist, Clark was a strong advocate for baptism by immersion arguing that the practice of sprinkling infants was quite unknown in apostolic times.[21] In June 1876 he made a wager in the Congregational "Christian Witness" journal,

> Will you permit me to make a proposition and an offer to all ministers of religion in Tasmania, especially to those who are so fond of talking of "interpolations," and passages that are "apocryphal," "supplementary," "not in the original," "not genuine," etc. Let them unite and expunge from the New Testament all passages to which they object, treating of baptism, or bearing upon the subject, and having thus cleared away the stumbling-blocks so obnoxious to them at present, let them produce one single precept or example within the boards of that same Testament, as authority for the sprinkling of an infant. To the first individual who discovers one such verse I hereby offer a purse of one hundred sovereigns. The offer will stand open for six months, to afford time for research. I send my name, Mr. Editor, as an earnest of my good faith, and when the authority is produced you may publish it.

Clark's reply to the Rev Joseph Black, MA, refuted what the paedobaptist charged.[22]

During Clark's time the property was improved, and all debts cleared. He was a gifted pastor and solid worker in the Sunday school. He welcomed the celebrated Baptist public lecturer and elocutionist, the Rev Charles Clark of Albert Street Baptist Church in Melbourne, who gave recitals on the works of Charles Dickens, Oliver Goldsmith and others.[23]

*1-4 Charles Clark*

## The Rev William George Gillings

The Rev William George Gillings replaced Clark, commencing in June 1877 and served there until March 1880. He continued Grant's endeavour of Sunday afternoon services in Mrs. Elizabeth Noakes' Assembly Rooms in Longford.

---

[21] LEx 9 March 1875 p3.

[22] The Christian Witness 8 June 1876 p5, 15 June 1976 p5.

[23] LEx 19 February 1876.

Wrote the Launceston Examiner of this endeavour,

> He is, I should think, a very sincere, intelligent, hard-working gentleman, and reminds me of the late lamented Rev James Martin, of the Baptist Church, Collins-street, Melbourne. As may be expected, the fact of Mr. Gillings going to Longford, to try and effect the conversion of the heathen there, rouses the ire of some ill-disposed persons, notwithstanding he takes care not to interfere with any services which ministers of other denominations may be holding. Luckily Mr. Gillings is not a man to be daunted by any such opposition, and there is no doubt he will do a lot of good."[24]

Gillings' years at Perth were momentous because of the visit to the colony of the Rev Charles H. Spurgeon's son, the Rev Thomas Spurgeon, and the English evangelist, Henry Varley. These two involved themselves in the Baptist work in the colony on numerous occasions.

Time and time again the Gibsons invited other graduates from the Pastors' College and many more followed. Due to the Gibsons' efforts the town took on certain characteristics and some were critical.

*1-5 Thomas Spurgeon*

Perth is a sanctimonious place. If any people in the world are blessed with spiritual advisers Perth is, but some of them, the Pharisees say, "I thank the Lord I am not as other men," but "as no roads so rough as those that are newly mended, so no person is so intolerant and bigoted as a neophyte."[25]

## The Rev Robert Williamson

The next to minister was the Rev Robert Williamson, from May 1880 to August 1884. He arrived from Parramatta in NSW and upon his arrival such was his health that many thought he would not live long, but as the years progressed his health improved dramatically. Three years after his arrival Dr. Harry Benjafield of Hobart reported, "By the way, if his friends in England and Scotland saw him now, they would scarcely believe he was the same bent, consumptive man as landed here a few years ago."[26]

---

[24] LEx 5 April 1878 p3; the Rev James Martin died on a bush walking holiday in Tasmania on 3 February 1877.

[25] LEx 16 March 1880 p2.

[26] Dr Harry Benjafield's 1883 Assembly report on the Tasmanian Baptist Churches.

Journalist Henry Glennie, pen name "Silverpen", mentioned Williamson in his article, "Evangelism at Tabernacle - Evangelising at Deloraine". Williamson had been guest speaker. Glennie wrote,

> Pastor Williamson is, I judge, one of those hard-headed Scotchmen (sic) who would never venture to advance a statement or theory he could not fully prove; and from the beginning to the end of his address he stuck to his text, and proved (at any rate to my satisfaction) that his heraldship was a direct commission from Heaven to lost men and women with which he was entrusted, and that the Book and its teachings revealed the facts he advanced to every one of those present. There could be no mistaking his plain common sense. Said he, "All have sinned. The lamb was slain for sinners. The reconciliation was made between God and man; accept the remedy provided, and life, eternal life is the result." Pretty plain that; no mystification about it. "If any are willing, now and here (said he) to accept Jesus, stand up."[27]

A year later, this time "Quince", a Daily Telegraph journalist, visited the old Baptist Chapel in York Street expecting to hear the Rev William White but Williamson was filling in while White was elsewhere.[28] Quince confirmed what Silverpen had observed,

*1-6 Robert Williamson*

> ...his address was more of a persuasive appeal than a sermon. There was none of the firstly, secondly, and thirdly about it. Mr Williamson has a very pleasant and effective way of driving truth home by illustrating his subject of discourse as he proceeds with word pictures of everyday life. So homely and telling were the lights and shadows of his illustrations, that the congregation occasionally had in a good-natured way (of course) to smile at the apt remarks made. There could, however, be but one opinion of their telling character, Pastor Williamson is, to my mind, thoroughly earnest about soul-saving.

Quince also added in the same column,

---

[27] LEx 16 December 1882 supplement p1.

[28] Obviously the Spurgeon men had no qualms about preaching in Particular Baptist Churches as their mentor, the Rev C H Spurgeon, confessed that he was Particular even though altar calls were made at his Metropolitan Tabernacle in London.

I cannot but think, however, that the Baptist denomination is going in the future to make a brave stand for God and his truth in Tasmania, and no one who wishes the onward progress of the gospel-car will, I opine, say ought else to them than God-speed. Their notions of immersion by water are, to many minds not with them in church-fellowship, thought scriptural. Hard-headed non-Baptists may argue out the sprinkling theory as long as they like, but if we take the literal meaning of the passages relating to Baptism, as recorded, we must come for the conclusion, no matter how prejudiced we are, that dipping, not sprinkling, is the mode of baptising taught in the Scriptures.[29]

## The Rev Rides Cooper

Then the Rev Rides Cooper followed, commencing on 4 February 1885. He arrived in Tasmania on the SS Liguria with fellow student the Rev Harry H. Driver and Spurgeon's sickly son, the Rev Thomas Spurgeon. This was Spurgeon's third visit to the colony for health reasons. Cooper had been selected by Spurgeon at the request of William Gibson Senior to take charge of the Perth Church.[30] During Cooper's time there were 800 inhabitants in the town, which was said to be the cleanest, healthiest and godliest on the island. All those employed by the Gibsons at Native point and Scone were required to be in attendance at the Perth Chapel on Sundays. The Perth Church was now conducting services on Sunday afternoons at the Council Chambers in Evandale for a constituted Baptist Church had been formed there in October 1884.[31] Further Perth meetings were being held at the "Snake Banks" farm with Pastor Harry Wood [32] By April 1885 the Perth Church's Blue Ribbon Mission was growing in strength with a total of about 100 "putting on the Blue Ribbon".[33] On Easter Mondays the annual treat to the children attending the Baptist Sunday school, and to all others who wished to attend, was hosted by William Gibson Senior and his wife

*1-7 Rides Cooper*

---

[29] Daily Telegraph (Launceston) 25 June 1883 p3.

[30] LEx 6 February 1885 p2; WY Fullerton, *Thomas Spurgeon, a biography* (London, Hodder and Stoughton 1919) p117; S&T December 1884.

[31] Mercury 23 Feb 1885 p4; LEx 18 October 1884 p1; Daily Telegraph (Launceston) 9 August 1888 p3.

[32] LEx 24 December 1885 p2.

[33] LEx 1 April 1885 p2.

Mary Ann in a paddock near the township, where over 300 old and young assembled to have a day of fun and frolic. At the close, nearly all assembled in the tent and several of Sankey's hymns were sung, and short addresses were delivered by Cooper and the other preachers present. Three cheers would be given for the Gibsons "in a very enthusiastic style".[34] Cooper stayed for only two years before transferring to the mainland to pastor the Portland Baptist Church. At his farewell his wife was given a sewing machine from the children of the Sunday school and Cooper himself a purse of sovereigns as well as a Bible from the Young Men's Bible class. It was reported that Cooper had been very successful in keeping together his congregation, the neat Baptist Church being always well filled. He had laboured

> in season and out of season, and been instrumental in doing much good, especially amongst the young. He is an indefatigable worker, and at visiting he has no equal. His ministrations at the dying bed were exceedingly valued. Nor were his visits confined to members of his own church. He attended to the spiritual wants of all as occasion required and was welcomed by all. The poor, the weak and infirm

had ever in him a kind, sympathising friend.[35]

He baptised nine believers and by his leaving ten names had been added to the church roll.[36]

Cooper was followed by William Compton. Many consumptives survived the voyage to the sunny Australian colonies only to die shortly after arrival, Compton being one of these, dying in Perth on 27 August 1887 aged thirty-three years.[37] The vacancy left by Compton was filled by the Rev John Edwin Walton.

## The Rev John Edwin Walton

The church in Perth again approached Spurgeon and he offered them this time the Rev John Edwin Walton; again Gibson Senior paid the expenses of bringing him and his wife Hannah and their family to the colony. At the Waltons' welcome Gibson said, "I had written to a minister asking him to come and take oversight of the church, but he (Spurgeon) could not come and had done the next best thing."[38] Having just partially recovered from an attack of inflammation of the lungs, Walton's medical adviser recommended that he accept the offer. Walton had always wished to see the Colonies, so, hoping to return

---

[34] Mercury 15 April 1885 p3.

[35] Mercury 23 February 1887 p4.

[36] Pastors' College Annual Report 1886.

[37] Day-Star September 1887 p139.

[38] Day-Star June 1888, edited.

in about ten years, either for a trip, or to remain in England, he and the family made for Tasmania at the end of 1887. He commenced at Perth on 22 January 1888 and during that year the foundation stone was laid for the octagonal shaped Tabernacle on 8 August.[39] Finally,

> on November 9th (1890) the fair temple, long in building, the centre of many hopes, and the subject of many prayers, was filled with its final glory – the glory of the Lord of Hosts in the midst of His worshipping people.[40]

An organ fund was soon commenced, and bazaars were conducted at Perth's Victoria Hall for that end.[41] The Victoria Hall was a gift to the town by William Gibson Junior.[42] One scribe described the Tabernacle thus: "The roof put me in mind of the dome of St Paul's, minus the cross, a pretty place outside, the grounds nicely kept, and inside cheerful and attractive."[43]

Another wrote,

> Perth is made a sort of Baptist capital, with a kind of Baptist Cathedral, through the munificence of Mr. and Mrs. Gibson. Perth always seems so restful, so neat and clean - an ideal abode of saintly spirits, waiting for the coming of the Lord.[44]

On 27 June 1892, the Church suffered the loss of Gibson Senior.[45]

During Walton's ten-year ministry eighty-two persons joined the church, and nearly a hundred others professed Christian commitment. The membership at the end of 1890 stood at 100 and at 131 in 1897.[46] In the fairly compact township he adopted the plan of visiting every family and these visits were appreciated by the poorer inhabitants through Gibson's daughter-in-law, Elvina Gibson, by making her his "almoner".[47] In 1900 evangelist and temperance advocate, Henry Varley, stated that the drunkenness, disorder and crime had gone from the town. He attributed this to the strong Baptist presence.[48]

With regards to the finances of the Church, no balance sheet was ever distributed to the members; such matters were secret.[49]

---

[39] Day-Star August 1888.
[40] Day-Star May 1890.
[41] Day-Star December 1890.
[42] "Tasmanian Towns in Federation Times by Laurie Hoare, self published p243.
[43] Day-Star August 1891.
[44] SB 13 Nov 1901 p256.

[45] For expansive details of his life see Spurgeon's Men thesis.
[46] Day-Star February 1891; September 1897.
[47] An almoner is a chaplain or church officer who originally was in charge of distributing money to the deserving poor.
[48] Daily Telegraph (Launceston) 31 January 1891 p4.
[49] Day-Star June 1892.

Work amongst young people was an especial feature of Walton's ministry. A Young People's Meeting, with a well patronized Penny Savings Bank attached, became exceedingly popular and useful with an attendance of seventy-eight in July 1890.[50] This was before the advent of the Young People's Senior Christian Endeavour Societies. At these Young People's meeting they were warned of "the evils of sin and intemperance". About ninety on average were attending each week in 1897.[51] It was amongst these young church-going people that temperance preaching bore most fruit as they were confirmed in total abstinence and total abstinence was seen as being one and the same as being a Christian.

A Women's Christian Temperance Society was also formed. Temperance was a major issue at this time and was strongly supported by the Baptists; they saw it as an outreach issue.[52]

Another means which Walton used to help educate folk was the formation of the "Reading Circle" which had its meetings at Scone House, William Gibson Junior's residence.

Representatives from most of the wealthy families in the neighbourhood attended and the works of Tennyson, Ruskin, Carlyle, Emerson, John Foster and others were studied. A Children's Ministering League was also inaugurated, and classes to help young preachers. Mission stations were opened, one fortnightly for a time at Cleveland in its chapel in 1890 run by a Strict Baptist, another fortnightly at Epping in the hotel and another for a time at Snake Banks. Then there was another at the Nile and one at Lymington. About forty-five children were attending the Sunday school at Cleveland where a Band of Hope was commenced.[53]

After ten year's ministry at Perth, Walton was farewelled, on 10 November 1897.[54] The church requested him to reconsider but he had long cherished a return to the homeland.

*1-8 Rev John Walton*

---

[50] Day-Star August 1890.

[51] Day-Star October 1891, April 1897.

[52] For Walton's attitude to the place of women in the Church see Manley p309.

[53] Day-Star August 1890, September 1890, January 1891, October 1892, February 1893, March 1893, July 1893.

[54] LEx 6 November 1897 p8.

## The Rev Henry Clark

The Rev Henry Clark commenced at the Perth Baptist Church on 19 July 1898. He continued the Debating Society which met in Perth's Victoria Hall on Friday evenings, admission being by a silver coin. The first subject in his time was, "Is agriculture more beneficial to Tasmania than mining?"[55] He supported the Lodge of the Independent Order of Rechabites, speaking at their Sunday church service parades, the Tabernacle being the destination from the Victoria Hall each member dressed in full uniform. He preached powerful sermons against the evils of strong drink contending that "wine and strong drink were not needed to give people health and strength but that on the contrary, they were always pernicious and deadly in their effects."[56] The congregation grew, and the membership reached 134. There was a large choir, and the Sunday school could boast of 180 scholars. But all too soon, in June 1900 he preached farewell sermons to large and attentive congregations.[57]

## The Rev Stephen Howard

In 1901 the Rev Stephen Howard transferred from the Kew Baptist Church. But it appears initially that Howard's pastorate at Perth was only "for a time".[58] Howard continued the weekly Perth Debating Society in the Victoria Hall in the evenings with subjects such as "Should women propose?" Other subjects were, "Should counsel defend an accused person of whose guilt he was aware?" and "Should Vaccination be compulsory?"[59] More than once he suffered a "sharp attack of illness" which incapacitated him. He and the Rev Walter J. Eddy of the Launceston Tabernacle were appointed Joint Editors of the "Southern Baptist". The census in 1910 indicated that there were four Baptist Church members within each thousand of the population.[60] Howard

*1-9 Perth Baptist Tabernacle: "a kind of Baptist Cathedral"*

---

[55] LEx 8 August 1899 p6.

[56] Daily Telegraph (Launceston) 25 October 1899 p6.

[57] Daily Telegraph (Launceston) 19 June 1900 p3, on 17 June.

[58] LEx 9 April 1901 p5.

[59] LEx 31 May 1901 p3, 2 November 1901 p5, 14 June 1902 p6, 25 July 1903 p6.

[60] Our Yesterdays Vol.10 p29.

involved himself in the public meeting to change the name of Perth as it clashed with that of Perth in WA.[61] Mary Ann Gibson died on 12 January 1903 aged ninety-two years. The Church wrote, "We cannot lament that angels have borne her into the 'eternal rest'." At Blackwood Creek many lamented her passing as she had "been a good friend to the people of this place, and many were the cases of distress, etc., relieved by her." For years, she supplied blankets and warm clothes every winter.[62]

## The Rev Alfred Metters

The Rev Alfred Metters commenced at Perth on 23 October 1904. There the predictable cycle of anniversaries, harvest festivals, church picnics, Trafalgar Day demonstrations and fairs coupled with the Band of Hope and the Christian Endeavour meetings took place. Soon he gave a stirring temperance address at nearby Longford Baptist Church, the temperance theme being dear to his heart.[63] He maintained the numbers. A year from his commencement the Temperance Band of Hope children numbered 100.[64] Musically capable, he not only rendered solos but also would conduct the children in their singing for their Sunday school anniversaries accompanied by the organ and violins.[65] His calibre was so recognized that in April 1905 he was appointed editor of the State Missionary journal, the Day Dawn. Also under his pen was the month-by-month denominational journal the Baptist Church Messenger. Later both journals combined with the "Tasmanian Day Dawn" mast head and in some small way it became a rival for Tasmanians to the Australian Baptist "which was not creditable" to them. As to the scarcity of Tasmanian news in the "Australian Baptist", the opinion was expressed that the fault lay with the churches in not sending reports to the State editor.[66]

*1-10 Alfred Metters*

Further he was made Tasmanian contributing editor for the Southern Baptist, the journal which only five years earlier was the source of much trouble between the Tasmanian, Victorian and South Australian Associations. A scholarly

---

[61] LEx 18 August 1903 p6.

[62] Day-Dawn January 1903; NWA&EBT16 January 1903 p3; Daily Telegraph (Launceston) 19 January 1903 p3. AB 18 November 1947 p1.

[63] LEx 31 October 1904 p7.

[64] LEx 16 October 1905 p3.

[65] LEx 30 November 1905 p6.

[66] AB 14 November 1916; 30 Oct 1917.

person, he gave a lecture on James Russell Lowell and his works.[67] So begins one of Lowell's poems,

> Not failure, but low aim, is crime.
>
> Not what we give, but what we share,
>
> For the gift without the giver is bare.
>
> Books are the bees which carry the quickening pollen from one to another mind.

On Sunday 28 February 1906 Metters preached farewell sermons to large congregations; he was transferring to the Devonport Church[68] since it would provide a suitable winter climate and a more active sphere than Perth.[69] Metter's ministry was a settled ministry, not the excitable one of an evangelist which might explain the Perth church report issued on his leaving,

> The general feeling was that Mr Metter's work in Perth was preparatory for better days to follow, and confidence was expressed that our new pastor (Harry Wood) would reap where another had sown.[70]

# Appendices

## Appendix 1: Charles Cater

The Rev Alfred Grant's place in Perth was soon taken by Rev Charles Cater, late town missionary of Launceston, who had commenced with the Mission in 1866.[71] He was of a sensitive and retiring nature and was hardly fitted to gain a high position in the rough life of the Colonies, but his consistent life won the respect of all who knew him.

The Caters were originally from London and they had nine children. He attended the church of the Rev J. Harrington Evans. Cater was "well instructed in the doctrines of grace", this being a code for a strong Calvinist. He was also connected with the church under Baptist Wriothesley Noel. Noel was an unusual Baptist leader in England. An evangelical Anglican and member of the aristocracy, he resigned from the Church of England and became a Baptist in 1848 and pastor at the John Street Baptist Chapel in London. Noel was not a Strict and Particular Baptist so with his attendance at John Street Cater had evidently moved into mainstream Baptist life.[72] In London he became a London City Missioner. Their twenty-year-old daughter Hannah was the first to immigrate to Sydney, in 1857 and her parents followed the next year. In November

---

[67] Daily Telegraph (Launceston) 25 May 1905 p2.

[68] LEx 30 January 1906 p1.

[69] SB 30 January 1906 p28.

[70] Day-Star March 1906.

[71] The Ballarat Star 27 October 1871 p2.

[72] Notes by Dr Ken Manley.

1862 they commenced a branch church to the Clarence Town Baptist Church, at Glen William, a farming locality on the Williams River. The work languished on his departure, possibly to Tasmania.[73] In 1864 Cater was appointed missionary to the Launceston City Mission and Elizabeth was appointed "Bible Woman". In February 1869, lack of funds forced the Mission to dispense with Elizabeth's services although they retained Charles. They were members of the York Street Baptist Chapel with the Rev Henry Dowling as Pastor. In September 1869 they resigned from the Chapel as there was a concerted effort by the Revs Samuel Cozens and Daniel Allen to have the York Street Chapel revert to a Strict Church. In 1871 Cater became pastor at the Williamstown Baptist Church in Victoria.[74]

After the Perth pastorate in Tasmania for 1872, Cater pastored the Deloraine Baptist Church in 1873, again for a year. But the Launceston City Mission was again in need of a Missionary and so Charles and Elizabeth accepted the call from June 1875. He retired in April 1879 and died on 16 July 1888 at the age of seventy-nine years. Elizabeth died in Ballarat on 6 May 1890.[75]

## Appendix 2: The Rev William Clark

While the scholarly and popular pastor, the Rev William Clark, began his ministry in Tasmania, it was in Victoria that he provided outstanding leadership to the Baptist Association.

William Clark was born in London on 15 January 1839 and spent his boyhood in the city. Clark came under the spell of the Rev C. H. Spurgeon and upon his conversion experience "at once began to tell others of his new-found joy" of knowing Christ. On Spurgeon's advice he entered the Pastors' College. In 1867, during the later part of his course, he was sent to open a preaching station at Finchley Common and Spurgeon supported

*1-11 Ballarat Baptist Tabernacle*

---

[73] The Recorder February 1989 p6.

[74] Baptist Union of Great Britain Handbook for 1872.

[75] The Mercury (Hobart) 10 May 1890 p4.

him with £250 from his purse.⁷⁶ This new cause was a group which had broken away from the St John's Lane Baptist Church and at first met in the Corn Exchange and later the Assembly Rooms. Why the split occurred before Clark's arrival is not known,

but it took place during a church service. The disruption was so bad that the local Police Superintendent came to keep order. To stop the dissatisfied group being heard, the harmonium was played at full volume to drown the speaker, or a hymn was announced to achieve the same result. Those who went to the Corn Exchange took the Communion Plate with them. Threats of legal action were a regular feature of Church Meetings at the St John's Lane, but nobody was sure where the Communion Plate was.

Under Clark's care a good congregation had gathered and he oversaw the commencement of a building fund. Following Clark's leaving, another student or graduate from the Pastors' College was appointed and it was during this person's ministry that the two churches were reunited. This was based on changes introduced by Clark at the Assembly Room Church. Clark had been selected by the Rev C. H. Spurgeon and Dr. William Landels for the Tasmanian Perth church in 1874.⁷⁷

*1-12 William Clark*

**Following Perth in July 1876** he began his long and fruitful ministry at the Dawson Street Tabernacle, Ballarat. He followed the Rev Alfred W. Grant who had left dispirited a year and one half earlier. But before Clark could settle in, he had to respond to a report in "The Tasmanian" that he approved additional alcohol booths at the Annual Perth Boxing Day Regatta. His name was used in justification of providing these increased facilities. It was asserted that Clark a year before had said that "he had never witnessed a more decorous and temperate meeting."⁷⁸

At Ballarat, as in all his churches, Clark was an untiring visitor, "his geniality and unfailing humour made him popular everywhere."

---

⁷⁶ The Victorian Freeman November 1893 p247.

⁷⁷ Information supplied by Raymond Davis of the Baptist Church in Middleton Cheney UK; The Herald 5 June 1911 p3.

⁷⁸ The Tasmanian 18 November p6, 25 November 1876 p11; The Cornwall Chronicle 22 November 1876 p3.

Annually the church celebrated his tenure. In his time 210 persons, including many young people joined the Church. In this country centre he married Scot Eliza Stalker (1851–1933).[79]

Clark strongly supported the visits of Scottish Temperance Advocate and evangelist, Dr. Alexander Neill Somerville[80] and Evangelists Margaret Hampson and Emilia Louise Baeyertz. These two women were a departure from the norm. In her campaigns Hampson commended the Blue Ribbon Gospel Temperance Movement. Clark was honorary Secretary of the Ballarat Mechanics Institute.[81] At the time, with Clark being the Secretary of the Ballarat Ministerial Association, the question of the use of Bibles in State Schools was a fiercely debated issue.[82]

The £1000 debt on the property was cleared and the facades painted. In respect to the latter, as the painting work proceeded, "Vagan" a journalist described the edifice thus,

> The Baptist Church in Dawson-street has a forlorn appearance. It resembles a building which has been baptised with fire, water and hail. The rough brickwork smuttered with mortar, the Corinthian pillars bare and naked, the entablature scowling down upon the lower parts of the building are like a giant, angry and wrathful with himself and the world in general through exposure and long neglect; but old things are to be hidden under the skilful treatment of the plasterer, and in the future this church will be one of the handsomest in the city.[83]

The Ballarat Church "enjoyed quiet prosperity". Other pastorates for Clark were Crimea Street Baptist Church in St. Kilda (1885 – 1892) and North Carlton Baptist Church (1892 – 1906). He was appointed chairman and then Secretary of the Victorian Baptist Association, the latter from 1906 to 1912.[84] Later he became President of the Victorian Churches and Secretary of the Baptist Union of Australia. He was in constant demand for church and Sunday school anniversaries. On medical advice he retired in his 74th year. On 15 March 1917 Clark died suddenly during a communion service at the Armadale Baptist Church. He was seventy-eight years of age, at the time the oldest minister in the denomination.[85]

---

[79] The Ballarat Star 16 April 1880 p2. Eliza died at Malvern, Vic.

[80] See Defending "A Christian Country" by Walter Phillips, University of Queensland Press p59ff.

[81] The Ballarat Courier 28 July 1877 p3; The Argus (Melbourne) 20 January 1885 p6; The Ballarat Star 11 September 1877 p2.

[82] The Ballarat Star 27 August 1879 p2, 25 August 1879 p3; Wilkin p58.

[83] Bendigo Advertiser 26 July 1879 p1.

[84] For the Rev Walter J Eddy's appreciation of Clark on his retirement as Secretary of the Union of Victoria, see SB 25 January 1912 p52.

[85] Sea Lake Times and Berriwillock Advertiser 24 March 1917 p3; Wilkin p153.

## Appendix 3: Rev George William Gillings

In the Rev George William Gillings we meet a man of predetermined mind, an evangelist who early was willing to work in the monotonous northern regions of Victoria without creature comforts but as the years progressed became preoccupied with the doctrine of the Second Coming.

George William Gillings was born in 1821 and christened at St George's, Hanover Square, London. He married Harriet Dorothea Jones in 1852 at Camberwell, London. Harriet was born 8 July 1827 at Bishopsgate, London, to a Baptist family and she attended Sunday school. Her birth registration listed her as Nonconformist. While she and George were ministering in 1861 at Dorking[86] thirty-five kms south of London, George Muller's biography, "The Lord's Dealings with George Muller", had a great impression on both of them. They were then baptised. It was reported that Harriet in her baptism, "inwardly to her last breath, knew that 'she and Christ were one'." Further they both

*1-13 George Gillings*

began to see that George Muller was right, "that the Lord Jesus was actually coming". Then two other books made a deep impression on her, namely, Wesley's work on "Christian Perfection" and "The Life of Hester Anne Rogers". The account of Harriet's life states, "she left commercial life for the ministry in 1855" and became a public speaker of some note. In one of her articles, "Women's Ministry: Its Legitimacy and Power", she said, "It is of the Lord that His handmaidens shall preach, teach, and &c, in public."[87]

Following their migration to Australia, Gillings pastored for six years from September 1871 the Hargreaves Street Baptist Church in Bendigo. During his time there the large schoolroom below the church was installed and other extensive improvements effected. A keen evangelist, Gillings wanted nothing to "retard" the Lord's work, so no offering or communion was taken during the evening evangelistic services. Communion became "open", and an organ was purchased.[88]

At the 1875 annual meeting of the Victorian Baptist Association it was

---

[86] The 1861 UK Census has them living at Dorking in Surrey.

[87] The Victorian Baptist August 1890 p122, January 1892; Hester Anne Rogers was a Methodist writer.

[88] Bendigo Advertiser 29 March 1890 p3; Our Yesterdays Vol 18, p56.

resolved, on the motion of Gillings, "this Association, having taken into consideration the pressing need for evangelistic work in the bush, would urge the subject upon the attention of the Victorian Baptist Home Mission Committee". As Dr Basil Brown records,

> Some months later, Gillings himself was prevailed upon to engage in such a ministry for a brief period. Gillings, provided with a grey mare and wagonette, drove into the country districts to the north of Sandhurst (Bendigo), which was then being settled as the result of favourable land laws. As he journeyed, he sought-out the lonely settlers, preaching to them whenever a congregation could be gathered together, and bringing the Word of Life to one and all in personal conversation. At length he reached Echuca, a town on the Murray River. On May 1, 1876, Gillings began services in the local town hall. During the following weeks congregations increased so that the building was inconveniently crowded. Gillings resigned from his church early in 1877 so that he might engage in missionary work for the Society. Unfortunately, ill-health put this out of the question and he was obliged to take up pastoral work again, (this time) at Perth, Tasmania.[89]

**Following his time at Perth**, Gillings was the first minister of what was to become the Pakington Street Church in St. Kilda. As it was yet to build its own building, they met in the Town Hall for five years. When he left in 1887 for missionary work in Bangalore, India, there was a church of 117 members with 250 Sunday school scholars.[90] Prior to his departure, itinerant evangelist, the Rev Henry Hussey, conducted a mission at the St. Kilda Town Hall at Gillings' invitation and he records in his diary spending the early part of one week revising for the press Gillings' book, "The Days of the Son of Man: are they to be?" He added to his diary the line, "Mr. Gillings, the author of several works on prophecy."[91]

Since the early 1870s Gillings had made a name for himself with his lectures and writings on the Second Coming of Jesus.[92] In Gillings' view there was no cure for all of society's ills; Satan rules this world by God's permission and the only hope lay in the Second Advent of Christ.[93]. In his End Time messages he gave startling and authenticated accounts of the rapidly growing strength of Anarchy and the godless and the insurrectionary aims it has in view ...

---

[89] Basil Brown, Members One of Another p61.

[90] Wilkin p73. The current church building in Pakington Street was erected in 1915.

[91] Hussey, Henry, Colonial Life and Christian Experience (Adelaide, Hussey & Gillingham, 1897) chapter 22.

[92] Bendigo Advertiser 5 November 1870 p2.

[93] Manley p400.

the education of the young and the luxury of Victorian society which provided the soil in which these dangerous principles too easily took root.[94]

One of his bestselling books was, "Our Lord's Return, or, What is 'Maranatha?' A Dialogue."[95] Spurgeon in London was not impressed with Gillings' over-emphasis on the Second Coming. He wrote,

> There are good brethren in the world who are impractical. The grand doctrine of the second advent makes them stand with open mouths, peering into the skies, so that I am ready to say, "Ye men of Plymouth, why stand ye here gazing up into heaven?" The fact that Jesus Christ is to come is not a reason for stargazing, but for working in the power of the Holy Ghost. Be not so taken up with speculations as to prefer a Bible reading over a dark passage in the Revelation to teaching in a ragged-school or discoursing to the poor concerning Jesus. We must have done with daydreams, and get to work. I believe in eggs, but we must get chickens out of them. I do not mind how big your egg is; it may be an ostrich's egg if you like, but if there is nothing in it, pray clear away the shells. If something comes of it, God bless your speculations, and even if you should go a little further than I think it wise to venture, still, if you are more useful, God be praised for it. We want facts — deeds done, souls saved. It is all very well to write essays, but what souls have you saved from going down to hell?[96]

Gillings was appointed the accredited agent and a leading speaker of the "Melbourne Prophetical Conference" of 1887 and thereafter lectured in the churches on the event. A second conference took place in 1890. He was also a speaker at the Prophetic Conference held in Launceston in September 1888. The subject of The Second Coming of Jesus was given great emphasis and heartily endorsed at the time in the churches with Gillings a welcomed speaker on the subject.

At their farewell from the St. Kilda congregation, it was said of Harriett,

> Mrs. Gillings, we also tender our heartfelt acknowledgments for her earnest and faithful co-operation with you in seeking to gather in, to teach, and to train, the youthful part of the congregation for the service of Christ. Few pastors are favored with partners capable of rendering like efficient service ... Many mothers amongst as have acknowledged the value of her truths and stresses the sudden return of Jesus. It is a check against worldliness.

---

[94] Day-Star Aug 1888 p121.

[95] Chicago, Bible Institute of Colportage Assn. (c1901). The book is a fireside chat between a father, his daughter and her cousin on millennial

[96] S&T April 1874.

exposition of the Word, her interest in the welfare of their offspring, and her desire and prayers for their salvation; although the kindness thus rendered have been with impaired health, and often amid much bodily pain.[97]

After the death of Harriet on 16 July 1890 in Geelong,[98] Gillings lived in India. There he married missionary Rosa Steer on 24 May 1892 at Ebenezer Baptist Church, Bangalore, South India.[99] Some years later Rosa had the sad task of writing a funeral notice for the Bangalore papers. She was a woman of letters for the notice is beautifully crafted. It reads:

> "Mrs. G W Gillings respectfully informs her friends of the passing of her beloved and esteemed husband on July 16th, 1915, in the 95th year of his natural life, the 75th year of his spiritual life and the 60th year of happy service for his Divine Master, the Lord Jesus Christ. He is not dead but sleeping 'through Jesus' 'until the day break'."[100]

## Appendix 4: The Rev Robert Williamson

Like so many migrants the Rev Robert Williamson from the Pastors' College survived tubercular

*1-14 Crimea St Baptist Church, St Kilda*

infection and lived a long and productive life.

Robert Williamson was born in 1848 at Port of Menteith, Perthshire, Scotland and baptised at the Stirling Baptist Chapel in Scotland by the Rev Dr. James Culross who became Principal of Bristol Baptist College. Williamson entered the Pastors' College in 1871 from Stirling. Following his studies at the College, he became pastor of the Paradise Row Chapel in the Essex town of Waltham Abbey from 1873. He married Margaret Easdon Hamilton on 13 August 1874 at Stirling. Margaret was born in 1850 at St Ninians, Stirlingshire.[101] Ill-health forced his resignation from the pastorate in 1877 and in failing to recover his health, he like many other Englishmen of the time, sought it in sunny Australia. Arriving in Sydney in September that year[102] he had letters of commendation from

---

[97] Weekly Times (Melbourne) 23 June 1883 p11.
[98] Bendigo Advertiser 23 July 1890 p2.
[99] The Argus (Melbourne) 17 July 1890 p1; The Herald (Melbourne) 1 July 1892 p2.
[100] Source: John Sampson, former Victorian Baptist Historical Society archivist.

[101] Family History research by Barbara Coe.
[102] For 1880-1889 25% of College Graduates went overseas. Pastors' College Reports 1879-89, 1915-16.

the Revs. C H Spurgeon and George Rogers, the latter the Principal of the College. He gained secular employment but the opportunity for Christian ministry was realized with the offer of the pastorate of the Parramatta Baptist Church the following year even though the financial position of the Church was weak. It seemed that his health improved for a time, but in January 1880 illness forced him to seek rest and a change in Tasmania. He returned to Parramatta but ill-health continued and medical advice forced him to resign the pastorate and accept an invitation from the Perth Church.[103]

**Following the Perth pastorate** Williamson moved to the Kyneton Baptist Church in country Victoria commencing in 1886. He filled the appointment of a trustee of the Kyneton Savings Bank.[104] The Kyneton church reported in March 1885 that Williamson was having "premonitory symptoms of a return of illness from which he suffered most seriously some years ago ... and will in all probability return to Tasmania, the climate of which suited him better than either that of New South Wales or Victoria." He concluded at Kyneton by mid-1886.[105]

He was welcomed at the South Yarra Baptist Church on 30 November 1886 where he would spend the next five years.[106] He returned to the Perth Church in Tasmania in 1892 as an interim for some months.

On 11 April 1893 he was welcomed as pastor of the Crimea Street Baptist Church, St Kilda, a Particular Church which was part of the Baptist Union of Victoria. The communion table was enclosed by a small fence complete with railing signifying it was very particular about who participated. Among those who spoke on the occasion of Williamson's welcome was the Rev William Clark, Perth Church's former minister as well as Crimea Street's pastor, the latter from 1885 to 1891. Clark spoke of work in Crimea Street, "where there were a lot of well-to-do people living in fine houses, and also perhaps people who were not well-to-do living in fine houses."[107]

A journalist called on the Church and subsequently presented his report in The Prahran Telegraph. Apart from his comments on Williamson, his

---

[103] For more on Williamson at the Parramatta Baptist Church, see H Watkin-Smith, Baptists in the Cradle City. The Story of Parramatta Baptist Church 1838-1986 (Eastwood, Baptist Historical Society of NSW, 1986).

[104] The Kyneton Observer (Vic) 10 May 1887 p2.

[105] Victorian Freeman, March 1885 p59; for a sermon given during his time at Kyneton see "Supplement to the Victorian Freeman" December 1884 p8; The Herald (Melbourne) 31 July 1886 p4.

[106] The Telegraph, St Kilda, Prahran and South Yarra Guardian (Vic) 27 November 1886 p5; The Prahran Telegraph (Vic) 24 October 1891 p2.

[107] Chronicle, South Yarra Gazette, Toorak Times and Malvern Standard (Vic) 15 April 1893 p3.

account of the actual sermon was more his take on what it ought to have said than on Williamsons' own rendering. On Williamson and the congregation, he wrote,

> I have an impression that the gentlemen himself has suffered from ill health and is far from robust even now. The congregation on Sunday was scanty, and the choir, accommodated at the rear of the church, thin but sweet, being led by a skilful young lady organist. The congregation did not attempt to sing much, though the tunes were easy. Possibly the exertion would have been too much. But the one prayer of the service was made by a member of the congregation. The Rev R. Williamson is a fine looking man of middle age, possessed of a good deliverance and a forcible style. There is neither in his speech nor appearance very much of the cleric. He eschews white "choker" in his dress, and affectations in his manner. The preacher asserted that men would hardly take the trouble to make gods for themselves but simply treated God with contempt - a statement I fancy altogether too sweeping ... The preacher proceeded to draw a line between the chosen of God and those outside the pale ... It was a short sermon but there was a great deal in it.[108]

*1-15 Robert Williamson later in life*

The financial collapse of the 1890s impacted on the Church and Williamson resigned in February 1899 after seven years of ministry. His salary had been halved the previous year as had that of the caretaker and the church still had a debt of £471 owing on the building.[109]

He then filled in for two years as a supply at various churches. In January 1901 he was offered the Baptist Church at Latrobe and its outstation of Sassafras but declined due to ill health. Finally that month he accepted the pastorate of the Hamilton Baptist Church but there bouts of ill-health interrupted his ministry and on 20 March 1902 he was forced to relinquish his charge. He then supplied churches as far away as Goulburn in NSW and then took charge of the Sheffield Baptist Church in Tasmania.[110]

---

[108] The Prahran Telegraph (Vic.) 28 November 1894 p3.

[109] Our Yesterdays Vol. 24, 2016, p20.

[110] Hamilton Spectator (Vic) 8 January 1901 p2; The Australasian (Melbourne) 19 October 1901 p5; Goulburn Evening Penny Post (NSW) 30 July 1903 p2.

## Appendix 5: The Rev William Compton

A number of migrants did not survive the ravages of tubercular infection and English born the Rev William Compton was one of them.

William Compton entered the Pastors' College in 1876 from the Congregational Church, Worthing, a seaside town fifteen kms from Brighton. Following College he was pastor of the Hove Baptist Church for four years and the Stoke Road Baptist Church, Gosport, for three years. The Sword and Trowel reported "His hopeful disposition and unconquerable spirit battled the disease so long." With his wife already dead, he sailed for Tasmania in 1887 leaving his two little children behind hoping that the climate would enable him to continue preaching. Even in the months before his death in Tasmania, he was planning his return to "dear old England". The Sword and Trowel in 1887 reported his passing saying, "He has been laid to rest in a foreign land," and added that his fellow students in Tasmania had "little thought that he would follow them out here to die." The journal continued, "We helped him to go out in the hope that his valuable life might be lengthened for a few years, but his departure was delayed too long (and) he gradually faded away." It was anticipated that Spurgeon back in London would take Compton's children into his Stockwell Orphanage.[111]

## Appendix 6: The Rev James Rides Cooper

The Rev James Rides Cooper was one of the sixteen English Baptist men from the Pastors' College who were sent out to minister in Tasmania. Three of them returned home after a number of years of effective ministry, which was not only in Tasmania but in other colonies as well; Cooper was one of them.

Cooper was born on 16 September 1856 "of pious parents" at Staines-upon-Thames not far from the present day Heathrow Airport. Being fond of study, he wanted to become a teacher but ended up being apprenticed to his eldest brother, a coach builder. About sixteen years of age, he came to a personal faith in Jesus and moved home and attended Spurgeon's Metropolitan Tabernacle. It was because of one of Spurgeon's texts, "Who is on the Lord's side?" that he resolved to be baptised on the 27 May 1876 and came into membership.

On each Sunday morning and afternoon he taught a class in the Almshouses Sunday school, and in the Sunday evenings associated with other young men of the same Bible class in open-air preaching in the New Kent Road.

---

[111] S&T May 1878, April 1882, 1887 p599; Day-Star September 1887; LEx 30 August 1887 p2.

Medical worries took him back home to Staines-upon-Thames. On his recovery, he moved to Peterborough in eastern England, its Baptist Church being under the ministry of the Rev Thomas Barrass. He taught Sunday school, and again with other young men, engaged in open-air preaching. He also preached at a branch chapel at nearby Stanground. There he preached his first sermon from the words, "Where art thou?" Like many other preachers before, he started well, but suddenly a rush of self-consciousness, or a lack of ideas, brought him to an abrupt pause. The embarrassing silence was at last broken by the preacher exclaiming, "I do not know what to say; but I do love my Saviour, and wish that you loved Him, too."

As his preaching improved he was sent as a supply to Pinchbeck some thirty kms north of Peterborough, where finally he was invited to become pastor and he ministered there for eighteen months before seeking formal training for the ministry. In January 1882 he entered the Pastors' College. While still a student, Cooper was sent to establish a Baptist Church at Aldershot, fifty kms southwest of London and soon a chapel was built.

In 1885, at the request of Spurgeon, he and his wife, Bessie (nee Pomeroy), left for Tasmania for two years at Perth after a pastorate at Batley, Yorkshire.[112] On his voyage out, leaving on 12 December 1884 with his wife, the first organist of the Aldershot Church, they had two travelling companions: the Rev Harry H. Driver who was returning to New Zealand after his course at the Pastors' College, and Spurgeon's son, the Rev Thomas Spurgeon. Cooper recalled some of the experiences of the voyage,

> We had much happy fellowship, and (Thomas') gentle kindly way made him a favourite with those whose goodwill was to be welcomed. It was our custom to join in devotional fellowship day by day in Tom's cabin. The four of us read together a Psalm and then the exposition of it from his father's "The Treasury of David". At Naples fortune favoured us - we were able to spend eight hours ashore.

They spent Christmas Day in the Suez Canal. Wrote Spurgeon,

> So lovely a morning I have seldom seen; even Australia and New Zealand could scarcely rival it. Happy children romped about us with the presents Santa Claus had placed in their hung-up stockings.

They arrived at Adelaide on 20 January 1885, and were heartily welcomed, and then it was on to Melbourne. As the Tasmanian ship did not leave Melbourne till after the Sunday, all three preached in different churches in Melbourne. William Gibson Senior, his son, and

---

[112] S&T April 1884.

all the Baptist ministers of the Island welcomed them to Tasmania. Spurgeon then continued his journey to New Zealand. Cooper's daughter, Marguerite May, soon joined her family in Tasmania.[113]

In 1887, Cooper commenced at Portland, Victoria (1887-96). Soon a very substantial hall was purchased for a church for £800.[114] In 1897 Cooper returned to England and held pastorates at Helston, Cornwall (1898-1901), Castle Donington, Derby (1901-08), Clay Cross (1908-14) and at Freedom Rd., Walkley, Sheffield (1914-1923) and Foxton Baptist Church (1923-1929). Bessie died in 1913. He retained fond memories of his time in Tasmania and Victoria.[115] He died on 15 May 1937. One of his sons, J. Roy Cooper, who trained at the Baptist Rawdon College, entered into Christian ministry.[116]

## Appendix 7: The Rev John E Walton

The Rev John Edwin Walton's ability as a preacher and pastor was recognized by church-goers and others alike. A scholar of some note, he cared for young and old alike and his ministries were "characterised by steady, but continued progress, rather than revivals and reactions." He gave eighteen of his best years to the work in Tasmania. With his last years in Queensland and NSW, he was typical of so many outstanding Tasmanian Baptist ministers who began their Australian pilgrimage in Tasmania and then contributed greatly to mainland Baptist Associations.

Walton, born in 1856 at Clay Cross, Derbyshire, was the first child of Baptist Edwin and Hannah Walton; four sisters followed. During an address of a Sunday school teacher who said that it had been stated that only one out of every nine scholars became followers of the Lord Jesus Christ, Walton inwardly cried, "Lord, may I be one of the saved!" He was scarce nine years of age. But it would be in his thirteenth year that he came to a conversion experience. His mother noticed the change, and said to him "I don't know how it is, for some time you have been quite mopish and now you are singing all the while." "I have good cause to sing mother," the boy replied, "for Jesus has saved me, and I belong to Him." "If that be so," she rejoined, "you should attend the prayer meeting at the church." This he did. The grave seniors were surprised to see one so young in their midst but a thrill of joy and sympathy shot through the whole gathering when the lad's voice was heard in prayer, when, after a few sentences, he broke down in

---

[113] Fullerton, WY, Thomas Spurgeon, a Biography (London, Hodder and Stoughton, 1919) p117; see also "Outward Bound" by Harry H Driver S&T 1885 p227ff.
[114] Wilkin p48.

[115] 1930 letter AB p259.
[116] Baptist Union of Great Britain Handbook 1937; S&T 1897 p534.

tears. To the Sunday school teacher especially, it seemed "a token for good", and so it was.

About seven months later he was baptised by the Rev George Slack of Derby and brought into church membership at the Clay Cross Baptist Church. By letter writing, by tract-distribution and conversation, he now sought to win others to Jesus. During his teenage years, beside his daily employment, he immersed himself in the life of his church and began to teach in the Sunday school. He had four secretaryships to attend to, viz., Sunday school, Band of Hope, the Young Men's Mutual Improvement Society and the Rechabites. For the most part, every evening was fully spent in some form of Christian service. In time he began to conduct services in the surrounding villages. At the young age of nineteen he applied to enter the Pastors' College but the death of his father meant he had to bear the burden of the family's support. His ability as a preacher was first recognised by a Rev Mr. Williams. A year later, upon his mother's remarriage, he entered College and studied there for three years. In 1883 at Chesterfield, Derbyshire, he married Hannah Taylor. In January that year Walton also began a five-year ministry at Balsall Heath, Birmingham. But he suffered "an attack of inflammation of the lungs" and was forced out to the colonies.[117]

## Appendix 8: The Rev Henry Clark

The Rev Henry Clark, was a pastor at heart who truly exemplified the maxim, "A house-going minister makes a church-going people". Theologically, he remained true to the Spurgeon orthodoxy whether it be in the church or with the Protestant Defence League. He was another of the many Tasmanian Baptist ministers who began their Australian pilgrimage in Tasmania and then contributed greatly to mainland Baptist Associations.

*1-16 Henry and Ada Clark*

Henry Clark was born in Edinburgh on 1 July 1862, within a short distance of the house where John Knox lived. He was brought up in a distinctively Christian home and attended a Presbyterian Sunday school. At the early age of eleven years Henry attended for two years a small bush school. His first job was to look after and do the chores in a doctor's house and then he began as a storekeeper. While weighing

---

[117] Daily Telegraph (Launceston) 9 September 1904 p2; S&T 1900 p489ff.

# Lessons from our first 20 years

*1-17 The Rev Henry Clark (third from left in the front row) with the staff of Perth Baptist Sunday School*

something in the store one day, the customer remarked, "My word, you're very exact in your weighing, and you don't give any over-weight." To this young Clark replied, "If I give you more than the weight you are paying for, I should be robbing my employer; and if I gave you less than you are paying for, I should be robbing you."

Driving to the Anglican Church service one Sunday, his employer, who was a Methodist quite unexpectedly asked, "Harry, don't you think you are old enough to join some Christian church?"

Nothing more was said, but the question never left him, and three weeks later, at a Methodist "love-feast," he made his decision to become a Christian, and at the close of the service applied to join the church.

As the result of his father's death, the Clark family returned to Scotland to obtain assisted passages to New Zealand to join the elder brother and sister.

There he took up Sunday school teaching. About eighteen years of age, he commenced preaching amongst the Methodists, and when twenty-one became a probationer in the Methodist ministry with charges in Geraldine and district, South Island, and Fielding and district, North Island. After being a Home Missionary for over three years, he resigned his position as a Methodist minister, and severed his connection with the Methodist Church in consequence of a change of conviction concerning baptism. In New Zealand he preached among Maoris and was baptised.[118]

In 1886 he returned to London and entered the Pastors' College. He was a student pastor at the Queens Road Church, Broadstairs, Essex, and remained on at the Church after College.

He migrated in 1891 to Adelaide preaching on the voyage but suffered badly with rheumatic fever. In April 1892 he was very ill. He remained for six years in Adelaide and then in 1893 he transferred to the pastorate of the Harris Street Baptist Church in Sydney. The work immediately prospered in his hands both in Sunday services and in the Sunday school which had now a larger staff of teachers than they had

---

[118] AB 12 July 1932 p3.

had for a long time. In the first two years he baptised forty candidates. In his five years there the membership increased from sixty to over 200. Conscious of the physical, it was reported that in his opinion "there are so many Christians suffering from fatty degeneration of the heart that an ambulance society is needed in most churches to carry them about." He married Ada Stone on 28 March 1894.[119]

While in NSW he was honorary Secretary of the Baptist Union Home Missionary Committee. He was also a member of the Petersham Loyal Orange Lodge, No. 46. Clark was farewelled from the Harris Street Church on 19 June 1898.[120]

After two years at the Perth Church Clark returned to NSW and accepted the pastorate of the Newtown Baptist Church. He also provided leadership to the NSW Baptists. After a three years' successful pastorate, he accepted a call from the West Melbourne Baptist Church and commenced in July 1904. If one goes by the press records of his time in Melbourne, one would have to conclude that most of his efforts were spent with the Victorian Protestant Defence Association (VPDA), of which he was founder and first President for two years and then Grand President and President of the local branch. The VPDA was part of the Loyal Orange Institution of Victoria which gloried in the Protestant Reformation and attacked the Roman Catholic Church ceaselessly and also at times attacked Socialism, it attacked the Labor Party too.[121] The VPDA sought the teaching of Scripture lessons in State schools. There were those who were glad to see Clark, this "High Panjandrum" (a person who has or claims to have a great deal of authority or influence), leave the state when he did.[122]

In 1907 he commenced at the Burwood Baptist Church in NSW and resumed his position on the Home Mission Committee. But by his early fifties his health was poor and a number of short pastorates was his lot. They were at the Bourke Street Broken Hill Baptist Church, at Goulburn and at the Wellington Baptist Church, the last for seven months as he again had to retire owing to ill health.[123]

In 1921 he was appointed President of the Baptist Union of NSW for the

---

[119] Evening News (Sydney) 27 July 1892 p2, 6 April 1894 p3; Daily Telegraph (Launceston) 20 May 1893 p9, 21 December 1895 p13, 28 May 1898 p5.
[120] Goulburn Evening Penny Post 14 October 1893 p2; Daily Telegraph (Launceston) 5 August 1895 p3, 18 June 1898 p5.
[121] Daily Telegraph (Launceston) 18 July 1903 p7; Punch 21 July 1904 p33; North Melbourne Courier and West Melbourne Advertiser 20 January 1905 p2; The Age 30 August 1906 p4, 5 September 1906 p9; The Herald 14 January 1907 p4.
[122] Geelong Advertiser 31 January 1907 p4; Labor Call 30 May 1907 p8.
[123] The Sydney Morning Herald 2 October 1908 p10; Goulburn Evening Penny Post 18 April 1912 p4, 1 May 1913 p4; Wellington Times (NSW) 5 November 1914 p4, 22 July 1915 p8.

second time and in his Presidential Address attacked Higher Criticism.¹²⁴ Higher Criticism was a new type of interpretation of Scripture which for the first time applied rigorous historical and critical methods to the study of the Bible. With its emphasis upon the human origins of the Bible and abandonment of the concept of biblical inerrancy it was having an increasing impact at the time. Over the years he also held the office of President of the Christian Endeavour Union in NSW. In 1923, Clark took up the position of Commissioner for the Baptist Church House and Soldiers' Memorial Fund following three years in the pastorate of the Granville Baptist Church being its pioneer Pastor. Then, in 1924, he was appointed Superintendent of the Baptist Union Home Missions in succession to Dr Arthur John Waldock.¹²⁵ Other pastorates in NSW were Bexley and Drummoyne both in Sydney from 1919 and Wollongong.¹²⁶ He retired in 1923 and died on 22 June 1942, at eighty years of age.

## Appendix 9: The Rev Stephen Howard

Growing up in rural South Australia, Stephen Howard entered the Baptist ministry at the mature age of thirty-three years and remained in the ministry until retirement. He served in three states but poor health dogged many of his pastorates. Although lacking in formal ministerial training, he proved a hard-working pastor and an able preacher.

Stephen Howard was born in England in December 1841, the son of farmer Nicholas H Howard and Elizabeth (Bessie). The family migrated to South Australia on the ship "Three Brothers" in 1849 and settle on a farm at South Rhine on the Murray Flats. Howard Senior gathered a few Christians around him and formed a Baptist church. Stephen was soon called to help as a lay-preacher.

*1-18 Stephen Howard*

In Adelaide Howard met and married English born Elizabeth Royal in August 1867. She had arrived from England with her family in 1848. It was claimed that in

---

¹²⁴ Petras, Michael, Extension or Extinction, Baptist Growth in New South Wales 1900-1939 (Sydney, Baptist Historical Society of New South Wales, 1983) p122.

¹²⁵ The Sydney Morning Herald 20 September 1921 p8; AB 10 July 1923 p4; The Sydney Morning Herald 19 August 1897 p5; The Cumberland Argus and Fruitgrowers Advocate 10 November 1923 p2; The Baptist Church House was the former Bathurst Street Church in Sydney which was handed as a gift to the Baptist Union; The Sydney Morning Herald 1 November 1924 p11.

¹²⁶ AB 30 June 1942 p2; Newcastle Morning Herald and Miners' Advocate (NSW) 13 December 1919 p5.

1851 Bessie's mother had made the first load of cheese ever sent out of South Australia and it was forwarded to the Victorian Diggings.[127]

In 1874, when the Rev David Badger was forming churches in the recently opened up Northern areas, the Association invited Stephen Howard to assist by taking charge of the newly-formed Jamestown Church. Even though Howard had had little (if any) formal education and no training in ministry (which fact he felt keenly to the end of his days), he accepted the invitation and a wiser choice could not have been made.[128] Yet Badger let it be known that it would not be advisable for the Church to send young ministers to do the work, for then they had little chance to improve their minds in the way of studying.

Every Sunday Howard had to preach three times and ride from thirty to forty kms but for three out of the four weeks little more than Sunday services were his lot.[129] In this Northern Area of the State there were four stations: Jamestown, Georgetown, Laura, and Terowie. Howard was the Vice-President of the Jamestown Mechanics Institute with its large hall and he was involved in other institutions such as the local hospital.[130] Unfortunately poor health brought about his move from Jamestown in July 1880. In South Australian Baptist history, Howard's name will always be linked to that of the Rev David Badger (1827-1890).[131]

After a "critical and protracted illness", he accepted an invitation to the pastorate of the Church at Gawler in the northern part of the State. At first, he was unable to undertake all his duties until he regained his strength. There were some seventeen district organizations under his supervision by 1881. By his third year, while there had been thirty church members added to the church, losses meant they were in a stagnant state. Poor health again brought about his move from Gawler. His lecture at the time on the "Uses and Abuses of the Present Life", received wide coverage.[132] The family then moved from South Australia to Victoria for Howard to pastor the struggling bayside Brighton Baptist Church in Melbourne (1886-1894). He commenced the Endeavour Society which had lapsed although the Sunday school continued to prosper

---

[127] The Mount Barker Courier and Onkaparinga and Gumeracha Advertiser 11 December 1908 p3.
[128] AB 29 July 1939.
[129] The South Australian Advertiser 16 October 1875 p1; Adelaide Observer 7 October 1876 p19.
[130] Evening Journal 30 September 1876 p3; South Australian Register 4 August 1877 p7; The Express and Telegraph 3 August 1880 p3.

[131] Gordon Grubb, letter of 28 January 2022.
[132] Christian Colonist 13 October 1882 p5, 27 July 1883 p3; Bunyip 22 June 1883 p2, 19 December 1884 p4; Evening Journal 13 January 1885 p2.

Lessons from our first 20 years

*1-19 Perth Baptist Church Sunday School Picnic*

but Church growth was again minimal.¹³³

Howard then pastored the influential Kew Baptist Church for nearly six years commencing 24 October 1894 but growth was again minimal.¹³⁴ Full transcripts of some of his sermons were published in the Melbourne newspapers. He was appointed President of the Baptist Union of Victoria for 1898/99 and thus took part in the Parliamentary Commission into scripture lessons in State schools.¹³⁵

**Following his time at the Perth Church in Tasmania**, Howard transferred back to South Australia to pastor the Grange Baptist Church in Adelaide (1905-1906). He then took charge of the Stepney Christian Church also in Adelaide (1907-1911) and facilitated the church rejoining the Baptist Union of South Australia. It belonged to the "Christian" churches in South Australia which were a small grouping of churches that were independent in polity and baptistic in belief. It entered the Baptist Union in 1912.

A move followed to Melbourne where for a short time he pastored the Box Hill Baptist Church. He retired from the regular ministry in 1914 yet for five years took an active part in a Union Church in the Dandenongs just out of Melbourne and was Superintendent of the Upwey-Belgrave Inter-denominational Mission all the while associating with the Kew Baptist Church where he took a leading part in the life of the Christian Endeavour Society and was a frequent preacher. This second association with the Kew Church lasted more than twenty years. At a meeting of one of the branches of the Protestant Federation, which was almost exclusively devoted to Conscription and the denunciation of Archbishop Mannix, Howard characterised the Roman Catholic Church as the huge political organisation whose final purpose was to shatter the British Empire. Bessie died on 19 May 1939 at ninety-four years of age and three months later Stephen died on 13 August 1939. He was at the time the oldest Baptist minister in Victoria. He had served his pastorates well.

---

¹³³ Wilkin records that the church greatly prospered.
¹³⁴ A History of the Kew Baptist Church 1856-1981 by Jill Manton p18.
¹³⁵ The Australasian 1 May 1897 p5, 4 September 1897 p5, 19 March 1898 p5; Leader 7 April 1900 p24.

They were survived by three daughters.[136]

## Appendix 10: The Rev Alfred Metters

Alfred Metters who was forever involved in various Baptist causes, served in four states. His visit to the Island State prior to his two pastorates there, revealed the deep theological division between the Tasmanian, Victorian and South Australian Associations. His literary skills were over many years employed in journalistic articles and in poems. In his military chaplain role of many years he was untiring in his attention to the men.

Metters was born in Melbourne in 1863, the youngest child of bricklayer James and Susan Metters. The couple arrived in Victoria some time before December 1854 and Alfred followed his brother Frederick to Adelaide in February

*1-21 Laura Baptist Church, SA*

*1-20 Kapunda Church, SA*

1883. Alfred was soon involved in various Baptist causes. He had become a Christian through the work of the YMCA. Frederick patented his "top fire" stove design in 1891 and founded his own business which eventually became Metters Limited. Alfred became Secretary to the Gospel Temperance Mission and preached the Temperance cause for the Blue Ribbon Army of which he became President in 1884. He was also closely involved with the YMCA and the Band of Hope. In 1885 he began studying for the ministry at Union College, a joint venture of the Congregational, Presbyterian, and Baptist denominations. A quality which marked him throughout his whole career was his thoroughness which showed itself in his student days. In 1888 he began his ministry as pastor at the Goodwood Baptist Church. In 1889, satisfying his literary skills, he became manager of "Truth and Progress", the State Baptist newsletter. In 1890 in the mid-north of South Australia he and the Rev E. J. Henderson, pastor of the

---

[136] The Herald 21 October 1913 p8; The Argus (Melbourne) 16 March 1921 p13; The Age (Melbourne) 13 November 1917 p8; Victorian Baptist Witness September 1939; History of the Kew Church by Jill Manton; AB 13 June 1939 p4.

Baptist church at Laura, exchanged pulpits.[137] In February 1892, he relinquished the pastorate of Laura and Appila for Jamestown, Georgetown and Cloverhill, which he resigned from in November that year and took charge of the Hill Street Baptist Church at Kapunda. He resigned that post and returned to Goodwood early in 1886 which the following year combined with Wayville. He married Ottilie Caroline Strempel on 29 August 1888. His next posting in late 1898 was to Mount Barker but he was suffering ill health and resigned in May 1900 rather than face another cold winter in the hills. He was given a short-term posting at Magill. While in Mount Barker, he founded a Berean Association.[138]

Having turned down the call to the Tasmanian Latrobe Baptist Church in May 1901, he accepted a call to Katanning, Western Australia, and in 1902 was appointed Superintendent of the Great Southern Railway Home Missions and Vice-president of the Baptist Union of WA. He transferred to Fremantle in December 1902 and shortly after was elected Secretary of the Baptist Union of Western Australia while retaining the Vice-Presidency, followed by the Presidency in November. His health had broken down in Western Australia which led to his relinquishing both the Fremantle Church and the State Presidency and for a time he contemplated leaving the ministry. In March 1904 he returned to South Australia.[139] In Adelaide Metters represented the British and Foreign Bible Society and undertook various preaching roles for the Baptist Churches. He soon recovered from failing health and in October 1904, he accepted a call to Perth in Tasmania.[140]

## Conclusion

Tasmanian Baptist Statistics reveal a disturbing decrease in church membership and active participation from a peak in 1982 with 2,200 members to 1,200 members in 2020. This decline can be attributed in large part to the increasing number of Australians who express no interest in organized religion, something like 45% in 2022. It is not just about young adults, but also about people of all ages in our churches. Sadly many have dropped out and will not be coming back and many have died. Further the volunteers who used to carry multiple positions in the church are now looking to do just a few things if any. Our regular attendees are becoming semi-regular. Our fringe folks are fading away.

---

[137] South Australian Weekly Chronicle 26 September 1885 p12, 18 February 1888 p9, 12 April 1890 p8; Observer 9 March 1918 p29; and generally from Wikipedia, the free encyclopedia.
[138] Kapunda Herald 17 January 1896; Mount Barker Courier 10 January 1901.

[139] Western Mail 11 May 1901 p73; The Register 7 March 1903 p8; The West Australian 14 November 1903 p9, 19 March 1904 p7.
[140] LEx November 1904 p3; 24 October 1905 p8; The West Australian 27 October 1904 p3.

One or two of our churches are moving toward a more socially oriented mission. Its lay people and leadership are committing themselves to working with the underprivileged. For them the Christian Gospel must not only be applied to the salvation of the individual but also to the salvation of society.

While very few, if any in our churches are greatly focused on the sweet by and by, the End Time and its hopes, a number appear aimless when facing the grind here and now. Every one of our churches needs to discover what it means for it to be a church in its post code; to make changes to worship, programs and ministries best needed to reflect and meet the needs of the communities around them; in short they need to adapt or die. For most it means a contemporary service and small group ministry.

The local church is important for it is where love and grace can be demonstrated. It is also the place and space where faith can be formed, life shared, and ministry be conceived. Helping people grow will result in Church members taking their faith into the community.

Further to Tasmanian Baptist statistics, while we all willingly admit that denominational loyalty is no longer what it was once, denominationalism will not fade from the scene any time soon because denominations offer answers to life's questions and a place of belonging. In respect to the churches by 1900 there is neither evidence as yet that congregations were looking for change in worship and preaching style nor evidence that they wanted inclusive language.

# Chapter 2 Blackwood Creek

## Introduction

More than one hundred years ago a little weather-board church at Blackwood Creek was "a silent witness for Christ to the settlers of the lonely bush." It nestled among the foot-hills of the Western Tiers, that magnificent range of mountains that straddles the centre of Tasmania.[141]

The chapel had the distinction of being the first outpost of the Spurgeon work in Tasmania. It was opened on Sunday 21 November 1880 by the Rev Thomas Spurgeon, assisted by Pastor Harry Wood. Spurgeon and Wood were both on holiday from New Zealand and were staying with the Gibsons at Native Point. Spurgeon was in the antipodes because of Tuberculosis and Wood was working in a pastorate at Willoughby Street, Thames, New Zealand.

## William Ross

The work owed much of its origin to the tireless labours of a local identity, Christian layman and Bracknell storekeeper William Ross. In the 1880s, Ross walked many miles through the bush at night to conduct morning services in the rough bush huts that were the dwellings of the settlers who worked in gravel pits and on the roads. As the story goes, he would often spend the greater part of Saturday night in prayer in the bush, emerging next morning to conduct the Sunday services "with his clothes saturated by the heavy dew from the undergrowth". For a time he used his own bush hut as a chapel before using a saw mill as a chapel.[142] Prior to his time with the Baptists, he and his family ran the Bracknell Primitive Methodist Sabbath School,[143] but he threw his lot in with the Baptists with the opening of the Brumby Bush (now Blackwood Creek) Baptist chapel.[144] At the time Blackwood Creek was a rough and godless place,

*2-1 Blackwood Creek Baptist Chapel*

---

[141] AB 29 November 1900.
[142] Day-Dawn May 1905.
[143] The Tasmanian (Launceston) 19 December 1874 p4.
[144] LEx 24 October 1878, p2 and 30 January 1879 p3.

the only roads being rough corduroy bush tracks. The soil is mostly heavy clay and without this the roads in winter would have been impassable. At the Longford Baptist church in January 1886 he "recited a soul-stirring incident connected with spiritual success attained in the backwoods."[145]

The chapel was made possible through William Gibson Senior and Junior's generosity; it cost £100. The foundation stone had been laid on Sunday 9 May 1880 a day when "it rained, blowed and snowed and ... closed with some vivid flashes of lightning". The Rev Robert McCullough late of Spurgeon's College preached. The next day celebrations continued in the presence of "a goodly number" including some visitors from further away and refreshments were provided in the afternoon as "the party sat down to tea".[146] Mr. Whitchurch was the building contractor, assisted by H. Gee.[147] While the Gibsons bore the building expenses, others including Ross, Charles Hodgetts, Donald Campbell, Dargaville, Frankcombe, Denman and Smith gave freely for fencing, catering, and the like.[148]

Pastor Harry Wood, during his ministry at Longford from October 1883 to August 1887, and from January 1901 to October 1906, worked closely with Ross.[149] In fact he found in him a soul mate. Wood, who was poor in health, said of the district, "To travel two or three hundred yards was a real shake up for a sluggish liver." The Rev Wesley Bligh, an early Tasmanian Baptist historian, recorded that it was a frequent thing to hear the shooting of kangaroo and wallaby in the thick scrub near at hand at the time of the services at the Blackwood Creek Chapel and to him this indicated that Sundays were held in little regard by the inhabitants.[150] The cottages were of a primitive type, built of slabs with earthen floors and hessian partitions. Bligh added, "But the people were hospitable, as only the poor know how to be, and welcomed (a) preacher."

*2-2 William Ross*

---

[145] The Tasmanian (Launceston) 9 January 1886 p14.
[146] LEx 21 May 1880 p3, 5 June 1880.
[147] LEx 13 November 1880 p2.
[148] LEx 8 January 1881 p2.

[149] LEx 13 November 1883 p3; Bligh pp25ff. Report of the BUT Conference of 27 May 1884.
[150] The account of the Blackwood Creek Baptist church is greatly drawn from Bligh's, Altars of the Mountain

## The Rev George Lake

The Rev George Lake, Baptist colporteur[151] and evangelist, was associated with both the Blackwood Creek Church and the Longford Church all the while working closely with Wood, while undertaking his colporteur work in the north of the colony as early as October 1884.[152] Lake was the speaker for the Blackwood Creek Sunday School anniversary in April 1885.[153] He was also one of the speakers for the laying of the foundation stone ceremony at the Bracknell Baptist Church in August 1884 and for its opening.[154]

Of a colporteur it was reported in February 1886,

> A book-hawker in journeying from Perth to Longford yesterday afternoon came to grief in one of the back streets of the first named township as he was driving his stock along in a four-wheeled vehicle. The horse, from some cause unknown to "your own" set off at a lively pace, eventually throwing the driver off on terra firma, scattering his Bibles, albums, etc., broadcast along the road, and galloping away with the shafts and the two fore wheels until suddenly run into a gorse hedge by a few of the more peaceably disposed and less frantic inhabitants of the village. Proprietor or bailee of goods arrived in due course to the spot named, took charge of his refractory steed, and set about repairing damages, himself and quadruped very little (frights excepted) the worse for their unexpected "country outing".[155]

On 1 January 1887 at the Longford Tabernacle, George married Ada Susan Hortle, the daughter of Thomas William and Elizabeth Hortle, a leading family of the Longford Tabernacle. Harry Wood officiated.

It must be noted that there is no suggestion that his vehicle was a mobile preaching platform for open-air preaching.

By the middle of 1887 Lake was stationed at Bracknell, designated Home Missionary and also given oversight of the Blackwood Creek work.[156]

At the Blackwood Creek chapel anniversary in 1887, more than 200 gathered for the occasion coming from as far away as Perth and Longford. For such occasions "two

---

[151] A colporteur is a door-to-door and/or travelling vender of goods, in this case Biblical literature.
[152] LEx 8 October 1884 p116, January 1885 p3.
[153] Daily Telegraph (Launceston) 6 May 1885 p3.
[154] Daily Telegraph (Launceston) 14 September 1885 p3, 11 November 1885 p3.
[155] LEx 27 February 1886 p3.
[156] LEx 9 July 1887 p3, 14 November 1887 p2.

waggonette loads would come from Longford Baptists".[157]

One wonders what prompted the Gibsons to be involved in this "Bush Mission" work: was it that they knew William Ross or was it on the recommendation of Harry Wood, Gibson Senior's beloved son in the Faith?

At the formation of the Baptist Union in May 1884, Blackwood Creek was one of the constituent Baptist Churches and was at the time under the care of the Perth Church.[158] Later it was attached to the nearer Longford Baptist Church. After the opening of the Bracknell Church on 8 Nov 1885, it was finally attached to the Bracknell Church.

A revival was experienced at the Blackwood Creek Chapel in the winter of 1886. The Rev John Alfred Soper of Petersham, New South Wales, was spending a holiday at the Longford Baptist manse and happened to accompany Wood to Blackwood Creek for an evening service. It was said that the power of God was so manifest in that meeting that three times the preacher closed it, but the people refused to leave. They continued until midnight and as Wood and Soper left the building they passed some of the men who had been at the meeting (now) on their knees, earnestly seeking God in prayer. Wood and Soper arrived at the Longford Manse at 2 am. with "hearts full of praise to the Lord for what we have seen of the Grace of God."[159]

## William Kenner

From June 1890 school teacher William Kenner was appointed Home Missioner to the district with the assistance of two lay preachers.[160] Of Kenner's work it was reported that there was "considerable awakening of interest on the part of the unconverted and a good degree of teaching and help bestowed upon the believers in response to the teaching of their educated Pastor. Since the chapel was without a baptistry, baptisms were conducted in the Liffey River at nearby Bracknell.[161] In 1891 the Sunday school witnessed for the first time "believers' baptism" conducted in a river.[162]

A plot of ground adjoining the Blackwood Creek Church was purchased in 1905 from Mr. B. Francombe for £1-10s as a cemetery for the district. This piece of "God's acre" became the quiet resting place of many of the sturdy pioneers of the district.

---

[157] Day-Star December 1887, December 1889.
[158] Report of the Tasmanian Baptist Union Conference Conference of 27 May 1884.
[159] Bligh; Day-Dawn May 1905.
[160] Day-Star May 1891.
[161] Day-Star April 1894.
[162] Day-Star May 1891.

## Vincent George Britton

Another man who made a great impact in the district was Vincent George Britton who was accepted for Home Mission Service in September 1898. When he commenced only twenty-five attended the Bracknell and Blackwood Creek Churches and further, the buildings were in a state of disrepair. After only a few months congregations were taxing the capacity of both buildings. At Blackwood Creek the building was soon extended by four metres to allow for increased attendances. The Baptist Association provided £40 to that end.

The Rev Wesley Bligh who knew Britton personally said of Britton that he was physically suited for the work. He was of,

> Short, stocky build, but was a man of great strength. His physical strength and prowess made him respected amongst the hardy, rough pioneers, many of whom literally feared to match their strength against his. He was an expert horseman and would "break" horses that other men feared to ride. His genial disposition and his deep human sympathy and understanding soon won for him a response in the hearts of the people and gave him ready access to their homes.

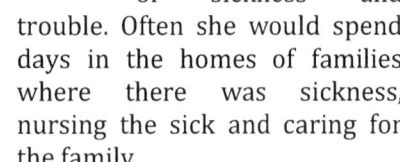

*2-3 Vincent G Britton*

Perhaps his most outstanding qualities were a deep and tender sympathy with the poor, and an intensely practical approach to all life's problems.

Old and young, rich and poor, land-owner and cottager, V.G. Britton was the friend of all. Although an ardent Baptist he was unsectarian in his sympathies. His wife Elizabeth (Ida) (nee Whiting) shared with her husband the strenuous life of these pioneering days. She was the personification of kindness and was on constant call in times of sickness and trouble. Often she would spend days in the homes of families where there was sickness, nursing the sick and caring for the family.

Britton carried out the first baptisms, those of Mr. and Mrs. Philpott Senior, George and Charles Philpott and Mr. Ferguson and son Joseph Ferguson on 8 June 1900. The first wedding was on 11 July 1900 between John William Upton and Mary Ann Philpott.

Once the building work had settled, the Launceston Christian Mission Church brass band would again visit from Launceston on Good Fridays. It visited the district as early as 1887.[163]

## The Upper Liffey Baptist Chapel

Part of this Baptist "Bush Mission" venture was the erection of another chapel, this time at Upper Liffey then known as Mountain Vale when there were only bush tracks and it was hard to travel even on horse back. The foundation stone was laid on 17 March 1881 and the building opened on 21 August 1881. It was not a large structure and was in fact blown over in May the following year. Fifteen years later this Upper Liffey work flourished under Britton's leadership and it became necessary to erect a new building. Work on this replacement took place in 1902 under his command with the help mainly of local voluntary labour and it opened on 7 September with about 150 persons present; a Sunday school attached to the work had already commenced.[164]

That year the total membership of the District church was thirty and 130 children were in attendance at its Sunday schools.[165]

*2-4 Mountain Vale (Upper Liffey) Primitive Methodist Church*

At the conclusion of his time in the Bracknell District at the end of 1904, Britton passed the examination in General Theology and was ordained to the Christian ministry.[166]

The Primitive Methodists had already established their chapel at Mountain Vale in 1867 on land donated by James Green a saw miller, who wanted church services for his employees. It was capable of accommodating seventy persons. They replaced it with a better structure on 27 October 1872. This was capable of accommodating 100 persons, and erected at a cost of £100 and still in use in 1900. In the same year the Primitive Methodist Chapel at Bracknell was enlarged to double its original size. Both chapels

---

[163] Day-Star December 1887; Day-Dawn February 1902.
[164] Daily Telegraph (Launceston) 14 June 1902 p 5, 12 September 1902 p4; AB July 1930 p54.
[165] Day-Dawn May 1902.

[166] Day-Dawn January 1905. In 1995 when the tiny Blackwood Creek Chapel was no longer in Baptist hands; it was given a new lease of life and a new name: the Blackwood Creek Community Church. It was the dedication and enthusiasm of the Blackwood Creek community which brought it back to life. SB 31 January 1905 p28.

were under the care of the Longford Primitive Methodist Church.[167]

# Appendices

## Appendix 1: William Ross

Shop keeper and farmer William Ross was well known in the Bracknell district. For a good number of years he was a zealous labourer in the interests of the Baptist churches. It is said that even the Primitive Methodist Church at Mountain Vale owed its existence to his efforts.[168] His daughter played the organ at the Bracknell Primitive Methodist Church.

2-5 Memorial to William Ross which hangs in the Blackwood Creek Chapel

When the roads were bad and vehicular traffic impossible, Ross would often walk from Bracknell to Blackwood to conduct services, returning home afterwards.[169]

Practically he was the means of obtaining roads and a school in the area.[170] Described as indefatigable, and so he was to his very end, he expressed his desire to work as Colporteur at a meeting of Baptist Union Council in April 1903.[171] He was a member of The Bright Future Lodge, I.O.G.T. His life size portrait was hung in the Templars Hall.[172] The day his house burnt down in 1878, they found him half a kilometre away putting in potatoes. A few years later his boy died of severe burns from another event. Ross died on 23 April 1904 at Perth "after a long and painful illness".[173]

## Appendix 2: Colporteur and Evangelist the Rev George Lake

The Baptist Union of Tasmania, which considered colportage

---

[167] Daily Examiner (Launceston) 21 November 1874 p11; LEx 23 March 1867 p4; Daily Telegraph (Launceston) 11 September 1900 p4, 7 May 1904 p6; The Tasmanian (Tas) 15 May 1875 p4; LEx 20 August 1872 p2; only the cemetery ground remains today; Weekly Examiner (Launceston) 28 December 1872 p12; Stansall Tasmanian Methodism 1820-1975.

[168] Daily Telegraph (Launceston) 7 May 1904 p6.

[169] Daily Telegraph (Launceston) 29 April 1904 p4.

[170] Cornwall Advertiser (Tas) 21 October 1873 p2.

[171] Tasmanian Baptist Union Council Minutes p 366/11.

[172] The I.O.G.T. was the International Organisation of Good Templars founded as the Independent Order of Good Templars, a fraternal organization which is part of the temperance movement, promoting abstinence from alcohol and other drugs. LEx 2 December 1876 p5, 23 August 1877.

[173] LEx 24 October 1878 p2; The Mercury 12 August 1882 Supplement p1; Daily Telegraph (Launceston) 29 April 1904 p4

essential for the growth of the work, especially in country districts, sent £50 to the Pastors' College in 1884 for the passage of a Colporteur. In sending out the Rev George Lake, the College provided him with a well-assorted stock of books from its depot. William Gibson Senior had a major part in bringing Lake to the colony and William Gibson Junior assisted in maintaining him, providing a bequest of £100 per annum for the work.

Lake was born in 1854 at High Laver, Essex, England, the son of William Lake and Martha Saville.[174] He arrived in Launceston in January 1885 and his work extended to Blackwood Creek, Fingal, Deloraine and the North West Coast.[175] In 1885 it was reported that Lake visited forty-six townships, delivered 160 gospel addresses, sold 1,600 books, 240 Bibles and New Testaments, 466 cheap Testaments and 12,000 scripture text cards. His task was to visit the lonely dwellers in the bush and not only sell his Bibles but also if the opportunity arose "to speak to men about their souls" but he did not preach baptism.[176] It was said of him that he "was a man of little education, but sincere and enthusiastic".[177]

*2-6 George Lake and the Gospel Van*

At the end of 1888, Lake and his wife Ada transferred to Melbourne and he began work with the "Evangelisation Society of Victoria".[178] Following Lake's leaving, at first it was proposed that "a bush missionary to minister in the scattered districts of the colony" be sought. The following year William Gibson Junior offered £60 per annum for a replacement for Lake.[179]

In 1889, Lake joined the staff of the Victorian Baptist Home Mission and began work in Warracknabeal. Soon there were three places of worship in the area. On 27 April 1890, a church building called the "Crymelon Baptist Tabernacle" was opened at Crymelon Dam. The other two places were Brentwood and Peppers Plains. A church site was also secured in Warracknabeal itself. His time at Warracknabeal proved that he was impetuous and a difficult man to work with. He was at times

---

[174] Family History research by Barbara Coe.
[175] Day-Star 12 August 1884; S&T December 1884; Day-Star 27 May 1884; LEx 16 January 1885 p3, 7 April 1886 p3.
[176] LEx 18 October 1884 p1, 7 April 1886 p3.
[177] Our Yesterdays vol 1 1993 p16.

[178] Day-Star August 1889 p125; LEx 19 March 1889 p2, 27 April 1889 p6; Ovens and Murray Advertiser (Vic.) 8 June 1889 p2; The Argus (Melbourne) 9 December 1889 p8.
[179] LEx 11 April 1888 p3, 31 May 1889 p3.

an "excitable, spasmodic brother who will do nothing except spontaneously on the immediate inspiration of the Spirit". He even purchased a buggy and harness at a cost of £35, raising the money by loans from Methodists and Presbyterians which exasperated his Supervisor, the Rev John Hughes Jones. But Jones did admit that there was a basic goodness about Lake despite his irritating ways. On a hot Sunday Lake could ride for fifty miles to preach at three services. Further Ada was delicate in health and found conditions in the Wimmera very severe, and their children were often ill and another was on the way.[180]

Then in January 1892, he took up with the Rev J. B. Sneyd in the Tatura and Shepparton districts making use of the Kyabram Mechanics Institute building. In 1893 he was pastor of the Daylesford Baptist Church. In November 1898, Lake was thanked for being co-pastor of the Coburg Baptist Church.[181]

The Rev George Lake died on 8 December 1933 at Black Rock, Victoria.[182] Ada died 6 January 1943 at nearby Brighton.[183] They both were buried in the Cheltenham Cemetery. They had three daughters and two sons: two children born in Tasmania, two in Warracknabeal and the youngest in Richmond, Victoria.

## Appendix 3: William Kenner

In his forties public school teacher William Kenner brought an educated pastoral ministry to a couple of small Baptist country churches before facilitating a Baptist fellowship further afield.

Kenner, a Londoner born in 1847, arrived in Australia in 1856 with his parents.[184] They settled in Penguin, Tasmania, and by 1870 William associated with the local Congregational Church under the charge of the Rev I. B. Palfreyman and he also associated with Thomas Hainsworth who would play a leading role in the Latrobe municipality and in the Latrobe Baptist Church in later years. Hainsworth ran Temperance meetings in his Penguin schoolroom at which Kenner would speak.[185] In 1870 Kenner expressed his strong Temperance stand by placing a poem in the Launceston Examiner,

> God bless our Temperance band,
> And may't still increase,
> Like mountains may it stand
> Till drunkenness shall cease,

---

[180] Our Yesterdays vol.1 1993 p16; Wilkin p99.
[181] Kyabram Union (Vic) 15 January 1892 p2; The Coburg Leader (Vic) 19 November 1898 p1; Daylesford Advocate, Yandoit, Glenlyon and Eganstown Chronicle (Vic.) 2 April 1914 p3.
[182] The Argus (Melbourne) 11 December 1933 p1.

[183] The Argus (Melbourne) 8 January 1943 p2.
[184] South Australian Register 27 August 1856 p20.
[185] The Cornwall Chronicle (Launceston) 23 April 1870 p13; LEx 11 August 1870 p4, 26 December 1871 p2.

And drunkards give their practice
o'er, (no more.
And touch the dangerous draught
O may the drunkard see
The folly of his way,
From poison's draught now flee,
Ere drink its victim slay;
And join us with their hands and heart,
And never from our cause depart.
Strong drink has thousands slain
With its deceitful scare;
No longer may it reign
Is our united prayer.
O may intemperance have an end
Hear us, O God, our heavenly friend.[186]

Kenner was vice-band leader that year for Palfreyman's Band of Hope meetings.

In 1871 Kenner worked for the Tasmanian Education Department as a teacher at the new Castra Road School for two years prior to the Sassafras appointment.[187] The Sassafras school was conducted for a time in a church building and in late October there were "twenty youngsters of both sexes in attendance and Kenner expected that as the warmer weather came on and the roads dried, the number of scholars would increase."[188] On his application he stated that he was General Baptist. In 1875 he commenced teaching at the Sprent and Abbotsham Schools.

He lived in a "lean to" on the sunless side of the Abbotsham School which commenced with just five children from one family and he spent Monday, Wednesday and Friday mornings here, and Tuesday, Thursday and Saturday mornings at Sprent. At the Abbotsham school reunion fifty years later one old scholar said, "He was loved and esteemed by the children. Roads were few in those days, and the teacher had to ride through mud and slush." An old resident of the district wrote of Kenner,

> The spirit of Him Who made the stupendous sacrifice is the spirit that ruled the whole of the life of this first teacher of the Abbotsham School, making him kind, courteous, faithful, courageous in duty, conscientious, thorough and honorable in all his dealings. Forty years later the good little man, only shoulder high beside some who had been his scholars, found love and reverence the reward of his faithful labor, and tears of gratitude trickled down his face.

On 10 June 1875, he married Mary Emily Button whose family attended the Perth Congregational Church and of which her father, T. L. Button, was a deacon and the Sunday School Superintendent. The next day he attended the day school with his bride and presented an apple and a bun to each child. The residents of Abbotsham soon found that a half-

---

[186] LEx 21 July 1870 p3.
[187] The Tasmanian (Launceston) 2 September 1871 p13.
[188] The Cornwall Chronicle (Launceston) 31 October 1873 p3.

time school did not meet the requirements of the rapidly developing district and pressed for a full time school. It was on 1 April 1876, that the schools commenced with daily programmes, and Kenner remained on until the end of 1878.[189]

In 1879 and 1880 he taught at the Leven School near Ulverstone. Mary became a teacher's assistant at the Leven School.[190] Kenner was headmaster at Sassafras State School from 1881 to the end of 1889.

He fell foul of the Department when he conducted the morning service at Sassafras Wesleyan Chapel adjacent to the school on 2 April 1882 and was told not to do so again and he agreed but he did so again when replacing the appointed preacher, William Bonney who due to illness was unable to attend. Kenner filled this preaching appointment at short notice informing the Department of the same and came close to dismissal.[191] This was a violation of an old British law which forbade teachers from preaching within five miles of their schools, now seven miles in Tasmania. Originally this was an attempt to curtail the Scottish Covenanters. There was an earlier case when school teacher, Mr. A. C. Wellard, preached at the Dunorlan Wesleyan Church. Wellard was a preacher of many years standing in the Deloraine area, but when reproved he ceased from preaching. The Kenner case was reported in the press even as far away as South Australia. This must have been the first case of the infringement of religious liberty in the history of the Colony. The "Mercury" and "South Australian Register" took up the cause of religious liberty, and so too did the Harrington Street Baptist Church and the pastor of the Davey Street Wesleyan Church. Thanks to his openness with the Department, he was not dismissed and the archaic law fell from use. This upheaval became a victory for religious liberty in the area of servants and masters.[192]

In 1889, Kenner was moved to the Bracknell public school and soon became Home Missionary to the Bracknell Baptist Church remaining until the end of August 1898. Upon taking up the work at Bracknell, the Union Council requested that he also have oversight of the Blackwood Creek Church. In May 1898, Union Council thought fit to place Bracknell and Blackwood Creek under the Rev A. John Casely at Longford but Kenner disagreed and henceforth resigned.[193] It could have been from this incident that it was said that Kenner was not an easy man to get

---

[189] LEx 10 July 1875 p4, 7 May 1935 p5; Advocate (Burnie) 4 May 1935 p4, 20 May 1935 p6.
[190] LEx 14 June 1878 p3; Mercury (Hobart) 27 June 1879 p2.
[191] LEx 27 April 1882 p3.

[192] South Australian Advertiser 20 July 1892; Rowston, Baptists in Van Diemen's Land Part 1 p98.
[193] BU Council Minutes April 1890 p7/23, p187/24, p189/29.

on with but his farewell from the Sassafras School argues strongly against this. At the Sassafras Baptist Chapel he was Secretary of the Church and President of the Band of Hope, the latter for five years. Years later he was Sunday school Superintendent at the Perth Church.[194] William Kenner died on 10 May 1916 at sixty-nine years of age having resided in the Forth and Leven districts for a period of over fifty years. There was much regret as he was very highly respected. Mary died on 9 April 1928. [195]

## Appendix 4: Vincent George Britton

From altar boy to the "Battle-worn and battle-scarred Baptist Bishop of Tasmania", Vincent George Britton's story is exemplary.

Britton (affectionately known amongst his intimate friends as "V.G.") was born at Scotchtown, near Kempton in the midlands of Tasmania on 11 February 1866. His parents were Roman Catholics. He was instructed in all the rites and ceremonies of that Church, and became an "altar boy, serving at the celebration of mass". At the early age of thirteen he left home to make his own way in the world.

He became a "half-deck boy" on the ship "The Islander". His duty was to look after the quarters of the boat steerers and harpoonists and his adventures took him as far as Java although most of the whaling expeditions were carried out off the coast of New South Wales. He was at sea under whaling conditions for some years.

The family had removed to Dysart, then known as Constitution Hill where an Englishman named Speak, a Particular Baptist and former member of Harrington Street Baptist Chapel, Hobart, had built a small chapel which still stands. Young Vincent was occasionally attracted to these services and so came in touch with Baptists.

Wesley Bligh picks up his story and gives an account of his conversion,

> He proceeded to Launceston where he entered into business as a butcher. During a visit to the city by the Rev George Grubb, M.A., a (Keswick) missioner from England, who was engaged in evangelistic work, he attended some of the meetings held in the Albert Hall. During the course of a powerful address on "The man without a wedding garment", he was led to make a definite decision for Christ. "I felt", he said, "that I was the man without the wedding garment."
>
> He was baptised by the Rev A. J. Clark and joined the Launceston Baptist Tabernacle. He became a teacher in the Sunday school and a worker in the Launceston City Mission. Here he came into

---

[194] The Colonist 21 September 1889 p20; Day-Dawn February 1902; LEx 18 September 1889 p2.

[195] NWA&EBT 11 May 1916 p2, 13 May 1916 p2, 12 April 1928 p2.

*2-7 Band of Hope Member's Card*

contact with the Rev Robert Marshall, then City Missioner.

The City Mission was the centre of great activity at that time. Bands of Hope, teas, evangelistic services and special meetings for sailors were among its many aspects of service. He was engaged in this work for about seven years.

About 1898, he felt a desire to enter the ministry. He was, at this time, a married man with two children. He made application to the Council of the Baptist Union of Tasmania and was accepted for service as a Home Missionary.[196]

What Bligh didn't note was that Britton's parents were former convicts. They were married in 1853 in the Catholic Church at Kempton, where young Vincent was christened in 1866.[197]

Now in his late twenties in Launceston, he relished the opportunity to be involved in the Temperance Band of Hope meetings. These meetings gave the opportunity to speak publicly and earnestly of the things that mattered to him; that was their attraction. Over five years he associated with six Band of Hope Societies and they included the Sandhill Church Band of Hope. This church was part of the Presbyterian Chalmers Church circuit. Then there was the Lawrence Vale Band of Hope. The Lawrence Vale Church in South Launceston was a preaching station of the Launceston Wesleyan Circuit. He chaired the Paterson Street and Invermay Wesleyan Church Bands of Hope. In Launceston there was also the Presbyterian St Andrew's Band of Hope, the Christian Mission Church of Henry Reed Band of Hope, the Chalmer's Presbyterian Church Band of Hope, the Launceston Temperance Hall Band of Hope, the Congregational Churches of Christ Church Band of Hope and Tamar Street Band of Hope. He would attend more than one Society some weeks at the end of his day's employment, but his greatest allegiance was to that of the Launceston City Mission Band of Hope under City Missioner Marshall as Bligh notes.[198] Among those who gathered there at the City Mission

---

[196] Bligh.

[197] From descendent Bruce Walkley Leichhardt, NSW. The carved sternboard of the whaler Islander on which young Vincent ran away to sea at the age of thirteen is on display in the Maritime Museum of Tasmania in Hobart.

[198] LEx 6 May 1893 p4, 19 July 1894 p4, 12 October 1894 p5, 20 May 1896 p4; Daily Telegraph (Launceston) 29 May 1896 p2, 7 August 1896 p2.

Band of Hope was Miss Mary Ann (known as Susan) Lamb of the Launceston Tabernacle, later missioner for the Launceston Tabernacle at its outreach in Invermay known as the "Inveresk Baptist Mission".

In 1898, Britton had some doubts when he accepted the position offered of a Home Mission pastor to the Bracknell and Blackwood churches; he doubted that he was capable of fulfilling the call. He wrote to the Secretary of the Council of the Baptist Union of Tasmania, the Rev John Edwin Walton,

> It gives me great pain to have to withdraw from the position accepted by me as missionary at Bracknell/Blackwood. I feel I would do wrong in God's sight and hinder his work in that place if I finally took up the work. I feel I am not competent to teach Christianity. I have never had any experience in such work. I have devoted my time to Evangelistic work, and am certain that I would be trying to teach those that could teach me.
>
> I have also family reasons for withdrawing which, if I did not consider, would put me in a false position ... I am grieved at letting it go so far, as it may cause you great inconvenience, but, it is better not to start when I have no hope of success.
>
> I feel condemned in having accepted the offer. I do hope you will consider it as charitably as you can, and forgive any trouble that you may be put to. God shows me that I must be content in the work as I am and I would do wrong in going out when I ought not. I will tell Pastor Wainwright all about it and must bear all responsibility. I had made arrangements to leave here but my conscience condemns me for it. I have not been educated enough and I did wrong in applying for work to the council. I hope you will not think harshly of my actions, but will see it as I do.

*2-8 Typical source for poems and short stories used at Band of Hope meetings and the Gospel Van*

Two weeks after writing the letter of resignation, he had a change of heart. He had been assured of the correctness of his move and he wrote again,

> I am sorry that I let the Devil have even the semblance of a victory over me. As soon as God had shown me that I was to take the work, Satan commenced and sought to prevent me from going on with it. I wrote to you almost in desperation so greatly had

Satan upset my mind. But thanks be to God, He has given me the victory. The path is plainly set before me, and I have been taught my first great lesson, upon the need of perfect and implicit obedience to God's will. Oh, how I have been sifted, tossed and troubled, but Jesus speaks, Peace be still. I interviewed Pastor Wainwright and he could not see anything but the obstacles of Satan in it. I do feel my entire weakness, but God is greater than I. Pray for me. Oh that God may strengthen me in this work. I do feel my need of Divine Assistance and only in His Power can I dare go forth.

## Conclusion

At the Education session of the Baptist Assembly in 1944[199], a champion for a trained ministry presented himself in the person of the old stalwart, the Rev V. G. Britton. With so many extra-mural[200] men in its ministerial ranks, there were oft-times some controversy on the question of ministerial training when the Education Committee presented its report. On this occasion, somebody pointed to the great work accomplished by its veteran brother during his long ministry in the State without the benefit of a ministerial training, whereupon Britton got to his feet and made an impassioned appeal for the fullest possible education for every man entering the ministry. Britton said that he would refuse to go into the work now as ill-equipped as he entered originally. He added that the whole standard of secular education had advanced so far over the last half-century that every minister should be given the very best training available. Sadly today some still think they don't need to be trained and subsequently have little time for serious theological reflection, saying "What's the use of it anyway?" Anti-liberalism, doggedness in a number of churches on biblical inerrancy, wide contentment with an untrained ministry and local preachers can still be said to be part of our identity as Tasmanian Baptists, agreeing with George Barna, the American church commentator, "seminarians ... are taught how to exegete Scripture and teach ... but they are not synonymous with leadership."[201] Yet we are challenged to a higher standard of education for the ministry, for more business-like methods from the leaders of our churches, for more self-denial on our part for the outreach, local and overseas, for missionary enterprise. The work is not ours; it is that of our Lord.

---

[199] AB 7 November 1944 p2.

[200] Extra-mural indicated a course of study for people who are not full-time members at a university or other educational establishment.

[201] Barna, George, "The Second Coming of the Church" (Word Publishing 1998) p27. Biblical inerrancy is the belief that the Bible "is without error or fault in all its teaching". Exegesis is a critical explanation or interpretation of a text.

# Chapter 3 Bracknell Baptist Church

## Introduction

In contrast to present day social life, early settlers in the towns like Bracknell had no outside entertainment. Indeed, as one settler in the small town of Yolla remarked, "There was nowhere to go and we were too busy creating our livelihood."[202] As a settlement developed so did social life which was mainly centred on the churches. The common bond of daily hardship was lessened by opportunities to exchange ideas and share experiences, happy or otherwise.

At first in Bracknell folk gathered at the Primitive Methodist Chapel. This Methodist work began with the Longford minister, the Rev William H. Walton, preaching in a barn from 1863. As the congregation grew a foundation stone for their chapel was laid on 14 October 1864 and the chapel was open by Christmas. Yet by 1876 "unsectarian" Gospel services were held in the Good Templars Hall every Sunday, being available for any Christian worker "without regard to sect or denomination".[203]

## Baptist Beginnings

The permanent Baptist work in Bracknell began as an outreach from the Longford Baptist Church in 1884,[204] and it was initiated by both local William Ross, and the Pastor of the Longford Baptist Church, Harry Wood. They began by conducting services in the Bracknell Temperance Hall, the Good Templars Hall as it was known at the time. The foundation stone for the present Bracknell Baptist Church building was laid in August 1884 by Wood's wife, Elizabeth; the building yet another gift from William Gibson Senior of Native Point, Perth. Even though it was a simple weatherboard construction above a stone base, it was deemed a Tabernacle and was officially opened on 8 November 1885.[205]

The church was conducting a Sunday school prior to the opening

*3-1 Bracknell Primitive Methodist Chapel*

---

[202] Pegus, Margaret, Yolla – The First Century p18.
[203] LEx 21 July 1885 p4, 17 June 1876 p5.
[204] Day-Star May 1887; Report of the BUT Conference of 27 May 1884.
[205] Daily Telegraph (Launceston) 11 Nov 1885 p3.

of the new building. The first official anniversary of the Sunday school was held in November 1887 with about forty children present and the collections for the day "consisted principally of the smallest silver coin of the realm" which was to be expected.[206]

## The Rev George Lake and Teacher William Kenner

The Rev George Lake, Baptist colporteur and evangelist, designated Home Missionary, was given oversight of the work and that of Blackwood Creek in 1887.[207]

Home missionary, William Kenner, followed Lake in the oversight of the two Churches commencing 1 June 1890 but after eight years in August 1898 he resigned and Home Missioner Vincent G. Britton was appointed in his stead.[208] The Bracknell–Blackwood Creek Church was constituted in November 1889 with twenty-eight members, 138 scholars in the Sunday school, a week-night meeting, and a Bible class, as well as a monthly Temperance meeting.[209]

## Home Missioner Vincent G. Britton

Vincent G. Britton who had been assistant pastor at the Launceston Tabernacle from 1891 to 1893 arrived at Bracknell with his wife, Ida, and their two children in September 1898. The Home Mission Committee which was formed in 1895 had directed him there. To begin with he faced small congregations.

During his time in the Bracknell Circuit he purchased his trademark Magic Lantern, the forerunner of today's digital projector, to illustrate his lectures and so began his decades of entertaining and educating people with his commercial slides. With this innovative instrument he became a regular visitor to churches and other public places, even the Launceston Benevolent Asylum. The use of these illustrated lectures had

*3-2 Bracknell Baptist Tabernacle*

---

[206] LEx 21 April p3.

[207] LEx 9 July 1887 p3; 14 November 1887 p2; for George Lake's contribution to the Bracknell Church and for his life story see chapter 2, the Blackwood Creek Church.

[208] Day-Star May 1891 p452; AB 29 September 1898.

[209] SB May 1900; Day-Dawn June 1900.

a drawing appeal at the time and their use would continue until his retirement in 1934. The subjects could be as diverse as the life of the Baptist preacher the Rev C. H. Spurgeon, views of London and the Middle East landmarks, the evils of gambling and the temptation of strong drink.[210] In 1904 he became a member of the Launceston photographic club where members would display their recent homemade lantern slides. Such camera clubs offered a support network of enthusiasts' facilities and equipment. Part of the evenings would be spent in judging the lantern slide competitions. Through the club Britton would have been given a wide choice in subject matter to purchase.

But sometimes there were problems in the use of the Magic Lantern in churches. The first problem is that they could explode and when they did people went for the doors.[211] Then some people would object to their use as once happened when organs were introduced into church services. At Deloraine Baptist Church discussion arose as to whether an offer to exhibit magic lantern slides be accepted by the church or not and the decision was made that it was not advisable to accept the offer. "One brother withdrew from church membership because of this decision" but by 1894, the magic lantern was acceptable.

With Britton's appointment Bracknell became the first official Tasmanian Baptist Home Mission station. Within a few months of his appointment there were some remarkable results with enlarged congregations and the undertaking of necessary maintenance. The floor of Bracknell's Tabernacle was renewed and the roof resheeted; a large vestry was also added. Within eighteen months he baptised nineteen people in the Liffey River. A baptistry was finally installed in the Church in July 1903. Britton carried out deputation work for the Home Mission and was seen by the Bracknell folk as "their missionary".[212]

Bligh told of Britton's "deep and tender sympathy with the poor" and of his "intensely practical approach to all life's problems." In the Bracknell Church an easy rocking-chair was placed near the platform "where invalids or convalescents could sit in comfort, and mothers with restless babies have the opportunity of soothing them!"[213] Bligh wrote,

> On one occasion (when) he was distributing Christian literature to homes in Bracknell, he called at the home of a bigoted Irish Roman Catholic woman who

---

[210] Daily Telegraph (Launceston) 17 February 1904 p4, 20 October 1902 p2.
[211] LEx 18 November 1904 p4; National Advocate (Bathurst, NSW) 28 April 1908 p2.
[212] SB 4 May 1899 p97, 3 May 1900; AB 14 July 1903; 3 May 1900; Day-Dawn September 1900.
[213] AB 18 November 1947 p1.

manifested a profound resentment. Later he heard that this woman's son was ill and called to inquire whether he could render any assistance. He was met at the door by an irate woman who ordered him to leave and finished her invectives by spitting in his face. Quietly wiping his face, Britton retired. It was late at night, but he saddled his horse and rode fourteen miles to Longford to procure the necessary medicine for the sick man. When he returned in the small hours of the morning, he received a very different reception. A much chagrined and humbled woman profusely apologised and thereafter became one of his ardent friends."[214]

While services were already being conducted at the Upper Liffey Chapel, regular services were commenced at the Cluan State School. In later years a Church would be built.[215]

In May 1899, the Launceston Examiner ran a report on the successful Baptist ministry of Robert Walker, eldest son of Charles Walker of Cressy who went to study at Spurgeon's College and who had recently taken up the pastorate of the Broadway Baptist Church, Chesham. This English Church experienced a revival not long after his arrival.[216]

In November 1899, the Bracknell Church was constituted with twenty members. Soon a new stable was erected and a Sunday school recommenced. In 1903, the former hotel next door to the church, on the corner of Louise and Elizabeth Streets, was purchased by Joshua T. Soundy of the Hobart Baptist Church for use as the Bracknell manse and then was sold onto the Church for £100 less than he bought it.[217]

## Robert Steel

Britton was succeeded in 1903 by Robert Steel who was willing to work for the Home Mission at Bracknell for £35 in his first year when the going rate was £2 a week; the offer was

*3-3 Bracknell Church Manse at the corner of Elizabeth and Louise Streets*

---

[214] Bligh.

[215] Cluan is a settlement at the foot of the Cluan Tiers, at the edge of some of the richest agricultural country in the Island; HM Council Minutes p 345/21 meeting April 1902.

[216] LEx 17 May 1899 p7.

[217] HM Council Minutes p248/24, p312/31, meeting October 1901; AB 29 November 1900; SB 10 May 1904 p114.

accepted.[218] Three years later, in June 1906, Ernest Albert Salisbury, who had been previously been assisting at the Christian Mission Church in Launceston, was appointed assistant to Steel but remained only for three months; he was soon sent on to the Ulverstone Home Mission work under the supervision of the Rev James Palmer of Latrobe. At the end of his time at Ulverstone, Salisbury returned to Bracknell for the year 1910 and then he was sent on to Wynyard.

In April 1906, the Bracknell Church held its first "Annual Flower and Produce Sale of Goods Show" and this became an annual event for the residents in the district. It was held at the local Bracknell State School to begin with and later in the local Town Hall. It continued for near twenty years. The proceeds were used to support the Baptist foreign and home missions.[219]

In 1906, as part of the Baptist work in the district, construction began on the erection of a church just ten kilometres away in rural Cluan. To begin with the church fellowship met in the local Cluan State school room with Harry Ratcliff and deaconess Miss Mary Ann (Susan) Lamb both from the Launceston Tabernacle, and others taking services.

Mr. H. Masters was appointed contractor of the ten by six metre structure while Steel himself contributed as "the foreman and the architect". Mrs. J. Hummel of the Hobart Baptist Church sent in £10, the same Mrs. Hummel who left the princely sum of £1,000 to the Australian Baptist Missionary Society on her death. James Leonard, who originally offered a sheep, gave £1 instead. Susan Lamb and her Bible class also sent in £1.[220]

*3-4 Cluan Baptist Chapel with Rev Albert Butler and Mrs Dunkley*

In 1906 the Baptist State paper, the "Day Star", reported,

> By October, the building was in the course of erection. Frank Page and six out of his eleven sons were part of the working bee. Joining them were Mr. L. Hall, Mr. N. Gibson and Tom Lockhart, the last with "his fine

---

[218] HM Council Minutes p 368/19 dated April 1903.

[219] The prize winners are listed for the first couple of years, see LEx 20 April 1905 p3, 10 April 1906 p3.
[220] Day-Dawn May 1906.

pair of bullocks and block and tackle".

They put in a day's work grubbing and clearing the ground ready for the building, with Steel in command. The youngest of the working bee was fourteen, while the oldest, Mrs. Page was seventy years, and she did more work than any other man. It was just like a picnic, and didn't we enjoy it, though Mr Steel did not the next day. He was so stiff with using the axe and the pick, but (he) is to have a go a little more at the foundations."

Over the weeks ahead, Mr. Cummins carted the stone for the foundations, George Cummins fenced the ground for free, Mr. C. Gibson carted the sand, J & T. Gunn of Launceston donated the lime, Mr. E. Masters put in the lime with the assistance of Steel who mixed and carried the mortar. James Leonard gave six fir trees and offered the church half an acre of more land. James Lockhart (brother to Tom) gave the church a front porch. Mr. Edward Masters built the footings gratis. Mr. F. Smith donated a large gate.

For the opening, Mrs. Cummins gave two offering boxes, Mrs. L. Heazlewood donated a pulpit Bible and Mr. L. Hall donated the hymn books. Miss E. Bird lent the church her organ for twelve months.[221]

The building was opened officially on Sunday 25 November 1906 with a customary tea meeting held the following Wednesday. The "Day Star" continued,

> The weather was perfect for the opening day. People from all over the surrounding district attended and young folk arrived on their bikes. When asked where they were going to, the cyclists replied, "to the opening of the Cluan Baptist Church!" Many at Whitemore wanted to come but there was no conveyance until James Leonard came to the rescue with horses and a wagon.

It was a wet day for the Wednesday tea meeting but the weather did not stop twenty-one visitors coming from the Henry Reed Mission Church in Launceston with the express purpose of entertaining the guests that evening.

The fund-raising continued the following Wednesday. It commenced with the Page brothers playing the Liffey Baptists at cricket; the Page boys won. Races and "lollie scrambles" for the children followed. Following the evening meal, a concert concluded the day.

Early in the New Year the Cluan Church held a sale of gifts at Weedon's store in Glenmore to reduce the debt. Readers of the "Day

---

[221] Day-Dawn October 1906.

Star" were asked to send in "fancy work, fowls, geese, turkeys, ducks, sheep, produce, silver and gold, or coppers – even the smallest donation will be thankfully received." The fund raisers' motto was, "Ask and it shall be given."[222] Good stewardship continued. Within six years the building was debt free.

A couple of years later Steel himself added a vestry to the building. The Band of Hope meetings became a feature of church life. Steel was assisted in preaching by visiting speakers from the Launceston Baptist Tabernacle; its Pastor, the Rev Stephen Sharp was his supervisor. An appeal was made for a trap "which is sorely needed" and a widow sent in 2s 6d from her earnings at the washtub. The cost would be about £17 and within six months £9 was in hand.[223]

Many years later Ron Churchill related just how colourful a person Steel was,

> One time some young fellows were playing up (at the Bracknell Church). He told them to stop or he would put them out. Evidently they tested his sincerity for they continued, so Robert kept his word. One young fellow ran out of the church with Robert in hot pursuit. He chased him down the street and then the young fellow thought, "If I run through the hotel he won't chase me." So he ran through the hotel - with Robert after him! The youth jumped over a fence out the back of the hotel. He knew what was there and jumped well out, but Robert jumped over - and into a ditch of water over his knees! That stopped the little chase, but the next day Robert visited the boy's parents for lunch. Steel told me he did not say anything to the boy's parents as the boy was sitting at the table shaking, so he reckoned he was punished enough! Apparently another chase occurred at the Sassafras church after a Harvest Home sale of goods.[224]

Great assistance was given to the Cluan work for over forty years by Theodore Ernest West and his wife Charlotte. West was a most acceptable lay preacher and a man of irreproachable character. His assuring manner, his charitable disposition, and his sterling Christian qualities, won for him the esteem of the whole district. As a girl Charlotte attended the York Street Baptist Chapel, Launceston, under the ministry of the Rev Henry Dowling by whom her father and mother had been married, and where her father had been Sunday School Superintendent and her mother organist for many years. Later, Charlotte attended the Memorial Baptist Church, Launceston, where she met and married Theodore, the Rev George

---

[222] Day-Dawn April 1907.
[223] Day-Dawn March 1908, October 1906, April 1907, November 1906.

[224] Hemsley, Jennifer Around the Country Circuits, p89.

Soltau officiating. Charlotte was organist at Cluan for years.

At the beginning of 1909, after three years ministry at Blackwood Creek, Bracknell, Liffey and Cluan, Steel was transferred to the Home Mission Church at Wynyard. At the farewell at Cluan the congregation all joined in singing, "For he's a jolly good fellow" and hoped that "the day is not far distant when they will see their Pastor back again." At Bracknell Britton "spoke in the highest terms of the generous qualities and Christian character of Mr Steel" and he was presented with a volume of "Wright's Biblical Treasury and Concordance".[225]

*3-5 Robert Steel with his mother & sisters*

## Appendix: Robert Steel

By the time Robert Steel had reached normal retiring age, he had spent nearly thirty-three years of his working life in the Baptist ministry in Tasmania. Yet he still continued on in the official ministry with his hands-on approach. From an early age the Church had become dear to him as he gladly participated in its many activities. From the year he commenced in the pastoral position, it would be thirty-five years before this Association acknowledged him in ordination and when it did probably few churchmen were better known in Northern Tasmania.

Robert Steel was born in 1875, one of a family of eleven children. He was eight years of age when his family arrived in Hobart from Leeds Yorkshire, England. The family soon moved to Launceston. He learned the carpentry trade from his father and together they worked on many Launceston projects, among them the installation of cross-arms on the poles along the middle of Brisbane Street that were to carry the first electricity lines to the town. He attended the Memorial Mission Church Sunday school, and earned a reputation of being one of the bad boys but the church became dear to him; it was his spiritual birthplace. He became a keen worker for the church and taught at Sunday school; sometimes he preached.[226]

He was a keen participant in the Church's monthly and lengthy Temperance Band of Hope meetings, sometimes acting as chairman. At twenty-six years of age Steel approached the Baptist Union Council indicating that he was willing to work with its Home

---

[225] Day-Dawn March 1908; Daily Telegraph (Launceston) 19 January 1909 p7, 27 May 1902 p3

[226] LEx 29 October 1907 p6, 26 February 1901 p7.

Mission. For reasons yet unknown, he went to live in the tin mining town of Derby in North East Tasmania and took an active part in local community affairs and was preacher at church services.[227]

## Conclusion

As we see from the text Home mission work meant supporting small groups of denominational loyalists in new settlements. Most denominations had their own Home Mission where pastoral aspirants could try their wings. Early in the piece Tasmanian Baptists saw the value of such work. Its aims were to establish new churches, missions and conduct Sunday schools, to carry on evangelistic work and to publish and circulate Baptist literature. Through it there was the romance of the exploration of new districts

As early as 1900 it was said of a Home Missionary that he "had to be made of soldier stuff, and be upheld by Divine love and the omnipotent Spirit, to hold on his way and keep his appointments at all seasons, and spread sunshine among his people."[228]

The Home Missioner had to learn on the job especially at places like Yolla which enjoyed the distinction of being "God's country training ground". Their ministries at these Home Mission churches seldom lasted for more than a year as they were there to gain pastoral experience before College training. Lacking in academic skills as they were would have been to his flock's benefit as rural Christians are generally conservative theologically and cling to traditional ways. Likely, the young apprentice would have just regurgitated what he had learned from the preacher of his home church. As Graeme Garrett wrote, "People want their pastor to be like them; not too far above or below, not too far ahead or behind."[229] Yet for the Home Mission recruit his first year would either make or break him.

In 1909, the first Home Missionary Superintendent was the Rev Frederic Joseph Dunkley. His supervision was needed as this work was taking place away from suburban areas. He held a small church and was paid jointly by that church, the Home Mission and the Association's Sustentation Fund. In 1913, Dunkley was followed by the Rev Vincent George Britton. During their time outstations were opened and as a result a steady stream of Tasmanian young men began training for the ministry. Important centres such as Devonport began as a Home Mission Church. In time, struggling churches were brought under the wings of the Home Mission. Dependent as they were on the Association's support, they

---

[227] LEx 21 June 1901 p4; HM Council Minutes p 268/1 dated Oct 1900; Daily Telegraph (Launceston) 28 October 1902 p3; The Mercury 7 September 1903 p6; LEx 13 March 1905 p7.

[228] Australian Baptist 29 November 1900.

[229] Paper, "Church Growth: Some Questions"

received financial aid but in return they submitted control to the Home Mission. Many of the Home Mission churches had numerous outstations. It was hoped that these outstations would supplement the necessary staff for both our home and overseas fields and they did. By 1926, the Home Mission Churches had twenty-eight outstations.

Three decades on in the 1950s, the long term Home Mission churches finally found financial self-sufficiency. It took Deloraine eighty-four years since its constitution to do so and Latrobe a similar number. Although these churches were now only receiving relatively small subsidies, their dependence finally ceased.

For some Home Mission churches the financial support from the Association became addictive and year by year their growth was minimal so much so that these churches depleted the Association's coffers without benefit. It was not until the late 1970s that the Association dispensed with the Home Mission all together.

Summing up, even with the enormous surges of the 1880s and the 1950s, the pattern of our denominational growth has not really changed. There has been a steady growth but it has been slow and our growth more often than not has not kept pace with the growth in the population. It appears that when the economy is buoyant, our Tasmanian Baptist church membership grows but when hard times come, the work stagnates. Our fortunes appeared linked with the economy and so we appear destined to remain a union of small churches, especially outside the four main population centres. The Rev D.F. Mitchell, who pastored the Hobart Tabernacle in the mid-1920s, said that the Baptist Home Mission achievement will always be the result of heroic sacrifice. Citywide Church in Hobart and a number of other churches, illustrate this truth. Churches in the Island State owe much to these pioneer ministers who spared not themselves in order to minister to the people and to gather them into fellowship. The work also owed much to men of substance, such as business man Joshua T. Soundy who gave liberally for the erection of church buildings and the support of the preachers.

# Chapter 4 The Christian Mission Church

## Introduction

The old Christian Mission Church sanctuary at Launceston, an historic centre of evangelistic zeal, is one of the most capacious and stately of churches in Australia. Names connected to it in the past are now half forgotten: Dr. Grattan Guinness, and his son, Dr. Harry Guinness, Daniel Walter Hiddleston, George Grubb, Mrs. Baeyertz and Pastor George Saltau to name just some. It was in this church, too, that George Craike commenced in his youth as an assistant to Joseph Tanner Piercy.

Wesleyan Missioner Henry Reed (1806-1880) returned to Tasmania from England in December 1873 full of religious zeal. He began street preaching and used his wealth gained through whaling, sealing and general trading to purchase for a mission, Parr's Hotel in Wellington Street, Launceston. He had the shed long used as a skittle alley behind the hotel renovated and installed with seats and thus the Christian Mission Church became a reality in July 1876. In 1877, a year or two after purchasing the property in Wellington Street, Reed ungracefully resigned as a member of Paterson Street Church to which he had given £500 for its erection as he objected to the collection being taken up after his sermon because he wanted monies merely placed in a collection box. He was also troubled by other matters such as the church's administration and thus he felt bound to carry on his mission work in his own way "according to the light that was given him". Further, Reed regarded infant baptism as unscriptural, convinced of baptism by immersion.[230] Reed replaced the skittle alley with a brick building, opening it on 6 June 1880. He himself preached the first sermon sitting in an armchair because he was too ill to stand. He died on 10 October 1880 and henceforth his widow, Margaret,

*4-1 Christian Mission Church Launceston with the two storey Parr's Hotel on the left*

---

[230] Hudson Fysh, 'Henry Reed (1806-1880)', Australian Dictionary of Biography, vol. 2, 1788-1850, pp. 371-372; Hovenden, 'Methodism in Launceston 1864-1890', BA Honours thesis, University of Tasmania, Hobart, 1968, p13, pp48-57; LEx 11 July 1876, p2.

then sixty-four years of age, took charge of the work.

## The Rev John Henry Shallberg

Late in December 1879 the Rev John Henry Shallberg was appointed Pastor of the Church, soon to be known as the Christian Mission Church. Shallberg never held back from working with the other churches and their pastors in their shared concerns for the town. He also lectured under the auspices of the Tasmanian Teetotal Society.[231] But he lasted barely seven months in the Pastorate resigning because he felt he could not maintain an independent position on account of interference with his work; he was not happy being a subordinate with Margaret Reed, it was unsettling for him. As a newspaper correspondent recalled,

> I remember the same trouble arising at a church in one of the country districts some considerable time ago, where either two or three pastors resigned through the interference with their duties by a wealthy patron, and if I remember rightly a sort of conference was held, at which a distinct understanding was arrived at, and peace reigned afterwards.[232]

Following Shalberg's leaving, Welsh evangelist Emilia Louise Baeyertz held a mission at the Church accompanied some evenings by the Rev Alfred James Clark of the West Melbourne Baptist Church.[233] During his life Henry Reed encouraged her in the work.[234] A reporter from the Launceston Examiner attended one evening and made his report,

*4-2 Evangelist Emilia Baeyertz*

> Mrs. Baeyertz is a lady of prepossessing manner and appearance, while her voice is soft and musical, and her articulation clear and emphatic. Her discourse was most eloquent and persuasive, and as she warmed with her subject, and related thrilling and affecting narratives, she carried her audience with her, and loud sobs could be heard from various parts of the church.[235]

---

[231] LEx 6 December 1879 p2, 5 March 1880 p2.
[232] The Mercury 6 July 1880 p3.
[233] LEx 12 February 1881 p2.
[234] THRA P & P 49/3 "Mrs Baeyertz, the "Jewish Lady evangelist from Melbourne" by Elizabeth Wilson.
[235] LEx 28 June 1886 p2.

## The Rev Daniel Walter Hiddlestone

In 1881, during the time of the weatherboard pavilion, Margaret Reed appointed the singing preacher, the Rev Daniel Walter Hiddlestone of Melbourne, to replace Shallberg. Hiddlestone's wife and two children soon followed.[236] Hiddlestone, a preacher with well thought out sermons delivered "with much pathos and power", was described by a journalist as,

*4-3 Henry Reed*

> an extempore preacher with a forceful and earnest delivery, in a voice which though not particularly powerful is sufficient to fill the Pavilion without effort. His language is extremely simple, but considerable care is exercised in the choice of words most appropriate to the concise, but full expression of the idea he intends to convey. His power of description is of high order ... His sermons are strictly confined to gospel lines.[237]

By May 1882, the Christian Mission Church, in partnership with the Rev Robert Williamson of the Perth Baptist Church, was conducting fortnightly Gospel services in the Evandale Council Chambers with a congregation of about forty.[238] The following year they erected an "Evangelistic Hall". For its erection the Baptists bought the land, while Margaret Reed paid for building. Yet by 1887 services had reverted to the Evandale Council Chambers.[239]

Further, Hiddlestone worked closely with the Baptists when it came to conducting evangelistic missions. It could be said that he and Harry Wood were inseparable in such ventures.[240]

Henry Glennie, aka "Silverpen", a feature columnist with the Launceston Examiner who was supportive of the temperance cause, recorded his impressions of Hiddlestone when he heard him sing at the Deloraine Baptist Tabernacle,

> Then a sweet singer of Israel, Pastor Hiddlestone, from Launceston, sang accompanying himself on the organ - a most plaintive touching song, "Where

---

[236] Weekly Times (Vic) 14 May 1881 p22; The Argus (Melbourne) 21 June 1881 p4.
[237] LEx 5 May 1887 p3, 10 May 1887 p3.
[238] The Tasmanian (Launceston) 27 May 1882 p21.
[239] LEx 26 July 1883 p4, 20 October 1883 p2, 26 October 1883 p3 and 27 October 1883 p2; The Mercury (Hobart) 30 May 1887 p 3.
[240] LEx 18 July 1884 p4.

is my wandering boy tonight?" I could see the mothers all over the congregation wiping away the silent tear. The song, so simple and so sympathetic, touched the heart-strings of many a mother as she thought of her dear boy away from home. Go on singing the gospel Pastor Hiddlestone; there is real power in gospel singing. Preaching is good, and often effective, but give me the Songs of Zion, sung with sweetest sympathy, echoing and re-echoing in the heart - resurrecting old thoughts of childhood and innocence - vibrating like an Eolian harp - down to the very bottom of the soul, and forcing the devil out at the bayonet's point. "I like the singing," said one to me, "it does me good, like." "I feel better for that song," said another; "Wasn't it natural - the poor mother anxious about her absent boy." "My poor mother," said a third, "no doubt often thinks of me," and then the tears down the cheek of the big burly fellow told the effect it had on him. "If I only got a poor sinner to think and feel," said a venerable divine, "my work of getting at his heart is easy."

4-4 Dan Hiddlestone

"Silverpen" continued, this time attending to Hiddlestone's preaching,

> Pastor Hiddlestone spoke with great earnestness and power. It would seem that this "herald" is used at the meetings as the clincher of the rivets. He does the winding-up business, and always does it well. Full of illustrations, his addresses are peculiarly telling, his manner pleasing, and the arguments used by him indisputable. His farewell song last evening was one of those musical gems not to be forgotten, breathing a spirit at sympathetic lovableness that took the audience by storm. As he concluded the tears fell fast; young and old seemed to feel the holy influence pervading the meeting.

With Hiddlestone who had come with his brass band of ten performers to Deloraine, "Silverpen" concluded,

> There seemed to be no proselytising; no urging persons to join the ranks of the Baptists, or join the Tabernacle, but the simple asking all those out of Christ to accept Him as their Saviour, and be at peace, and the kindly invitation to the members of all the other churches to assist by their prayers the work of "soul

## The Christian Mission Church

saving". I know there are those who laugh and jeer at any special effort to do good, if not done in orthodox fashion; but when we hear, as I have done, at Deloraine of men giving up their evil ways - renouncing the devil and all his works - drunkards saved from the curse of strong drink, husbands and wives reunited, and living only to do good, young men openly professing to have taken the life offered to them by believing in Jesus, and hallowing by their lives and conversation that a great change has passed upon them. These effects following the "Royal Proclamation" issued by these "Heralds of the cross" are in themselves evidence that their labours have not been in vain and that they have not spent their strength for naught. I like to see and hear of "signs following", the special efforts of God's servants. I don't care a "red cent" who they are or what they are called, but I confess I do not admire the old devilish spirit of narrow-minded jealous bigotry exhibited by other professedly Christian churches, because these Tabernacle folk are successful in their efforts, giving hearing to the deaf, strength of limb to the lame and halt, and eyesight to the spiritually blind, and with this intent are using somewhat outré (or so it may appear) means in order to accomplish their ends.[241]

Most churches at the time had their own regular "Gospel Temperance and Band of Hope" meetings and the Christian Mission Church was no exception. These churches sought to bring the Gospel and temperance together because, as they saw it, temperance depended not so much on human will but divine grace thus making temperance the agent of a man's redemption.

The Christian Mission Church had been conducting services and a Sunday school at Ravenswood for a number of years and the school attracted a good number of children. Finally, its new building was opened on Sunday 25 March 1883. On the next evening 200 men, women and children sat down to "tea". Their Church Band played for the occasion. The 10 x 5 metre building, set on stone foundation walls with its fireplace, nine windows and two doors, cost £80, and the fencing and out-offices added £20 more. By the end of the extended weekend, a debt of only £25 remained.[242]

Just after Hiddlestone's arrival, a weatherboard structure, "the Pavilion", with seating for nearly 1000, was erected on the Wellington Street site by covering the chapel-yard and providing seating; it opened on 23 July 1882. From then on an average of 600 would regularly worship there on Sunday

---

[241] The North Coast Standard (Latrobe) 14 October 1891.

[242] The Tasmanian (Launceston) 31 March 1883 p346.

mornings. In the evenings it was so full that chairs were placed down the aisles and then still "hundreds were still unable to obtain admittance."[243]

"Silverpen" visited Christian Mission Church in October 1882 and spoke of the Pavilion and the service, the entrance of the Pavilion being off Wellington Street. He began by saying that the entrance was "more like the carriage right-of-way to a hotel than the 'Come in and be saved' road into a Mission Church".

Inside "Silverpen" found a modern walk-about-pulpit with its cabinet organ and above were the words "Jesus only. Mighty to save" in large letters. He wrote,

> What cheerful news thought I to the poor heavy laden sinner dropping in, out of, it may be curiosity, or a wish to pass an hour away on the Sunday morning, the day of rest to all Christian nations. All round the building appropriate texts of Scripture are displayed. Streams of decently-dressed women and men came pouring in till the front part of the hall was well filled; then the school children filed in, and before the beginning of the service the place was crowded, forms along the aisle assisting in the stowing away of the people. ... many there were not church goers all their lives.

He noted,

> Mission Halls now-a-days are in towns and cities I have visited, filled with too respectable a looking class of people. In fact, to be plain, not the persons for whom Mission Halls are built and mission services held. It is said many go to these places because they get "cheap gospel." No collection seems to be the order of the day. Others go because they have an itching ear, and like to hear plain talking on Bible subjects. But I opine mission services are intended for the lower strata of society, who do not feel they would be comfortable in a church sitting alongside persons dressed better than themselves and as a consequence in the Mission chapel they feel at home, and not embarrassed because their coats are greasy or their dresses and bonnets faded and worn.

Following hymns, a prayer and the reading of the Scripture, Hiddlestone preached. Wrote Silverpen further,

> The preacher understands his business, as he himself said speaking as "a dying man to dying men". I liked the service from beginning to end. The preacher is a plain, earnest speaker on Gospel topics; keeps nothing back, nor hesitates to thunder out the sinner's doom if unrepentant. "Take" and "have" seem to be the

---

[243] The Pioneer journal of the Christian Mission Church June 1887 p1; Frank Dexter in his history of the Memorial Church omits any reference to the weatherboard pavilion.

burden of this gospel song. At the close of the service the unusual announcement was made that a whole night prayer meeting would be held on the following night, refreshments provided about midnight ... I doubt not many will have reason in the sweet bye and bye to thank God for the establishment of the Launceston mission to the poor, conducted as it is by earnest men believing and practising the truths they preach.[244]

He wrote again in 1883,

> The Rev Mr. Hiddlestone has a fine Band of Hope; the roll numbers several hundred. I was favoured by Mr. Hiddlestone with a couple of their medals, and very pretty they are. Clasps are attached for wearing on the breast. There are three degrees in the Band: blue, scarlet, and purple. Those joining receive the blue, after a certain time of trial they get the scarlet, and then the purple. The officers wear gilt medals. Large quantities of temperance fly-leaves and tracts are regularly sent out from England by Mrs. Reed.[245]

By 1884, the Christian Mission Church had 300 members.

Even though Hiddlestone had settled into the task, by July 1885 he was obliged to leave the colony for health reasons. He had already been through a time of severe illness staying at Margaret Reed's residence to recuperate. He travelled to South Australia and stayed with his brother, the Rev William Robson Hiddlestone, also a "Singing Evangelist". For a time it appeared he had regained his health but on 3 May 1887 he succumbed to acute inflammation of the lungs and died. He left behind Alice and their six children; he was only thirty-three years old. He also left behind a beloved congregation of fully 1,400 persons. The day the news of his death reached Launceston, the Church bell tolled at various intervals.[246] Alice died on 21 September 1907 aged fifty-one years.[247] Finally, in memory of her husband, Margaret Reed replaced the pavilion with the present Memorial Church. The imposing

*4-5 Dr. H G Guinness*

---

[244] LEx 21 October 1882 p1.
[245] The Tasmanian (Launceston) 10 February 1883 p160.
[246] The South Australian Advertiser 25 July 1885 p4; South Australian Register 5 May 1887 p4; Daily Telegraph (Launceston) 1 September 1886 p2, 9 May 1887 p3; Evening Journal (SA) 5 May 1887 p3; Border Watch (SA) 7 May 1887 p2.
[247] The Argus (Melbourne) 23 September 1907 p1.

edifice was in the course of erection in 1889 being built at a cost of £8,900 and seating for 1200.[248] Once it was opened, the Pavilion was removed to a site at Trevallyn for use by the Church for its open-air services.

## The Rev George Soltau

After five months as a co-worker with Moody and Sankey in London, the Rev George Soltau and his wife, Grace, accepted an invitation from the Church. They left London for Melbourne by the Iberia on 8 July 1886 and brought with them their children accompanied by a nurse and the Rev W. R. Thompson and his wife. Thompson was a student from the Rev Henry Grattan Guinness's College and he was engaged by Margaret Reed for country work.[249] The party arrived in Launceston on 27 August 1886; the Soltaus would remain for seven years in Launceston. His opening services at the Church took place the next day. The Soltaus' welcome coincided with an extended time at the Church of the evangelist, Emilia Louise Baeyertz. She was engaged by the Church for two months prior to Soltaus' arrival to help maintain the congregation's numbers and her biography states that she "had the joy of handing over to him a congregation of 1800 and 300 professed converts."[250] Also present in Launceston at the time was Dr. Henry. G. Guinness, the son of the same name.

Within a month Soltau and Guinness were also conducting "men's only" meetings as Baeyertz was holding "women's only" meetings. At these men's meetings Guinness spoke of the havoc wrought by impurity, that is, of the visiting of "houses of ill-fame". Soltau also related his knowledge of prostitution in London and commended the English Social Purity Alliance.[251] Soltau also delivered his lectures to men only at the Salvation Army Barracks.[252] Dr. Guinness' used explicit language at these "men's only" meetings and gave the opportunity for those gathered to sign a "social purity pledge". He dealt dramatically with the subject of lust as Walter Phillips in his book, "Defending 'A Christian Country'" explains,

---

[248] LEx 25 July 1882 p2; the foundation stone was laid on 19 July 1883, see LEx 24 May 1884 p2 and 27 May p2. The opening took place on 3 July 1885, see LEx 3 July 1885 p3; 4 July p2; 6 July p2. It would be known as the Christian Mission Church until 1935 and then it was renamed the Memorial Baptist Church.

[249] Mataura Ensign (NZ), vol. 17, issue 17, 11 June 1895 p5; LEx 16 July 1886 p2, 19 August 1886 p2.

[250] THRA P & P 49/3 "Mrs Baeyertz, the "Jewish Lady evangelist from Melbourne" by Elizabeth Wilson. LEx 28 June 1886 p2, August 1886 p2.

[251] The Contagious Disease Act, initially passed in 1864 by the Parliament of the United Kingdom with the goal of preventing venereal diseases within the armed forces, was reformed the first time in 1866. The Act of 1866, worked to spread the jurisdiction of this legislation to more naval ports, districts, and army towns and even the civilian population—with a new goal to regulate prostitution in general.

[252] LEx 25 March 1887 p2, 26 November 1886 p2.

Drawing on his medical experience, as well as the fund of bogus information given out by crusaders against sexual licence, he warned of the dire consequences, especially venereal disease, of giving in to "youthful lusts". He aimed to persuade or frighten youth from all forms of sexual gratification outside marriage and to practise extreme abstemiousness within marriage itself. Guinness medical lecture, which took nearly two hours to deliver, produced such an effect that at some meetings young men were carried out fainting.253

*4-6 George Soltau*

It was this aspect of his messages that drew criticism in the press,

> If Dr. Guinness had acted upon the advice of the Melbourne papers he would have ceased to hold forth on "Medical Talk" (which he is pleased to style his lecture), but some men are too conceited to profit by good advice, let it come from whence it may. To my mind I cannot conceive anything more revolting than a man standing up before his fellows pandering to the viciousness of those who live upon excitement. "Medical talk" indeed, before a mixed audience of men and boys, many of whom went for a treat, and they got it dished up to their liking; the coarser the language, the more indecent the gesture, and the more disgusting the subject, the better it was appreciated. Here strip, my children, here at once leap in; here prove who best can dash thro' thick and thin. If Dr. Guinness is so desirous of imparting such knowledge, why does he not modestly form a private class for such instruction? But no, there are those who must cry aloud from the house-top, they must come to the front even if their topic for the evening is filth ... I notice Mr Soltau is to improve and enlarge upon Dr. Guinness' address next week. According to Dr. Guinness, his friend Mr Soltau is a finer exponent of vice than himself, but if he has the least respect for our children he will pause before he ventures to further pollute our community.254

---

253 Phillips, Walter, Defending 'a Christian Country': churchmen and society in New South Wales in the 1880 (Brisbane, University of Queensland Press 1981) p71.

254 Daily Telegraph (Launceston) 15 October 1886 p3, 16 October 1886 p29, 20 October 1886 p2; LEx 16 October 1886 p3, 21 October 1886 p2.

Soltau delivered a number of sermons dealing with the question, "Is there a Lake of Fire?" These sermons were illustrated by long charts being enlargements of designs drawn by his father. In England and America his lectures had attracted large audiences.[255]

Soon after Soltau's arrival the Church and the Salvation Army conducted together night time torchlight processions through Launceston with the procession concluding at the front of the Launceston Baptist Tabernacle. The subsequent meeting in the building would often result in a packed house. At the time the torchlight procession was just one technique for reaching people outside the church, especially the poorer classes. The entertainment also included street marches, brass bands, open-air preaching and big choirs all to attract folk into the meeting house. Soltau also held twice a week in the City Park a series of undenominational religious meetings for children. The question of Liquor Licensing laws was also much on his mind.[256]

It was publicly noted in the press that since the death of Henry Reed, the character of the Church had greatly altered in that it had become middle class,

> That members of other churches crowd out the poor; that it is a Baptist Church; that the meetings are lengthened too far into the night, and young females kept from their homes in the name of religion."[257]

During Soltau's time, Margaret Reed and her daughter, Annie, left for London in March 1887 for Annie's marriage to Dr. Henry Grattan Junior.[258]

Soltau worked closely with the Rev Alfred Bird of the Baptist Tabernacle. Evangelists Mateer and Parker held a fortnight's series of services at the Christian Mission Church in February 1887. Soltau engaged in open-air preaching at Cataract Hill, speaking on temperance matters. Being a vigorous, forcible and earnest speaker, coupled with a good voice and sympathetic manner, he was within a year holding the largest Sunday evenings and week night services in Launceston.[259]

Yet Soltau could at times be outlandish in his assertions. One such statement: "Launceston was ten times more degradingly immoral than the majority of old world cities"

---

[255] The Ballarat Star 19 November 1894 p2; Mount Alexander Mail (Vic) 9 October 1894 p2; LEx 12 March 1887 p2.
[256] LEx 16 October 1886 p1; Daily Telegraph (Launceston) 30 November 1886 p3, 5 March 1887 p3.
[257] LEx 23 October 1886 p3.
[258] Daily Telegraph (Launceston) 30 March 1887 p2.
[259] LEx 28 February 1887 p2; The Mercury (Hobart) 31 May 1887 p2.

drew the ire of the town's citizens.[260]

"Tommy Trot", feature writer for the Launceston Examiner, also took a disliking to Soltau and saw him as tough on the youngsters in his charge. Attending the Christian Mission Church one Sunday he wrote,

> No one has a right to turn a chapel into a circulating library, especially during divine service, and when the literature is of a light and frivolous character. Nor is it the proper thing for young men to "smirk", as pastor Soltau hath it, at girls on the opposite side of a gallery, nor for the latter to "frivol" in a similar way. Still more is it a heinous sin to be inattentive to the sermon; but on each of these points a slight difference of opinion exists between the reverend gentleman referred to and an irreverent section of his large congregation. Still, though I am an old stager now, and have given over the giddy ways of thoughtless youth, I can hardly see that the conduct of these culprits was deserving of the anathemas which were hurled directly at their heads. After rebuking them for their inattention, Mr. Soltau assured them that some of their number had undoubtedly had as much of heaven as they would ever get, and proceeded to impress upon their memories (with an air of "put this in your pipe and smoke it") the passage and "these", laying particular stress on the word "these" and pointing to the portion of the gallery in which the sinners were located, "these shall go away into everlasting punishment," which he further explained meant "a long, long hell." As he did not add any consoling remark those unfortunate lads and lasses must have gone away with the pleasing reflection that, if their aggrieved pastor's prognostications were correct they were safe to undergo particular Hades in the near or distant future. Don't you think you were a little too rough, Pastor Soltau?[261]

If Soltau was tough on the youngsters in his own congregation, and he was, he breathed hell-fire on the Roman Catholic Passionist Fathers, a small-scale charity first established in Hobart in 1856 and now in Launceston. The Roman Catholic Press in Melbourne chided him for his outbursts,

> We shall not notice the ravings of the charitable pastor (Soltau) regarding the Passionist Fathers' mission, though many testimonies in reference to these ravings have reached us. The pastor's mouthings on Romish superstitions remind us of the baying of a dog that howls himself into a swoon while the moon at which he bays sails her peaceful and tranquil course through the silent stars in the

---

[260] LEx 24 December1887 p10.

[261] LEx 28 March 1888 p3.

overarching canopy of heaven. We pity him and his audiences. The bigotry of (this) one and the folly of the others pass our comprehension. Tonight I went to hear Pastor Soltau, whose unchristian remarks might be considered too bad, indeed, for the dark ages. He predicted (amongst fierce denunciations of the Passionist Fathers) that "there would be a visitation of the wrath of God on Tasmania for this grievous and sinful mission." I was upset to know that we have a man amongst us who is evidently so void of Christian love, and, at the same time, laying claim to be a minister of the "God of Love". May the Lord lead him out of the darkness and bigotry into His most marvellous light, and, above all, grant him the grace of Christian charity.[262]

It was also noted that Soltau lashed out when there was anything to lash out about, and exposed fearlessly the sins of the day, and the worldliness amongst its members, because "people wanted Barrabas rather than the Saviour."[263]

But Soltau achieved both approval and disapproval with a throwaway line at a church service a week before a Christian Convention in Launceston, namely that an earthquake shall occur in Launceston. In fact a sharp earth tremor did take place on Wednesday morning 27 February 1892 at 3am; the Convention was to commence the next day. One of the Convention speakers, Keswick missioner the Rev George C. Grubb, wrote triumphantly,

> The Lord made His presence and power manifest in many ways, not only at the convention meetings, but also by giving us a slight repetition of Acts xvi. 25, 26; for "at midnight ... there was a great earthquake," which lasted about thirty seconds. The whole town was shaken, clocks stopped, chimneys fell, and people were rocked in their beds. Many were much alarmed, while several of the convention Christians rushed to their windows and looked out, thinking that the Lord was coming, and said, "Praise the Lord!" while several unconverted yielded to God. Strange to say, Pastor Soltau, who had been mainly instrumental in getting up the convention, had, on the previous Sunday, prayed, "O Lord, if nothing but an earthquake will awake these people, send us an earthquake.[264]

Soltau now claimed that he had now a full demonstration of the power of God to answer prayer. The response in the newspapers was immediate. Wrote one,

> He (Pastor Soltau) prayed for the Almighty to send an earthquake

---

[262] Advocate (Melbourne) 31 October 1891 p17.
[263] The Ballarat Star 19 November 1894 p2, 22 November 1894 p3.
[264] The Rev George C. Grubb in his book, "The Same Lord".

to wake up the people during the convention. He had answered his prayer. Now, apart from the inhumanity of the petition, what arrant blasphemy it is for a man to imagine such a thing as that the Almighty would answer such a prayer! What damage such preaching does to the cause of the Gospel! ... if Pastor Soltau will persist in doing so, please, Mr Editor, ask him to arrange for them to come off at a stated time, but not at midnight, as our dressing-gowns are not always handy.[265]

Another wrote,

> We suddenly find we have a man amongst us with power to call forth earthquakes ad lib. Had he only asked for them to call along gently at first, gradually increasing in force, thereby rousing the sluggard in faith, I would not have thought so much of it; but to drop on to us at 3 am, with such a clatter is rather too bad for a start.[266]

And again,

> It appears we have to thank this worthy for the earthquake shock the other morning. He considered the people required rousing up in connection with the convention meetings, and prayed for a shock, and along it came. We would suggest that if Parson Soltau really wants to do good for the masses that he help along social reform. First fill the bellies of the starving workers, and then try the old intimidating dodge to get them into the fold.[267]

And further,

> I would like to know if this is not rank blasphemy, I would also ask if this minister of the Gospel is not answerable for the damage done to our hospital, and the fright sustained by its inmates. Is he not also answerable for a recent death which occurred on the same morning as the earthquake and which death was traced back to the system. Perhaps a shock similar to this reverend gentleman while roaming our hills carrying a lantern at night would restrain his ardour as regards praying for evil to happen to his fellow men.[268]

And more,

> Now, my good saint, whoever you are with conceit enough to think that the Lord would answer such a wicked prayer, allow me to tell you that I do not believe a word of it for two reasons: God would never terrify a host of good people that night who fell asleep under the shadow of the

---

[265] Daily Telegraph (Launceston) 30 January 1892 p5.
[266] LEx 1 February 1892 p3.
[267] The Tasmanian Democrat (Launceston) 6 February 1892 p2.
[268] The Tasmanian Democrat 6 February 1892 p4, edited.

"everlasting arms", for the sake of gratifying the desire of any enthusiast, nor is it likely that such a prayer was uttered at all, for no sane man with a spark of the Master's spirit in his breast would dare to invoke supernatural agency to overthrow a city, however corrupt it be. "Vengeance is mine," saith a high authority. Instead of praying for an earthquake to overwhelm Launceston, methinks a righteous man would plead for its safety, as did holy Abraham for the Cities of the Plain in the olden time. [269]

And more:

The humane pastor is reported to have said he was doubtful as to the prayer being answered at the time of giving utterance to it. He now learns for the first time what a vastly important personage he is in the eyes of the All-Upholder (to use Goethe's expression), when hundreds of miles of the solid crust of this planet are set in motion in response to his entreaty to bring the great majority of the inhabitants of this city to a sense of their sinful condition ... no doubt the sharp earth shock lately experienced will go down in our local seismologist's diary as the "Soltau earth tremor of January, 1892" ... He now would be as renowned amongst the credulous, the illiterate, as the famous oracle of Delphi amongst the ancient Greeks, and would probably be held in the same reverence and awe ... Perhaps the earthquake shock of the 27th ult. is really a tardy response to a prayer offered by Pastor Soltau when his mind was so disturbed in connection with the outbreak of Roman Catholic activity in the mission field (by some of the Passionist Fathers). As Pastor Soltau seems to have been the cause of the late earthquake cannot he be held responsible for the damage done?[270]

And finally,

Pastor Soltau has "built himself an ever-lasting name". I should not be surprised to hear now that he had prayed again, fervently, imploringly for another earthquake to come and shake down and swallow in oblivion that same name. Says the poet, "some people are born great, others achieve greatness, others have greatness thrust upon them." The pastor has achieved by one prayer a name that hundreds of laboriously chiselled sermons could not have made for him. The Melbourne men's little practical joke is delightful, I think; they have formed a syndicate, and through a local firm of solicitors have served Pastor Soltau with a writ for £200,000 damages alleged to

---

[269] Daily Telegraph (Launceston) 6 February 1892 p5.

[270] LEx 6 February 1892 p7.

have been sustained through the earth-quake.[271]

After a vigorous ministry of seven years in Launceston, Soltau was farewelled on 26 October 1893. He was to join his brother, Dr. Henry Soltau, at Madras, Southern India, and starting thence was to conduct missions throughout India. He told the gathering, "God had told (me) about four months ago that He would send (me) to India, and (I) had answered that (I) would gladly go." He conveyed his belief that he was more fitted for mission and convention work than that of the pastoral ministry.

Further, it was noted that the Christian Endeavour Society, which had spread all through Tasmania, "might justly call Pastor Soltau its head, for he was the father of the movement in this colony."[272] Christian Endeavour proved for many young people their first opportunities to give leadership and speak publicly. Dr. Soltau was on the Board of the North African Mission and was acquainted with the likes of Doctor Barnardo.[273]

Soltau's wife, Grace, also had an outstanding ministry in Launceston. At the Church she ran her own Bible class.[274] She became the first President of the Tasmanian Women's Christian Temperance Union after Jessie Ackermann's revitalizing visit in 1892. Grace strove to encourage the Tasmanian WCTU members saying, "I get many confessions of ignorance and inability" but "I believe our Union is a great education for women with a niche for everyone." Nor did she downplay the difficulties: "We are sure to receive many rebuffs, sneers and incredulity that women will have the courage to continue." She presented a Tasmanian progress report at the first inter-colonial convention in Victoria.[275] She was responsible for Launceston's first successful rescue home. The last of their nine children, the twins Theodore and David were born in Launceston in 1890.

## The Rev Charles Mortimer Cherbury

The Rev Charles Mortimer Cherbury, retired Pastor of the Collingwood Tabernacle, well known in Northern

---

[271] The Mercury (Hobart) 26 February 1892 p4. For the Melbourne men's little joke see Table Talk (Melbourne) Friday 4 March 1892 p1; for a further send up of the lawsuits, see The Tasmanian Democrat (Launceston) 13 February 1892 p3.
[272] LEx 27 October 1893 p5 yet the Day-Star claims this for Robert McCullough in its May 1889 issue p66.
[273] Articles in the North African Mission Journal include, "Circles of Divine Power and Love" and "Following Fully". Dr. Soltau travelled widely, in

Burmah, China, India and Africa, being a pioneer missionary among unevangelised tribes in Burmah.
[274] LEx 3 March 1887 p 2.
[275] "The Foundation of the Women's Christian Temperance Union in Australia," by Alison Alexander, Tasmanian Historical Studies Vol.7 no.2, 2001.

Tasmanian for his many annual holidays in the State over many years, was invited for an interim pastorate of the Church and he arrived in April 1894. He preached regularly, twice each Sunday as well as at other times in the week giving lectures both at the Church and in other Baptist churches and officiating at marriages. But the drive of the earlier Cherbury had gone. He preached his farewell sermons on 25 November as reported in the newspapers,

> The Rev C. M. Cherbury of Melbourne, who has supplied the vacant pulpit of the Memorial Church, Wellington-Street, since April, will return to Victoria in a few days and is advertised to preach two farewell sermons to-morrow. Mr Cherbury states that his health, which had broken down through many years of close application to his various works in Melbourne, is rapidly improving, and that he has thoroughly enjoyed the beneficial influence of the salubrious climate of Tasmania and the friendship accorded to him by the church and congregation inasmuch as everyone has made his stay most agreeable to him and his work light by the kindly co-operation he experienced.[276]

## The Rev Henry James Lambert

In March 1894 the Rev Henry James Lambert of South Australia preached in the Launceston Tabernacle, in the Christian Mission Church and elsewhere in the town until finally in December he was offered an interim at the Christian Mission Church. He participated with other Baptist, Wesleyan, Congregationalist and Presbyterian clergy in the annual United Christian Conference over two days in February, his subject in two parts being "Rivers of water", John 7.38. The point being that Christ was the head of the river, and the believers the channel in which the Holy Spirit flows. He conducted Bible classes at the Girls' Industrial School on weekdays.[277]

*4-7 Charles Mortimer Cherbury*

---

[276] Daily Telegraph (Launceston) 24 November 1894 p4.

[277] Daily Telegraph (Launceston) 1 December 1894 p 5; LEx 15 February 1895 p4, 13 June 1895 p4.

The Church always welcomed those who in their own way were busy on Christian mission. In 1895 an evangelistic service entitled, "The deepening of the spiritual life", was conducted by Miss Vaughan Barber and Miss Johnson, both of London. These young women were on a tour through the Australian colonies for the purpose of promoting Christian work among police. They were from the International Christian Police Association making the police men their special care. A Melbourne branch was soon to be formed.[278] Lambert concluded at the Church in January 1896.

## The Rev Joseph Tanner Piercey

Early in 1896 the Rev Joseph Tanner Piercey of Hobart was approached by the Christian Mission Church to become Pastor for twelve months and three months into this appointment Margaret Reed endorsed him as Pastor. The Christian Mission Church had a very large and growing congregation at that time and he resigned from the Primitive Methodist Church to take up the appointment. His resignation raised concern among the Primitive Methodists.[279] He would spend the next eight and a half years in Launceston.

*4-8 Henry Lambert*

Apart from Sunday services at the Christian Mission Church, there was also a wide range of associated activities. Piercey's own description of the work included this statement, "After much prayer and hard work, the congregation began to increase, and in two years we had the joy of preaching the old, old story to 1,000 every Sunday evening." His report also added,

In connection with this large sphere of work there was the oversight of a large Sunday-school (300 scholars), young men and young women's Bible classes, with Chinese classes, open-air services and with early morning and evening prayer-meetings every Sabbath. The week-night services were numerous – prayer meetings, Christian Endeavour (senior and junior) (120 in each), Chinese classes for reading and writing, brass band, sewing meetings, Bible and local preachers' classes, with Saturday open-air services. Besides these, there were four outstations at which the Gospel was preached

---

[278] LEx 11 September 1895 p4; The Mercury (Hobart) 4 May 1894 p3.

[279] Secretary's Annual Report ending 31 January 1896; LEx 21 May 1896 p4; Bendigo Advertiser 8 February 1896 p5.

every Sabbath, with mid-week services. A students' class for candidates for foreign missionary work was also conducted, some of whom are now in preparation for the field.[280]

At the end of his first two years "the work has gone apace, the congregations having increased and everything bearing a healthy tone." Well over a year later it was reported that Piercey's ministry "is full of success and blessing ... that the large building seating 1,200 was now comfortably filled on Sunday evenings," and finally, "Mrs Henry Reed, of Mount Pleasant, also referred to the work of the pastor and his wife in very encouraging terms."[281]

During his time Piercey also conducted evangelistic missions in Hobart, Scottsdale, Perth, Chudleigh and Hagley, and further afield, in Geelong. By 1902, he was increasingly associating with Baptists, speaking at their services and even speaking at one of their Annual Assemblies, obviously at one with them and naturally on their stance on baptism; the Christian Mission Church practised baptism by immersion. In July 1902, the Church involved itself in the United Evangelistic Mission of the Dr. Reuben A. Torrey and his song leader Charles Alexander. Torrey was superintendent of Moody's Bible Institute in Chicago.[282]

But by 1903, he was suffering declining health and Margaret Reed indicated in June that his time had come to leave. As Robert Evans writes in his book, the Evangelistic Society of Victoria,

The records reveal that Piercey enjoyed the confidence of most of the people; it was Margaret Reed who wanted his resignation. At the church meeting dealing with his reappointment, she said, "Mr. Piercey's health was much impaired and he was not fit to carry it on without someone to assist him and I am not led to engage another assistant.[283]

*4-9 Joseph T. Piercey*

But he already had an assistant in George Craike. Robert Evans continues,

> Here is also revealed Mrs. Reed's power in the situation. In her

---

[280] *Southern Cross* 16 March 1906 p245.

[281] LEx 7 February 1898 p4; *The Mercury* (Hobart) 30 September 1899 p2.

[282] *Southern Cross* 16 March 1906 p245; *Daily Telegraph* (Launceston) 11 April 1902 p3; LEx (Launceston) 23 April 1902 p2, 26 May 1902 p4, 30 June 1902 p4.

[283] Elders' Minutes Book, June 1904.

view, her considerable wealth, and having paid for building the church, seems to have given her the right to decide whether extra staff would be employed. Perhaps she would also have to provide the wages for a helper, although such a large and strong church should have had no trouble getting the money, if such was necessary. She apparently considered that she had this right, and the people seemed to accept this, although no other Protestant church would ever allow itself to operate under such dictatorial restrictions. It seems that she had already decided Piercey's fate, by saying that he was no longer fit for the work.

*4-10 Mrs. Margaret Reed*

At the July meeting, it was stated that Mrs. Reed had contacted her daughter to look out for a suitable new pastor. A decision was made at that meeting to invite the Rev Edward Isaac to be the new pastor. Isaac was well known in Australia, having been a Baptist pastor in Melbourne for some years. He duly arrived from England the following year.[284]

The secretary composed an appreciation of Piercey's work,

It is with great regret we have received the resignation of our Pastor who has so long occupied the pastorate of this church. During his ministry he has been the means in God's hands of leading many souls into the kingdom, and has done a noble work for his Master. We too feel that much of his worth and value will be the more apparent and the more appreciated when they no longer have the means of enjoying them. May the prayers of God's people follow him and bring blessing on him and his through all the future years.[285]

When Piercey concluded at the Church in October 1904, Margaret Reed absented herself from his farewell. Piercey had encouraged and helped many young men to prepare for the Christian ministry.[286] He moved to become the pastor of the Burnie Baptist Church.

---

[284] For an extensive work on the Evangelistic Society of Victoria, see the self-published books of Robert Evans.
[285] Extract from Elders' Minutes July 1905.
[286] Daily Telegraph (Launceston) 28 September 1904 p5; The Herald (Melbourne) 29 April 1912 p3

## Assistant Pastor George Craike

In May 1903, George Albert Craike from the Hobart Baptist Church was welcomed as co-pastor to the Rev Joseph Tanner Piercey. Craike intimated that he had been about to leave for America to study for the ministry when he accepted the call. During his time he also preached at the Church's outreach mission at Summerhill and involved himself in the Band of Hope.[287]

In February 1904, a newspaper journalist visited the Church early for a Sunday evening service with Craike speaking and left his impressions of what took place prior to the service,

> Long before the hour advertised I was in waiting at the Reed Memorial ... and was struck at once by the evidences of energy and healthy organization for which it is noted. Already officials and workers are about their duties. One kindly conducts me to the schoolroom, and informs me that there are about 300 scholars taught in the Sunday school; he draws my attention to the programme of the Christian Endeavour Society; and gives me a cordial invitation to be present at that society's anniversary to be held next Sunday. This gentleman is about to start out with printed notices of the forthcoming service to distribute then broadcast, and invite all and sundry to be present. In an adjoining vestry is being held a "yoke-fellows" meeting; the members thereof having taken tea together on the premises, are now engaged in prayer for the Divine blessing on the evening service. In other rooms are heard voices raised in sacred song, and my guide informs me that another meeting for prayer is being held presumably by the sound of the voices, this meeting is for ladies. Passing on to the "minister's vestry", I am courteously received in by elders and deacons, who are busily engaged in preparation for their duties, but find time to answer my questions. This is just what it purports to be, a mission church pure and simple. It has a rather elaborate constitution, published in pamphlet form, consisting of a "Declaration of Faith and Order," and strictly defining the place and duties of all church officers and members. The financing is of the simplest kind; there is no "collection" (other churches take note!), and no registered list of subscribers. All moneys for the support of the church work are raised by means of boxes for voluntary offerings placed in the porch, and held at the doors during the dispersal of the congregation. No appeal for contributions is made from the

---

[287] LEx 27 June 1903 p4; Daily Telegraph (Launceston) 30 May 1903 p4, 26 October 1903 p2.

pulpit, and one does not hear the word money so much as mentioned. In the morning the "Pioneer Hymn Book", compiled by the late Mr. Reed, is used, but at the evening service Sankey's hymns are the vogue. Entering the church, I note that preparations have been made for the administration of the Sacrament, a table at the front of the platform being spread with an ordinary white table cloth, on which stand the vessels for use, silver or plated chalice, containing the wine; four goblets, and four plates of similar material for the distribution of the bread. While the congregation is assembling there is considerable whispering and even audible conversation to be noticed, and the whole atmosphere is more suggestive of energetic business life than of the reposeful quiet usually associated with worship. This is inevitable in a congregation gathered in the manner above described, and does not disturb me, as it would in differently constituted congregations. Energy, activity and earnestness of purpose are the orders of the evening, and no one is concerned about dignity or aestheticism. At two minutes to 7 comes the first item of service. The choir, about 20 in number, has assembled on the platform, and the choirmaster invites us to join in singing the hymn beginning "All hail! the power of Jesu's Name". The choir rises, the congregation remains seated, and instead of the almost universal voluntary, the hymn is sung to the accompaniment of the organ, a powerful two manual, assisted by cornet and violin. During the singing, Mr. Craike enters the pulpit Bible in hand. A large congregation has assembled, filling probably 900 of the available 1400 seats, and at the conclusion the leader rises to announce the first four verses of the hymn "Abide with Me". The singing is hearty and congregational, being forte, if not fortissimo all through, and is followed by the invitation from the Minister "Let us approach God in prayer". This is announced as an "Evangelistic Service" on the printed slips before referred to, and the prayer is in keeping with the announcement. Almost all through it has to do with sin and salvation from sin; at times it becomes an utterance of warning and exhortation rather than petition for, the people, though towards the close "the needy and the poor, the afflicted and the dying, and those looking upon the faces of the departed dead are remembered." The announcements follow another hymn, and seem to occupy considerable time and at the close of these we had another token of the heterogeneous character of the congregation. Another hymn precedes the reading of the lesson.

The journalist liked the style and content of Craike's sermon and also his voice which "has pleasing qualities, and he uses it naturally and without effort or strain." Concluded the journalist, "If Mr. Craike fulfils the promise of his youth, I prophesy for him a very successful future as a missioner."[288] In 1905 Craike entered the Pastors' College in London.

# Appendices

## Appendix 1: The Rev John Henry Shallberg

Late in 1876 the German Baptist, the Rev Johann Heinrich Schallberg (anglicized to John Henry Shallberg), arrived in South Australia from England, and for the first few weeks preached in various churches sometimes conducting services in German for his German fellow-colonists. For the next sixty years he was untiring, assiduous and yet unpredictable in evangelistic ministry in the Australian colonies.

He was born in 1851 on one of the German Islands in the Baltic Sea and educated in Schleswig-Holstein. He evaded service in the Franco-Prussian army by moving to Hamburg, and ultimately to London sacrificing "his property in Germany rather than be a party to slaying his Christian brethren." In London, he attended Spurgeon's Tabernacle and missioned among the poor in the East End of London.[289]

In South Australia Shallberg engaged in evangelistic and ministerial work at Terowie,, a small town in the Mid-North region located 220 kms north of Adelaide commencing on 3 December 1876. There and elsewhere he would give his lecture on "The East End of London" touching upon his mission work and the present drunkenness in that part of London with its 10,000 public-houses – "10,000 too many, and if he had his own way he would burn

*4-11 John H. Shallberg in his army days*

*4-12 Terowie Baptist Church SA*

---

[288] LEx 23 February 1904 p7. The journalist also included his impression of the sermon.

[289] Daily Mercury (Qld.) 9 October 1914 p6; LEx 20 October 1880 p2; North Melbourne Advertiser 10 February 1882 p3.

them all." On the other side of the picture, he pointed out that a good work was being done by rescue organizations and he alluded to the exertions of missioners Moody and Sankey. After four or five months, he moved to the Baptist Church at Hindmarsh.[290] On 10 February 1878, he preached his farewell sermons as he could not "work with profit and comfort". He now involved himself with the South Australian Total Abstinence League and fulfilled pulpit appointments and preached at open-air services, the last in the Adelaide Exhibition Grounds.[291]

Finding no openings in South Australia to his satisfaction, he moved to Victoria and engaged in evangelistic work, and worked with C. Edwin Good preaching in a Gospel Tent in Collingwood, with considerable success. This work also took him to the Hargreaves Street Church in Bendigo where he as likely met his future wife, local Anna Archer (née Bell). They married in June 1880. Within a few months they sailed to Tasmania for evangelistic and temperance work.[292]

**Following his time at the Christian Mission Church**, Shallberg transferred his services on Sunday evenings to the Oddfellows Hall soon

*4-13 Christ Church Congregational Church, Launceston*

"gaining a large and attentive congregation". With Ned Kelly presently awaiting trial in Melbourne, one of his lectures was "The Kelly Gang, or the spirit of outlawry". George Pullen worked with him. Shallberg had the support of the United Christian choir and an ensemble of musicians. The singing of Sankey hymns was his preferred choice. On Sunday afternoons he gave open-air addresses at the Cataract Gorge where some five or six hundred people would gather, some on the hillside, some on the roadway and some on the bridge

---

[290] Northern Argus (Clare, SA) 8 December 1876 p2; Evening Journal (SA) 31 March 1877 p2; South Australian Chronicle and Weekly Mail 1 September 1877 p21; The South Australian Advertiser 21 September 1877 p6; Bunyip (SA) 28 September 1877 p2.
[291] The Express and Telegraph (SA) 13 February 1878 p1; South Australian Register 16 April 1878

p6; South Australian Chronicle and Weekly Mail 1 June 1878 p10; Christian Colonist (SA) 25 October 1878 p1.
[292] Sandhurst became Bendigo in 1891. Christian Colonist (SA) 23 May 1879 p1; Bendigo Advertiser (Vic) 19 June 1879 p3; LEx 18 October 1879 p2; The Argus (Melbourne) 14 June 1881.

below. Oddly, he believed that anyone who has witnessed the attendance and interest in connection with the open-air gatherings on the Cataract Hill "will not believe that the inhabitants of Launceston are dead to the spirit of our forefathers."[293]

But by the end of October 1880 he relinquished the work at the Oddfellows Hall for health reasons leaving the work in the hands of City Missioner the Rev Robert Marshall and others. Finally, the Odd Fellows Hall work was disbanded and those who made up the congregations were urged to join other churches.[294] He then preached for a time in Hobart at St Andrews Church. His lectures on London as "the modern Babylon" continued.[295]

Shallberg's next pastorate was the Brunswick Baptist Church in Melbourne. For a time progress looked good and a school hall was erected but by March 1884 the relationship had deteriorated and a slanging match took place in a church service between Shallberg and a couple of the deacons whom Shallberg publicly named and "personal injury could have ensued".[296] The falling out between Shallberg and the church was widely reported in the colony's papers. Dr Marita Munro explains what happened,

> Apparently simmering tension had eventually erupted between Shallberg and some of the deacons, leading to Deacon Frith calling for the pastor's resignation and accusing him of defamation. Shallberg was accused of bringing a charge against Brother George Burton from the church platform before the congregation on Sunday 24 February 1884, claiming that Burton had not contributed financially to the church for some months. Burton had refuted the charge and had Frith declare to the church members that he (Burton) had contributed over £37 and the family over £57. A motion of sympathy for Burton was carried overwhelmingly for the false charge laid against him. Shallberg resigned on 9 March 1884. He was not present at the next church

*4-14 Brunswick Baptist Church*

---

[293] LEx (12 July 1880 p2, 26 July 1880 p2, 25 August 1880 p2, 10 September 1880 p3.
[294] LEx 5 January 1881 p3.
[295] LEx 19 January 1881 p3; The Mercury (Hobart) 18 August 1881 p 2.

[296] North Melbourne Advertiser 10 February 1882 p3; Leader (Vic) 29 March 1884 p30; The Tasmanian 8 March 1884 p23. "Our Yesterdays" Vol.22 p36f.

meeting and refused to pass on the Minute Book to the Secretary so that a full account of the special church meeting could be recorded. His resignation was accepted 61 in favour, 23 against.[297]

Shallberg departed and commenced an eight month ministry at the Presbyterian Church at Sale in country Victoria. In March 1886, he accepted the call of the Durham and Kerang Presbyterian congregations and was ordained to the ministry of the Presbyterian Church. He added to his responsibilities in July 1887 with the Presbyterian Church at Macorna, near Swan Hill. He then transferred to the Presbytery of Seymour which took in Shepparton, and became outspoken on public issues.

In October 1896, he began Sunday evening services in the Melbourne Theatres of the Bijou, the Theatre Royal and the Gaiety "in order to reach the large masses who have social and political anarchy poured down their throats on the Yarra-bank and elsewhere on Sundays" and those who were non-church goers. By 1902, he was based in country Victoria in Donald. He caused a stir when he wrote a home-truth article on how, "We poor ministers have to square our teachings with the tastes of those who supply our bread and butter." From 1910 to 1915 he was in charge of the Streatham Presbyterian Church near Ararat. On 7 August 1915, his younger son, Reginald Shallberg, 2nd Lieutenant in the 8th Battalion, twenty-one years of age, was killed at Lone Pine, Gallipoli.

The Rev John Henry Shallberg died in October 1944 aged ninety-three years. He served in Christian ministry for fifty-four years.[298]

## Appendix 2: The Rev Daniel Walter Hiddlestone

Itinerant evangelist Dan Walter Hiddlestone, thoughtful and passionate, well filled the criteria Mrs Margaret Reed sought for those who would take the mantle of soul-winner for her Christian Mission Church but sadly he suffered failing health.

Hiddlestone and his older brother, William Robson, were brought out by their parents from England to Tasmania when they were very young. Their father was "noted for his prayerfulness, spirituality and earnestness; his mother was a sweet singer, whose services were much sought after and highly appreciated."[299] Daniel was born in 1846 at Newcastle-upon-Tyne and William was born in 1855 at South Shields. The boys spent their childhood in Hobart with William later employed at "The Mercury" office. Then the family moved to the mainland and settled in Emerald Hill (South Melbourne) where their aged father ran a family grocery store and

---

[297] "Our Yesterdays" Vol.10.
[298] Advocate 18 October 1944 p2.

[299] AB 25 September 1923 p9.

more than likely Dan worked in the business. At the young age of eighteen Daniel was associated with the Emerald Hill Total Abstinence Society and was the President of the Band of Hope. Dan married young and his wife Alice gave birth to a son in March 1875 while they were living at Emerald Hill. The next year their father died insolvent.[300]

Early in 1879, Daniel and W. Corrie Johnston embarked on a three week's evangelistic tour through Queensland, opening their campaign in Ipswich. The afternoon meetings were for the children from the various Sunday schools while the evening meetings were for adults.[301] Johnston wrote of their mission,

> In the heat of summer in Queensland, during the months of January and February, two of us conducted meetings nearly every night and twice on the Lord's Day. We visited about ten thousand homes, did the necessary writing in connection with receiving and transmitting the names of about seven hundred subscribers, wrote articles and notes for two numbers of "Words of Grace".[302]

Hiddlestone and Johnston continued their Gospel tent ministry campaigns in Brisbane, Sydney, Melbourne, Adelaide and other population centres all the while selling Bibles and religious literature. In Adelaide, they erected their tent in Whitemore Square and on Sunday afternoons gave Bible readings and in the evenings preached and sang the Gospel; Johnston undertook the preaching and Hiddlestone the singing. In Melbourne they ran their meetings in a Gospel Hall.[303]

## Appendix 3: The Rev George Soltau

Christian Brethren missionary, evangelist and Bible expositor, the Rev George Soltau who had missioned in England, Scotland, Ireland, Canada and the USA was a trophy for Mrs. Margaret Reed and her Christian Mission Church. Coupled with his impeccable international connections, his engagement ensured that her Church would remain one of the leading churches in Launceston. Even though he was a forceful "speaker with good descriptive powers", he could be coarse and

---

[300] Daily Telegraph (Launceston) 26 September 1923 p4; The Record and Emerald Hill and Sandridge Advertiser (Vic) 15 October 1874 p1, 12 June 1873 p2; The Age (Melbourne) 6 March 1875 p4; Advocate (Vic.) 29 July 1876 p16.
[301] The Week (Qld) 4 January 1879 p15, 4 January 1879 p15. Johnston was a freelance evangelist in the late 1870s and early 1880s, having declined ordination or a licence to preach as a Presbyterian, "preferring to hold himself free for evangelistic work". He had taken gospel missions in Victoria, South Australia and NSW. In 1876 he started producing "Words of Grace", an evangelistic newspaper. The paper was handed out on visitation as much as for Christians' edification. Source: "Wandering stars, the impact of British evangelists in Australia".
[302] Christian Colonist (SA) 4 April 1879 p2.
[303] Evening Journal (SA) 28 March 1881 p3, 2 April 1881 p1; The Age (Melbourne) 23 April 1881 p7.

crude at times exhibiting a propensity for the bizarre.

Soltau was born in Devonshire, England, in 1847, the son of the Rev Dr. Stanley Soltau who was pastor of the First Evangelical Church of Memphis for twenty-five years. George commenced employment with the Civil Service at Whitehall remaining for ten years while devoting his spare time to "slum work" in the city thus gaining experience in what William Booth termed the "Submerged Tenth". He married Grace Elizabeth Tapson on 12 March 1874 at Trinity Church, Paddington, London.[304] They joined Dr. Barnardo's staff taking charge of the Village Home for girls at Ilford, a London suburb, and they remained with Barnardo's for seven years with Grace's health forcing their resignations. He then worked as an itinerant evangelist.

**Following his time in Launceston**, and true to his word, Soltau never returned to the pastoral ministry but concentrated on evangelistic missions which soon took place in Melbourne and in the Western district of Victoria. In Melbourne at the South Yarra Baptist Tabernacle, he conducted an eight-day mission with "enthusiastic meetings each evening". During the pastorate of the Rev John Alfred Soper at the Ballarat Tabernacle Soltau also conducted an eight-day mission which was well reported in the local press. During this mission he also preached a number of times at Lydiard Street Wesleyan Church (now Ballarat Uniting Church). Other missions took place in Geelong. He lectured on the Tabernacle of Israel. He also continued his engagement with the annual Christian Conferences in Melbourne and Geelong.[305] These missions illustrate his original and topical sermon subjects such as the sermon on popular fallacies.

He was quoted as saying:

- I must do my best and God will do the rest.
- It's never too late to mend.
- If I turn over a new leaf, I shall have a better chance.
- No one can know for certain that he is saved till he comes to die.[306]

Another topical sermon subject was "Closed for Stock-taking",

The heart was compared to a warehouse, with various stock. It was pointed out that man was responsible for the use of his stock, and the hearers were urged to at once enter into an investigation of affairs. The leading creditor - the Holy Spirit - was regarded as inquiring into the methods of our life business: "What class of goods have you been dealing with?" was the first question. Many must say, "I have been living for myself, for the pleasures of this life." The second

---

[304] Family Research by Barbara Coe.
[305] The Prahran Telegraph (Vic) 11 August 1894 p3; The Age (Melbourne) 16 August 1894 p6.
[306] Geelong Advertiser (Vic) 29 August 1894 p3.

question was: "What stock have you got in hand?" The best that a man could present was his honesty, his prayers, his good deeds, good intentions, and good resolutions, and they are all corrupt and worthless. The third question was "How do the books stand? How much do we owe God for all his mercies, the common and daily mercies? Alas! there had been no return. Indeed His gifts had been often used against God." The fourth question was, "What can be done?" They could not compound with the Divine creditor. They could not slip off to another land and start again. Wherever they went their creditor was there, and they could not start under another name.[307]

During the Depression of the 1890s he blamed Australians worship of

> a god of leather, the football, and a smaller god of leather, the cricket ball; and when 2000 men go to see Carbine off to England, and you can't get 200 men to a prayer meeting, no wonder God has smitten Victoria with a depression such as that colony has been experiencing.[308]

In 1895, he conducted missions in New Zealand.[309]

It appears that they returned to England in 1895 where Grace helped run a children's home. That year their fourth son, John Leonard (Jack) died at Mildmay, Middle Brighton. The Rev George Soltau died on 4 October 1909 in Los Angles, USA, after a brief illness aged sixty-two years.[310] In her later years Grace lived in Colchester, England, with her physician daughter Dr Eleanor Soltau, who was director of a Tuberculosis hospital. Grace died in Halstead, Essex, in 1940 aged ninety-four years of age.[311]

## Appendix 4: The Rev Charles Mortimer Cherbury

The Rev Charles Mortimer Cherbury of the large Collingwood Tabernacle celebrated due to its welfare arm, became well known to the Northern Tasmania Baptists during his annual holidays. It was in his retirement that he was invited to take an interim ministry at the Christian Mission Church.

Cherbury received part of his education at the Universities of Leyden and Utrecht. In his youth he travelled to South America, Java and

---

[307] Geelong Advertiser (Vic) 30 August 1894 p4.
[308] Table Talk (Melbourne) 5 July 1895 p1.
[309] LEx 8 May 1895 p4.
[310] The Argus (Melbourne) 17 November 1909 p9.
[311] Alexander, A., 'A Turning Point in Women's History? The Foundation of the Woman's Christian Temperance Union in Australia', Tasmanian Historical Studies, Vol.7, No. 2 (2001). Jordan, R., White-Ribboners: the Woman's Christian Temperance Union of Tasmania, 1885-1914, Unpublished BA Hons thesis, University of Tasmania, 2001. The Argus (Melbourne) 17 January 1895 p1. Family Research by Barbara Coe.

Sumatra. He arrived in Australia in 1861. In 1864, he became an Anglican minister but now, "no slave to orthodoxy", he gravitated to the Baptists while at Beaufort in a Victorian mining district situated on the Western Highway midway between Ararat and Ballarat. He was baptised in the Dawson Street Tabernacle. That year he formed a Baptist Church with sixteen members and opened a Chapel in November 1864, taking occasional services at Ararat.[312] This was followed by a pastorate at the Castlemaine Baptist Church commencing 6 March 1870. From 1873, he was pastor for two years of the Baptist Church, George Street, Fitzroy. During Cherbury's time there were 340 children on the Sunday school roll with thirty-one teachers. He now began his monthly annual holiday sojourns to Tasmania and would undertake speaking engagements in the Northern churches at which he would at times both "sing and preach" the Gospel. He was advertised as an "evangelist of Melbourne" and "a minister belonging to the 'Christians', Melbourne'". Over the course of his six-week holiday in 1876 in northern Tasmania he took part in no less than sixty-five services.[313]

*4-15 Cherbury's Collingwood Tabernacle*

On his retirement from George Street Church, he began in January 1875, his life work in a more independent stance in Collingwood, one of the poorest portions of the city. Assisted by the Albert Street Church, he rented a building in Gold Street as a public place of "unsectarian" worship.[314] Within two months the church saw 250 present for a "tea meeting" with the building comfortably filled every Sunday. As were most Baptist ministers of the time, he was a loyal member of the Loyal Orange Institution of Victoria being a member of the Good Templar Order: No. 1 Pioneer, Melbourne, and became one of its chaplains.[315] He was also a temperance lecturer.

---

[312] Victorian Freeman 9 October 1864; Baptist Union Handbook 1866 p135; Wilkin p62, 65. The Beaufort work ceased after Cherbury left.
[313] Utrecht is a city in the Netherlands. The Age (Melbourne) 29 March 1871 p2; Mercury and Weekly Courier (Vic) 27 May 1882 p3; The Ballarat Courier 29 January 1870 p2; Mount Alexander Mail 8 March 1870 p2; The Age (Melbourne) 28 May 1873 p2; LEx 22 November 1873 p2, 7 March 1876 p2; Weekly Examiner (Launceston) 4 March 1876 p15; Weekly Examiner (Launceston) 8 April 1876 p9.
[314] Wilkin p173.
[315] Mercury (Fitzroy) 13 March 1875 p2; The Age (Melbourne) 13 July 1875 p2.

Within three years he had a large mission hall to accommodate 500 persons with its coffee room, its reading room large enough to seat 230 persons, and its smoking room all at a cost of £2000 in nearby Sackville Street. This became the weatherboard Collingwood Tabernacle which soon had to be enlarged to seat 1500 people.[316] He later established in 1880 the soon to be well-known Homes of Hope for Destitute Children. Of the home it was reported,

> The religious training will be of an evangelical, though undenominational character, under the supervision of the honorary superintendent Mr. Cherbury, and the matron Mrs. Aubrey. The home will be supported entirely by voluntary contributions, and, in time, it is hoped to make it self-supporting by establishing a competitive scheme of industry among the children, by teaching them to make useful and ornamental articles, selling these and depositing one fifth to the children's credit in the Savings Bank, and devoting the remainder to the general maintenance of the home.[317]

After five years a new Home of Hope was constructed of stone in Easy Street Collingwood at the cost of £1,600 to accommodate twenty-eight boys and girls. In 1889 an Ocean Grove home was erected for the Home of Hope's sick children.[318]

Later he established the Pilgrim's Rest for Aged Destitute Gentlewomen and his name often went before the Victorian public as he appealed for funds for these institutions.

He was confronted with a usurper following his twelve month much needed break in London after ten years of ministry in Collingwood. The Tabernacle had been given over to the care of the Rev John Alexander Dowie of Sydney, a prophet and healer. Dowie sought to supplant the pastorate from Cherbury.[319]

Cherbury's annual holiday visits to Tasmania continued and he inevitably became well known especially with the Perth Baptist Church which often ran fairs to raise funds for his Home of Hope.[320] In June 1890, the constant load of being Pastor of the Collingwood Tabernacle, now one of the largest in the district having a Sunday school with children numbering 600 and being Honorary Superintendent of

---

[316] The Argus (Melbourne) 2 February 1878 p6; Gwyneth Long, 'True to Life: A Story of the Rivett Family', typescript, 1992, p5ff; Mercury and Weekly Courier (Vic.) 27 November 1880 p3.
[317] Weekly Times (Melbourne) 20 March 1880 p7.
[318] Geelong Advertiser 18 December 1889 p4.

[319] Mercury and Weekly Courier (Vic.) 27 May 1882 p3; Camperdown Chronicle (Vic) 13 September 1882 p3. For Dowie's account of his time at the Collingwood Tabernacle see "Sin in the Camp".
http://www.deadandburiedpodcast.com
[320] LEx 12 May 1887 p3.

both the Home of Hope and the Pilgrim's Rest for Aged Destitute Gentlewomen took its toll and he relinquished all his responsibilities.[321]

Following his interim ministry at the Christian Mission Church, Cherbury associated with the Congregational Church in Collingwood and officiated at the Beechworth Congregational Church during the absence of the Rev A. Rivett, his son-in-law, husband of Elizabeth Mary Ann. In his twilight years he lived with the Rivetts in Sydney. He died on 14 November 1917 aged eighty years. The Rev T. A. Eunson followed Cherbury at the Collingwood Tabernacle and his pastorate there lasted almost thirty years. The Home of Hope orphanage was closed in 1925 and the weatherboard Collingwood Tabernacle was demolished.[322]

## Appendix 5: The Rev Henry James Lambert

When a leading Baptist of long-standing was admitted into the ministry of another denomination, serious questions were generally asked. It happened with the Rev Henry James Lambert of South Australian, pioneer pastor of the influential Norwood Baptist Church in Adelaide and one time President of the South Australian Baptist Union. His change was much to the vexation of fellow Baptists. In time he became the Moderator for the Presbyterians in South Australia.

Lambert was born in London on 26 March 1836. He received his theological training at Regent's Park College commencing in 1859, and after his ordination he took charge of the Islington pastorate in London where he had a congregation of 1,000 members. This was followed by a pastorate at Milton and then Union Chapel, King's Lynn, Norfolk. During a visit to England, South Australian Sir Charles Goode was so impressed with this eloquent preacher that he successfully persuaded him to come to Australia. Lambert commenced at the newly opened Moonta Baptist Church in South Australia on 18 March 1866. He soon became Vice President of the town's Mechanics Institute. Sunday attendances doubled within the first year. Services were also regularly held at the mines where the great bulk of the population resided. But within eighteen months he was farewelled as he took charge of a gathering of Baptist folk at Norwood, commencing 29 March 1868; thus began a twenty-one year ministry. About twenty-three members of the Flinders Street Church residing in the locality united to form the Church which was constituted on 18 December 1869 and within two years of Lambert's ministry there were eighty-eight members. The following month, while they were still meeting in the Town Hall, the foundation stone was

---

[321] The Herald (Melbourne) 21 June 1890 p3

[322] The Evening Echo (Ballarat) 17 November 1917 p3; Wilkin p173.

laid for their new sanctuary. He also lectured at the Adelaide Theological College, and took a great interest in the Norwood Public School over many years.[323] He represented the Baptist Association in its discussions with the Congregationalists on how both denominations might work together in spreading the Gospel in scattered areas. He was the Secretary of the Independent Order of Good Templars Grand Lodge of South Australia.[324] In 1871, he married Helen Garrett, a daughter of deceased Tasmanian Presbyterian, the Rev James Garrett, M.A. Lambert concluded at Norwood 10 December 1888.

In South Australia he twice held the position as President of the Baptist Union (1869/70 and 1876/77) He was Secretary of the Baptist Association for many years and Editor of its journal, "Truth and Progress", and up to this time still lectured at the Adelaide Theological College.

After seven years at Norwood there were 168 members on the roll with an average attendance of 168 scholars every Sunday in its Sunday school.[325]

In his retiring speech at Norwood he said,

> He was not leaving because he was tired of the people, but he believed the chief reason that induced him to forward his resignation rested in the fact that during the last three or four years he felt that he had lost the grip of the people. Other things might have discouraged him, but it seemed that the people had become too used to him. They wanted new views, someone to deal with them in a more modern way, but perhaps not better.[326]

He then returned to England where he hoped to resume ministerial work but in fact returned, this time to Victoria. On 26 November 1890 a Church was constituted at Clifton Hill with forty-two members principally from George Street Baptist Church, Fitzroy, and Lambert was chosen pastor and remained for two years.[327] In 1892, he took charge of the South Melbourne Baptist Church for two years.[328] At

---

[323] The Freeman of 11 October 1865; South Australian Register 12 March 1866 p2, 29 September 1888 p7, 11 January 1870 p6, 16 April 1869 p3, 10 April 1873 p6; Moonta is a town on the Yorke Peninsula; South Australian Weekly Chronicle 7 July 1866 p3; The Adelaide Express 25 October 1866 p2; 4 April 1868 p3; Adelaide Observer 15 December 1888 p28; Evening Journal 25 January 1870 p3.

[324] The International Organisation of Good Templars (IOGT; founded as the Independent Order of Good Templars), whose international body is known as Movendi International, is a fraternal organization which is part of the temperance movement, promoting abstinence from alcohol and other drugs.

[325] South Australian Register 11 November 1874 p4.

[326] Evening Journal (Adelaide) 10 December 1888 p3.

[327] Wilkin p134.

[328] Evening Journal (Adelaide) 19 October 1888 p2, 21 October 1892 p4; The Advertiser (Adelaide) 10 October 1889 p6; South Australian Chronicle 18 October 1890 p9; South Australian Register 3 May 1892 p3.

the time the South Melbourne Church was in the midst of a densely populated area.

**In June 1896, following his time in Launceston,** Lambert was admitted into the ministry of the Presbyterian Church in South Australia. He said that he had changed his view on the question of baptism, and was willing to accept the doctrine, discipline and government of the Presbyterian Church. He now believed that baptism by immersion should not be the basis of church membership and he did not consider that to be a just ground for a separate denomination. For the latter, he must have known after near three decades in Baptist circles that the doctrine of believer's baptism set Baptists apart from other churches.

His Baptist colleagues in South Australia were mystified when they learned second-hand that

> Rev H. J. Lambert is reported to be knocking at the door of the Presbyterian ministry. It appears to us that it would have been a courteous act to intimate to his Baptist brethren, with whom he has been so long associated, his intention of leaving them, and on what grounds. We have not heard that he has done so, and we are left to wonder what can have worked the change in his views.

Did he never hold sincerely that the Baptist doctrine of baptism, for instance, was scriptural, or has he now discovered that our Lord did institute the baptism of infants? A man may pass from one to another among many of the denominations without any scruples of conscience, or feeling he has anything of importance to give up, but it cannot be so on leaving the Baptists.[329]

In South Australia he served the two Presbyterian pastorates of Spalding, and from 1901, that of Wallaroo.[330] He was appointed Moderator of the Presbyterian Church of South Australia in 1905 and 1906 and was now designated "the Right Rev H. J. Lambert, M.A.". In these years he took a more active role in the Orange Movement, being Chaplain of the Loyal Hopetown Lodge. He resigned from the Wallaroo pastorate in June 1907 and went on the supply list.[331]

In his retirement he attended St. George's Presbyterian Church at St. Kilda, where he was an elder. The Rev Henry James Lambert died on 14 July 1924, at eighty-nine years of age. He and his wife, Helen, are buried at a homestead near Cressy, Tasmania.[332] One of their daughters Ada a'Beckett, M.Sc., was the first woman to be appointed a lecturer at the Melbourne University and

---

[329] SB 14 May 1896 p1.

[330] Spalding is a town located 171 kms north from Adelaide. Wallaroo is a port town on the western side of Yorke Peninsula in South Australia, 160 kms northwest of Adelaide.

[331] The Advertiser SA 4 June 1896; Chronicle (Adelaide) 12 September 1896 p15, 6 May 1905 p45, 10 February 1906 p17; The Kadina and Wallaroo Times (SA) 18 July 1906 p4; The Mail (Adelaide) 8 December 1917 p7.

[332] The Observer (Adelaide) 26 July 1924 p38.

pioneer of the Kindergarten Training College in Victoria.[333]

## Appendix 6: The Rev Joseph Tanner Piercey

The versatile Joseph Tanner Piercey walked an interesting path on his journey from being a Primitive Methodist to a Baptist with some years in between at the Launceston Christian Mission Church. In time the call to be an evangelist overtook all pastoral interests.

Piercey was born in Geelong on 24 April 1856. His father, also Joseph Tanner Piercey, had been an officer in India, but was now employed in Australia as a mounted policeman. His mother was Jessie Berrell.[334]

During his childhood, the family moved to northern Tasmania. At the age of eighteen, Piercey made a Christian commitment as he attended the Primitive Methodist Church. He immediately commenced gathering the district's children to teach them to read and to give them Bible lessons. He also worked amongst the poor in Launceston. In 1879 he became a probationer pastor and was soon sent to the Ballarat Circuit for two years working mainly at Sebastopol. There he associated with Baptist the Rev William Clark who on a visit to the local Primitive Methodist Church said that he had a liking for the Primitives for three reasons, "Firstly, because they made a good strong noise; secondly, because they gave one a very strong and warm shake of the hand; and thirdly, because they invariably asked one home to tea."[335]

In September 1880, Piercey was moved back to Tasmania, and began work for two years with the Church in Penguin. He tried to establish a Primitive Methodist work at the Mount Bischoff Mine and for some months he lived at the Mine securing the use of a billiard hall for the meetings.[336] Soon, a little wooden chapel was built there and this church joined with other Primitive Methodist churches to form the Waratah Circuit. The following year he was sent to the Penguin circuit, and after eighteen months a church building was erected costing about £400 which was filled every Sunday evening.[337] On his leaving to the Benalla Circuit, it was reported, "He came as a one year probationer, but had successfully passed three years examinations in the two years, and was now at liberty to take to himself a wife," which he soon did in

---

[333] The Argus (Melbourne) 18 February 1927 p14; LEx 25 May 1948 p2.
[334] Death entry. Register entry 3870, District of Whitfield, Victoria.
[335] Devon Herald (Tas) 15 February 1879 p2; The Ballarat Star 24 July 1879 p2.

[336] The Mercury (Hobart) 15 September 1880 p2; LEx 21 April 1883 p1. The Mount Bischoff Mining Company established the township of Waratah as their centre of operations in 1880 and immediately the Wesleyans opened a work in Waratah. A Century of Tasmanian Methodism by C C Dugan p74.
[337] SB 10 April 1906 p91.

Launceston when he married Sarah Jane Dally on 16 April 1883.[338]

He was ordained in February 1883 in Ballarat. The Superintendent for the district, the Rev Heathershaw, delivered the charge,

1) They (the candidates) were to have a firm basis for their religious belief. They were to guard against theological Goodwin Sands.
2) They were to be careful to have clear, sound, utterances on matters affecting the salvation of the soul. No Delphian oracle-like sentences, but sharp and incisive, like a "Thus saith the Lord."
3) They were to pay attention to themselves, in order to avoid selfishness and the assumption of a stiff, inflexible attitude, as though error on their part was impossible.
4) Make human nature a study, with a view of adopting methods of winning individuals to goodness and God. Grip the meaning of the Apostle's words, "I seek not yours, but you." The many-sidedness of some men is not hypocrisy, but the varying aspects of their nature, like the varied aspects of a landscape. Christ admired the good, even in so imperfect a character.
5) Educate the people to work. The boast of the early Methodists was that they were at it, all at it, and always at it. Do not attempt to do everything yourselves. A church to be healthy and successful must work.[339]

While he was in the Benalla Circuit with its twelve preaching places and a parsonage heavily in debt, the debts were reduced and the buildings improved. He was there for three years (1883 – 1886).[340]

Talbot followed, part of the Maryborough and Talbot Primitive Methodist Church circuit. He remained a fourth year on the circuit as superintendent.[341]

Piercey's next appointment was in the Longford Circuit, Tasmania, which included Bracknell. He began in April 1889. While by 1886 there had been 100 members, six local preachers, five class leaders, three churches, four Sabbath schools, nineteen teachers and 149 scholars, in September 1889 the Launceston Daily Telegraph noted, "It may not be out of place to notice the great improvement in the attendance since the Rev J. T. Piercey commenced his labours in the circuit." An Orange man and their Grand Chaplain, he spoke at the Anniversary and the Bi-Centenary of

---

[338] LEx 17 April 1883 p1.

[339] The Ballarat Star 21 February 1883. The Goodwin Sands is six miles off the coast of Deal in East Kent, England. It is one of the most treacherous stretches of sand in Britain lying as they do in the middle of the English Channel in the narrow Straits of Dover. More than 2,000 ships are believed to have wrecked there.

[340] The North Eastern Ensign (Benalla Vic.) 23 March 1886 p3.

[341] Bendigo Advertiser (Vic.) 14 June 1886 p2; The Ballarat Star 13 September 1888 p2.

the Battle of the Boyne. He worked closely with the Baptists in the district.³⁴²

In April 1892, Piercey began what was to be his last appointment in the Primitive Methodist Church, this time in Hobart, going through to January 1896.³⁴³ While the Church met in its church building in Collins Street, he quickly became involved in evening services in the Town Hall. At the Church chairs soon had to be placed down the aisles, and the gallery, which was closed for years, was reopened. Reported the Launceston Examiner,

> The Rev J. T. Piercey is meeting with very great success in his work in Hobart. The church in Collins-street has long become too small to hold the many anxious hearers who crowd to hear the earnest messages of the pastor, so that last November he started, his "forward movement" in the Town Hall by holding the Sunday evening services there, and although Hobart is favoured very much just now by the visit of several earnest evangelists, Mr Piercey preached last Sunday evening in the Town Hall, when he was greeted by a large congregation.³⁴⁴

In 1894, the Church commenced a mission in Sandy Bay. Piercey was also a keen amateur photographer and joined the local Photographic and Art Association which took in the technology of lantern slides shown by limelight. In 1895, he began using this technology as an aid in presenting the Gospel message but five years later he suffered serious injuries as the result of a lantern exploding - a fractured right arm, the thumb of his left hand displaced, both lips cut and his face disfigured. He also enjoyed raising poultry for agricultural shows. He joined in with the Hobart Ministers' Association; the Congregationalist the Rev G. W. Sharp was amongst them. In the midst of the national Depression of the 1890s, he joined the Committee to look into the unemployment problem.³⁴⁵

Through October and November 1894 he took a short tour of New Zealand to conduct evangelistic meetings. In November 1895, he conducted a Gospel Mission in the Christian Mission Church and the pastorate there followed.³⁴⁶

## Appendix 7: Assistant Pastor George Craike

The Rev George Albert Craike of the Hobart Church became one of the outstanding ministers in the Australian Baptist churches fulfilling the promise of his youth. In N.S.W.

---

³⁴² Daily Telegraph (Launceston) 13 April 1889 p2, 11 September 1889 p2; The Colonist (Launceston) 19 July 1890 p22; LEx 26 June 1891 p2.
³⁴³ LEx 3 March 1892 p2.
³⁴⁴ Tasmanian News (Hobart) 11 July 1892 p2.
³⁴⁵ LEx 23 July 1900 p7, 25 January 1895 p5, 7 August 1902 p3; NWA&EBT 16 June 1900 p2; The Mercury (Hobart) 29 May 1893 p4.
³⁴⁶ LEx 6 November 1895 p4.

particularly he became one of the foremost preachers.

Craike, born in Hobart in 1879 to William Craike and his wife Ruby, was among the many scholars in the Hobart Baptist Tabernacle Sunday school. He was converted under the Rev James Blaikie and became a teacher in the Sunday school and was active in other church work. He manifested notable preaching gifts and was known as the "boy preacher". As early as October 1898, he gave a paper at the Half Yearly Baptist Assembly taking for his subject, "How to get and keep young men." On Good Fridays he was among those who spoke at the anniversaries of the Baptist Chapel on Constitution Hill. He involved himself in the Y.M.C.A. and Christian Endeavour work in Hobart.[347]

In 1905, following his time at the Christian Mission Church, Craike entered the Pastors' College in London. Fellow student, the Rev W. Cleugh Black, in a personal tribute, said of him:

> We occupied the same room in the college house, studied in the same library, walked together to our lessons, and listened to those evangelical giants of London, Campbell Morgan, John Henry Jowett, Sylvester Horne, and Dr. F.B. Meyer. We spent our holidays at springtime in Surrey, when the snows covered the old Cromwellian battlefields of Hampshire, and at last left England together with the college farewell hymn "Hallelujah for the Cross" ringing in our ears. Together we rambled over the ruins of ancient Pompeii, sailed through the tropics, strolled through the spicy Cinnamon Gardens of Ceylon, and came at last to our desired haven, to the land of the Southern Cross; and, throughout all these journeyings, I was in the presence of one of God's gentlemen.

In October 1908 Craike completed his studies and was ordained. He preached in Spurgeon's pulpit in London. He returned to Hobart to marry Ruby Morgan, the daughter of John Morgan and his wife, also from Hobart Baptist Church. They were married on 5 March 1910 by the Rev Frank W. Boreham.

The Burnie Baptist Church took the opportunity to engage him as assistant as he was soon to return to England to minister to the Zion Baptist Chapel, Chesham, Bucks. He preached his closing sermons at the Christian Mission Church on 28 January 1912. While at Zion he conducted a number of missions in England and Scotland.[348]

With his wife he returned to Tasmania for health reasons. On 28 April 1912, Craike commenced at the

---

[347] The Mercury (Hobart) 27 October 1898 p3, 12 August 1901 p2, 29 October 1902 p4.

[348] NWA&EBT 27 August 1909 p2; The Grenfell Record and Lachlan District Advertiser (NSW) 8 August 1929 p6; The Mercury (Hobart) 23 October 1929 p16.

Devonport Baptist Church in Tasmania which held afternoon services at Spreyton. He preached to large congregations. Foundation member of the Hobart Baptist Church, Samuel Bulgin Pitt, was present and remarked that,

> I have known Mr Craike when a boy, and had watched him during the many years that he had studied. They would find that Mr Craike was a fluent speaker and full of words.

In his reply to the Devonport Church Craike said,

> Folks would evidently think that I am a model sent out from England, but I am only a man. I have come to preach an old message, which had lost none of its efficacy, and the people would find lodging for it somewhere. I have travelled 12,500 miles to take over the pastorship, and I trust I will save a soul for every mile I have travelled.[349]

He soon converted the midweek evening service into a Bible school commencing with lectures on Genesis and those evenings attracted a good following. He was a welcome speaker at the Young Ladies' Social Circle.[350]

At a Temperance meeting he quoted David Livingstone's last letters relative to slavery – "All I can say in my solitude is, 'May Heaven's rich blessing come down on every one - American, English, Turk - who will help to heal this open sore of the world.'" At the end of 1912, there were 108 scholars on the Sunday school roll. As a visiting speaker he often lectured on the subject, "People I have met" in an interesting and amusing way.

In April 1913, the Devonport Church farewelled John Pearson Harrison, son of Rev Samuel Harrison, who was leaving for England to study for the ministry. Craike was appointed Tasmanian editor of "Australian Baptist". With the World War looming, he became a chaplain to military forces.[351]

Craike's lecture on butchery of all the Protestants of Paris on St. Bartholomew's Day was carried by the "Watchman", the weekly newspaper of Australian Protestant Defence League.[352] Craike initiated the Devonport Ministers' Fraternal Association and became its secretary. Craike's final Sunday at Devonport was on 28 February 1915 as he was transferring to Clifton Hill in Melbourne. The Church Secretary, A. J. Stokes, said on his leaving that

---

[349] NW Post 19 January 1912 p2, 20 April 1912 p2.
[350] NW Post 15 June 1912 p2, 23 May 1914 p2; NWA&EBT 19 September 1912 p2.
[351] NWA&EBT 26 September 1912 p4, 3 December 1912 p2; Daily Telegraph (Launceston) 24 March 1913 p2; NW Post 1 May 1913 p2; LEx 21 November 1913 p6.
[352] Watchman (Sydney) 18 June 1914 p5; The Watchman represented the interests of the APDA whose mission was to "preserve and defend the general interests of Protestantism against the encroachments of Rome in matters religious, political, social and commercial."

## The Christian Mission Church

when Craike arrived "the congregations were small and the position of the church was not the best. Now it was thoroughly sound."[353]

The Clifton Hill Baptist Church had been opened in 1890 during the pastorate of the Rev Edward E. Harris at George Street and the Rev Henry James Lambert had become its first Pastor. Craike was following the Rev Horace H. Jeffs who had been at Launceston Tabernacle as had Harris. Commencing in March 1915, he found the church in good shape. One of Craike's first tasks during these difficult war years was to unveil a roll of honour containing the names of twenty-nine young men who had enlisted from the church and Sunday school. He became a sought-out preacher for other churches anniversaries and special occasions. He was an excellent speaker, "lucid, forceful and impressive; and he knows exactly when to introduce a pathetic, humorous anecdote or incident."[354] At Clifton Hill he was the founder of the well-known Men's Morning Meeting which became so popular in many churches.[355] A manse was also purchased during his time.

In October 1918, he accepted a call from the Baptist Church in the Sydney suburb of Petersham and commenced in March 1919. He again initiated the Men's Morning Meeting which brought many men into the life of the church. Craike believed strongly in sporting clubs for the young. At an early stage he saw the vast possibilities of the "wireless". During the epidemic of 1919, he introduced individual communion cups. He kept people involved in the life of the church by finding jobs, small and large, for them, in accordance with his maxim, "use or lose". His series of sermons on Sunday evenings, "Portraits of unpopular people", was well reported on. He could be blunt at times, and his bluntness was exhibited back in his Christian Mission Church days when he upbraided in the sermon some who slipped out before the sermon was finished, namely,

> Some of you are guilty of this tonight! Have you ever thought, "How you can make light of God?" By getting up and going out at 20 minutes to 8 tonight. It is to the eternal shame of those who make light of the Man who, with pierced hands, comes pleading to them.[356]

At the Diamond Jubilee of the Newcastle Baptist Tabernacle he said,

> One of the weaknesses of the church today is that there are so many tired people in it. If members of this church were

---

[353] NW Post 12 February 1915.
[354] The Herald (Melbourne) 29 November 1915 p3; Shepparton Advertiser (Vic.) 3 June 1918 p4.
[355] AB 22 August 1939 p4.
[356] The Sydney Morning Herald 5 April 1919 p7; The Daily Telegraph (Sydney) 7 March 1921; LEx 23 February 1904 p7.

going to do anything in the years to come to get over that tired feeling, he would urge them to try the tonic of prayer ... other sections of members retard church life, among them, he was sorry to say, were to be found the deacons and Sunday school teachers of yesterday.[357]

He contributed articles regularly to papers in New Zealand and N.S.W. He was the first Baptist minister to broadcast in N.S.W.[358] He undertook a mission at the Auckland Baptist Church in 1928.

In his ninth year at the Petersham Church it was recorded,

> Petersham Baptist Church is one of those near-suburban churches where "standing room only" might always be posted up in the porches as a warning to latecomers. It is one of the most popular churches in the metropolitan area. It is a family church. A large proportion of the men meet on their own at 10 a.m. and later file into the church, and take their places with their wives and children. It is a unique sight these days when the old family pew largely has ceased to be a sign manual of church attendance. Yesterday the minister (Rev G. A. Craike) commenced the ninth year of his ministry at this Boulevard church, and the congregations were even larger than usual. Mr. Craike is an attractive preacher, with a pungent, alliterative style, which holds the listener's attention.[359]

On 22 October 1929, he died tragically after a nervous breakdown a few months before. His death was a sad loss to the Baptist denomination. His death badly affected his wife and she died after long and severe suffering in May 1930. The Rev W. Cleugh Black said further of him,

> He was ever a devout soul, a true evangelical mystic. Whatever his faults (and that he had them is but to say that he was human, like us all, for the heavenly treasure is always contained in earthen vessels) he loved his Lord, and on a memorable day in college, made his consecration vow, and framed it in familiar triangular fashion. "I will be," said he, "a man of vision, a man of passion and a man with a mission," and for twenty years, in his pastorates ... he kept his sacred vow, for he was a visionary, and at times, like Enoch, walked with God. He had, like Paul, a passion for souls."

While at Petersham Craike wrote a little book titled, "People at Wit's End Corner" based on a series of

---

[357] The Newcastle Sun (NSW) 12 October 1921 p3 edited.
[358] The Grenfell Record and Lachlan District Advertiser (NSW) 8 August 1929 p6.

[359] The Daily Telegraph (Sydney) 7 March 1927 p8.

sermons preached in 1929 as P. G. Young explains,

> They are the declination of peoples met in other lands who have experienced in days of sunshine the presence and pleasure of the great Joy-bringer - He was there: it is the testimony of many who have proved, even though they have descended to sorrow's greatest depth - He was there, the great Friend and Comforter. There are chapters on, "Worse off People", "People Who Fall Out of Love", "People Not Understood", "People at Life's Breaking Point", the latter recalling to us the story of Elijah, Jacob, Job, men who in their extremity took the extra step and were met by the angel of God.

Craike's life was a life richly endowed. His was a unique personality and he exercised a distinguished ministry.[360] When Ruby died the Rev F. W. Boreham reflected on her passing,

> In my Hobart days, Ruby Morgan was one of our brightest and best workers ... Ruby shone most attractively in the Christian Endeavour. She made us all feel that, to her, Christ was wonderfully real; and she would think nothing a trouble that would enable her to impress some other mind with a sense of her Saviour's grace. She is still remembered in Hobart as one of the fairest ornaments of the spiritual life of the congregation. She radiated hope, brightness, and faith.

Hobart church member John Chamberlain added, "Our beloved friend is gone, but her influence shall remain 'until the day breaks, and the shadows flee away.'"

Ruby's dearest theme was the Second Coming of Jesus, and her only desire was that she might be "caught up" to meet him but that was not to be.[361]

## Conclusion

The preaching once heard from evangelists of the past such as Henry Varley, which was used so effectively to tell people about Jesus, has lost its persuasiveness in part because the language of religious experience is increasingly unfamiliar. If we keep using methods that worked for them to talk to non-church attenders about Jesus, we might see some fruit, but we can be quite certain that we'll lose the vast majority, and we'll lose the vast majority under the age of thirty-five. Further, even the great and thoughtful preaching of that era such as sought after by Congregational Church preachers will not fill a church, as much as we wish it would and think it should. What is more, it is harder today to

---

[360] AB 19 May 1936 p4.
[361] AB 26 May 1936 p4.

[361] LEx 23 August 1884 p2.
[361] Bendigo Advertiser 16 September 1887 p2.

put together a good twenty minute sermon than a prattling forty-minute conversation. On the sawdust trail it was a case of bringing folk to Christian faith in a limited time frame.

So in the post-Christian, postmodern age in which we live, this method of evangelism has to change in order to keep the mission alive. Here are a few pointers and they have more to do with the subject of evangelism generally than the week by week preaching in church.

"Embracing the question is as important as giving an answer. Evangelism used to be mostly about helping people find answers but, often, in the process of providing an answer, we fail to really embrace or honour their question.

**"Steering the conversation is better than pushing for a conclusion.** We should not step away from people's questions. We need to learn to listen without judgment. We need to affirm a person's intentions.

"Being open is more effective than being certain. We can be certain. Ultimately, we must be certain because our faith is certain. Our faith stands on a sure and certain ground. But, when talking to others, coming across as certain is far less effective than coming across as open. The person who is always certain thinks they're being convincing when the opposite is often true.

**"Arrogance, smugness and superiority are dead.** For too long putting the case for Christianity has been carried with a tone of arrogance, smugness and superiority. It was the case with Billy Sunday. There was a triumphalism in his words. This triumphalism continued in "Moral Majority" and today continues in the preaching of imaginative TV preachers. Arrogance is so ingrained in many Christian cultures that Christians don't even see it or hear it anymore. Humility is attractive. Humility is what makes Jesus so much more attractive to people. Spreading the kingdom does not mean hell-fire evangelism; it means living a Christ-like life.

**"The timeline is longer.** We like to conclude everything in about thirty-five seconds; revivalists did, within the hour. Increasingly, evangelism doesn't work that way. People who come to faith when pressured often leave it after a few years. And that, conversely, the people who come to faith in their own timeline tend to be flourishing years down the road.

It kind of took the disciples three years to figure out who Jesus was, didn't it? We need people and leaders who will take the time to go on a journey with people."[362]

But for the revivalists such at Billy Sunday, it all had to be done in the time frame of the particular revivalist meeting – hear the message, respond to the message, acknowledge your sin, repent and commit. It is true we are not to lose our sense of urgency in the mission, as also we should not raise doubts where there are none, but we need to give people space and we need to give the Holy Spirit time to do His work

---

[362] For this quote I am indebted to Carey Nieuwhof who is pastor of one of the most influential churches in North America.

# Chapter 5 Deloraine Baptist Church

## Introduction

The town of Deloraine has the distinction of being one of the earliest settings of Baptist work in the colony. The first services were commenced at Deloraine by the Rev Henry Dowling from Launceston. They were held in the Government School rooms during September 1859 and continued intermittently until 1860 when land was purchased in West Barrack Street. On 1 February 1863, Dowling opened a new chapel and two days later assisted in the constitution of the church. The chapel at 73 West Barrack Street is "very small, only the size of a room" and is still there today. The baptistry was outside in the grounds, for had it been inside it would have taken up half the building."[363] On 19 January 1864, when the first baptismal service was administered, it caused considerable interest.[364] The Baptist chapel was the third Church in the town, the first two being the Anglican Church which opened on 29 April 1845, and the Wesleyan Methodist Church which opened on 7 December 1856. The Methodist Church was capable of accommodating 120 persons and cost £600. Soon it had its own cemetery.[365]

From 1860, the pastor of the Deloraine Baptist Chapel was blacksmith, Jesse Pullen, who had arrived in Hobart as a Wesleyan in 1822 carrying his Wesleyan class ticket.[366] In 1848, he accepted an appointment as an agent of the Colonial Missionary Society in Hobart. Later that year he was an itinerant preacher for the Congregationalists at Richmond, Sorell, Cambridge, Pontville, Bagdad and further afield. About the year 1851, while working in the northern part of the colony, he associated with

*5-1 The Chapel at 73 West Barrack Street*

---

[363] Day-Star August 1891, p498.
[364] Australian Evangelist February 1863.
[365] The Courier (Hobart) 15 April 1845 p2, 8 May 1845 p2; LEx 23 April 1945 p1, 11 December 1856 p3; Stansell p65.

[366] A Wesleyan Class was a group of up to twelve worshippers, who would meet together for prayer and bible study. The Class Leader was often responsible for hosting this group, and gave out class tickets, or membership cards to members of their class. These tickets could be withheld from those unworthy of being called Methodists.

Mary Ann Gibson who at the time was living at Eskdale with her husband, William Senior, and Pullen adopted Baptist views and was baptised.[367] He became their chaplain on their grazing property.[368] Pullen's talents were best "among Sawyers, Splitters and little Farmers" and Dowling ordained him to the Christian ministry. This tough-minded but hard-working pastor commenced in Deloraine in 1866 but died in 1871 and the Baptist work lapsed not long after even though it had had the support of the Pastors at the York Street Baptist Chapel in Launceston.[369] The names of several of the early Trustees of the property were Henry and John Tidey, William Abey, William and Thomas Clarke, Henry Dowling, James Davies, Walter Ridley and Henry Jones. At least two of these, John Tidey and William Abey were associated with the new Baptist work.[370] In 1880, approximately 500 people lived in the district and there was no regular postal service.

## The Rev James Samuel Harrison

The Rev James Samuel Harrison, a world famous evangelist, recommenced the work at Deloraine in 1879. He had arrived in Melbourne on 16 December 1878 with the Revs Thomas Spurgeon and Robert McCullough. Spurgeon went on to Auckland in New Zealand.

*5-2 Henry Varley*

Harrison's coming was preceded by evangelistic missions being conducted in towns across the colony by the likes of English evangelist, Henry Varley, with his non-denominational stance, the newly arrived Church of Christ evangelists and the Open Brethren Assembly folk. In Deloraine, Varley and his colleagues made use of the Pavilion in the Public Gardens and Spurgeon and the Rev George W. Gillings, Pastor at Perth, assisted him. As part of this

---

[367] Australian Evangelist, 1861 p157 and February 1863, and further based on research on Jesse Pullen by Glenn Pullen, file Archives Office of Tasmania. On 26 August 1851 he submitted his final report to the Colonial Missionary Society from Cleveland. See Jesse Pullen in Tasmania, 1822-1871, by Glenn Charlton Pullen (Hobart, 1983), p12. Pullen file TSA.

[368] TL Pullen, From Little Acorns, being The Pullen Story in Tasmania, with occasional excursions into mainland Australia (1974).

[369] The Cornwall Chronicle (Launceston) 7 October 1870 p3.

[370] For more on Pullen and the early Baptist work in Deloraine, see Rowston, Baptists in Van Diemen's Land Part 1 and Spurgeon's Men MA thesis.

Deloraine mission, conferences were open to Christians of all denominations except the Roman Catholics. To handle the extra numbers attending from Launceston, special trains were scheduled.[371]

Harrison began regular weekly services in Deloraine in the Town Hall because the original 1863 Baptist chapel was far too small.

> TENDERS, addressed to W. Gibson, Esq., Native Point, Perth, will be received up till Saturday, April 3 (inclusive), for the erection of Baptist Chapels at Longford and Deloraine.
> Plans and specification can be seen on application to Rev. C. Cater, Longford, S. Shorey, Esq., Deloraine, and at the office of the undersigned. Tenders must specify time required. The lowest or any tender not necessarily accepted.
> HARRY CONWAY,
> Brisbane-street,
> 46235)      Launceston.

*5-3 Launceston Examiner 30 March*

Within six months, on 9 June 1880, the foundation stone for one of Gibson's Tabernacles was laid by Mary Ann Gibson. William Junior, her son, addressed the meeting and shared what his parents wanted to say,

> They wanted no credit for their liberality. If they had strong hands or warm hearts, if they had wealth, they wished to lay it all at the Saviour's feet. They might erect buildings, but unless Jesus was in them, their labours would be in vain. They might lay foundation stones, but unless

they had that other Foundation Stone which the builders rejected, but which had become the Head of the Church, all would be useless.[372]

The Rev Thomas Spurgeon conducted the opening services and was in Longford the following week for the opening of a second Tabernacle in Tasmania.

The Deloraine Church building, a substantial brick structure picturesquely situated on a block of land facing the Meander River, just downstream from the bridge, was the gift of both William Gibson Senior and Junior. The building has an open baptistry and seats about two hundred people. Tradition records that the Tabernacle was paid for by the sale of a Merino ram.[373]

Journalist Henry Glennie, pen name "Silverpen", mentioned the Deloraine Tabernacle in his article, "Evangelism at Tabernacle - Evangelising at Deloraine". He wrote,

> When I heard of the Tabernacle builders, the Messrs. Gibson, and saw the three beautiful structures erected at Longford, Perth, and Deloraine respectively by them, I could not but be reminded of the scene on the Mount of Ascension and the offer then made, "Let us build three

---

[371] LEx 20 April 1878 p2, 27 April 1878 p2.
[372] LEx 10 June 1880 p3

[373] This is questionable; see Spurgeon's Men MA thesis for a discussion on this.

# Deloraine Baptist Church

*5-4 Deloraine Tabernacle facing the Meander River*

Tabernacles; one for Thee, one for Moses, and one for Elias." As I arrived by train and left the car, the first object that attracted my attention was the Tabernacle. The outside resembles the one at Longford, and as I looked across the River Meander I could not but think the site was wisely chosen, and the surroundings quite in keeping with a place of worship. Just before the building the rippling stream murmurs its song of gladness, and the green sward, with the ti-tree and wattle growing in profusion on the river's bank, gives you the notion of a resting place - a camping ground where the traveller, dust-stained and weary, may be for a while at rest[374]

The church was constituted on Monday 27 December 1880 with nineteen persons forming the membership. The constitution of the church simply read: "For the present the Bible is our only guide as to Church Matters. We expect it will be enough." Harrison's words typified what was important to these early Tasmanian Baptists. Nearly twenty years later the President of the Union, Scotsman Everard Duthoit, whose heart burned with the desire to see the gospel as preached by Baptists spread through Tasmania, introduced his address with these words, "Dear friends. I am so accustomed to use my Bible that I can scarcely talk without it. But if you will have a president's address you shall have a president's address: but it will be very much like a Bible reading."[375]

*5-5 Samuel Shorey's Flour Mill (now Harvey's Roller Flour Mill, Deloraine)*

---

[374] LEx 16 December 1882 supplement p1.

[375] SB April 1898, 4 May 1899 p1. For sermon by Duthoit see SB 15 December 1898 p284.

Messers Tidey and Olson were elected deacons. Another ten members were added in the same year. Harrison departed at the end of 1880 feeling that his call was to evangelistic work and that with the Rev Edward Isaac.

## Pastor Harry Wood

The same day the church was constituted it also extended an invitation to Pastor Harry Wood to accept the pastorate. Wood had recently left Saddleworth in South Australia. Soon after the Rev C. H. Spurgeon wrote,

> Mr. Harry Wood, who has left Saddleworth on account of the excessive heat, has had the same joyous experience (as Harrison) since he took charge of the work at Deloraine. Our son (Thomas) says, "Mr. Gibson will feel amply rewarded and ready for more service and sacrifice."[376]

Wood was installed as Pastor on 14 March 1881 with a stipend of £170 per annum and "with board and apartments", the latter being one of the dwellings of the Sunday School Superintendent, Samuel Shorey who was the owner and operator of Deloraine's flour mill.[377]

Wood recorded something of his own early days at Deloraine,

> My beloved friend, the Rev J. S. Harrison, was much used of God to open up the sphere during his short ministry. The new converts were well grounded in the truth; there was no rubbish to be removed. Many were brought to Christ and were baptised and joined the church. There were several instances in which whole families were converted and there were some remarkable conversions, especially among the men at the saw-pits at Quamby Bluff. The Baptists were not understood in those days and were the sect everywhere spoken against. But these were days of power and blessing.[378]

Wood was very much "a Bible only" man. At the 1881 annual meeting of the Deloraine Branch of the British and Foreign Bible Society held in the Tabernacle, Wood addressed the meeting giving "evidence of the power and worth of the Bible, and stating his personal knowledge of persons who had been converted simply by reading the Bible."[379]

Wood, like his mentor, the Rev C. H. Spurgeon, had no time for Higher Critics of the Bible. Wood stood by the text no matter how unlikely it

---

[376] S&T.

[377] Shorey's mill is situated in West Parade and was built in the 1850s; it is now Harvey's Mill. It made Shorey a wealthy man. Built of bluestone and brick structure, with walls 610 mm thick, it produced flour, oatmeal and rolled oats. He was a member of the first Deloraine Council of 1863. In

1886-87 he and his wife Esther moved to Melbourne to live in "Deloraine Terrace", a row of five two-story terrace houses which are now heritage listed at 499-507 Royal Parade, Parkville.

[378] Pioneer Work for the Lord in Tasmania by Harry Wood.

[379] LEx 20 April 1881 supplementary p1.

would have been the case. At the Sunday school anniversary of the Launceston Tabernacle in 1889, he told the children, "The iron did swim," dwelling on the axe head incident referred to in 2 Kings adding, "The miraculous was a means adopted by God in conversion of most unlikely circumstances to accomplish his purposes." Wood and his fellow Pastors' College men were generally totally out their depths in endeavouring to comment on Higher Criticism. They were not learned on such details and stood with their mentor.[380]

Even so, or because of this, Wood's ministry, though brief, made a profound impression upon the folk in the district and many were added to Church membership. Prominent family units at this time were the Sherriff, Tidey and Cornell families. There were difficulties and financial stringency at the time. To obtain a church organ, a voluntary subscription list was opened, each member having to pay one penny per week. The church gave Samuel Shorey a bill of sale on the organ to be paid in two years.[381]

In July 1881, Spurgeon further recorded, "There has been a glorious revival at the Deloraine Tabernacle, which is one of the chapels built by his friend and ours, Mr. Gibson, of Perth, Tasmania." Wood concluded his time at Deloraine in December 1881, having decided to return to England to complete his college studies and to be married.[382]

## The Rev Edward Vaughan

The Rev Edward Vaughan, another student from Spurgeon's College, commenced in December 1882. He was said to be "a zealous evangelist". His stipend was £200 per annum including house rent, with six weeks' notice on either side to be given to terminate the pastorate. He baptised a dozen folk in his first year. The Rev Charles Pickering who worked with Vaughan in the Goulburn Valley[383] from January 1885, wrote of him,

> It was not intellectual culture, scholarly attainments, literary brilliancy, and thrilling eloquence that Mr. Vaughan was known and beloved so much as for those Christlike qualities which live long after he who possessed them has passed away. It must not be imagined, however, that our brother under-estimated the value of educational equipment for Christian service. When the Divine call came to him to preach the gospel he keenly felt the disadvantage at which he was

---

[380] LEx 11 November 1889 p2, 16 September p3, 21 September 1885 p3, 24 September 1885 p3.
[381] Church Minutes of 11 March 1881.
[382] Wood sailed on the "Barque Berean" on 20 December 1881 departing from Launceston and arriving at Gravesend on 18 March 1882 having experienced a "good passage", from his diary.
[383] Hughes p131; the Goulburn Valley is an area stretching from Seymour in central Victoria right up to Echuca on the Murray River.

placed owing to not having received a thorough schooling in early life, and in order to rectify this deficiency he entered the Pastors' College, where he studied for three years. But the passion of his heart was to win souls for Christ, and hence burning fervour was the leading characteristic of his preaching. Those who attended his ministry looking for the refinements of high culture were doubtless disappointed, but those who desired "the sincere milk of the Word," were edified. Mr. Vaughan was a man of one book. The Bible was his companion. The copy of the sacred volume which he used in his study is marked throughout, and a careful examination of his "marking system" shows that he pondered over the Word of God not only constantly but most intelligently. To some hearers his preparations for the pulpit would appear somewhat loose. He was not a writer of sermons. His manuscript notes were the merest skeletons. To have fettered himself in the "sacred desk" would have been death to his power. Liberty was essential to his success as a preacher and this he enjoyed in a more than ordinary degree. Though small in stature our brother had a "big heart".[384]

Journalist Henry Glennie, mentioned Vaughan in his previously mentioned article, "Evangelism at Tabernacle - Evangelising at Deloraine", a joint church venture. He wrote,

Pastor Vaughan gave a capital address at the start - subject, "What must I do to be saved?" Full of fire and earnestness, he eloquently portrayed the prison scene where the incident occurred, causing the query to be asked, and urged in a most telling and effective way those feeling the burden of sin to not only ask "What must I do?" but to follow the advice given, "Believe and be saved." There seemed to be no proselytising; no urging persons to join the ranks of the Baptists, or join the Tabernacle, but the simple asking all those out of Christ to accept Him as their Saviour, and be at peace, and the kindly invitation to the members of all the other churches to assist by their

*5-6 Edward Vaughan*

---

[384] SB 4 February 1897.

prayers the work of "soul saving.[385]

A year later, in June 1883, a third journalist gave his impressions of Vaughan. The journalist, pen name "Quincy", visited the York Street Baptist Chapel one morning to find its Pastor, the Rev William White, absent and Vaughan filling in. Quincey writes on Vaughan's ministrations that day,

> The opening prayer of the preacher is by far too long for the beginning, middle, or latter end of a service, and as a consequence is wearying. The range of subjects prayed about are too expansive, too much wandering away from the congregation present, not enough of that special - Bless me, even me, oh my Father - pleading about it to satisfy the longing soul. But the right "grit" shines out occasionally, showing that the heart of the prayer leader and preacher is right with the prayer hearer, although he occasionally allows himself to wander in rambling words and strange utterances. The subject of discourse was calculated to create a soul longing for something, and that something attainable. The text - 'Oh; satisfy me early with Thy mercy, that I may rejoice and be glad all my days." The preacher evidently a matter-of-fact man - forcible and argumentative - but to my mind lacking in sympathetic pathos, and not calculated to draw the silent tear and touch the strong heart. Pastor Vaughan, I have heard to much better advantage than on this occasion. I confess the text was treated with a considerable amount of intelligent word-picturing and, on the whole, would please a mixed congregation, but it lacked something to my mind. The backing-up quality used was not as effective as it might have been. Had the discourse been as telling as the application very little fault could have been found. The preacher said many good things, and said them well, showing that his Spurgeon College training has in this respect, fitted him for a good reasoner, if not a very eloquent preacher. I take it Pastor Vaughan is more effective as a preacher when there is more excitement about. The sermon, notwithstanding what I have said, was above the average in

*5-7 William Gibson Senior*

---

[385] LEx 16 December1882 supplement p1.

thoughtful argument and eloquent utterance, and quite repaid me for my first visit to Pastor White's Baptist Chapel, York-street."[386]

During Vaughan's time, Gibson made it possible that a baptistry be installed in the Tabernacle. In July 1884 Temperance lecturers, R. T. Booth and T. W. Glover, under the auspices of the Local Option League, visited the township and made use of the Town Hall; Vaughan participated. Glover praised those who made the effort on such a cold night commenting, "If he was a resident of Deloraine with his family, it would take something more than a Temperance meeting to cause him to leave his own fireside."[387] Booth and Glover's mission won 200 converts in the town adding in number to the many non-drinkers in the town. Vaughan's Church already had a large "Blue Ribbon Army".[388]

On 13 October 1884, after two years of ministry Vaughan resigned. The church asked William Gibson Senior to "make up the deficiency in his replacement's stipend for "the church is not prepared to call a man if such a guarantee is not given." Vaughan apparently resigned because of the strong action taken by Gibson, whatever it was. "This unsettling time in the church's life apparently resulted from undue discipline by the church and the poor public relations which resulted."[389] For a short time Wood of Longford attended to the pastoral oversight. Vaughan had taken up work as a Victorian Baptist Home Mission agent working in Shepparton.

## The Rev Alfred Hyde

Vaughan's replacement was the Rev Alfred Hyde who had just arrived in the colony from the Pastors' College, London. He preached his first sermon at the Tabernacle on 31 October 1885. On 3 January 1886, the church held its anniversary and on the following day there was a Public Tea Meeting which was followed by the Pastor's Recognition Service.[390] Hyde would not have been more than twenty-five years old. By the end of the year he had become the Secretary of the Baptist Association. Tasmania would prove for him to be God's training ground and by the time he took up long term pastorates in South Australia, he was an outstanding church planter. For Hyde a prosperous church was "Bible-loving, trusting and prayerful."[391] The newly

---

[386] Daily Telegraph (Launceston) 25 June 1883 p3.
[387] LEx 12 July 1884 p1.
[388] Daily Telegraph (Launceston) 18 August 1884 p3.

[389] From an earlier history of the church; LEx 2 May 1885 p1.
[390] Daily Telegraph (Launceston) 31 December 1885 p3.
[391] The Tasmanian (Launceston) 9 January 1886 p14.

constructed Sunday school building was opened early in 1885.³⁹²

In February 1886, a vote of thanks was conveyed to William Gibson Senior for his generosity in building a stable free of all expense to the church. Public teas were held at Easter time commencing in 1886 and continuing through until the time of World War 1.

By May 1886, the Church was conducting monthly Blue Ribbon meetings which took the form of concerts with folk contributing recitations, solos, song renderings and choir items. A temperance message would also be given and folk would be invited to take a blue ribbon to signify their vow to refrain from alcohol in any form. A Miss Parker recited the "Teetotal Mill":

> Two jolly old Topers once sat at an inn, discussing the merits of Brandy and Gin; Said one to the other. "I'll tell you what Bill, I've been hearing to-day of the Teetotal Mill."

The temperance theme was a very common one. Alcohol was seen as mainly, or solely, responsible for criminal behaviour. The poem the "Teetotal Mill" was named as a cure for disease, marital problems, bad language, financial troubles and weakness, alcohol having been the root cause of these ills. The question of a Local Option for Deloraine was also raised at this May meeting.³⁹³

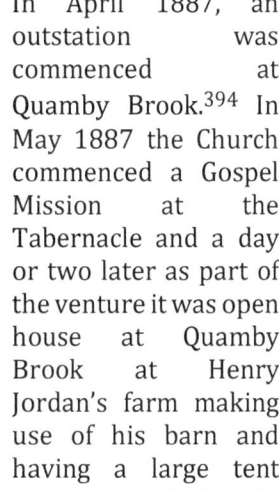

*5-8 Alfred Hyde*

In April 1887, an outstation was commenced at Quamby Brook.³⁹⁴ In May 1887 the Church commenced a Gospel Mission at the Tabernacle and a day or two later as part of the venture it was open house at Quamby Brook at Henry Jordan's farm making use of his barn and having a large tent erected. In 1887 Hyde moved to Longford; his success at Deloraine was limited.

## The Rev Herbert Davies Archer

The Deloraine church then communicated with William Gibson Senior to ascertain whether he would assist with the Rev Herbert Davies Archer's stipend if Archer was willing to come. Gibson wrote in reply,

---

³⁹² LEx 16 December 1884 p3.
³⁹³ Daily Telegraph (Launceston) 20 May 1886 p3.

³⁹⁴ Day-Star April 1887.

Lessons from our first 20 years

*5-9 Sunday School at one of Deloraine's outstations: the Quamby Brook Chapel*

... I feel quite as much interest about the Church at Deloraine as the Perth Church, it is all the Lord's work, and being one of his servants he will expect me to do all I can to further His work, whenever the opportunity offers; I am very thankful He has permitted me to do some little in His Name and trust that it might all be done for His glory. My advice to the Church is to invite Mr. Archer for a short time with a view to the Pastorate, mentioning the salary, say One Hundred and Fifty Pounds per annum; if the Lord should prosper his ministry and finances increase, then the salary might be increased if the Church think it best. I will still continue to assist in raising his salary, that is, if they strive to help themselves. The assistance the different Churches may require will soon be in the hands of the Union as I am now making over Six Thousand Pounds the interest of which will be for that purpose. Praying the Lord's blessing may rest on every member of the Church and that they may be all brought to love Him more, and serve Him faithfully, not looking to man, but to Jesus, is the prayer of yours, Sincerely, In the Lord, W. Gibson.

Gibson Senior was speaking of a recently formed Sustentation Fund, the interest from which was to be used in the founding of new churches and in aiding weak ones. It was substantially formed in 1887 by his and his son's gift of the said amount.

Archer began at Deloraine 4 September 1887. Wood advised him, "... the Gospel needed to be preached with some bite in it in these times. The Lord make you a new, sharp threshing instrument having teeth," obviously referring to the text of Isaiah 41.15. During Archer's five years at Deloraine, he and his wife, Rosamond Augusta (nee Spong) whom he married on 30 July 1889, added two children to their family but Archer was of frail body and delicate health and remained so to the end of his days.[395]

During Archer's time, Messrs J. Tidey, Orchard, Sherriff, Wilson,

---

[395] BCC August 1924 p3; Bligh p50; Day-Star August 1889 p125; Rosamond was the eldest daughter of the Spong family of the Hobart Church.

Cornell and Propsting formed the first Church mission band.

On June 1887 it was agreed to erect a small chapel at the Quamby Brook outstation but this never eventuated and the old chapel near the childhood home of William Bligh was to be used instead. By now William Ross formerly of Blackwood Creek, a man deeply involved in the bush mission life of any church he associated with, was part of the Deloraine Church. Ross' enthusiasm for the work of the local church was not shared by many; it was proving difficult to find a Church Secretary or Treasurer. The one who took on the task of being Secretary would have the added task of Treasurer thrust upon him.

In 1889, an outstation was commenced at Dunorlan and in 1892 another one at Circular Pond.[396] The Deloraine Church welcomed the return of the Thomas Glover Temperance Mission in July 1889. That year a Sunday school was prospering at the Church's outstation at Dunorlan and a chapel was envisaged.[397]

Archer remained until September 1892. His Deloraine ministry suffered removals, failures and discouragements even though the Sunday school was the second largest in the district with its sixty or so scholars.[398] He moved on to Longford.

## Harry Wood's Return

In January 1893, as an agent for the Baptist Union, Pastor Harry Wood was asked after leaving Sheffield to return to Deloraine, but upon arrival he found things had greatly changed for the worse. In his short memoir he wrote,

> After leaving Sheffield I was asked to return to my old ... at Deloraine, alas, to find things had greatly changed for the worse. The church was in a low state, the people dispirited, my health was not too good. During the time we were there God was pleased to bless and revive the work. We would have been content to remain.[399]

Within his first year a roll-revision deleted twenty names from the church roll. But as in keeping elsewhere, with Wood being a "favoured son" among the many of the Spurgeon students in the colony through the generosity of the Gibsons, renovations were carried out to the Tabernacle and an increase in the congregation began. In May 1893, a special service for young men saw seventy in attendance. Wood was facilitating open-air preaching. The comment made that "the church was still

---

[396] Daily Telegraph (Launceston) 5 May 1887 p3; Day-Star December1889, June 1892.
[397] Day-Star May 1889 p67.
[398] Day-Star May 1890, May 1891.
[399] Pioneer Work for the Lord in Tasmania by Harry Wood.

working on the old Gospel lines" was true. In 1894, Wood was recognized as pastor and the steady increase in numbers continued.[400] He received a tempting invitation from Auckland, New Zealand, requesting him to permit his name to be placed before the Church. There the membership was 270, and a large building in a growing city offered wider scope for his work. His salary would have been in the vicinity of £300. He declined the offer.[401] He also received a call from the Hobart Baptist Church but again he declined. In April 1895, Wood was asked to transfer to Latrobe and Sassafras.[402]

## The Rev Samuel Archer Harris

Wood was followed by the Rev Samuel Archer Harris, the son of the Rev Edward E Harris who happened to be pastor of the Cimitiere Street Baptist Tabernacle in Launceston. Harris began his ministry at Deloraine on 22 September 1895. He had just been married to Annie Butler on 12 September 1895. Annie was one of the principals of the non-government Glenthorpe College, Regent Street, Ascot Vale in Victoria.[403]

5-10 Howard Elliott

Harris cycled the district to visit and to perform weddings and the like. On one occasion he had to carry his bicycle for two miles to perform a wedding and do the same on the way home.[404] He concluded his first pastorate in January 1898 and they moved to the Sydney Baptist Church in Mullens Street Balmain.

## The Rev Howard Leslie Elliott

The Rev Howard Leslie Elliott was invited to the oversight of the Deloraine Baptist Church initially for a period of twelve months, commencing on the 1 June 1898 and under the supervision of Wood at Latrobe.

Elliott's ministry at Deloraine continued smoothly for three years with anniversaries, United Evangelistic missions, the monthly meeting of the Band of Hope,

---

[400] Day-Star June 1894, February 1893, July 1893, April 1894, September 1894; The Mercury (Hobart) 24 May 1893 p2.
[401] Bligh.
[402] Daily Telegraph (Launceston) 12 July 1894; SB p101.

[403] The marriage took place on 12 September 1895. The 1894 photograph was taken in the first year young Harris, just 25 years old, was at the Victorian Baptist College in Melbourne; The Argus (Melbourne) 27 December 1895 p3.
[404] LEx 30 August 1897 p7.

*5-11 Main Street of Deloraine*

Christian Endeavour, and church picnics[405] until late in 1900 when he publicly got involved with the "Free Education" question and said things that went too far. The report of the well-attended Deloraine Town Hall meeting mentioned that the opinion of the gathering was that Elliott had insulted Tasmania when he stated that "50 per cent of the natives (that is, the young people) were uneducated".[406] A D.D. Griffin arose and congratulated the audience as being the most orderly ever congregated in the town hall even though Elliott had made "such ridiculous and wild statements". Elliott retorted, "Mr Griffin has got hold of the wrong end of the stick." Griffin replied, "But the big end." When another in the gathering challenged what Eliott had said, Elliott apologized and withdrew the statement. He was then asked, "You withdraw unconditionally?" Elliot succumbed, "Yes, I was evidently in error." But the damage was done. Then Elliott intimated that he would preach on the matter but did not when persuaded later by friends not to do so. Within days stones were thrown through four large glass windowpanes of the Tabernacle.

Elliott added to it by a letter to the Daily Telegraph in that he responded to a correspondent with these words,

> Your correspondent stands on the eminence of assurance, and like Goliath of sacred history cries, "Send me a man to fight with me that I may give his flesh to a Launceston audience, and his

---

[405] Daily Telegraph (Launceston) 11 September 1900 p4, 19 June 1900 p4.
[406] According to the Australian Bureau of Statistics in 2021 47 per cent of Tasmanian's adult males and 53 per cent of females are considered "functionally illiterate". They struggle with the basic skills needed to read a form, a recipe, a brochure or understand a newspaper article so back in 1900 Elliott was not that wrong.

bones to the local bone dust factory."[407]

Upon hearing that the Church was disturbed and as there were unfavourable reports in circulation, the Baptist Union Council asked Wood to look into the matter. The outcome was that Union Council suggested that it was advisable that Elliott resign "as he had raised bad feelings in the town which resulted in vandalism being enacted on the Tabernacle."[408] Elliott concluded at Deloraine on 24 July 1901 and transferred to Hendra, Queensland. Yet the end of his time in Deloraine was not all loss; on 31 July 1901 he married Samuel Shorey's adopted daughter, Bertha Kate.[409] On their leaving the following minute was recorded, in part,

> That Miss Shorey's resignation as a Sunday school teacher be accepted, and her request for a letter of dismissal be granted, and that we express our very high esteem of her faith and invaluable work in the Sunday school and church.

But history would repeat itself. His intense personality and passion for lost causes expressed through public statements brought about the cessation of his pastoral ministry in Christchurch, New Zealand.

The activity of the Deloraine church has never been just confined to the Deloraine township. The church exercised an evangelistic, preaching and teaching ministry when it sent out teams of lay preachers into the surrounding districts for the purpose of conducting services. These Church's pastors rode on horseback for miles or hired a "gig" to arrive at services in farm houses and the Church's rural chapels. There were some remarkable conversions among timber workers, bushmen, farmers and mill-hands alike. In certain cases, whole families were won.

## William Henry Short

In his beginning at Deloraine, William Henry Short's work was considered by Union Council to be not equal to what the pastorate required and so Council appointed the Rev George Mackay of Devonport as honorary Pastor.[410]

Yet early in 1902, Short was admitted to the status of Home Missionary and the appointment was extended for a further period of twelve months.[411] At the Church,

---

[407] Daily Telegraph (Launceston) 3 November 1900 p5, 13 November 1900 p3, 15 November 1900 p4.
[408] Council Minutes p238/6 dated January 1900, p293/26 dated April 1901, p296/26 dated April 1901.
[409] Daily Telegraph (Launceston) 6 August 1901 p4. Bertha's birth parents were George and

Catherine Reeman. Family History research by Barbara Coe.
[410] Council Minutes 268/10 – meeting October 1900, p 276/9 dated January 1901.
[411] SB 14 May 1902 p111.

Short ran a series of Literary and Musical competitions which closely resembled Temperance Band of Hope meetings with their recitations, solos, duets, impromptu speeches and temperance addresses.[412]

The 1934 history of the Church records,

> William Short used to ride to the (outstation) church and walk straight up the aisle long after the (evening) service had commenced. In his hand, he still carried his riding whip and, beneath his arm, he clasped firmly his Bible. The clatter of the spurs, not yet removed from his boots, announced his entrance. His day had begun early in the morning, and his ride into the country was long and hard; the service had been commenced as usual by a church deacon. Once, during the service, Mr. Short glanced out through the window. There he could see his horse struggling and, suddenly, the congregation was startled by a loud "Whoa" and the clatter of boots and spurs as the preacher ran down the aisle to rescue his choking horse.

Short remained at Deloraine for another eighteen months as Home Missioner. He left the work in good heart. He commenced services at Chudleigh which saw conversions and baptisms. He was transferred to Wynyard under the supervision of the Rev Joseph Tanner Piercey of Burnie.[413]

## The Rev Vincent George Britton

At the commencement of his pastorate at the Deloraine Church on 25 October 1905, Vincent George Britton was ordained to the Christian ministry. Within a month he had conducted two Temperance meetings. Apart from the use of Magic Lantern pictures, the forerunner of today's digital projector, the balance of the Temperance meetings resembled Band of Hope meetings with solos, duets, recitations and the taking of the pledge. These were the commencement of the Church's monthly Gospel Temperance meetings.[414]

During his three years at Deloraine and elsewhere, he also made good use of his phonograph. He commenced a Ministering Children's League on Saturday afternoons. He brought folk together on work day evenings for socials with songs, choruses, recitations and dialogues.[415] On one such evening he gave an illustrated lecture on the Charles Monroe Sheldon novel, "In

---

[412] LEx 27 September 1904 p3, 23 December 1904 p7.
[413] LEx 16 November 1905 p 4.

[414] Daily Telegraph (Launceston) 27 October 1905 p5, 25 November 1905 p9.
[415] The Mercury (Hobart) 16 May 1906 p2; Daily Telegraph (Launceston) 4 August 1906 p5.

His Steps".[416] On another evening the poem, "The Newsboy's Debt", by Hannah R. Hudson was recited.[417] One night, an illustrated lecture was given on "Ben Hur", part of a vocal and elocutionary programme. At times Britton involved the wider community. He arranged a concert in the Quamby Brook chapel involving the local State school and its school teacher. In July 1907, 250 people attended the annual evening of entertainment in connection with the Sunday school anniversary in the Tabernacle. At times he used the net proceeds of concerts to assist folk in need. In 1908, he was also the honorary pastor of the Bracknell District Churches. His time at Deloraine concluded in January 1909 as he transferred to the Sheffield Baptist Church.[418] Within a year of his leaving, membership had declined considerably, chiefly by removals from the district and by deaths.[419]

# Appendices

## Appendix 1: The Rev James Samuel Harrison

Sometimes, those who were not suited to the pastoral work of the local church became pastors. There were reasons: the need of financial support to carry out what was for them the more pressing need, evangelism or a question of health. These matters played out in the life of the Rev James Samuel Harrison, a celebrated evangelist from the Pastors' College who always knew that his call was to evangelistic work.

Harrison was born in Marylebone, London, in 1853. His parents were nominally members of the Church of England. He was the subject of religious impressions from early childhood as seen when he was about ten years old. He attended a Gospel service for children and being deeply impressed by the earnest addresses given, sought help from his mother but she was not capable of providing it. Yet his ambition was to be a missionary as the story of missionary toils, perils and triumphs stirred him greatly.

---

[416] *In His Steps* is a best-selling religious fiction novel first published in 1896. The book has sold more than 50,000,000 copies, and ranks as one of the best-selling books of all time. This novel introduced the principle of "What would Jesus do?" which articulated an approach to Christian theology that became popular at the turn of the 20th century.

[417] *The Newsboy's Debt*, Harper's New Monthly Magazine May 1873. Plot: a gentleman trusts a newspaper boy to get change, which he was to bring to the office. The lad, however, is run over and sends his brother to say that when he gets well he'll work to refund the money lost at the time of the accident. Daily Telegraph (Launceston) 14 August 1906 p6.

[418] Daily Telegraph (Launceston) 6 September 1906 p3, 27 July 1907 p5, 5 November 1908 p7; LEx 17 September 1906 p3, 23 April 1908 p6, 7 January 1909 p5.

[419] SB 6 January 1910 p 19.

Employed in Swansea in his nineteenth year, he responded at a Gospel service, the preacher being Oscar T. Snelling. Harrison later recorded that the words of a hymn echoed in his head, "I was filled with joy unspeakable and full of glory: Heaven came down my soul to greet, and glory crowned the mercy seat."

He moved to Bristol and attended the church of George Muller engaging in Sunday school and tract distribution, Y.M.C.A., cottage meetings and open-air preaching. At twenty-two years of age he decided to devote himself entirely "to the ministry of the Word" and began with three years of preaching in the villages of Gloucester, Somerset, Wiltshire and Dorset resulting in many responses.

In 1877, he entered the Pastors' College but studied with some difficulty because of the lack of his general education. In April 1879 he accepted the pastorate of Montague Street Baptist Church, Blackburn, prior to accompanying Spurgeon's son, Thomas, and the Rev Robert McCullough to Tasmania. William Gibson Senior paid for the passages of Harrison and McCullough on the basis that they accept pastorates in the colony. Harrison's acceptance of the offer also had to do with health. The ship, the *Sobraon,* arrived at Melbourne on 16 December 1879. Harrison began at Deloraine but by the end of one year, in December 1880, he acknowledged that his call was to evangelistic work. He wrote to the Rev Edward Isaac, a Pastors' College colleague, asking him to join him in Melbourne that they might work together as evangelists in the Australian Colonies and Isaac agreed.[420]

*5-12 S. J. Harrison*

Then Harrison alone travelled on to New Zealand to conduct a mission at the Rev Thomas Spurgeon's Auckland Church. He then returned to England; and, in the spring of 1882 conducted missions in various parts of England and Ireland, and especially at Frederick Charrington's Great East-End Hall. But inevitably the strain of incessant work, added to a cold and sunless summer, "eventuated in a severe-nervous prostration" and Harrison embarked once more to Australia.

After a time of evangelising in Victoria, he visited Launceston and there met his wife Anna Louisa Kidgell, and they married on 14 May 1885. The pastorate of the Aberdeen Street Baptist Church, Geelong, followed commencing April 1885. As

---

[420] S&T October 1879, November 1882, 1899/560ff.

*5-13 Aberdeen Street Baptist Church, Geelong*

Geoff Holland records in his history of the church,

> Both Harrison and the congregation were encouraged by the immediate results of his ministry: numbers increased; £500 was paid off the debt in a few weeks; and many were converted and added to the church. But he had not fully recovered his strength and was too dependent on piety and enthusiasm. The Rev Alfred Bird had warned him that he was facing a breakdown, and he did, suffering a complete collapse. His anxious wife took him to Tasmania to recover, but the damage had been done. He told the church his health was failing and that he needed complete rest ... he resigned (after only two years), to the sorrow of many friends he had made in Geelong.[421]

Anna and her ailing husband then returned to London. In 1892 he commenced a ten year stint as an evangelist preaching many times at the Great Assembly Hall, Mile End Road, at Dr Barnardo's and in other large halls, Anna at times assisting with singing.[422]

They then returned to Australia and in 1897 he became Pastor at the Ashfield Baptist Church in Sydney. On returning to England he had pastorates at New Malden (1909-13), Gipsy Road, Norwood (1913-17), Ilderton Road, Bermondsey (1918-21), Bristol Road and Weston-Super-Mare (1922-23). Anna died on 29 December 1921, aged sixty years.[423] He remarried in 1923, this time to Sarah Isaac, the widow of the Rev Edward Isaac. Victorian Baptist archivist, John

*5-14 Auckland Tabernacle NZ*

---

[421] Aberdeen Street Baptist Church: The Colonial Years.

[422] S&T 1903 p562; Geoff Holland asks, "Was his health the only reason he resigned from the Aberdeen Street Baptist Church?

[423] BCC March 1922 p4.

Sampson, writing on Sarah, reveals something of their courtship,

> In 1922 Sarah was corresponding with Rev Harrison. He was looking for a new church and she gladly helped by putting an announcement in the Australian Baptist saying that he intended to return to Melbourne in October 1922 with his stepson, son of his first wife. But her plan did not work out as Rev Harrison secured a position at Bristol Street Baptist in England and started there in January 1923. Soon after, however, we find that she had another announcement in the Australian Baptist in January 1924. This one gave the good news that he had arrived in Melbourne at the end of 1923, that they had married and were living in her house at 180 George Street Fitzroy. I suspect that when it came to marriage; she was not the passive object of Rev Harrison's quest but took the initiative. In an article Sarah made the following observations, "People set a very high ideal for the minister's wife. She has many domestic duties over and above those in a private home. She cannot get help due to the high cost of wages for maids, the high cost of living and low stipends. Her children and the life of the home are her responsibility. She is expected to visit the sick. She is expected to take a Sunday school or Bible class. And she is expected to foster missionary activity in the church.

*5-15 Great Assembly Hall, Mile End Road, Aberdeen*

In 1927 Harrison accepted the invitation of the West Hawthorn Baptist Church remaining there until his death on 30 November 1935; he was eighty-five years old.[424]

## Appendix 2: Pastor Harry Wood

In Pastor Wood we have the essence of the Spurgeon man in Tasmania – a zealous and able evangelist, holding tenaciously to the theologically conservative views of his mentor, the Rev C. H. Spurgeon, and devoted to the Christian ministry forever spurred on by the memory and love of this same mentor.

Harry Wood was born at Brighton, England, on 16 March 1854 into a

---

[424] Wilkin p131; The Australasian (Melbourne) 7 December 1935 p14.

large family. He was raised as an Anglican. At an early age he was sent to work to augment the family income. At sixteen years of age, following a serious illness, he made a Christian commitment at a gospel meeting and took to "soul-saving". He worked among the young male flower sellers, offering them carbonated lemon drink if they attended meetings. Encouraged by clergy, business men and others he gathered a number of workers around himself and together they ran gospel meetings. Such were the demands of all this that he eventually devoted all his time to these ventures. Two of those won over entered into Christian ministry while others moved to better employment. Wood was finally baptised in Bond Street Baptist Chapel, Brighton, and his name was placed before Spurgeon. There had been prospects of him training for the Wesleyan ministry but the matter of believer's baptism had arisen. The outcome was Wood's entrance into the Pastors' College in 1877 or 1878.[425]

In 1879, while studying at the Pastors' College, as extracurricular activities, he became a member of its Evangelisation Society, but his frail physique would not stand the strain of study and of missions and an inevitable breakdown followed. His doctor ordered him to "the Colonies".[426] Spurgeon spoke of him as being "highly esteemed by us all." He said,

*5-16 Harry Wood*

I had hoped that his career, which had begun with great promise, would have continued in his native land, where we greatly need such a zealous and able evangelist as he has already proved himself to be ... I love him much in the Lord ... I commend him to the hearty confidence and loving hospitality of all my brethren in New Zealand and elsewhere. New Zealand will gain by our loss ... Go forth, my brother. You are so well known to me that I think I see you (especially your distinguished head of hair), and I look you in the face with a tear of love in separation, and say, God bless you, Wood! Go, and blaze away for your Lord.[427]

He sailed to New Zealand in May 1879. Once he had recovered from sea-sickness, he conducted weekly church services on board until they

---

[425] LEx 6 November 1889 p2; 'Our Own Men and their Work', S&T 1896 pp. 561-565.
[426] Bligh.

[427] The Rev James E. Walton. S&T 1896/p561-565, Bligh; Spurgeon, a new biography by Arnold Dallimore p114.

reached Auckland. There he received an invitation to preach at the Willoughby Street Baptist Church, Thames, with a view to the pastorate. But with the climate's excessive heat proving unbearable, he moved to Saddleworth in South Australia to pastor its Baptist church. Commencing in May 1880, the cooler climate markedly restored his health and the work itself revived under his ministry. The membership trebled, the chapel debt was paid off and a fund was commenced for necessary building alterations.[428]

But in Saddleworth his health deteriorated again. There he received a letter from the Rev Thomas Spurgeon who was spending a holiday in Tasmania with William Gibson Senior and his wife Mary Ann at their Perth home, "Native Point".

Wood accepted Spurgeon's invitation and concluded his ministry at Saddleworth in October 1880.[429] One of Wood's letters to home tells of their first meeting,

> My first meeting with our beloved President (William Gibson) was on his (Spurgeon's) second visit. On arriving at Perth station a young gentleman came to the carriage window and inquired for me by name. It was

*5-17 Saddleworth Baptist Church, SA*

> Mr. Spurgeon, and he got into the carriage and rode with me to the next station, where he had just time to catch the return train to Perth. We were only about a quarter of an hour in each other's company, but he won my heart, and the friendship commenced in the railway carriage grew and deepened with the years.[430]

On 21 November 1880, Wood assisted Spurgeon at the opening of a Baptist chapel at Brumby's Creek (Blackwood Creek).[431]

Wood concluded his time at Deloraine in December 1881, having decided to return to England to complete his college studies. There, on satisfactory completion of his studies, he was ordained at the College. On 19 April 1882, he spoke at the Subscribers' meeting in the College's Lecture Hall. The next day Spurgeon and his wife and their son Charles entertained him for dinner.

---

[428] Bligh; S&T April 1880, July 1880, July 1881, November 1880.
[429] S&T April 1880; Bligh calls Thomas "his friend" but Thomas and Wood were only known through Thomas' brother Charles.
[430] WY Fullerton, Thomas Spurgeon – a biography p95.
[431] See chapter two.

That evening Wood preached at the Metropolitan Tabernacle thus having as a student, the rare distinction of taking Spurgeon's place in the pulpit. On several occasions he preached at the Rev Archibald G. Brown's East London Tabernacle.

In July 1882, Wood and Harrison conducted missions at Frederick Charrington's Great Assembly Hall, Mile End Road, East London. They also spent a fortnight missioning at Coleraine, Ireland. Back at the College, his address at the (Annual) College Conference was reported by "The Christian" as one of the main features of the gathering. On 26 September 1882, he married Elizabeth Childs with Spurgeon officiating.

In a later tribute Wood spoke of Elizabeth's early years and how they met.

> As a young woman my dear wife attended a Mission Hall where I conducted services while in business in my native town of Brighton, England. It was there she commenced her Christian life and work for God, and it was there we became interested in each other. Like myself, my beloved wife was not "free born", i.e., we were not born and reared in a Baptist home and Church. Our people were strictly Church of England. She saw believers' baptism to be the Christian's duty and privilege. In her home and village Baptists were only the name of a strange people, dissenters from the established Church. There being no Baptist Church in the village, she worshipped with the Methodists, and became a teacher in the Sunday school, but always was known as a Baptist. When I returned to England (in 1882) I made for a village in Hampshire. I called at the comfortable old farm house. It was a surprise visit, and in the afternoon, asking for my friend, her mother informed me she was away at the Methodist Church helping the children practise their hymns for the Anniversary. I learned she was one of the most active workers, and beloved by all, but still regarded as a member of the baptised Church of Jesus Christ.

On 19 October 1882, they left Gravesend for Melbourne. On board they conducted "Gospel" services and Blue Ribbon Temperance meetings. Wood explains,

> Numbers signed the pledge and donned the colours. My little wife pinned on every badge. When we had exhausted the blue ribbon, which we had brought with us for temperance work, she cut up the blue ribbon from off her bonnet. We reached Melbourne on 1st of December.[432]

---

[432] "Leaves from my life story" – a tribute to my wife by Harry Wood, BCC December 1926 p4.

Once in Melbourne Wood assisted the Rev A. J. Clarke, his colleague from the Pastors' College, at the West Melbourne Baptist Church. From January 1883, he was given oversight of West Melbourne's branch church at Williamstown. He commenced a Gospel Temperance work which had wide implications. In a report to the Pastors' College, he explained, "In less than six months the press acknowledged the effect for good the movement had had upon the community. It is little better than three years since it was started. I think its members number some thousands."[433] Press notices were frequent and, for reasons unknown, the temperance work created quite a furore. But in July 1883, they relinquished the work and made for Tasmania. They had received urgent letters from William Gibson to return to "the tight little island". Gibson's letters were coupled with a letter of call from the Longford Baptist church dated 14 August 1883, offering him the pastorate cognizant of his delicate state of health and allowing him leave to be "free as the Lord's servant to arrange your meetings and do your work as you feel best able."[434]

## Appendix 3: The Rev Edward Vaughan

The Rev C. H. Spurgeon's Pastors' College did not attempt to produce scholarly pastors but "soul-winning" pastors. It was happy to train men with a limited formal education or no education at all and so assist those who were already preachers whether they were delivering an address in mission halls, at ragged schools or on street corners. But they had to have the gift of preaching.[435] Edward Vaughan was one of these. Even though he never proved an articulate preacher having made up for his deficient schooling in early life, he proved a zealous evangelist and thus would have pleased his mentor.

Edward Vaughan was born on 23 June 1852 in London. As a nineteen-year-old, he entered the Pastors' College from the Vernon Baptist Chapel, King's Cross, Pentonville, where he had become a Christian.[436] He had left school early to support himself because of the death of his parents. He spent three years at the Pastors' College and had a keen loyalty to the Baptist denomination. His first pastorate, lasting three years and commencing in 1874, was with working folk at the small Baptist church in Surrey Lane, Battersea, London, conducted in a

---

[433] S&T 1896/p561-565; Pastors' College Annual Report 1886.
[434] S&T 1896/p561-565; Bligh. For Wood's time at Longford, see chapter 6.
[435] AB 19 September 1956 p2.
[436] Table Talk (Melbourne) 21 June 1889 p1; Living Stones, A History of Vernon Baptist Church, King's Cross, by Rev Arthur Thompson.

temporary iron chapel. The church continues today.[437]

Because of his health he departed for Sydney but was waylaid at Adelaide, arriving in September 1878 carrying recommendation letters from Spurgeon and the London Baptist Association. He soon found a settlement as pastor of the Baptist Church in the circuit of South Rhine, Eden Valley and Salt Creek.[438]

On 14 October 1879, in South Australia he married Emily Whiting of Battersea who had journeyed from England for their marriage.[439] Emily was born in 1848 in Bromley, London, the daughter of Jonathan Whiting, a ginger beer manufacturer, and Sarah (nee Simpson). In 1871, the family lived at High Street, Battersea. In South Australia Vaughan associated with Harry Wood at the Saddleworth Church. Under Wood's ministry the membership in the circuit had grown to a total of ninety-four by 1882 with many baptisms. In the area the Seventh Day Adventists had been busy proselytising much to the Baptists' detriment. Vaughan was making full use of the Magic lantern with lectures such as "England Past and Present".[440]

In December 1881, Harry Wood, Vaughan and Emily sailed together to Tasmania and while Wood eventually returned to South Australia, the folk at the Deloraine Tabernacle met their new pastor and his wife.

Following his time at the Deloraine Church, Vaughan took up work as a Victorian Baptist Home Mission agent working in Shepparton. He was appointed for twelve months working with the Rev Charles Pickering beginning in January 1885. He began weekly prayer meetings in his own home and hoped to be able to open a Sunday school and requested a tent for church services. He established a Ministers' Association but the numerous churches in Shepparton and elsewhere were competitors for the allegiance of a relatively small population. Following his leaving, the work was scaled down.[441]

Vaughan then moved to the pastorate of the Victorian Baptist Home Mission Churches of Eaglehawk and White Hills. He was under the supervision of the Rev Dr Thomas Porter of the Hargreaves Street Church.

In July 1888 Vaughan moved briefly to take charge of the South

---

[437] S&T 1878 p254, p446.

[438] The South Australian Advertiser 10 October 1878 p5, 7 January 1879 p6; The Express and Telegraph (Adelaide) 2 December 1878 p2; Christian Colonist (SA) 20 December 1878 p1.

[439] The South Australian Advertiser 15 October 1879 p4.

[440] The South Australian Advertiser 3 November 1879 p16; South Australian Chronicle and Weekly Mail 9 October 1880 p24; Christian Colonist (SA) 13 October 1882 p5; 16 September 1881 p3.

[441] Our Yesterdays Vol. 6 p25ff.

Australian Minlaton and Minlacowie Baptist Churches on the central Yorke Peninsula staying until 10 December 1891. Hughes records,

> He was a zealous evangelist and he revived the circuit. A revival occurred in the year – people had never seen anything like it elsewhere in Australia. In 1890 he baptized 40 converts in Minlaton.[442]

He then moved to Mannum on the west bank of the Murray River. But in a year it was advised that Emily find a cooler climate and Vaughan accepted a call to the Sheffield Baptist Church, Tasmania.[443]

## Appendix 5: The Rev Alfred Hyde

Alfred Hyde's entry into the Pastors' College was typical of so many in that it was preceded by engaging as an evangelist with one of the English Evangelistic Societies. Candidates for entry had to be preaching regularly over the previous two years,[444] and had to be men "touched with live coals from off the altar". After a time in Tasmania, his work and that of his wife Sarah in South Australia bore much more fruit as they had the gift of being church-planters.

Hyde was born in 1860 and as a young man attended Regents Park Chapel and evangelized in London with the London Evangelistic Society. He entered the Pastors' College in 1882 and stayed until 1884. During his College years he had a student pastorate at the Woolwich Baptist Church in South East London. He arrived in Australia in October 1885.

## Appendix Six: The Rev Herbert Davies Archer

The State Education Department teacher Herbert Davies Archer gained distinction in Tasmanian Baptist ranks as being the first Tasmanian to be educated at the Pastors' College in London. Although he would have been far better educated than his College peers who were mainly from the labouring class, he would have felt at home as he was (and remained) a "lover of the old Gospel". During his subsequent ministries his educated ministry was evident but he suffered a life-time of poor health and succumbed to an early death after pastorates in four states.

The name "Archer" ranked high in the Deloraine district's early community life. Settling at "Chestnut", just beneath Mother Cummin's Peak in the Western Tiers, his father, William Archer, carved a home out of the bush and reared a family of seven daughters and six

---

[442] Hughes p131.
[443] The Argus (Melbourne) 12 December 1881 p4; Evening Journal (Adelaide) 3 January 1882 p2; Bendigo Advertiser 20 March 1886 p3; South Australian Weekly Chronicle (Adelaide) 4 August 1888 p22; 5 December 1891 p4; South Australian Register 15 December 1892 p6.
[444] S&T December 1874.

sons. He became the first Warden of Deloraine. In 1882, young Archer matriculated at the Launceston Church Grammar School. In 1885 he resigned from the teaching staff of the Education Department to undertake a two years course of study at the Pastors' College, London.[445] Years later he spoke of the Friday afternoon student muster to whom Spurgeon himself would speak,

> Punctually at three o'clock he would enter. His advent was the signal for every man to rise and welcome him by cheers and clapping, which, when the president was seated, would take the form of beating the desks, to which sometimes he protested by putting his hands to his ears, and bidding someone open the windows for fresh air. His first words were always cheerful, and sometimes quaint. Mr. Spurgeon was never long on the platform before there would be laughter from the benches ... He knew we had been grinding away all the week at our studies, or should have been, and that many of us would be preaching on the coming Sunday, and so his words were cheering and helpful withal. He ever aimed, too, at preparing us for our future life work. Almost every student would be seen with his note-book, jotting down for future reference, and so gathering together a thesaurus of pointed and pungent sayings.[446]

He returned in 1887 to take charge of the Deloraine Church he knew so well, remaining until 1892. At the time it was noted of him, that he was "A real Tasmanian, the pioneer we trust of a band of our (men) whom God shall raise up as pastors of the Baptists of this their native land."[447] His ministry was considered very acceptable and he took his place well in public affairs.

## Appendix 7: The Rev Samuel Archer Harris

Samuel Archer Harris, son of a Baptist minister, a graduate of the Victorian Baptist College, was one of the first trained men not to have come from the Pastors' College. He was also the first of those who served in Tasmania to move to the Presbyterian Church ministry.

Samuel, son of the Rev Edward E Harris, was born on 2 March 1866 as part of the extended Harris family in Geelong district. He would have been at Portland when his father was Pastor of the Baptist Church there, from 1880-84. It was during the time his father was pastor of the George Street Baptist Church, Fitzroy (1884-1894) that Archer, a member the West Melbourne Baptist Church, worked with the Victorian Home Mission in northern Victoria.[448]

---

[445] Wood, BCC August 1924 p3.
[446] Day-Star December1893 p171.
[447] Victorian Freeman May 1888 p90.
[448] Harris was with the Mission in 1890.

In 1891, he entered the Victorian Baptist College and remained in training until 1894.[449] Following his initial pastorate at Deloraine Baptist Church, he and Annie his wife transferred to the pastorate of the Mullens Street Baptist Church, Balmain, Sydney, remaining until December 1903. His next pastorate was the Grafton Baptist Church also in NSW, remaining until September 1905. They then transferred back to rural Victoria and were stationed at Cohuna. In 1907, Harris undertook an interim pastorate at the Mount Gambier Baptist Church. Following this appointment, they moved back to the Kerang area and attended the Macorna Baptist Church. In 1910, they moved States and Harris commenced at the Ororoo Baptist Church in South Australia and established a preaching station some miles out at Wynflete.[450]

Major changes took place in their lives as they spent the nine months from July 1913 in New Zealand, this time not in the pastoral ministry but working in the "No Licence" campaigns. The other change was they became Presbyterians. On their return to Victoria, Harris was appointed organiser of the Victorian Alliance "No Licence" campaign which entailed extensive travel. This work continued until June 1917 when Harris took up Presbyterian Home Mission work in the Traralgon district of Victoria. In May 1923, Harris took leadership of the Wodonga Presbyterian Church. In 1925 he was employed again as a Presbyterian Home Missioner, this time to Golden Square, a suburb of Bendigo. This Home Mission work continued in Ararat from June 1930 and in June 1931 to Pomborneit Mission.[451] On 30 June 1931, Annie died. She was born in County Armagh in the North of Ireland in 1862. In her eulogy it was said that for thirty-five years no minister could have had a more devoted or efficient helper. Annie had taught Bible classes, prepared teachers for examinations, trained children for Sunday school anniversaries, at times was choir leader and conductor and often soloist at services and occasionally preached. She was head of women's guilds and a most enthusiastic worker for the WC.T.U. They had one child, Howard

*5-18 Young Samuel Harris during his Baptist College years*

---

[449] A report says he resigned from College but subsequently carries the title of Rev from then.
[450] Hughes p123.

[451] Pomborneit is a rural locality in western Victoria situated on the Princes Highway between Camperdown and Lake Corangamite.

Archer Harris. The Rev Samuel Archer Harris died on 27 April 1949 at Ringwood, Victoria.[452]

## Appendix 8: The Rev Howard Leslie Elliott

The Rev Howard Leslie Elliott, a foundation student of the Queensland Baptist College who showed early promise as a leader in Church circles and whose discourses were eloquent and impressive, twice in his ministry, once in Tasmania and once in New Zealand, suffered greatly from his bad case of plain-speaking.

Elliott, a native of Maldon in Victoria, born on 10 March 1877, was the son of prominent townsman J Elliott, J.P. Young Howard was educated at both public and private schools and subsequently studied under private tutors and ended his student years at St Andrew's College, Bendigo. He was converted under the ministry of the Rev John McNeil and associated with the Wesleyans. Once convinced that baptism by immersion was scriptural, Eliott was baptised by the Rev T. Beeson of the Maldon Baptist Church. Elliott became the first secretary of the New English Baptist Church in Maldon. On his application to minister in Tasmania, the Baptist Council wrongly believed that he lacked formal Theological College training and only studied theology under the tutorship of Beeson.[453]

Following his time at Deloraine, Elliott moved in September 1901 to the Hendra Baptist Church in Queensland for a three months' engagement which led to the pastorate itself. Now as a leader of the denomination, at the Queensland Baptist Half Yearly Assembly in 1906 he presented a well-thought out paper titled, "Our Suburban Churches and our Denomination Position" lamenting the lack of Baptist Church growth in the population centres. Still in Queensland, in May 1909, after seven and a half years at the Brisbane Clayfield Baptist Church, he and his wife Bertha and their four children were farewelled to New Zealand. These years in Queensland had passed without adverse incident and the Clayfield Church had grown under his direction.[454]

5-19 *Maldon Baptist Church, Vic*

---

[452] Camperdown Chronicle (Vic) 7 July 1931 p1; The Argus (Melbourne) 28 April 1949 p13.
[453] HM Council Minutes p193/23 October 1898; Queensland Baptist 1 March 1902 p35; AB 8 November 1921 p4.

[454] The Queensland Baptist 1 November 1901 p145, 1 March 1902 p35; 1 June 1909 p535.

He had accepted the pastorate of the Mount Eden Road Baptist Church, Grafton, Auckland. The Rev T. J. Malyon Principal of the Queensland Baptist College had preached at the Church early in 1901 so he might have commended Elliot to the Church.455 The Oxford Terrace Baptist Church in Christchurch followed.

*5-20 Oxford Terrace Baptist Church, Christchurch*

In New Zealand, as a member of the Grand Orange Lodge, Elliot became chief spokesman for the Protestant Political Association of New Zealand and subsequently became well-known as a sectarian preacher and social reformer. He believed that the Roman Catholic Church was attempting to capture control of the NZ Labor Party and accused the Pope of having started the First World War. Among his many other claims was the erroneous allegation against the Post-Office, namely that the Auckland Post Office had assisted unduly in delaying the distribution of Protestant mail matter. This claim resulted in a Parliamentary House of Representatives enquiry in 1917. He was publicly horsewhipped by a returned soldier as a protest against aspersions he was alleged to have cast upon the soldier's sister who had drowned; she was a Roman Catholic nun. Elliott was much denounced for his anti-Catholic remarks in the Roman Catholic newspapers. Elliott was in line to become the President of the Baptist Union of NZ but henceforth ceased to be a credible candidate. The Australian newspapers reported widely on this incident. Elliott, whose discourses were eloquent and impressive, suffered from a case of straightforwardness at times. He needed to take to heart the words of the evangelist of the time, William Graham Scroggie, whose final pastorate was at Spurgeon's Tabernacle (1938–1944), "Let us clearly understand that the interests of Christ and His Word are not served by raw haste, violent denunciation, presumptuous ignorance, or uncharitableness of spirit." The Oxford Terrace Baptist Church finally released him from his position. He never pastored a church again. After a time back in Adelaide, the family returned to New Zealand where he became proprietor and managing editor of the New Zealand Financial Times. The Rev Howard Leslie Elliott died on 11 November

---

455 The Malyon connection is a suggestion by Rodney Kirkpatrick, Queensland historian.

Queensland Baptist April 1909 p479, 1 June 1906 pp83–86.

1956 at Te Awamuta, Waikato.[456] For all their joys and regrets, Bertha forever kept in touch with the folk at the Deloraine Tabernacle. She died in Napier, New Zealand, on 22 June 1958 aged eighty-seven years. Elliott and Bertha had three daughters and two sons[457]

## Conclusion

Those Tasmanian Baptists who preceded the Spurgeon men who began arriving from 1869, the Particular (Calvinist) Baptist forebears with their sectarian ways, found the going hard. As they held to their distinctive beliefs, seeking to be unspotted by other Christian groupings, they saw little success. Their internal divisions over who could and who could not of their own number participate in the Lord's Table greatly destroyed their internal fellowship. They were eventually left behind. They had envisaged themselves as guardians of pure Christianity, sealed off from worldly ways and from critical scholarship, observers of strict spiritual discipline amidst the slackness of what they thought generally passed for Christianity.

Yet many of the Spurgeon men continued their ways with their combative anti-liberalism and insistence on biblical inerrancy; after all Spurgeon himself their Chairman was very much against Higher Criticism. Spurgeon also held that he was a Calvinist but he wasn't in a strict sense and his men in Tasmania gave no hint that they agreed with him on this matter; they were strident evangelists.

One of the Spurgeon men, the Deloraine preacher, the Rev Edward Vaughan, was in agreement with the Particulars in that he was a man of the Bible; it was his constant companion.

Of course life was simpler in those days, hence our early forebears were able to focus on only three aspects in ministry: be Baptist denominationally which meant emphasizing baptism by immersion, preach the Gospel just as their Chairman preached it and plant churches, the last thanks to the Gibsons.

For years we too have heard the same cry, "Be missional" but sadly the gospel today means different things to different folk in our Tasmanian Baptist Churches. For a few it is an inerrant Bible with its "young earth", one of the tenets of Fundamentalism, and for many more it is an awakening to the truth of God's preference for the poor and Jesus' passion for "the little ones": the need for justice and sharing thus attending to that deprived person who hangs around the church. These

---

[456] Press (NZ) 13 November 1956 p9.

[457] "A Handful of Grain, The Centenary History of the BUNZ" p96f; Freeman's Journal 12 April 1917 p10; The Evening Star 4 August 1917 p2; New Zealand Tablet 20 September 1917 p37; The Catholic Press 11 October 1917 p27; The North Western Courier 17 October 1917 p2; Truth 17 August 1918 p6; Tasmanian Family History Society.

say that by their actions they preach the gospel. Of the former, it is generally admitted that the doctrine and infallibility of the scriptures throughout their entire extent can no longer be held. It does not follow however that God is not in these writings. True, as a people we Tasmanian Baptists continue very much the Spurgeon emphasis on valuing the Bible highly and like him we are conservative in our theology yet I wonder if we have arranged ourselves into discrete enclaves that have little to say to those who think otherwise and show little incentive to try, hence we veer toward associating only with those who think and believe as we do and seem to have forgotten why they exist. Any organization must be crystal clear about its purpose and focus to be successful. "If you're stuck in the past, you will decline because effectively you're locking yourself into a certain way of doing things, and everyone else moves on," it is said. Yet on a positive note we are those who want the traditions of the church to continue and be honoured and celebrated and so we have infused some of the best things of our traditions into our current worship practices.

Still the resulting intolerance for differences or diversity which currently exists does not assist us in our denominational mission. We need a renewed effort to rediscover and reclaim the nature of the gospel itself, what it was, what it is and what it might be in and for our community of faith.

# Chapter 6 Longford Baptist Church

## Introduction

Longford is a small town twenty-four kms south from Launceston and five kms west from Perth.

Baptists became known at Longford through the work commenced in 1869 by the Rev Alfred Grant, the first of the Pastors' College men to arrive in Tasmania. During his two-year stay at Perth and at the invitation of Mrs Elizabeth Noakes, the builder and owner of the Longford Assembly Rooms, Grant commenced "unsectarian worship" on Sunday afternoons. After his first lecture which was "tolerably well attended", she offered him the main room free of charge for regular afternoon services. Grant had the support of William Gibson Senior.

Longford's Primitive Methodist minister, the Rev Samuel Ironside, did not think that "Mr. Grant's meetings in the afternoons would take one from either the Wesleyan or Primitive congregations". The Wesleyan Methodists had opened their chapel in 1837 at the cost of £1,000 while the Primitive Methodist Church had commenced in March 1861.[458] Unbeknown to Ironside and other non-Baptist clergy, Grant's ministrations in Longford set the ground work for the beginnings of a permanent Baptist work in the town.

Grant's work was continued by the Rev George William Gillings and his wife Harriet, also of the Perth Baptist Church.

## The Rev Robert McCullough

Robert McCullough, who barely saw out his two years of study at the Pastors' College, arrived in Tasmania on the last day of 1879. His first sphere of work was at Longford.

Discussion took place about erecting a place of worship in the town. McCullough's first Sunday

*6-1 Longford Assembly Rooms*

---

[458] LEx 5 January 1870 p5. The Anglicans commenced in Longford in 1831. LEx 28 March 1861 p4; Stansall p53.

services were held in the same Assembly Rooms, again free of cost. The week-night gatherings took place in the Rechabite (now Druids') Hall.

McCullough had many discouragements from the other churches in the town mainly on the question of baptism. Baptists had been the first church grouping known to introduce baptism by immersion to Van Diemen's Land and this went back to the 1830s, but there was little outcry against the practice until these decades when Disciples of Christ, the Brethren evangelists and McCullough's Baptists began work in areas already occupied by churches that did not practise baptism by immersion.

The Baptists soon learned that they were a despised sect, as reported in the newspapers of the day. Public baptisms resulted in reactions from the Wesleyan and Primitive Methodist Churches who saw them as intruders. They felt obliged to defend their own church's practices.[459]

On his second Sunday, McCullough preached in the Assembly Rooms again "to a large congregation" and informed the gathering that the Baptists intended to build a place of worship as soon as a suitable site could be procured. This was not good news to the Longford Wesleyans who were erecting their own church building which was opened on 18 July 1880.[460]

The foundation stone of the Longford Tabernacle was laid by Mary Ann Gibson on 11 June 1880. The tradition continues today that as with the Deloraine Chapel that Gibson sold merino rams at the Royal Melbourne Show for 1,000 guineas and one also paid for the Longford Tabernacle.[461] The church was constituted in March 1881 with thirty-eight members.

In the next year, twenty-six members were added to the roll. A manse was built next to the Tabernacle with William Gibson Senior and Junior bearing the expense. One of the first candidates for baptism was Eva Richardson and she became McCullough's wife. By the time he departed to begin a work in Hobart, there was a growing Sunday school and a large and earnest band of church

*6-2 Robert and Eva McCullough*

---

[459] S&T College Annual Report 1886; for a full study of the public debate in Longford see Spurgeon's Men MA thesis.

[460] LEx 14 January 1880 p3, 17 April 1880 p3. Stansall p53.

[461] This tradition is discussed in Spurgeon's Men MA thesis p94.

workers. In the Pastors' College report of 1886 he wrote, "When I left there was a good church in a flourishing condition. It is flourishing still. Many there are dear to my heart who came out of the world, gave their hearts to the Saviour, and helped me in the work of the Lord." This popular minister, in part through the liberality of the Gibsons,[462] was farewelled on 30 September 1883.

## Pastor Harry Wood

Pastor Harry Wood received a call from the Longford Church which was aware of his delicate state of health and he commenced there on 13 November 1883. He worked with William Kenner and William Ross at Bracknell and Blackwood Creek Baptist Churches, Bracknell being an outstation of the Longford Church while Blackwood Creek was under the care of the Perth Church.[463]

**6-3 William Gibson Jnr and wife Elvina**

At the time Wood began, there were unhappy divisions among the Longford Baptists: the church was in a low state. But under his leadership the work prospered and outstations were opened at Bishopsbourne and Illawarra. Aggressive evangelism was his style and at the time he had a love for the text Luke 5.12, "Lord, if thou wilt, thou canst make me clean."[464]

Wood's well-organised monthly Temperance Band of Hope meetings in Longford led hundreds of adults and children to join the Blue Ribbon Army. At one Longford Band of Hope meeting ninety-eight responded and thus "exhausted the supply of blue provided for the occasion." Reporting on another of Wood's temperance meetings, this time in country Beaconsfield, the Launceston Examiner reported that this chosen one of Spurgeon "quickly established himself as a favourite with the audience by his denunciation of the liquor traffic." At the annual yearly Assembly of the Baptist churches in 1886, Wood was reappointed as Superintendent of the temperance work of the Association, the temperance roll standing at 1318 persons.[465] But success in gaining pledges and at giving out Blue Ribbons was not always assured. At a Temperance Demonstration at the Longford Tabernacle in November 1884, the pledges were not forthcoming nor were Blue Ribbons being given out

---

[462] Pastors' College Annual Report 1886; LEx 10 May 1882 p3.
[463] LEx 13 November 1883 p3; Bligh pp25ff. Report of the BUT Conference of 27 May 1884.
[464] Pioneer Work for the Lord in Tasmania by Harry Wood; Daily Telegraph (Launceston) 6 December 1883 p3.
[465] LEx 14 November 1883 p3, 18 July 1884 p4; BUT report of Assembly 1886.

due to the recent drive in the township by Evangelist and Temperance campaigner Thomas Burnett, for he had "evidently cleared out the local market for the present."[466] Because of Wood's temperance work and his devoted Band of Hope Secretary, Mr. F. Clark, there was a strong temperance influence through the whole district and as many as 500 people would "sit down" to their Annual Band of Hope Tea meetings with the different churches in the town joining in. It was noted that no other Tasmanian town had so many wearers of the Blue.[467] The full title for the movement was "The Gospel Temperance Blue Ribbon Band of Hope" and this was aptly applied in that it was maintained that the temperance habit could not be maintained without God's help.[468]

A Sunday school hall was erected at a cost of £400, a gift of Elvina Beaumont Gibson, William Gibson Junior's wife.[469] When Wood concluded his ministry at Longford in August 1887, he left a strong self-supporting church of eight-six members and a large Sunday school.

Wood had responded to a call to the Launceston Tabernacle but the Longford folk didn't want to lose him. During his time at Longford, Wood was absent at times due to ill health.[470]

## The Rev Alfred Hyde

The Rev Alfred Hyde who arrived from the Pastors' College in 1882, transferred from Deloraine to Longford in July 1887. The text for his opening service was Psalm 20.5, "In the name of our God we will set up our banners."[471] A notable event on Show Day in the second half of the year was the visit of the Rev George Soltau and his Christian Mission Band from Launceston. This team held an open-air meeting immediately after the Show. In the evening the team made a torchlight procession through the town and the "usual" evangelistic meeting was held at the Tabernacle. Several members of the Mission Band were

6-4 "The Blue" Band of Hope medal

---

[466] LEx 6 November 1884 p3.

[467] Daily Telegraph (Launceston) 4 November 1884 p3, 28 January 1885 p3; LEx 19 August 1904 p6; Pioneer Work for the Lord in Tasmania by Harry Wood.

[468] Daily Telegraph (Launceston) 30 January 1884 p2.

[469] AB 1929 p81.

[470] Daily Telegraph (Launceston) 28 January 1885 p3, 24 August 1887 p2; LEx 2 July 1887 p3.

[471] LEx 6 September 1887 p3.

among those who gave addresses. Also present in the town was colporteur the Rev George Lake and his work was appreciated.[472]

At times the Sunday school of the Perth chapel made visits to the Longford Tabernacle to perform choral items under the leadership of school Superintendent William Edward Watkins, "helper in the (Perth) church work in every way" with his wife at the organ. Elvina Beaumont Gibson, William Gibson Junior's wife and a Miss Inglis would give a duet.[473]

Under Hyde's ministry numbers increased for both Sunday and week-night services and his ministry was appreciated. But six months before his leaving there were only fifty-seven Sunday school scholars on the roll and the Band of Hope had been disbanded. At the end of October 1888, the reporter for the Launceston Examiner suggested Hyde's leaving would be beneficial both to pastor and people. All that could be said was that the church was in a "depressed state" and that there had been a lack of progress.[474] The "Day Star" reported on the Church in the New Year saying, "There is nothing of interest to record." It added an anecdote of a Christian sailor who had lost his leg and reading between the lines, the report was saying that Hyde's time at Longford was an abject failure.[475]

## The Rev Henry George Blackie

The Rev Henry George Blackie transferred from the Latrobe Church in December 1888 and stayed for three years. The manse underwent painting and wallpapering prior to the family's arrival. In that regard the local newspaper suggested that "a little attention to the garden ground attached would also conduce to its advantage, and redeem it from the appearance of growing wild."[476]

Under his ministry and that of his wife Louisa the work of the Church prospered as it did for them at Latrobe but with Longford it took some time. Blackie had acquired a reputation as a preacher and was known for his readiness to assist in every good work.[477] On occasions an open-air Sunday night service was held in front of the Tabernacle and it drew a large audience. Yet on one such evening there was an added difference: Blackie had the loan of the "Ballarat Bible van",

> imported some three years ago by Mr Henry Owen Taylor Friend and after a protracted and

---

[472] Day-Star November 1887.
[473] Day-Star December 1887.
[474] Day-Star May 1888, December 1888; LEx 19 September p4.
[475] Day-Star May 1889 p67. The report was likely written at the time of Hyde's departure.

[476] LEx 2 January 1889 p4; Daily Telegraph (Launceston) 12 December 1888 p1.
[477] Daily Telegraph (Launceston) 8 December 1888 p1; Day-Star September 1890.

sensational journey from Launceston, it was safely delivered in the Tabernacle grounds on Saturday, and on Sunday evening, after the usual service inside (the Tabernacle), it was used for the first time, being placed in front of the Tabernacle, and, of course, it attracted considerable attention, the lamps being lighted, and a small harmonium and a choir stowed inside. The platform was occupied by Pastor Blackie and Messrs. Lake and Stokes. Lake was visiting from Victoria.[478]

**6-5 Henry G. Blackie**

As a member of the United Friendly Societies, Blackie took part in its annual demonstration on the day after St. Patrick's Day. The day began with a procession through the main streets headed by the Longford Band. Then a sermon at the Tabernacle followed. A "reforming" took place and there would now be a march to the Assembly Rooms so folk could "partake of a sumptuous repast". Then the procession once again "reformed" and headed by the band, made its way to the Show Ground, where the usual sports were held.[479]

In May 1889, the Church formed a choir of fifty persons. The Church's new schoolroom was opened in October 1889. A Tract Distribution Society, in vogue during McCullough's time, was recommenced.[480] In the town at the time were the Seventh Day Adventists, "under the leadership of Messrs Israel and Foster". Reported the "Day Star", "What can be said of all their rank Arminianism and heterodox teaching concerning conditional immortality? The Lord save the people from their meshes is the earnest prayer of many."[481]

On return with his family from an annual holiday in Melbourne, one of the Blackie twin boys died and he was buried at the Perth Cemetery.

---

[478] Daily Telegraph (Launceston) 7 February 1889 p4; LEx 6 February 1889 p2; Day-Star January 1890.

[479] The Mercury (Hobart) 23 March 1889 p1.

[480] LEx 13 May 1889 p3, 10 October 1889 p2; Day-Star December 1889.

[481] Day-Star December 1889. This is one of the few mentions of Arminianism versus Calvinism in the sermons and speeches of Spurgeon's men in Tasmania. Although their mentor proclaimed that he was a Calvinist, in fact at times in practice he denied it; his College men made little of Calvinism and the Spurgeon's Calvinism went into eclipse following his death. In fact by Spurgeon's death the debate between Calvinists and Armenians was a thing of the past. The Spurgeon men in Tasmania in fact showed no sympathy for the struggling Particular (Calvinist) Baptist Chapel in York Street Launceston. Without acknowledging it, the Spurgeon men were Arminian in practice. In Sydney some years later the SDAs were fined for working on a Sunday, Day-Dawn 10 September 1894 p65.

*6-6 The Longford Tabernacle*

## The Rev Herbert Davies Archer

The well-educated Rev Herbert Davies Archer from the Deloraine Church followed Blackie at Longford. At his commencement on 4 September 1892, he preached on the text of Zechariah 4.6, "Not by might nor by power, but by My Spirit, saith the Lord of Hosts." The church's anniversary services in January 1893 saw large congregations. Archer became President of the local library. He presided over the first meeting of the Longford United Band of Hope and Total Abstinence Society that was held in the Longford Temperance Hall.[483]

The Rev Thomas Spurgeon again visited Longford in April 1890 and with Wood, the church conducted an evangelistic mission to "excellent congregations". The gloom in the Tabernacle was dispelled early in 1890 with the installation of "truly splendid" lamps at the cost of £25. A branch work was commenced at Woolmers in the little chapel on the estate. Between thirty and forty persons would gather there on Sunday afternoons. At the end of 1891, the Blackies were farewelled with every blessing trusting that their new abode, Albert Park on the edge of the city of Melbourne, "would have all the advantages of residence in a good city and a wide sphere of labour."[482]

During the Longford flood of July 1893, he assisted in every way he could. Near the end of 1893 renovations were undertaken on the Tabernacle.[484]

On 4 July 1894 Archer, "a lover of the old Gospel", preached final sermons as he was returning to the mainland as Tasmania was too cold for him; he had to leave before winter set in.

---

[482] LEx 12 March 1890 p2; Day-Star March 1890, September 1891, December 1891 p562.
[483] LEx 6 September 1892 p2, 3 January 1893 p6, 6 July 1893 p4; Daily Telegraph (Launceston) 25 April 1893 p1.
[484] LEx 22 July 1893 p6, 16 November 1893 p5, 4 September 1894 p5.

The Longford Baptist Jubilee history of 1931 records, "His thoughtful ministry drew some of the most influential people of the town and district to the services." Archer had been appointed by the Victorian Home Mission to work in the Koroit district, in Western Victoria.[485] His final text for the Longford congregation that morning was Habakkuk, 3.2, "O, Lord revive Thy work," and the closing hymn of the evening was Sankey's, "God be with you till we meet again."

After his departure the Longford Church suffered a serious set-back. The Presbyterians, some of their best supporters who had sent their children to its Sunday school, withdrew on the arrival in the town of the Rev Alexander Hardie, a member of the Free Church Presbytery. The Baptist work now plateaued.[486]

## The Rev John Macallister

The Rev John Macallister, late of the Presbyterian Church in NSW but now a Baptist, commenced in September 1894. But the church failed to recover. As for the Sunday school, with the aim of countering the easiness with which some were receiving prizes at the end of the year – children knew when that was and when the annual picnic was to be held and would attend briefly to gain the benefits that long term scholars rightly received - Macallister informed the children that in the future the maximum number of marks to be obtained during the year would be 1000, and those scholars who did not gain 500 would not be entitled to a prize at the next anniversary.[487] It was a problem faced by most Sunday schools at the time.

*6-7 John Macalister*

As well as the Sunday school, a quarterly church service was held for the children on a Sunday afternoon. At one, called "a friend in need service", the children were asked to contribute to the fund for the support of over 5000 inmates of Dr. Barnardo's Homes in England. Macallister's address was from Matthew 25.40. "He dwelt on the importance of kindness to others, showing that the ground work of their future happiness or misery depended almost wholly on the treatment of Christ himself in the person of his suffering children."[488]

---

[485] LEx 24 April 1894 p5, 14 February 1895 p4; The Tasmanian (Launceston) 14 July 1894 p16.
[486] Heyer, J, The Presbyterian pioneers of Van Diemen's Land (Launceston, Presbytery of Tasmania, 1935) p177; Day-Star June 1894.
[487] LEx 23 April 1895 p2.
[488] LEx 10 July 1895 p7, 15 July 1895 p3.

In July 1895, new seats were acquired for the church. The following month he preached on Numbers 31.23, "Everything that may abide the fire, ye shall make (it) go through the fire, and it shall be clean: nevertheless it shall be purified with the water", the subject being "An Unpleasant Text". He said,

> even though to worldly and sinful men this was one of the most unpleasant texts in the whole Bible, yet it is God's truth, and God's truth must be heard, and men must be told whether they like it or not, that every mean, selfish, foul sin they commit is sure, here on this earth, to come home to them in some way with compound interest. After a very solemn and impressive discourse the preacher appealed earnestly to those who were suffering by the disappointment, the unsatisfied craving, the gnawing shame of a guilty conscience, to see the awful heinousness of sin and turn before it be too late, before their sin find them out, breaking their hearts and leaving them in a state of stupid despair and discontent.[489]

The newspaper report added that a large number remained for the prayer meeting, and many resolved to decide for Christ.

Macallister was appointed to Union Council in April 1895 but in fifteen months from his arrival he preached his final sermons at Longford, in June 1896. Following his leaving the Church was at low ebb. The faithful few met for prayer and hoped for brighter days. What was happening nationally: a fall-off in capital inflow from Britain, adverse movements in the terms of trade and drought, accentuating and prolonging the depression, was being mirrored in Longford Baptists' experience. There is no evidence that Macallister was being treated poorly by some in the Longford congregation but more likely he felt that he was a fish-out-of-water among the Spurgeon men and if so, the likes of Harry Wood would have had no wet eyes on seeing him leave. Macallister transferred to the Kyneton Baptist Church as an interim pastor.

*6-8 Cornish miner, Billy Bray*

## The Rev A John Casley,

The vacancy at Longford was filled by former Congregationalist, the Rev John Casley. He commenced on 14 August 1896 and he found a small congregation without a Sunday school. With the Church's finances in

---

[489] LEx 2 August 1895 p3.

such a poor state, the filling of this vacancy was made possible with moneys from the Sustentation Fund. For his first twelve months he worked under the supervision of the Rev John Walton of the Perth Church. For a time the Church revived and prospects looked brighter. Casley took a keen interest in the Local Traders' Association.[490]

Casley also relished giving public lectures. A favourite subject of his was a two-part one on Cornish miner Billy Bray and he delivered this lecture at various venues. Casley would relate one of Bray's favourite sayings which he used when people complained about his enthusiastic singing and shouting, he would reply, "If they were to put me in a barrel, I would shout glory out through the bunghole! Praise the Lord!"[491] Other lectures of Casley included "Eccentric characters I have met" and his popular "Strange Tales of John Ashworth."[492] Casley had a good voice, a pleasing manner and was a fluent speaker. He possessed great descriptive ability,

*6-9 The Longford Manse*

was abounding in humour, and was always at home with his audience; he was easy to follow. Throughout his life he had an interest in "manly sports" and was an expert lawn bowler.[493]

Casley was an engaging speaker. He gave a lecture at the Longford Tabernacle one evening titled, "Jokes and Jokers". There was a good attendance. After giving the definition of a joke, he gave numerous illustrations of jokers, "keeping his audience in a thorough good humour from start to finish." There was a six penny entry fee.[494]

He gave his farewell sermons on 15 January 1899 as he transferred to the Sheffield Baptist Church. In

---

[490] Day-Star February 1899; LEx 2 June 1897 p6, 15 November 1898 p3.
[491] The Mercury (Hobart) 8 April 1897, p3; It must have made a great impression on Harry Ratcliff of the Launceston Tabernacle because he gave the lecture at Longford ten years later, see LEx 4 September 1908 p8.
[492] LEx 10 November 1897 p7, 7 August 1897 p9. John Ashworth was the founder of "the Chapel for the Destitute" in Rochdale, Manchester, England, in the mid-1800s.
[493] Chronicle (Adelaide) 12 August 1916 p50. For a reasonably full transcript of one of Casley's sermons, see LEx 19 June 1897 p3. The sermon closes: Jesus Christ lays the obligation upon us, "Go ye into all the world and preach the gospel to every creature." We owe allegiance to him. One Sabbath day a man was seen carrying his bed through the streets of Jerusalem. The strictly orthodox Sabbatarians said, "It is not lawful for thee to carry thy bed." Mark the man's reply, "He that made me whole, the same said unto me take "up thy bed and walk." I like that man's logic. It meant this, "He that made me whole, shall he not command me? He that gave me the power, shall he not direct that power? He that made me whole said unto me." Is that what Jesus Christ has done for you, "Made you whole?" Is it? "Then let him command, direct, control you. Let your willing feet in swift obedience run to do his will. "Whatsoever he saith unto you, do it."
[494] LEx 9 September 1897 p7, advertisement 29 September 1897 p1.

Longford he did a "splendid work" among the poor, and left a fair sized Sunday school and congregation. Peace and harmony again reigned.[495]

From then on the Longford Baptist work languished; it was difficult to get preachers. There were few scholars attending the Sunday school. The Sunday morning and evening services ceased; only an afternoon service was held. The income for one year at this time amounted to £11 8s. The Rev Henry Clarke of Perth did all he could to help by visiting the few members left and taking the Sunday afternoon services as often as practicable.

The Longford work did not revive. It was suggested by Union Council that the property be sold and the proceeds used for work elsewhere. The proposition did not materialise on objection by some Council members, so the buildings remained in Baptist hands. For some time Gilbert E Moore ministered to the church, but ultimately he joined the Methodists as resident Home Missionary.[496]

## Pastor Harry Wood Returns

Near the close of 1900 Pastor Harry Wood, who was at Burnie, became seriously ill. It was decided to ask Wood to occupy the vacant Longford manse. On his return in January 1901, after fifteen years' absence, having left the church when it had a large membership, there were now only five members on the roll and an average of twelve persons attending the Sunday services. The Sunday school was in a moribund condition. His stipend for the first year was £120 which he received as a grant from the Sustentation Fund of the Union. It was all the Fund could provide; the weekly offerings were needed to pay for the supplies and to meet current expenses. At the time Wood wrote,

> It was a trial of faith but the Lord did not fail us. He was our Bank and our Banker. The Longford church had been without a minister for a long time ... my old sphere was in a state of heartbreaking desolation. The property had well nigh gone to ruin. Fences were down, gates off the hinges, shingles off the roof of the Tabernacle; the Manse which had been let to an R. C. Constable was in a fearful state. The entrance to the Tabernacle and paths were grown with weeds. The once fine, large stable was in a state of collapse. Only a Sunday afternoon service was held (there was) no week night meeting, or Sunday school. Finances were at low ebb. I shall never forget the

---

[495] Day-Star February 1899. Yet an earlier church history of the Longford Church suggests that the Longford work under Casley in fact had made little headway although Casley had a certain appeal.

[496] HM Council Minutes p228/6 – meeting October 1899; LEx 15 July 1905 p6, 17 November 1919 p6.

first Sunday morning when I sat up in bed and held a little service in the manse. We all literally wept when we remembered Zion.[497]

For a while he was unable to do very much. In time he recovered sufficiently to take a number of services and arrange for speakers with the result that the people began to return. Further his presence seemed to be an attraction to the place. An earlier history record well sums up the situation,

> Behind all the struggles was the undaunted personality and high character of the loved and invalid pastor who as his health improved entered more and more into the service of the people entrusted to his care.[498]

The Rev Vincent George Britton who was then stationed at Bracknell, came to the rescue. The long-closed baptistry was re-opened. Britton assisted with the baptisms and week-night meetings. He also was preaching as often as possible and helping greatly in the Band of Hope meetings which again became crowded. The Sunday school recommenced and prospered, the prayer meetings grew. Again with Britton's help, the whole of the Church property was put in a state of good repair, including the matter of resheeting the Tabernacle roof with sheet iron. New gates and fences were erected.[499] So the work revived. Also, practical interest was again taken in Foreign Mission work. When the last report of the five years' work of Wood's ministry was read at the Union meeting in Launceston, the whole Assembly rose and sang the Doxology for the blessing God had given to the Church.

# Appendices

## Appendix 1: The Rev Robert McCullough

In the Rev Robert McCullough we follow a Pastors' College man who spends his days in Tasmania and South Australia faithfully serving his Lord with everything within him. His contribution to the Baptist churches over fifty-four years of ministry was immense.

McCullough was born in 1853 at the village of Randalstown, on the banks of the Maine River, County Antrim, Ireland. His father was a farmer on the Shanes Castle Estates and had descended from the old yeomanry of Ulster. Robert was brought up in the Anglican Communion and had the Bishop's hands laid upon his head in confirmation. In his early days, Robert saw not a little of the factional fights between the Orangemen and the Ribbonmen.

After passing through the classes of the Anglican school in the neighbourhood, he found employment at the Old Bleach Irish Linen Company. Acting as time-

---

[497] Harry Wood, Pioneer Work for the Lord in Tasmania.

[498] Longford Baptist Church's Jubilee History.

[499] Bligh.

keeper, he had to be at the office at 6 a.m. and remain until 6 p.m. In addition to keeping the books of the head office, he was in daily contact with all parts of the works and his prospects were bright.

The first time he heard of Baptists was when the Rev Grattan Guinness and his wife visited the North of Ireland holding evangelistic services. The Baptists were then disrespectfully called "Dippers" and it was whispered among the youth of the neighbourhood that these strange people had in their churches a hole in the floor full of water into which people went down and were dipped. Sometime after this, there came a stranger, and asked if he could stay one night at the McCullough's farm house. He was made welcome but it was soon discovered that he was one of those dreaded "Dippers".

The visitor was asked why they baptised people by immersing them, and they were told that they tried to follow Jesus, and that Jesus was immersed in the Jordan. The answer made a lasting impression upon McCullough. When, at the age of nineteen he responded at a revival meeting, he looked into the question of baptism anew and found from the New Testament that the despised "Dippers" were right. Feeling that it was his duty to cast in his lot with them, he joined the little Baptist Church gathering about five miles from his town to which he had to walk each Sunday. The severance from the Anglican Church, the church of his fathers, to which he was much attached, did not come easily.

At the Baptist meeting he began "exhorting" as was the custom with the Irish Baptists. He was led on to conduct services and, notwithstanding his busy life, he preached almost every week in various districts. His spare time was given to study under the direction of his pastor, the Rev W. S. Eccles. Friends for some time urged him to devote himself to the ministry. After nine years at the Old Bleach Irish Linen Company he resigned to enter the Pastors' College and he was presented with a gold watch. It was his full intention to minister in Ireland, but he was suffering from tuberculosis and as his studies at the college drew to a close, the cure lay in migrating to Australia. He sailed with the Revs. Thomas Spurgeon and James Harrison, Harrison sharing a cabin with Spurgeon. Following his time at Longford, McCullough was given the

6 10 Robert McCullough

Longford Baptist Church

task of raising a new Baptist Church in Hobart.⁵⁰⁰

## Appendix 2: Pastor Harry Wood

Following Wood's departure from Longford his health continued to decline. Month by month the Baptist publication of the "Day Star" reported on the state of his health. In 1902 unable to preach, all he could do was visit. His apology was received at Assembly after Assembly. For the next five years he battled his way back to health, and finally made an appearance at an Assembly in November 1905, his first appearance in five years. There he delivered a brief address. The last Assembly he attended was in Burnie in November 1906.⁵⁰¹

Early in 1906, by the unanimous decision of the Perth church he was asked to pastor them and Longford at the same time. But his health was such that he relinquished the Longford component in October 1906. But after a little over a year of ministry at Perth, he was obliged to resign from the pastorate. He never regained his health sufficiently to undertake a pastorate again. He recorded his sense of loss,

> For 27 years I have laboured in the gospel in Tasmania, and have never been without a church till the present time, and the thought brings a feeling of sadness into my heart. Gladly would I have served the Church at Perth, if God so willed, for I love the place and the people.⁵⁰²

Following his joint pastorate at Longford and Perth in 1907, his health continued to cause great anxiety In February 1908 he suffered a mental breakdown.

*6-11 Harry Wood "Locked indoors by Giant Ill-Health"*

Wood retired to the cottage "Ebenezer" which the Baptist Association had provided, a gift given by Mary Ann Gibson.⁵⁰³ He remained until after the death of his wife Elizabeth on 9 June 1927.⁵⁰⁴ Just prior to her passing, Wood penned a tribute to her,

> Having a working knowledge of medicine in country districts where there was no doctor, she has rendered good service to the

---

⁵⁰⁰ S&T.

⁵⁰¹ Day-Dawn March 1901, May 1901, July 1901, December 1901, May 1902, June 1902, February 1906, April 1906.

⁵⁰² SB 1 October 1907 p226.

⁵⁰³ Daily Telegraph (Launceston) 23 March 1910 p8.

⁵⁰⁴ LEx 10 June 1927 p1.

sick, especially among the children. My dear wife has never sought the limelight or a foremost position, her quiet, Christian influence still lives in the churches where we were privileged to minister the word of life. She has been a true Phoebe, a servant of the church. As my true yoke-master in my long term of physical weakness she has been to me as God's good angel.[505]

Subsequently, he went to live in High-street, Launceston. He was a confirmed invalid "Locked indoors by Giant Ill-Health". For the last ten years of his life he barely left the house yet exercised a correspondence ministry.[506] Yet surely there alone in his rooms he would have reflected on the day he stood with the Rev C. H. Spurgeon in the Metropolitan Tabernacle pulpit as Spurgeon sent him forth; that was his day of glory and it would have forever impelled him on. He died in Launceston on 29 June 1935, after thirty-two years of incapacitation from any public work.

Wrote his biographer, the Rev John E. Walton,

> Twice he has been called to the Presidency of the Baptist Union of Tasmania. Thrice he has preached the annual sermon. He is as true as steel to "the old-time religion". The ideal minister is evangelist, expositor and pastor, all in one; and Brother Wood has these gifts in a remarkable degree. He visits his flock persistently, and quickly catches at events of joy and sorrow to win influence for his Lord. He is equally at home with the unlettered labourer or his cultured master; with the small audiences of the bush, or the crowded ones of the city. He has a bright and racy quality in him; a very genius for description and appropriate gesture; a quick facility of illustration and sparkling epigram; a pleasing voice and ready utterance; and, withal, a special gift in prayer.[507]

Years earlier he had been capable of entering fully into children's sports to such an extent that he seemed one of them.[508] While in Sydney in July 1886, Wood conducted a Mission at the Petersham Baptist Church. Present was Henry J. Morton, later President of the Baptist union of NSW. A little lad in 1886, Morton accepted the call to the ministry. Morton forty years later wrote to Wood,

> You will not recollect the little lad who was only one of many who heard the call that night, but both the occasion and the preacher are one of my most vivid memoirs of childhood. The subject was "Stumbling Blocks" and the

---

[505] Leaves from My Life Story – a tribute to my wife, by Harry Wood, BCC December 1926 p4.
[506] BCC September 1926; Rev John Complin, BCC July 1935.
[507] S&T 1896 p561-565.
[508] LEx 9 April 1885 p2.

message was simple enough and winsome enough to be understood and accepted by a little child.[509]

In a letter to the Treasurer of the Baptist Union of Tasmania in 1935, months before his death, Wood wrote, "I am the only survivor of the fifteen brethren that met to form our Tas. Baptist Union in the large vestry of the Launceston Tabernacle on May 27th 1884." Throughout his ministry he had received many tempting offers to much larger and more lucrative spheres both from the Mainland and in New Zealand. On several occasions he was asked by the leaders and supporters of the Tasmanian Baptist denomination not to leave the colony.[510]

## Appendix 3: The Rev Henry George Blackie

The Rev Henry George Blackie was the first pastor of the Albert Park Baptist Church in Melbourne. He commenced there in January 1892 and remained until February 1894.

*6-12 H G Blackie's advertisement of Nov 1902*

During his time a branch church was formed in the Clarke Street Hall, Port Melbourne.[511] In his final year he was running the Hygienic Tea and Coffee Co. at 30 Queen Street Melbourne. He made a visit in May 1894 to Auckland, New Zealand. Later that year in an address given at Shepparton in Victoria, he spoke of how "Methodists were like kittens with their eyes closed and Baptists were like kittens with their eyes opened". He took an interim pastorate at the Ashfield Baptist Church in 1894 and commenced at the South Melbourne Baptist Church later that year remaining until February 1898 and resigned for health reasons.[512] He then withdrew from being recognized as an ordained Baptist pastor of any Baptist Association. The family moved to New Zealand and by 1908 in the South Island he was taking preaching opportunities whether it be found in Baptist, Primitive Methodist or Congregational Churches. He died of a heart attack on 6 April 1916 while in membership with the Auckland Tabernacle; he had been ailing for

---

[509] Henry J Morton, letter of 11 July 1925. For Wood's use of Drummond's story of the coachman and "throw the reins to Christ" which makes the point of ceasing to try to live in one's own strength, see The North West Post (Formby) 11 July 1895 p4.

[510] Letter to W. D. Weston, April 1935; Wood never used the title, "Reverend" preferring "Pastor". Pioneer Work for the Lord in Tasmania by Harry Wood.

[511] Wilkin p132.

[512] SB 17 February 1898 p48.

some time.513 He was spared the pain of losing two of his four sons in France in the war. But not so his second wife, Louisa, who lost one son. Louisa died on 17 June 1923, aged sixty-five years. Blackie in all had seven children, three with Louisa.

## Appendix 4: The Rev Herbert Davies Archer

In Victoria the Rev Herbert Davies Archer took interim pastorates at Newmarket and Moonee Ponds. He was then appointed by the Victorian Home Mission and Church Extension Committee to the Koroit district.514 On the first Sunday school anniversary following his arrival there was, a very interesting flower service. The church was tastefully decorated with wreaths and festoons of flowers, while the platform (occupied by the scholars) presented a gay appearance as each child held a bouquet. Mr Archer had ... for his address a cross, composed of scarlet flowers, betokening the Cross of the Lord Jesus Christ, whose blood was shed as an atonement for our sins; bunches of white and blue flowers, representing purity of life and heaven respectively, while a wealth of yellow flowers was used to tell of the crown of gold which awaits the faithful followers of the Saviour.515

During his pastorate the Koroit building was moved to a more central position in the town and church buildings were erected at Grasmere and Rosebank.516 By 1898, he was stationed at the Castlemaine Baptist Church and remained there until October 1905 when he accepted the pastorate of the Granville Baptist Church in NSW. But just over a year later, in December 1906, he accepted the pastorate of the historic Bathurst Baptist Church. At the Masonic Hall in April 1907 he gave a well researched lecture on the "Growth of Roman Catholicism"; the paper was published by the Australian Protestant Defence League. Keble and Newman were mentioned.517 In

*6-13 H G Blackie's gravestone*

---

513 Victorian Baptist 1894 p244; AB 2 May 1916 p3.
514 The Tasmanian (Launceston) 14 July 1894 p16; LEx 14 February 1895 p4.
515 Mount Alexander Mail (Vic) 22 November 1897 p2.
516 Wilkin p75.
517 Mount Alexander Mail (Vic.) 22 February 1898 p2; The Sydney Morning Herald 21 October 1905 p11; Australian Town and Country Journal (Sydney) 28 November 1906 p5; Watchman (Sydney) 18 April 1907 p8

1909 he suffered typhoid fever and some months later preached his farewell sermons. He spent a time at Culcairn in the south-east Riverina region of New South Wales, then he began at the Beryl Street and Gypsum Street Broken Hill Baptist Churches in June 1913 after a time at the Brocklesby and Goombargona Baptist Churches in NSW[518] but once again poor health brought about a pastorate of just over a year to a close. The Angaston Baptist circuit in SA which included Angaston, South Rhine and Eden Valley Churches followed in November 1914 but he only stayed for two years. In 1915 he had published the poem, "Out of the Depths." He was beginning the last decade of his life. The fourth verse reads,

> When buoyant youth no more is ours,
>
> When weak'ning age decays our pow'rs;
>
> When sickness drives us from the field,
>
> Where once we fought, but did not yield,
>
> Keep us, O Lord, still trusting Thee,
>
> With whom, for aye, is verity?[519]

He took charge of the Black Forest and Richmond Baptist Churches commencing March 1916.

In October 1918, he was seriously ill and ceased that ministry. Pastorates followed at Edward Town, SA, in 1918, Leeton NSW in 1921, for two years, and Hornsby also in NSW in 1923 but throughout these years poor health continued to hamper his ministry.[520]

Archer died at his residence "Deloraine" in Hornsby on 31 May 1924, aged sixty years. Harry Wood who had the highest regard for Archer wrote, "Archer was also minister of the Longford Church for several years, which (his ministry there) rank(s) among the brightest and best in its history. He did good work, too, for the denomination as Secretary of the Tasmanian Baptist Association."[521] His wife Rosamond died on 9 December 1936 survived by their two daughters.[522] Archer was the President of the Tasmanian Baptist Association for 1893/94.

## Appendix 5: The Rev John Ferguson Macallister[523]

In the Rev John Ferguson Macallister we have a Presbyterian who had

---

[518] AB 3 June 1913.

[519] AB 26 October 1915 p6.

[520] National Advocate (Bathurst, NSW) 24 February 1909 p2, 28 June 1909 p2; Barrier Miner (Broken Hill, NSW) 5 June 1913 p1; The Advertiser (Adelaide) 1 August 1914 p23; Newcastle Morning Herald and Miners' Advocate (NSW) 28 November 1914 p13; The Register (Adelaide) 26 February 1916 p5; The Mail (Adelaide) 26 October 1918 p11; AB 23 August 1921 p5, 27 November 1923 p10.

[521] The Daily Telegraph (Sydney) 3 June 1924 p8; Archer's obituary by Harry Wood, BCC August 1924 p3.

[522] The Sydney Morning Herald 10 December 1936 p10.

[523] Research by Daryl Lightfoot, Research Officer Presbyterian Church of NSW discovered that there are questions about

come to understand New Testament baptism as being that of believers and by immersion. In Tasmania he entered into a Baptist Association tightly controlled by men from the Pastors' College. More than likely to his dismay he found his culture and theirs did not correspond.

Macallister was born on the Isle of Skye, Scotland, in 1861. He migrated to the Australian colonies for the benefit of his health. He had married Mary MacDougall, the daughter of Archibald MacDougall, draper of Glasgow, on 10 April 1884.[524]

In Queensland he attended the Presbyterian Divinity Hall in Brisbane for eighteen months, and then returned to Scotland to finish his studies, purportedly taking his M.A. degree at Glasgow University. He then returned to Australia and was employed in Presbyterian Home Mission supply work in New South Wales and Victoria until his views on baptism changed. Once baptised by immersion, he sought admission into Baptist ministerial ranks.[525] Tasmanian Baptist Union Council received his credentials at a meeting on 10 October 1894.

In December 1896 he proceeded to Perth, WA, to undertake the headmastership of a new college and preached at times in the churches. In October 1898 he was commended by the Baptist Union of Western Australia for work on the Kalgoorlie goldfields. In his subsequent years he reverted to the Presbyterian Church and migrated to New Zealand. There, from 1899, he worked at Owaka and Waiwere South in Presbyterian Churches until 1906.[526] A number of pastorates followed in NSW Presbyterian Churches: Junee (1911-12) and Berry (1912-14). He resigned from the ministry on 14 September 1915[527] to enlist in WW1 together with three of his sons. On his return he devoted himself to assisting unemployed returned soldiers.

Fittingly he wrote the song, "Australia's Crowning Hour",

> Ye that have faith to look with fearless eyes
> Beyond the tragedy of world at strife
> And know that out of death and night shall rise
> The Star of ampler life

---

Macallister's story, namely, "Falsely claimed to have attended and graduated from University Glasgow and to have been licensed by Free Church Presbytery, Glasgow. He was deposed by Presbytery of Sydney 14.9.1915 because of falsehood and contumacy. Further his post-war assertions of being a member of a specific unit OAS, being wounded in action, etc. None of this could be substantiated by official records and he was later declined membership of the unit association."

[524] Brisbane Courier 20 May 1884 p3.
[525] The Sydney Morning Herald 14 April 1894 p10.
[526] History of the Presbyterian Church of NZ 1840-1940 by John Rawson
[527] The Challenge of the Years, a History of the Presbyterian Church of Australia in the State of NSW by CA White.

No senseless lust of cruel strife sent thee
To die ten thousand miles across the sea
Your country's call a nobler fairer holy creed
Set soul a flame and inspired that deed
Rejoice whatever anguish rend the stricken heart
That God has given you a priceless dower
To live in these great times and have your part
In freedom's crowning hour
That ye may tell your sons who see the light
High in the heavens their heritage to take
"I saw the powers of darkness put to flight
I saw the morning break
I saw the morning break!"[528]

Then ill-health, caused by disabilities suffered during the war, forced him to retire. The Rev John Ferguson Macallister died in Sydney on 13 September 1938.[529]

## Appendix 6: The Rev A. John Casley,

The Rev A. John Casley who early in life ministered in both Wesleyan Methodist and Independent (Congregational) Churches was one among many who at the time were taken by the truth of baptism as given in the New Testament, and joined the Baptist denomination. Although he was not scholarly, he exercised a unique ministry which he brought from his earlier traditions. Limited pastoral openings in Baptist circles in time drew him back to minister in Congregational Churches.

Casley, born in 1856 and christened at St Just, the largest Wesleyan Chapel in Cornwall, England,[530] came to Australia from Cornwall in 1878. In 1881, at Ballarat, he married Ann Jones who was born at Wolverhampton, UK. He was accepted as a probationer for the ministry in February 1883 with the United Free Methodist Churches and was posted to Lai Lai, Victoria. By 1886, he was ordained and moved to Tasmania taking charge of the Ebenezer Free Methodist Chapel, Murray Street, Hobart.[531] In Hobart he was chaplain of the Loyal Orange Lodge. A year later he took charge of the Carlton and Bream Creek Congregational Churches, a posting lasting eighteen months. He presided at an Edith O'Gorman lecture in the Tasmanian Hall in 1887. Edith, Sister Teresa de

---

[528] Song/music by Charles Davis; words by F Macallister. Call number MUS N mba 783.2421599 D261.
[529] BUT Council Minutes p89/31; LEx 11 February 1897 p5; The West Australian 17 April 1897 p4, 26 October 1898 p3; Daily Advertiser (Wagga Wagga, NSW) 28 September 1936 p6;

Obituary, The Sydney Morning Herald 16 September 1938 p17.
[530] Family history research by Barbara Coe.
[531] Bendigo Advertiser 15 February 1883 p3, 17 February 1883 p2; Tasmanian News (Hobart) 17 April 1886 p1; Day-Star October 1886 p151.

Chantal, was known as the "Escaped Nun".[532]

In April 1888, he moved back to Victoria to take charge of the Castlemaine Congregational Church. Then in May 1891, he moved again, this time to Newcastle, NSW, to pastor the Wallsend Congregational Church and happened to associate with a leading Baptist preacher in Newcastle at the time, the Rev Stephen Sharp. At times Sharp gave him the opportunity to preach in Baptist Churches.[533]

In 1893, he transferred to the Islington Congregational Church in Newcastle and concluded three years later, on 29 March 1896 as he took the step of becoming a Baptist. Following his time at Longford, he was officially welcomed at the Sheffield Baptist Church on 14 March 1899.

## Conclusion

Through his Pastors' College, Spurgeon set himself the task of producing preachers of the gospel: not scholars but those who could "get to the hearts of the masses, to evangelise the poor - this was the College ambition, this and nothing else," Spurgeon wrote. For this purpose if it was necessary to allow a "lowering of the average of scholarship, so be it," he continued. Spurgeon was only interested in inculcating certainty, otherwise faith could be weakened and resolve dispersed.[534]

The men from the Pastors' College firmly retained his thinking on the interpretation of the Bible, standing firm against all the modernist thinking associated with Higher Criticism.

Higher Criticism was primarily an effort to determine what the Bible was in itself, independent of all formal pronouncements about it by the Church. It was seen as a necessary tool to enable intelligent churchgoers to make sense of the Bible but the Pastors' College men resisted the overwhelming trend to accept liberal theology. It was enforced by their sense of loyalty, community and fellowship.

For them this Higher Criticism undermined the doctrine of biblical infallibility which was entrenched among general chapel attendees. They had that fear that Higher Criticism would upset the faith of their congregations.

For those who were accustomed to thinking of the Bible as totally reliable in all matters, the new Higher Criticism seemed to

---

[532] Tasmanian News (Hobart) 24 September 1886 p2; The Mercury (Hobart) 8 February 1887 p3; LEx 14 June 1887 p2.
[533] LEx 5 March 1888 p2; Newcastle Morning Herald and Miners' Advocate (NSW) 12 August 1893 p 6.

[534] Willis B Glover, Evangelical Nonconformists and Higher Criticism in the Nineteenth Century (London, Independent Press, 1954). pp163, 191.

challenge the very basis of their faith.

Higher critics were applying the same methods of textual, historical and literary criticism to the Bible as were applied to other literature.

The Pastors' College men could not accept that this could go hand in hand with doctrinal orthodoxy. What modern scholarship they had been introduced to was given only to counter Higher Criticism.

They could not see that Higher Criticism was potentially liberating for Christians who wished their faith to be intelligently grounded and intellectually honest. This meant that they could not adequately address the intellectual struggles of their increasingly well-educated populace in a positive way. Unfortunately, from the late 1880s any person young or old in Tasmanian Baptist churches who was troubled by aspects of the Bible and its relationship to modern science would have found it difficult to find a sympathetic Baptist Pastor prepared to resolve their difficulties.

So Tasmanian Baptists were never brought to see that once the idea of infallibility of the Biblical text is jettisoned, one can come to a true appreciation of the Bible literature and its claims. If they had come to this place, they would have had to agree that Higher Criticism could no longer be dismissed on theological grounds. Fortunately, from the 1880s, many evangelicals outside Baptist circles accepted the validity of Higher Criticism, but not of the most radical kind.

The acceptance of Higher Criticism made Christianity less vulnerable to the attacks of the free thinkers and removed many of the difficulties which faced better educated members of the Churches. Tasmanian Baptists still have to learn that all truth is of God and sadly the fundamentalism of this time has continued to somewhat shape our churches; its influence continues. Yet Christianity sustains no harm if it be shown that snakes do not talk and that world was not made in six days.

# Chapter 7 Launceston Baptist Church

## Introduction

Wrote a Baptist scribe in 1898,

> Launceston is so important socially, commercially, and religiously that it claims, as a matter of right, equality with the capital in Baptist Union matters. It claims to be the finest governed municipality, under the Southern Cross. Who has not heard of its Cataract Gorge, gorgeous with flowers, its splashing cascades, and rushing river, struggling to reach the sea, as if in a hurry, at the last, to make up for its many quiet meanderings? How majestic the basaltic and perpendicular cliffs in their pillared strength appear! The winding walks, the cozy nooks, the feathery ferns, the open glades by the wide basins, the rustic huts, beautiful trees, sunny reaches, and gloomy shades, the Swiss cottage and artistic bridge, all showing how wonderfully well man can co-operate with God to train wild nature into lovely form and entrancing beauty! ... In this well-churched electric-lit city we met at the Tabernacle.[535]

## Launceston in the 1880s

In 1886, the Rev William White, pastor of the York Street Particular Baptist chapel, Launceston, wrote, "The erection of the large buildings by Henry Reed and Gibson meant the death knell for York St. Few care for the Particular Baptists' tenets." At the time Tasmania had a population of about 104,000 with about 16,000 in Launceston. Of these about seventy-five per cent were Protestant, about sixty per cent were literate and about fifty per cent were born in the colony. A few years earlier the fifteen churches in Launceston saw a

*7-1 The Congregational Church met in Milton Hall, on the right*

---

[535] SB April 1898.

regular attendance of 5,000 and could claim an attendance of 3,000 on Sunday evenings.[536]

The effects of the Wesleyan revival in England in the eighteenth century had filtered through to Launceston and new church buildings were in the course of erection. The Princes Square Congregational Church, meeting in Milton Hall, was one of those churches with a new sanctuary in the course of construction.[537] Moreover, the Salvation Army had recently arrived in the town and had by 1884 purchased land in Elizabeth Street for the erection of a circular circus tent capable of seating 1000. In the following year, with great success, they erected a citadel.[538]

As a population centre, Launceston was naturally a focus for evangelistic effort. Controversial English evangelist, Henry Varley who had no time for prudish pastors, visited there and the northern parts of the island in 1878; he also visited in 1888 and 1889. Itinerant female evangelists, Margaret Hampson and Emilia Louise Baeyertz, both visited, Baeyertz a number of times commencing in 1878. At this time the long awaited new translation of the Bible was released in the form of the Revised Bible. It had the possibility of replacing the archaic King James Version of 1611.[539]

The Temperance Movement had by the 1880s found its way to the young in the churches through their Blue Ribbon societies. Temperance Halls were a feature of most population centres. The Bible Societies, the Town Mission and other forms of Christian endeavour enjoyed a good following being supported by all the non-Roman Catholic denominations. Men and women of all Protestant and Anglican persuasions freely associated at such gatherings. Furthermore, the street parades of the Sabbath schools featured in the church calendar year. The *Cyclopedia of Tasmania* in 1900 recorded that Tasmania "has now a larger proportion of church-going people than England, a much larger number of Sabbath school attendants, and a degree of active benevolence, social prosperity, and even moral development ..."[540]

About six blocks away from Reed's church, William Gibson Senior had purchased land in Cimitiere Street for a new Baptist Tabernacle.[541] The

---

[536] York Street Baptist Chapel Minutes (Tasmanian State Archives) 1886 p401; LEx 3 August 1875 p2, 3 May 1881 p3, 13 July 1887 p2, 24 May 1881 p3, 8 June 1883 p3.
[537] Anne Bailey, "Launceston Wesleyan Methodists 1832-1849: contributions, commerce, conscience", PhD thesis University of Tasmania, Hobart, 2008. The foundation stone of Princes Square Congregational church was laid on 8 March 1883 and the building opened in October 1885. See LEx 9 March 1883 p3, 20 October 1885 p3.

[538] LEx 24 May 1881 p3, 19 January 1884 p2, 22 January p2. Barbara Bolton, Booth's Drum: The Salvation Army in Australia 1880-1980 (Sydney, Hodder and Stoughton 1980) p164.
[539] LEx 4 March 1878 p2, 5 March 1878 p316, April 1878 p3, 5 July 1884 supplement p1.
[540] Cyclopedia of Tasmania (Hobart, Maitland and Krone, 1900) p389.
[541] Craig Skinner, Lamplighter and Son (Nashville, Broadman Press, 1984) p74 suggests that the Tabernacle was erected in the hope that

tender for the Tabernacle had been accepted in February 1883. The foundation stone was laid on 7 June 1883. Gibson consulted with the Rev Charles H Spurgeon in London about a minister and Spurgeon chose the Rev Alfred Bird.

As Pastor White correctly noted, his York Street chapel was being eclipsed by both the new Tabernacle in Cimitiere Street and Henry Reed's Mission Church in Wellington Street, the latter only a city block away from the York Street chapel.

With their completion, Launceston was able to boast of four churches each able to hold 1000 persons.[542]

## The Rev Alfred Bird

The Rev Alfred Bird arrived in Launceston on 20 February 1884. The difficulties faced were many. There was no building committee for the edifice, only an architect and the Senior and Junior Gibson donors.[543]

*7-2 Alfred Bird*

So, there in Launceston with a large and unfinished edifice, Bird commenced services in the Mechanics Institute, retaining the hall until 24 May 1884.[544] When the Launceston Tabernacle was completed it was capable of seating 1,200 but the church membership stood at only thirty-six. Spurgeon's son, the Rev Thomas Spurgeon, constituted the church with its new Tabernacle on the 14 July 1884. The edifice had cost William Gibson Senior and his son, William Gibson Junior £5,719 with additional costs for the school rooms and the manse bringing the outlay to nearly £11,000. On 25 May 1884, the Tabernacle was officially opened by Spurgeon.

A Sunday school was formed on 27 August 1884 with twenty-seven scholars. A building to house the school was completed by the end of the year.[545] In 1884, a journalist with the Launceston Daily Telegraph profiled Bird,

---

Thomas Spurgeon would be its first pastor. Skinner says, "Thomas had refused (the position) a year prior to the building dedication." Skinner offers no source for this statement. But by midwinter 1881, Thomas had accepted the permanent pastor position at the Wellesley Street Baptist church, Auckland. (Auckland Tabernacle leaflet, 'Shapers of Baptist Life' #4); S&T January 1882.
[542] LEx 15 April 1886 p3.

[543] LEx 5 June 1883 p2, 7 June 1883 p2, 8 June p34; S&T 1884 p432.
[544] LEx 5 June 1883 p2, 7 June 1883 p2, 8 June p3, 21 February 1884 p2, 12 March 1884 p3; S&T 1884 p432.
[545] LEx 24 May 1884 p3; the manse was a purchased building - Daily Telegraph (Launceston) 2 May 1884 p2, 28 July 1884 p3, 16 December 1884 p3, advert 26 May 1884 p3.

He is tall and well-built, of fair complexion, and light coloured hair and beard; his expression kindly, yet resolute, and his features intellectual, with a forehead of unusual height and width; his delivery is fluent and clear, given a voice which fills the building with ease, while his deportment ... is full of earnestness, it is here that his chief defect appears: often in the minor parts of his sermon his earnestness would reach its highest pitch, and would be succeeded by a period which logically required a still greater degree of emphasis, but to which the preacher was incapable of rising.[546]

In 1885, the Church commenced a Mission at Ravenswood in a hall for Sunday services and a Sunday school.[547] Bird strongly supported the visit to the town of the Temperance Mission of the American Mary Greenleaf Clement Leavitt in February 1886. Leavitt was an educator and successful orator who became the first round-the-world missionary for the Women's Christian Temperance Union. Leavitt's crusade was followed in the next month by that of the meetings of Richard T. Booth which Bird chaired. Hard on the heels of these two was Dr. Henry Grattan Guinness, the son of Henry Grattan Guinness who was an Irish Protestant preacher, evangelist and author. Again Bird chaired a number of Guinness' lectures in April 1886. In July, Bird, with others, gave lectures in a series of meetings for men only on the "Wordless Book", first used by the Rev C. H. Spurgeon in 1866. The Wordless Book had become a very popular tool used all over the world to explain the plan of salvation to children using the gospel colours.[548]

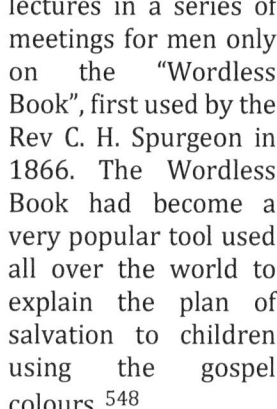

*7-3 Mary Clement Leavitt*

Bird, as with other Pastors' College men in Tasmania during these years, was for aggressive Christianity and was focused on the sin of man with salvation offered through Christ. They were not learned on the details of Higher Criticism being uncritical in their use of Scriptural texts, completely rejecting both the methods and conclusions of modern biblical scholarship and seeking refuge in giving numerous lectures

---

[546] Daily Telegraph (Launceston) 28 July 1884 p3; LEx 31 March 1884 p3.
[547] LEx 30 December 1885 p2.

[548] The Tasmanian 27 February 1886 p7, 17 July 1886 p28; LEx 3 March 1886 p3; Daily Telegraph (Launceston) 31 March 1886 p3.

*7-4 Sketch of the Launceston Tabernacle*

in Second Coming hopes.[549] In 1885, Bird commented on an article written by Congregationalist, the Rev George Clarke, on the inspiration of the Bible by saying that "the spiritual man discerns that all scripture is given by inspiration of God and so frees men from unbelief." Bird was totally out of his depth in endeavouring to comment on what was being discussed and therefore completely missed what Clarke was trying to say. For Bird and his colleagues, the other evils of the age foremost in their minds were "the Social evil, secularism, the love of pleasure, and Popery".[550]

During Bird's time a two-day conference to form the Baptist Association was held in the vestry of the Tabernacle; it was commenced on Tuesday 27 May 1884. Those present were William Gibson Senior, the Rev Robert McCullough now of Hobart, the Rev Albert Tucker of the Strict and Particular Baptist chapel in Hobart, the Rev Robert Williamson of the Perth chapel, the Rev Albert Bird, the Rev William White of the Strict and Particular Baptist chapel in York Street, William Gibson Junior, Dr. Harry Benjafield of Hobart, Thomas W. Hortle, A. Frosting, A. C. H. Hodgman, William Stokes of Longford, the Rev Robert Marshall of the Launceston City Mission and the Rev Thomas Spurgeon.

Bird concluded his ministry in Launceston in April 1887.[551] There were now 101 members on the roll, fifty-one of whom had been baptised by Bird. There were 190 Sunday school scholars. Further, there were weekly prayer meetings with fifty in attendance, Zanana Mission meetings, "Blue Ribbon Union Band of Hope" meetings, sewing meetings, a weekly tract distribution, open-air preaching and a young people's "Christian Band".

According to Wood, Bird was a gifted preacher who had laid a good foundation in Launceston but Wood held that Bird never drew large congregations and the latter was his reason for his resignation after three years. Wood was wrong; he had a habit of putting people down as he elevated his own successes. Within three years from 1884 a total of 200 were weekly attending Bird's Sunday services.[552]

---

[549] LEx 26 July 1884 p2, 16 August 1884 p2, 2 August 1884 p2, 20 March 1886 p2.
[550] SB 2 May 1895 p109.
[551] LEx 20 April 1887 p3.
[552] Pioneer Work for the Lord in Tasmania by Harry Wood.

## Pastor Harry Wood

Wood concluded his ministry at Longford in August 1887, having responded to a call to the Launceston Tabernacle. Wood began on 4 September 1887 and was appointed as permanent pastor on 19 July 1888. Wood's first candidate for baptism was a young man, Andrew Duncan, who years later became a generous benefactor of the Baptist Association's Home and Foreign Missions.[553]

Baptist baptism was a strong point of Wood's ministry as it was with all of the Pastors' College men. The Baptist publications would report that at baptismal services Wood would often give "a masterly exposition of the subject". In 1887, at the Sunday school demonstration of Queen Victoria's Jubilee, the school was the second largest in the city numbering over 400 children but the claim of 400 needs to be weighed against newspaper reports one of which speaks of 228 scholars and another of 169 scholars.[554]

In 1888, forty-one persons were added to the church's membership and of these a total of twenty-one were baptised by Wood.[555] There was now a Mutual Improvement Society for young men, a Temperance work which sought to "rescue the perishing", a mission work at Inveresk and a "Track Distributors scatter seed" band. Further, a Bible-woman was "stirring up the people in their homes". Wood's celebrity status was enhanced by his portrait in oils displayed in the Brisbane Street shop window of Craw and Ratcliff; it was painted by A. W. Barrett. In April 1890, the church was looking into beginning an outstation in Scottsdale.[556]

Wood's health began to deteriorate towards the second half of 1888 as he completed his first year at the Tabernacle. He took his annual holidays but he returned in a weakened state. A year later, following his holidays at the end of 1889, he was too unwell to preach on the first Sunday of his return. His poor health continued throughout the year. By May 1890, his doctors forbade him to preach. He finally resigned in July making possible an extended time of rehabilitation and the possibility of entry into a lesser sphere of work which turned out to be in Sheffield. With 148 members on the roll, he left behind the largest Baptist church in the colony.[557]

---

[553] LEx 5 September p2; Day-Star August 1888; Bligh.
[554] Pioneer Work for the Lord by Harry Wood; LEx 11 November 1889 p2; The Colonist 17 November 1888 p3.
[555] Day-Star July 1888 May 1889.
[556] LEx 18 July 1884 p4, 20 April 1887 p3, 7 September 1889 p2; BUT report of Assembly 1886; Day-Star June 1888; The Colonist 19 April 1890 p28.
[557] Day-Star October 1888, March 1889, May 1889, December 1889, January 1890, May 1890; Devon Herald (Tas) 18 December 1888 p2; Daily Telegraph (Launceston) 1 July 1890 p3; Pioneer Work for the Lord In Tasmania by Harry Wood.

Lessons from our first 20 years

## The Rev Alfred James Clark

The evangelist, the Rev Alfred James Clark, was welcomed at the Tabernacle on 17 December 1890. In his reply that evening, Clark said that "he had not come to find any new thing in the Bible, but would preach the old truths." There was some feeling that Clark was running away from his post in Sydney but this was countered by the Rev John Alfred Soper (NSW) who said this was not so. The Tasmanian Baptist Union Council had its own doubts. It proposed, "That a letter be written by the Secretary to the Executive Committee of New South Wales to ask why the letter of transfer in connection with the Rev A. J. Clark was so brief and curt." Clark was referred to as "the big gun from Sydney". It was also mentioned that in the colonies "Tasmania is a land of clover for Spurgeon's men and it looked like they had come to possess the land"; in fact they had. After only a month under Clarke's lead, congregation numbers nearly doubled.[558] Clarke's Temperance emphasis continued with vitality. In his first year in Tasmania he was elected to Union Council for twelve months. As a Spurgeon's man, his credentials were impeccable and with the Tasmanian Baptist Association still largely controlled by his London College brethren, how could they deny him a place, even on Council? He engaged in a very public and lengthy debate in the newspapers with "Mode" and with the Presbyterian, the Rev John Lyle, on the matter of the form and purpose of baptism. The Congregationalist, the Rev Frederick Hales, refused to engage in the debate as in his view nothing would be gained. The debate lasted from April to June in the Launceston Daily Telegraph.[559] But within the leadership of the Launceston Tabernacle, strained relationships had surfaced early; notable office bearer William Dubrelle Weston was excommunicated within six months of Clark's arrival. In June 1891, Henry E. Ratcliff resigned as secretary and deacon and W. L. Stokes as choir leader and deacon. Further, the Union Bank wanted to know who would be responsible for the Church's overdraft. A number of troubled members wrote to the Baptist Union Council informing it of the Church's problems but the

*7-5 Alfred James Clark*

---

[558] LEx 18 December1890 p2; Baptist Union Council Minutes 5 March 1991 p12; Day-Dawn December 1890, January 1891, April 1891.

[559] The debate begins in Daily Telegraph (Launceston) 3 April 1891 p4.

diaconate members saw this as a regrettable action as the matter should have been first brought to them. Clark was instructed not to visit the twenty-seven estranged; this was to be left to the deacons but subsequently those estranged requested that there be no visitation at all. Four deacons were stood down at the Annual Meeting held in Clark's first year. Union Council minutes saw it in a harsher light, "Two of the deacons had been voted out." It further noted that "in fact 4 deacons were involved." Council requested that the deacons and all male members meet with Pastor Harry Wood, the Revs Robert McCullough, John E. Walton and William Gibson Junior.[560]

Outwardly there was no evidence of an inner turmoil. The statistics for the first year stated that while thirty-one had been added to the membership, thirteen by baptism, seventeen were removed from the roll; financially there was a positive report. In the first half of 1892, baptisms continued with thirty-five in April. There was a glowing Annual report given in August 1892. In the second half of 1892, 400 to 500 attended its Gospel Temperance Coffee Supper. There was an increase of twenty-eight in membership for 1892 but by the end of February 1893 the divided diaconate was stood down.[561] Finally, the real situation was disclosed in the Church's report to the Day Star,

> If all were accepted that emanates from the unruly member no man can tame, an unfavourable impression might be made upon the minds of some, but we are confident that truth must prevail, and while we are badly reported the Lord is dealing with us in a marked manner, both wounding and binding up. The Church officers recently elected have handed in their resignations, which have been accepted, and three brethren have been appointed as acting deacons ... Our Sunday

*7-6 Baptist Union Council of 1889: Front row: JT Soundy, W Gibson Jnr, R McCullough, HG Blackie. Middle Row: J Chamberlain, AJ Ratcliffe, unknown, A Hyde, SB Pitt, H Wood, WJ. Murphy, JE Walton. Back Row: AJ Stokes left end, WD Weston right end, of those unidentified – HD Archer and Dr Benafield*

---

[560] Baptist Union Council Minutes p41/29, p52/10, p62/17, p67/15; Deacons' Minutes 25 June 1891, July 1891 21 November 1891, 21 August 1893.

[561] Day-Star 4 June 1892, May 1892, August 1892, September 1892, February 1893; Church Meeting minutes 27 February 1893.

school is reported as looking up, but a superficial view would seem to contradict this is in consequence of a complaint as to the management; the superintendent and secretary have resigned.562

Clark informed Council of his resignation and was farewelled on 26 November 1893.563

As Wesley Blight wrote in his 1935 thesis, "Altars of the Mountains",

> The state of one's health was not the only difficulty faced by the Spurgeon's men in Tasmania. Success in ministry could often be assured, but there was always the possibility of pastoral failure. In 1893, the Launceston Tabernacle sustained a severe set-back during the pastoral settlement of the Rev Alfred James Clark. For month after month the Baptist journal, the Day Star gave a glowing report of the Launceston work, but unbeknown to the wider Baptist church family, the true state of the church was not being disclosed due to the failure in leadership, the church was disrupted and the congregation scattered. At the conclusion of the Assembly held in Launceston in 1894 following Clark's departure, a whole day was devoted to humiliation and prayer. By now

the Council of the Union had assumed control and taken measures for the resuscitation of the work. At the end of the decade Weston was Editor of the "Day Dawn" and in 1901 he became the Union honorary legal adviser.

## The Rev Edward E Harris

With the Launceston Tabernacle in disarray in 1894, Clark having resigned, the deaconate disbanded and a large number of members having departed, the Baptist Union Council engaged the Rev Edward E. Harris to take oversight of the church for twelve months on a salary of £300, £100 of which was promised by William Gibson Junior. Fifty notices were placed in shop windows advertising the welcome "tea" with 300 tickets printed at a shilling each but only 170 attended. Weston soon returned and was appointed Church Secretary.564

Weston penned these words on this disruptive time,

> As a Tasmanian Baptist, I should like to bring to remembrance the signal service almost unnoticed that Harris rendered to the Tasmanian Baptist Church. Owing to circumstances which need not now be retold, the church at Launceston was literally in ruins. There was scarcely a congregation in the

---

562 Day-Star September 1893.

563 Baptist Union Council Minutes p70/19; Church Minutes 15 December 1893; LEx 27 November 1893 p5.

564 Church Minutes 2 April 1904; LEx 17 November 1894 p4.

city where our members were not found. In the leading Wesleyan Church for a time they formed a majority of the choir. The collections had fallen to less than a third of the usual. There was little of a congregation and as little money. Our brother was invited by the Council of the Union to take the oversight, and if possible secure the return of the lost sheep to the fold. In this work he displayed - with his discreet and much esteemed wife - such tact and grace, that in the course of his pastorate the church was fully re-established. No Tasmanian Baptist can forget the debt of gratitude owed to our brother for his success in the most trying and difficult work a minister can be called on to undertake. W.D.W.[565]

The Launceston Examiner reported,

Tabernacle Christian Endeavour Society after a very severe attack of decrepitude, nearly ending in dissolution, has assumed a good position, and under the presidency of Rev E. Harris, a thorough (Christian) Endeavour man, coupled with the exertions of a conscientious secretary, is likely to assume an even better place, though the membership is still a score less than formerly. The last two quarterly reports show a great improvement.[566]

Finally in May 1895, Harris was appointed permanent pastor. As in other churches, Harris worked closely with the Young Men's Christian Association.[567]

In 1894, the local newspaper, the Daily Telegraph, ran a forum for two months titled, "the Pulpit at Fault" commencing in September with a letter by Joseph E. Clark in which he criticised the pulpit for "not openly and honestly avowing the change of belief which has come about to a more or less extent in all churches," for not making "good use of the position it holds in leading mankind into the newer and truer light of advanced religious thought and conviction." The main subjects dealt with were the personality of the

*7-7 Edward E Harris*

---

[565] AB 18 June 1929 p12. Written following Harris's death in May 1929, edited.
[566] LEx 21 May 1894 p3.
[567] Tasmanian News (Hobart) 15 May 1895 p1; The Age (Melbourne) 16 August 1894 p6.

*7-8 Launceston Tabernacle Sunday School picnic in 1902 at Kilafaddy*

devil and future punishment.[568] Harris responded by means of his sermons.

Harris always highly valued the Christian Endeavour Societies in his churches and within the Launceston Church there was no exception. The growth in societies had been phenomenal on the mainland but they had only commenced in Tasmanian in 1892. Now there were five such societies in Launceston with a membership of 1,500. Harris continued the use of a Young Men's Improvement Association. He also exhorted his congregation to pay attention to the signs of the time. For him, they were the overthrow of the power of Islam, the return of the Jews to Jerusalem and the increase of missionary effort on the part of the Christian Church spoken of centuries ago. He also held that in respect to "The Marriage in Cana of Galilee" when Jesus performed the miracle of turning water into wine, the latter was not intoxicating.[569]

After his nearly two years at Launceston, the church membership stood at 142 and there were 211 Sunday school scholars with twenty-two teachers. The Sunday school at Trevallyn had closed because the promoters had left the colony. Sunday school scholar numbers rose to 240 a year later. Harris was appointed President of the Baptist Union of Tasmania for 1897/98 but within months, on 26 September 1897, he preached his farewell sermons at the Tabernacle; he was transferring to West Melbourne. The pulpit at the Tabernacle was to be supplied by the Rev George Wainwright who had lately arrived from England for the benefit of his health; he had been ministering at the nearby Perth Church.[570] At the time the Launceston Church was the most important in the denomination.

## The Rev George Wainwright

The Rev George Wainwright began at the Launceston Tabernacle on 13 March 1898. During his time he was appointed to the Union Council and

---

[568] The letters in the Daily Telegraph (Launceston) began on 18 September 1894 and concluded on 27 October.

[569] LEx 18 October 1894 p7, 16 March 1896 p5, 7 January 1895 p7; The Mercury (Hobart) 4 April 1895 p3.
[570] LEx 21 October 1895 p5, 1 July 1896 p5, 19 October 1896 p5, 27 September 1897 p5.

made Editor of the Day Spring journal. One of Wainwright's favourite lectures was on "Eccentric Preachers", especially Billy Bray the unconventional Cornish preacher. Wainwright quoted from some of these ministers' sermons and writings.[571] Wainwright's assistant was George Vincent Britton who was also employed with the Launceston City Mission.

Work continued with the Church's Percy Street Mission, situated about a kilometre south of the Tabernacle where on Sundays a Sunday school was conducted in the afternoon, a Gospel service in the evening and a Gospel Temperance service every second Friday evening. Britton involved himself in this work. Wainwright's farewell took place on 13 April 1899.[572]

## The Rev Walter J Eddy

The Rev Walter J Eddy began as a temporary to the Tabernacle on 7 May 1899 and was officially welcomed as Pastor on 10 July 1899. A few months later at the Sunday school anniversary, the Tabernacle was well filled on the Sunday with over 2000 for the day. That year in the school, there were 107 boys, 113 girls and thirty-two teachers. At the Percy Street branch there were fifteen boys and fifteen girls, a grand total of 250 scholars and thirty-two teachers which indicated that some of the teachers were at times on duty more than once for any given Sunday. Among his many lectures on Sunday evenings was a number on China. The Tabernacle's Young Men's Institute conducted a weekly evening meeting of the Debating Society. Eddy, its President, received questions on diverse topics in advance and would seek to answer them; his opinions were open to debate.[573]

*7-9 Walter Eddy*

In 1900, he was appointed Secretary of the Baptist Union. He edited the "Day Dawn and Baptist Church Messenger" journal which for some years had a regular issue of 3,000 copies. He was also the Tasmanian editor-in-chief of the "Southern Baptist". With William Gibson Junior and W.D. Weston he worked on a scheme for the modification of Tasmanian Baptist Church government. He was one of the Secretaries of the Torrey-Alexander Mission of 1902 from which the Launceston Church received

---

[571] The Mercury (Hobart) 7 April 1898 p3; LEx 14 October 1898 p4.
[572] LEx 13 May 1898 p4, 26 August 1898 p4, 14 April 1899 p7.

[573] LEx 9 May 1899 p4, 16 October 1899 p6, 30 August 1900 p6, 31 August 1900 p4.

*7-10 Bloomsbury Baptist Church, London*

valuable additions to its membership. In order to assist him in his increasing work, the Launceston Church appointed a salaried Bible woman and Church visitor. He took strong interest in the work of the Christian Endeavour movement. In July 1899, the first Baptist Union Education Committee was formed, its members consisting of the Revs. Eddy, Clark, Walton and Messrs. Weston and Duthoit. Eddy was appointed honorary Pastor of Bracknell and Blackwood Creek in April 1900.[574] In Launceston, Eddy joined the Northern Tasmanian Camera Club which would have assisted in his preparation of illustrative lectures, one such lecture entitled, "Cornwall and the Cornish".[575] During Eddy's time the work steadily progressed, and the membership increased considerably. In January 1901, the Church created a memorial fund for the Rev Robert Marshall, a long-standing member of the Church and former Superintendent of the Launceston City Mission who died in November 1900.[576] His death preceded that of Queen Victoria for which Eddy preached fitting sermons on 27 January 1901. Eddy was the Honorary Secretary for the Queen's Memorial Service held at the Town Hall.[577] In 1902/1903 Eddy was elected President of the Baptist Association which involved visitation of churches across Tasmania.

Eddy was farewelled on 9 August 1903 to the Parkside Baptist Church in South Australia. In his farewell addresses he said he would have been glad to have remained in Launceston, but "for the doctor's opinion that his health would not be good here." He had suffered continual trials in health for "the climate that was evidently unsuited to the constitution of his family." Even so the conclusion of the four years' pastorate the Church both numerically and financially had advanced most considerably.[578]

# Appendices

## Appendix 1: The Rev Alfred Bird

Born in a Baptist family and raised in a Baptist Church, Alfred Bird had taken to evangelizing as had most Pastors' College students before he

---

[574] Council Minutes p 259/26.

[575] LEx 21 September 1899 p4.

[576] LEx 17 November 1899 p5, 19 January 1901 p8, 23 April 1902 p1; NWA&EBT 6 April 1900 p2.

[577] For a précis of one of the sermons see LEx 28 January 1901 p6; Daily Telegraph (Launceston) 14 February 1901 p2.

[578] LEx 10 August 1903 p4; *The Australasian (Melbourne)* 22 August 1903 p47. SB 1 September 1903 p195.

entered the Pastors' College. He was greatly influenced by the Rev C. H. Spurgeon and practised aggressive Christianity and as typical of the ethos of the College rejected much of the conclusions of modern biblical scholarship. He also made a strong emphasis on the Second Coming. He was one of the few College men who arrived without health problems and was gifted with a large building seating 1,200 and just thirty-six members and all the Church had to do was fill it on Sundays.

Bird was born on 19 October 1848 at Hammersmith in London. His parents were members of the West End Baptist Church, Hammersmith, of which his grandfather was pastor. The family moved to Camberwell where they attended the ministry of the Rev Dr. Edward Steane (1798-1882). He attended the Coldharbour Lane Sunday school. He was first sent to a preparatory school at Brixton, and afterwards to the City of London School. At fourteen years of age he entered a City warehouse to work. He entered the Pastors' College in August 1867 from the Baptist Bloomsbury Chapel, Central London, which was under the pastorate of the evangelical and forceful ministry of the Rev Dr. William Brock. At Bloomsbury, he was involved with tract distribution and invited young men whom he met in the street to Bible class. He also became a Sunday school teacher and an open-air preacher. When friends urged him to devote his life to the Christian ministry, he undertook a twelve months' evangelistic tour in two neighbouring areas of London.

In 1868, after he had been in the Pastors' College for twelve months, Spurgeon suggested that he should attempt to continue a new cause meeting at the Luxemburg Hall in the thickly populated suburb of Dalston Junction of Northern London; it had been commenced by another of the College's students. During Bird's ministry a roomy and comfortable building was erected in Ashwin Street, Dalston, but the building had cost £5300, including land, with only £800 in hand. Spurgeon writing in the "The Sword and the Trowel" was not impressed,

> We are glad to see one of our students so zealous and useful, but we do not see how this project can be carried through: nor should we like to be thought responsible for its having been undertaken. To trust God is one thing, but to build a chapel on trust is quite another. With this enterprise our College has had nothing to do, as we judged the scheme to be beyond the means of the people, and therefore imprudent.[579]

After several years at Dalston Junction, he became pastor of an already settled work at Commercial Road, Oxford, where in his last year

---

[579] S&T August 1878.

ill health was his lot. At Oxford he undertook University subjects.580

Then followed the Clarence Street Baptist Chapel at Penzance, Cornwall (1877-79). His next charge was at Middleton Cheney, North Hamptonshire (1879-80). The final English pastorate before his leaving for Australia was at the seaside resort of Sandown, Isle of Wight (1881-83). The church began as a Union Church under Bird's and Spurgeon's guidance in the old Town Hall. Bird was now a married man. He and his wife, Annie Eliza, had a one year old daughter, Maud, and a servant.581

Writing from Whitchurch in 1907, Bird remembered every detail of the Macedonian call which brought him to Sandown,

> I well remember the letter summoning me to Westwood (Mr Spurgeon's home in Upper Norwood), and my subsequent interview with the beloved and revered C H Spurgeon, in which he told me that he wanted to see a Baptist church established at Sandown and that he had fixed on me for this work, and that I was to look to him for the maintenance of my family. As I had other plans for the future I demurred, but all objections were overruled in his own inimitable way.582

The work began in an upper room over a mineral water factory and a building fund was commenced. The church was constituted with twenty members and a chapel seating 320 persons erected in Pell Street at a cost of about £1,000.583 Among Bird's first-fruits was the conversion and baptism of a young Army officer of Anglican upbringing. He was Captain Dixon Edward Hoste, stationed at Sandown Barracks. Hoste resigned his commission in order to serve with the China Inland Mission, becoming one of the famous "Cambridge Seven" which included C. T. Studd and the Rev W. W. Cassels (afterwards Bishop). Hoste served in China from 1885 until shortly before his death in 1946, aged eighty-four years. He had followed Hudson Taylor as General Director of the Mission in 1901.

Once chosen for the Launceston Tabernacle work Bird and his family sailed on the "John Elder" in January 1884.

**Following his time at the Launceston** Tabernacle, Bird began as Pastor of the Dawson Street Tabernacle, Ballarat, in May 1887 but a call had been extended to him earlier in November 1885 when the pastorate became vacant. This first

---

580 Daily Telegraph (Launceston) 28 July 1884 p3.
581 S&T April 1882; 1881 Census.
582 His Excellent Greatness – The Story of Sandown Baptist Church and its Ministers, 1882-1982.
583 S&T 1883.

call he declined.[584] In his one-and-a-half years at Ballarat the Sunday attendances were not nearly as large as it was felt they ought to be. In order to attract larger congregations to the evening services a bold step was taken - all the seats in the church were declared to be free and unallotted and the collection abolished. It was hoped that this startling innovation would have the effect of attracting all sorts and conditions of people to the church services who were repelled by pew rents, private cushions and offering baskets.

As with most men of the cloth in Ballarat, he supported the town's Benevolent Asylum, the Y.M.C.A. and the City Mission. In Ballarat, he also strongly supported the crusades of evangelists, Henry Varley and Mrs Emilia Baeyertz, the latter having a strong Second Coming flavour. Bird always played a leading part in Prophetic Conferences in which it was admitted that some people will get "unhinged" by studying the truth of, "He that shall come will come, and will not tarry." (Hebrews 10.37) At such conferences Bird associated with the Revs. George William Gillings formerly of Perth and James Blaikie. Blaikie was destined for Hobart. Bird confessed that in "the truth of the Lord's personal second coming he had found the clue, or the key, which interpreted the whole Bible; before (that) one-half of it was to him as a sealed book." Bird's opinion, said one who heard him some years earlier, was that "they were living in a time of much darkness and evil and the devil would have the last word, the last power". The listener added that he heard no sound of victory, no mention that "God would stamp out of existence altogether of evil, and bring the whole world to submission to his feet."[585]

Bird's brief pastorate of twenty months in Dawson Street terminated in January 1889 as he responded to a call from a new Baptist work in Melbourne.[586]

While forty-three new members were added to the Ballarat Church during Bird's pastorate, only seven were baptised which suggests that the large majority of them had transferred from other Baptist Churches. At Ballarat, Bird followed William Clark from the Perth Church in Tasmania.

Bird's last charge in Australia was a new work at Auburn. Baptists in the district in 1888 had resolved to establish a Baptist Church in their midst. They purchased the old Congregational Chapel and invited Bird to be their pastor. During his time at Auburn, on 22 May 1890, Bird formed the first Australian China Inland Mission Council, and invited Hudson Taylor to visit Australia to confirm the work. Bird

---

[584] Daily Telegraph (Launceston) 25 November 1885 p2.
[585] Day-Star April 1886 p58.

[586] The Ballarat Star 24 March 1888 p4, 7 October 1887 p4, 8 December 1887 p4, 28 January 1889 p2.

became its first Honorary Secretary and during his first year in that office, twelve missionaries were sent out. Bird had attended a China Inland Mission (CIM) conference at the Launceston Christian Mission Church. There he and other delegates met Henry Reed's daughter, Mary, who had returned from China and she spoke of the need in that Oriental country. Deputation for the Mission took Bird interstate. At Auburn in 1889, Bird also commenced the first Branch of the Christian Endeavour Society in Australia and the movement quickly spread through the colonies. By 1893, there were forty-three societies with a total membership of 1,588 in Victorian Baptist churches. Total membership rose to 3,000 members in the next twelve months. The Christian Endeavour movement bridged the gap between the Sunday school and the Church. Its work and that of the CIM occupied a good part of Bird's time. His wife, Annie, strongly supported him in these areas and at one CIM meeting where young women were being sent off to China, she chaired the meeting.[587]

*7-11 West Melbourne Baptist Church*

Although he was not known for public humour, in October 1893 it was asked of him,

> Was it the Rev A. Bird, Baptist minister of Hawthorn, or another clergyman of that denomination who has caused a sensation by preaching a sermon on the elopement of a pious young married man with a giddy member of his church choir? Both parties are musical, foolish and romantic, but it is a pity that a sensible clergyman should have taken public notice of a silly escapade, which rightly belongs for consideration to the Divorce Court rather than the pulpit.[588]

Bird was elected President of the Baptist Union of Victoria in 1895. At the end of January 1896, the family returned to England where Bird began deputation work for the CIM.[589] He also held pastorates again at Clarence Street, Penzance, Isle of Wight (1896-1902), and then at Brannockstown (1902-1904), and finally at the Whitchurch Baptist Church, Harts (1905-1910).

In 1910, through the decay of the optic nerve, he became totally blind, but still continued to engage in Christian activity. In 1917, he approached Dr. Frederick B. Meyer with reference to the formation of a society for heralding the imminence of the Lord's Return, and the result

---

[587] S&T 1896 p369; AB 18 January 1927 p4; Manley pp119, 350; The Kerang Times 28 September 1894 p2; The Ballarat Star 8 June 1892 p4.

[588] Table Talk (Melbourne) 13 October 1893 p3.

[589] The Daily Telegraph (Launceston) 1 February 1896 p10.

of that appeal was the inauguration of the Advent Testimony and Preparation Movement.[590] After forty-two years of ministry he retired and he died on 19 November 1926, at the age of seventy-eight years. Annie survived him but their four children had already died.[591]

## Appendix 2: The Rev Alfred James Clark

Pastors' College evangelist, the Rev Alfred James Clark, believed in aggressive evangelism As with so many, health reasons brought him to Australia and his success as an evangelist continued as he at times pastored leading churches in two States with outstanding results. But the winning run came to an end when he took the leading Baptist Church in Tasmania and sadly he left it in a state of disrepair. Following this, although he had other pastoral successes, he was and remained essentially an evangelist.

Clark who was born in Wiltshire in 1848, entered the Pastors' College in 1875 from the Metropolitan Tabernacle. He and the Rev J. Manton Smith became the Pastors' College Evangelists with Spurgeon's blessing and so from 1877 for the next two years they preached and sang the Gospel in various parts of the country. They began at Stockton, Hartlepool and the neighbourhood where they remained for a month or more. Their work also involved street preaching. They also ministered in Reading, Redruth, Truro, Hayle, Penzance, Trowbridge, Leicester, Falmouth and Landport. But in 1878, at Bacup in Lancashire, Clark's health failed and he was ordered to the Australian colonies. Through Spurgeon, an invitation came from the West Melbourne Baptist Church. Clark accepted, migrating in 1878 and travelling with the Revs. Thomas Spurgeon and James Harrison. They left England by SS Sorata on 30 November.[592]

Clark, a man of rare power and success, was welcomed at the West Melbourne Church on 19 October 1879. At the welcome he told those gathered that "he had told Mr Spurgeon before leaving England that if he found himself among a people who would not work he would soon return because he held that the preacher could do nothing without the co-operation of the church."[593]

By August 1880, he had baptised sixty-nine persons, and had received eighty-seven into membership. He began monthly evangelistic song services specially intended for non-churchgoers. Such were the numbers that many could not gain

---

[590] D W Bebbington, "Baptists and Fundamentalism" p310.
[591] AB 18 January 1927 p4.
[592] S&T September 1877 p334, August 1877, January 1878, October 1878, June 1879, 1882 p444.
[593] Geelong Advertiser 7 November 1879 p2; The Argus (Melbourne) 18 October 1879 p6, 31 October 1879 p3.

admission. As a consequence, the Church rented the local Hotham Hall and held services there. It was hoped that Clark would become as popular in Victoria as Spurgeon was in England, or as Dr. T. de Witt Talmage was in America. At first it was decided to enlarge the chapel to seat 950 people, but soon a new structure was planned to be called the Victoria Street Tabernacle and to cost between £6000 and £7000.[594] The Church began a new work at Footscray and various other good works were inaugurated or extended.[595]

Clark made a number of visits to Tasmania. As Temperance advocate, he spoke at Rechabite and Victorian Alliance meetings. His message was simple, "We do not ask that all public houses shall be closed, but that power shall be given to the ratepayers to close them if they so desire." Under his leadership the "bit of blue" – the Blue Ribbon - made its appearance in Melbourne. He spoke at rowdy meetings in opposition to what was seen as a violation of the Sabbath: the trustees of the Public Library were taking steps in opening the Picture Gallery and Museum on Sundays. At the Melbourne Temperance Hall this "gentleman of full habit and of strident voice" was on the committee for the visit of evangelist Mrs Margaret Hampson.[596]

After four years at West Melbourne and with 300 being added to the Church during his pastorate, Clark resigned so that he might devote himself entirely to evangelistic work. He helped found the "Evangelization Society of Victoria" which sent forth evangelists throughout the colony "at the invitation of, and in co-operation with the existing churches to preach the Gospel not only to those who never enter a church, but also to the many who do. Their preaching was to be so simple and so clear that everyone could understand." By the first half of 1885, his fellow missioners were Arthur E. Eustace, James S. Harrison, H. Robertson, H. M. Axthelm, Dr. Henry Guinness of London and G. Williams. They conducted fifty missions in eighty-four places with an attendance of 106,440. These missions, incorporating Mrs. Yarcoa's Mission Band, were in conjunction with Baptist, Wesleyan, Congregational and Presbyterian Churches.[597]

---

[594] S&T October 1880; The Age (Melbourne) 13 December 1879 p4; The Mercury (Hobart) 2 February 1880 p2; The Grafton Argus and Clarence River General Advertiser 21 June 1880 p3; Cootamundra Herald 17 July 1880 p6.

[595] Our Yesterday's Vol.10 p85.

[596] The Argus (Melbourne) 16 August 1881 p4, 23 June 1883 p12; The Age (Melbourne) 24 August 1881 p3, ; The Kyneton Observer (Adelaide) 13 July 1882 p2; The Riverine Herald 23 April 1883 p2; The Horsham Times 8 May 1883 p2; The Herald (Melbourne) 19 June 1883 p3.

[597] S&T September 1883; The Ballarat Star 7 August 1886 p2; Weekly Times (Melbourne) 5 March 1887 p11; The Argus (Melbourne) 29 August 1885 p12; The Herald (Melbourne) 22 September 1885 p2. For an extensive work on the Evangelistic Society of Victoria, see the self-published books of Robert Evans.

Outside one of Clark's missions in Yackandandah in northern Victoria, lively youths struck up and sang the ditty as they marched down to the township, "Little children should be there, with hob-nailed boots and carroty hair. If you want to go to Heaven when you die, you must wear a collar and a tie."[598]

At one of Clarke's missions the congregation was asked to sing the song, *Waiting and Watching.* The words were:

> When my final farewell to the world I have said, / And gladly lie down to my rest:
>
> When softly the watchers shall say "She is dead", / And fold my pale hands o'er my breast: / And when with my glorified vision, at last, / The walls of that city I see,
>
> Will anyone then at the beautiful gate
>
> Be waiting and watching for me?

It was this gospel song that led James McQueen to faith. McQueen had emigrated from the Isle of Skye to Australia in 1857 but sadly his young daughter had died. McQueen was forcibly reminded that he had a daughter, a "dear lassie" who would be waiting and watching for him and that if he did not come, she would be disappointed. These thoughts seem have awakened him to a sense of his need of conversion. He was baptised, and soon was serving as treasurer of the Goulbourn Valley Baptist Church.[599]

At the end of 1886, Clark resigned from the Society and accepted the pastorate of the newly built Burton Street Tabernacle at Woolloomooloo, NSW. He began in January 1887. There he took a special interest in the children of the poor, the working children in the area and the Aboriginals generally. He worked in Temperance and with the Local Option League. In the constant controversy between those interested in the drink trade, either as producers, retailers or consumers, and those who maintained that the traffic was wholly evil and required absolute suppression, Clark said that the time had come when it was not a matter of regulation but of prohibition.[600]

He took time away for a mission tour of New Zealand. He also delivered lectures, one subject being, "Noah's

*7-12Sketch of the Burton Street Tabernacle, Sydney*

---

[598] Ovens and Murray advertiser 22 November 1884 p1.
[599] Manley pp276.
[600] The Daily Telegraph (Sydney) 11 April 1887 p5, 30 December 1887 p1, 17 January 1888 p5, 24 January 1888 p5, 5 April 1889 p3; The Burrowa News 14 December 1888 p2.

Ark; and what became of the Carpenters?" It was noted that Clark "has a happy, and, we should imagine, an effective knack of getting at the feelings and consciences of his audience."[601]

Clark's pastorate at Burton Street concluded on 1 December 1890. The pastorate had been an absolute success. The new building, first envisaged as only being half completed, was fully built. There were only fifty members when he commenced and the membership rose more than threefold and the overall debt was less than £1000. As Colin Scott recorded,

> One enthusiastic church member heralded him in the NSW Baptist as "a pastor not only the equal of any of the Baptist ministers in the colony, but in his own life as a plain, earnest, and eloquent preacher of the old-fashioned Gospel, probably he will be without equal."[602]

Clark's successes came to an end for a time when in 1890 he accepted the pastorate of the leading Baptist Church in Tasmania.

In December 1893, following his time in Launceston, Clark accepted the NSW pastorate of the Burwood Baptist Mission, a committee which was soon to open a new building. But such was Clark's appeal that the missions he and others ran had to be held in other venues to handle the numbers.[603] His areas of interest continued at the Burton Street Tabernacle, including the matter of strong drink and politicians who loved the grog. At a public meeting in regards to the Local Option question, to many cheers he said,

> Good laws could never be made by bad legislators. They could not get a clean thing out of an unclean, or figs out of thorns, or grapes out of thistles, and never could a colony be governed in the best interests of the people by men honeycombed by immorality or shattered by drink. In all other walks of life it was required that men should be sober, and therefore why not in the most important case of all

*7-13 Hargreaves Street Baptist Church, Bendigo*

---

[601] The Daily Telegraph (Sydney) 27 February 1888 p3; Newcastle Morning Herald and Miners' Advocate (NSW) 20 June 1888 p5; The Recorder October 2003 p6.
[602] The Recorder, July 2003 p6, "A History of the Burton Street Baptist Tabernacle".
[603] The Australian Star 5 November 1890 p3; The Sydney Morning Herald 9 December 1893 p10; The Daily Telegraph (Sydney) 19 February 1894 p6; The Recorder April 1995 p4.

- the case of the men who made the laws of the country. They must say that immoral men and men who could stand on the floor of the Legislature tottering with drink, whether in the Ministry or out of it, (they in fact) should not be allowed inside Parliament (Cheers.) He hoped this question of the morality and sobriety of candidates would be kept steadily to the front at the elections. There was something wrong when many of the men in the Legislature were living in debauchery and soaking in drink, while the people were starving and the nation going to beggary for all they cared.[604]

In March 1895, Clarke began in Leichhardt, a suburb in the Inner West of Sydney. He would only remain for fifteen months conducting mission-oriented services in the Town Hall on Sunday afternoons and evenings. The events were well structured with Duffield's twenty-piece orchestra and a choir and the services attracting sizable congregations, especially in the evenings with the room "filled to the doors" month by month. The work came under the title of "The Forward Movement".[605]

Clarke's next placement was with the Hindmarsh Baptist Church in a suburb of Adelaide. He commenced in August 1896 and he remained for twelve years. The Church would serve as his base and a good part of his time was spent away on missions or advancing the Orange Lodge Order; he was its deputy Grand Chaplain of South Australia. His attention continued with the Temperance movement. But his public figure was clearly seen as he vigorously championed Protestantism. A number of his public statements were seen as intemperate to the extreme. He pandered to Protestant bigotry and was openly mocked. Wrote the Sydney Truth, a "scandal sheet",

> Rev A. J. Clarke, of Adelaide, is a holy Christian man. On Sunday week he fulminated against his fellow Roman Catholic Christians. He urged that they should be boycotted from all public positions, and that Protestants should deal only with Protestants. Next thing, some fierce Protestant Christian will be urging that all Roman Catholics

7-14 Alfred Clark and his wife Jane Clark

---

[604] The Sydney Morning Herald 30 January 1894 p3.

[605] The Sydney Morning Herald 28 May 1895 p6; The Australian Star 27 July 1895 p3, 13 August 1895 p3.

*7-15 Aberdeen Street Baptist Church 1853*

be burnt at the stake. Then we'll rise up and howl, in a raspy voice, "Let brotherly love continue".[606]

Such was the offensiveness of many of his Orange Order speeches that on a speaking engagement at Petersburg on his way to Broken Hill, he was refused entry to the Baptist Church and that of the Anglican parish hall: "His reputation had gone before him, and all respectable people held aloof."[607] He was riding the high wave of the Loyal Orange Institution which had seen impressive growth in second half of the 19th century.

After a pastorate of twelve years at Hindmarsh, Clark accepted a call to the Hargreaves Street Church in Bendigo. It was remarked correctly on his leaving Hindmarsh that he had noted ability as a preacher but there had not been the success of earlier pastorates. At his close the church had a liability of £62 and it was serious enough that "the church for a time would do without the services of a settled pastor". Maybe if they had had a "settled pastor" for twelve years, then they would not have been in this state! Yet he continued his concern for the unemployed.[608] Clark was farewelled on 7 October 1908.

Before he officially commenced at the Hargreaves Street Church on 18 October 1908, he held a three-week evangelistic mission. Clark was Labor in his political leanings and nearly joined the Party and this came out in the mining city with an address which drew a sympathetic note from many a worker. The address, "Employer and Employed", drew much public comment in the press. It echoed his concern for the poor and the unemployed in earlier years in Sydney. In this explosive address he hinted that a resident Methodist minister had been involved in underhand dealings. The Preacher in question was the Rev Henry Worrall and the insinuations brought forth great indignation.[609] During Clark's time the schoolroom underneath the church sanctuary was completed at a cost of £815 and the Jubilee of the church was celebrated.

---

[606] The Advertiser (Adelaide) 24 July 1903 p6; Port Adelaide News 23 April 1904 p6; The Areas' Express 15 July 1904 p3; Truth 24 July 1904 p1.
[607] Southern Cross 14 July 1905 p10.

[608] The Advertiser (Adelaide) 12 May 1903 p7, 8 October 1908 p8.
[609] The Bendigo Independent 10 August 1908 p3, 24 February 1909 p5, Bendigo Advertiser 7 April 1909 p3; For Worrall see ADB and The Bendigo Independent 19 April 1910 p3.

In October 1910, Clark relinquished this pastorate to return to South Australia, as the state of his wife's health demanded it. For a time he ministered at the Mount Gambier Baptist Church and then the Stepney Baptist Church, the latter for three years. Clark died on 14 April 1916 in Adelaide aged sixty-eight years. His wife Jane (nee Hook, born in Heddington, Wiltshire) died on 3 April 1915, also in Adelaide.[610] Both are buried at Woodville cemetery, Adelaide. In Robert Evans' view, Clark's story shows that he was an evangelist at heart and being a pastor gave him no lasting fulfillment.[611]

## Appendix 3: The Rev Edward E. Harris

Australian born the Rev Edward E. Harris was brought to Tasmania to oversee one of the leading churches then in total disarray. His contribution to the Tasmanian Baptist cause here, as elsewhere, was immense. He returned to further pastor other leading mainland Baptist churches.

Harris was born in July 1854 in Geelong and raised in a godly home to parents Thomas and Caroline Harris. In his teens Edward was a Sunday school teacher at the Aberdeen Street Baptist Church and he was just about to give up when he was converted and baptised at the age of twenty-one years by Rev W. C. Bunning.[612] He and his sister Elizabeth then started a Sunday school in Marshall Street with about twelve scholars and he was an occasional preacher at outstations of the Church. With a number of others he formed a Y.M.C.A. He spent six years in the hardware trade.[613]

In 1877, after he had studied under Professor Gosman and the Revs. John Reid, A. Harper and D. Mercer at the Congregational College as a Baptist student, he was among the first to enter the Baptist Theological College.[614] On the completion of his three year college course, he married Ruth Pearson.

His first pastorate was the Portland Baptist Church and he was welcomed on 1 February 1880. There he was ordained by the Rev Samuel Chapman, his pastor at Collins Street Baptist Church while he was in College. He gathered together about seventy young men averaging perhaps eighteen years of age to create a fellowship for them. His addresses to them "were humorous, the tendency of the teaching being to incite to patient

---

[610] The Advertiser (Adelaide) 5 April 1915 p8; The Express and Telegraph (Adelaide) 5 May 1916 p1.
[611] The Advertiser (Adelaide) 15 April 1916 p8; Robert Evans, The Evangelisation Society of Australasia p37; AB 2 May 1916 p3.
[612] Amelia Baeyertz was baptised on same occasion.
[613] Our Yesterdays Vol. 9, Life of Thomas & Caroline Harris.
[614] Wilkin p83. His fellow students were F. J. Wilkin, A. Steele, C. Hardy, and A. Dakin. AB 15 October 1902 p233.

labour, mental improvement, and honest perseverance in all things." Harris served as Secretary to the Portland Free Library. His lengthy sermon on the current matter of the opening of libraries and museums on the Sunday was given full press. His position on the observance of Sunday was later reflected in his joint letter to the St. Kilda Municipal Council during his time at George Street, Fitzroy. The letter objected to the watering of streets "on the Sabbath". This protest succeeded and the watering on Sundays ceased; the sanctity of the Sabbath was preserved.[615]

In December 1883, he resigned the pastorate of the Portland Baptist Church for a move to the George Street Church. The Rev Frederic J. Wilkin later wrote:

> It seemed a big venture for a young preacher to follow the Rev Dr. T. Porter, but the renowned Rev Samuel Chapman had endorsed the call, and events

proved that no mistake had been made. Crowded congregations, largely attended, fervent prayer meetings, outdoor preaching, and a constant stream of conversions gladdened all hearts.

He was thirty-one years of age when he commenced on this vigorous ministry during which there were many additions to membership. A mission hall was erected in Yarra Street near Hoddle Street, East Collingwood, and opened in 1886 to cater for a large Sunday school. In 1885, Mrs. Emilia Baeyertz held an evangelistic mission at the Church. The Church also commenced a work at Clifton Hill. He was Secretary of the Baptist Union of Victoria and he followed this with being Secretary of the Baptist Home Missionary Society. In 1890, he was appointed President of the Baptist Union of Victoria. As with Portland, he fostered a Young Men's Society at George Street. By the time of the anniversary of the Church in 1887, its debt was cleared.[616]

Harris was a man of decided views. He had no time for

> the ridiculous assumptions in regard to the Church and to apostolical succession, the pernicious teaching about the efficacy of sacraments, the proud arrogance of so-called priests who "lord it over God's heritage",

*7-16 George Street Baptist Church, Fitzroy*

---

[615] Hamilton Spectator 14 January 1882 p2; Portland Guardian 14 December 1882 p2, 26 June 1883 p2; The Telegraph, St Kilda, Prahran and South Yarra Guardian 5 November 1887 p6.

[616] The Herald (Melbourne) 8 August 1885 p2, 23 January 1886 p3; The Argus (Melbourne) 15 July 1887 p9, 13 November 1890 p6; Mercury and Weekly Courier (Vic) 24 June 1887 p3, 16 September 1887 p2.

the absurd mummeries of ritualists with whom vestments, and candles, and crucifixes, genuflexions, and positions, play such an important part in the worship of God; the introduction of the confessional, and the ill-concealed sympathy with Roman Catholicism.

Further,

the Ritualistic movement began ... by Keble, Hurrel Fronde and Newman was inspired by a hatred of the Reformers, a contempt of the Evangelicals, and a desire for corporate re-union with Rome.[617]

Yet Harris had humility about him. To a group of fellow Baptist Pastors he confessed,

after preaching he often felt it would have been better had he not preached at all, and he at times felt as if he did not care if he never preached at all again. He could not account for this except there was so much in their work that tended that way.[618]

The Fitzroy City Press recorded the Sunday school anniversary in June 1891, in which there were 396 scholars on the roll,

On the platform that most zealous of pastors, the Rev E. Harris, was in his element, tried friends on the platform with him, and on every hand beaming faces around, and all on the alert for the pleasant sayings and songs which make the evening a subject of annual and pleasant anticipation to youth and adult alike.[619]

**After his time in Launceston** the West Melbourne pastorate proved another successful pastorate; it lasted six years. The Church, a long time without a settled pastor, had drifted into a very unsettled state, losing considerable membership. Many, while not altogether leaving the church which in numerous cases they were brought up in, attended other places of worship in the neighbourhood. At his welcome he urged them to "put things of the past aside, to let old wounds heal, and look forward to what he was sure was going to be a prosperous and happy future." He also took on the task of being honorary pastor of the Bacchus Marsh Church and was present for the opening of its rebuilt building which used materials from the old. In West Melbourne he was appointed President of the North and West Melbourne Christian Citizens Association. One of the preachers at Bacchus Marsh was his daughter, Ann Whalley. He was an organizing secretary of the evangelistic committee of the Council of Churches for the 1902 Torrey-Alexander Simultaneous Mission in Melbourne. In 1902, he

---

[617] SB November 1895, 27 October 1908 p258.

[618] The Herald (Melbourne) 12 November 1888 p6.

[619] Fitzroy City Press 5 June 1891 p2.

was also President of the Victorian Council of Churches.[620]

The Baptist Aberdeen Street Church in Geelong was his next pastorate. He was welcomed to this his childhood church on 13 December 1903 and would stay until 1915. As elsewhere he ran a Young Men's Guild. The congregation formed another church, this time at Belmont with eleven members.[621] He was secretary of the Geelong Council of Churches. He strongly advocated the placing of the Christian scriptures in State Schools. In 1911, Harris began to teach at the Baptist College once a week and remained on the staff for a number of years. At a Summer School of Theology for ministers, home missionaries and students of the churches he gave a lecture on "The Book of Revelation".[622]

By July 1913, his physical strength began to fail and he took an extended holiday and was finally farewelled on account of his health on 11 April 1915. The church unanimously agreed that his stipend should continue for six months after termination. He lived quietly for some years in Camberwell since his health was not up to pastoral service yet in 1925 he took on being interim pastor at South Melbourne and then being pastor of the Box Hill Baptist Church and was present for the laying of the foundation stone for Box Hill's new building. He died 10 May 1929.[623] Ruth died at the age of eighty-six. Such was their influence that all their children became church members during his ministry at Belmont and three of his sons, namely Edward Chapman Harris, Frank and Samuel Archer Harris were all ordained to the Christian ministry and their daughter Ann Harris became the founding principal of Newtown Ladies' College in Elizabeth Street, Geelong.[624]

---

[620] North Melbourne Gazette 22 October 1897 p2; North Melbourne Courier and West Melbourne Advertiser 22 June 1900 p2; The Bacchus Marsh Express 11 April 1903 p2; Weekly Times (Melbourne) 3 May 1902 p13; The Age (Melbourne) 22 October 1902 p7. The Simultaneous Campaign was a new strategy whereby teams of evangelists led missions in local areas while Chapman and Alexander conducted a meeting at a large central venue.

[621] Wilkin.

[622] Geelong Advertiser 14 November 1910 p2, for the content see 11 October 1911 p5.

[623] Geelong Advertiser 5 July 1913, 12 April 1915 p4; AB 22 February 1921 p6; The Argus (Melbourne) 16 February 1925 p14; The Reporter 20 February 1925 p4; Harris was buried in the Box Hill cemetery.

[624] AB 1933 p124.

# Appendix 4: The Rev George Wainwright

Acknowledged English Baptist, the Rev George Wainwright arrived from the home country in 1898 and took a short pastorate for the Launceston Tabernacle and then held short pastorates in Victoria and New Zealand before returning to England for further pastorates. He then arrived back in Tasmania for another pastorate where he met his sad demise.

Wainwright was born in 1852 in Stubbin, a colliery village near Barnsley which was a large market and college town in South Yorkshire, England. Stubbin is between Leeds and Sheffield. He was raised in Manchester until the age of fifteen. In 1867, he was apprenticed to the grocery trade in Douglas, Isle of Man and joined the Presbyterian Church under the Rev James Fettes; he became a Sunday school teacher.

Removing to London, he preached his first sermon in 1873. There were present two members of the Metropolitan Tabernacle, one of whom thus counseled the young preacher, "A good message brother. Get a few of the corners knocked off and you will do well!"

The magnetism of Spurgeon's Tabernacle drew him into its ranks.

*7-17 George Wainwright*

Baptised in 1873 by the Rev James Spurgeon, he was "received" by the Rev C. H. Spurgeon with the text, "God make thee strong in the Lord, and in the power of His might!" Occasional preaching and attendance at the Bible-class of Elders Bowker and White followed. Then as a member of Birmingham Baptist Christ Church, he became a regular preacher at the Farm Street Mission Hall. At the end of 1873, he entered the Pastors' College.

After two years in College, a call from the Aldershot Baptist Church was accepted. It was here he married his first wife. Dissatisfied with results at the Church after the first year, he transferred to the Waterbeach Baptist Church in April 1877 and remained until the end of 1878. Then he accepted a call to Stockton-on-Tees and, in 1884, in the last six months of his ministry over sixty persons were baptised.

After a brief ministry at Grosvenor Street, Manchester, Wainwright walked away with 100 members in 1886 and he formed the Coupland Street Church. Two years later his health drove him South to a ministry at the Westbourne Baptist Church where the West Cliff Tabernacle was erected.

After nine years of service he was directed to Australia. Accompanied by his daughter Edith, he arrived in August 1897. He was invited to the Perth Church in Tasmania. He and Edith stayed with the Gibsons at Scone. The remaining family arrived in January 1898. Another short pastorate followed, this time at the Launceston Tabernacle.[625]

Following his resignation at Launceston Tabernacle, Wainwright held short pastorates first in Victoria at the Fenwick Street Baptist Church, Geelong, and in New Zealand at the Dunedin Baptist Church. The family then returned to England and did not return to Tasmania until August 1917. Daughter Edith met Joshua T. Soundy's son, John; they married in South Africa. On his retirement, Wainwright associated with the Hobart church and with the formation of the Sandy Bay Baptist Church, he became its first pastor in a temporary capacity, beginning on 28 September 1921. Following the death of his wife, Harriett Ann, seventy-four years of age in 1928[626], he returned to England. Soon he returned with a new wife, Marie, and took up the work again. Marie proved a great help to the Sandy Bay church and became its Secretary.[627]

On 25 July 1931, Wainwright was tragically killed on a dark, rainy night while crossing the street near his home.[628] Marie continued as Church Secretary. One of his daughters, Madam George, had outstanding musical ability.

## Appendix 5: The Rev Walter J Eddy

Of the Rev Walter J. Eddy Australian Baptist historian Gordon Crabb wrote,

> When the life and ministry of the Rev Walter J. Eddy is researched, a very impressive figure emerges. Eddy was a tireless, energetic, and indefatigable man, totally committed to serve both his Lord and the community. He had a strong social conscience, demonstrated by his secretaryship of Geelong Female Refuge and was committed to training young people through agencies like Christian Endeavour and Sunday school. His social conscience for those who were marginalised was shown through his work

7-18 *The original Fenwick Street Baptist Church, Geelong, on the left and the 1911 building on the right*

---

[625] *The Australasian (Melbourne)* 2 October 1897 p5; The Mercury (Hobart) 19 March 1898 p2.
[626] The Mercury (Hobart) 13 January 1928 p1.
[627] G. D. Hooper, Bournemouth West.
[628] Advocate (Burnie) 27 July 1931 p5.

with the Mission for Lepers (Leprosy Mission).⁶²⁹

Eddy was born at Liskeard, Cornwall, on 30 December 1859.⁶³⁰ His father, Peter Eddy, at the age of eighteen years, preached at St. Just, the largest Wesleyan Chapel in Cornwall. Subsequently he became a skilful mining expert and was known as "Captain Peter".

Young Eddy's mother was a Baptist, and Walter accompanied her to the Baptist Chapel at Liskeard. Eddy received his early education at Castle Academy and Dobwall's House, and at the age of fourteen years was converted in the Wesleyan Chapel, Trevelmond. On leaving school, he was apprenticed to a chemist at Looe, and there joined the Congregational Church engaging in active Christian service. Before he was nineteen years old his employer died and for eighteen months he managed the business for the employer's widow. Eddy always felt grateful for his business training. In 1880, he removed to London, and for two and a-half years was one of the chemists in New Bond Street. In 1881, he was baptised and joined the Bloomsbury Chapel Baptist Church in Central London of which the Rev J. P. Chown was pastor.

For a number of years the question of the ministry occupied his mind. Finally, the reading of the life of Rev Dr. William Brock (1807–1875), the first minister of the Bloomsbury Chapel (1848–72), an abolitionist, biographer and supporter of missionary causes combined with other circumstances, led to Eddy's decision to devote his life to the ministry. In this decision he received the hearty support of the Bloomsbury Church. In July 1882, he was accepted as a student of the Regent's Park College, Oxford, of which the Rev Dr. Joseph Angus was the Principal. A fellow student was Samuel Pearce Carey, later of Collins Street Baptist Church, Melbourne. At the close of the first year Eddy's College career was cut short by an attack of inflammation of the lungs, contracted after mission services in the slum kitchens of South London. A trip to Australia was urged by the doctors, and in 1883 he arrived in Melbourne.⁶³¹

His first pastorate was the Maldon Baptist Church with which Newstead and Daylesford Churches were afterwards connected. During

*7-19 Daylesford Baptist Church, Victoria*

---

⁶²⁹ Correspondence January 2022.
⁶³⁰ Table Talk (Melbourne), 26 December 1889 p2. Eddy was born about twenty-five years after the Cornish revival. Family History research by Barbara Coe.
⁶³¹ SB 16 April 1902 p90. 17 December 1902 p278.

this time he married Eliza (Lillie) Sarah Mackenzie on 19 November 1895 at the Baptist Church in Cecil Street, Prahran; her father, the Rev John J. Mackenzie, was the Baptist minister at Prahran. After working this large circuit for a time, Eddy and his wife removed solely to Daylesford where a church was built and opened in 1887.[632] The Daylesford Baptist church was built in Camp Street at a cost of £700. But when Eddy left the district, the circuit was disbanded. For Eddy the climate of the Daylesford district was too severe, and so a call to Fenwick Street Baptist Church, Geelong, was accepted. He began on 7 October 1888, aged just twenty-nine years. He spent nearly eleven years at the church which was crowded with strenuous, successful labour. During that period the membership was doubled and a new school premises was erected. Eddy engaged in several departments of philanthropic work outside the Church, among them as honorary Secretary of the Chinese Famine Relief Fund for Geelong and representing those who faced serious allegations at the Police Court. He also set up a female refuge in Geelong and became its secretary. Eliza was on the Ladies Committee. Eddy was ever ready to assist with the Y.M.C.A., the Geelong Town Mission of which he was secretary, and the Baptist Union in its work for the denomination at large. He also took a keen interest in the photography of the time. He gave a lecture entitled, "Through the Mallee and Wimmera with a camera," illustrated by his own slides. He was also a member of the Geelong Field Naturalists' Club taking a keen interest in seaweed.[633] After a pastorate lasting eleven years, he accepted a call to the Launceston Tabernacle which at the time was the largest Baptist Church in Tasmania.

**After his time at the Launceston Tabernacle**, he accepted a pastorate at the Parkside Baptist Church in South Australia following the Rev Robert McCullough. In a telegraph to the Church in accepting the invitation to the pastorate he planned to send two biblical verses: "Now God Himself, and our Father, and our Lord Jesus Christ, direct our way unto you. And the Lord make you to increase and abound in love one toward another and toward all men even as we do toward you." (1 Thessalonians, 3.11 and 12) Mistakenly, he had the misfortune to send a reference to 2 Thessalonians 3.11 and 12: 'For we hear that there are some which walk among you disorderly, working not at all, but are busy-bodies. Now them that are such we command and exhort of our Lord Jesus Christ that with quietness

---

[632] The Telegraph, St Kilda, Prahran and South Yarra Guardian, 28 November 1885 p4, 5 December 1885 p4; Wilkin says that when Eddy was pastor of the Maldon church he proposed that a circuit be formed on Maldon, Newstead and Daylesford.

[633] Geelong Advertiser 4 October 1888 p2, 14 June 1889 p4, 10 November 1890 p2, 11 February 1891 p2, 8 August 1891 p2, 5 August 1893 p3, 26 August 1896 p3, 1 July 1897 p4, 20 April 1898 p2.

they work and eat their own bread."⁶³⁴

Fortunately, the error was quickly rectified and at his official welcome to Parkside on 3 September 1903 he was able to draw from his error to praise the work of the Church and to challenge them to a productive ministry together.⁶³⁵

He said,

> I admire the efforts made towards Baptist federation; the work of the ladies in the church; their liberty and freedom, especially from theological and doctrinal trammels. I am pleased to be among those who did not ask me to "utter" any shibboleth before joining them, but have left me plenty of room to grow. You must give to others the liberty they claimed for themselves. The God who had found room in the New Testament for such diverse natures as Paul and James found room in our church for such different natures as Spurgeon and Dr. Clifford. There were differences we must not minimise. I have come to the conclusion that the other churches, when focusing into a sentence what the Christian ought to be, use Baptist phraseology. If they stuck to their position they would find as the years went by that the other churches would seek them and co-operate with them.⁶³⁶

It was during his time at Parkside that Eddy showed interest in the Australian Protestant Defence Association (APDA). In giving a lengthy address on "Priestcraft and National Life", he compared the progress of Protestant countries with those dominated by Rome. In January 1905, the Parkside Church formed a circuit with the Wayville Baptist Church. As with many a pastor at the time, he rendered solos at public gatherings.⁶³⁷ As elsewhere, he played a major part in the Christian Endeavour Movement. In 1906, he was President of the South Australian Baptist Union. Eddy created a Men's Mutual Club comprising two societies: namely, a Sunday afternoon class and a literary and debating society which

*7-20 South Yarra Baptist Tabernacle*

---

⁶³⁴ Zeehan and Dundas Herald 18 September 1903 p2.
⁶³⁵ The Express and Telegraph (Adelaide) 4 September 1903 p2.
⁶³⁶ The Register *(Adelaide)* 8 September 1903 p6 - edited. Trammels are restrictions or impediments to freedom of action and

shibboleth (a difficult word to pronounce) is a choice of phrasing or even a single word that distinguishes one group of people from another.
⁶³⁷ Watchman (Sydney) 19 November 1904 p8; The Advertiser (Adelaide) 3 January 1905 p6, 14 October 1905 p10, 29 January 1906 p3; Chronicle (Adelaide) 19 August 1905 p13.

*7-21 Inside the Launceston Tabernacle*

met weekly on Tuesday evenings. He formed the same at the South Yarra Church, Melbourne, which he accepted in January 1907.[638] At Parkville, he was on a salary of £200 per annum and with six children; the family could not survive.[639] In his reply at the South Yarra welcome he said that he was a great believer in foreign missions; at Parkside, contributions to missions the previous year had increased five fold. He asked the South Yarra congregation to give him plenty of time for study. Further, he informed the folk that he relied on the church and congregation for much help and co-operation and if they did this they would get ten times as much out of him. Finally, he also informed his flock that he would only give to outside Christian work any time he could spare from his church ministerial duties. It is a promise he didn't keep when he accepted the appointment as Secretary of the Victorian Council of Churches. It was a time-consuming task beginning with the arrangements of a united church service to mark the death of King Edward VII.[640]

The Secretaryship put before him many far-reaching and time-consuming social questions which the Council had to rule on such as matters of the Art Union lotteries, the push for the government to appoint a censor to prevent the importation of indecent visual material, the question of the Tattersall's Sweeps and the giving of prize money for boxing contests. He retained his association with the Australian Protestant Defence Association.[641] For the second anniversary of the Church's Mission Sunday school in Prahran, held in the Prahran City Hall, the Rev Vincent G Britton was the speaker. Britton told his hearers that he had been converted in a mission hall. His address was in the form of an acrostic on Jesus as the children's Friend: **F**aithful, **R**eal, **I**nterested, **E**ternal, **N**ear and **D**ear.[642]

---

[638] Malvern Standard 20 April 1907 p2, Malvern Standard 23 February 1907 p3; The Register (Adelaide) 13 February 1907 p5.
[639] SB 26 February 1907 p54.
[640] The Herald (Melbourne) 13 May 1910 p8; Leader (Vic) 27 February 1909 p22.

[641] The Herald (Melbourne) 12 July 1910 p5; Bendigo Advertiser 14 July 1910 p5; The Age (Melbourne) 29 July 1910 p6, 30 October 1909 p14, 30 October 1909 p14; Daily Telegraph (Launceston) 3 August 1910 p5). He retained his association with the Australian Protestant Defence Association.
[642] Malvern Standard 8 April 1911 p3.

In November 1910, Eddy was appointed Vice President of the Baptist Union of Victoria but became acting President in the New Year, this again taking him away on many a Sunday. And before the year was out, he had accepted a recall to Fenwick Street Baptist Church in Geelong with its newly built structure next to the original edifice; for Eddy a second term of four years. The church had not forgotten him. He resigned as Secretary of the Victorian Council of Churches as he was now President of the Baptist Union.[643]

He was welcomed at Fenwick Street on 3 December 1911. Early in 1913, the Church participated in the Dr Wilbur Chapman Crusade in Geelong, but in August 1913, Eddy accepted the General Secretaryship for the Australian Auxiliary of the Mission to Lepers and was farewelled from the Church on 6 November 1913. The object of the Mission was to preach the Gospel to the lepers; to relieve their sufferings, supply their wants, and, if possible, cure their disease; to rescue and educate their untainted children and to rid the world of leprosy.[644] He held the position with the Mission until his 72nd birthday in 1931. Because of the character of this work, he preached from pulpits of many denominations across Australia. At one of his meetings, after his visit to India to see the work first-hand, he told his audience that night,

> I was travelling from Calcutta to Gaza in the company of an educated Hindu, we chatted about our work. He was greatly interested in Australia, and wanted to know how we lived there, what we ate and drank, &c. He was a bit disgusted, though too polite to show it much, when I told him we were fond of beef! ... Presently the train rattled past a large field with scores of cows in it, and a fine block of buildings at one end. "What is this place?" I asked of him. "That is a cow hospital," he replied, and explained that when the cows were of no further use they were sent to such a hospital, and the well to-do Brahmins contributed for their support, so that they might be cared for and die in peace. I could not help saying: "Pardon me, but this is a surprise to me. You maintain hospitals for cows, but you do not provide homes for lepers! Is not a man better than a cow!"[645]

In 1928, the Australian Arm of the Mission was accommodating 6,700 lepers in the Indian Leper Mission homes. Eddy explained, "We are not merely pulling men out of the fire, we are putting the fire out."

After retiring from the Mission to Lepers, he became General Secretary

---

[643] Bendigo Advertiser 4 May 1911 p7; *The Australasian (Melbourne)* 16 November 1901 p5; Leader (Vic) 28 October 1911 p38.

[644] Sydney Morning Herald 24 July 1920 p7.
[645] Chronicle (Adelaide) 28 July 1923 p39.

of the Australian and New Zealand branch of the Sudan United Mission until he accepted the pastorate at Ashburton Baptist Church in 1935, remaining until 1938. He and Eliza were now frail and in their 70s and Eliza died on 5 March 1937. Not long afterwards a bronze tablet was erected in the wall-less church in the leper village of Makutupora, Central Tanganyika in her memory as was the installation of seating. The church itself was erected in memory of her husband. The Rev Walter J. Eddy died on 16 June 1947, aged eighty-eight years.[646]

## Conclusion

Disputes destroy our churches from the inside. Often, things degenerate to the point that many pull out of the church, while others show their worst selves in such a way that their actions cannot be undone. Full-scale congregational conflicts require years for recovery. As Bill Wilson, feature writer for the Baptist Global Press put it, "The Bible predicts that when God's people turn on themselves, the inevitable result of that is the sins of the mothers and fathers are visited upon their children and their children." He adds, "Church conflict is a gift that keeps on giving for years to come." A recent American church survey found that 80% of pastors expect conflict within their church and 40% report serious conflict with a parishioner at least once in the last year.

Those who are called in at such times to deal with the situation, such as the Rev Edward E Harris was in 1894, are often called in late in the proceedings. The next time we are tempted to turn on a Christian brother or sister, let us remember that Jesus has a higher calling for the church that bears his name. It starts with us: let us put down our weapons and call a ceasefire to the battles inside our churches. We have much more important and life-giving tasks before us.

---

[646] The Argus (Melbourne) 31 May 1928 p7, 18 June 1947 p4; The Mercury (Hobart) 11 May 1925 p3; The Age (Melbourne) 8 March 1937 p1; LEx 5 May 1932 p10, 6 March 1937 p9; The Herald (Melbourne) 19 June 1937 p20.

# Chapter 8 Hobart Baptist Church

## Introduction

The Hobart Baptist Church for many years was one of the two leading Churches of the denomination but it was somewhat isolated in the south of the Island. When Annual Assemblies took place in Hobart, it was quite an adventure for the delegates to just arrive. As A. E. B explained in 1897,

*8-1 Construction of the Hobart Exhibition Buildings*

A fair muster left Launceston by the afternoon express, and the time passed pleasantly in singing and conversation until we reached Parattah, where we stopped for tea. The line from there is rather zig-zag, in and out, following the indentations of the mountains, doubling back to get round a gorge. The motion of the train somewhat resembles that of a steamer coming across the Straits, and the effect is very much the same. Everybody was glad to see the lights of the city come into view, and to be relieved of the confinement of a stuffy railway carriage.[647]

## Hobart's Beginnings

After a number of successful years in Longford it was laid on the Rev Robert McCullough's heart to attempt, without any promise of financial support, to start a new church in Hobart. As he said in later years, "There had been one of the hyper-Calvinistic school, but it was broken up, and I decided to start a new work."[648] William Gibson Senior again came forward and gave him an assurance that if the contributions of the new congregation were not sufficient for his support, he would stand by him and make up the difference.

On taking up the work in the southern capital, McCullough was not going to be alone. Hobart homeopath, Dr. Harry Benjafield, supported him all the way. Among those who were also willing to stand behind him were Hobart businessman, Joshua Tovell Soundy

---

[647] SB March 1897.

[648] South Australian Register 13 November 1900 p4.

and Victorian pioneer Baptist, Samuel B. Pitt.[649]

McCullough's work in Hobart began in the Exhibition Building on 7 October 1883.[650] Dr. Benjafield, under the direction of Gibson Senior, rented it from the Hobart Corporation at the weekly rental of fifty shillings.[651] McCullough's preaching drew Baptists who had been scattered about among other denominations. Its mid-week services were held in the Berean School Room just off Upper Liverpool Street.

Shortly afterwards, the first baptismal service was held in the Exhibition Building. The baptistry was a zinc-lined carriage case which had been brought out from England by A. G. Humby, a carriage builder who had joined McCullough's Baptists. Humby's business, the "London Carriage Works", was in Macquarie Street.[652]

At the Exhibition Building in November 1883 McCullough gave a lecture on the reformer Martin Luther and the Reformation. At least 600 persons gathered, many from the Methodist churches. The lecture was accompanied by a choir. The Mercury reported,

His lecture upon the whole was fair and temperate, and was altogether devoid of that hot-headed exaggeration which is often heard from the lips of evangelistic preachers. There was as a consequence an absence also of the unrest and disapproval which such addresses invariably provoke, and the audience throughout was quiet and attentive applauding the lecturer at frequent intervals.

McCullough concluded his address with these words,

Truth could not be stilled. If one man with a Bible could do so much, what could not thousands of men do, similarly armed? Taking Luther as an example, he could look calmly forward to the day which must assuredly come when truth would be triumphant.[653]

Among McCullough's sermon titles were: "People who turn the world upside down", "The Jolly Tar's Motto", "After the Bottle" and "The True Blues". Dr Benjafield preached at times and a couple of his sermon titles were, "Drowning Troubles" and "From Bad to Worse".

Gibson Senior instructed McCullough to secure a suitable site

---

[649] Samuel B. Pitt had the distinction of meeting William Knibb, James Smith of Delhi, and John C. Page, all famous missionaries, Daily Herald (Adelaide) 1 November 1913 p3; SB May 4 1899 p97.
[650] The Mercury (Hobart) 6 October 1883 p2, advert 20 October 1883 p1.
[651] LEx 26 September 1883 p3.
[652] Advert 27 June 1884 p1, 27 June 1884 p3.
[653] The Mercury (Hobart) 13 November 1883 p3.

for a church building and inform him of its location and the price for which it could be purchased. Subsequently, Gibson sent a cheque for £950 for land in Elizabeth Street which had a residential dwelling well back on the block.

On Saturday evenings, late night shopping existed and McCullough proceeded with his handbills around the block formed by Liverpool, Murray, Collins and Elizabeth Streets. He introduced himself as a student of the Rev C. H. Spurgeon, reckoning folk would be able to evaluate rightly from this the content of his preaching.[654]

On the Sunday afternoons, if there were any steamers in port, McCullough would go aboard with three or four choir members and hold a service. McCullough also visited the Immigration Depot at the top of Argyle Street, where newcomers to Hobart were first settled and invite them to his services.

On 25 January 1884, Richard T. Booth, a reformed drunkard himself, and his co-worker, T.W. Glover, commenced a three-week Blue Ribbon Gospel Temperance Mission in the Exhibition Building. A 400-voice choir accompanied the mission and McCullough and his people were involved. Over the period of the mission 3,562 pledges and 5,497 ribbons were taken. 1000 attended a farewell tea arranged by Dr. Benjafield.[655]

In April 1884, Evangelist and Temperance Campaigner, Matthew Burnett held a mission at the Exhibition Building.[656] Further the various denominations arranged for a mission to be undertaken by Mrs. Margaret Hampson of New Zealand, and the Exhibition Building was suggested as a venue. So it was of the general view that McCullough had turned the Exhibition Building into a Baptist Church and even someone on the Council confirmed this when he remarked, "The Exhibition Building is none other than a Baptist Church!" And when the question of Mrs. Hampson's accommodation was considered, opposition was raised to Dr. Benjafield's offer to provide such freely on the ground that he was a Baptist! This unfriendly spirit further manifested itself when two ministers who had received tickets for a "tea meeting" returned them with the remark that they were sure that a mistake had been made in supplying them.

At the time a detractor wrote of one of Mrs. Hampson's meetings in NSW,

> Last night the vast floor space of the Exhibition building proved insufficient to accommodate the thousands who were anxious to hear Mrs. Hampson's first address. The other third (of those who attended) would represent

---

[654] The Mercury (Hobart) 4 October 1887 p3.
[655] Tasmanian News (Hobart) 1 March 1884 p3.

[656] Tasmanian News (Hobart) 3 April 1884 p3; The Mercury (Hobart) 11 April 1884 p3.

non-church goers, whose presence illustrated the power of curiosity as a motive. They went to hear a woman orator with an intercolonial reputation, and to see a vast crowd and perhaps some religious excitement ... Her theology is the familiar theology of Evangelical Churches, but she has completely mastered it. Her voice is marvellously strong, but not as marvellously sweet. Her throat and lungs must be of remarkable strength and capacity. Her sermon lasted an hour or more, and was delivered with impassioned energy. An admirably distinct enunciation made it possible (the building having been draped so as to stifle the echoes) for the entire audience to hear almost every syllable. Most of the preachers of Sydney, if they tried to speak in such a building at Mrs. Hampson's pitch and place would have to be carried off the platform in about 15 minutes ... The lady has no freshness of thought, coins no original phrases, but has an easy command of the thoughts and phrases of the school of Christians to which she belongs. Some of the descriptive passages were very realistic, and some of the appeals were tremendously earnest, but there was nothing to stir the brain of a thinking man or woman. Mrs. Hampson disclaimed any intention of "working upon the emotions" of her audience; but that was just what she did, and nothing more. There was just as much truth in her message and wisdom in her methods as there are in the message and methods of every Evangelical Church in Sydney.[657]

The Hampson Mission ran in the Hobart Exhibition Building from 11 to 25 May.[658]

At the end of June 1884, after McCullough's folk had had use of the building on Sundays for nine months, the City Council threw out the Baptist seats making plain that they were no longer welcome. Prior to this the Town Clerk had informed the Baptists that the quarterly rent, already £2, "would be almost doubled in the next quarter". The Mayor had other things in mind: the Corporation wanted the use of the building in July for a "Ye Old English Fayre".[659]

The following Sunday, 29 June 1884, the congregation arrived to find the pews piled up on the pavement and the doors locked. The church was now homeless. The seats were carted away and stored. On the following Saturday there was no usual mention in the religious notices section in the Mercury newspaper of the Exhibition services

---

[657] The Maitland Mercury and Hunter River General Advertiser (NSW) 20 September 1883 p6.
[658] The Mercury (Hobart) 5 May 1884 p3, 10 May p1.
[659] The shops and stalls in the market were converted into the Old English shop styles. There were Maypole Dances, Punch and Judy Shows, and other side-show attractions.

but McCullough placed this advertisement:

> PASTOR McCULLOUGH'S SERVICES. Being TURNED OUT of Exhibition Building, our things put in the streets, and now being STOPPED with our NEW Building, after obtaining permission to build, we can have NO SERVICE on SUNDAY. R McCULLOUGH.[660]

An attempt was then made to rent the closed St John's Presbyterian Church in Macquarie Street, but to no avail. The request to use the Temperance Alliance rooms in Macquarie Street was ultimately granted for a few Sundays.

With the land in Elizabeth Street now theirs, Dr. Benjafield suggested that a temporary edifice be erected until a school room was built. Accordingly, a structure was erected of such a character that it was facetiously called a "shedifice" while others called it the "tin chapel". Services began therein on 24 August 1884.[661]

The building was a piece of patchwork from floor to roof. It had a sawdust floor with duckboards laid down the aisles. The walls of sawn timber were covered in ragged tarpaulins with old iron here and there, a wisp of straw jammed in the gaps to keep out the wind. There were several windows. The unlined walls inside were decorated with texts. A raised platform at the western end was utilised by both preacher and choir. Benjafield lent the timber for the platform with the stipulation that no nails were to be used. The preacher entered at the western end through a door covered by a curtain. Under the platform was Humby's coach case as a baptistry.

In high wind the iron and tin rattled and drowned out the preacher's voice and when it rained the women put up their sunshades and umbrellas while the remainder of the congregation moved "well into the centre of the building to avoid a baptismal sprinkling".[662] At night, the building was illumined with candles stuck between nails on crossed pieces of wood hung from the roof. The structure stood at the street front.

*8-2 North Hobart area prior to the purchase of the Church land*

---

[660] Tasmanian News (Hobart) 28 June 1884 p 2.

[661] The Mercury (Hobart) 23 August 1884 p1.

[662] The Mercury (Hobart) 4 October 1887 p3.

# Lessons from our first 20 years

*8-3 The School Room*

The Church had sent a letter to the Council asking for permission to erect this structure. As there had been no time to wait for the next Council meeting, the Town Clerk gave permission for works to proceed. But because of some private complaints the Council stepped in by serving a notice that the Building Act had been infringed and that work cease immediately. About £80 had been expended on the structure which only took six days to erect.

Despite the Council threat, the "shedifice" was completed and occupied for five months. The northern church paper, "The Pioneer", wrote approvingly,

> brother McCullough preaches in a building which is certainly a curiosity in this colony. We have been in bush chapels, but never one to equal this for cold, damp or rough appearance. On a warm evening there is a good congregation, but when it rains the people are huddled together in the centre to escape the wet. Under such circumstances great success could hardly be expected. Mr. Spurgeon says, "You cannot get souls saved where there is no fresh air," and we suppose the same might be said where there is too much air. But the Lord has been blessing, and a great interest is manifested in the meetings. As the weather improves, the rude building will be more suitable.

The Sunday school had commenced during the occupancy of the Exhibition Building with four teachers and thirty pupils. Humby was the first Superintendent of the School. On 20 February 1884, the formation of the church took place in the dining room of Dr. Benjafield's house.

With the Sunday school now meeting in the "shedifice", children in the thickly populated North Hobart area, mostly of a poorer class and somewhat destitute of religious privileges, were attracted but were an unruly lot at first. By the end of its first year of meeting in the "Shedifice", the school had thirteen teachers and 142 pupils. The front two rooms of the rear house were finally assigned to the Sunday school with the balance of the house occupied by a caretaker.

Finally on Saturday 1 November 1884, the church inserted a notice in the Mercury,

The Baptist Tabernacle, Elizabeth Street. "Anyone who has any regard for the fitness of things will rejoice to learn that this unsightly "shedifice" is soon to be removed to give place to a better structure, the foundation stone of which will be laid on Tuesday afternoon next at four o'clock. The ceremony will be followed by a tea and public meeting. A special train is being arranged for to bring friends and ministers from the North, and a large and successful meeting is anticipated."

The foundation stone of the new school room was laid by Mrs. Amelia Benjafield on 5 November 1884 in the presence of 150 spectators. The building, to accommodate about 400 persons, would cost about £400. The collection placed on the stone included a £50 cheque from Mary Ann Gibson.[663]

Four months later, on 21 March 1885, another notice appeared in the Mercury:

> Hobart Tabernacle Schoolroom: Those who complained of the temporary Tabernacle in Elizabeth St. as an eyesore, will be pleased with the neat edifice that is now almost completed on the ground. As the beginning of a large and costly building in contemplation, the Baptists are so far to be congratulated. The present structure is only intended for a school room at a future date, but it is really very suitable for a place of worship for some time to come ... The opening services will be held tomorrow and a tea-meeting on Monday, March 23. The stone for the building was obtained from the quarry on Dr. Benjafield's property on Mt. Stuart Road.[664]

For the inaugural tea 150 people turned up and for public meeting about 300 attended. It was stated that the Gibsons, Senior and Junior, had each given donations of £450 and that, with the money in hand, there was £400 to pay off. William Gibson Senior of Native Point himself was present. The "shedifice" had been demolished four weeks earlier and the services subsequently held for the intervening period in the old Harrington Street chapel. The new work in Elizabeth Street attracted the attention of the German Baptists who had purchased land in Glenorchy and had for baptisms made use of the Harrington Street chapel. They made application to become a branch church and on 30 July 1885 they were accepted but by 1889 a number had fallen into Seventh Day Adventism.

Following the occupancy of the School Room, the membership increased steadily and it soon became overcrowded. Yet with the Tabernacle envisaged, some wanted things to remain as is, "When we

---

[663] Tasmanian News (Hobart) 5 November 1884 p4.

[664] The Mercury (Hobart) 21 March 1885.

move into the larger building will we be as much at home in it as we are in this? It will be too big and we won't be able to get to one another so easily." The number of members on the roll at this time was forty-nine, showing an increase of twenty-seven since the commencement of the church. The great question occupying the minds of the members was that of funds. Generally speaking the congregation was not composed of persons of means.

Again the Church turned to William Gibson Senior since he had frequently expressed a wish that a building capable of seating a large congregation should be erected in the Capital. McCullough, Soundy and Pitt visited and again Gibson suggested that plans for a suitable building should be submitted to him.

Following this Dr. Benjafield obtained plans of the Baptist Church, Stockport, England, which was the newer class of Baptist Church building in England and Hobart architect George Fagg, a church member, adapted them to the site. Gibson gave his approval and enclosed a cheque for £1000 with a note, "the money would not build a palace but it would build something better than a barn." This gift was shortly followed by one of the same amount from his son, William Gibson Junior of Scone. This was in keeping with his son's earlier promise to match pound for pound the giving of his father.

The tenders were called by November 1886. For some reason fresh tenders for revised drawings were called for, returnable by 12 July 1887. Stabb Brothers Builders were awarded the contract, but the whole of the work was not included in this contract. The gallery, designed to seat 300, the seating, the baptistry, and other works were excluded, but provision was made for the footings of the gallery columns for the time that a gallery was needed.

The foundation stone was laid on 5 October 1887 in the presence of about 300 people with the placement of historical items underneath. Present was Mary Ann Gibson who performed the usual ceremony saying,

I pronounce this memorial stone of the Hobart Tabernacle well and truly laid. We raise the building for the worship of our God, for the preaching of the everlasting Gospel, for the conversion of sinners, and the building up of the Lord's people. We may raise the edifice, but God alone can build the Church.

**8-4 Laying the foundation stone of the Hobart Tabernacle**

The monies given that day included a cheque from this cautious seventy-eight year old lady.[665] Her trip to Hobart had necessitated a train journey for this. It was told that as the train neared the Rhyndaston Tunnel she drew from her bag a candle, which she lit. After emerging from the tunnel she blew out the candle and replaced it in her bag saying to her amused fellow passengers, "We never know with whom we may be travelling these days."

*8-5 The Stately Hobart Tabernacle*

A tea and public meeting followed the laying ceremony. "This ornament to the City", erected at considerable cost, was finally opened for public worship on 20 January 1889. The guest preacher for the day was the Rev Samuel Chapman of the Collins Street Baptist Church, Melbourne. Services at both morning and evening worship were filled to capacity.

On its opening the Mercury reported that all that had been anticipated of the perfect adaptability of its new building as a place of worship was amply fulfilled.

> Designed on perfect architectural lines, chastely decorated, lofty, well lighted, comfortably seated and with specially good acoustic properties, the interior is all that a place of worship should be ... Externally, the edifice forms a striking addition to the public buildings of the city.

Builder David Williams Junior constructed the seating. The organ was the gift of grocer Mr. Henley. The Secretary, Samuel B. Pitt, donated the pulpit Bible. The beautifully moulded capitals on the two pillars, one on each side of the pulpit, were the gift of the Architect. Joshua T. Soundy paid for the iron railing, gates and gas pillars in the front of the church building.[666] Years later, no less an authority than the Encyclopaedia Britannica, said that the building was the finest classical facade in the Southern Hemisphere.

---

[665] The Mercury (Hobart) 6 October 1887 p3.

[666] The Mercury (Hobart) 20 November 1886 p2, 29 November 1886 p3, 12 July 1887 p 2, 7 July 1887 p1.

At a special church meeting held on 20 October 1890, a letter was read from McCullough,

> Dear Brethren,
>
> I am sorry to have to inform you that I shall cease to be your Pastor in six weeks from this date. Your surprise at my taking this step cannot be greater than my own. It has been brought before me that I do not work hard enough, and that it is through me that there is not more success in the Church, and further, that my wife both by her dress and behaviour gives general dissatisfaction in the church and is looked upon as a hindrance to the work. As I do not know to what extent these feelings may prevail, there is no other course open to me as an honourable man, than to tender my resignation.
>
> The Hobart Church is dear to my heart - the Lord only knows how dear. I have given a few of the best years of my life for it, and now I only separate myself because I am led to believe that it will be better without me.
>
> I have no other door open for me at present and do not know where I shall be going, so it cannot be said I am influenced by offers from other quarters.
>
> I pray that God may bless you abundantly and guide you as to your future. Kindly remember me in your prayers. All this has come so suddenly that it has been almost too much for me.
>
> I remain, Yours in Christian love,

In a speech of considerable length, one member defended McCullough and moved the following resolution, "That this meeting now assembled sincerely sympathizes with the pastor and urges him to reconsider his resignation." This motion was seconded and many members spoke specially in its favour. At that juncture, Dr. Benjafield stated that he was the writer of the letter to the Pastor containing the allegation referred to in the letter of resignation. After attempting to justify his position, the resolution that McCullough stay on was put to the meeting and carried by a majority of twenty-seven to two. Dr. Benjafield then handed in a letter resigning his position on the diaconate. At the next meeting McCullough withdrew his resignation.

It was reported at the Annual church meeting in 1891 that the membership, whilst steadily increasing, had not continued to grow as in previous years. Of those who joined the church, "more than half as many have gone away as have been added." It was a year "not all sunshine, or all cloud and shadow, but a mixture of both."

In 1889, the Church had an outstation at Bismarck near Collinsvale with twenty members and a work in Sandy Bay. In April 1891, McCullough initiated the formation of the first Christian Endeavour Society in Tasmania.[667] The church was also conducting a Mutual Improvement Society and a Young Men's Bible Class. There were 250 children enrolled in the Sunday school with twenty-two teachers and an average attendance of 157.

The men and women of the Tabernacle worked hard at "Sale of Gifts" fairs in aid of the Building Fund.[668] The church welcomed visiting evangelists such as Englishman Henry Varley for his fortnight's mission at the Temperance Hall. The Baptist choir members were involved.

Among the other visiting speakers were internationally acclaimed Temperance speaker, the Rev Mark Guy Pearse. Pearse was from the East End of London and he preached with "a burning conviction which thoroughly possessed him." Another was Baptist Missionary, Miss Alice Pappin, a South Australian school teacher from the North Adelaide Church working in Fureedpore, India. She wore Indian native costume at her meetings. The church hosted the Annual Assembly Baptist Union Meetings which meant the re-erection of additional passenger platforms at the Hobart railway station.

McCullough was on the board of the Ragged School and supported, with Joshua T Soundy, the "Discharged Prisoners' Aid and Rescue Society". McCullough took part with the Hobart clergy for "A Day of Humiliation and Prayer". This was prompted by the prevailing sickness and depression of the 1890s which was gripping the country.

The Pastor's report, given in January 1894, spoke of a very disappointing year as far as the work was concerned. The financial position was getting worse - the debt on the property was considerable. Only three new members had been added to the roll for the whole year. Further, the 1890s saw disastrous bank failures with speculators losing fortunes which meant money was tight. He submitted his resignation letter stating how sorry he was to be obliged to leave the work here but, as the finances were getting lower and lower, there was nothing left for him but to release the church of his services.

This "Gentle Shepherd"[669] preached his farewell sermons on 11 March 1894. Days following the farewell sermons, folk assembled on the wharf to bid farewell to him and his wife and family. As the S.S. "Ophir" left the wharf, the company, some with tears in their eyes sang part of the hymn "God be with you till we meet again" amid long continued waving of hats and handkerchiefs.

---

[667] Day-Star May 1889 p66, but the LEx 27 October 1893 p5 states, "The Christian Endeavour Society, which had spread all through Tasmania, might justly call Pastor Soltau its head, for he was the father of the movement in this colony."

[668] For McCullough's attitude to the place of women in the Church see Manley p309.

[669] The Mercury (Hobart)

# The Rev Robert McCullough's "Day Star"

Two years after the formation of the Baptist Association it was resolved to circulate an undenominational religious paper under the editorship of McCullough but upholding "those doctrines which Pastor C. H. Spurgeon has so long and fearlessly proclaimed in England". The journal made clear, "Our fighting will not be on behalf of any sect, but on behalf of all Christians." The first issue was released in January 1886. The leading newspapers were all sent copies and the response was that "the local church news given, besides an amount of readable matter, (was on) the whole comprising a very creditable production."[670]

McCullough remained its editor for nearly its whole life. For years it began with an illustrative portrait and biographical sketch of the life of a well-known, earnest and successful Christian such as Hannah More and contained a sermon by the Rev C. H. Spurgeon. Apart from religious news, it expressed the views of Tasmanian Baptists on the social issues of the day. It attacked literary fiction calling it "literary garbage which finds favour among a large section of the community."[671] But there was little interest in the "Day Star" beyond the Baptist fold. Complained McCullough,

*8-6 Amy Sherwin*

> When we started, our intention was honestly to represent all evangelical denominations but they held aloof from us. They would give us no encouragement. They ignored us. Can we be blamed, then, if our views and some of our statements are more particularly for the care of the one denomination that reads us? If we should in the course of time be forced to become denominational, we remind other denominations that, through their own indifference or narrow-mindedness, they have thrown away a good chance of having a Tasmanian paper to help them. We should rejoice to see all the Churches working unitedly both to manage and support a paper that would faithfully witness for the things most surely believed among us.

After just eighteen months there were moves to cease publication as the circulation was not large but the leading newspapers approved of the paper as did many fellow Baptists

---

[670] The Mercury (Hobart) 13 January 1886 p2.

[671] The Mercury (Hobart) 15 February 1887 p2.

and so it continued with a 1000 run.[672]

The August 1887 issue dealt "earnestly with heterodoxy, intemperance, the Christian Chinese, church missions and many other subjects all of special interest in the advancement of a healthy emulation in the work of true religion." The Mercury's newspaper verdict was, "The extract matter is, as usual, well selected, and items of local interest are concisely given."[673]

McCullough received some feedback for his criticism of Amy Sherwin, the "Tasmanian Nightingale", an Australian soprano singer. He wrote,

> Her career has been highly creditable to herself all through ... we are not surprised that the people should feel proud of her. But is she doing right? Should not that charming gift of song be consecrated to Him from whom it has come? If she were to sing for Jesus instead of the world's silly ballads, her popularity would be none the less, but how much greater her usefulness, and how much more solid the honours. Alas! this applause that rings in her ears to-day, what comfort will it bring when the dying hour has come? There will be sweeter voices yonder than Amy Sherwin's now. What if she find herself out of tune and unable to join in the melody of Heaven?[674]

Of all those who replied was no other than the Rev William White of the York Street Baptist Chapel, Launceston,

> For my part I would rather she sung as now she does sing, the purest of worldly songs, believing that she would grieve God far more if she sang the Lord's songs in a strange land.[675]

McCullough even criticised one of England's leading Congregationalist, the Rev Robert W. Dale, doubting the doctor's soundness in doctrine; Dr Dale visited Hobart late in 1887.[676]

On Spurgeon's secession from the Baptist Union of England, McCullough wrote,

> He may possibly have erred, but all will admit that he acted with the purest motives. After all, the secession from the union is a small matter. The main thing is the bold attack that he has made on the false and dangerous teaching that so many are receiving as Christ's. The result will be a distinct separation between true and false doctrine, and, perhaps, the restoration of many whose feet have been set in slippery places. The battle will be severe, many will be wounded,

---

[672] LEx 15 April 1887 p3, 6 June 1887 p3.
[673] The Mercury (Hobart) 11 August 1887 p2.
[674] Day-Star August 1887; LEx 27 August 1887 p2.
[675] LEx 30 August 1887 p3.
[676] Day-Star September 1887.

Mr. Spurgeon himself suffering most of all; but the end will be victory for Christ and more honour and love than ever for His faithful and much honoured servant.[677]

McCullough, like Spurgeon, was of the view, "The New Theology must be opposed if Christianity is to retain its position as an unerring guide to happiness and heaven."[678]

McCullough didn't mince words when it came to politicians,

> Politics are left to the worst men, and the good hold themselves aloof ... The last Parliament was without an atom of religion, inasmuch as nothing was attempted for the preservation of good morals, drunkenness was encouraged, gambling was left untouched, and on the whole the tendency was in an irreligious direction.[679]

Overall its fourteen years the "Day Star" was seen as "that excellent little Tasmanian monthly".[680] The Rev Edward E. Harris of the Launceston Tabernacle took over editorship for its final year. It was Harris who asked through the "Day Star" whether travelling evangelists, who had of late abounded, really did any good to the cause of true religion. At the time evangelistic theology was infamously individualistic. He wrote,

> A great deal of frothy momentary excitement has been engendered, but where are the converts? Is there an abnormal increase of membership in the churches? Are they able to report larger congregations? Admitting that the answers to these questions may be disappointing (for people) ... chase after wandering lights, and their church finances turned topsy-turvey ... from these intermittent exaltations?[681]

Writing from South Australia where he was now based, McCullough agreed,

> In religion there are special missions and meetings in rapid succession. The McNeil and Burke mission drew together the largest crowds that have been seen here at evangelistic services. The outcome is, alas, disappointing. The people came, were amused, entertained, instructed, and no doubt deeply impressed, but we cannot hear that Sunday congregations are any better, or that any church has had its membership increased through the visit of these gifted evangelists. Evangelistic work is overdone, and men are becoming on one hand too much accustomed to gospel appeals

---

[677] Day-Star January 1888.
[678] Day-Star July 1888.
[679] Day-Star May 1891.
[680] LEx 14 June 1892 p2.
[681] Day-Star October 1894.

and on the other lulled into a state of carnal security by listening to preaching that robs the Bible of its authority.⁶⁸²

In 1894, the "Day Star" merged "its light in the greater glow of the arising Southern Baptist."⁶⁸³

## The Rev Morison Cumming

In November of 1894, the church extended a call to the Rev Morison Cumming who was in South Australia from England to see his parents and hoped to stay there.⁶⁸⁴ He participated in the opening of the new Norwood Baptist Church in Adelaide of which his father was the architect.⁶⁸⁵ After negotiations involving his stipend at the Hobart Baptist Church, he accepted the invitation saying, "I have felt greatly drawn to the work at Hobart, and trust there is set before me an open door which no man shall shut. May the Master help me to rise to the greatness of the opportunity." He immediately returned to England to fetch his family and was expected in Hobart in the New Year.⁶⁸⁶

Cumming received a great welcome at Hobart and commenced his ministry on 25 February 1895. A good preacher and one sound in doctrine, "Not one who belonged to the new school on doubting theology", he was seen by The Mercury as "a Pastor up to date". The newspaper reported,

His eloquent opening address received an enthusiastic applause. He assured the other ministers of churches present that he wished to be an earnest comrade in arms with them. He was proud of being a colonial born, and rejoiced to be called to minister among a colonial people. It was a painful wrench to say "good-bye" to the old country after so many years in it but both he and his wife could make a home wherever he found loving hearts, or wherever was planted Christ's flag. He came as their pastor and not as a priest - all

*8-7 Morison Cumming*

---

⁶⁸² LEx 13 November 1894 p5.
⁶⁸³ This proved a mistake. The leading Baptist Churches of Hobart, Launceston, Devonport and Burnie sent in reports but the smaller Churches increasingly failed to do so. The same happened eight years later when the Australian Baptist took the place of the SB.

⁶⁸⁴ South Australian Register (Adelaide) 28 June 1894 p7.
⁶⁸⁵ Christian Colonist (SA) 8 June 1894 p6; The Advertiser (Adelaide) 26 June 1894 p6.
⁶⁸⁶ South Australian Register (Adelaide) 12 October 1894 p4; The Mercury (Hobart) 16 February 1895 p2.

were priests who were believers. He trusted he should prove their friend as well as their pastor, being wishful to share in their sorrows as well as in their joys. The members of the Church and congregation, however, should remember that the pastor and deacons were not omniscient, or knew without being informed that sickness was in their houses. On the spiritual side, he hoped to be able to lead them. His main business was to preach and cling to the truth, and to what Rowland Hill called "the three R's." He did not believe in divorcing the secular from the sacred. He came to them also as a prophet and a teacher, believing in the Holy Ghost and the golden days to come. He was glad as a colonial to come to minister in this colony. It was somewhat depressed at present, commercially, but they must not be discouraged on that account and think that God had forgotten them. He pleaded with them to look at the bright side of things, for this was the right side.[687]

8-8 Collins St Baptist Church, Melbourne

And in time it was seen that not only did they have a good pastor, but also a good pastor's wife. In June, Hannah formed the Women's Guild with a foundation membership of forty. Its special object was that of reaching women of all classes and conditions. Help was also to be given to many mothers in the neighbourhood.

Cumming entered the work but did not seem to settle down. He resigned on 14 October 1895. He was compelled to return to England with deep regret. The present trying conditions in the colony made him feel that he must give place to a man of few responsibilities. The Woman's Guild regretted very much the loss of its President and founder and the church, for its part, wished Cumming and his devoted wife and family every good wish. Relations had been of a very hopeful character.[688]

The real reasons for his leave are not given. Samuel B. Pitt was soon to record,

> We could almost wish that a veil could be drawn over this part of our history. Mr. Cumming's ministry only lasted about six months ... Mention must however be made of this fact, viz., that the

---

[687] The Mercury (Hobart) 22 February 1895 p3.

[688] The Mercury (Hobart) 4 October 1895 p2.

Church faithfully fulfilled all its obligations to the departing minister, and whatever were his reasons for his actions, no blame could be attached to the members of the Church.

The answer to why he felt compelled to relinquish the work probably lay in the birth of their first son on 17 June 1895, Howard Cumming, and Hannah's need to be with her English family at this time.

## The Rev James Blaikie

The Rev James Blaikie, "a cultured Scotchman of noble bearing," a man with "a large brotherly heart, wise counsel, and sanctified cheerfulness",[689] became the Hobart Church's third pastor and began in August 1897. In his straightforward evangelistic messages Blaikie worked on the principle that the "Bible is our only guide"; he was fundamentalist in his preaching which came out in his response to a sermon in December 1900.

In November 1900, the Rev Samuel Pearce Carey of the Collins Street Baptist Church preached a sermon to a Victorian Baptist Assembly. Its main theme dealt with certain narrow views concerning the Bible,

> The modern attitude to the Scriptures should be welcomed ... (We are not to hold) that every line of the Bible should be regarded as though it had come by direct dictation from the Holy Ghost; that every word is recorded as the utterance of a man of God would be infallible; that every historical statement should be inerrant; that every prophet's prophecy should get its literal fulfillment.

He continued,

> We have been called away from what has been ill grounded theory to a thorough, patient facing of facts, and I am well convinced that this more inductive scientific method of approach of every biblical problem has come out of the signal good providence of God. We are sure to modify many of our traditional judgments about the book, just as we have modified many of our conceptions as to the material universe.[690]

Upon learning of Carey's sermon, Blaikie wrote an article titled, "The Old Landmarks",

> Instead of the Bible being God's Word, as our fathers believed it, it only contains it, and only what the critics are pleased to select as suitable. Instead of authenticity, which was considered fairly settled a century ago, the critics are casting about for authors in all directions, until poor Moses and Isaiah have to take a back seat. Instead of the old fashioned

---

[689] SB 1 November 1904 p245.

[690] SB 13 December 1900; The Argus (Melbourne) 16 November 1900 p6.

*8-9 Constitution Hill Chapel*

belief of the plenary inspiration of the Scriptures, so firmly held by the old Protestant Church a few generations ago, we have a censorship of what we might call "inspired scholarship," that treats the Bible as a chemist treats a heap of ore that only yields a few ounces to the ton. History, prophecy, and miracle contain but little that is reliable by the time it has gone through the crucible of the Higher Critic.

He added,

> The bulwark of our evangelical faith is an implicit reliance on an open and inspired Bible. But the Bible of the Higher Critic order shakes faith at its foundations, and opens wide the door for rationalism and sacerdotal authority. If half of the Bible history is doubtful, if the miracles are incredible, if part of Genesis be but a poem or allegory, Abraham a "free creation of unconscious art," the narratives of the Hexateuch "the fruit solely of late Jewish fancy," &c., is it any wonder that men turn a deaf ear to the claims of the Bible when they learn on such good authority they are quite baseless."[691]

Our leading Australian Baptist historian, the Rev Dr. Ken Manley, sees a close connection between the Spurgeon tradition (as seen best in Tasmania) and the later fundamentalism to emerge clearly in the second decade of the twentieth century in North America. He writes,

> The Rev James Blaikie, a Spurgeon's man in Tasmania in the 1900 debate about Higher Criticism in the (Tasmanian, Victorian and South Australian) Southern Baptist, sounds exactly like the later fundamentalists when he deplored the loss of old landmarks and opposed claims made for "'inspired scholarship".[692]

Blaikie was saying that he lamented the attempts of some who analysed the Scriptures to determine which part was inspired and which was not.[693]

---

[691] SB 13 December1900 p279; LEx 16 September 1891 p2.

[692] Chapter by Manley, *Prophecy and Passion: Essays in Honour of Athol Gill*, edited by David Neville. Adelaide: Australian Theological Forum, pp358ff.

[693] LEx 16 September 1891 p2.

In 1901, the seventh Hobart Baptist Church anniversary was held and in the annual report it was stated that twenty-two new members had joined the church during the past year, seventeen of them being baptised, an increase of thirteen to 167. The finances were in a sound and healthy condition. The Sunday school was well attended while the Christian Endeavour Society had a membership of 100. The church continued to support its branch church at Constitution Hill. Ten out of the twenty original members were still on the church roll. One, Joshua T. Soundy, had been in office as Deacon from the beginning and had been Treasurer for fifteen years.

In August 1904, Blaikie presided over the opening of a Baptist Church at Sandy Bay making it the twelfth Baptist Church in the State.[694] During his time at Hobart he was twice President of the Baptist Association, 1900/1901 and 1904/1905.

Sunday observance remained a community issue at the time, especially in regard to the running of Sunday trains, as did the social evil of gambling, with Tattersall's being the main culprit with the latter. In 1905, Blaikie became secretary of Hobart's Citizens' Moral and Social Reform League but expressed the view that its influence would be far greater if it had amalgamated with the Workers' Political League.[695]

Blaikie penned a number of letters to the Mercury on various subjects. One, in February 1898, spoke of "Black Tuesday", 1 February 1898, when fire engulfed Tasmania while in Victoria 2000 buildings were destroyed and twelve lives lost. The disaster which was described as unparalleled in the history of the Tasmanian colony was, according to Blaikie,

> an act of God. Being so, we ought, in a public way, to acknowledge God, or we as a people will miss the benefit of distress, for is it not written, "When His judgments are abroad in the earth, the inhabitants of the world learn righteousness."

Blaikie concluded by pleading for public and national prayer as "the sin of the nation is at the back of all this desolation". A month later he wrote again, this time softening his approach by requesting books for those who suffered in the fires.

Another letter put the case for uniform shop closing hours while a fourth deplored the nation's low birth rate. He made it clear that he was well aware of the difficulties the churches were facing created by science, Higher Criticism and general unbelief, and yet he was sure

---

[694] The Mercury (Hobart) 5 August 1904 p4.

[695] The Mercury (Hobart) 8 April 1905 p5.

that "the old time power was omnipotent".⁶⁹⁶

At the end of 1899, Tasmanian Baptists were casting a wide net. The cry went out,

Baptists are now in the field. Now is our opportunity; if we keep on delaying our chances are small. We ought to follow our people and carry out our commission.⁶⁹⁷

*8-11 Lilly Soundy's Bible Study Class with George Craike sitting to her left*

The West Coast is in our judgment the greatest home mission field in Tasmania. It is a wide open door for a great and prosperous work.

"Whom shall we send, and who will go for us?" Now that we have a Union evangelist we hope steps will soon be taken to begin a work in, say, Queenstown, with its 10,000 inhabitants. Gormanston, Lyell, and Queenstown are practically one. There should be no difficulty in getting a footing there. A great many

*8-10 Dr. Harry Benjafield*

From late June 1901, Blaikie spent a month on the West Coast at Zeehan at what was now the Baptist Mission following the input there of the Rev Thomas Vigis of the Burnie Church. At the 1900 Annual Association meeting the year before the cry had been repeated, "We want to take possession of the West Coast for Christ. Our Home Mission wants extension."⁶⁹⁸ No permanent work resulted.

The aged Blaikie was farewelled from the Hobart Church in February 1906. During his time 102 persons had been baptised and 151

---

⁶⁹⁶ SB 15 May 1901 p118.
⁶⁹⁷ SB 4 January 1900 p1.
⁶⁹⁸ SB 28 August 1901, May 1900.

added to the church membership.[699] His next appointment was in Castlemaine in Victoria.

# Appendices

## Appendix 1: Dr Harry Benjafield

Dr. Harry Benjafield arrived in the colony in April 1873 having studied at both London and Edinburgh Universities and graduating Bachelor of Medicine and Master of Surgery from Edinburgh University in 1871.

In Manchester he married Amelia Pywell, daughter of the Rev J. Pywell, Baptist Minister of Zion Chapel, Stockport. As soon as he saved enough money, he bought passages to Australia, embarking on 22 February 1873.

On arrival in Hobart Town, he opened the first homeopathic pharmacy in the city. As a medical man, he did a roaring trade and the business proved a lucrative practice. He had landed with £20 and by 1883 he had gathered £20,000.

In 1879, he built his residence, "The Willows", a substantial structure midway between the city and New Town. In the eighties he established a dairy farm and traded under the name, "The Tasmanian Milk Company". He was one of the first to advocate the export of fruit to London.

He was also a convinced Baptist. Benjafield professed that, on arrival, he wandered from one church to another seeking vainly for a congenial spiritual home, but without success, longing for a Baptist Church in the south of the State.

He was a man who believed in the Bible and was against modern thought in the churches. In regard to his own baptism, he confessed that that was the means of him being able to do what little good he had done.

Benjafield was in correspondence with William Gibson Senior over a new Baptist work in Hobart, having been told by Gibson of his own desire to form an open communion work in the town. Once McCullough arrived, Benjafield was behind the new Baptist venture in the south.

## Appendix 2: Joshua Tovell Soundy

Joshua Tovell Soundy was born in 1840 in Bicester, Oxfordshire, England. As a young man, he did not demur when he was found a job as apprentice to a draper at a shop near his home. He married Elizabeth Johnson on 12

*8-12 Dr Joshua Tovell Soundy*

---

[699] SB 30 January 1906 p20.

November 1867. Four and a half years after his marriage, now with one child, he fell ill with Tuberculosis and he received medical advice that a sea voyage to Australia could give him a few more years. One of his advisers was Dr. Harry Benjafield.

In 1872, and living in Hobart, one of his many jobs in Hobart was as an assistant in the leading colonial drapery establishment of Andrew Mather yet he looked around to establish a drapery business of his own. The search took him to Parramatta in N.S.W. and to Ballarat in Victoria.

The family then tackled the long voyage back to England and he was soon back in the drapery business in his own shop at Dorchester, Dorsetshire, about thirty kms from Bicester. He and his wife Elizabeth became members of the Baptist Church there. The business prospered but the English climate slowly began its insidious attacks on Joshua's fragile constitution. In 1882, his doctor advised him that he should leave before the English winter and try life again in Tasmania. The family, by now comprising five children, arrived in Hobart on 16 February 1883 and determined to settle. With a horse and trap, he commenced hawking drapery around Hobart and further afield, not only making a living but also steadily establishing his name and a reputation of fair and honest dealing. Within a year, he bought one of a pair of conjoined cottages in Elizabeth Street, North Hobart, establishing his first shop in the basement. He then purchased land over the road and built a solid, city style, three level stone edifice with shop and dwelling.

Now using a wagon fitted with specially designed lock-up tin trunks, he carried his drapery lines further afield to the Southern Midlands, the Huon, the Channel and the Tasman Peninsula.

On McCullough's arrival in 1883, his support for the preacher and the new work was given unreservedly. His gifts which would be liberal and frequent, would be given unostentatiously. The Hobart Church and the Baptist Churches of the State would, in time, rejoice that God gave such a man to his work and service.

Soundy's answer to struggling churches 100 years ago was not as some suggest: longer pastorates. Rather Soundy wanted the church officers to tell their pastor straight out to "go" if the Church was dwindling month by month; they were not to be kept on. Said Soundy,

> "They don't like to speak so plainly; and the minister often hangs on till the place that was once fairly filled is almost empty, except the few who cling to the dear man; or to the bricks and mortar, out of a kind of sympathy. My views may differ from many, but I think our country Churches could have someone to go round once or twice a year, and see how the Church and minister are

getting on, and not go by reports in papers or on paper, for, alas! too often they are highly coloured. And when a leakage commences, if it is the fault of the good brother, tell him in a business way that a change will benefit the people, and most likely do him good too. We have Churches, if this plan had been adopted, would have saved the Union pounds; the Churches would have been stronger to-day, and supplies would have had a fair congregation to preach to instead of empty seats. We know of men where the Church has grown with them, and they are growing wide in the Master's service. Some of the Colonial Churches are adopting a plan which perhaps we hardly like, but it will help the Church over the difficulty of telling the pastor to go. The plan is to engage them a year at a time, so each yearly meeting they are re-appointed, or in plain words re-engaged. Some ministers object to it, but good men will not mind. It does some trees good to transplant them several times, especially if the soil does not suit them, and the same with pastors; and some will say "officers of the Church, I quite agree to that, then who is to blame?"

- The Church, for not telling the pastor to go.

- The pastor, for hanging on.

- The Union, for not looking to them both.

But I cannot see what the divorce has to do with the subject. If the Church is married to the pastor instead of Christ, the sooner they are divorced the better.

There would not be any Baptist work or Baptist building in Tasmania in Soundy's time in which he would not have had some part financially. He worked with a singleness of purpose, for he regarded himself as a servant of God in all that he did.

## Appendix 3: The Rev Robert McCullough

Following his time at Hobart, the Rev Robert McCullough received a call from the Parkside Baptist Church, Parkside being an inner suburb of the city of Adelaide, and he was welcomed on 3 May 1894.[700] He would labour there for nine years

*8-13 Parkside Baptist Church SA*

---

[700] The Advertiser (Adelaide) 4 May 1894 p7.

during which he entered fully into the life of the South Australian Baptist Association. McCullough became acquainted with Morison Cumming at the State Assembly meetings and sometimes shared the preaching. It is more than likely that the recommendation for Cumming to pastor the Hobart Church came from McCullough himself. McCullough was soon appointed to the editorship of the South Australian Baptist journal, "Truth and Progress" working with the Rev E. H. Ellis who was his fellow student at the Pastors' College. Also McCullough became editor of the new "Southern Baptist".[701] In a paper he had published in the "Southern Baptist" in June 1895, McCullough of whom it was said at the time, "His tastes all run in a literary channel," wrote on "The ministry of the future". He dealt with three aspects - the anti-clerical, the up-to-date, and the spiritual. In part he said,

> Antiquated fossils are not the class of men who will constitute the ministry of the future. What was wanted was an army of educated well-read men, men who could speak on almost any subject, who were up-to-date in matters concerning the temporal as well as the spiritual welfare of the people. The intellectual enlightenment of the people had become so advanced that ignorance and the use of bad grammar in the pulpit tended to drive people from rather than attract them to the churches, and in order to keep pace with the times the ministers must be good speakers and well versed in all the topics of the day. At the same time he contended that the ministry would have to maintain its spiritual tone if it was to accomplish all the good that was expected of it.[702]

8-14 Rev F W Boreham

This article shows there was a shift in his outlook. In his early years in Tasmania McCullough held the view the Bible said all that needed to be said and one had to take it on face value, word for word. There was no need for any creative and imaginative approach. There was little openness to stories, poetry and new ways of viewing things. To stand apart and critically evaluate a text was unheard of and only led to doubt and disbelief. It was considered that the Gospel must

---

[701] The Advertiser (Adelaide) 26 June 1894 p6; South Australian Chronicle (Adelaide) 13 October 1894 p9; Adelaide Observer 26 September 1896 p15.

[702] South Australian Chronicle (Adelaide) 22 June 1895 p11; Critic (Adelaide) 17 November 1900 p8.

be preached faithfully in all its simplicity, with the results left to God.

This shift in his outlook came to the fore in May 1906 when he returned to Hobart to preach for the month at the Hobart Tabernacle, while the Church waited for the arrival of the Rev F. W. Boreham. Present at Boreham's reception he said,

> He had widened his views since he had been away, and had come to the conclusion that goodness was worth more than doctrine or creed. While still holding fast to the faith as it had been handed down to him, he had come to recognise that they were all pressing forward to a heavenly home, and that the differences between them were not so great as some people thought. He felt less and less inclined to judge and condemn other people, and more and more inclined to feel a bond of brotherhood with those who entertained different views on some points, but who were yet engaged in the same grand work.703

This was echoed in 1912 when he commented on a South Australian Ministers' School he had just attended,

*8-15 North Adelaide Baptist Church*

> In the early days there was sometimes a feeling of alarm when opinions were freely expressed which threatened to upset old views. But it is now recognised that we can only get at the truth by everyone speaking out just what he thinks.

John Walker adds,

> McCullough was a widely respected conservative and so this endorsement meant much ... Conservative–evangelical ministers who remained in South Australia for long periods of time during the first quarter of the twentieth century were not in charge of large and influential churches.704 The ministerial career of McCullough exemplifies this trend ... Another conservative minister with a

---

703 The Mercury (Hobart) 5 May 1906 p5, 18 May 1906 p7.

704 John Walker's, 'The Baptists in South Australia', p52.

similar career path was Thomas Vigis.[705]

While at Parkside in 1895 McCullough was on the committee of the Adelaide City Mission. For the year 1900/1901 he was President of the Baptist Association and as President he and his wife attended in NSW the inaugural ceremonials of the Commonwealth.[706]

In 1902, the Parkside Sunday school had an average attendance weekly of 145 scholars with thirty-five scholars added that year.

After nearly nine years in the pastorate he resigned "for family reasons" but in November 1903 he accepted the oversight of the Baptist Churches at Morphet Vale and Aldinga until 1906.[707]

Then, in August 1906, he accepted the pastorate of the Mitcham and Coromandel Valley Baptist Churches. With the jubilee of the Coromandel church approaching in September 1908, fund raising began for the purpose of rebuilding the Coromandel Valley church building which was "altogether too small for the requirements of the congregation". Two years later the replacement building was opened. By March 1914, over £700 had been spent on buildings and a new Sunday school at Mitcham was being erected.[708]

At a Baptist Ministers' School in May 1912, McCullough gave a paper on "The seven ages of a Baptist minister". It dealt with phases of his life from student days to old age. At the Union Assembly in September 1912, he spoke of his own church, "Originally there was only a home mission church, assisted by the union, but this year, with a membership of only fifty-eight, they had been able to send £100 for foreign and home mission work."[709] After twenty-one years in South Australia, McCullough accepted a call to the Burnie Baptist Church in the North West of Tasmania.

## Appendix 4: The Rev Morison Cumming

South Australian born, the Rev Morison Cumming, who was filling an important pastorate in England, accepted the pastorate of the Hobart Baptist Church but relinquished the position within six months because of what seems to be a family matter.

Cumming was born in South Australia on 30 May 1851, the first child of Scottish parents, James Cumming and his wife, Helen (nee

---

[705] SB 23 May 1912 p329, see John Walker chapter 2.
[706] The Advertiser (Adelaide) 5 July 1895 p6; Adelaide Observer 22 September 1900 p 45, 5 January 1901 p18.
[707] The Register (Adelaide) 14 May 1902 p6; Evening Journal (Adelaide) 1 December 1902 p1, 13 November 1903 p1.

[708] South Australian Register 31 May 1851 p2; The Register (Adelaide) 2 August 1906 p4, 19 July 1924 p4; The Advertiser) 30 November 1907 p10l; Daily Herald (Adelaide) 28 February 1914 p3.
[709] The Express and Telegraph (Adelaide) 10 May 1912 p4; The Advertiser (Adelaide) 19 September 1912 p19.

Cumming). In November 1860 the family with three children sailed for London and in Glasgow James received his early education under Dr. Morison. In October 1864, they were back in South Australia and attending the well-to-do North Adelaide Baptist Church where James was a deacon. He was a leading architect in Adelaide who specialized in Church buildings. He was also Treasurer of the Baptist Union of South Australia Missionary Committee and took an interest in the South Australian Evangelical Alliance.[710]

When Morison was eighteen he gave a paper to the Mutual Improvement Association at the North Adelaide Church on Saint Paul at Athens. In Adelaide, following his father's footsteps, he studied to be an architect and in 1870 won an award for the best mechanical drawing, original or copy at the South Australian Society of Arts.[711]

His early conversion in North Adelaide led to his taking a deep interest in preaching. He eventually entered the Pastors' College in London in 1874[712] and became student secretary to the Rev Charles Haddon Spurgeon.

*The Sword and the Trowel* in December 1875 reported,

> On Friday, November 5, a great meeting was held at the Tabernacle to bid farewell to the Pastor, and to aid the College. Five of the students, Mr. Tooley, Mr. Cummings, Mr. Mackey, Mr. Fitch, and Mr. Josephs, addressed the meeting with remarkable power. The enthusiasm for the College which they stirred up among the friends was delightful to witness.

*8-16 Garland St Baptist Church, Bury, St Edmunds*

His first pastorate at the young age of twenty-six years was at the London Association Church at New Barnet, which he entered in March 1877. Professor Rogers and Professor Gracey, both of Pastors' College, took part in the proceedings.[713] Three years later he became pastor at Bury St. Edmunds at the Garland Street Church. In fourteen years of vigorous ministry,

---

[710] Adelaide Observer 3 November 1860 p4; South Australian Register (Adelaide) 12 February 1864 p2, 11 September 1869 p3; The Adelaide Express 23 November 1866 p3.

[711] Evening Journal (Adelaide) 22 December 1869 p2; The South Australian Advertiser (Adelaide) 28 January 1870 p3.

[712] Day-Star 10 November 1894 p83.

[713] Evening Journal (Adelaide) 27 July 1877 p2.

Cumming raised the membership of his church to 550. He had married Harriet Lester, born in Poplar, London, but she died on 9 June 1892. He remarried, this time to Hannah Tillotson of Stockwell, London, on 20 November 1894.[714]

In 1894, Cumming was on leave of absence from the Bury St. Edmunds Church and in Adelaide when he accepted the call to the Hobart Church.[715]

Following his short time at Hobart, he returned to England, accepted the charge of the Baptist church at Honor Oak and took a prominent part in public life. He became President of the Camberwell, Peckham and Dulwich Free Church Council, and after nearly ten years at Honor Oak he transferred to Priory Street Church, York, for one year. He then went to College Street, Northampton, as successor to the Rev Philip H. Smith in October 1909 and remained there for ten years. Then he accepted a call to the pastorate at Bushey, Walford, where he did good work until stricken with an illness. He partially recovered, and then went to live at Felixstowe in Suffolk where he died on 22 December 1923 aged seventy-two. He was buried in Bury St Edmunds Cemetery, St Edmundsbury Borough Suffolk.[716]

## Appendix 5: The Rev James Blaikie

The Rev James Blaikie, another Pastors' College man in the antipodes, remained committed to his conservative roots and fundamentalist ways for all his colonial pilgrimage as he dispensed blistering fire on any espoused Modernist, yet his kindly ways and evangelistic zeal won many to his Saviour.

*8-17 James Blaikie*

Blaikie was born in Edinburgh in 1850[717] and early showed a talent for speaking and a desire to serve in the ministry. He entered the Pastors' College in London in 1875 from the large North Frederick Street Baptist Church in Glasgow. Blaikie's first pastorate was that of the Bank Street Baptist Church, Irvine, North Ayrshire, Scotland, from December 1876. In 1881, he and his wife Jamesina Falconer now had a son James.[718]

Blaikie was obliged to resign his charge at Irvine through ill-health

---

[714] Evening Journal (Adelaide) 25 July 1892 p2; The Mercury (Hobart) 18 January 1895 p2, 5 January 1895 p4.
[715] South Australian Register (Adelaide) 12 October 1894 p4.
[716] AB 1923 13 February p4.
[717] 1881 Census says 1848.
[718] Jamesina (nee Grant) was born at Forres, near Elgin. The Mercury (Hobart) 4 January 1907 p5; S&T January 1877 p225; 1881 Census.

and the family made its way to Australia leaving in June 1882. He soon "quite recovered his strength" and accepted the pastorate of the Kew Baptist Church in Melbourne, commencing as an interim in October but soon was made permanent pastor. Blaikie immediately associated with his Baptist brothers and sisters in the colony and at a Baptist Union Association meeting in May 1883, Blaikie gave a paper on "Evangelistic work".[719]

At a Local Option meeting in Kew in July 1893 Blaikie spoke,

> hopefully regarding the cause of total abstinence, and drew a vivid picture of the evils of intemperance. He argued that "the sight of means to do ill deeds makes ill deeds done," and that the existence of so large a number of public houses was one of the causes of so much intemperance. The local option principle was a grand one, and was receiving support throughout the United Kingdom.[720]

For the 1886 Annual Report of the Pastors' College he wrote of the Kew Church,

> The border of this land has been to me the hem of the Master's garment, making me whole. I preached the first Sunday after my arrival, and right on, and a month afterward was invited to the pastorate of the church at Kew, where I have laboured ever since with joy and reward. The Church, which then had a membership of between forty and fifty persons, met in a small wooden building but they had nearly finished a neat brick building, with accommodation to seat 300 worshippers ... The Church here had been rent many times by internal strife, but there had always been a few faithful to the Lord and to the Victorian Baptist Association, under whose auspices the work had been begun fifteen years previously.
>
> At the time of my advent these few were in great trial of many afflictions through recent dissension; but, by the blessing of God, one difficulty after another has been overcome, inch after inch has been gained, and to-day we have nearly treble the membership of three years ago. Last year I received twenty-nine into fellowship. We have a Sunday-school, with corresponding increase, a "Model" church building, and the promise of better and greater things at no distant future. We have been enabled to organize and direct earnest efforts for grasping and holding the non-church goers, of whom there are

---

[719] S&T December1882; The Ballarat Courier 16 May 1883 p3; the full text of this paper is found in The Victorian Freeman July 1883, p116.

[720] The Age (Melbourne) 10 July 1883 p6.

at least seven thousand in our town of ten thousand people.[721]

Blaikie was acutely aware of what was happening in the colonies and particularly was taken by the treatment being meted out to the Aborigines in Western Australia. He knew of David Carly's letter of protest to Lord Derby, the Secretary of State for the Colonies in respect to the treatment of the natives especially in Broome where they were being enslaved for work on the pearl industry and where the authorities were turning a blind eye to inhumane treatment and even the murder of some. Blaikie wrote to Carly in March 1886 offering his sympathy,

> Dear Mr. Carly, coming as your letter did after Mr. Gribble's communication, it served to intensify in my mind the sad conviction of our colonial sin in relation to the native races. I am glad of the faithful witness you bear against the evil as it exists in high places, though you have to suffer in soul and substance in the cause of righteousness. I trust that your letter to the Home authorities may cause investigation to be made, and that the offenders, in the interests of humanity and religion, may be punished ... But this sore evil cleaves so closely as you contend to the ruling classes that it is a hard thing to effect any change. The difficulty is illustrated in Mr. Gribble's case. A noble stand he is taking, but if he has to stand almost alone, the cause of the blacks must inevitably go to the wall. No doubt God can find a Moses when he wills an Exodus, but, humanly speaking, in judging from past and present experience, it looks as if our mission here was not to try and civilise or save the blacks, but destroy them ... The Lord lay not this sin to our charge. If the Judgment Day of the blacks has come, ours will hasten on as white transgressors ... I pray God to help you in your all but single handed fight against this evil, and bring about a day of salvation. - Believe me, yours in the fellowship of holy warfare.[722]

Contravention to Local Council by-laws did not deter Blaikie from open-air preaching in forbidden places which in Kew was in the front of the public buildings at a major road intersection. In March 1889, he drew police intervention and comment in the local Council chambers. In the course of his preaching, he called the Mayor atheistic and impugned his honour.[723]

Between his commencement at the Kew Church on 29 October 1882 and his leaving, the church had had sixty-three baptisms and the membership grew from fifty-three to 133. A brick

---

[721] College Annual Report 1886.

[722] The Daily News (Perth, WA) 16 February 1905 p2.

[723] The Age (Melbourne) 14 March 1889 p7.

Sunday school hall was opened in December 1890. A Young People's Society of Christian Endeavour commenced the same year.[724]

After a ministry of nine years at Kew, Blaikie was invited to the Auckland Tabernacle then vacated by the Rev Thomas Spurgeon who returned to London to fill his father's pulpit at the Metropolitan Tabernacle. Blaikie commenced in 1892. The following year he commenced a weekly market-day service for farmers in the City Hall.[725] In New Zealand he filled the office of President of the Baptist Union.

Possibly the church folk at the Hobart Baptist Church might have first heard of him from a Mercury newspaper story in 1894.

> SANKEY AND MOODY V. MONKEY, the Auckland correspondent of the Christchurch states that recently when Pastor Blaikie, of the Tabernacle, proceeded to hold his usual open-air services in front of the City-Hall he found a man with a barrel-organ and a monkey in possession. The blending of sacred and secular music was so irresistibly comic that a crowd of several hundred people soon assembled. The young lady who played the harmonium for Pastor Blaikie had no chance against the barrel organ, aided by the meretricious attraction of the red petticoated, cocked hatted monkey, but was encouraged to persevere by the choir singing "Hold the fort". At this stage Constable Eastgate put in an appearance, but, finding both parties had permits, he adopted a policy of masterly inactivity, and retiring, left the solution of the difficulty to the "survival of the fittest". The crowd began to take sides, one portion being for the pastor and the other for the barrel organ man, and more particularly the monkey; so that there seemed a probability of a serious street quarrel. Constable Howell, who was unaware that Constable Eastgate had been about, came on the scene, and, witnessing conduct which he thought likely to create a breach of the peace in a public thoroughfare, interposed, and requested the barrel organ man to move on. Then after some parley, he did. Some of the tradesmen in the vicinity complain that these street services in the middle of the day interfere with business.[726]

After ten years in Auckland, Blaikie resigned due to ill-health.[727]

Following his leaving the Hobart Baptist Church, Blaikie's next appointment was the Castlemaine

---

[724] A History of the Kew Baptist Church 1856-1981 by Jill Manton p15.
[725] The Daily Telegraph (Sydney) 13 May 1893 p9.
[726] The Mercury (Hobart) 10 May 1894 p2.
[727] The Daily News (Perth, WA) 30 May 1896 p8.

Lessons from our first 20 years

*8-18 Castlemaine Baptist Church*

Baptist Church in Victoria commencing as an interim in April 1906 but soon a permanent call was issued to which he agreed. He immediately suggested several alterations and improvements to the building and the cost of the alterations and improvements were soon fully met. The congregations greatly increased and the building was thoroughly renovated. He continued his tirade against social evils, this time against gambling at sporting ventures. In October he conducted a fortnight's mission at Eaglehawk just outside Bendigo.[728] But late in the year he was seriously ill from gastritis and heart weakness and died on 2 January 1907. He was only fifty-seven years of age. He was buried in the Boroondara General Cemetery at Kew.

A thanksgiving service for his life was held at the Hobart Tabernacle with the pulpit draped in black cloth and appropriate hymns sung. At the close of the service the "Dead March" from "Saul" was played. The new minister, the Rev F. W. Boreham, preached an impressive sermon. He likened Blaikie to the patriarch Enoch who had "walked with God".[729] At the Kew Church the Rev W. H. Holdsworth, MA, said of Blaikie,

> The brilliant man, the intellectual man will soon be forgotten, but the kind man will be continually remembered, and Mr. Blaikie was wonderfully kind, and the fragrance of his tireless, unselfish life will long linger.[730]

His wife, Jamesina died in Fairfield, Victoria, in 1932, aged seventy-nine years.

## Conclusion

Our Baptist contribution to this island has not been a spectacular part yet it has had a part. It has not determined the life of too many people, yet without our Baptist contribution many a life would have been different; it has never

---

[728] Mount Alexander Mail (Vic.) 24 March 1906 p2, 4 August 1906 p51, 8 September 1906 p2; The Mercury (Hobart) 4 January 1907 p5; The Bendigo Independent 15 October 1906 p3.

[729] The Mercury (Hobart) 7 January 1907 p 5; full transcripts of Blaikes' sermons can be found in the SB, "Landmarks" 13 December 1900, p233, "What Hath God Wrought!" 17 September 1902.

[730] SB 15 January 1907 p15.

conquered the land but it has held a place. It is a mistake to write down our contribution. Our churches and pastors have not appeared in the towns and cities without effect. But it need not be said that what worked in the past is likely to pull us out of our 21st century nosedive. Sadly, what we read here about the Hobart Baptist Church, the Christian Mission Church and others, the ways of the past are unlikely to provide the paths into the future. So we need to ask whether our church life today suggests an addiction to the past. We need to ask, "Are we seeking to reach a world that no longer exists?" The remedy is not a case of technical changes in the worship service – such as conversational sermons, a new minister or some other simple fixes which will turn things around. Today requires a creative use of buildings as ministry tools, collaborative partnering, re-thinking building construction/renovation, and engaging with the local community to infuse Gospel salt and light where it is desperately needed. Our former self-sufficient churches are discovering they no longer can be all things to all people. Whether we like it or not, our churches are being forced to consider new forms. If the change inside the church isn't equal to or greater than the change outside our walls, irrelevance is inevitable.[731] But sadly for a number of our churches the only one source of troops to man the work is the old, those who served greatly in the past and feel that it is time for retirement.

While our history tells of uneven progress, and obviously not all that it could have been of late is as it should be, as a denomination we have as it were a strong network in terms of buildings and people both of which allow us to continue to grasp the unique opportunities in the beautiful island; let us not too readily yield to the spirit of defeatism.

We need at times to ask the hard questions of our Churches such as:

- How many disciples have each of your staff and lay leadership core nurtured this past year?

- How many new Christians beyond the church walls has your church reached through each activity over the past year?

- How many new non-threatening, comfortable entry points have you created to attract, incorporate or disciple new believers and new members?

- How much time, energy and money do you spend on reaching out versus the amount you spend on reaching in?

- What changes have your congregation put into practise to meet the needs of your changing community outside the church walls?

---

[731] Carey Nieuwhof.

Lessons from our first 20 years

# Chapter 9 Latrobe Baptist Church

## Introduction

A Baptist scribe wrote of Latrobe in 1896,

> The town of Latrobe is embosomed in encircling hills, backed with high ranges over 4000 feet (1200 metres) high, which for half the year are covered with snow. There are glittering patches still visible, which show how reluctant stern winter is to give way to smiling spring. The district is noted for its fine fertility, and the river Mersey which meanders by the town, teems with splendid fish.[732]

*9-1 Thomas Hainsworth*

When Baptists first became known in Latrobe in the second half of the 19th Century, the town which had a population of less than 3000, was noted for its over representation of religious denominations. The Church of Christ (Disciples of Christ) was showing the lead followed by the Independents (Congregationalists). The Church of Christ had opened a church in Latrobe in 1872 with Mr W. Moffit, also of the Church of Christ, active for some years at the nearby New Ground (Moriarty) chapel. Of the other churches, the Church of England had been at the nearby New Ground (Moriarty) since 1851. Its small Saint Luke's Church opened in Latrobe on 6 May 1868. The Wesleyan Methodists were working in the town from 1853 and their small weatherboard Church, removed from Sherwood (Tarleton), was opened on 24 October 1869. The foundation stone of its brick replacement was laid on 9 July 1879.[733] The Congregational Church under the charge of the Rev John Bennett opened in April 1878.[734] The Salvation Army was busy in Latrobe in December 1883.[735] By early 1887, Presbyterians had commenced

---

[732] SB October 1896.

[733] The Sherwood Wesleyan building was built in the 1850s. Devon Herald 12 July 1879 p2. Tasmanian Methodism, Stansall p69.

[734] Launceston Examiner 4 April 1878; The Mercury (Hobart), 12 September 1903 Supplement: Centenary of Tasmania p3.

[735] Daily Telegraph (Launceston,) 28 December 1883 p3.

services in Latrobe. Then there were the Open Brethren.[736]

According to local personality Thomas Hainsworth, Bennett was "an eloquent preacher and popular lecturer and classical scholar who had been heard in two hemispheres, and we all know what he has done to advance Latrobe, morally, socially, religiously and intellectually ..."[737] For more than a decade Bennett publicly combatted the re-baptisers as the paedo-baptist churches of Latrobe did not take kindly to the Disciples of Christ and Open Brethren evangelists questioning their practices. The majority of people in the town had been at least christened. The Disciples of Christ, the Open Brethren and the Baptists were all called "re-baptisers".[738]

Thomas Hainsworth, one of Latrobe's leading citizens, was headmaster of Latrobe's public school. He arrived in Latrobe a Wesleyan and when he and Bennett engaged in a number of very public feuds through the local newspaper over the nature of the temperance movement, Bennett attacked Hainsworth with a most revealing epithet, "Noble Thomas Hainsworth! – would that your 'double immersion' had made you another man!"[739] It appears that Hainsworth had been re-baptised by immersion by either the Open Brethren or the Church of Christ.

The re-baptisers who baptised by immersion on the declaration of faith insisted that if members of another denomination came to see baptism as a matter of personal obedience, what else could they do? The Church of Christ received some support by an advertisement in the *Devon Herald* in June 1881 in the form of a lengthy play on the "Trial of Simon Peter".[740]

## The First Baptist Presence in Latrobe

As early as 1884 the Baptists had also infiltrated the area but it would be some years before a Baptist church would form. In November 1884, a number of Baptists in the town wrote to the Baptist Association asking for help and suggested that evangelistic work be carried on in their midst.[741] And in late 1885 the Launceston Examiner confirmed the Baptist presence by reporting,

> FORMBY (Devonport) November 16 – An excursion of the members of the Baptist

---

[736] DS December 1892; LEx 20 January 1887 p3.
[737] DH, 24 July 1885, p3, 24 April 1888, p2.
[738] DH, 18 January 1887 p2 and 21 January 1887 p2. For the actual debate see DH 1 February 1887 p2; CC Dugan, A Century of Tasmanian Methodism, 1820-1920 (Hobart, Tasmanian Methodist Assembly, 1920), p. 74.

[739] DH, 28 January, p3; 11 February, p3 and 14 February 1880, p2, 13 August 1881, p3. Eventually the Hainsworth family played a leading part in the Latrobe Baptist Church.
[740] DH, 4 June 1881 p3.
[741] LEx 18 October 1884 p1.

*9-2 Gilbert Street 1912*

community, numbering from 30 to 40 persons, arrived today by the river steamer Thistle from Latrobe. After proceeding to the buoy they landed, and spent a pleasant day in rambling and picnicking on the beach, returning in the evening to Latrobe.[742]

A letter rebutting the size of the Baptist body and its claims soon followed,

> You have received a curious statement from Formby the other day, viz. that 30 or 40 of "the Baptist community" from Latrobe alighted here per "Thistle" for a picnicking. Your readers ought to be informed that there is no such body as a "Baptist community" in Latrobe, but an individual who gathers 2 or 3 others to his house to "break bread", and teach that immersion saves men, and they are alone the church of Christ – sentiments which every intelligent Baptist abrogates. These occasionally beat the bush and pick up innocent strangers, as recently, and go a-picnicking. – Baptist.[743]

In response a further letter appeared early in December,

> I was much surprised and grieved at reading the letter signed "Baptist" in the open columns of your issue of 27th. Surprised to find we had such a man in Tasmania, and grieved to think he had been allowed to give publicity to such deliberate misrepresentations. First he says there is no "Baptist community at Latrobe, only an individual who," etc. (here "Baptist" vents his personal petty spleen in a few false remarks), and "these (the individual) beat the bush," etc., which seems to me to be much like carrying out the old command of "Go to the highways and hedges". Now for the truth of "Baptist's" letter. This individual gathers others to his house to 'break bread' — no harm in that all must admit — and teach that "immersion saves men!" A wilful misrepresentation. They teach that baptism with faith and repentance, or as the outcome of

---

[742] LEx 17 November 1885, p3; Formby was the earlier name of Devonport.

[743] LEx 27 November 1885 p3.

these and as an act of obedience, saves men. They teach "He that believeth and is baptized shall be saved". Baptists teach the same, else why do they baptise? This scribe continues, "They teach they alone are the Church of Christ." Another misrepresentation. They say that only those who take the Bible for their guide constitute the Church of Christ, or Christians, and they refuse to accept any other name than Christians, or members of the Church of Christ. — Yours, etc., CHRISTIAN.[744]

This Baptist "presence" in Latrobe commenced a Sunday school in November 1886.

On January 1887, a debate took place in the Odd Fellows Hall between the Rev George Bickford Moysey of the Disciples of Christ, and Congregationalist, Rev John Bennett, on the question of baptism. Moysey needed some help during the debate because he "persisted in reading quotations from the lexicons".[745]

In the public press those who were opposed to the Church of Christ asked Moysey if the Church of Christ held that it is essential to salvation that everyone should be immersed. Furthermore, do the Disciples of Christ preach all persons that die, or have died in the past, without having been baptised by immersion, are inevitably damned?[746] The Baptists too were attacked publicly. In response in 1891 Samuel B. Pitt wrote,

When (the Baptists) first started (at Latrobe), a resident minister who thought them intruders preached against them in the open-air, and said this doctrine of (the Baptists regarding baptism) was of the devil.[747]

*9-3 Rev G. Moysey*

## The Rev Henry George Blackie

By 1887 the Rev Henry George Blackie, one of the five Pastors' College men in the colony, was appointed to supervise the Baptist work in Latrobe thus making the Baptists the eighth official religious group in the town. Latrobe at that

---

[744] LEx 5 December 1885 supplement p1.

[745] Devon Herald (Tas) 18 January 1887 p2 and 21 January 1887 p2. For the actual debate see Devon Herald (Tas) 1 February 1887 p2.

[746] Devon Herald (Tas) 4 February 1887 p2.

[747] Day-Star August 1891, p499.

time had a population of less than 3000. Under his ministry and that of his gifted wife, Louisa Rose (nee Murphy), the Church was constituted on 28 March 1887. Louisa frequently took services.[748]

Blackie also had another reputation: he was the only Tasmanian Baptist pastor who smoked and he was happy to boast of the fact. Some commented that his sermons didn't end up in smoke. His mentor, the Rev C. H. Spurgeon, also smoked yet Spurgeon did it to the "glory of God".[749]

In March 1888, and before a crowd of 300, Blackie "dipped" six of his converts in the River Mersey. For the Latrobe Baptists at the time there was no alternative but to conduct baptisms in the open-air. Further baptisms followed.[750]

## The Rev Alfred Hyde

The move from Longford to Latrobe proved beneficial to the Rev Alfred Hyde but he came as an interim. A week before he commenced, on 19 December 1888, he married Sarah Elizabeth Shute of Devonport.

In Latrobe the Baptists continued to use the Odd Fellows Hall. Off duty local constable Smith enjoyed Hyde's messages and one Sunday he noted,

> I rather enjoyed the address, which partook more of the character of an evangelistic appeal than a set sermon. The change was, however, very agreeable to me, and I must say I go with the pastor in putting the great questions he deals with plainly and unmistakably to his hearers. He does not mince matters, but sets before them what may be called unvarnished truths, and if they then make the fool's choice it is no fault of the preacher. It is as much the duty of the teacher to exhibit to his hearers the blackness of the outer darkness, to be the portion of the wanderer as to show the promises of everlasting bliss laid up for those who make a straight course for the kingdom; and from the few opportunities I have had of listening to Pastor Hyde I judge that he appreciates this consideration.[751]

The Odd Fellows Hall situated at 54 Gilbert Street was built in 1882 and extended in 1888. It was the largest building in town and was always a popular venue. For these reasons the Baptists were wise to book it for Sunday evenings. During the week the Baptists also used it for their Band of Hope meetings where solos,

---

[748] Day-Star May 1887, January 1892. Louisa was born on 3 March 1858 Kent England. LEx 16 October 1886 p2. There's no evidence of his first wife Sarah and Louisa were sisters.
[749] Day-Star February 1888 p25.
[750] S B Pitt in Day-Star, August 1891; Day-Star 29 March 1887 p2, March 1888 p43.
[751] Devon Herald (Tas) 26 Feb 1889 p2.

# Lessons from our first 20 years

*9-4 Sunday School at Devonport. John Chamberlain and Harry Wood standing in back row*

vocals, instrumentals, recitations and dialogues were given by a variety of participants. This most popular programme was varied with humorous temperance dialogues, an indispensable part of the monthly gatherings. Thomas Hainsworth and his family were keen supporters. In six years 579 names were appended to the Blue Ribbon pledge list.[752] A number of churches had their own Band of Hope meetings in Latrobe. There were also temperance societies, local option leagues, Rechabites, and other similar institutions for the suppression of "demon drink". But in 1889, W. K. Goodson, a temperance lecturer at the Latrobe Odd Fellows Hall claimed the smallest attendance ever seen, through his neglect in making himself known to the temperance advocates in town. It was reported, "Mr. Goodson must have some pluck to have given a two hours' oration to an audience of four persons."[753]

In early May 1889, there were thirty-five Latrobe Baptist Church members[754] and services were also commenced at Spreyton. Hyde barely lasted a year before transferring to Formby (Devonport) and as at Longford, he made little headway.

## John Chamberlain

On April 1890, layman from the Hobart Tabernacle, John Chamberlain, commenced his ministry at Latrobe.[755] Now as an accredited pastor of the Baptist Association,[756] he took on the role of being Secretary of the Association and co-editor of its monthly, the "Day Star".

He had requested a pastoral position from the Association but after a

---

752 The Mercury (Hobart) 14 January 1889 p4; LEx 19 Aug 1889 p3.
753 Devon Herald (Tas) 12 Mch 1889 p2.

754 Devon Herald (Tas) May 1889 p67.
755 Devon Herald (Tas) July 1890.
756 LEx 9 April 1890 p3.

refusal he was given Latrobe.[757] William Gibson Junior in his address at Chamberlain's official welcome on 8 June 1890, "maintained the right of the Baptists to a place in Latrobe", and "dwelt upon the steadfastness of those who had held to the cause under adverse circumstances."

Chamberlain continued with his public lectures this time in the Latrobe Odd Fellows Hall and they were the means of drawing folk to Sunday services. One entitled "Backbone" "dwelt upon the necessity of backbone in character, which gave the mutual courage to adhere to a principle, and steer a straight course without swerving from the paths of rectitude and honour." He concluded, "Religion should be the very marrow of the backbone."[758] Within a year Chamberlain was proving a very popular preacher attracting "very good congregations". An apt lecture in late 1891 was "Leaking Money Bags, or Thoughts on Bank Failures," as bank failures at the time occupied a large share of public attention.

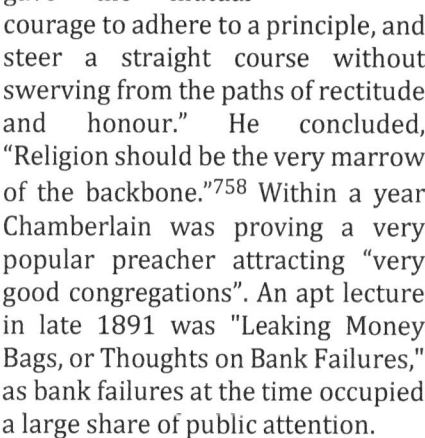

*9-5 John Chamberlain*

In Latrobe there was such a turnout of children and adults for the annual Baptist Sunday school picnic in 1890 that the Baptists declared that the event was "an evident sign that the Baptist cause has gained considerable favour in this district." The churches looked to youth as a significant supplier of church members and regarded Sunday schools as "feeders to the churches". Christian Endeavour also helped greatly in this regard.

Late in 1891, Chamberlain, in partnership with Harry Wood the "popular Baptist preacher from Sheffield", conducted a series of evangelistic services in a Sassafras Chapel known at the time as the Skelbrook Baptist Chapel. Two years earlier Henry Rockliff had offered this his Sassafras chapel to commence a Baptist work in the area and soon Sunday morning services were being conducted on a fortnightly basis. Within a year services became weekly and have continued as such ever since. In 1900 the present building replaced the Skelbrook Baptist Chapel.[759]

---

[757] BU Council Minutes p277/23 dated Jan 1901.
[758] Day-Star July 1890; LEx 9 April 1890 p3; The North West Post (Formby) 1 February 1890 p2, 5 September 1891 p2, 20 July 1892 p2, 4 February 1891 p2; for a transcript of one of his sermon see The North Coast Standard 16 January 1892 p4.

[759] Day-Star, December 1890 p380; The North Coast Standard 7 November 1891 p2; The North West Post (Formby,) 9 January 1897 p2. As for the origins of the Sassafras Baptist Church A. F Dyer writes, "In 1865 Henry Rockliff had a small chapel built on part of his land for the use of Protestant denominations, but in 1876 the Methodists built their own church a short distance

Early in 1889, William Gibson Junior had purchased a block of land for £500 near the Post Office in Gilbert Street, Latrobe's main street, and had architectural drawings prepared for a Tabernacle. The Launceston Examiner reported that the architect, F. W. Heaps, had informed the newspaper that in fact the drawings were produced not in 1889 but in 1887 and its design was "a new one for Tasmania, the form of the inside of the building being circular." Gibson Junior denied that he ordered plans in the earlier year.[760]

*9-6 Latrobe Tabernacle*

Yet even with the purchase of land the Latrobe Baptists that year commented in the "Day Star", "Doubtless if there had been a Tabernacle at Latrobe, as in the sister township, the work would have been as successful, and carried on with greater efficiency."[761] They repeated the same message in the "Day Star" of January 1890,

> Our difficulties are many, and we find it a great drawback having to worship in a public hall that is used for all sorts of purposes, but we are full of hope that the Lord (one could add, "and Mr. Gibson") may clear the way, so that a Tabernacle at Latrobe may be a fact.[762]

Again, in February 1891, they complained, "A building is our urgent need, in order to consolidate our work and establish it on a thoroughly satisfactory basis." There was also the need of a manse.[763] But the progress of the Church that year was such that Union Council at its May meeting discussed the possible dissolution of the work.

This was the pattern of some of the churches at the time, appealing regularly for Gibson Junior's financial assistance and such appeals bordered on manipulation and badgering. These appeals suggest a culture of dependency. And the setting up of the Sustentation Fund in 1887 had not

---

to the north of Rockliff's chapel. The Baptists eventually took over Rockliff's church, but they replaced it some years later by a new building." With the Pioneers p83.
[760] LEx 27 April 1889 p3, 27 April 1889 p3, 27 April, p3 and 4 May 1889, p6.

[761] Day Dawn and Baptist Church Messenger May 1889 p67.
[762] Day-Star January 1890 p221.
[763] Day-Star February 1891 p411; BU Council Minutes p67/21, p25/19.

lessened this dependency. Even so at Latrobe, the foundation stone for a Tabernacle was laid on 15 October 1891. Early in 1892, Chamberlain's congregation bid farewell to the Odd Fellows Hall as that year the Tabernacle was finally opened on 31 January being a gift of Gibson Junior.[764]

Added to Chamberlain's responsibilities was the care of the Devonport Churches.[765] For some reason or reasons Chamberlain's ministry was not seen as successful even though he was good preacher, preached a sound Gospel, had a ready pen, had a good acquaintance with literature and was a true and loving brother to all he dealt with. Moreover there had been a meaningful increase in the church membership. The church had experienced financial restraints possibly due to the economic depression of the decade and there could have been other tensions. He was farewelled on 28 October 1894 yet through his local employment continued his association with the Church until his death.[766]

## Pastor Harry Wood

Pastor Harry Wood wrote in his memories at the time, "Council desired us to go to Latrobe as the cause there was in danger of becoming defunct. They could get a minister for Deloraine but no one would look at Latrobe." He began at Latrobe on 9 July 1895. Wood continued,

> The Tabernacle (though comparatively a new building) was in bad disrepair. The services, attended by the faithful few, were held in the vestry. There were outstanding church debts. There was one good brother who acted as a Deacon, and only thirteen people attended my welcome. The only house that could be secured was a large brick building that was so damp and out of order it could not be let. I was receiving £20 a year less than the Minister who left the church on the rocks.

Wood felt that there was a spiritual death in the town.[767]

The Latrobe Baptist people were unanimous in their desire for his settlement, and the Council anticipated that his ministry would lead to speedy development of the Baptist work.

His first year saw a steady increase in the congregation. In his first thirteen months thirty were added to the church membership. In his three years he baptised more than

---

[764] North Coast Standard 23 January 1892 p2; Day-Star November 1891.

[765] The North West Post 7 May 1892 p2.

[766] Day-Star April 1892, October 1893 p145, November 1894; The North West Post (Formby) 30 October 1894 p4, 10 October 1893.

[767] Devon Herald (Tas) 6 July 1895 p2; SB 1 August 1895; The North West Post (Formby) 13 July 1895 p2; Pioneer Work for the Lord in Tasmania by Pastor Harry Wood.

forty people.[768] By the end of 1898 there were eighty-two Sunday school scholars on the roll.

In regards to the church property two years after his arrival, apart from a new front street fence,

> The building (has been) put into thorough repair. Externally the front coping has been recemented, and internally a varnished native wood dado has been run round the chapel; the walls and cornices have been decorated with a neutral tint and appropriate shadings. Along the back of the platform the motto, "Holiness unto the Lord," has been tastefully printed in blue and imitation gold. And to complete the list, the wheezy and uncertain old instrument has been replaced by a rich-toned Bell organ.[769]

In eighteen months they had also a new manse which had been built by J. T. Farmilo of Launceston. At the Sunday evening services the building was often full. The money for the most part for the restoration had been raised in the district. The outstation at Sassafras experienced a revival.[770]

But Wood's health problems continued. His doctor's verdict on one occasion was that he was minus half his left lung and was suffering with vascular weakness of the heart. Near the end of his time at Latrobe he accepted a call to return to Launceston Tabernacle but then he withdrew the offer.[771]

At the end of December 1898, he was compelled to rest as he was threatened with an attack of paralysis. Even though he now absented himself from Assemblies, he was appointed President of the Baptist Association for 1897/98. He was farewelled from Latrobe on 25 April 1899.[772]

## William Henry Short

For family reasons Baptist layman and artist William Henry Short of Castlemaine, Victoria, arrived at Devonport with his wife and family of four children in March 1900 and sought employment in the Baptist churches.[773]

After some weeks assisting at the Devonport Baptist Church he became the interim at the Latrobe and Sassafras churches commencing in April 1900 and stayed to March

---

[768] Day-Star January 1896, February 1896), April 1896, May 1896, July 1896, September 1896, December 1898; North West Post (Formby)17 November 1896 p2; SB 2 December 1897.
[769] SB 29 October 1896 p240.
[770] Daily Telegraph (Launceston)16 December 1895 p2; Pioneer Work for the Lord in Tasmania by Pastor Harry Wood; SB 29 October 1896 p240.

[771] BCC September 1926; W. Bligh; The North West Post (Formby) 9 December 1897 p2.
[772] Day-Star December 1898; The Mercury 28 January 1898 p4; NWA&EBT 26 April 1899 p2.
[773] Union Council meeting of July 1900; Council Minutes 262/10. SB 13 Dec 1900 p278

*9-7 Winding Track by William H. Short, 1891*

1902. The Rev George Mackay at Devonport was his supervisor. The Latrobe pastorate had been vacant for nearly a year. The basis of his employment was that he would stand aside if the Council found someone else. At the time Union Council was seeking for the Church another Pastors' College single graduate for two years but the reply was not encouraging as the College "did not know anyone suitable". The Council reported in the Southern Baptist, "We seem to be making progress backwards. The harvest is plenteous, the labourers are few. Half-a-dozen God-sent men from the old land would be a great Nineteenth Century blessing." Perth, Longford, Latrobe and Burnie were without pastors.[774]

Short, well-educated theologically and an experienced Biblical preacher, fitted easily into the role of pastor. His sermon subjects included, "Was Jesus the Son of God?" "How shall we Escape?" and "Is Life Worth Living?" He participated in the First Annual North-West Coast District Christian Endeavor Society Convention which drew in about a dozen societies of the affiliated Churches. When not busy with church life, he was out painting and drawing. Soon his work was displayed in a shop window in Stewart Street, Devonport, among them, "A Quiet Morning on the Mersey at High Tide", "The Don Heads at Even", "A Bend in the Mersey looking towards Spreyton" and "Scene on the Spreyton Road near Devonport". He also displayed his works at local Horticultural Society shows. Some of his works were taken to England by the Rev John E. Walton for exhibition as illustrative of the natural beauty of Tasmania. Short's pastoral ministry was encouraging with baptisms.[775]

One evening at the Devonport Baptist Church he chaired the Young Men's Mutual Improvement Society. The impromptu speaking subjects were: "Why we oppose strong drink?" "Bodily exercise", "Should women enter Parliament?" "Should bachelors be taxed?" "The rival claims of Devonport and Burnie", "Is

---

[774] The North West Post (Formby) 3 March 1900 p3; 10 March 1900 p3; NWA&EBT 7 April 1900 p2; BU Council Minutes p276/9, p276/19 and p292/8.

[775] NWA&EBT 18 April 1900 p4, 21 April 1900 p2, 26 April 1900 p2, 5 May 1900 p3, 31 July 1900 p2.

marriage a failure?" "Should ladies ride a bike?"[776]

Short remained at Latrobe until his replacement arrived from the Pastors' College, London, having being selected by the Revs Thomas Spurgeon and John E. Walton; the Rev Robert Williamson was chosen. But it happened that Walton took the position himself and commenced in August 1901. In response Short accepted a Home Mission position at Deloraine for twelve months.[777]

## Rev Albert Metters and a sermon on Hell

On 24 March 1901, a Baptist from South Australia, the Rev Albert Metters, preached at the Latrobe Church and its outstation, Sassafras. He had been invited to its pastorate but in his trial sermon he denied the existence of a literal fiery hell. After he discussed his teaching with some church folk, he discovered on returning to South Australia that members of the Tasmanian Baptist Union Council now required assurances from him on two doctrines, namely: "The universal Fatherhood of God" and "The final destiny of the wicked". He was also asked to give a promise not to interfere with the closed membership policy of the Tasmanian churches. The SA Baptist Churches at the time had a strong tradition of open membership churches.

Metters resented this as he had already given his assent to Tasmania's doctrinal position. Having heard about the matter and aware of Metter's thoughts, Samuel Bulgin Pitt from the Hobart Baptist Church wrote tersely in the *Southern Baptist* paper saying, "Tasmanian Baptists as a rule cannot support preachers who do not clearly proclaim ruin through sin, redemption through the blood, and regeneration by the Spirit."[778]

Hobartian Joshua T. Soundy agreed with Pitt and defended Tasmania's conservative doctrinal position. Then in the *Southern Baptist* a savage attack was unleashed on Tasmanian Baptists under the pseudonym of "Old Baptist",

It is a marvel that no one in Tasmania protests against such bigotry. Is there no party in Tasmania bold enough to protest

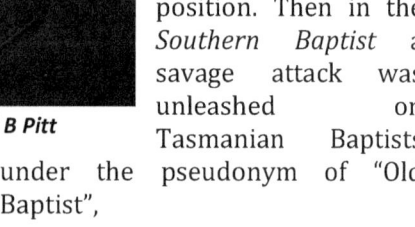

*9-8 Samuel B Pitt*

---

[776] NWA&EBT 24 September 1900 p2.
[777] LEx 13 February 1901 p4, 23 April 1902 p 2; NWA&EBT 14 February 1901 p2.
[778] Council Minutes p 293/ff dated April 1901; SB 15 May p109, 17 July 1901, p168.

against certain narrow-minded men making the Baptists of that Island ridiculous in the eyes of the intelligent religious public of Australia?[779]

Then Pitt complained again in the Southern Baptist,

> South Australian Baptists find grave fault with us Tasmanian Baptists. In the "Southern Baptist" we are charged with being "illiberal", "unreasoning", "bigoted", and "narrow-minded!" We simply reply "speaking the truth in love" we will continue to contend earnestly for the faith which was once for all delivered unto the saints.[780]

Another shot was fired by Everard Duthoit of the Hobart Baptist Church who suggested South Australians should relinquish their input into the Southern Baptist journal and revert to their "old regime under Truth and Progress (backwards)". But Metters did receive numerous letters from Tasmania expressing regret. Furthermore, the Council itself formally apologised to him and expressed its full confidence in him as a minister.[781]

In the very next issue was a selection of letters bluntly headed,

"TASMANIA v. SOUTH AUSTRALIA". William Gibson Junior, as President of the Union, reacted to letters of Duthoit and others and insisted they did not represent his views or the majority of Tasmanian Baptists.[782] In the end Metters declined the call to Tasmania and accepted another, to Katanning in Western Australia.

After all this the editors understandably resolved to terminate the correspondence on the subject of Higher Criticism. Tasmania's connection with the Southern Baptist ceased at the end of 1902 but some local Tasmanian church news entries were made. There had been no meeting of minds, there was no way forward. In 1900, Tasmania wanted six more men from the old country who thought just like they did. Dr Harry Benjafield in his Presidential speech to Assembly in 1888 had expressed how Tasmanians thought,

> As a denomination, God being with us, we stand by the old truths and walk in the old ways, still believing that "straight is the gate and narrow is the way which leadeth unto life." If with me you endorse those views - and I know you do - why we embrace a Christianity which to-day is very unpopular, and we have to consider how our church - but now in its infancy - shall grow up to exercise a wide and beneficent

---

[779] SB 28 August 1901 p203f.
[780] SB 11 September 1901 p216.

[781] SB 11 September 1901 p216, 16 October 1901 p 240.
[782] SB 2 October 1901, 16 October 1901 p240.

## The Rev John Edwin Walton

A welcome at the Latrobe Baptist Church was tendered to the Rev John Edwin Walton and his family in August 1901. The family had just returned from England. An outreach was commenced in 1902 to the young people in the South Spreyton area and soon church services began with fifty folk in attendance. The Church had been expecting the Rev Robert Williamson but his health prevented him taking the position. In April 1902, the Latrobe Church had fifty-four church members and eighty-one Sunday school scholars with eight teachers while circuit church Sassafras had thirty-six Sunday scholars with six teachers. In June 1900, it was noted that the Sassafras Church had twenty-five members.[784] The Temperance Band of Hope meetings recommenced at the Tabernacle in May 1902. On a Sunday in January 1903 memoriam services were held in the Latrobe Church, as in other Tasmanian Baptist Churches, to give thanks to God for the life of Mary Ann Gibson; she died on 12 January aged ninety-three years.[785]

The church socials in connection with the anniversaries and the like provided excellent vocal and musical programmes involving all the church folk and the Latrobe orchestra, all accompanied by brief addresses. Among those participating were Walton's five daughters: Mabel, Annie, Eva, Lucy and Edwina. At the Latrobe Sunday school anniversary held near the time of his departure were 100 scholars accommodated on the tiered platform and ninety-four book prizes awarded; credit in part to the Sunday school Superintendent, Mr J. Clark.[786]

*9-9 Mary Ann Gibson*

Walton's interests included competition poultry. In the local court he represented young offenders and on one occasion in

---

[783] LEx 11 April 1888 p3; For a chapter on this incident see "Spurgeon's Men.

[784] SB 14 June 1900 p140. Does this indicate that the the Church was constituted before this time?

[785] Day-Star March 1902, May 1902, Oct 1902; Daily Telegraph (Launceston) 19 July 1902 p5, 21 January 1903; For the contribution of the Gibsons to the Baptist denomination in Tasmania see "Spurgeon's Men chapter 6. Their son, William Gibson Junior continued their legacy.

[786] Daily Telegraph (Launceston) 30 November 1904 p6; NWA&EBT 12 August 1903 p2, 9 December 1903 p2, 30 November 1904 p2.

pleading for mitigation of the sentence of a young man he suggested the offender be given the option of a fine or of leaving town. In February 1904, the Church celebrated the centenary of the colony of Tasmania. As in earlier pastorates, Walton's ministry was "distinguished by steady progress". His sermons were marked by "very striking and original illustrations".[787]

The way forward in accepting the pastorate of the Jireh Baptist Church in Brisbane near the end of his ministry at Latrobe was prepared by a glowing reference in a Brisbane newspaper which was unusual for one just visiting the city on sick leave and so happened to attend the Queensland Baptist Association meetings and preach the Association Sermon and also preach on four Sundays at the Central Brisbane Tabernacle!

His farewell at Latrobe was the largest gathering of a religious nature seen in the town for some time. The Congregational Minister, the Rev J. G. Wright, said that he considered Walton to be "the best type of a Baptist minister he had met during his eighteen years in Tasmania." He continued, "He was a consistent man, not fool enough to think that he only had the truth, and nothing but the truth. He was a true man and also a sympathetic man." Tributes were also made to his wife Hannah and to their daughter, Annie who had given wholehearted service as organist for some years.[788]

## The Rev Charles Palmer

In early 1905, Palmer and his wife, Phoebe, having ministered in NSW and Victoria, now began their time in Tasmania. The Palmers would spend their next ten years on the island. They were welcomed to the Latrobe Baptist Church on 19 March. At the welcome Palmer's past experience in home mission work was mentioned and it was hoped that because of this he might be of great service to Tasmanian Baptists. In his response to the welcome, he said he too had that hope and that his ministry would be "a season of spiritual prosperity, and

*9-10 Charles and Phoebe Palmer*

---

[787] LEx 24 September 1903 p6; NWA&EBT 7 October 1903 p2, 23 February 1904 p2, 21 February 1905 p3; The Telegraph 9 September 1904 p2.

[788] The Telegraph (Brisbane) 9 September 1904 p2, 10 October 1904 p5. In later years Annie was organist at the Concord Baptist Church, for twenty-three years, see AB 23 June 1936 p4. September 1904 p4; NWA&EBT 22 February 1905 p4.

... a time of blessing akin to the Welsh revival."[789]

While at Latrobe, Palmer acted as pastor-superintendent of the new work in Ulverstone which took in Upper Castra and Penguin; he visited quarterly. On the 6 August 1906, Ernest Albert Salisbury was appointed to the Ulverstone work for three months. The South Spreyton Mission and the Sassafras Baptist Church were also under Palmer's supervision.

Palmer gave his support for the newly created branch of the Latrobe Citizens Moral and Reform League of Tasmania which also had branches in other centres. The former pastor of the Latrobe Church, John Chamberlain, was its treasurer. Apart from supporting the Local Option Bill for the area, the Latrobe League sought "to promote temperance and social purity, to oppose all forms of gambling, and to obtain an improvement in the general, moral and social condition of the people."[790] In June 1906, Palmer was one of two of the Baptist delegates to the inaugural meeting of the Tasmanian Council of Churches, the other delegate being Samuel Bulgin Pitt.[791] Palmer had "green fingers" and participated in the Latrobe Horticultural Society. He was the President of the Baptist Union of Churches for 1908/1909.

Palmer was present for the official opening of the Spreyton Church building on 4 August 1909 which was now under the control of the Devonport Church.[792] Present too was the Rev Vincent G. Britton who remarked that when he visited the North-West Coast ten years ago it was but a wilderness. The Spreyton building was he said, a child of the Devonport Church and it would be used by the State school children on week days "instead of the present pokey room in which the children now meet." [793]

While at Latrobe, the Church was the venue for a Baptist Assembly and the correspondent to the Hobart Mercury likened Palmer to "Gaius, the hospitable entertainer of pilgrims to the Celestial City, with his trusty helpers to extend a welcome to the travellers".[794]

In Latrobe, Palmer's son was more than a shop keeper; he was also an evangelist like his father. In May 1911, Palmer Junior conducted a fortnight's mission at South Spreyton and Melrose with the result that seventy-six professed conversion! To Palmer Senior was entrusted the memorial address for the late King Edward VII held at the Odd Fellows Hall in Latrobe on

---

[789] NWA&EBT 21 March 1905 p2, 29 March 1905 p2.
[790] NWA&EBT 11 December 1905 p4.
[791] The Mercury (Hobart) 6 June 1906 p6.
[792] SB 13 July 1909 p172.
[793] The North West Post (Formby) 5 August 1909 p3; NWA&EBT 21 April 1910 p2.
[794] The Mercury (Hobart,) 8 April 1910 p8.

Friday 20 May 1910, a day of mourning across the country.

Palmer's closing words to his Latrobe flock on his leaving were, "I have preached to you as a dying man to dying men, and have urged you to do as the Israelites did in the wilderness when the brazen serpent was held up - to look and live." After six years at Latrobe, in June 1911, Palmer began his ministry at the Burnie Baptist Church.[795]

# Appendices

## Appendix 1: The Rev Henry George Blackie

The Rev Henry George Blackie, a Pastors' College man with a pastor's heart was also an evangelist. Further, he had fulfilled his missionary aspirations before arriving in Tasmania. Wherever he went he took with him his most valued assistant, Lousia, his wife.

Blackie was born on 20 March 1857 at Stepney, a district in the East End of London to Henry George Blackie (1831–1907) and Mary Elizabeth Luke (1821–1881). As a twenty year old he entered the Pastors' College in 1875 coming from the prosperous North Frederick Street Baptist Church in Glasgow. He had also spent time in Edinburgh and been associated with the Plymouth Brethren. In 1877 the Lall Bazar Baptist Church, being William Carey's Church in Calcutta, wrote to the Rev C. H. Spurgeon requesting a graduate from his College. At the time the Church was the English speaking Church of the Baptist Missionary Society in the city. The College paid for Blackie's passage and that of two others on the steamer "Daiunda" and they arrived at the end of 1877.[796] Blackie was officially welcomed on 11 December 1877 by about 300 people.

*9-11 Henry G. Blackie*

This was his very first pastorate and Lall Bazar would be a fitting training ground. In 1878, the church membership grew by thirty-eight but only by six in 1879. Most of those admitted were soldiers, fourteen from the 54th Regiment. There were also six sailors from the ship the "Great Victoria". Blackie had a sphere of great usefulness before him in Calcutta as the *Sword and the Trowel* reported in September 1879,

> From Calcutta we have an earnest appeal for more Christian

---

[795] LEx 16 May 1910 p7; The North West Post (Formby) 17 June 1911 p2; Daily Telegraph (Launceston) 23 May 1910 p5; NWA&EBT 13 June 1911 p3, 6 May 1911 p4.
[796] S&T Nov 1877.

workers in India. Mr. Blackie is doing what he can, for beside his pastorate at the Lall Bazar, he has been teaching native boys and girls in the mission schools, he is secretary and treasurer of the Benevolent Institution, and secretary of the Baptist Indian Mission, and the Calcutta Temperance League. He is hoping soon to be able to labour entirely amongst the natives.[797]

Blackie obtained access to the Zenanas as a medical missionary. But as a male he had no personal access to his female patients for when his services were required, the tongue or pulse of the patient was examined through a hole in the curtain, and he was in blessed ignorance as to the age or symptoms of those he was treating.[798]

Blackie married Sarah Ann Murphy on 16 September 1878 at the Lal Bazar Baptist Chapel.[799] They had four children: Ruth born in Calcutta, Harry Francis born in Croydon, England, William Bruce born in Darjeeling and Owen Campbell born in Calcutta.[800]

Then suddenly at the end of 1879 he severed his connection with the Church and was farewelled on 30 November to take up the Pastorate of the Baptist Church in Colaba, Bombay. He became Secretary of its school.[801] His reports to the Pastors' College included a mention that westerners in India can experience tropical rheumatism, fever, dysentery, boils and sunstroke, some of which he and others there with him experienced.[802]

Then his theological views changed and he reconnected with the Plymouth Brethren and returned with his wife and an infant to England. They returned as Plymouth Brethren and remained in Calcutta for two or three years but on a visit to Darjeeling his wife died. Twenty years later a ground mound was all that was left where her remains were buried in the Darjeeling Cemetery. Throughout his life Blackie kept in touch with friends at the Bombay Church.[803] Blackie arrived in Tasmania in October 1886 and he was accompanied by Baptist, the Rev W. J. Murphy and Murphy's daughter, Louisa. Blackie and Louisa were married on 4 November 1886.

## Appendix 2: John Chamberlain

Well-liked public lecturer, John Chamberlain, had aspirations to

---

[797] S&T sept 1879.

[798] LEx 12 April 1888 p33; the word Zenana means a secluded room. It was the place where the wives of a chief lived in such entire seclusion as not be allowed to see any male person.

[799] Sarah was born on 9 June 1855 at Plumstead, Kent.

[800] Family history research by Barbara Coe.

[801] The Bombay Church, English speaking, was established in 1867 in Byculla. It was then moved to Bombay Central and in 1911, to Colaba.

[802] S&T July 1880.

[803] S&T 295/1887; From the book "The Story of the Lall Bazar Baptist Church, Calcutta Being the History of Carey's Church from 24th April 1800 to the Present Day" by Edward Steane Wenger, ch 41.

become a Baptist Pastor but they ceased after his one attempt at Latrobe. Even so, he continued contributing greatly to the work of the Baptist Association and, on a community level, in Latrobe.

Chamberlain was born at Brighton, England, in 1859. In 1883, at Manchester, he married Alice Hartley. The family migrated and arrived in Hobart and joined the Baptist Church. He first lectured in the Church School Room in July 1887. He proved a popular lecturer, well-liked by the Mercury, and the subject of his lectures included, "The Defeat of the Spanish Armada and the Protestant Revolution in 1688", "The Old Flag and those who fought under it" and "John Bunyan". He also gave lectures to aid various causes.[804] He was baptised on 22 July 1888. He was well-educated and at times preached instead of the Rev Robert McCullough. On 19 September 1888, with the oversight of the Hobart Church, he commenced a mission at Sandy Bay but the work lapsed after Chamberlain's removal to Latrobe. He ministered at Constitution Hill just out of Hobart in the second half of 1889.

Following his resignation as Pastor of the Church in 1894, Chamberlain became clerk of Latrobe Municipal Council and his public lectures continued. One of his sons, Henry Morgan Chamberlain died at twenty-four years of age; he also had been a council clerk of the Latrobe Municipality. John Chamberlain died on 24 August 1928. He had taken an active part in public affairs, had been secretary of the old Town Board and the Council Clerk since the inception of local Government. He was also a Justice of the Peace. His literary efforts often appeared in various journals. During the War he gave lectures in aid of various patriotic funds. He was an enthusiastic member of the Latrobe Horticultural Society and the Latrobe Bowling, Football and Cricket Clubs. There was a large turnout for his funeral.[805] He was survived by his widow, Alice, their son John Harley and daughter Alice Miriam. Two sons, Henry Morgan as mentioned, and Philip Lionel and daughter Mary Ethel predeceased him.[806] Alice died on 13 September 1943, about ninety years of age.

*9-12 John Chamberlain in old age*

---

[804] LEx 14 September 1889 p2 in aid of the London dock labourers; The North Coast Standard 21 November 1891 p2 in aid of the Devon Cottage Hospital funds.

[805] NWA&EBT 14 May 1909 p2, 5 September 1911 p2; Advocate 25 August 1928 p2, 27 August 1928 p2.

[806] Advocate (Burnie,) 25 August 1928 p215, sept 1943 p2.

## Appendix 4: William Henry Short

William Henry Alexander Short, an outstanding landscape painter and serious Bible student of Baptist persuasion arrived in Tasmania possibly to find part-time employment with the Tasmanian Baptist Home Mission and practise his artistic skills in Tasmania. He found a niche in a couple of the Baptist churches for some years before returning to Victoria where he engaged further in ministry and artistic endeavour. Short was born in 1868 in Melbourne. He was the son of William Howes Wackenbarth Short and his wife Caroline. They arrived in Victoria in 1852 and soon settled in Ballarat.

Short Senior was a serious landscape painter and travelled widely in Victoria[807] and took up teaching art in what he called the Austral Studio, in Bendigo. Later he opened classes in Castlemaine and Ballarat.[808] His works are in the Ballarat Art Gallery.

William Henry Alexander Short also became an artist. In later years Wesley Bligh in "Altars of the Mountain" wrote, "Mr. Short was an artist of some considerable merit. Some of his work, depicting

*9-13 Baptist Union Council of 1889: Front row: JT Soundy, W Gibson Jnr, R McCullough, HG Blackie. Middle Row: J Chamberlain, AJ Ratcliffe, unknown, A Hyde, SB Pitt, H Wood, WJ. Murphy, JE Walton. Back Row: AJ Stokes left end, WD Weston right end, of those unidentified – HD Archer and Dr Benafield*

Tasmanian scenery, may still be found in homes in the Island state."

William Henry Alexander Short married Margaret Amy Field on 8 February 1897 in Melbourne. Amy was the daughter of Samuel and Jane Field.[809] The Fields had arrived from Chatham in Kent, England, in 1878. They were living in Devonport in Tasmania when the Victorian family arrived in 1900.[810]

## Appendix 5: The Rev John E. Walton

On leaving Latrobe, Walton's designated pastorate of Brisbane would be for him a larger and more important sphere than what he was leaving behind. In this way he was typical of so many outstanding Tasmanian Baptist ministers who began their Australian pilgrimage in

---

[807] The Argus 4 February 1892 p 4.
[808] The Bendigo Independent 4 June 1897; Mount Alexander Mail 18 February 1898 p2.
[809] The Bendigo Independent 10 February 1897 p2. Family research by Barbara Coe.
[810] NWA&EBT 27 April 1909 p3.

*9-14 The First Kerang Baptist Church*

## Appendix 6: The Rev Charles Palmer

The Rev Charles Palmer, self-taught with a strong belief in Home Mission work, made a lasting contribution in Victoria, NSW and Tasmania.

Palmer was born in Huntingdon, England, on 10 April 1849. He was largely self-taught. He was brought to a Christian commitment under the ministry of one of Spurgeon's students, and was baptised in the river Cam, the main river flowing through Cambridge in eastern England. He found employment in the coprolite-extraction industry, coprolite being a particular phosphate. He married Phoebe Ann Frear at Chesterton, Cambridgeshire, on 27 March 1870.[812]

On the eve of their departure for Australia in 1873, he attended the Metropolitan Tabernacle service, and he had the opportunity to speak to the great preacher. Afterwards

> the young man from Waterbeach knelt side by side, and he was commended to God and to the Word of His grace. Surmising that the intending emigrant was not overburdened with wealth, Spurgeon slipped half a sovereign into his hand at parting, and with

Tasmania and then contributed greatly to mainland Baptist Associations. His final day at Latrobe was on 19 February 1905 but he left with failing health and hoped that Brisbane would have a beneficial effect. While twice he had been chosen President of the Baptist Union of Tasmania, he soon became a member of the Queensland Baptist Union Council and also its President. At the end of 1909, he accepted a call to the Harris Street Baptist Church in Sydney. He remained there for two years but it was failing health that elicited his resignation. He died on 21 September 1914 in Homebush, New South Wales, aged fifty-eight years. At the Latrobe memorial service conducted by John Chamberlain, the pulpit was draped in black, the sheet tied to the railings with white bows. On 6 October 1916, Hannah died, aged sixty-three years in New South Wales.[811]

---

[811] NWA&EBT 11 February 1905 p2; LEx 11 February 1905 p5, 7 October 1914 p4; The Daily Telegraph (Launceston) 23 September 1914 p8, 7 October 1916 p8. Family details by Barbara Coe.

[812] Phoebe was born in Waterbeach. Family research by Barbara Coe.

it the preacher's hearty "God bless you".[813]

The family, now with daughter Bertha, arrived in Queensland on 15 November 1873 on the Gauntlet and in time moved to the Western District of Victoria where he associated with the Primitive Methodists.[814] He was regarded as "enthusiastic, warm-hearted and likeable, being possessed of vocal powers of no mean order". In October 1880 at Kerang, Palmer joined the Northern Victorian Baptist Home Mission as a bush missionary to assist its first missioner, the Rev George Slade.

Then in September 1881, the Rev Frederick J. Wilkin arrived to head up the work and Wilkin extended Palmer's time for twelve months at a salary of two pounds a week plus allowances for horse-keep and stationed him at Boort. By now he was one of three young men with the northern Mission training for the ministry. The work progressed with buildings erected at Cohuna, Minindee, Benjeroop and Barraport at a total cost of £400.[815] At the Annual meeting of the Victorian Baptist Home Missionary Society in 1885, Palmer explained his method of gaining support for the work. He had gone through the country and asked the farmers in the denomination to give the proceeds of one acre of their lands to the Society. So far he had met with good support, for he had obtained the promise of 24 acres of land.[816]

On deputation in November 1883, he spoke at the anniversary of the Footscray Baptist Church which was a Home Mission Church. He kept in touch with early acquaintances in the Primitive Methodist Church, speaking at their anniversaries, thus "cemented old friendships and formed new ones". He was then based at Koroit in 1886 but this was not to his liking as his family was 190 kms away living in Kerang.[817]

Palmer was appointed Pastor of the Home Mission work at Footscray for some two years (1888-1890). Services were held in the new Blue Ribbon Hall, Leeds Street, and a site for the Footscray Church building was purchased in Paisley Street. The new Church building was officially opened on 2 March 1890.

By 1893, Palmer had moved interstate and took charge of the "Burwood Baptist Mission" in NSW commencing in August. The fellowship met in the School of Arts. Soon he took on the role of mission evangelist among the NSW Baptist churches being first based at

---

[813] AB 20 June 1916 p3.
[814] Goulburn Herald (NSW) 12 April 1899 p3; Hamilton Spectator (Vic) 4 September 1877 p4.
[815] The Age (Melbourne) 29 May 1885 p6; Kerang New Times (Vic) 20 October 1908 p3.

[816] The Age (Melbourne) 29 May 1885 p6.
[817] North Melbourne Advertiser 16 November 1883 p2; Hamilton Spectator (Vic) 26 April 1887 p4; correspondence between Palmer and the Mission.

Petersen and then Carlton on the Illawarra Line. In 1896, he became the first pastor of the Carlton Baptist Church.[818] At his induction he remarked,

> They would not find him eloquent. He was a simple-minded but, he trusted, a faithful-hearted man. He had come to preach the Gospel of Jesus Christ. He would never preach at them, but if they came and told him that his remarks had hit them he would say "thank God". Anything he could do to help them, to sympathise with them in their afflictions, he would do.[819]

The Goulburn Mission followed and in his farewell speech on 22 May 1900, after three years in the pastorate, he said to this fellowship of little means, "During twenty years in the ministry, Goulburn was the first charge in which he had not been instrumental in either erecting or enlarging a church." He added, "There were at least 100 volumes in his library, gifts received from friends in Goulburn."[820]

Palmer was next welcomed as pastor at the Bathurst Baptist Church on 27 November 1900.[821]

At a religious service in Bathurst following a Protestant Demonstration of the Bishop Ridley Loyal Orange Lodge 259 in July 1903, Palmer read a paper entitled "The Qualifications of an Orangeman." By mid-1903, he had returned to the Baptist Mission at Carlton.[822]

## Conclusion

It was almost impossible to escape the influence of religious conviction in a society whose very customs and attitudes – for instance in respect to Sunday observance, abject poverty, alcohol and recreation – were so largely shaped by it. The Churches in Latrobe, as elsewhere, commenced in such an environment working very well in the suburbs and towns playing their pivotal role in the community for decades. They were more than just places of worship, they were a stronghold of "the old values" which supported wholesome human behaviour, while preaching the Good News of Jesus, a message of love and liberation which the human race still craves.

They were, in fact, the social hub of the community: a special place where people would travel sometimes long distances to gather in a communal sense and educational pursuits. For many in the farming districts, the Sunday services were the few times during

---

[818] The Daily Telegraph (Sydney, NSW) 5 August 1893 p13; Bathurst Free Press and Mining Journal (NSW) 14 December 1896 p2.
[819] Goulburn Evening Penny Post (NSW) 27 May 1897 p4.
[820] Goulburn Herald (NSW) 23 May 1900 p2.
[821] National Advocate (Bathurst, NSW) 28 November 1900 p2.
[822] The Sydney Morning Herald (NSW) 27 July 1903 p4; The St George Call (Kogarah, NSW) 16 April 1904 p4.

the week that they travelled into "town", making it a grand occasion and a major day out. Further, there were church tennis and cricket associations which in many cases were the main sporting associations. As such they were the social hubs all year round. Many of the churches, especially in larger centres, were vast edifices with seating for hundreds, filled every Sunday.

These churches were often of architectural merit, often one of the finest buildings in the town. In the 19th century, and into the 20th century, local newspapers advertised the Sunday services and then sometimes on Mondays gave a summary of the content of the sermons.

Oratory was regarded as a gift and sermons could extend well beyond today's twelve or twenty minutes lasting up to forty minutes in length.

The clergy were among the best educated in the community with the actual pulpits occasionally towering over the congregations. Decades beyond the time frame of this book, changes took place as pastors sought to better engage with their congregations. By the 1960s formality no longer reigned and for the congregation, it was a case of "come as you are" and sadly families were now beginning to lose their church connections. But being the social hub there were many disengaged Christians filling up seats. They attended, but they didn't serve, didn't give and didn't invite anyone to come with them. They simply attended.

Today, where those sixty-five years and over constitute about 15% of the local population, they comprise more than 70% of worshippers in an average Tasmanian Baptist Church. Somehow, the local church needs again to become the focal point of community, providing people with meaning and belonging and being cared for and having a sense of mission and be known to be that. Churches need to ask if they are providing a great experience and offering engagement but how do we bring that about? We don't provide that by being a church online or by offering a consumer Christianity which asks, "What's in it for me?"

# Chapter 10 Sheffield Baptist Church

## Introduction

A Baptist scribe journeying to Sheffield for a Baptist Association Assembly in 1897 quoted the English writer and philosopher John Ruskin as he spoke of the town,

> The township of Sheffield lies in a small valley among mountains which rise between three and four thousand feet above the sea. It is seven miles from the railway, and from the station there is an ascent of 800 feet. Old Mount Roland rears his towering head with solemn dignity like a patriarch above the hills at his foot. The fertile farms are set on land which at one time seems to have rolled and heaved in awful convulsions, and in a moment made rigid, keeping forever the tokens of its former labour and distress. A strong, lion-hearted race inhabits these highlands of Tasmania. Men with a nobler weapon than the sword have hewn out for themselves homes amid the giants of the forest, and let in God's fertilising rain and sunshine to bless the work of their hands. And in the doing of this bravely, hopefully, trustfully, they have found that "to watch the corn grow, or the blossoms set; to draw hard breath over the plough or spade; to read, to think, to love, to pray, are the things that make men happy." This conquest of the soil by vital human energy marks the unconscious greatness of some of these men; happier and more independent than Kings are they, and they know by experience Ruskin's dictum, that "God has placed man's real happiness in the keeping of the little mosses of the wayside, and of the clouds of the firmament. Now and then a wearied King, or a tormented slave, found out where the true kingdoms of the world were, and

*10-1 Christian Brethren Sunday School*

possessed himself in a furrow or two of garden ground, of a truly infinite dominion." The religious and social life of such a people is bound to be simple, strong, sincere, unconventional, impatient of formalism, professionalism, and vapid sentimentalism.[823]

*10-2 The original Sheffield Tabernacle: "Now what to do as Sunday school is over for the day?"*

Apart from the Christian Brethren work in the district, which began in 1873, the Wesleyan Methodists commenced services about 1860 with the preacher being Jesse Pullen. They erected a chapel in 1867 and replaced this with a weatherboard Sheffield chapel in 1882, opening on 25 November 1882.[824] By 1888 the Wesleyans circuit had outstations at Barrington, Railton and Wilmot. Then there was the Salvation Army which began in Sheffield in 1883.

## The Rev Henry George Blackie

and the 1888 Mission at West Kentish

The Rev Henry George Blackie, the Secretary of the Baptist Union, was invited to hold an evangelistic mission in the Kentish Christian Brethren Gospel Hall situated about three kms from Sheffield. While he was in the midst of the mission a number of the Brethren arrived from Victoria and scolded their local brothers for allowing this Baptist Minister to conduct meetings in their hall. They closed the mission down.

Apart from the Christian Brethren work in the district, which began in 1873, the Wesleyan Methodists opened their Sheffield chapel much earlier, in 1867, having begun in the district in 1863. Now, in 1888, they had outstations at Barrington, Railton and Wilmot. About 1,500 people lived in the district in 1888.

Blackie returned to the area in April 1890, accompanied this time by John Chamberlain of Latrobe and Pastor Harry Wood. They made use of the Roland Hall in Sheffield and from these meetings in time a fellowship

---

[823] SB 4 November 1897 p243. The writer was most likely the Rev John E Walton stationed at Devonport at the time. Walton included Ruskin in a "Reading Circle" at Perth, Tasmania.

[824] LEx 2 December 1882 p3. Stansall p70.

formed numbering twenty persons.⁸²⁵

## Pastor Harry Wood

The Sheffield Fellowship requested that Pastor Harry Wood, "the Evangelist of the Baptist denomination of Tasmania", be sent to them to carry out a pastoral ministry amongst them. The Baptist Council then wrote to Wood who had just resigned from the Launceston Tabernacle,

> ... we understand that you are willing (at least for a time) to take up quieter work in the country. We think it well to ask you definitely if you would be willing to accept an appointment to labour at Sheffield and are also cognizant of the danger of our undertaking being relinquished and another denomination allowed to enter the field because of the difficulty of securing the right man to represent us there.⁸²⁶

On hearing that their request was going to be fulfilled, the "Day Star" reported, "The Sheffield folk have been ever since expecting him ..."⁸²⁷ Wood commenced on 7 September 1890 and William Gibson Junior sent a cheque to cover the cost of a four-room cottage which Wood had rented. He recalled his beginnings in Sheffield,

> Sheffield has a warm place in my heart. It was one of the roughest pieces of work the Lord called me to in Tasmania and one of the happiest and most encouraging. When sufficient strength was regained I was asked to open up work in the Sheffield district. A greater contrast to the work in Launceston could hardly be imagined. We (Baptists) were a comparative stranger. Our first meetings were held in the open air, then we rented the dingy old Skating Rink for Sunday services and soon a Sunday school was formed. Outstations were opened at Promised Land and Paradise.⁸²⁸

Early in 1891, the Baptists had the largest gathering in the district and possibly because of this a familiar message was soon reiterated in the April edition of the "Day-Star", "that local (Sheffield) Baptists thought that matters (regarding a chapel) were moving too slowly." Gibson Junior then purchased land in the

*10-3 The Sheffield Baptist Sunday School*

---

⁸²⁵ Day-Star April 1890.
⁸²⁶ Association Council letter of 22 August 1890.
⁸²⁷ Day-Star September 1890, October 1890.
⁸²⁸ Pioneer Work for the Lord in Tasmania by Harry Wood. AB 1 January 1905 p4.

township for a Tabernacle.[829] He also paid for the erection of the weatherboard Tabernacle capable of seating 250 and it was opened on 10 May 1891. The builders were Roe Brothers. At the same time an outlay of £400 was made for three acres of land and a house as a residence for Wood.[830] Of the furnishing of the Tabernacle, Gibson Junior's wife, Elvina, presented a full set of lamps, while the local people supplied the seats.

Soon the Sheffield Church had four outstations. The first outstation was at Promised Land, the regular services commencing on 20 December 1890 in Angus McNab's old barn with stables on one side and a piggery underneath. In winter it was extremely cold, as the wind whistled up through the boards and the only light was through a large opening in the side of the building. Subsequently McNab gave land and a Tabernacle was built, the locals doing all the carting for free. On 18 October 1891, the building was opened for public worship and, next day, a monster public tea and meeting was held.[831] Over the years it was referred to by some of the old timers as "the Tab on the hill".

The second outstation was at Paradise and commenced in Mr. Treloar's large kitchen. Once the numbers grew, the Baptists moved to Treloar's rough building that was used for drying bacon and then erected a wooden paling structure on land provided by Mr. R Manning. The other station was at Beulah. Wood also met with young men at Barrington.[832]

The Anglican Canon Missioner of St David's Cathedral, Canon A. W. Icely of Sheffield, took offence at Wood's teaching on baptism. In defending his own church's practice in respect of baptising children it was purported that Icely said, "unbaptised infants are no better than dogs" for which he was taken to task by Wood. A lengthy public dispute followed between Icely and Wood. What Icely meant to say was, "If your child remains unbaptised there is no difference in this matter of giving the name between the child and my dog here for instance."[833]

After two years in Sheffield, Wood's health deteriorated again. At an Assembly meeting at Latrobe in October, Wood, the first speaker, wisely curtailed his address. Wood retired from Sheffield at the end of the year. To his credit, all the

---

[829] A Short History of the Sheffield Baptist Church of 1918; Day-Star March 1888, April 1890, May 1891, June 1891

[830] The Colonist 6 December 1890 p12; Day-Star June 1891; Daily Telegraph (Launceston) 14 May 1891 p2.

[831] Daily Telegraph (Launceston) 25 April 1891 p3, 27 June 1891 p4; Day-Star January 1891, November 1891.

[832] Daily Telegraph (Launceston) 27 June 1891 p4; Pioneer Work for the Lord In Tasmania by Harry Wood; Day-Star February 1891, January 1892; K. R. von Stieglitz p46; Icely denied he made the statement, see Day-Star May 1891 p452.

[833] Day-Star March 1891 p428, July 1891 p482, August 1891 p501, September 1891 p524, December1891 p574; LEx 18 July 1887 p2; SB 1891.

properties were now free of debt. He was then asked to return to his former church at Deloraine.[834]

## The Rev Edward Vaughan

The Rev Edward Vaughan arrived from the South Australian Baptist work at Mannum on the Murray River and ministered at Sheffield from 1893 to July 1896 commencing with a six month probationary period. During his time his wife, Emily, and their two daughters went to visit the "old country" for the good of her health. The Church became a constituted Church of the Baptist Association in April 1893 with thirty members. Services started at Staverton in1895. Services and Sunday school commenced at Nook in 1895. Vaughan became President of the Baptist Association in 1895/96 and as such Vaughan was signatory to the Baptist Association's protest in the midst of the Tattersall's Consultations in a concerted effort to prevent Tasmania becoming "the gambling hell of the Southern Hemisphere."[835] Legalised gambling began in 1893 by legalizing the V.D.L. Bank lottery. The next year a Totalisator Bill was offered and adopted; it was hard to refuse it. Two years later (1896) Tattersall's Sweeps, denied a home in all the States, was welcomed to Tasmania. A Christian Endeavour society started in 1896. Vaughan's pessimistic views about society and human nature continued,

> Godliness is pushed out of politics and social life and though men were better educated they were more indifferent than ever ... the State was rapidly approaching that of the times of the decline of the Roman Empire.[836]

His fellow missioner earlier in Northern Victoria, the Rev Charles Pickering, wrote of Vaughan's situation at this time,

> ... The hilly nature of the (Sheffield) district which had to be traversed, the dampness of the climate and a protracted series of evangelistic services enfeebled our brother's health, and apparently undermined his constitution. A heavy cold was followed with what seemed to be haemorrhage of the lungs. His removal became imperative.[837]

Vaughan tendered his resignation yet it was proposed that the resignation be not received until he had a holiday; he needed a warmer climate. He was presented with a purse of gold.[838] Not long after he wrote to say that it was impossible

---

[834] Pioneer Work for the Lord In Tasmania by Harry Wood; Day-Star November 1892 p162.
[835] South Australian Register 6 January 1893 p7; South Australian Chronicle 9 September 1893 p23; Day-Star June 1892; LEx 12 April 1893 p5; SB 27 February 1896 p37; Wellington Times and Agricultural and Mining Gazette (Tas) 14 January 1896 p3.
[836] Day-Star April 1896.
[837] SB 1896.
[838] Church Minutes 18 June 1896.

for him to return. He then accepted the pastorate of the Castlemaine Baptist Church and commenced on 11 November 1896 but he died of heart disease two months later, on 18 January 1897. He was forty-four years of age.[839] The folk of the Sheffield Church hung a marble tablet in their sanctuary in his memory. His wife Emily soon returned to England with their two daughters to live with her parents. One daughter, Sarah returned to Australia and marry. Emily and her second daughter, Nellie May remained in England and Emily died on 26 March 1918 in London.[840]

## Pastor Albert E. Blackwell

At the welcome of the Rev Albert Edward Blackwell and his wife, Ethel Winifred (nee Wortley), to the Sheffield Church on 17 February 1897 for twelve months, Albert was attired in Indian costume and related some thrilling experiences of his mission work in India. The Blackwells had just married in Victoria on 19 January 1897.[841] At the end of the twelve months, Blackwell was ask to stay on without limitation of time yet the church would not hold itself responsible for any fixed salary but on the basis on what was in collection.[842]

*10-3 Young Albert Blackwell*

But by May 1898. there were strained relationships between Blackwell and church leadership and so he soon resigned from both the Church and the Baptist Union Council.[843]

## The Rev John Casley

The Rev John Casley was officially welcomed on 14 March 1899 at the Church's Anniversary tea meeting. Present was Miss Ellen Arnold, the first missionary to serve with the Australian Baptist Missionary Society; she had just returned from India. Casley stated that if the Sustentation Committee could not increase the grant to Sheffield to £60 per annum, he would not be able to support his family. Casley also requested one month annual leave. It was decided that Casley be paid all offerings less current expenses at the end of the month, possibly a

---

[839] Minutes 13 July 1896; Mount Alexander Mail (Vic) 13 November 1896 p2; The Age (Melbourne) 17 January 1897 p6.

[840] SB 4 March 1897 p54; Williamstown Chronicle (Vic) 5 September 1936 p5; UK National Probate Calendar 1918 p149.

[841] The Age (Melbourne) 27 January 1897 p1.

[842] Daily Telegraph (Launceston) 20 February 1897 p7; Minutes 16 September 1897.

[843] Council Minutes p187/15 – meeting May 1898; p189/17 – meeting July 1898.

continuation of the arrangement that existed for Blackwell.[844]

Troubles between Casley and the Union Council continued over whether the horse allowance should be paid to him as the animal he was using was only on loan. His Union sermon for the Association meeting in April 1900 was titled "Words of Cheer for Ill-used and Discouraged Workers." Whether he was preaching to himself we cannot say. As with many of the men from the Pastors' College, he lectured on the Rev C. H. Spurgeon, "the People's Preacher". His other subjects varied: "Eccentric Christians I have met with, heard of and read", "Strange Tales", the perennial "Billy Bray" and "John Ashworth's Strange Tales from Humble Life".[845] His many addresses were reported to be "powerful" and "impressive". In October 1902 the Rev James Blaikie of Hobart and the Rev George Mackay, in conjunction with Casley, conducted a mission at the Sheffield Church. The Southern Baptist reported,

10-4 Missionary Miss Allen Arnold

Our missioner brethren ... have day by day waited upon God in prayer, with a fervency and earnestness that would take no denial, with the result that both Sheffield and the mission cause at Promised Land have received a wave of blessing. Above sixty souls were born into the Kingdom as the result of this mission.[846]

Missions aside, whatever troubles there were in 1903 for Casley we don't know, but at a meeting of the Sheffield deaconate in March that year, the meeting unanimously sympathised with Casley and his wife "assuring them of the unabated confidence and the deep sympathy". At an Association Council meeting the following month Casley's "grievous trouble" was raised and also the fact the Church was not happy with him. The Council Secretary also read a letter from Casley in which he asked to be relieved of the pastorate of the church. Farewell socials were tendered Casley and his wife at the church and its outstations in June and he informed Union Council he wanted to remain on the accredited ministers' list and take the position

---

[844] NWA&EBT 17 March 1899 p2; Church Minutes 1 January 1899, 16 February 1899.

[845] LEx 7 April 1899 p6, 27 April 1900 p3, 1 September 1900 p8; NWA&EBT 1 April 1901 p4; Daily Telegraph (Launceston) 13 June 1901 p2.

[846] SB 1 October 1902.

of a "traveller", that is, take interim pastorates. He had further trouble with the church over his removal of the manse furniture which in fact belonged to the church! [847]

## The Rev Robert Williamson

The Rev Robert Williamson was invited to the pastorate in 1903 and the Church was willing to pay him the sum of £80 for the first twelve months (exclusive of the Sustentation grant). This amount continued until his leaving. In 1908, Williamson's resignation was accepted with regret "owing to circumstances in which he was separated from his family through their residence in Victoria and this church wishes to record their appreciation of his able, godly and self-denying work as Pastor of the church for the past four and one half years." He was presented with a purse of gold coins at his farewell.[848]

## The Rev Charles Henry James Warren

The Rev Charles Henry James Warren of Queensland commenced at the Sheffield Church in June 1908 with the church paying half of his removal expenses from Queensland. But in December, due to his ill-health, he was moved to the Home Mission Church of Ulverstone.[849]

## The Rev Vincent G. Britton

The pattern of church life that the Rev Vincent G. Britton had set for himself at Deloraine continued when he began at Sheffield in January 1909. In fact, his winning formula and his "happy knack of drawing together forces, and spurring them on to undertake ... things" and his "consistent visiting" brought new life to the Church and its eight outstations at Staverton, Paradise, Railton, Nook, Promised Land, Beulah, Lorinna and the Claude Road township. The distances were considerable: Lorinna was forty kms from Sheffield and Staverton was on the way. Services started at Railton

*10-6 Staverton Chapel*

---

[847] Church Minutes 9 March 1903, 19 October 1903, 16 November 1903; Council Minutes 364/24, 371/10 1903.

[848] Church Minutes 16 November 1903, 2 February 1905, 20 February 1908, 15 March 1908.

[849] Church Minutes 3 June 1908, 1 December 1908.

in July 1910 on Friday evenings in the old billiard room. The Nook service was held monthly. The expense incurred by the preachers in keeping bicycles and horses in good order was considerable; hundreds of kms had to be travelled every month in visitation and preaching. In some cases to be on time for the 10am Sunday morning services the preacher was required to leave on Saturday by horse and stay overnight and then leave the service immediately so the 3pm service could be attended elsewhere. A new Tabernacle was opened at Staverton practically free of debt on 12 February 1911. It was well built and furnished throughout. Angus McNab was the builder; the painting was done by Mr. Colledye. Mr. G. Robson supplied the seats. Mr D. Davis gave the land, and others did a large amount of work in clearing and the like. In all only about £160 was spent.[850] A chapel was also erected at Beulah with folk from Perth, Hobart and Launceston helping financially.

Britton's reputation seems to have preceded him. At one of the first of the evening services he took in the Sheffield Tabernacle there was an overflow. Not long into the pastorate he applied to the local Council to have a gas street lamp installed opposite the Baptist Tabernacle. This was granted and one of the councillors remarked at the Council meeting that he was for the motion because "he would like to see a street light in the town somewhere!" Britton appeared to have taken upon himself at times to light the gas lamp for in October 1909 as he was attending to what was a pressurized lamp, the generator exploded with the cover hitting his head with force.[851]

Over the years Britton was closely associated with the local Methodist Pastor, the Rev A. P. Watsford. Sometimes they would share the preaching at United Evangelistic Meetings.[852]

In 1910 the news of the Oxford Movement in the Church of England had reached this island colony and Britton joined with many fellow concerned Protestant clergy at the Devonport Town Hall to hear the Baptist Christopher Stark deliver a lecture on the principles of Protestantism titling his message, "Our Glorious Heritage, is it in Danger?" Stark based his concern on what he had read in the 1899 book by Walter Walsh, "Secret History of the Oxford Movement".[853]

---

[850] NWA&EBT 16 August 1910 p2; The North West Post (Formby) 16 February 1911 p2.

[851] Daily Telegraph (Launceston) 27 March 1909 p9, 12 October 1909 p4; The North West Post (Formby) 8 February 1909 p4. Britton's many road accidents appear to show that he was prone to them.

[852] The North West Post (Formby) 14 June 1911 p2.

[853] This work from 1899 provides documentation on the 19th-century infiltration and internal takeover of Oxford University and also the Church of England by Jesuit clerical spies and other agents of the Vatican. Walsh identified such turncoat notable clerics as Newman, Pusey, Keble,

In 1910, a further development in Britton's life began which had important implications for the denomination: he began to train young men for the ministry. That year chicken farmer Ernest Charles Walsh became his assistant in the Sheffield District. He worked with Britton until the end of February 1912 and then was placed in the Wynyard-Yolla district. Pastor Harry Wood's son, Fred J. Wood, replaced Walsh at Sheffield for two months until he departed to go to the Pastors' College in London. Mr. Howe replaced Wood but lasted only a couple of months; obviously Britton advised him to enter secular employment. Louis Harding of Waratah then became Britton's assistant.[854] Britton continued for many years this task of training the young men.

Britton's success with the Magic Lantern and gramophone had a limited life but for a time the years were his. In June 1912, Wright's Picture Company had arrived in Railton to provide for a night's good entertainment in the Roland Hall. It attracted a large audience and announced that the company would give similar entertainment fortnightly throughout the winter months.[855] At Sheffield, Britton took note of how many of the young people were leaving the area to find employment.

## Pastor William Llewellyn Heaven

Pastor William Llewellyn Heaven commenced in the Sheffield circuit on 29 December 1914, the circuit now comprising Paradise, Lower Barrington, Staverton, West Kentish, Nook and Promised Land. He had not as yet satisfied the educational requirements required by the Home Mission Committee. The Church replied to the Committee protesting of "Pastor Heaven being regarded as a Home Missionary in charge". Early in 1915, S. R. Bannister was appointed assistant to Heaven but at the end of May Heaven reported that Bannister had resigned because he was unfit for the work. A letter of sympathy at his forced retirement was sent to him.[856]

*10-5 William & Mary Heaven*

---

and others - the so-called "tractarian" Anglican Church leaders, as they were then called; The North West Post (Formby) 5 July 1910 p2.
[854] The North West Post (Formby) 18 September 1912 p2.

[855] The North West Post (Formby) 5 June 1912 p2.
[856] Church minutes 1 June 1915.

Heaven was then provided with another Home Mission assistant, this time from the Staverton Church but the assistant, Mr Loone, was farewelled for the War effort in June 1916. After two years in the pastorate Heaven had been taken to the peoples' hearts and they staged a surprise social presenting him with a Holman Pronouncing Bible which was inscribed on the fly leaf, "To Rev W. L. Heaven, a token of esteem and goodwill, from the deacons, members and friends of the Sheffield Tabernacle after a successful two years' ministry, Sheffield, Feb. 1, 1917." In May that year, Heaven and the local Methodist Pastor, B. L. Semmens, debated at the Sheffield Municipal Hall the subject of baptism, the proceedings opening and closing with the National Anthem. Such was the need of the hour that at the close of a Sunday school concert Heaven finished the evening with an appeal for national and individual repentance.[857]

In these years the Church welcomed back those from the Front, among them local lad Private Harold Claude Reinmuth who had spent over two years service at the front and was invalided with a shattered right arm. This was followed by an evening in the Town Hall for the purpose of helping to fill the Christmas boxes for the Tasmanian soldiers. The evening was presided over by Heaven. In October Heaven gave £1 to the General War Fund in the Kentish Municipality. The Church celebrated its 25th anniversary in 1918. On 25 April, an "Anzac Remembrance Evening" was held at Staverton with Heaven chairman by request, and gifts were given for the troops and items were performed. Heaven "delivered a stirring address suitable to the occasion."

Throughout these years functions at Sheffield and at the outstations were greatly supported making a constant demand on Heaven's services. He was greatly loved by his people. Finally on 6 July 1919 a "Signing of the Peace Treaty" thanksgiving service was held in the Sheffield Town Hall following the arrival of the good news.[858]

In the middle of August 1921, the Sheffield Ministers' Fraternal commenced united prayer meetings four times a week culminating with a ten day mission in November, the speaker being the former Captain of the HMAS Australia, Stoker Stephens.[859] After seven years at Sheffield, a farewell social on 15 March 1922 was tendered to Heaven and, Mary, his wife as they were moving to the Bracknell District Churches. Heaven commenced in there in March 1922 and stayed for nearly three years. He was farewelled at a Boxing Day gathering in 1924 with about 200 present thanking their "popular minister" for

---

[857] The North West Post (Formby) 26 June 1916 p4; NWA&EBT 6 February 1917 p2, 8 August 1917 p2; Daily Telegraph (Launceston) 15 May 1917 p7.

[858] LEx 9 August 1917 p3, 8 July 1919 p3; NWA&EBT 11 August 1917 p4, 11 October 1917 p3, 30 April 1918 p2.

[859] AB 11 October 1921 p6.

the "earnest work performed for the past three years." He had written to the Home Mission Committee saying that he was considering resigning and would find another area of employment and he did in Victoria. On his departure to the mainland he was also farewelled from a number of the outstations.[860]

## The Rev Henry Saunders

In January 1914 the Rev Henry Ebenezer Saunders was called to the Sheffield Baptist Church. He provided a steady ministry of services on Sundays some involving travelling to the various outstations, one being situated at Nook which was a Union Church; it had opened in June 1914. That month, Saunders paid a visit to the Beulah district and "was delighted to find that a labour of love had been going forward at the local Baptist church. A number had given their evenings, and had lined the Church in a very creditable manner indeed." But within a year the outbreak of World War I marked the end of his pastorate and he made an early departure for Queensland. As reported, "A removal from the bracing climate - especially of this corner of Tasmania - is absolutely imperative on account of Mrs Saunders' health."[861]

# Appendices:

## Appendix 1: The Rev Albert E. Blackwell

The Rev Albert Edward Blackwell was another with missionary aspirations but financial restraints crippled their fulfillment and his early ventures into pastoral life in the home country did not look promising either but he persisted and displayed natural leadership ability and became a sought after pastor for the rest of his days.

Blackwell was born in Albury, New South Wales, on 27 January 1872 to Richard Thomas Blackwell and Lucy Hunter. In 1891, Albert was on the committee of a temperance club "run on new lines" in Prahran, Melbourne, as a counter

*10-6 Henry and Frances Saunders*

attraction to the public bar. In his early twenties he was preaching in Melbourne Baptist churches and was involved with Christian Endeavour. As a Baptist Missionary

---

[860] Advocate (Burnie) 20 March 1922 p5, 6 January 1925 p4; LEx 31 December 1924 p2; HM Minutes p112.

[861] Daily Telegraph (Launceston) 29 September 1914 p4; The North West Post (Formby) 15 June 1914 p2, 4 June 1914 p2.

Society designate for India, he was among the first students to enter the newly opened Baptist College in Melbourne in 1895 and took time off studies to lecture on India in the churches. He was also the first graduate for missionary service. Sixty-seven years later he was the only surviving foundation student.862

Blackwell went to India in late 1895. As Basil S. Brown records,

> Unfortunately, because of the economic depression in Australia, the finances of the mission were giving great concern and a year later it became necessary to terminate Blackwell's probation because he could not be maintained.863

Back home by July he gave lectures on India both in Melbourne and Tasmania.864 Reported the Launceston Examiner,

> There was a fairly good attendance at the Tabernacle last evening, when the Rev A. E. Blackwell delivered a lecture on missionary work in India, illustrated by limelight views. Mr. Blackwell, who spent some considerable (sic) time in the Indian mission fields, principally at Barisal, under the auspices of the Victorian Baptist Missionary Society, gave an interesting account of his labours. The natives were very anxious to hear the word of God and learn the English language, and were apt to learn.865

*10-7 Rev A. E. Blackwell*

**From Sheffield** Blackwell transferred to the Baptist Church at Balmain in Sydney, and was welcomed on 20 October 1898. Through the years he continued his interest in the Christian Endeavour movement and in the overseas missionary ventures becoming secretary of the Foreign Mission Committee for NSW. He

---

862 The Argus (Melbourne) 29 January 1872 p4; The Prahran Telegraph (Vic.) 17 October 1891 p2; The Age (Melbourne) 17 June 1893 p12; The Ballarat Star 9 September 1893 p4; Williamstown Chronicle (Vic.) 23 February 1895 p3. Wilkin p112 – Errol St was purchased in 1912; Geelong Advertiser 21 September 1895 p3; AB 18 July 1962. Family History research by Barbara Coe.

863 The outgoing group usually went in late October or early November in order to arrive in the cool season, and to be in attendance for the combined Annual Missionary Conference. As a single man Blackwell would then have been assigned to live with a missionary for his training in language and work, rather than go to the Mymensingh station. From Five Barley Loaves, Rosalind Gooden; "Members one of Another" BS Brown p87, 90.

864 LEx 27 October 1896 p1.

865 LEx 29 October 1896 p5.

stayed at Balmain until the end of 1901.[866]

He soon accepted the pastorate of the Hargreaves Street Church in Bendigo and remained until January 1908. The mining town held a special spot for him as his mother, Lucy Blackwell, lived there and the Bendigo Congregational Church was the church of his grandfather, Richard Blackwell, an honoured deacon and someone highly esteemed in the district.[867]

One evening Blackwell preached on the subject, "What Baptists believe." He listed the five principles:

- The first principle is that Christ Jesus is vested with all authority.
- The second principle is that the Scriptures are the sole guide in all matters of faith and practice.
- The third principle of Baptist belief is the right of private judgment.
- The fourth principle of Baptists is that we believe in maintaining the purity of Christ's church.
- The fifth principle of Baptist belief is that we believe in the priesthood of all believers.

He closed by saying,

> Baptists say to any priest, Anglican, Catholic, or any other who dare to get in their way, "Stand, aside, by the blood of the eternal covenant, we have access right to the very throne of grace, right to the very heart of God!"[868]

Blackwell failed to annunciate a sixth principle: it is the gathered church in which members seek the mind of Christ together. The life of the church is not determined by the pastor or any other person or persons within the church or outside the church. Baptists do not have bishops.

Blackwell was also very clear on what conversion meant,

*10-8 Rev E. McIntosh Brown, with dog-collar, standing in the ruins of the Tabernacle*

---

[866] The Australasian (Melbourne) 29 October 1898; Australian Town and Country Journal (Sydney) 15 October 1902 p11.
[867] The Australasian (Melbourne) 21 February 1903 p49; Mount Alexander Mail (Vic.) 20 October 1906 p2; Bendigonian (Bendigo) 13 January 1916 p20.
[868] Bendigo Advertiser 29 June 1903 p6.

There is but one word, with its compound, used in the New Testament to designate conversion. It means to reverse, to turn back and turn around. When a man becomes converted he reverses his mode of life, he has been living to please himself, now he lives to please Christ. He has been living in sin; he turns round about, and follows the path of holiness. He has been turned away from Christ; now he turns back to Christ. Paul lived the first half of his public life in utter hostility to Christ: he became a converted man, and then he lived to serve Christ. His life from being self-centred became Christ-centred, "Not I, but Christ." This is conversion.[869]

"Is Cricket preferable to Football?" was one of the subjects at Blackwell's Bendigo Baptist Mutual Improvement Society debates. Blackwell played a leading part in the Bendigo Ministers' Association and was President of the "Bendigo Rescue Home". Blackwell closed his ministry at Bendigo at the end of January 1908.[870]

His next Church was the Melbourne Newmarket Baptist Church from March 1908 to May 1912. At Newmarket he published a letter sent by the Rev J. Tyssen, vicar of St. George's Church of England, Maldon, to one of his former parishioners, a young man who had come to Melbourne seeking employment. At Newmarket this young man had been "converted in true Baptist fashion" and applied for baptism and church membership. Tyssen ordered him to come home at once.[871]

Ethel's weekly girls' Bible Class at Newmarket numbered around forty young women. She selected three of them to attend with her a lecture at the Collins Street Church on kindergarten work and the three began a kindergarten as part of the Sunday school and had over eighty children between the age of four and eight.[872] During their time "the church reached its peak in attendance at all services, yet by the end of his term signs were appearing of the church's slow decline."[873] By late 1911, Blackwell who was now a

*10-9 Ethel Blackwell and her Newmarket Young Ladies' Bible*

---

[869] Bendigo Advertiser 22 August 1906 p6.
[870] The Bendigo Independent 2 December 1905 p4; Bendigo Advertiser 9 July 1907 p2, 24 December 1907 p3.
[871] Watchman (Sydney) 9 September 1909 p5.
[872] Our Yesterdays Vol.8 p35.
[873] "A Cause in their Neighbourhood", a history of the Newmarket Church by Mark and Sue Garner, p13.

man of high standing in the Victorian churches and was a sought-out pastor, received in one month two calls, one from Albert Park in Melbourne and one from Warrnambool in country Victoria. He chose the latter. During his time the foundation stone was laid for a new badly needed Warrnambool Sunday school hall. He resigned in August 1915 because of poor health, yet before Blackwell lay another thirty-five years of ministry; commencing with some years of interim pastorates among them the South Melbourne Baptist Church.[874]

In May 1924, Blackwell accepted the pastorate of the Dawson Street Baptist Tabernacle, Ballarat. During his time in this provincial city he was appointed President of the Baptist Union of Victoria. In his Presidential Address he gave a "a vigorous advocacy of two basic Baptist principles; namely, the freedom of each individual in his conscience before God, and, the Bible as authoritative, inspired source of faith and practice."[875]

In August 1928, he became Associate Secretary in Australia for the Mission to Lepers with the Rev Walter J. Eddy as General Secretary. He became its General Secretary in December 1931, relinquishing the

*10-10 The Newmarket Baptist Church*

pastorate at Ballarat and moving to Brisbane.[876]

He resigned from the Society in June 1933 because of ill-health and was inducted as pastor to the Country Victorian Warracknabeal Baptist Church where he remained until June 1935.[877]

The Melbourne Regent Baptist Church followed from July 1935 to November 1938. While at Regent he was again elected President of the Baptist Union of Victoria. Williamstown Baptist Church was next commencing in December 1938 and concluding in April 1941. Blackwell then became pastor of the Colac Baptist Church and

---

[874] The Colac Herald (Vic.) 27 October 1911 p4; The Argus (Melbourne) 26 October 1911 p8; Warrnambool Standard (Vic.) 27 April 1914 p4, 12 August 1915 p4; Weekly Times (Melbourne) 26 October 1918. In April 1914.
[875] The Herald (Melbourne) 3 May 1924 p18; The Age (Melbourne) 19 October 1927 p12. AB 11 August 1971 p15.

[876] The Age (Melbourne) 30 December 1931 p6, 20 December 1928 p14.
[877] The Herald (Melbourne) 5 January 1934 p7; The Argus (Melbourne) 8 July 1933 p10, 29 June 1935 p21.

superintendent for the Home Mission work in the district.[878]

Then from 1943 to 1945, at the commencement of his retirement, interim ministries followed in Melbourne at Box Hill, Elsternwick and Surrey Hills, and one at the Country Church at Kerang in 1947. Another interim ministry began in March 1950 at East Ringwood Baptist Church.[879] Ethel died on 11 July 1944.[880] The Rev Albert Edward Blackwell spent his final years at the "Strathalan" Baptist Aged People's Home in Macleod[881] and died on 2 July 1971. They had two children. Unaware of the reasons that lie behind a poor performance in a person's beginnings, we may think that is all the person is capable of, until the master-touch of some unexpected circumstance catalyses what has been there all the time, and makes an unpromising life a means of blessing to many.[882]

## Appendix 2: The Rev A. John Casley

For some years following his leaving the Sheffield Baptist Church, the Rev A John Casley worked as a wholesale Travelling Agent in the North West of Tasmania. He remained on good terms with his fellow Baptists but took church services where they were offered in Baptist, Congregational and Methodist churches. In his secular business dealings, he was fined one shilling for not having his name painted on his dray. He was finally welcomed back to the Congregationalist fold in July 1906 when he became assistant Pastor at the Latrobe Congregational Church. Even so, his travelling salesman pursuits continued but in a lesser way. In July 1908, he was called out for selling tea packages on Sundays when in fact all he was doing was delivering the packages to someone who would be attending the same church as him. By March 1908, he was stationed at the Esperance and Hastings Congregational Mission in Tasmania. In March 1912, he was transferred to Renmark, South Australia, to work with the Parkin Mission.[883]

In April 1914, he took charge of the Torrensville Congregational Church in South Australia and the work prospered greatly under his ministry. He also did excellent work at the Halifax Street Mission, which was associated at the time with Stow Church.[884] In 1916, he took the oversight of the Croydon Church in

---

[878] The Argus (Melbourne) 22 May 1935 p6, 16 November 1937 p12; Williamstown Chronicle (Vic.) 5 November 1938 p8; The Herald (Melbourne) 31 July 1941 p17.

[879] The Argus (Melbourne) 22 June 1943 p2, 25 August 1945 p2, 5 April 1947 p15, 4 March 1950 p11.

[880] The Herald (Melbourne) 12 July 1944 p4.

[881] AB 1971 21 July p14.

[882] From an Age Saturday Reflection by Robert Brown.

[883] NWA&EBT 27 June 1903 p4, 12 August 1903 p2; LEx 13 July 1906 p7; The Mercury (Hobart) 23 July 1908 p6, 30 May 1908; Renmark Pioneer (SA) 15 March 1912 p8.

[884] Originally an initiative of Flinders Street Baptist Church.

conjunction with his pastorate at Torrensville. A new structure at North Croydon was erected as the result of his energy and zeal. He concluded there in February 1921. He then took the temporary oversight of the Congregational church at Beachside Semaphore in 1921, and later the Cheltenham Congregational Church. He died in South Australia on 14 November 1924, aged sixty-eight years. At the time it was said of him, "He was not a scholar, but was abundantly endowed with virile common sense and interpreted the Christian teaching in a large and humanistic manner. His sermons at times were eloquent and his pulpit readings were a treat to listen to."[885] Anne died on 13 June 1926 in Adelaide in her sixty-seventh year. They had had two daughters, Edith Mary and Bertha. Anne "was a worthy helpmate to a much-loved pastor".[886]

## Appendix 3: The Rev Robert Williamson

The Rev Robert Williamson commenced at the Brighton Baptist Church in Melbourne on 7 April 1908. In 1912, he was called to give evidence in the Tasmanian Government Enquiry over the Ownership of the York Street Chapel, Launceston. In his fifth year the Brighton Church celebrated its sixtieth anniversary. In his eighth year he resigned through ill-health.[887]

Like so many migrants Williamson survived tubercular infection and lived a long and productive life. The Rev Robert Williamson died on 20 August 1916 at sixty-eight years in Brighton, Melbourne, leaving his wife Margaret, a son, Leonard Robert, and four daughters, Christina, Margaret, Elvie and Emonia.[888] Margaret died on 11 February 1927 at Malvern East, Victoria.[889]

## Appendix 4: The Rev Charles Henry James Warren

The Rev Charles Henry James Warren arrived from Queensland in 1908 to work with the Home Mission but two short placements, both curtailed for health reasons, saw him soon depart.

Warren was born on 3 July 1873 at Geelong. He married Laura Isabella McInnes eldest daughter of Duncan and Laura McInnes on 15 February

---

[885] Daily Herald (Adelaide) 11 April 1914 p 3, 29 July 1922 p8; The Advertiser (Adelaide) 5 August 1916 p12; The Register (Adelaide) 5 February 1921 p10, 17 November 1924 p8; Murray Pioneer and Australian River Record (SA) 28 November 1924 p16.
[886] The Advertiser (Adelaide) 14 June 1926 p8.
[887] SB 28 April 1908; LEx 13 January 1912 p3; see Rowston, Baptists in Van Diemen's Land Part 2; The Herald (Melbourne) 16 September 1912 p3; Weekly Times (Melbourne) 20 May 1916 p8.
[888] Daily Telegraph (Launceston) 2 August 1884 p3; Bligh p53.
[889] The Argus (Melbourne) 14 February 1927 p1.

1899 at Elsternwick, Victoria.[890] They trained at the Queensland Baptist College offering themselves for missionary service but due to lack of financial support from the mission concerned, in June 1901 he entered the home ministry provisionally at the Ryan Street Home Mission church in Charters Towers. But Laura aged twenty-five years, "an earnest Christian worker", died on 25 January 1902 at the manse. He himself suffered typhoid fever in February 1903 during the epidemic. In August 1904 he was farewelled from the church; he had now married again, this time to Amy Edmonds on 13 August 1903 in Brisbane. Amy was born on 29 May 1872 in Brighton, Victoria. Then, in October 1904, his next placement was Sandgate, a northern coastal suburb in the City of Brisbane. The Church had 130 scholars attending the Sunday school. Even though he was ordained, he was still studying at the Queensland Baptist College. He concluded at Sandgate in November 1906 and moved to Nundah Baptist Church, Nundah being an inner suburb in the City of Brisbane. This was but a short pastorate as he transferred in June 1908 to Tasmania to work with its Home Mission and he was placed at Sheffield.[891]

## Appendix 5: The Rev Henry Ebenezer Saunders

The Rev Henry Ebenezer Saunders, like a number who ministered in Tasmania, began with the Victorian Home Mission in the Mallee. In the Sheffield Church he was at the centre of its Pentecostal revival. He remained a Baptist minister in full standing for forty-nine years.[892]

Saunders was born on 15 October 1876 in Coburg, Victoria, to Thomas and Maria Saunders. They had five sons and four daughters. Henry was converted under the preaching of the well-known Presbyterian evangelist, the Rev John MacNeil. Shortly after his conversion, in June 1903, Henry was placed for a short time by the Victorian Baptist Home Mission with the work in the Mallee, in the district of Barraport which was part of the Kerang circuit.[893] Then, in June, under the supervision of the Rev Frederick John Wilkin of the Footscray Baptist Church he ministered jointly at the Samuel Chapman Memorial Church in Ross Street, Port Melbourne, and in Yarraville and commenced ordination studies. The Yarraville work was just beginning.[894] On 20

---

[890] Family history research by Barbara Coe.

[891] The Telegraph (Brisbane) 11 September 1901 p7; The Evening Telegraph (Charters Towers) 27 January 1902 p2; Gympie Times and Mary River Mining Gazette (Qld.) 3 February 1903 p3; The Northern Miner (Charters Towers) 4 August 1904 p7; The Brisbane Courier 29 May 1905 p4, 28 January 1905 p16; The Telegraph (Brisbane) 5 October 1904 p4; NWA&EBT 2 June 1908 p3.

[892] AB 30 March 1960.

[893] SB 16 May 1905 p1.

[894] Independent (Footscray, Vic) 30 May 1903 p2.

February 1903, he married Frances Manson Robertson, daughter of the evangelist James Robertson.[895]

In 1905, Saunders was returned to Barraport. In June 1908, he moved to Queensland to Home Mission Beaudesert Baptist Church sixty kms from Brisbane, staying for over two years. A breakdown in health had necessitated the move.[896] He became very good friends with evangelist the Rev Wilfred Lemuel Jarvis.

He began at the Moonah Baptist Church in Hobart in September 1910 which was under the charge of the Rev F W Boreham of the Hobart Baptist Church. Again, it was for health reasons that he had been compelled "to seek the cooler air of Tasmania".[897]

This year Harry Wood commented that since his arrival on the Island in 1881 to the end of 1909 he has seen no less than thirty-eight ministers come and go in the Tasmanian Churches. The Editor of the Southern Baptist responded to his words by saying,

> The Churches in Tasmania evidently cannot complain of

*10-11 Laying the foundation stone at Spreyton 4 Aug 1907*

monotony in the matter of their ministers. It would probably make for the welfare and stability of the work if the pastorates generally were of a somewhat longer duration. Perhaps these frequent changes are not wholly the result of the migratory instincts of the ministers.[898]

By November 1911, Saunders was stationed at the Latrobe Baptist Church with its outstations of Sassafras and South Spreyton. South Spreyton was the scene of a remarkable achievement of planned co-operation – the building of a Church in a day in April 1913. [899]

In March 1913, what was probably the first ordination service was held under the auspices of the Tasmanian Baptist Association. Saunders and Jack Fisher were ordained in the Launceston Tabernacle. Previous Home Mission pastors had been

---

[895] The Age (Melbourne) 7 March 1903 p5.
[896] Kerang New Times (Vic) 3 February 1905 p2; The Brisbane Courier 16 June 1908 p4.
[897] SB 14 April 1910 p144; The Mercury (Hobart) 1 October 1910 p6.
[898] SB 6 January 1910 p29.
[899] NWA&EBT 18 November 1911 p4; LEx 12 April 1913 p6.

granted full ministerial status, but so far as the records show this was the first ordination service.[900]

In 1915, following his time at Sheffield, Saunders, having been rejected for military service, accepted the pastorate of the Gympie Baptist Church in Queensland but soon moved to the Albion Church and then to short term pastorates for some years. With his passion for social righteousness, he was appointed General Secretary of the Citizens' Six O'clock Closing League but was unable to devote full time to the duties of his office owing to illness. He also took a leading part in the Temperance Movement as Secretary of the Queensland Temperance Alliance which worked for the Local Option Legislation and with the Y.M.C.A.[901] He also organised War Savings Groups.

Saunders returned to Tasmania, to the Sheffield Baptist Church in May 1923. At the Baptist Assembly in February he spoke on the liquor business and Prohibition in America and of the good that Prohibition had done. At one of the Sheffield Sunday school anniversaries, a Miss Crack was awarded a special prize for having to walk the furthest distance to Sunday school for the past two years and having the best attendance; her home was four miles away. That month a stable was erected at the Paradise Church.[902]

But at the outset of his pastorate at Sheffield, Saunders requested that his son, Neil, be appointed assistant pastor in order to ensure that the various outposts of the church could be adequately supported. In his youth Neil was greatly influenced by the Pentecostal movement through a friend in the Queensland Y.M.C.A. who demonstrated the extraordinary gifts of speaking and interpreting tongues. His friend claimed that this was his baptism in the Holy Spirit. Neil's Pentecostal experiences in turn influenced his father's theology and behaviour. One thing is clear: by the time of the commencement of Saunders' second term in Sheffield, they were both distinctly Pentecostal in outlook.

Within two months a revival started suddenly. The Minutes of the Deacons' Meeting of 21 July 1923 reads,

> Pastor Saunders reported a great revival at Staverton and Beulah there being 80 converts. We thank God that everywhere our churches, outstations and centre are showing increased activity since the coming of Pastor and Mrs Saunders and family.

By late September, Saunders reported having conducted a successful mission at Cethana, twenty kms from Sheffield, where "a time of great blessing was

---

[900] Bligh.

[901] The Brisbane Courier 31 March 1916 p8, 15 September 1916 p11; The Daily Mail (Brisbane) 24 February 1917 p4.

[902] Advocate (Burnie) 11 April 1924 p7, 12 November 1924 p4, 24 December 1924 p4.

experienced". This was soon followed by forty-nine applicants for membership and four for baptism and membership. It was around this time that the Diaconate recommended to the church that Neil Saunders be formally appointed as assistant pastor. In the Sheffield Baptist Church News October 1923 a glowing report was given to the congregation of the continuing revival,

> The result has been a great outpouring of God's power to save, as we know of no less than 108 persons who have yielded their lives to Him ... four baptismal services in three months with 10 sisters and 19 brothers baptized ... great power and blessing.

The glowing report in the Australian Baptist gave more detail,

> Our pastor, his wife and son, commenced a series of special meetings at Staverton and Beulah, two of our outposts, on Sunday June 17, and concluded on Wednesday, July 11. The mighty power of God fell on both places, especially at Staverton. At Beulah 22 publicly confessed Jesus as Saviour and Lord. At Staverton, 54 made the great confession. Special meetings were started at Promised Land (another outpost) on July 15, concluding on August 3. The mighty power of God fell on the people, and 29 dear souls came forward in response to the appeal, and publicly confessed Jesus as Saviour and Lord. Four dear souls had previously confessed at Sheffield, making a total of 109. Thirty-two of these converts have applied for baptism, and been baptized, and quite a number of others have also applied for baptism.[903]

Days later, it was estimated that 119 persons had accepted Jesus as their Saviour. But coinciding with the revival was a serious division in the church. At the centre of the division were three influential deacons. The main cause of division was that some were rejoicing at the conversions and renewal and others were concerned at its seeming excesses. Even so, the revival resulted in an increase in the number of members at Sheffield by fifty-nine, along with "a wonderfully improved spiritual tone of the outstations" and a marked increase in the church's finances.

The split resulted in the three deacons resigning and making a complaint to the Baptist Association. In addition, they raised a number of complaints which, writes Dr Adams who wrote a treatise on the revival, "Were all designed to undermine the ministry of both Henry and Neil Saunders." Four church members resigned, including the Secretary of the diaconate. Also, the Baptist Association appears to have cautiously sided with the former deacons. Consequently, in January

---

[903] AB 2 October 1923 p10.

1925, Henry submitted his resignation which took effect in May 1925.[904] This was preceded by the resignation of his son, Neil.

Of this revival, Dr Adams writes further,

> The Saunders strong evangelicalism with a passion for Keswick style holiness, evangelistic fervour and ardent commitment to dispensational premillennialism had brought them to experience empowerment attributed to the baptism of the Spirit with the evidence of speaking in tongues, but a relationship between Pentecostal pneumatology and Evangelical revivalism, which was evident in the revival, was a concept too difficult for traditional Evangelicals to accept.
>
> Through (the Rev.) E. B. Woods, the Pastor of Burnie Baptist Church, the Baptist Union made an effort to ensure there would be little room for a repeat of any Pentecostalism within the Baptist churches of northwest Tasmania. In a message on the "The Personal Ministry of the Holy Spirit", E. B. Woods taught the traditional Reformed view that regeneration is the Baptism of the Holy Spirit and he attacked Pentecostals and Pentecostalism. Further, Woods taught the Reformed view that the filling of the Holy Spirit is part of sanctification: "The secret of a Spirit-filled life is that we 'trust and obey' the Lord Jesus Christ as our Saviour and Master." Woods further surmised that little groups within the Christian Church fasten on to a few familiar New Testament phrases such as "The baptism of the Spirit", and make them into something like the watchwords and badges of a party. "This is the mistake of the Pentecostalist Church," added Woods. He continued, "The doctrine of the Holy Spirit has been taken up into the clouds, too often regarded as a matter for a select few, who can give more time and trouble to the cultivation of the Spiritual life. It has been connected with certain mystical notions which soar far above the heads of the average Christian and relate themselves somehow to the experiences of Pentecost. There is a craze for supernatural signs." Woods concluded that Pentecostalism was similar to the ancient mystery religions and modern day Theosophy.

Dr Adams concludes,

> This reassertion of traditional pneumatological teaching seems to have had the intended effect of curbing Pentecostal excess. Certainly the brief flirtation with Pentecostalism around the Sheffield district through the Saunders family did

---

[904] *Advocate* (Burnie) 27 May 1925 p4.

not result in any lasting movement. The district, in time, saw an increased "the close-the-ranks against Pentecostalism". Even to this day there is no Pentecostal church in Sheffield.

This staunch Evangelical opposition resulted in Tasmania being the last state in Australia to see the establishment of a formal Pentecostal church, and additionally, ensured that the Sheffield Revival (the first "Pentecostal" revival in Tasmania), was conveniently forgotten and remained hidden as part of the spiritual history of Tasmania.[905]

Writing in the Australian Baptist on the Tongues subject, Woods began his cutting article with these words,

> "Tongues" Menace. Here, on this North-West Coast of Tasmania, a promising work of God among our Methodist friends has been seriously menaced by an outbreak of "Tongues," and what looks like an attempt to introduce Pentecostalism, with its blighting, soul destroying influence into this district. It is our experience that wherever this movement gets a footing among the churches, it causes division and confusion (as did of old); and that when it passes (as it usually does), it leaves nothing but an aftermath of spiritual wreckage and reaction.
>
> The whole contention, that we can only be sure of having received the fullness of the Spirit by giving the supernatural sign of speaking in "tongues," is absolutely destitute of any basis in the Scriptures. It is a monstrous assumption, and a shameful reflection, not only upon all the earnest and devout believers of all the ages, but upon the great outstanding soul-winners, such as D. L. Moody, C. H. Spurgeon, General Booth, Wilbur Chapman, Dr. Torrey, Gipsy Smith, etc., who, repudiating such extravagant notions, have been used of God for the salvation of countless souls throughout the world. In view of such facts it can only be characterised as a subtle species of that Pharisaism which "puffs up" and does not "edify," either its votaries or its victims. I do not think, indeed, that our Baptist folk in these regions are in much danger of being ensnared; for they are, on the whole, too level-headed and warm-hearted, and I trust, too well grounded in the everlasting gospel.[906]

The Sheffield Baptist church and the Baptist Association were quick to invite back those who had resigned from membership and restore the

---

[905] "Lucas, an Evangelical History Review" No. 11, June 2018; Tasmanian Baptist Advance 2019. Tasmanian Baptists were given a fresh warning against tongues and the Pentecostals in 1931 after there had been a movement among the Methodists in the North West of the State. See AB 29 September 1931 p6, re Manley.

[906] AB 29 September 1931 p6.

former deacons back into office. There were those who felt the loss of Saunders' departure and even a decade later, remembered the revival fondly.

Following their removals, Neil was accepted as a student Pastor at Maldon Baptist Church in Victoria. He later became a Pentecostal evangelist and author. He then moved to a Presbyterian ministry where he had an influential career. There is no record of the occurrence of any Pentecostal activity on his part as a Presbyterian.[907]

Saunders Senior transferred to the Rainbow Baptist Church in Victoria for two years. From Victoria he returned to Queensland. There is no report of any Pentecostal activity in Henry's pastorates in the Sunshine State. His wife became the Queensland secretary of the Oriental Missionary Society. He saw out his days in active service in the Churches, namely at the Denison Street Rockhampton Baptist Church and as Superintendent of the Wood Street Mission. He was President of the Central Queensland Christian Endeavour Union. Because of ill health he resigned from the Rockhampton Church in January 1929. His next church was the Lanefield Baptist Church in Brisbane but again, this time in February 1949, he resigned because of ill health. Advancing years gradually slowed the tempo of Henry's energies. His death came after a brief illness on 26 February 1960. He had been a Baptist minister in full standing for forty-nine years.[908]

## Appendix 6: Pastor William Llewellyn Heaven

Following his leaving Sheffield Baptist Church, William Llewellyn Heaven only stayed for eighteen months at the Victorian town of Hopetoun which serves as the major service centre for the Southern Mallee area. He returned to Tasmania in June 1926 and to the Home Mission. He was stationed at Wynyard commencing 18 June. In August 1926 he preached an appropriate sermon, that of the Prodigal Son, he in a sense being the Prodigal Son.[909] He was appointed President of the Baptist Association for 1928/1929. As Secretary of the Minister's Fraternal Association in Wynyard, he wrote to the Table Cape Council,

> The Christian ministers of Wynyard wish to affirm the principle of the necessity of a stricter observance of the Lord's Day, as the Christian Sabbath. We view with alarm the growing disregard and lax observance of it in our district, believing that the

---

[907] Lucas June 2018.
[908] The Argus (Melbourne) 11 June 1925 p12; The Telegraph (Brisbane) 4 November 1933 p5, 28 January 1939 p22; Morning Bulletin (Rockhampton, Qld.) 19 June 1936 p11, 27 February 1937 p10; Daily Mercury (Mackay, Qld)

10 July 1937 p8; The Courier-Mail (Brisbane, Qld.) 30 May 1942 p4; AB 30 March 1960.
[909] Daily Telegraph (Launceston) 26 June 1926 p7; HM Minutes p122; Advocate (Burnie) 16 August 1928 p11, 1 November 1928 p4.

desecration of the Lord's Day is both dishonoring to God and inimical to the best interests of the community. We desire the co-operation of your council as far as may be toward that end.[910]

A couple of years later, in August 1931, the Ministers' Fraternal successfully lobbied the Table Cape Council to ban Sunday trading. Heaven's sermons were well reported in the local Advocate newspaper.[911]

The Home Mission Committee at this time was obviously not happy with Heaven's work and the Wynyard Church on hearing of this, sent an objection to what had been stated. Even so, in November 1931 the Home Mission Committee minutes record that the Committee was still not happy with the progress of the work and a year later, after six years at Wynyard, they transferred him to the Yolla Baptist Church, the Church to which those who were seeking to enter the ministry were usually sent to see if they were making the right life choice.[912] Farewell sermons were preached at Sheffield on 31 July 1932.

When Heaven commenced at the Yolla Baptist Church in August 1932, he was forty-four years of age. In April 1933, the Church and its outstations of Henrietta and Oonah, sent a protest to Parliament regarding the moving of the closing hour of liquor bars from 6pm to 10pm,

> That the members and congregation of this church are strongly opposed to any extension of hours of trading of hotel liquor bars, and take this opportunity of protesting against any attempt by Parliament to alter the hours unless it receives a mandate from the people of the State.[913]

Again, this time for 1933/1934 he was appointed President of the Baptist Association. Heaven conducted the funeral of Isabella Smith, the wife of Daniel Smith of "Sea View" who died on 1 November 1936. The Smiths had donated the land on which the Yolla chapel stands and it was in their dining room that services were held once the fellowship moved from the local school room. Heaven was farewelled from Yolla in June 1938 and he retired from the Christian ministry. The Baptist Union of Churches made him an Honorary Life Member after his thirty-six years of ministry having arrived in Tasmania twenty-nine years earlier; he was seventy-

---

[910] Advocate (Burnie) 13 November 1928 p16.

[911] Advocate (Burnie) 11 August 1931 p4. For one of Heaven's sermons in the series titled, "The Message of the Church" see Advocate (Burnie) 8 May 1929 p11. He asks and answers, "Do I belong to the Methodists, the Church of England, the Salvation Army, the Gospel Hall. His answer: "They are mine, as all other teachers under Christ are."

[912] HM Minutes p153, p166; see Laurence F Rowston, "God's Training Ground, the History of the Yolla Baptist Church".

[913] LEx 27 April 1933 p5.

one years of age. He had always been in charge of Home Mission causes.

Following his retirement, the Rev William Llewellyn Heaven and his wife Mary visited New Zealand. He died on 10 July 1944, seventy-seven years of age and had been in failing health since his retirement. He left behind Mary and their three sons, Ron, Bert, and Cliff; and their daughters, Muriel E. Bye and Daisy J. Hamilton.[914] He was buried in the Wynyard public cemetery. Mary died in 1958.

## Conclusion

As folk built their homes in the Sheffield District, in the "land of pork, peas and potatoes", there was also the desire to have a "House of God," a place where they could meet for fellowship and worship. There a number of them could experience the religious life they had known in England. I am referring to what could be called "the Myalla miracle" as given in this account. At Myalla some distance from the Sheffield township, a group of men of Baptist persuasion erected a Sunday school hall which would serve as a public school during the week and also a house of worship on Sunday. Within six months twenty-five children were attending the Sunday school. Then an approach was made to the Education Department for a State School teacher and soon one was provided. Allowing valuable space to sit empty six days a week is poor stewardship. Inward-focused churches that exist primarily for the benefit and use of their members are institutions of the past. Outward-focused churches that embrace their communities flourish. Effective churches have created multiple options to connect on days other than Sunday and offer their buildings as gifts to the community at nominal fees.

---

[914] Advocate (Burnie) 27 October 1933 p12, 2 November 1936 p2, 19 May 1938 p6; LEx 16 June 1938 p4; BCC July 1938 and August 1944.

# Chapter 11 Devonport Baptist Church

## Introduction

The Devonport Baptist History of 1948 sets the scene for a Baptist Church in the town sixty years earlier.

*11-1 Formby's original Anglican Church*

> Formby, a tiny village on the West (of the Mersey River), Torquay on the East. No port, no railway, unformed streets, no communal lighting, no modern amenities. There was no resident minister, no church building. Sunday services were held irregularly in the Protestant Hall, and sometimes in a building near where the Formby Hotel now stands. The Esplanade was the river bank, covered in shingle and unlighted. So Winter evenings were not conducive to attendance.

It was wrongly reported in 1885 that there were in Formby and Torquay sixteen church services every Sunday. A more correct report was given in 1888, that there was only one church and one shepherd who occasionally preached to about a dozen people. A later report in 1891, appears to be correct but it refers only to Formby. It reads, "We have Church of England, Wesleyan, Baptist, Congregational, and Salvation Army." But the report added, "All feebly supporting resident ministers."

The Anglicans had established a Church at Torquay (East Devonport) in the 1860s and their "temporary Mission Church" was opened in Brooke Street on 15 May 1887.[915] In 1860s, Congregational services began in Thomas Hainsworth's school room in Torquay and a Congregational Church building opened on 26 November 1871 on land given by George Best.[916] Best had commenced the first Congregational Sunday school in the town.[917] Wesleyan Methodist services in Torquay commenced in

---

[915] Information on 1860s church from Duncan; The North West Post (Formby) 12 May 1887.
[916] George Best associated with the Rev Henry Dowling when Dowling first arrived in VDL. See Baptists in Van Diemen's Land Parts 1 and 2.
[917] LEx 5 December 1871 p3, 21 August 1889 p3.

*11-2 Torquay's Wesleyan Methodist Church*

the courthouse in 1857 prior to the opening of their building on 29 August 1858. Wesleyan Methodist services also commenced in Formby the same year but their Formby building did not open until 6 October 1889.[918]

Before the Baptists arrived in Formby it was considered that those who lived there and further afield in the North West, that is, "the people behind the mountains", "live in almost heathen darkness for want of the Gospel light."[919] The Baptists were going to bring that light.

## Baptist Beginnings with the Rev Albert Hyde

The first Baptist service in Formby was held on 22 August 1888 in the rear room of Daniel Cowle's Hall with Pastor Harry Wood as preacher. Present were eight men and three women. Part of the minutes of the meeting read as follows:

There were present Messrs. Cowle, Carter, Pratt, Hiller, Priest, Marshall and Pierce, and three women: Mesdames Pratt, Marshall and Pierce; also Mr. Adams of Launceston. Mr. Marshall was voted to the chair and read the advertisement convening the meeting and also stating its object, which was: To take into consideration the further development of Christian life and work, and also the advisability of establishing in Formby a Sabbath Morning Service. After Mr. Marshall had addressed the meeting and prayer had been offered ... Mr. Pierce proposed and Mr. Hiller seconded the following resolution: That a Baptist service be held on Sunday morning. This proposal was adopted and a committee consisting of Messrs. Pierce, Hiller, Marshall and Priest was appointed to carry out the resolution.[920]

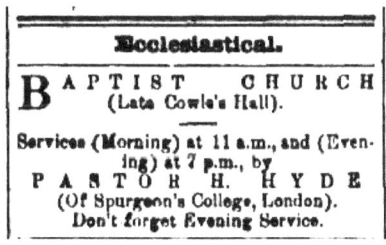

---

[918] The North West Post (Formby) 1 December 1908 p3; Cornwall Chronicle (Launceston) 18 August 1858 p7. Stansall p67.
[919] LEx 4 July 1885 p4, 21 February 1891; in The North West Post (Formby) of 30 March 1889

p2, only four services were advertised. Day-Star April 1890; SB 16 June 1898 p134.
[920] The Devonport Baptist History of 1948; The Mercury (Hobart) 12 February 1887 p1.

This structure recently built by Daniel George Cowle, on the corner of Stewart Street and Rooke Lane, was at that time referred to as the "Protestant Hall" because it was being used by Protestants. Cowle associated with the Baptists for some years assisting them greatly.[921]

*11-3 East Devonport: Torquay*

Since Cowle's Hall was in use by others on Sunday mornings, Wood took his small gathering down to the lower end of Stewart Street to the newly built Saloon of William Buck. Although it had a hairdressing saloon in the front, it served until 1900 as a general meeting place. At the first service in the Saloon Wood sat near to the billiard table and took as his text Luke 22.31, "Satan hath desired to have you, that he may sift you as wheat." The hymn, "To God be the Glory" followed. [922] Here they met for a time.

Then the Rev Albert Hyde of the Latrobe Church was commissioned to replace Wood and oversee the work while continuing his work at Latrobe; he commenced on 4 November 1888 but there was no remuneration for his efforts from Formby.[923] The Daily Telegraph gave some free publicity,

> Mr. W. G. Buck ... has now completed his billiard room and haircutting saloon ... The building is of brick ... The billiard room is now being used on Sundays as a place of worship. Pastor (Hyde) under the Union of Baptists of Tasmania, holds services every Sunday at 3 p.m. I wonder if any of the naughty youths, in looking at the billiard table on Sundays, wish they were having a game. It is to be hoped not.

In time the Baptists reverted to Cowle's Hall, it and Buck's Saloon being just two of the few halls in

---

[921] Daniel George Cowle was one of the best-known of Devonport's public men. He figured as being one of those advocating the extension of the railway to Formby from Deloraine, and gave the address of welcome to the Minister of Lands and Works on the occasion of the celebration of its opening. He for many years figured in every public movement at Devonport, being a member of the Road Trust and afterwards of the first Town Board, while he also figured as judge of the regatta events. He was a justice of the peace for many years. Advocate (Burnie) 26 January 1927 p2. In time Cowle added an abutting hall to the rear of the building and this was used by the Technical School (note of June 1892) and this abutment was demolished when the erection of the Tabernacle commenced. See the laying of the foundation stone photograph which shows only part of the rear hall demolished. Cowle's Hall itself was retained and formed part of the Baptist property. Years later when the Town Council purchased the Tabernacle, Cowle's Hall was demolished to make room for a toilet block.

[922] Advocate (Burnie) 24 July 1935 p2; The Devonport Baptist History of 1948.

[923] Day-Star December 1888; The North West Post (Formby) 3 November 1888 p2.

town used for recreational purposes.[924] The venture was the limit of Baptist work in that part of Tasmania at the time.

On 6 December 1888, the Church was formally constituted with a membership of eight.[925] R. W. Pierce, the local school master, was appointed Secretary and R. R. Marshall as Treasurer. The Church affiliated with the Baptist Union. Hyde's stipend was £40 per year. Every Sunday he rode to church on a horse, hired by the church for his use at three shillings per day.

By July 1889, the Baptists commenced a Sunday school and it soon had fifty scholars on the roll with eight teachers. The first anniversary of the Sunday school was held on 15 December 1889.[926]

They found Cowle's Hall to their liking and for a time Cowle made it rent free. The Devonport Baptists too had Latrobe's "cargo cult" mentality expecting the Gibsons to provide a building for them which eventually the Gibsons did in September 1889 by donating £450 of the £500 price tag for Cowle's Hall. The purchase took place in April 1889; it could comfortably seat 250 people and had two vestries.[927]

They soon erected a lamp outside with its rays shining directly on their church door, that is, on the door to Cowle's hall. The hall then was officially opened as a Baptist house of worship on 21 June 1890 and it became known as the "Baptist Hall". Cowle was still associating with the Baptists. The hall was nearly new and was in every way suitable for the Fellowship.[928] A new organ was soon acquired and a baptistry installed.

As the 1889 year drew to a close there was every sign of vibrant life. The Sunday school now had sixty-five scholars. On Monday evenings there was a prayer and Bible study. Wednesday evenings there was worship and singing practice. Friday evenings seventy were attending the young people's meeting at Hyde's residence.[929]

On 27 October 1889, the Church, still under Hyde's leadership, commenced Sunday afternoon services over the Mersey River in the Torquay Town Hall; the attendance was encouraging. No other regular afternoon church services were being held in Torquay at the time.[930] The Church also commenced monthly church services at Teasdale and Co.'s coal mine

---

[924] The North West Post (Formby) 22 September 1887 p2.
[925] Day-Star May 1889 p67. The foundation membership: Mr. and Mrs. Sicklemore, Mr. and Mrs. R W Pierce, Mrs. Hiller, Mr. and Mrs. R R Marshall and Rev Hyde.
[926] The North West Post (Formby) 17 December 1889 p2.
[927] The North West Post (Formby) 16 April 1887 p3; Day-Star August 1889 p125.
[928] LEx 1 July 1891, Day-Star May 1889, August 1889, May 1890; AB 31 May 1903.
[929] Day-Star October 1889.
[930] Daily Telegraph (Launceston) 29 October 1889 p2.

which was situated about one and a half miles from the Dulverton siding, itself three kms away from Railton. There they raised a little "Tabernacle in the wilderness". On 9 March 1890, they also commenced services at Ulverstone which eventually led to the formation of a Baptist Church. Then a branch work commenced at Spreyton in 1890 with Hyde still at Latrobe heading up the Devonport work and this also led to the formation of a church. In April 1890, the Rev Thomas Spurgeon preached in the Devonport Baptist Church.[931]

In 1890 a public vote was taken in the town on whether to unite Torquay and Formby into one estuary town and on its agreement the Formby Baptist Church changed its name to the Devonport Baptist Church.

For the public meeting of the Church's Anniversary in July 1890 Cowle was chairman. But by the end of the year the work faltered and evening services ceased. Hyde relinquished the oversight of the Devonport Church in April 1891 "in the hope that a more genial climate would be more favourable to his health, and restore him from the distressing malady to which he was subject."[932] For him "a sojourn in a warmer climate during the winter months (was) very desirable."[933] The secretary of the Church, R. W. Pierce, stepped down in April 1891 due to the loss of an eye. Hyde resigned in May 1891 for health reasons creating a pastoral vacancy for a year.

At this time Cowle made another generous gesture: the offer to the church to buy the adjoining land for £300; it had its own building. The offer was accepted and the church now had a schoolroom.[934]

The Launceston Examiner reported that for Sunday 4 October 1891 there was no Baptist service adding, "for want of both preacher and congregation". At the time the Church was using a Congregational preacher. A cry went out, "May we insert here (in our monthly report to Day Star) that any assistance from wealthy Baptists, in aid of a struggling church, will be thankfully received." The prospects were not sufficiently promising to induce the Council of the Union to settle a pastor even though Mary Ann Gibson gave £50 for the provision of

---

[931] The North West Post (Formby) 22 April 1890 p2.
[932] SB 31 March 1898 p82.

[933] Daily Telegraph (Launceston) 9 April 1891 p2; BU Council Minutes p24/2.
[934] The Mercury (Hobart) 10 April 1891 p4. This would have been the land on which the Tabernacle is built.

one. Latrobe's John Chamberlain, then commenced afternoon services and in January 1893, the morning and evening services were resumed.

By July 1893, other Baptist preachers were being utilised and the congregational numbers increased with the church full at times. One of these interims was the Melbourne Baptist College student, son of the Rev Edward E Harris, who stayed for the three months of his college vacation.[935] With his departure the church was practically closed and only occasional services were held. Many members had left; a few were "holding the fort". Further, Wood ministering at Latrobe declined the pastorate. Yet the Sunday school continued and its Anniversary was held in December 1894. Throughout all this, the Spreyton work, "this little cause", continued.[936]

## The Rev George James Mackay

In April 1896, under the supervision of Harry Wood now at Latrobe, George James Mackay "for a period of twelve months" was given the task of restoring the Devonport venture, restarting "as a mission station in connection with the Latrobe church." He had relinquished his position in the Hobart legal office. On 5 February 1897, Cowle's Hall which was closed reopened and afternoon services commenced with Wood preaching. The Sunday school recommenced with Edwin Thomas Clements as Superintendent.[937] Cowle's Hall was now designated the "Baptist Tabernacle". On 10 June 1897, the Devonport Church was reconstituted. Cowle's Hall was also thoroughly renovated using the rents of the brick hall adjoining the Cowle's structure.

*11-4 George James Mackay*

Mackay's gifts were many. He was "an acceptable preacher possessing qualities which made him a welcome guest in every farmer's house, an organist musical to his finger tips, capable of training a choir or, in Alexandrian fashion, compelling a congregation to sing." These valued abilities filled many with high hopes, that he would have a fruitful career. At Sunday school anniversaries Mackay "ably trained the children to sing their special hymns in a manner that reflected the

---

[935] The North West Post (Formby) 5 December 1893 p2.
[936] LEx 10 October 1891, 20 October 1891, 19 November 1892 p5, 11 December1894, 10 April 1896.
[937] Daily Telegraph (Launceston) 10 February 1897 p5; Day-Star March 1897; The North West Post (Formby) 15 June 1897 p2, 13 January 1898 p2, 27 January 1898 p2.

highest credit on the scholars and him." In December 1897, there were fifty-nine scholars on the roll with four teachers.[938] A month earlier Wood visited for a baptismal service and after he had explained at length the scripturalness of baptism by immersion,

> He then retired, and reappeared in a black robe, and descended into a tank of water in the centre of the platform. Three candidates, each attired in a long robe, were immersed, a verse of a hymn being sung as each was put under the water.[939]

In that short time the cause was completely resuscitated. The congregations became the largest in the town. Mackay's natural abilities and winning manner endeared him to his people even though he had arrived with no pastoral experience.[940]

At the commencement of 1898, Mackay resigned to take up two years of studies at the Baptist College in Melbourne. This was made possible by the generosity of Joshua T. Soundy. Fellow students who entered College in that year were Horace H. Jeffs, P. J. Masters, M. L. Murphy, E. L. Watson. In 1897, the Devonport church assumed full responsibility for the work at Spreyton. A few years later, in 1908, the Spreyton services enthusiastically recommenced. On 4 August 1909 the foundation stones were laid for the Spreyton building.

## The Rev John Edwin Walton

At the close of his ten year ministry at Perth in 1898, instead of returning to England as he had originally intended,[941] the Rev John Edwin Walton took up the Home Mission work in Devonport. Tasmanian Baptist Council had expressed strongly that he should remain in the Colony. He commenced on 6 February 1898.

During his two year Devonport ministry, he consolidated the work on ordinary church lines, with twenty members joining the church bringing the membership up to forty-three. At the commencement of his second year, the Launceston Examiner reported,

> The faithful preaching of the pastor had been much appreciated, and the need of a larger building on Sunday evenings is often felt. The Sunday-school was in a flourishing condition, the Endeavour Society had been well attended lately, and the work of

---

[938] Daily Telegraph (Launceston) 15 December 1897 p8.
[939] The North West Post (Formby) 6 November 1897 p2.
[940] The Mercury (Hobart) 20 January 1898 p4; A J Stokes' first-hand and lengthy account of the first years of the Church, see SB 31 March 1898 p82.
[941] Tasmanian News (Hobart) 14 September 1897 p4.

tract distribution had met with an encouraging reception by many who attended no place of worship.⁹⁴²

Monthly temperance meetings continued. There were 116 Sunday school scholars as against fifty-nine a year earlier. For special events the Church used the Town Hall. In Walton's second year a manse was provided through the generosity of Mary Ann Gibson, to the sum of £800,⁹⁴³ and she also gave £310 toward the cost of an envisaged larger place of worship which would become a reality in 1904.

In the local press Walton railed against "The Wicked Work of Palmistry." He wrote, "No two palmists will agree in the reading of the hand; how, then, can we trust them? The Good Old Book says it is wrong to consult these folk." At a Baptist Assembly later that year he continued in this vein on gambling, liquor traffic, and cigarette smoking by youths and also on sacerdotalism, "much to the delight of the delegates".⁹⁴⁴

J. H. Stephens of the Australian Evangelistic Society visited early in 1899 as did Miss Allen Arnold, returned Baptist missionary from India, who was visiting the churches. She had with her a number of children dressed in Indian native costume.

Walton was not one for Christmas observance insisting that there was no scriptural command for such and he was "not much in favour of church festivals of this sort".⁹⁴⁵

On his farewell meeting on 25 February 1900, the local paper said, "Broad-minded, liberal, and always ready with a hearty greeting, Walton has justly established himself as a favourite, and all denominations regret his departure." During his time the Church membership had grown to forty and the Church was packed on Sunday evenings.⁹⁴⁶ The Church, like many others, was making use of the Australasian Evangelistic Society.

In Tasmania, he was a member of the Council of the Tasmanian Baptist Union. He was chosen President twice, he was inter-colonial

*11-5 Rev John Walton*

---

⁹⁴² LEx 8 February 1899 p3.
⁹⁴³ NWA&EBT 13 January 1903 p2.
⁹⁴⁴ LEx 9 February 1899 p3; SB May 4 1899 p97. Sacerdotalism is the belief that priests are meant to be mediators between God and humankind.
⁹⁴⁵ NWA&EBT 17 March 1899 p2; SB 29 December 1898 p295.
⁹⁴⁶ Day-Star February 1898.

representative to the Victorian Baptist Union; and for several years he was Secretary to the Union, and Assistant Editor and then Editor of The Day Star (1887-1894). For the first five years of the Southern Baptist he was the Tasmanian Editor.[947]

Walton also was taking a leading part in the Christian Endeavour movement. He had been on the Council of the Australasian Union, and was first President for two successive years of the North-West Coast District Union of Tasmania.

Walton returned to England in May 1900 and was a delegate to the International Christian Endeavour Union meetings at the Alexandra Palace in London. In the years that followed it is impossible to assess what the Christian Endeavour Societies have meant to our churches. This Society provided a steady flow of young life with its fervour and expectation into the life of the church, young workers of incalculable value.

On the voyage to England he and others formed a Sunday school and a Christian Endeavour Society. He also conducted Sunday evening services and daily morning family worship.[948] The family returned to Tasmania in July 1901 for him to take charge of the Latrobe Church.

## The Rev George James Mackay's Second Devonport Pastorate

On returning to Devonport in March 1900, the Rev George James Mackay often made use of the Magic Lantern and gave a lecture on "Marvellous Melbourne". In the press he continued the fierce debate against Devonport's "sacrilegious" Sunday night concerts writing, "Are we, as citizens, joined to allow travelling companies to use our hall on Sundays to give concerts, which are far from sacred? Surely we can keep one day out of seven free from performances, such as was given last (Sunday) night." Later he questioned whether the Latrobe Federal Band should be allowed to hold sacred concerts on Sunday afternoons. He successfully closed down these Sunday performances. Mackay also headed up a protest against the opening of a new hotel in the town. For this he was accused of being a "meddlesome minister" and a "dog". Again, he and those who joined the protest were successful. At its outcome, it was reported that

> "the applicant thought so little of his prospects that he wagered a £1 to a shilling that he would be unsuccessful, so that he was as much surprised as other folk. He left for Launceston by the next

---

[947] LEx 14 December 1894 p5.

[948] S&T 1900/489; Tasmanian News (Hobart) 14 March 1900 p2; NWA&EBT 13 September 1900 p1.

train, carrying the plans with him."⁹⁴⁹

To a crowded congregation on one Sunday evening, Mackay spoke on "The Morals of Devonport" saying,

> Every week he had wives and children appealing to him for assistance, whose husbands and fathers had drunk their earnings instead of taking them home; private persons were also cognisant of an amount of Sunday drinking being carried on. Adultery and immorality, he declared, were only too common.⁹⁵⁰

*11-6 The laying of the Foundation Stone on 3 Sept 1903; Cowle's Hall to the left*

In 1903, Mackay and the Rev Samuel Harrison were instrumental in commencing a Baptist work in Ulverstone in the Town Hall. The town of Ulverstone witnessed a baptism by immersion, probably the first in the town.⁹⁵¹

In June 1903, the Devonport Baptist Church's Band of Hope and its Sunday school joined with the Devonport Rechabites, Good Templars, Salvation Army and other local Sunday schools for a torch-light Temperance Demonstration procession through the town.⁹⁵²

Mackay also commenced Sunday services at Forth in March 1904. On a Monday evening Mackay arranged an adult recitation competition and the response was that "Cowle's Hall" was so crowded that many were unable to gain admission.⁹⁵³ With his musical interests, Mackay became secretary for the examinations in the town held in connection with the Conservatorium of Music of the Melbourne University and in 1905 editor of the Baptist publications, "Daydawn and Baptist Church Messenger". He was also honorary secretary of the Devonport Benevolent Society, President of the Baptist Union in 1906. A lecture, "The Thrilling Account of Ten nights in a Bar Room" illustrated by a number of life size coloured pictures, was one of his favourites

---

⁹⁴⁹ NWA&EBT 11 October 1900 p2, 12 December 1900 p2, 16 October 1902 p2, 5 May 1903 p3; NWA&EBT 8 May 1903 p3, 13 September 1904 p2; The Mercury (Hobart) 8 August 1903 p6.
⁹⁵⁰ NWA&EBT 22 September 1903 p2.

⁹⁵¹ NWA&EBT 14 March 1903 p2; 11 August 1903 p2.
⁹⁵² SB 14 July 1903.
⁹⁵³ NWA&EBT 5 March 1904 p2, 13 July 1904 p2; LEx 5 November 1903.

Lessons from our first 20 years

during this Presidential year.[954] Mackay's work was so effective that the Church considered either to spend £400 to enlarge Cowle's Hall or spending an estimated £800 in erecting a new Tabernacle inclusive of extra land, furniture, etc. Two years before his leaving in February 1906, £860 had been raised for the latter.[955]

*11-7 The Devonport Tabernacle adjoining Cowle's Hall*

Having decided on a new Tabernacle, the two stones were laid by William Gibson Junior and Joshua T. Soundy, Soundy being the President of the Baptist Union. The giving for the day raised £60; it would be the largest church in Devonport. The additional land needed at the rear was purchased for £90.[956]

This new brick Stewart Street Church building was opened on 22 April 1904 by the Rev Samuel Pearce Carey of the Collins St. Baptist Church, Melbourne. The debt on the building at the opening was £840; it had cost £1226 with S. Priest senior, a member of the church, as the builder. At the end of 1898, again with thanks to the generosity of Mary Ann Gibson, the Church debt had been reduced but this structure which had been designed to meet the demands of a growing town for years to come placed it under heavy financial obligations and possibly without expressing it, it was built in the hope that Mackay would be staying on for a good number of years.[957]

When it came, Mackay's resignation was a "grievous" shock as it was understandably considered that his work in Devonport was not yet complete. This is a mistake many a church has made as the prosperity of the work at the time is based on a unique individual whose departure so often will bring a downturn. At his farewell it was reported that "during the whole of his ministry there had not been one jarring note in his

---

[954] Day-Dawn August 1905; "Ten nights in a bar room" is a melodramatic story by T. S. Arthur, published in 1854. It became a favourite text for temperance lecturers, and was popular in the dramatic version by William W. Pratt (1858). Its temperance song by Henry Clay Work, "Come Home, Father," begins, "Father, dear father, come home with me now, The clock in the belfry strikes one"; NWA&EBT 16 June 1905 p2.

[955] BU Council Minutes p263/26; NWA&EBT 4 March 1904 p2.
[956] SB 29 September 1903; The North West Post (Formby) 15 October 1891 p2, 3 September 1903 p2.
[957] SB 1 November 1904 p245; NWA&EBT 8 February 1899 p2; Day-Dawn 31 May 1900.

relationship with the church."⁹⁵⁸ He was farewelled on 4 February 1906.

## The Rev Albert Metters

On 4 March 1906, the day of the welcome to the Rev Albert Metters at the Church, a banner over the platform displayed the words, "Welcome to our Pastor".⁹⁵⁹ He had become familiar to them as a preacher during his time at Perth and even preached at Mackay's farewell. It was rightly said to those who had gathered that evening by the President of the Baptist Union of Tasmania, the Rev Robert Williamson,

> They would find Mr. Metters an honest man and an honest preacher; a fearless man, who would tell them the truth whether it pleased them or not, and who was above the little tricks of some ministers, and would not condescend to them to create a sensation. Mr. Metters was a man of stainless character, which was one of the first qualifications for a minister. He had done good work in Perth.⁹⁶⁰

The Rev Samuel P. Carey was the visiting guest to the Annual Baptist Assembly that year and he gave his own assessment of Metters,

> It was delightful to me to study Bro Metters. He has a Baptist's instinctive dread of exclusive restriction, and he watches "the seventy" (the leadership of the Mormon Church) as a cat a mouse. But his fighting is so frank, and so just-minded, unirritating and brotherly that he makes himself increasingly beloved and trusted all the time.⁹⁶¹

*11-8 Alfred Metters*

In his reply to the welcome Metters said he wanted to make his pulpit his throne, and to go amongst their homes, and deserve some of the nice things they had said about him."⁹⁶²

That month Harvest Festival was celebrated. Speaking with careful words on the parable of the Prodigal son Metters declared,

> The parable of .the prodigal son showed how the young man had sowed his wild oats, and had reaped the natural harvest. The same was being done to-day, but it all ended at the swine trough.

---

⁹⁵⁸ Day-Dawn November 1905; The North West Post (Formby) 5 February 1906 p2.
⁹⁵⁹ NWA&EBT 5 March 1906 p2.
⁹⁶⁰ The North West Post (Formby) 8 March 1906 p3.
⁹⁶¹ SB 15 May 1906 p122.
⁹⁶² LEx 9 March 1906 p3.

The earth was full of anomalies and one of these was the fact that there were both fullness of bread and starving people. There were certain modern conditions of life that fell far from the Divine ideal - an ideal that would some day be realised, when multi-millionaires and starving people would not always be. He was not a believer in the exaggerated form of Socialism, but he did believe there would be a different distribution of food by and by, not perhaps in the manner advocated by some ardent reformers, but in God's own way and in God's time. There was something seriously wrong in their social laws when one could starve and others have enough and to spare, and he believed that if a man was willing to work, there should be something for him to eat. It was not so to-day.

In poetical words, he continued speaking on God's goodness,

> Nature's witness to God speaks in the harvest: of His power, beneficence and purpose. Nature was a book of symbols, and testified to the unwearied energy of God. Harvest results largely depended upon the soil, and so we do not see more direct results from the preaching of the good seed, because men's hearts were not prepared to receive it. The purpose of God's goodness was to "fill our hearts with food and gladness," and to satisfy our heartbeat aspirations.[963]

Within the month he had written to the local press on subjects dear to his heart,

> The twin evils of strong drink and gambling are very properly linked together by your ardent eulogist of "Tattersall". If he will study history he will find that among the causes of national decay alcohol and gambling have ever ranked chief. Destroy the moral ideals of a people and it is only a matter of time when "Ichabod" must be written. The story of the rise of "Tattersall" reflects no credit on our financiers and statesmen.[964]

Metters was on the Committee of the Devonport Library. He also worked towards the realization of the Local Option for Devonport, which would put the control of the liquor traffic into the hands of the people and not the politicians; that the people should have a say on whether licences in their town be issued or not. In 1906, he was appointed Chaplain (4th Class) with the Chaplains' Department of the Australian Military Forces.[965] It was

---

[963] NWA&EBT 26 March 1906 p2.

[964] NWA&EBT 28 March 1906 p4; Ichabod is mentioned in the first Book of Samuel. On the day that the Israelites' Ark of God was taken into Philistine captivity, Eli's daughter-in-law names her child Ichabod, saying, "The glory is departed from Israel." Ichabod is a male given name from a Hebrew word meaning "without honour" and expresses regret at a loss of former glory or high standards.

[965] LEx 8 March 1906 p5, 21 June 1906 p3; The Mercury (Hobart) 13 April 1906 p6.

an appointment that followed him in his subsequent moves.

All too soon he resigned, in March 1907. The twelve months had been cordial and harmonious in every way but he had found the winter climate there as in Perth too rigorous for him. The church was also to lose his wife Ottilie who had worked with the Girls' Guild and the Bible Class girls on Sundays.[966] The debt reduction had been very much on the Church's mind with the installation of a debt reduction thermometer and the holding of fairs to bring it down and raise the thermometer's mercury. The Rev Frederick James Miles of Boulder Western Australia was Metter's replacement.

## Appendixes:

### Appendix 1: The Rev Alfred Hyde

Following his time at the Latrobe Baptist Church, the Rev Alfred Hyde commenced at the Hamilton Baptist Church in Victoria in August 1891. The energy he displayed in the work

*11-9 Hussey's Bible-Selling Book Store*

gave every reason to believe that he would remain with them for many years for the church prospered in every way following his arrival. He took an interest in every department of the church's work, including the branch at North Hamilton, and was the means of establishing a new branch with a flourishing Sunday school at South Hamilton. He was able to instil a spirit of work and enthusiasm into the young people and he formed a successful Christian Endeavour Society. Twenty-two persons, mostly young men, were baptised. His wife proved herself a true minister's helpmate, and, by unceasing efforts for the welfare of the church, won the esteem of all who knew her. But Hyde was compelled to leave in early 1893.[967]

At the time Henry Hussey recorded in his Diary,

> I made arrangements for another trip to Victoria, and left Adelaide by train on February 7, intending to try a different route to any I had taken previously. (In) Hamilton, I was met by the Rev A. and Mrs. Hyde. As Mr. Hyde was going to Portland, to conduct anniversary services there on the following day, it had been decided that I should occupy his pulpit. I took the morning and evening services, and lectured on the Lord's Coming in the afternoon, each gathering being largely attended ... Hamilton, I was informed, was too damp and

---

[966] Daily Telegraph (Launceston) 4 March 1907 p7; AB 13 November 906 p280.

[967] Hamilton Spectator 15 August 1891 p4, 13 April 1893 p3.

cold for him in the winter, and I strongly recommended the climate of South Australia as more likely to suit him. Shortly after I returned from Victoria, Mr. Hyde paid a visit to South Australia, and accepted the pastorate of the Baptist Church at Goodwood.

Hyde pastored the Goodwood Baptist Church from 1893-1898, with the 1895-1898 years part-time.[968] Like Hussey, Hyde was a strong Dispensationalist.[969] He spoke at the twenty-first annual Second Advent Meetings in Adelaide on the subject, "Christ is coming to complete our salvation," pointing to the resurrection of the body as the consummation of the "blessed hope" that would not take place till the second coming of Christ. In September 1901, in connection with another Second Advent Meeting, Hyde "discoursed on the beauty of the coming bridegroom."[970] In 1895, Hyde bought the stock of Hussey's Bible selling business in Flinders Street, Adelaide.

Hussey's Diary records the sale,

> I began the (1895) year in much weakness, and considered it necessary to make some change with reference to the Bible Hall. As time went on there were two applications made for the business ... In August I entered into, and concluded, negotiations with one of these (Mr. A. Hyde), who had a strong desire to be engaged in a business of this kind. Mr. Hyde having taken new premises in Flinders Street, opposite to Stow Church, arrangements were made to clear out (the stock) by the end of August ... My successor obtained much better premises at little more than a third of the rent that I had paid, which, of course, gave him a good start.[971]

Hyde was involved with the Flinders Street Baptist Church being chairman of the Young Men's Bible Class. His energy in these years showed no bounds. He was also reporter for the Southern Baptist and its business manager for the Baptist Union of South Australia. By December 1896, still as Pastor of Goodwood, he oversaw a new Church at Richmond. Even so he had to resign from the Goodwood Church in April 1896 because of poor health and reverted to just the Pastorate at the Richmond Church.[972]

He then pastored Hussey's Bentham Street Christian Church for twelve months following Hussey's

---

[968] The Advertiser (Adelaide) 22 July 1893 p6.
[969] Dispensationalism maintains that history is divided into multiple ages.
[970] The Advertiser (Adelaide) 6 September 1894 p6; The Register (Adelaide) 3 September 1901 p3.
[971] Hussey was required to restore his run-down premises before he left.
[972] The Advertiser (Adelaide) 8 January 1894 p6; South Australian Chronicle 20 April 1895 p7; South Australian Register 11 September 1895 p3; Adelaide Observer 19 September 1896 p14.

departure.[973] After Bentham Street, Hyde and his wife, Sarah, made considerable improvements to the Wayville Baptist Church.[974] The income from Bible sales and the sale of the business in 1913 allowed him now to work as worker pastor. For twelve months he was the honorary pastor for Black Forest Baptist Church in suburban Adelaide. Within the first year a building was erected with a church membership of twenty-seven and the Sunday school of 121 scholars with sixteen teachers.[975] Then two years later, he took on the growing sea-side resort of Brighton. Within the first year Hyde bought land for a church building, a Sunday school hall and a manse. The church was formed with nineteen foundation members. But again his failing health compelled him to relinquish the work. Tasmanian, the Rev Herbert Davies Archer followed him. Not long after Hyde spear-headed a branch church three kms along the coast at South Plymouth and donated £25 towards the purchase of land and soon a building was erected and a Sunday school opened.[976]

Then the Hydes involved themselves for nine months in the opening of the new Baptist Sunday School Hall at Seacliff and soon headed up a new Baptist cause at Brighton. They then returned to the Black Forest Church for just over a year. The Rev Alfred Hyde died on 13 April 1933 while in Sydney.[977]

## Appendix 2: The Rev George James Mackay

On the Church scene the Rev George J. Mackay was like a bright night time comet that blazed for many years but then went out. He first appeared on the Tasmanian Baptist scene when arrivals from the Pastors' College were dwindling in number. He was soon a celebrated evangelist and pastor in both Tasmanian and Victorian Churches and one wonders whether his time in War service dimmed the contrast between black and white and good and evil and made the old certainties less certain.

During the decidedly evangelical ministry of the Rev James Blaikie at the Hobart Tabernacle five members entered into full time Christian work. Two would have profound effect, one in Victoria and the other in New South Wales. One of these was George James Mackay who was employed in the legal profession for five years. He was born in Hobart on 9 January 1875 to George and Nellie Mackay. He came to the Hobart Tabernacle from the Primitive Methodists on their amalgamation of the Wesleyan Methodist and United

---

[973] The Express and Telegraph (Adelaide) 16 February 1901 p4; The Advertiser (Adelaide) 5 October 1908 p9.
[974] The Advertiser (Adelaide) 21 May 1910 p18.
[975] The Advertiser (Adelaide) 14 June 1913 p8; Hughes p182

[976] Hughes p185, 187; The Register (Adelaide) 15 January 1916 p5.
[977] The Mail 17 July 1915 p22, 16 November 1918 p11; Daily Herald (Adelaide) 25 December 1915 p7; The Express and Telegraph (Adelaide) 19 September 1916 p3; The Register (Adelaide) 7 February 1920 p10.

Lessons from our first 20 years

Free Methodist Church in 1902 and, further, his views on baptism had changed. He was converted when a youth under the preaching of the Rev Joseph Tanner Piercey. In 1896, he was secretary of the Christian Endeavour Union of Tasmania.[978] He became a member of the Hobart Baptist Church in February 1897, the same month he transferred to the Devonport Baptist Church to work under the supervision of Pastor Harry Wood. His soul winning zeal, his unmistakable fitness for the work of the ministry and his evangelical preaching had impressed the Baptists of Tasmania and especially Joshua T. Soundy of the Hobart Church. Mackay married Ellen Winter (1871–1947) on 18 July 1900 at Richmond, Victoria.[979]

**Following his pastorates at the Devonport Church**, Mackay accepted a call to the George Street Church at Fitzroy in Melbourne. At his commencement congregations only averaged about seventy but in less than six months they had increased to 600, quite filling the spacious building. During his time eighty persons joined the membership. On 3 July 1910, under denominational pressure, he assumed charge of the Home Mission Church at Northcote which had commenced four years earlier.

*11-10 Fairfield's Church Building-in a day*

In two years the cause was firmly established, and the membership more than doubled to sixty-six. The Sunday school had 212 scholars.[980]

While at Northcote in October 1911 Mackay and Rev Horace H. Jeffs of Clifton Hill Baptist Church commenced services in a private house in Fairfield. They then participated in the erection of a church building in one day with the foundations for the new church laid the afternoon of 11 October, and a week later 130 volunteers worked all day and finished the building by 10 pm. For the occasion the women prepared 1000 meals to feed the workers. The church at Fairfield was constituted in 1912.[981]

---

[978] Day-Star December 1896; Daily Telegraph (Launceston) 1 October 1896 p2; The North West Post (Formby) 27 January 1898 p 2; AB 4 October 1921 p6.
[979] The Age (Melbourne) 28 July 1900 p5.

[980] NWA&EBT 1 March 1906 p2 reporting on Mackay's private letters, 20 August 1906 p2, 14 October 1910 p3; Wilkin p167.
[981] Fairfield Baptist Church, source Darebin Heritage; Wilkin p171.

In August 1912, Mackay was appointed as Director of Victorian Home Missions and as such the following year he commenced services in the Sandringham Town Hall constituting the Church on 11 October 1914 with seventeen members. He withdrew from the Home Mission leadership position in January 1916 to work abroad as a chaplain to the A.I.F. Later during the War he was stationed at Broadmeadows Camp. In March 1918 he was appointed as temporary evangelist with the Victorian Baptist Union. In 1919, he resigned from ministry and entered business as an estate agent utilizing his legal background of earlier years. Even so he continued on as honorary evangelist with the Home Mission and was honorary pastor of the Sandringham Church from 1919 to 1923.[982]

In 1922, he stood as the local Democratic Nationalist candidate for Batman but was unsuccessful. In April 1924 he began a part-time ministry at the Westgarth Baptist Church. Then he was honorary pastor of the Albert Park Baptist Church from 1926 to June 1929. For fourteen years he was on the Loans and Sustentation Committee of the Baptist Union.[983] His love of singing came to the fore in concerts even before he enlisted in 1916 and then in 1924 he gave his time to Community Singing. It was reported of him, "whose voice and contagious mirth are known throughout the length and breadth of Australia and beyond ... the merry badinage of Mr. Mackay, even those who would tell one at any other time that they could not sing a note, were soon blending their voices with the ones of those of greater courage."[984] This interest took on intensity in the early 1930s with public gatherings sometimes numbering three times a week. He also had his own programme on Melbourne radio station 3LO. The Rev George James Mackay died on 21 January 1965 at Brunswick,

*11-11 The completed Fairfield's Church*

---

[982] The Herald (Melbourne) 10 June 1918 p4; The Argus (Melbourne) 26 March 1918 p6, 7 August 1923 p10; The Age (Melbourne) 14 March 1918 p8; Spectator and Methodist Chronicle 20 March 1918 p288; AB 4 October 1921 p6;The Rev JD Williams, a colleague of his both at the Hobart Baptist Church and in ministry in Victoria remarked in an interview with me that what drew him away from his early church pastoral work was that during the War he partook of what in earlier years he railed against at temperance meetings: strong drink.
[983] Newsletter of the Victorian Baptist Historical Society Issue 35, November 2001.
[984] The Age (Melbourne) 17 November 1922 p10; The Gippsland Farmers' 21 July 1914 p2; The Argus (Melbourne) 9 July 1924 p9; Frankston and Somerville Standard 21 December 1929 p1.

Victoria, aged ninety years. He was husband of Ellen, father of Lorna Kathleen, John Clifford, Keith Wilbur, and Hillis Jean. Clifford Mackay (1906–1985) became President of the NSW Baptist Union. Ellen died on 10 January 1947.[985]

## Appendix 3: The Rev Alfred Metters

Following his time at the Devonport Baptist Church, the Rev Alfred Metters and his family left for Sydney in March 1907 where he had been appointed to the Granville and Liverpool churches, experimentally made into one circuit.[986]

The politeness of the man was seen at a NSW Baptist Union Conference on "Oldest, and Old Theology" with the lead speaker the Rev John Urquhart of London railing against Dr. Marcus Dodds, Professor of New Testament Theology, Edinburgh. Urquhart said that Dodds had made it his business to upset the minds of his students and had said,

> We want an infallible book because we are idle and lazy, and will not search for ourselves, and we want something to compel the young people to believe without any exercise of their reason.

Urquhart continued, "It had to be remembered that these colleges were sending out men as missionaries in the foreign field, and to the pulpits as well." He went on to say that he had found in the hands of the students of the Baptist Union of New South Wales Professor Alexander Balmain Bruce's "Apologetics". "Selecting such a book for students to go through was disgraceful on the part of anyone," he concluded. In response a number saw the speaker as the Great Inquisitor, namely the Rev C. J. Tinsley who replied that Urquhart's address was destructive rather than constructive and the Rev Charles Pickering who said that Urquhart was wrong and the Rev Professor A. G. Gordon of the Melbourne Baptist College said that young men should be brought into touch with the books mentioned, but not necessarily to accept the views expressed there. Finally, the Rev H. S. Hughes (S.A.) said that he had absolutely no sympathy with Urquhart, "in fact, he had less sympathy with him than when he entered the church that morning." Metters merely commented that he glad he was abreast of the times, that he "was brought up as a sceptic - his father was one. However, he was in a position to be fortified against 'these errors'."[987]

Metters relinquished the pastorate of the Granville and Liverpool churches eighteen months later. He

---

[985] The Argus (Melbourne) 11 January 1947 p23.
[986] The Cumberland Argus and Fruitgrowers Advocate (Burnie) 27 February 1907 p3.
[987] The Daily Telegraph (Sydney) 28 September 1907 p11. The following year Urquhart commenced a "Bible Institute" at the Albert Street Church in Melbourne and in his magazine, "The Bible Investigator", continued his attacks of so-called modernists. Our Yesterdays Vol.10 p43.

was recognised as being the instigator in 1906 of Federal Congresses of the Baptist Church in Australia, first held in September 1908.[988]

He then received a call by the South Australian Hindmarsh Baptist Church, which he accepted in June 1909. He added the Prospect Church to his responsibilities in 1911. While pastor at Hindmarsh its finances improved sufficiently for considerable expansion to be undertaken. In 1912 he relinquished its pastorate yet continued his association with Prospect. He was a proponent of a referendum for compulsory Bible instruction in State schools, and for a couple of years organizing Secretary of the Scriptural Instruction in State Schools League. Writing under the pseudonym of "Cousin Felix" he was for many years the Editor of the Young People's Page, first in the *Southern Baptist* and afterwards in *The Australian Baptist*.[989]

By 1913, he had been elevated to the military rank of Captain (he had been a military chaplain since 1906), and then in 1915 re-graded from Chaplain 4th class to Senior Chaplain, 1st Class (Other Protestant Denominations), and promoted to Chaplain-Colonel in 1915. That year he wrote a poem, "A Song of the Wattle".[990]

I sing the song of the wattle bloom (air;
As it perfumes the spring-time
No discord I sound, no note of gloom,
When the wattle is everywhere.
Child of the bush is the wattle-gold, So radiant, happy, and free!
With wordless welcome its smiles unfold
As it wafts its message to me.
I sing the song of the wattle spray
When it yields its fragrance so sweet,
'Mid rustic silence, and on this day
In the home and the crowded street,
Bright are the orbs of the wattle flower
When gracing its green, leafy throne;
'Tis nature's gift from her lavish dower,
An Emblem - Australia's own!
'Mid halcyon peace or war's alarms,
Does its blossom speak joy to me;
I sing the song of the wattle's charms
In success or adversity!

Normally, home-based chaplains continued their usual pastoral duties. However, Metters, the resident chaplain at the Mitcham army camp, gave up the pastorate of Prospect Baptist Church in 1916 and was supported by the Other Protestant Denominations on a full-

---

[988] The Maitland Weekly Mercury 29 February 1908 p6; The Advertiser (Adelaide) 3 October 1908 p19.

[989] The Advertiser (Adelaide) 17 June 1909 p7, 18 April 1911 p5.

[990] The Port Augusta Dispatch, Newcastle and Flinders Chronicle 10 September 1915 p3.

time basis in his chaplaincy work. He was untiring in his attention to the soldiers, particularly the sick, in the various camps in South Australia. In February 1918, the Rev Alfred Metters was admitted to hospital in North Adelaide following a nervous breakdown, and died 1 March 1918 at the age of fifty-one years having never spared himself, having given his best and paying the price of an early death. Ottilie Caroline Metters died on 18 September 1953 at eighty-nine years and they are both buried in the West Terrace Cemetery, Adelaide.[991]

## Conclusion

Henry Clay Vedder's "History of the Baptists" up to 1900 traced the development of Baptist principles and the history of the Baptist churches from their beginnings. On the progress of the Baptists in Tasmania Vedder asked why the results had been meagre in our churches. He stated that Baptists started earlier in Tasmania than any other colony with but one possible exception, viz., New South Wales. "How is it that," Vedder asked, "after more than half a century, they have only nine Churches, of which only four are self-supporting after a sort.

"Specially, why is it that," he continued, "considering also the magnificent generosity of one family, we have no better record than nine Churches." The Baptist historian characterized the results as "meagre".[992] Kenneth Manley in his double volume on the History of Baptists in Tasmania gives his answer: "Baptists in Tasmania had erected the familiar denomination structures and were consciously united in their "safe" theological convictions."[993] It is my experience after living amongst Tasmanian Baptists for more than forty years that Manley's verdict still applies to us today.[994]

Even though Bollen in this work, "How British Christianity Came to Australia", put it differently,

> Nineteenth-century Australian churchmen talked of the Kingdom of God on earth; mid-twentieth- century churchmen have seen their hopes of Christian expansion blasted. They have inhabited a world in which expectation and reality, longing and actuality, have had no border, a hell of frustration and unfulfillment. The age of growth has been followed by an age of crisis and contraction, what least of all the churches were prepared for.

A most casual scrutiny of the Victorian Baptist churches in mid-

---

[991] Chronicle (Adelaide) 9 March 1918 p32. Ottilie Caroline Metters died on 18 September 1953 eighty-nine years and they are buried in the West Terrace Cemetery, Adelaide. I am indebted to Gordon D. Crabb for his assistance with the Metters' biography.

[992] SB 12 January 1899 p1.
[993] Manley pp116.
[994] Laurence F. Rowston.

20th Century reveals a number of Pastors from the Tasmanian Churches having come from across of the Strait. Further, in 1946, both Tasmania and Victoria embarked on a joint Home Mission venture for by now Victorian Baptist Churches knew that by assisting Tasmanian churches they would continue to build Victorian churches, and that applied too other States since Tasmanian Baptist Pastors would in time also be coming their way.

# Chapter 12 Burnie Baptist Church

## Introduction

With the founding of the Burnie Church in 1898 Tasmanian Baptists had reached their limits for a time as far as country Churches were concerned. As extensions were made in the next decade, they would be established near the population centres, at Elphin Road and Moonah, the first in Launceston and the second in Hobart. The Elphin Road Chapel was officially opened in 29 October 1905 and Moonah Church building on 30 June 1908.[995] The most well-established non-Home Mission Churches at the time were in Launceston, Sheffield, Devonport, Perth and Hobart. Yet there was no Baptist representation through the Midlands from Perth to Hobart, on the East and West coasts, on the Tasman Peninsula, in the Huon and Channel districts, and the Derwent Valley and Ouse districts; they were utterly neglected. But playing the blame game is not really fair. The population in places was extremely small and widely scattered in these years; in most districts there were too few Baptists to form worshipping congregations. Where there were only one or two Baptist families in a town, they didn't have the means to build a church or support a Pastor. Baptists would only flourish where numbers were sufficient which meant in large towns.

There were four church denominations in Burnie in 1899: the Anglican, the Gospel Hall, the Roman Catholics with its convent school and finally the Methodists. Yet with the Methodists there were three separate Churches

in their little town of Burnie! One church would have held them all. Each preacher told precisely the same old, old story. All the congregations would gladly have listened to any one of them. And yet there were three, not one. The causes which produced their separations in the Old Country have almost absolutely ceased to exist in Australia.[996]

*12-1 Burnie's Primitive Methodist Church*

---

[995] Daily Telegraph (Launceston) 30 October 1905 p5; SB 30 June 1908 p156.

[996] A Century of Tasmanian Methodism by C C Dugan p86.

In the town, the roads were not sealed thus there was plenty of mud in the wet weather as the many bullock teams churned up the soft surfaces.

## Baptist Beginnings

Early in 1898, the Revs. John E. Walton, Walter J. Eddy and George Wainwright came to Burnie to seek out Baptists for the formation of a Baptist Church; they conducted services for some weeks. Following this, in May 1899, a requisition signed by people in the town was sent to the Baptist Association headquarters in Launceston requesting that an official Baptist work be opened. They also asked for financial support.

The requisition signed by twenty-seven signatories read:

> The undersigned, either holding Baptist principles or practices, or else favourable to them, have been impressed with the necessity and importance of establishing a Church in connection with the Baptist Union of Tasmania at Burnie. We do not feel able to call a Pastor on our own responsibility, but if the Union can assist us in the establishment of a Church and in the selection and support of a Pastor, we pledge ourselves to do all in our power to carry on the Lord's work according to our faith and order in Burnie and its district. We here give a list of annual contributions already promised for this project, and we believe that after a cause is started, many others will come with us and help us. We feel we have no need to speak of the growing importance of our Township and district and the splendid scope for Christian work. We earnestly hope and pray that a favourable answer will be given to our request.[997]

It was the unanimous decision of the signatories that Pastor Harry Wood be appointed as the pioneer pastor. The requests were granted by the Baptist Association.

## Pastor Harry Wood

In 1899, at the end of four years of "strenuous and happy" ministry at Latrobe, Wood was asked by the Baptist Council to commence the new work. The pressure of the new cause at Burnie was so urgent that he allowed himself to be persuaded. In his memoirs he wrote,

*12-2 Harry and Emily Wood and family*

---

[997] Church Minutes.

It was at this time that heart weakness, from which I have suffered so long, began to show serious symptoms. My doctor advised me strongly, for health reasons, not to go to Burnie. A petition signed by a number of heads of families had been sent to the Council requesting that I might be sent to start a Baptist cause there. It was a big undertaking for a weakly man, but I felt it was the Lord's will I should go.[998]

*12-3 The Original Burnie Baptist Church*

Once again there was difficulty in securing a house. The only available house was a sub-standard four-roomed cottage at the far end of South Burnie. It was too small for a family of six people yet it had to do.

At his welcome he said, "It was not unusual for a minister to be idolised the first year, the second year criticised, and the third year scandalised; but in this instance the case was reversed."[999] Wood encountered opposition from other denominations. Some years later he recorded his early days there:

> When I commenced work here… there was a very strong spirit of opposition to the new Baptist cause, both from the church and the world. We were attacked by pulpit and press. We were looked upon as a new sect.[1000]

On the subject of baptism, animated discussions took place between Wood and other paedo-baptising Churches discussing the nature of baptism and to whom it should be administered. The controversies continued for months in the public press.[1001]

The Town Hall was hired for Sunday services. Week-night meetings were held in a rented building that had once been used by the Primitive Methodists. In the packed Town Hall with 400 attending, Wood conducted the first Baptist baptism in the town. The water was carried some distance in buckets to the temporary baptistry.

On 17 December 1899, six months after Wood had commenced, the church was formed with over sixty members. Another baptism of eight people took place on 10 June

---

[998] Pioneer Work for the Lord in Tasmania by Harry Wood.
[999] NWA&EBT 28 April 1899 p2.
[1000] S&T 1900 p323.
[1001] See Spurgeon's Men MA thesis for a discussion on this.

1900.[1002] There was now a thriving Sunday school with a fine missionary spirit but the Baptists were late comers in the town.

A site in Mount Street for the Burnie Church building and manse was purchased in part with a £500 donation from Mary Ann Gibson of Perth. In Wood's first year the work flourished and the membership stood at forty-two. But Wood's poor health continued. He could not preach in the last quarter of 1899. At the end of eighteen months his doctor advised that he leave as soon as possible so as to take a year's rest and to "be free from the anxiety incidental to pioneer work".[1003] Wood was farewelled on 28 November 1900.

## The Rev Thomas Vigis

The Rev Thomas Vigis was welcomed to the Burnie Baptist Church on 14 February 1901; he had previously been at the Rockhampton Baptist Church in Queensland. At the time the Burnie church had oversight of the Somerset work which was meeting in a drill hall.[1004] Vigis still enjoyed his game of cricket.

Together with the Rev James Blaikie of Hobart in June 1901, Vigis took time off to secure the Montagu Hall for Home Mission work in the west coast mining town of Zeehan.[1005]

During Vigis' time the two semi-detached cottages on the Burnie church site were demolished to make way for the erection of the weatherboard Tabernacle that could seat 260 persons and for the erection of a brick manse. The official opening of the church building took place on 5 May 1901 officiated by the Rev Dr. Silas Mead of the Baptist Church in Museum Street, Perth, WA. The manse was built for £420 and the wooden church building church for £530, the seats costing £65 of this amount.[1006] Because of his good knowledge of building construction, Vigis was a great help in the erection of the new structures. He also designed the church seats. Mary Ann Gibson gave another donation of £125 towards the building of the hall and manse.

Vigis ran a weekly Baptist Progress Society structured on discussion groups and musical items.[1007]

Vigis' pastorate was only for twelve months and he kept to that. On transferring to the Fenwick Street Baptist Church, Geelong, he refused to elaborate on why he would not stay longer.[1008]

---

[1002] The Mercury (Hobart) 13 December 1899 Supplement p1; SB 28 June 1900.
[1003] LEx 24 September 1900 p1, 12 November 1900 p6; SB 12 October 1899; Day-Dawn November 1900 p5.
[1004] LEx 12 March 1901 p7.
[1005] See page 120.
[1006] NWA&EBT 6 May 1901 p2; LEx 6 May 1901 p6.
[1007] NWA&EBT 21 September 1901 p2.
[1008] NWA&EBT 7 December 1901 p2.

## The Rev Samuel Harrison

In February 1899, the Rev Samuel Harrison of Sydney visited Tasmania and preached at the Church. He declined an invitation to the pastorate. When in November 1900 Pastor Harry Wood resigned the charge, it was rumoured that Harrison would fill the vacancy but this did not happen.[1009]

In March 1902, Harrison finally accepted and this was his second pastorate in the Australian Baptist churches. It is likely that he had family living in northern Tasmania. If so, it would have been part of the reason for his acceptance. The church membership, which stood at fifty-nine when he arrived, grew during his time and there was marked improvement in the financial state of the church.[1010]

In May 1903, the Rev Joshua T. Piercey of Christian Mission Church conducted a week's mission.[1011] That year Harrison was engaged in controversy through the columns of the "Burnie Times" in defending the right of Baptists to open a work at nearby Penguin. It was stated that the area was already well provided for in respect of churches.[1012] He further debated why Baptists baptise the way they do.

By 1903, apart from the services at Penguin, the Burnie Church had also commenced services at Wynyard and Stowport. In time, Devonport Baptist Church assisted with the Penguin services and Burnie assisted Devonport with the new work at Ulverstone.

*12-4 Samuel Harrison*

Harrison resigned from the Burnie pastorate in February 1904 because of severe ill-health. His doctors insisted on him leaving for a warmer climate and away from the seaside.[1013] On his leaving he asked for prayer for those who had written harsh things about him; he had received hate mail. Wrote one,

> no doubt some who attend his church are sheep, and they have to be watched and guarded by Shepherd Samuel against the wolf who desires to enlighten and

---

[1009] The Sydney Morning Herald 25 February 1899 p10; NWA&EBT 7 January 1899 p2,12 November 1900 p2; LEx 17 March 1903 p7.
[1010] NWA&EBT 10 March 1902 p2, 19 April 1902 p9.
[1011] LEx 2 May 1903 p6.

[1012] This is seen as a valid argument today by Baptist leaders which they take on board before they commence a new work in a given area. For an extended account of these matters involving Harrison see "Spurgeon's Men".
[1013] SB 10 November 1903; NWA&EBT 12 February 1904 p2; AB 15 May 1904 p64.

uplift them. I fear brothers like Samuel would reintroduce dungeons, racks, thumbscrews and the sword of annihilation; they would make the religion of our Redeemer a close preserve for tyrants, bigots and hypocrites.[1014]

The Burnie Church received sixty-three persons into church membership during Harrison's time and a good number of these were young men. On his leaving he added that if his health had allowed it, he would have been happy to spend another two years in the town.[1015]

## The Rev Joseph Tanner Piercey

Following his time at the Christian Mission Church in Launceston, the Rev Joseph Tanner Piercey was welcomed at the Burnie Church on 12 October 1904; he had preached there earlier. The Rev George Craike himself had preached at Burnie in June 1893 and maybe he was instrumental in bringing about the settlement. At the welcome Henry Dowling, the Sunday school Superintendent, referred to Piercey

*12-5 Joseph T. Piercey*

"as his spiritual father, having been led to Christ years ago by him." Dowling had first met Piercey at Waratah.[1016]

At the first Baptist Union Assembly after his installation at Burnie, Piercey preached the Union sermon "discoursing impressively on the theme, 'contending for the faith once delivered to the saints.'" In January 1905 English evangelist Henry Varley visited the Burnie Church and gave a lecture on "Billy Bray" and on another visit on the Second Coming of Christ. The proceeds went to the Church's purchase of an organ for its open-air meetings.[1017]

For more than twenty years from 1880 the hope for revival was very much a feature in Tasmanian church life. This emphasis on evangelism was unceasing in 1904 with a concerted effort to bring about conversions in the churches. It began that year in the Hobart Church in February with a fortnight mission with the American evangelist, the Rev D C Davidson M.A., as part of the Simultaneous Missions' Movement. At the Launceston Tabernacle, again from

---

[1014] NWA&EBT 4 December 1903 p4.
[1015] NWA&EBT 1 March 1904 p2.

[1016] NWA&EBT 6 May 1903 p2, 13 October 1904 p2; Day-Dawn 1 November 1904.
[1017] LEx 21 October 1904 p6; "Day- Dawn" January 1905.

early in the year evangelistic services were commenced every Sunday evening culminating with a United Churches' Mission in July. In August, Piercey conducted a mission at Chudleigh in the Deloraine Circuit. In October, he then assisted the Rev Walter J. Eddy in the Mission in Perth. This was followed by a Mission in September at Latrobe and Sassafras under the leadership of the Revs. Samuel Harrison and George Mackay. The same month another was conducted in the Bracknell District with the Revs. Stephen Howard of Perth and Eddy.[1018]

In March 1905, Piercey and the Rev George J. Mackay of Devonport conducted an evangelistic mission at the Penguin Fellowship which was under the care of the Burnie Church. In July 1905, Piercey conducted another mission, this time at Waratah where he had ministered in 1880. He concluded the mission in the Odd Fellows Hall with the lecture illustrated by coloured slides on "Ten Nights in a Bar Room". In September 1905, he won first prize in the Ulverstone Dog and Poultry Society competitions in the Indian Runner duck class with a fine bird. He was also Treasurer for the Emu Bay Horticultural Society.[1019]

The statistics for 1905 revealed 864 members in all the churches with 1353 Sunday school scholars being taught by 147 teachers.[1020]

In April 1906, after only sixteen months, Piercey preached farewell sermons departing to carry out evangelistic work under the auspices of the Melbourne based Evangelisation Society of Australasia. So it was that Piercey began his work as a full time evangelist commencing with a ten days' mission at the Launceston Tabernacle.[1021]

## The Rev Peter W. Cairns

The Rev Peter William Cairns, "one of Melbourne's prominent Baptist ministers and a cultured preacher with strong evangelistic tendencies", was welcomed at Burnie on 2 July 1906. He had just completed four years at the South Yarra Baptist Church in Melbourne.[1022] The Burnie Church still had its mission hall at Stowport.

Money matters were much in mind in 1906 as the Church inaugurated a giving system by which it was "intended to pelt the church debt to death with penny subscriptions!"

In 1909, Cairns became embroiled in a charge of plagiarism in respect to one of his sermons. The matter had followed him from his days at South Yarra and it had affected the confi-

---

[1018] Day-Dawn reports.
[1019] LEx 15 July 1905 p8; NWA&EBT 14 September 1905 p3, 31 October 1905 p4.
[1020] SB 2 June 1903 p122.
[1021] NWA&EBT 2 April 1906 p2; LEx 7 April 1906 p6.
[1022] LEx 15 May 1906 p1.

dence in him of his fellow Baptist ministers. After some considerable correspondence, the matter was finally resolved in his favour.[1023]

In 1907 the Burnie membership was seventy-nine and increased by ten in the next twelve months. There were 145 scholars in the Sunday school.

At the Baptist Assembly in April 1907, Cairns gave a paper, "Woman's Work in the Church" which he was asked to deliver again when he arrived back in Burnie.[1024]

At a Loyal Orange Lodge and Protestant Defence Association meeting in April 1907 Cairns, its chaplain, uttered the expected words for his address on "Defence or Defiance?"

The speaker's object was to show cause for defence on the part of Protestants against the placing of Roman Catholics in national power ... "We expect to allow Roman Catholics the freedom of thought, which we desire for ourselves, but not to allow them to secure the power of government."[1025]

A number of Cairns' addresses were put into leaflet form for distribution.[1026] He was now a sought-out preacher for anniversaries and the like. The Church farewell took place on 27 July 1909.[1027]

The Baptist churches at the time had amongst them another preacher of excellence, the Rev Frank William Boreham. At an Assembly in 1912, it was probably Boreham who said,

The great preacher has such a noble presence and delightful simplicity of manner, that before he begins to speak he has won all hearts. His voice has music in it, and astonishing carrying power. Quite in a conversational tone he speaks to us, and sometimes sinks his voice to a confidential whisper; but he was heard distinctly throughout the large building ... There (is) something hypnotic in the ease and massive simplicity both of matter and manner."[1028]

In 1909, the Church proposed a notice of motion protesting "against the Devonport Church resorting to

*12-6 Peter Cairns*

---

[1023] Victorian Baptist Historical Society newsletter June 1997.
[1024] The Mercury (Hobart) 3 April 1907 p7; NWA&EBT 11 April 1907 p2.
[1025] NWA&EBT 29 April 1907 p2.

[1026] The Bundaberg Mail and Burnett Advertiser (Qld) 26 August 1907 p3.
[1027] SB 10 August 1909 p199.
[1028] SB 11 April 1912 p232. Boreham as an usher at the Metropolitian Tabernacle in London

questionable means in raising money for God's work." Maybe it was Devonport's special thanksgiving offerings every Easter to reduce the debt?[1029] But Devonport was not the only Church seen at fault so the final motion contained these words, "We would earnestly urge the deacons of the Churches connected with our Union to advocate straight out giving." That year George Craike was assistant Pastor prior to his return to England to minister to the Zion Baptist Chapel, Chesham, Bucks.

## The Rev Oswald R. Linden

On account of his ill-health the Victorian Baptist Theological College sent its graduate, the Rev Oswald Rupert Linden, to Tasmania to act as pastor to the Church at Burnie for a period of twelve months. The interim was extended to fifteen months.[1030] This "most successful preacher" and his new wife, Beatrice Emma (nee Fyfe), were welcomed in January 1910. The Church's membership stood at about fifty. In 1910, Boreham now President of the Baptist Association, gave a number of public illustrated lectures at the Church.[1031]

A "surprise party" was held for Linden's thirtieth birthday at the manse with about forty friends and members of the church; the evening devoted to parlour games and songs. The senior deacon, Henry Dowling, presented Linden with a "handsomely bound" Strong's Concordance as "a slight token of the esteem in which he was held". Linden responded by remarking that the visit was a real surprise to him.[1032] As it happened, he and Edna were returning to Melbourne.

## The Rev Charles Palmer

In July 1911, within a month of the Rev Charles Palmer's commencement at Burnie, what the Rev George Mackay was doing in neighbouring Devonport successfully, Palmer was doing at a Temperance Rally in the Burnie Town Hall, that is protesting against the erection of a new hotel in the town as it was claimed the town already had enough. He cried,

> Every hotel in Burnie was more dangerous to the public morals and public safety than all the menageries in the world. Was it right to force on a town a hotel because it would be remunerative to a few? What would they think if they learnt that there were five wild animals planted in different parts of the town and that it was proposed to

---

often heard the Rev C. H. Spurgeon preach and Spurgeon "was heard distinctly throughout the large building".
[1029] Day-Dawn March 1909.

[1030] The Herald (Melbourne) 13 March 1911 p3. SB 20 January 1910 p51.
[1031] LEx 23 August 1910 p6.
[1032] NWA&EBT 9 November 1910 p2.

add a sixth - a lion with a shaggy mane and a brushy tail?[1033]

In Burnie he was a "fearless fighter" for the temperance cause yet his concerns were wider than just this issue; he had a pastor's heart and visited every house in the town.

As for the church building, in 1911 the original pulpit was given to the Penguin Church. Two years later the gas plant facilitating the church lighting was sold and electricity installed.

Palmer was a worker, but throughout his ministerial service it is suggested that there was a pattern to his work. He enjoyed relatively short stints with waning enthusiasm settling in as time went on but then came the desire to go elsewhere. Added to this, by 1914 relationships had become strained between Palmer and a number of the deacons so farewell services were conducted on 15 March 1914. He and his wife Phoebe returned to Sydney to live in Haberfield but within two years he died at the age of sixty-eight years, on 13 June 1916. He was buried in the Baptist section of the Rookwood Cemetery, Sydney.[1034] Phoebe Ann Palmer died on 10 July 1939 at Marrickville, NSW[1035] and was survived by their only son, Samuel Freer Palmer. Samuel trained at the Melbourne Salvation Army Training College, was appointed to a corps in New Zealand, where he served three years, and resigned in 1903 through illness.[1036] The Rev Charles and Phoebe had had four children, with Samuel, Minnie and Fanny born at Condah in Western Victoria.

*12-7 Charles Palmer*

## The Rev Robert McCullough

After twenty-one years in South Australia, the Rev Robert McCullough accepted a call back to Tasmania, to Burnie this time. Members of his wife's family lived there and it was time for Eva to enjoy a prolonged family reunion. At his first Tasmanian Baptist Assembly on his return, in November 1914, he mentioned, "The changes of twenty years almost made him feel a stranger," and he added that he had altered in many ways. Referring to the present war, he emphasized "the

---

[1033] NWA&EBT 12 July 1911 p4; LEx 3 August 1911 p6.
[1034] National Advocate; Daily Post (Hobart) 13 March 1914 p5; AB 31 March 1914 p9. Bathurst (NSW) 15 June 1916 p5.

[1035] The Sydney Morning Herald 11 July 1939 p10.
[1036] The Sydney Morning Herald 11 July 1939 p9, 11 April 1944 p8; AB 25 April 1944 p5.

necessity of realising that God was still living and acting." In Burnie he gathered together those of like mind and formed a Temperance Association. In August 1915 he and Eva received news of the death of their son, Private Charles Spurgeon McCullough, killed in action on 13 July; he was thirty years of age. Two of his brothers were also at the Dardenelles and one of them was severely wounded. Their son-in-law was also killed.[1037]

At his farewell in January 1918, McCullough said they were leaving "for family reasons" with South Australia beckoning. Eva had been an ardent worker for the Red Cross Society during the war period, and on their leaving she also received a public testimonial of appreciation for her services.[1038]

## The Rev Frederick Augustus Leeder

Following his leaving the Devonport Baptist Church, the Rev Frederick Augustus Leeder soon accepted a six months call from the Burnie Baptist Church but when the six months passed in April 1918, he stayed on.[1039]

As in so many towns and cities, the fourth anniversary of the entry of the British Empire into the war was celebrated by a day of intercession. The church services were filled to overflowing. While the services were intercessory asking for a speedy peace, there was underlying everything, a determination to see the war through to the end, and do everything possible for the bringing about of a victory for the cause of Great Britain and her Allies as various preachers expressed it, this is no time for the expression of feeble sentiment. We should enter the fifth year of the war asking the Almighty to arm us in crushing

*12-8 Frederick Leeder*

---

[1037] LEx 6 November 1914 p3; The Register (Adelaide) 10 August 1915 p6; NWA&EBT 3 March 1915, 26 October 1917 p2. For an Anzac sermon by McCullough see The Mount Barker Courier and Onkaparinga and Gumeracha Advertiser (SA) 1 May 1925 p3.

[1038] LEx 28 January 1918 p 6; The Mount Barker Courier and Onkaparinga and Gumeracha Advertiser (SA) 17 July 1925 p2.
[1039] NWA&EBT 6 April 1918 p4.

the Germans with their ambition of world conquest, for it is only by doing this that anything in the way of a lasting peace can be assured.[1040]

In Burnie, under the auspices of the Ministers' Fraternal Association, monthly united intercessory services were held in the town's theatre with Leeder presiding at times.

Orange man that he was, one of his sermons in Burnie was entitled, "The Papal Flag, Why Fly it in Australia?" He also had a dim view of drinking and dancing.[1041]

Leeder was farewelled from the Burnie Baptist Church to Melbourne on 29 January 1922. The local Presbyterian minister mentioned at the farewell that when "he met Mr Leeder in the street he associated him with the text in the Bible, 'Behold an Israelite indeed in whom there is no guile.'" It had been a successful pastorate.[1042]

## The Rev Edward Burchell Woods

The Rev Edward Burchell Woods was affectionately known either as "Daddy Woods" or the "old identity". Later it was ironically, "Rev Dr. Woods, Lord Bishop of the Island of Tasmanian".[1043] He was inducted into the Burnie pastorate on 11 June 1922.

*12-9 Edward Woods*

In September 1922, the Rev Wilfred Lemuel Jarvis conducted an evangelistic mission at Burnie making use of the Methodist Church building, the theatre and the Town Hall. For one of his messages he took as his theme, "Refuges of Lies",

Basing his address on the parable of "The Great Supper", he dealt in his own pungent way with the various excuses men make for refusing the offer of God's mercy, and showed the utter hollowness and unworthiness of those excuses as so many "refuges of lies".

Woods was chairman of the Burnie Tourist and Progress Association and Secretary of the Emu Bay Sick

---

[1040] NWA&EBT 5 August 1918 p3.
[1041] A precis of Leeder's address is found in Advocate (Burnie) 26 September 1921 p3.
[1042] Advocate (Burnie) 1 February 1922 p2; AB 7 March 1922 p7.
[1043] AB 1929 p165, 7 July 1931 p6.

and Benevolent Society.[1044] Over his years at Burnie Woods had numerous sermons published in full but he also had published some of his most provocative articles to which there were sometimes angry responses. Among the sermons were, "Absolution. New Testament Teaching", "The Sacrament of Penance", "The Menace of Communism to Christianity and the Empire", "Lessons from the Life of Gipsy Smith as I knew Him", "Christian Science", "The Claims of Theosophy", "Sabbath Law: A Reply to Seventh Day Adventism", "Churches and the Working Class" and "Churches and the Tongues".[1045]

At the Baptist Assembly in 1925 he gave a paper on "Fundamentalism: True and False". Commented the editor of the Australian Baptist, "The paper was a straight-out, stinging utterance by a scholar with a soul who always speaks his mind."[1046]

In 1923, under the urging of Woods, a day for conference and study for ministers in Launceston, which had been initiated many years earlier by the Rev Robert McCullough, was developed into an annual retreat and the Summer School of Theology. Later, the practice was followed by visiting country centres so that some of the smaller churches would be encouraged by the visitation of ministers from all parts of the State.[1047]

In September 1925, he began a series of messages on "Some Popular Mistakes about Religion", the first, "On Getting to Heaven". Another was "Christianity in Relation to Wowserism".[1048]

Shortly after Woods' arrival, the vestries of the church were extended to make room for the Sunday school. Later, the wooden piles on which the

*12-10 Laying the foundation stone of the New Burnie Baptist Church in 1925 by J. T. Soundy*

---

[1044] Advocate (Burnie) 13 June 1922 p7, 18 September 1922 p5.
[1045] Listed in order as given: Advocate (Burnie) 21 November 1922 p6, 20 March 1925 p6, 12 November 1925 p14; Daily Telegraph (Launceston) 22 April 1926 p6; Advocate (Burnie) 30 July 1926 p6, 15 December 1926 p13, 19 February 1927 p11, 2 June 1931 p2, 15 August 1931 p2; 27 November 1923 p7.

[1046] AB 17 November 1925 p7. For Woods' response to the Sheffield Pentecostal Revival of 1924 see chapter 10.
[1047] AB 31 July 1923 p10.
[1048] Advocate (Burnie) 30 September 1925 p14, 4 June 1927 p14.

church was supported were found to be decayed, and it was ascertained that it would be costly to replace them.

Woods suggested that thought be given to the erection of a new brick Church. At the time, £200 was owed on the property and a new church seemed out of the question.

However, owing to generous giving, the debt was wiped off. It was then decided that when £500 was raised or promised, a new building would be justified. In addition to finance, there were other difficulties to contend with. The heavy wooden building had to be moved from the street frontage to the rear of the site. This was done by two huge tractors, logs being used as skids. It was a fine feat and crowds came to watch it. This work was supervised by Church member Jim Baylis who had a good band of helpers.[1049] The old weatherboard church was remodelled to form vestries, a school hall, a kindergarten room and a kitchen. The balance of the £500 was eventually raised.

The foundation stone of the church was laid on 1 August 1925 by Joshua T. Soundy of Hobart, President of the Baptist Union.[1050] The new church, capable of accommodating 350 people, opened on 12 December 1925. Local J. C. Peace was the builder assisted by men of the Church, notable among them Henry Dowling as clerk of works, Fred Parsons as carpenter, Jim Baylis as bricklayer and Ray Haslock. It was completed at a cost of £1675. Seventeen years later the debt incurred was completely cleared.

It was the establishment of the Burnie Church as well as that of Devonport, Ulverstone, Penguin, Sheffield, Wynyard and Smithton that a third large centre of Baptists on the island had been created, and for that reason Baptists of the North-West Coast began to enjoy hosting the annual Association assemblies.[1051]

Woods was President of the Tasmanian Baptist Union for 1927/1928 and 1928/1929 and Union Secretary and Superintendent of the Home Missions for a number of years.

During his four months away in 1928, representing the State Baptists for the World Congress of the Baptist Churches in Toronto city, the Rev George Wainwright and Major Alexander F. Roberts-Thomson, the latter father of the Burnie Church members, John and Edward Roberts-Thomson, occupied the pulpit.[1052]

The Rev Edward B. Woods remained at the Burnie Church until 1932 and was farewelled on 12 June. His

---

[1049] LEx 3 LEx August 1925 p2, 10 July 1925 p2.
[1050] LEx 3 August 1925 p2, 14 December 1925 p2.
[1051] AB 8 November 1927 p3.
[1052] LEx 20 October 1928 p6; Advocate (Burnie) 15 June 1932 p11.

pastorate was one of the most successful in the life of the Church. His contribution to the denomination was immense and his departure to Adelaide sincerely regretted.[1053]

# Appendices:

## Appendix 1: The Rev Thomas Vigis

Not many Baptist ministers can claim to have held pastorates in five Australian states, but this was at the time the record of the Rev Thomas Vigis. Throughout his life he forever gave of his talents in improving the welfare of the towns in which he was resident. He worked at training young people in Christian living and ministry and his engagement with sport was to this end; Tasmanian's loss was other states' gain. He was an Australian Baptist leader wherever he went.

Thomas Vigis was born in November 1862 in Plumstead, Kent, England, and educated at the National School under the Rev W. McAllister, M.A., Vicar of East Plumstead. He came to a conversion experience when he was seventeen and was baptised the following year by the Rev J. Wilson, of Woolwich. Then at the age of eighteen he conducted evangelistic missions at Blackheath, Brighton, Plaistow and other centres near London in association with Dr. Thomas John Barnardo and the Rev Charles Spurgeon. He became a Baptist the same year. He trained for the ministry in London but one of his life's regrets was that his health broke down during his studies and prevented him obtaining his Degrees.[1054] In 1881, he had charge of the Baptist Mission at Hampton Wick, Surrey, under the auspices of the Kingston Baptist Church. He next settled at Petworth, Sussex, in 1882. Then his health broke down again and the doctors ordered him to Queensland, Australia. He arrived in Sydney in February 1886 and went immediately to Brisbane.[1055]

12-11 *Thomas Vigis*

---

[1053] LEx 13 June 1932 p5.
[1054] His associations suggest that he trained at the Pastors' College but the College did not issue written or printed certificates saying that a certain course of study had been completed or that the person had graduated, there were only internal assessments. See Bebbington, 'Spurgeon and British Evangelical Theological Education', Chapter 11 of Theological Education in the Evangelical Tradition, pp229f.
[1055] News (Adelaide) 18 September 1926 p4; the Laura Standard (SA) 22 November 1906 p3; The North Queensland Register (Townsville) 27 February 1899 p25.

He was soon participating in weekly evangelistic services held in the Theatre Royal. The speaker was usually the city missionary or someone from the Y.M.C.A. The services were backed by a lively United Evangelistic choir and had a temperance flavour with the offering of blue ribbons.[1056]

In November 1887, Vigis was appointed to the pastorate of the Rosewood Baptist Church in Ipswich. While on a holiday trip he took the first Baptist services at Townsville, on 29 January 1888. In December 1888, the Rosewood Baptist Church was admitted into the Baptist Association. Vigis was appointed Pastor but soon transferred north to inland Charters Towers, a much larger work "being principally foundation labour". He commenced in February 1889. Vigis became honorary Secretary for the School of Arts. He was also a patron of the Charters Towers British Football Association and referee for the games and Vice President of the Orpheus Choral Society.[1057]

After ten years at Charters Towers, he transferred to Rockhampton in March 1899. By now Vigis was "one of the most-deservedly popular clergymen in the North" and "one of the senior clergymen of the North".[1058] On 18 February 1892, he married Lilly Anne Jacobs; they had met at the Rosewood Baptist Church.

Vigis played with the Rockhampton Cricket club, was President of the Queensland Christian Endeavour Union and supported the W.C.T.U., the B.F.B.S. and Rockhampton Benevolent Society. In Queensland his work entailed travelling 1500 kms every month.[1059]

Just over a year later Vigis received a call to the Bathurst Street Baptist Church in Sydney but declined the offer. He obviously didn't give in to pride in respect to the NSW call but he did to the need of his wife's health. She had found in Queensland the summer heat unbearable so Vigis accepted the call to the Burnie Church in Tasmania; he had given some thought to Western Australia. His final service at Rockhampton was on 20 January 1901.[1060]

**Following his short time at Burnie**, he ministered in Victoria at the Fenwick Street Baptist Church in Geelong, from February 1902 to September 1904. A visitor described him as he entered the pulpit area on the a Sunday morning in late 1902,

---

[1056] The Brisbane Courier 15 February 1886 p4.

[1057] The Brisbane Courier 3 November 1887 p6; The Telegraph (Brisbane) 6 February 1888 p2, 16 February 1889 p5; The North Queensland Register (Townsville) 21 July 1897 p23, 30 March 1898 p38, 20 April 1898 p35.

[1058] The North Queensland Register (Townsville) 20 April 1898.

[1059] NWA&EBT 15 February 1901 p2.

[1060] Queensland Times, Ipswich Herald and General Advertiser 24 May 1900 p4; NWA&EBT 20 December 1900 p2; Morning Bulletin (Rockhampton) 21 January 1901 p5.

He comes upon the platform punctually. That is the sole remarkable thing about his coming in. Some ministers come in like lion-tamers, others like dancing masters, or with a "strut theatric," but Mr. Vigis came in without any sort of mannerism whatever. Dressed in faultless black, the only suspicion of clericalism is the small white necktie, tucked under his collar, as if he were half ashamed of this "last rag of Popery," as Spurgeon called it. In such a dress one may be taken or mistaken for an undertaker, a waiter, or a bridegroom adorned for his bride ... The text was from Luke xvii. 21-22. and was a plain, unadorned talk about the inwardness and spirituality of the Kingdom of God. There was nothing particularly forceful or original in it, but it was delivered in an easy and pleasant manner, which held the attention of the congregation.[1061]

Among the many programmes, meetings and commitments, Vigis lectured at the Victorian Union of the Normal College for Sunday school teachers which provided a two year study of Biblical History and Geography, "Christian Evidences" and the Theory of Teaching. This gave the teachers grounding for their Sunday work. In one year many of the teachers at the Fenwick Street Baptist Church took part. Vigis was also President of the Young Men's Mutual Improvement Association.[1062]

Vigis then moved to South Australia commencing with the Laura Baptist Church Circuit in October 1904. The circuit entailed the Laura, Clover Hill and Georgetown Churches and was part of the Northern District Baptist Association. These churches, which in 1906 had a combined membership of ninety-nine, belonged to rural towns in the Mid-North region of South Australia. He stayed on at Laura until April 1911. He formed a Baptist Social and Literary Society which Baptist churches outside the Laura Circuit joined. The Society had similar aims to his Geelong Young Men's Mutual Improvement Association. It so caught on that it took in non-Baptist Churches and was renamed the Northern Areas Literary Societies' Union. The evenings would include elocution, plays, recitation and singing competitions, something like the old "Band of Hope" meetings. Vigis was a young man's minister.[1063]

Four years from his commencement in the Laura District, the churches' combined membership had grown to 160, and the old structure of the Georgetown church was demolished and a new edifice constructed. The Laura building was painted and renovated. Vigis became the Secretary of the Northern District

---

[1061] SB 3 December 1902 p276.
[1062] Geelong Advertiser 16 December 1903 p2, 1 July 1904 p2.
[1063] Observer (Adelaide) 4 March 1905 p1; Chronicle (Adelaide) 16 December 1905 p41, 9 June 1906 p13.

Baptist Association and Secretary of the Baptist Union of South Australia. After six and one half years in the Circuit, in May 1911, he transferred to the pastorate at the Gawler Baptist Church. He was President of the local Union Cricket Club. The Church had its "Band of Hope". On his leaving in October 1917 it was said of him, "He is an excellent townsman and has used his influence in all matters pertaining to the betterment of the town and community".[1064]

Vigis accepted the pastorate of Mile End in Wright Street and remained there until 1927. With Mile End being an inner western suburb of Adelaide, he was appointed Honorary Secretary of the Association's Baptist Union's Young People's Department, Honorary Secretary of the City Mission, for seven years, and in 1924/1925, President of the Adelaide Council of Churches. Vigis was President of the Baptist Union of SA in 1926/1927. In 1925, the Baptist Churches at Mile-End, Southwark and Hilton joined forces forming what would be known as the Thebarton Circuit, under the supervision of Vigis assisted by students of the Baptist College.[1065]

On 29 November 1927, a public welcome was given to Vigis as he began as Circuit Superintendent of the three Broken Hill Baptist Churches – Chapple Street, Broken Hill South and Railway Town. He was now a proven leader and he retained this position until early 1935. During his time in Broken Hill the Chapple Street Church was destroyed by fire and then rebuilt at a cost of £1,700.[1066]

Finally, he returned to superintend the Adelaide West End Mission and the oversight of two small home mission churches, one at South Plympton and the other at Westbourne Park. He brought about the establishment of the Aboriginal Women's Home in Lower North Adelaide. He was keen in training the young people socially and intellectually as well as spiritually. He was still associated with the Mission when he died on 31 July 1936; he was seventy-three years of age. He left a widow, Lilly Anne, two daughters, Ellen and Lilly Irene, and one son. Lilly Anne died on 24 December 1942 in Adelaide.[1067]

## Appendix 2: The Rev Samuel Harrison

The Rev Samuel Harrison's magnificent story reveals the high cost some men paid when stepping away from the only denomination they had ever known and in which they were giving notable leadership. It happened to Harrison when he

---

[1064] Gawler is about forty km north of the Adelaide. Chronicle (Adelaide) 27 November 1909 p12; The Laura Standard (SA) 16 June 1910 p2; Bunyip (Gawler, SA) 19 October 1917 p4.
[1065] News (Adelaide) 28 August 1925 p11.

[1066] Barrier Miner (Broken Hill, NSW) 30 May 1928 p2.
[1067] News (Adelaide) 24 December 1942 p5.

saw what the true form of New Testament baptism was.

Harrison was born in Bradford, England, on 2 July 1861 and was brought up among the Primitive Methodists. In 1882, he married Martha Jane Kelly. Martha was the daughter of Pearson Kelly and Mary Hempsted and was born 9 June 1862. They arrived in Australia in 1883, and after a time of secular employment, he entered the Primitive Methodist ministry. In 1888 he was posted to Kempsey in the Bathurst district in the mid-North Coast region of New South Wales for his probationary service. The churches included Euroka just out of Kempsey, Upper Hickeys, West Kempsey and Northern Nambucca.[1068]

His sermons, many of which are printed in newspapers, were eloquent and learned; he had all the characteristics of a sought after preacher. In 1889, at the Annual conference of the Primitive Methodist Churches in the Newcastle District he gave a paper on, "How Can Our Scholars be secured for Jesus?" He was in his first year of probationers' studies and at examinations he gained high marks with much of the study done as he traversed his circuit on horseback.

At Euroka for its Church Anniversary in October 1899, 200 gathered for the tea meeting.[1069]

In 1891, at the annual social in connection with the Rechabite Benefit Society which took place in the Good Templar's Hall in Kempsey, Harrison "came forward with a song, the choir taking up the chorus" and he closed the evening with "a short but stirring address". In 1892, he was appointed joint editor of the Primitive Methodist publication, "Northern Light". Moves were afoot to amalgamate the three strands of the Methodist Churches in Australasian colonies – the Primitive Methodist, Wesleyan Methodists and the United Methodist Free Church.[1070]

Harrison was ordained to the ministry on 28 February 1892 which was immediately followed by his appointment as circuit minister in the Newcastle District which numbered thirty-seven chapels, ten ministers and 2,970 Sunday school scholars. At the time, the Rev A. John Casley was pastor of the Congregational Church in Islington and the Rev Stephen Sharp was the Baptist Pastor in the town.[1071]

But by April 1894, he was compelled to leave the Circuit through ill-health

---

[1068] Macleay Argus (Kempsey, NSW) 25 August 1888 p4.
[1069] Goulburn Herald (NSW) 12 February 1889 p2; Newcastle Morning Herald and Miners' Advocate (NSW) 13 February 1889 p3; Macleay Argus (Kempsey, NSW) 12 October 1889 p2.

[1070] Macleay Argus (Kempsey, NSW) 24 July 1891 p6; Newcastle Morning Herald and Miners' Advocate (NSW) 24 February 1892 p3.
[1071] The Sydney Mail and New South Wales Advertiser 27 February 1892 p496; Macleay Argus (Kempsey, NSW) 4 March 1892 p5; Newcastle Morning Herald and Miners' Advocate (NSW) 23 January 1893 p7, 26 July 1893 p7.

"in consequence of the strong sea air not agreeing with his constitution" and transferred to Forest Lodge, an inner-city suburb of Sydney.[1072] At his farewell he remarked,

> He had come among them to speak the truth, and plain truth was the grandest eloquence that God had given to man. Wherever he went he would preach the plain truth and nothing else. During the past six months he had not visited as frequently as he desired, but during his first 18 months no minister in their district had visited more than he had, and in visiting he did not think that merely call and say, "Good day!" was sufficient e'er leaving.

Then beginning in January 1895 he was moved to Granville, another suburb in the Inner West of Sydney.[1073]

On 5 May 1896, Harrison

> called his church officers together on Tuesday evening to inform them that he had resigned his pastorate, and severed his connection with the denomination. The rev. gentleman explained that he had been led of late to give much serious attention to the question of Christian baptism as it affected Church membership; and had in conscience felt bound to follow the Scriptural soundness of the doctrine of the Baptist Church. He had therefore decided to seek membership in that denomination. The rev. gentleman appeared to be much affected by the possible severance of his relationship with Granville.[1074]

He had heard an address on Baptist principles and his subsequent study of the New Testament convinced him that in respect to baptism, the Baptists were correct. What we know of Sharp leads us to conclude that Sharp would have had a lot to do with Harrison's change of thinking. Casley, Harrison and Sharp would all later be ministering among the Tasmanian Baptist Churches. On Sunday 24 May 1896, Harrison was baptised by the Rev Dr. Thomas Porter at the Petersham Baptist Church.[1075]

In all Christian grace the Granville Primitive Methodist Church farewelled Harrison in June. At the valedictory "the sitting accommodation there at being taxed to its utmost capacity", the opinion was expressed,

> There should be more religious tolerance, and that Mr. Harrison should be allowed to occupy the

---

[1072] Newcastle Morning Herald and Miners' Advocate (NSW) 5 April 1894 p3; the church was part of the Balmain Circuit.
[1073] The Daily Telegraph (Sydney) 23 January 1895 p7.
[1074] The Cumberland Free Press (Parramatta, NSW) 9 May 1896 p4.
[1075] The Daily Telegraph (Sydney) 30 May 1896 p13.

Primitive Methodist pulpit all the same.

Harrison in the course of his reply, responded,

> He felt that after all his struggles he was a step nearer God. He would have been glad to have remained on, but the laws of the Church were against that. The three churches under his oversight had raised over £400 during the past eighteen months; the membership had largely increased and the congregations had doubled. This was due to the church workers; for without them he could have done nothing. It was singular that their church - the most democratic - was the only one that did not allow freedom of conscience in this matter of baptism. But this must come sooner or later.[1076]

This graciousness on the part of the Primitive Methodist churches was further seen as Harrison was invited to speak at the Auburn Primitive Methodist Church in September that year for its Church Anniversary and that of the Wickham Primitive Methodist Church in October 1901.[1077]

In August 1896, he was inducted into the pastorate at Ashfield Baptist Church.[1078]

At the half yearly meeting of the Baptist Union of New South Wales in April 1898, Harrison gave an address, "Why I am a Baptist". Not long after he was appointed Secretary to the Baptist Home Mission which had twelve churches in its care.[1079] In March 1902 he resigned from the Pastorate of the Ashfield Church to accept the call from Burnie, Tasmania.

**Following his time in Tasmania**, Harrison returned to N.S.W. early in 1904 and became the first pastor of the Dulwich Hill Baptist Church. Under his leadership it became a strong church. Harrison's natural gifts as a preacher found their outlet through the Christian Endeavour movement and a preachers' class. His son, John Pearson, and four other members of this class graduated into the ministry. Harrison now moved to the Wellington Baptist Circuit in August 1909. At Wellington he again engaged in disputation in the popular press on the form of baptism and on the matter of farmers harvesting their grain on Sunday.[1080]

---

[1076] Evening News (Sydney) 3 June 1896 p7; The Daily Telegraph (Sydney) 4 June 1896 p5; Australian Town and Country Journal (Sydney) 6 June 1896 p8.
[1077] The Cumberland Argus and Fruitgrowers Advocate (Parramatta) 26 September 1896 p2; Newcastle Morning Herald and Miners' Advocate (NSW) 22 October 1901 p5.

[1078] The Daily Telegraph (Sydney) 29 August 1896 p11.
[1079] The Daily Telegraph (Sydney) 27 April 1898 p8; Australian Town and Country Journal (Sydney) 24 June 1899 p10.
[1080] The Sydney Morning Herald 21 May 1932 p7; Wellington Times (NSW) 2 September 1909 p2, 9 September 1909 p3, 11 November 1909 p2, 13 December 1909 p3.

The critical mail reflecting on his "desertion" some years earlier from the Primitive Methodists continued. Harrison's correspondence in reply was seen as "another opportunity of rubbing it into his old church." It was asked,

> What is the Rev Samuel Harrison after? Does he want some more Methodist scalps? According to your report of his remarks when the latest captured Methodist was baptised, Mr. Harrison was said to have emphasised strongly that baptism was not necessary to salvation, and that is exactly the position those outside the Baptist church take up. If it is not necessary to salvation why do they make such a mouthful of it, and try to lead people to believe that if they are not Baptists they will be shut out into outer darkness? Let the Baptists preach baptism in their churches by all means, let them try and convert the unconverted, but let them not concentrate their efforts on winning converts from the other churches. There are surely enough unconverted to absorb all their energies.[1081]

Yet a Presbyterian cautioned,

> The controversy has taken a personal tone, which is unchristian, and gives infidels an opportunity of exclaiming, "How those Christians love one another. This is not a time for Christians to wage war amongst themselves."[1082]

During his time at Wellington his son, John Pearson Harrison, returned from England and accepted the pastorate of the Mosman Baptist Church in Sydney before setting sail again to London to undertake a four year course of study at the Pastors' College.[1083]

Harrison's next pastorate for two years was at Hornsby commencing January 1911. During his time, the Church participated in "Simultaneous Missions" which were led by the American evangelists, Dr. J. Wilbur Chapman and Charles M. Alexander.

Then, in September 1913, he returned to Tasmania to pastor the Christian Mission Church in Launceston. During his thirty months the Church saw increased congregations and improved financial conditions.[1084]

In January 1917, he commenced at the Victorian coastal church of Warrnambool and remained there until March 1922.

Harrison's final pastorate was that of the historic Harris Street Baptist Church in Sydney commencing in March 1922. Being an inner city

---

[1081] Wellington Times (NSW) 24 November 1910 p7, 1 December 1910 p7.
[1082] Wellington Times (NSW) 15 December 1910 p4.
[1083] The Sydney Morning Herald 9 August 1913 p4; following the completion of his studies he took the pastorate of Harcourt Church, Dublin, Ireland.
[1084] LEx 19 February 1914 p4.

church, the focus of its ministry was tailored for its location made obvious in newspaper reports,

> In the evening, tea was provided for a hundred men from the ranks of the indigent. Pastor Harrison and the members of the Harris Street Church have been doing good and unostentatious relief work for several months, and have not only provided meals every Sunday for as many of the hungry as can be accommodated, but have been successful in finding employment for nearly thirty tradesmen.[1085]

This inner city church greatly revived under his care but in his tenth year this "tall thin man, always dressed in black" died on 16 July 1936 aged seventy-four years. It was reported, "Despite his gaunt appearance, he had a gentle and loving disposition."[1086] His wife, Martha, and sons John Pearson, George Edgar, Harold and daughter Alice Ella survived him. He was buried at the Rookwood Cemetery. Martha died on 20 May 1944.[1087]

## Appendix 3: The Rev Joseph Tanner Piercey

Following his time in Burnie, the Rev Joseph Tanner Piercey's work for the next twelve years with the Victorian Evangelisation Society took him across Victoria many times and also to Tasmania whether preaching in Baptist, Presbyterian, Methodist or Salvation Army churches and in the Town Halls of the many centres. He also took part in the Dr. J. Wilbur Chapman and Charles M. Alexander "simultaneous missions" around Melbourne. In 1910, Piercey began the practice of taking his daughter Muriel with him as soloist. He also worked with the singing evangelist, Amos Sidwell from the Hobart Baptist Church. One of Piercey's evangelistic sermons, "Guilty Nation Present Day Sin God's Unfailing Love", is found in the Melbourne Herald in April 1912 accompanied by Piercey's photograph.[1088]

On 19 July 1916, at Pozieres in France, his eldest son, Captain Hubert, fell shot through the head yet had a marvellous recovery.

Piercey retired from evangelistic work in 1917 and went to live with his other son, Hedley, in the Whitfield area of Victoria. He preached from time to time in the local Presbyterian Church. He died suddenly on 14 March 1921, at the age of sixty-five years.[1089] Sarah his wife died on 6 August 1951 aged

---

[1085] The Daily Telegraph (Sydney) 23 July 1923 p4.
[1086] Northern Star (Lismore, NSW) 21 October 1922; Baptist Recorder June 1986.
[1087] The Sydney Morning Herald 22 May 1944 p8. Family History research by Barbara Coe.

[1088] The Herald (Melbourne) 29 April 1912 p3.
[1089] I am indebted in part to Robert Evans for his chapter on Piercey as found in his history of Victorian Evangelisation Society. AB 22 March 1922 p6.

ninety-two years. They had had two sons and three daughters.[1090]

## Appendix 4: The Rev Peter W. Cairns

The Rev Peter William Cairns's story tells of the tortuous road some follow in their quest to serve their Lord, moving from Congregationalist, to Salvation Army Captain to Wesleyan Methodist and finally to one of Baptist persuasion. Scholarly, a preacher of note, caring, he lived a fulfilling life. His joy was to preach the gospel and he was only happy when telling of God's love.

Cairns was born in Glasgow on 20 April 1852. He was educated at the High School where he took prizes for all subjects dealing with History, Literature and Philosophy. He was a studious youth brought up in a Calvinistic home where the Bible was freely discussed and read. Later, he revolted from the Calvinistic idea of God's wrath "on the children of disobedience", and all his life long spoke, sang, and preached "The free unbounded love of God." He was immersed at the age of sixteen years, but attended the Congregational Church where he taught Sunday school, and worked in missions. He entered the Divinity Hall at eighteen years of age to study for the ministry and paid his way through. In 1873, he was working as a storeman when he married Jemima Struthus on 17 April in Glasgow. They emigrated to Brisbane in 1883 to lead the Salvation Army corps in Brisbane but the local leadership didn't know of this Captain's coming and resented his imposition as Salvation Army historian Garth R. Hentzschel explains,

*12-12 Peter W. Cairns*

Just 11 days after the arrival of Captain Cairns, the McNaught family (which was running things in Brisbane) expelled his party. A number of problems could have led to this decision. Although Cairns was commissioned and appointed by The Salvation Army he brought with him no official documentation from William Booth as it was the Divisional Commander of Scotland who farewelled the group ... there was a strong independent feeling in Queensland, and the Brisbane Salvationists wanted to answer to William Booth, not to officers in southern colonies ... Captain Cairns tried to find a suitable building to continue his work but the McNaught family had many

---
[1090] The Argus (Melbourne) 11 August 1951 p18.

friends in Brisbane and sat on committees of many of the halls, which squeezed out Cairns and his followers. Both parties believed they were representing William Booth's Salvation Army in Queensland so while the McNaught family continued to run the Army in Brisbane, Captain Cairns looked for other opportunities and commenced the work in Ipswich.[1091]

Eventually Cairns was vindicated when General Booth visited the colony in 1891 and met him personally thus,

> to clear away effectually any misunderstanding and doubt to their being the original officers sent out by General Booth to unfurl the flag and carry on the work of the Salvation Army in Queensland.[1092]

Obviously disillusioned with the cause, in 1893 Cairns became paid secretary of the Y.M.C.A. in Brisbane but in less than six months the organisation could no longer afford to employ him. Cairns moved to Ipswich no longer taking the title Captain.[1093]

The following year, still residing at Ingham, Cairns joined the Wesleyan Methodists as one of their clergy. By November 1895, Cairns was their only lay home missionary in the North, seeing success throughout the wide district lying between the Herbert and Tully Rivers with the work almost self-supporting; he was based at Herbert River.[1094] While there the area was suffering the scourge of ticks. He wrote,

> It makes one's spirit sad to look around on the deserted homesteads; and where once we heard the lowing of cattle, the crack of the stock whip, and the busy whirr of the cream-separator, there is now the silence of death. It makes one heartsick also to endure the almost unbearable stench; and when riding I have to cover mouth and nose with my handkerchief and look up to the hills, for on the right and left, before and behind, there are carcasses in all stages of decomposition. It is a blessing it is winter. As it is we have to close all doors and windows at nightfall and fumigate the house with sulphur.[1095]

---

[1091] Garth R Hentzschel, Executive Editor, The Australian Journal of Salvation Army History; Queensland Figaro (Brisbane) 27 January 1883 p14; Queensland Times, Ipswich Herald and General Advertiser 10 October 1891 p4.
[1092] The Telegraph (Brisbane) 12 October 1891 p2.
[1093] The Brisbane Courier 21 November 1892 p7; The Telegraph (Brisbane) 18 October 1893 p2; Queensland Times, Ipswich Herald and General Advertiser 2 March 1886 p3.
[1094] The Queenslander (Brisbane) 7 July 1894 p39; Queensland Times, Ipswich Herald and General Advertiser 19 November 1895 p5, Herbert River is 1200 km north of Brisbane.
[1095] The Telegraph (Brisbane) 16 June 1896 p2.

He came under the influence of the Baptist, the Rev William Whale of Brisbane, in respect to the form of baptism and in 1899 established a Baptist Church in Bundaberg under the auspices of the Home Mission of the Baptist Union of Queensland, commencing in August 1899. A month or two later he returned to Ingham to bring down his wife and their three daughters. The daughters had "earned an excellent reputation ... for their singing, and should prove a valuable addition to the ranks of our local vocalists." The following year he embarked on a series of lectures at the Bundaberg church, among them "John Wesley" and the "Immortality and Immateriality of the Soul". Even so he kept in touch with his fellow brother and sister Salvationists by speaking at their Annual Social meeting in June 1897.[1096]

At the Bundaberg church he formed a Young People's Total Abstinence Society. He was a member of the Hope Peace Lodge, I.O.G.T. He gave a monthly sermon to the young men in his church, which he would also undertake in subsequent pastorates and economically he would often reuse the same messages.[1097] In May 1899 he left for a visit to Melbourne to deliver the inaugural address at the Assembly of the Victorian Baptist Union, and, although not said, no doubt to enquire into a call from the Warrnambool Baptist Church in coastal Victoria.

In May 1900, after sixteen years in Queensland, Cairns was welcomed to the Warrnambool Church. In January 1902 he took issue

> with the granting of a licence to the local golf club for the sale of intoxicating liquors ... the turning of their park into a drinking shop for the benefit of a few, to whom was granted the privilege of using the people's park for their own pleasure.[1098]

In June 1902, in his third year in the pastorate, Cairns took his leave from the Warrnambool Church at "an overcrowded public meeting" to see him off and commenced in July at the 200 member South Yarra Baptist Church in Melbourne.

The local newspaper journalist, who specialized in writing community leaders' profiles, summed him up thus,

> The Rev P. W. Cairns is a Scottish gentleman in the prime of life, about 5ft 8in in height, of moderate build, active and energetic, greyish hair and moustache. He possesses no pulpit mannerisms, speaks distinctly, with a slightly Scottish accent, and with no hesitancy. He does not possess the failings of some parsons who endeavour to

---

[1096] The Bundaberg Mail and Burnett Advertiser (Qld.) 7 August 1896 p2, 2 June 1897 p2, 16 October 1896 p2, 4 June 1897 p2, 2 July 1897 p4; The Brisbane Courier 22 September 1896 p7.

[1097] The Bundaberg Mail and Burnett Advertiser (Qld.) 12 January 1898 p2, 24 April 1899 p2, 1 May 1899 p2; NWA&EBT 27 July 1908 p2.

[1098] The Ballarat Star 6 January 1902 p3.

mystify their people with many syllabled words. He knows what to say and he says it, without fear or favour of man. He is a good conversationalist, has a genial disposition, and possesses what is of considerable importance to every minister, a very devoted helpmeet in his wife ... Notwithstanding its evangelical aspect (of his sermon) there was nothing emotional about the preaching; it certainly was earnest and impressive, but it was withal a calm and dispassionate discourse, appealing alike to the heads and hearts of the hearers.[1099]

The matter of the Local Option movement was part of the church conversation. In Queensland he also gave a lecture on "The Kanaka and His relation to the Sugar Industry" at one of the Independent Order of Rechabite's meetings which showed how informed he was with the Queensland issues of the day.[1100]

In May 1906, Cairns and his wife took a holiday to Tasmania but what was not said was its other purpose, that of the question of the pastorate at the Burnie Baptist Church.[1101]

**From Burnie**, Cairns transferred to Western Australia. In August 1909, he commenced in the new pastorate of the Claremont Baptist Church; it would be a three-year stay concluding early in 1912. The matter of the Local Option again raised its head.[1102]

He then took charge of the Leederville Baptist Churches from April 1913 for two years. He was president of the W.A. churches in 1914. His retirement from the Leederville Church was brought about because of ill-health. He then took a brief interim pastorate at the Devonport Baptist Church. For the next ten years he worked in Victoria, first at Ballarat East from July 1915 for a year. During his next pastorate at Hamilton from September 1916 for three years, his son Andrew, upon winning a lottery in Queensland with a prize of £5000, bought the town boot shop for his father, "The Co-Operative Boot Supply". Andrew, an organist, now accompanied his father's singing during the services in the town. While at Hamilton, Cairns senior was also in charge of the Colac Baptist Church.[1103]

His final pastorate commenced in August 1922 at the Wangaratta Baptist Church remaining to August 1925. Just before he died he received a letter from someone whom he had helped,

> Dear Sir, It is my joy to be able to write and tell you that since your days in ... I have always carried a vivid memory of you. One

---

[1099] Prahran Chronicle (Vic.) 12 July 1902 p3.
[1100] The Argus (Melbourne) 22 March 1904 p7; Prahran Chronicle (Vic.) 29 April 1905 p3.
[1101] Prahran Chronicle (Vic.) 3 March 1906 p2.
[1102] The Reformer (Perth, WA) 29 October 1910 p2.
[1103] The Herald (Melbourne) 21 June 1915 p3; The Ballarat Star 17 April 1920 p1.

evening after you had been visiting us, I walked back with you, and when near the town, I told you that I could not feel as other Christians did, and had a feeling that I should be more advanced in the Christian life. Instead of receiving the sermon a youth expects from his minister, you put your hand on my shoulder and quietly remarked, "But you will some day." And so I am. The way through the wilderness has been long but the "milk and honey" of the Promised Land is now exceedingly sweet, and I desire no other food. Your sermonette has gone a long distance.[1104]

Cairns died on 30 November 1929, aged seventy-seven years. He was survived by his wife, Jemima, and son Andrew and two daughters.[1105] Jemima died on 14 December 1936.

## Appendix 5: The Rev Oswald Rupert Linden

The Rev Oswald Rupert Linden's story is one of those who after a number of effective pastorates returned to secular life and associated with a Methodist church because there was no Baptist Church as yet in what was now his home town.

Linden was born in Port Melbourne on 10 November 1883[1106] to Clarence and Henrietta Linden. Linden attended the Bethel Sunday school of the Seamen's Bethel Mission at Fishermen's Bend.[1107] Linden's life and that of the influential Rev Joseph H. Goble would soon intersect.

*12-13 Port Melbourne Baptist Church*

Goble had become a devout Christian in his mid-teens, and ascribed his conversion to the kindly reception accorded him at this same Seamen's Bethel Mission at the Bend. Young Goble began there as a cleaner and bell-ringer, then a Sunday school teacher and an open-air worker. By 1884 Goble was student pastor at the Baptist church in Footscray. His ministry was successful, but his health collapsed and in 1886 he had to withdraw. In 1892, now

---

[1104] AB 24 December 1929 p4.

[1105] The Age (Melbourne) 18 July 1925 p17, 2 December 1929 p10; AB 1929 p383.

[1106] Application papers to the Victorian Baptist Theological College year 1905.

[1107] Standard (Port Melbourne) 14 March 1896 p2.

married with a child, Goble was received into the fellowship of the Albert Park Baptist Church. That year a Baptist cause began at nearby Port Melbourne and Goble was one of the first Sunday school teachers. One of the Sunday school students was Oswald Rupert Linden.

Some years on, Goble now Senior Pastor of the Footscray Baptist Church, conducted a mission at his old Church, that of Port Melbourne Baptist, and through the mission Linden came to Christian faith. Goble now took a keen interest in Linden and Linden commenced attendance at the Footscray Baptist, becoming a regular lay preacher.

Goble's influence on Linden continued as in late 1903 when Linden was sent north for six months to take charge of a mission at Ryan Street Charters Towers Baptist Church in Queensland; the posting being for the purpose of pastoral experience.[1108] Such arrangements took place between the Baptist State Home Missions. Back in Victoria, he was assistant Pastor of the Lilydale Church for twelve months and on many a Sunday he was elsewhere preaching.

Linden then undertook ministerial training at the Victorian Baptist Theological College for four years. He had only reached sixth grade at State School so studies would have been a struggle.[1109] He was ordained at the Footscray Baptist Church on 12 January 1910.

**Following his fifteen month interim at the Burnie Baptist Church** in Tasmania, Linden's next posting was to the Elsternwick Baptist Church in Melbourne, commencing March 1911; it was a temporary pastorate.[1110] During this time he was Secretary of the Baptist Union of Victoria's Sunday School Committee, a task which entailed some travelling. At the Sunday school anniversary at the Williamstown Baptist Church, following one of his "clear-cut addresses", it was said of him,

This gentleman appears to have before him a great future. In his impassioned discourses he almost achieves oratory, so

*12-14 Oswald Linden*

---

[1108] Standard (Port Melbourne) 24 October 1903 p2.
[1109] From Linden's application to begin ministerial training.
[1110] The Herald (Melbourne) 20 March 1911 p3, 17 March 1913 p3.

lacking in the ordinary everyday divine. His sermon, "He is One Man in a Thousand," with its keen, logical deductions, was worth walking a long way to hear.[1111]

In April 1913, he took another interim pastorate, this time at the Warracknabeal Baptist Church. It was set for three months but his time there continued until September 1915. He became Vice President of the Wimmera Baptist Association. Then he enlisted for service with the Australian Expeditionary forces, and was selected for the Army Medical Corps. He left behind his wife Edna and their two daughters, Edna Beatrice and Lesley Joan, and a son. His posting took him to the Australian forces at Salisbury Plains, England. He was the men's chaplain. Linden of the 39th (Victorian) Battalion returned home "from France" in February 1918 to continue his ministry at the Warracknabeal Church.[1112]

By early 1920, Linden's life had taken a change of direction. He had possibly realized he was not called to the Pastoral Ministry after all. The family had moved to Mildura which had no Baptist Church so the family became involved with its Methodist Church. Linden accepted preaching appointments with the Methodists and the Presbyterians. He represented the RSSAILA in the Anzac Memorial services, the ANA Association at its gatherings, supported the local Hospital work and was secretary of the Mildura Recreation Club, and then its manager. He won a seat for two years on the Mildura Town Council. He became President of the Mildura Fruit Growers' Association. Beatrice died in Mildura on 1 January 1923 aged fifty-seven years.[1113] In 1925, Linden married Edna Florence Dowey (1901–23 February 1990).[1114] They had one child, Lesley Joan. In 1925, he also became the Canvasser for the Council's Electric Light Department. Then four years later Linden suffered the loss of his sixteen year old daughter, Edna Beatrice, on 6 April 1929. [1115]

Linden's own end came suddenly on 16 October 1934 when his utility truck overturned on the road between Mildura and Merbein through a collapsed back wheel. His companion, a tradesman, also died. Linden had been working as a garage proprietor.[1116]

---

[1111] Williamstown Chronicle (Vic) 18 May 1912 p3.
[1112] Warracknabeal Herald (Vic) 17 March 1914 p3; Weekly Times (Melbourne) 16 February 1918 p34.
[1113] The Argus (Melbourne) 3 January 1923 p1.
[1114] Table Talk (Melbourne) 2 April 1925 p17, Approaching Marriages.
[1115] The Age (Melbourne) 17 April 1923 p13; Sunraysia Daily (Mildura, Vic.) 15 March 1924 p6, 1 August 1925 p2; The Argus (Melbourne) 10 April 1929 p1.
[1116] The Age (Melbourne) 17 October 1934 p9; Sporting Globe, 18 March 1936 p13; After Oswald died Edna Florence married again in 1958 to Thomas Ernest Flower. Family history research by Barbara Coe.

## Appendix 6: The Rev Robert McCullough

Following his time at Burnie, the Rev Robert McCullough commenced at the Grange and Seaton Baptist Churches (1918-1924). Grange is a coastal suburb of Adelaide.[1117] McCullough was pastor for seven years.

McCullough began his ministry at Mt. Barker in November 1924 and here he would spend his final days. The next year, on 12 July 1925, his wife Eva died, of heart trouble and rheumatism, passing away quietly at the age of sixty-four years. McCullough and his remaining six children were left to mourn her demise.[1118]

In December 1929, he celebrated fifty years of Christian ministry.[1119] He could have been met on the rough country road, twelve kms out, pedalling away on his push-bike, to visit a member of his flock. His ministry was now of a quieter kind. Then on 18 September 1931

> He was found lying on the roadway unconscious, near his bicycle, at Western Flat, and his face was badly knocked about. It is surmised that he had fallen from his machine while visiting members of his congregation in the locality. He was picked up and taken to the Soldiers' Memorial Hospital at Mount Barker, where he lies in a critical state.[1120]

He had been knocked down by a motor car. He died on 11 October aged seventy-eight years. His remains were laid next to those of his wife in the West Terrace Cemetery, Adelaide. His ministerial service, extending over half a century, was seen as "rich and fruitful to a high degree, and beyond human evaluation." In all, he ministered for thirty-six years in South Australia and eighteen years in Tasmania.

## Appendix 7: The Rev Frederick Augustus Leeder

Scotsman, the Rev Frederick Augustus Leeder who served in Queensland, Tasmania and Victoria, moved through Presbyterian and Congregational Churches before settling with the Baptists. He was remembered as an outstanding pastor and expository preacher.[1121]

Leeder was born 9 May 1870 in Glasgow, Scotland, to Frederick George and Margaret Leeder. He trained for the Christian ministry at the Dunoon Bible Training Institute, a small theological training school near Glasgow. There in 1896 he

---

[1117] The Advertiser (Adelaide) 9 February 1918 p10.
[1118] The Register (Adelaide) 1 November 1924 p4; The Mount Barker Courier and Onkaparinga and Gumeracha Advertiser (SA) 17 July 1925.
[1119] News (Adelaide) 6 December 1929 p13.
[1120] The Mount Barker Courier and Onkaparinga and Gumeracha Advertiser (SA) 25 September 1931 p2.
[1121] AB 13 January 1954 p10.

married Katherine Kirke.[1122] He commenced his Presbyterian Church ministry in Australia, possibly in 1904 as an interim at Gin Gin and Isis stations in May, Isis being a suburb of Childers, Queensland.[1123] In September, he relinquished the work. At his farewell at Gin Gin the chairman,

> presented Mr. Leeder with a saddle, and in making the presentation advised him (Mr. Leeder) to stick to it. Mr. Leeder, in replying, spoke feelingly of his experience with Australian horses which has not been of the happiest description. The chairman commented further, "However he might get on with our horses remains to be seen; but in so far as the people are concerned he gets on all right, because he loves them, and loves his work; he believes in it, lives it, preaches it, and such enthusiasm is now, always has been, and always will be catching. Ah! yes, the great mass of mankind, notwithstanding croaking pessimists, are deeply and truly religious, clean-minded, and that immense silent longing for God so deeply implanted in the human heart, will yet have an answer by Jehovah sending such men as Mr. Leeder amongst us with the message of mercy; not stale, old, and useless formulas, but real live warm messages of sympathy, cheerful assistance, and God-like help."[1124]

He now concentrated on the Isis work.[1125] After two years there he planned to visit Scotland but first he moved to Maryborough and took interim ministries, first at St. Stephens Presbyterian Church, then at the Congregational Church, then at the Baptist Church and finally at the Taringa Baptist Church (a suburb of Brisbane), the last for three months. Present at the welcome at the Baptist Church in Taringa was the Rev Howard Elliot with whom he would soon associate in Tasmania. At the outset of his ministry at Taringa he was given a "most hearty and unanimous call to remain permanently as their pastor" which he accepted. Most likely the nature of baptism clearly played a part in his change of thinking as a few years later he spelled out clearly what the form of baptism should be.[1126]

Three months after the Taringa appointment, he was appointed to the Council of the Baptist Union of

---

[1122] 1896 Marriage of Frederick Augustus Leeder and Katherine Kirke in Glasgow, Scotlands People, SR Marriages 644/7 444.
[1123] The Brisbane Courier 23 April 1904 p16; Gin Gin is a rural town and locality in the Bundaberg Region.
[1124] Maryborough Chronicle, Wide Bay and Burnett Advertiser (Qld.) 14 September 1904 p4.

[1125] The Bundaberg Mail and Burnett Advertiser (Qld.) 12 September 1904 p2; The Brisbane Courier 1 October 1904 p16.
[1126] Maryborough Chronicle, Wide Bay and Burnett Advertiser (Qld.) 8 May 1907 p2; The Brisbane Courier 8 June 1907 p16, 6 June 1908 p16, 28 December 1908 p6; Warwick Examiner and Times (Qld.) 20 December 1913 p3.

Queensland.[1127] In December, he gave the closing address at the annual Boxing Day Convention under the auspices of the Queensland Evangelisation Society.

Six months after he had commenced at Taringa he married Miss Ethel Winnifred Meiklejohn, the daughter of the Rev W. D. Meiklejohn of Taringa, one time Moderator of the Presbyterian Church of Queensland. In October 1910, Leeder and Ethel took leave of the Taringa Church and set sail for Scotland; they returned by May 1911.[1128]

For the Leeder family, now three with a daughter, the next pastorate was that of the newly-formed Warwick Baptist Church. At the Loyal Orange Lodge Battle of the Boyne Celebration in Warwick in 1913, Leeder "delivered a very fine address, dealing with the watchfulness of Rome, through the medium of convents and Christian Brothers' schools, and warning Protestants against sending their children to such places."[1129] At the Baptist Assembly in September 1913 he stated,

> The Koran stayed at home but the Bible was for all peoples and all nations. Evangelisation was the first essential. It was possible to be a Baptist first and a Christian afterward but it was not after the mind of God. Souls perished, not only in Central Africa only, but in their own sunny Queensland. He urged them to go, support, and pray.[1130]

Three years after the opening of the Warwick Church, Leeder resigned for Tasmania had beckoned. He regretted, "The congregation had not grown much as he and they the congregation would have it." He had also been Secretary of the Warwick Branch of the British and Foreign Bible Society.[1131]

**After a short time at the Devonport Baptist Church,** he was offered the pastorate as the church had been without a settled Pastor for seven months; he accepted. There were 103 members on the roll and 109 scholars in the Sunday school with an average attendance of seventy children and thirteen teachers. The Church had outstations at Spreyton and Port Sorell. During his time he became President of the Devonport Tennis Club. In 1916, the Church farewelled its long-standing Church Secretary, Edwin Thomas Clements.[1132]

Leeder presided over a 6 o'clock Closing Devonport Campaign

---

[1127] The Telegraph (Brisbane) 9 September 1908 p3.
[1128] The Brisbane Courier 5 March 1910 p7; The Telegraph (Brisbane) 18 October 1910 p10; Maryborough Chronicle, Wide Bay and Burnett Advertiser (Qld.) 20 May 1911 p3.
[1129] Watchman (Sydney) 21 August 1913 p8.
[1130] Daily Standard (Brisbane) 25 September 1913 p2.
[1131] The Brisbane Courier 1 April 1915 p4.
[1132] NWA&EBT 29 September 1915 p2, 1 December 1915 p2, 10 February 1916 p4, 22 September 1916 p2.

meeting of about 250 people. It was reported, "Interjections were the order of the evening, but chiefly took the form of good-humoured banter. A few rotten eggs were thrown, but there was no general disorder." To that end Leeder hosted the visit of Temperance speaker, the Rev Charles E. Schafer of South Australia.[1133] A Young People's Improvement Society was formed to foster their mental and spiritual improvement. There was also a Church Debating Society overseen by Leeder. The Devonport Branch of the Women's Christian Temperance Union (W.C.T.U.) held regular meetings.[1134]

Leeder agreed with the sentiments of a Town Hall meeting when ministers of religion, waterside workers and friendly societies endorsed the call for men to enlist. There was no compulsory enlistment.[1135]

In ones and twos the soldiers returned from the War and were welcomed by the church. Upon Leeder's shoulders was the task of visiting the homes of those who would not return. In 1916, quarterly Church socials commenced for the congregation and friends. The Annual Church report for February 1917 disclosed a membership of ninety-five, a loss of eight. There was a credit balance in the bank, but the stipend fund was in arrears. An amount of £50 had been paid off the church debt.[1136]

In December 1917, Leeder resigned because "he felt that he was making no headway" and the farewell took place in January 1918. He soon accepted a call from the Burnie Baptist Church.

**Following his time at the Burnie Baptist Church**, Leeder's next pastorate was in Melbourne at the Yarraville Baptist Church commencing in March 1922. After three years, in July 1926, he accepted a call to the Ballarat East Baptist Church in Victoria Street. In Ballarat he became vice-president of the Council of Churches. Ethel died on 6 March 1933.[1137] In May 1935, after five years service in the Ballarat pastorate, he retired to live in West Preston where he died on 17 December 1953. The Rev Frederick Augustus Leeder was remembered as an outstanding pastor and an expository preacher.[1138]

---

[1133] NWA&EBT 6 March 1916 p2. A referendum was held in Tasmania on 25 March 1916. Alarmed by the poor response in South Australia for Eleven o'clock closing, the liquor interests concentrated upon Ten o'clock. Tasmanian electors gave 42,713 votes for Six o'clock closing, against 26,153 for Ten o'clock. See AB 27 October 1954 p7.

[1134] NWA&EBT 12 June 1916 p2; The North West Post (Formby) 15 June 1916 p2, 23 August 1916 p2.

[1135] NWA&EBT 20 September 1916 p2.

[1136] NWA&EBT 3 May 1916 p2, 5 October 1916 p2; LEx 22 February 1917 p3.

[1137] The Argus (Melbourne) 5 July 1926 p9; The Age (Melbourne) 7 March 1933 p1.

[1138] AB 13 January 1954 p10.

## Appendix 8: The Rev Edward Burchell Woods

The Rev Edward Burchell Woods in his pastorates contributed immensely to Australian Baptist Associations, especially in Tasmania; his departures were greatly regretted. His excellent educational qualifications, both in the arts, theology and Biblical studies contributed greatly to these outcomes.

Woods was born in 1861, a son of the manse. His parents were the Rev William Woods and his wife Hephzibah. His father held an important English pastorate and was for many years a member on the Council of the Baptist Union Great Britain.

In 1871, the Woods family lived in Sherwood, Nottingham. Edward had two brothers and two sisters attended by two household servants. The teaching profession claimed Woods in his early days, a mathematical master at Manor House School, Clapham in London.[1139] At the early age of nineteen he entered Regents Park College, London, under the principalship of the famous Dr. Angus. Unfortunately, through ill-health, he had several breaks, and actually had three separate terms in college before he was able to complete his studies. He finally graduated in Arts at the London University, and in Theology at St. Andrews. On 15 November 1885, aged twenty-four, he commenced his first ministry at Stalham, a market town and civil parish on the River Ant in the English county of Norfolk. In 1886 he married Janet Elizabeth Vynne in her hometown of Swaffham.

In 1891, the family with now three children lived in South Leicester, Leicestershire. His next pastorate for four years was in Manchester (1893-6). He stood on the same platform with the British statesman Lloyd George in support of Home Rule for Ireland. Once, as a visitor to the House of Commons, he sat near the youthful Winston Churchill.

In 1901 the family now with six children and two servants lived in Stalham, Norfolk, and Janet had died on 28 July 1896. He married again, this time to Henrietta Adams on 18 June 1901 at Heaton Moor. Henrietta was born at Whitley Hall, Manchester, on 20 January

*12-15 **Ballarat East Baptist Church***

---

[1139] The Mercury (Hobart) 27 October 1927 p3.

*12-16 Whyte's Causeway Church, Kirkcaldy, Fife*

1860.[1140] Then followed a pastorate of six years (1897-1902) at Clarendon, Leicester, which was a rising working-class suburb.

After a break down in health, he went to Switzerland in 1902 and became school master at the College Latin in Neuchatel, with a joint professorship in the Latin college for three years; he also preached in the Swiss language. While there he taught mountaineering and mountaineered himself.

A ministry in Scotland followed at Whyte's Causeway Church, Kirkcaldy, Fife (1905-1913). He was associated with the Free Church Movement. The Pleasant Sunday Afternoon Brotherhood movement, both in England and Scotland, received his warm support, the working men of Kirkcaldy presenting him with a handsome testimonial. The ministers of all denominations honoured him for his public service. Prior to World War I, for four and one half years he was minister of Cinnamon Gardens Church, Colombo, Ceylon. In Colombo, entrusted by the Government of Ceylon and the municipality of Colombo with the task of administering poor relief, and dealing with all who were stranded in the island during the war, all benefited by his secretarial gifts.

His three boys enlisted in the war, one being an Anzac, while two daughters were engaged in war work in London, and a third daughter was in Germany all through the war. By May 1918, one of the boys, Private Alan, returned home seriously wounded.

In 1918, the couple came to Australia to take charge of the Flinders Street Baptist Church in Adelaide for two months which was extended to five months commencing 5 May 1918.[1141] He was influenced to emigrate in part because his son who had emigrated some time earlier had now been invalided back home to Australia. But the French mail ship on which they were travelling, the Andre Le Bon, carrying a crew of about 800 and about 1,300 passengers, was wrecked off the coast of Singapore in April 1918. After a night of horror, Woods and Henrietta barely escaped with their lives.[1142]

---

[1140] AB 18 June 1901, 24 January 1933, 12 November 1935 p1.
[1141] The West Australian (Perth) 27 April 1918 p6; Observer (Adelaide) 25 May 1918 p39.

[1142] The Advertiser (Adelaide) 7 May 1918 p7; The Mercury (Hobart) 27 October 1927 p3; Advocate (Burnie) 7 August 1953 p6.

He also served for a brief period in the Petersham, Blackheath and Katoomba Baptist churches in NSW. He returned to the North Adelaide Baptist Church in March 1919 for nine months and sought to follow up every soldier who had had a connection with the church, about seventy in number.[1143]

To a Baptist Assembly at the close of the War, Woods had some hard things to say. He remarked that during the War,

> we were face to face with the opportunity on promoting vital religion, and bringing it back to the midst of their churches. There were gains to be registered from the terrible war they had just finished, in spite of the losses, anguish, and suffering. The war had pronounced judgment upon war for all time. Mankind had learnt generally its futility, folly, criminality, and its absolutely unchristian character. The shaking up of the churches from the war had been the very best thing that could have happened to them. The admitted comparative failure of the church to assist and attract the multitude and win them for Christ had had

12-17 Henrietta Woods

a powerful influence in creating that movement towards the union of churches. The condition of their church rolls filled him with dismay. If their church rolls were not regularly revised, and the revision kept up to date, their statistics were a fraud. How were they to deepen the sense of obligation towards those who came into their churches now when they saw the state of things that obtained already in the church?[1144]

There was little improvement in the churches as a consequence of the war. During 1920 and 1921 Woods was interim pastor at the Broken Hill, Black Forest and Edwardstown, Gumeracha and Kenton Valley Baptist Churches, all in South Australia. In May 1922, he accepted a call from the Burnie Baptist Church in Tasmania.

**Interim pastorates followed for Woods after his time at Burnie** commencing with the South Plympton and Hindmarsh Baptist Churches in South Australia and the

---

[1143] The Advertiser (Adelaide) 27 September 1918 p6, 1 March 1919 p12; AB 30 September 1919 p8.

[1144] Observer (Adelaide) 27 September 1919 p48.

Darling Baptist Church in Melbourne.[1145]

On 25 December 1932, Henrietta died; she had been in failing health for some time. She had had an active career in Christian work in England and South Africa, in the latter country residing with her uncle, Sir David Hunter, and rendering fine service in succouring soldiers during the South African War.[1146]

In May 1934, Woods began at the Sandy Bay Church in southern Tasmania and remained until February 1937. Interim pastorates took place in South Australia, Tasmania, Victoria and Queensland until March 1940 when he took charge of the Ulverstone-Penguin churches for five months. [1147]

In May 1939, he denigrated the Jehovah's Witnesses following an attack on the Churches by this deviant organisation.[1148]

His final pastorate was that of the Wayville Baptist Church in South Australia from August 1940 until he retired in 1947 having spent sixty years in Christian ministry. These final years in South Australia were the opportunity to visit earlier South Australian pastorates on the occasions of anniversaries and the like. He died on 2 August 1957 in South Australia aged ninety-six years. A man of strong theological conviction, he held always the sense of the enormous task before him and saw clearly the social and spiritual malaise of his day.

## Appendix 9: Edward Albert Joyce

The Burnie Baptist Church Sunday school was commenced by Edward Albert Joyce and it grew rapidly. Joyce became the Church's secretary upon its inauguration and remained in the position until 1944. He was elected a member of the first diaconate in 1899, an office which he held until his death on 2 February 1947.

He was born in Launceston where he served his apprenticeship as a jeweller and settled in Burnie in 1893 where he opened a jeweller's business in Wilson Street. Morning family worship was a feature of his family's life in "Wyona", their stately home in High Street. It is recorded that he was a person of a very helpful, kindly disposition, always keeping himself in the background,

---

[1145] The Advertiser (Adelaide) 16 July 1932 p7; News (Adelaide) 1 December 1933 p5.
[1146] The Mercury (Hobart) 27 October 1927 p3; Advocate (Burnie) 28 December 1932 p6.
[1147] The Mercury (Hobart) 16 May 1934 p9, 18 February 1937 p7; Advocate (Burnie) 13 July 1940 p6.
[1148] Advocate (Burnie) 31 May 1939 p11, 29 June 1939 p5.

and was only with great difficulty persuaded to speak in public. He was secretary of the Burnie Sick and Benevolent Fund for many years. When the Burnie Park was acquired by the Burnie Council, he presented its entrance gates to the municipality. He was twice married. His first wife was Fanny Clarke of Launceston. In 1907, he married Emily Pitt of Hobart. He was forever giving to the Church and, although at times the gifts came from an "anonymous donor", it was obvious from whom they came. It was related that during the depression of the thirties, a gang of about forty men was employed on the sewerage in his street. It was cold and wet and on two successive days he sent out hot tea, scones and cakes for the whole gang. He was for many years a member of the Council of the Baptist Union of Tasmania.

*12-18 Edward Albert Joyce*

## Appendix 10: Henry T. Dowling

Henry T. Dowling was Superintendent of the Sunday school for thirty-three years and for a greater part of that time, choirmaster. He and his wife were foundation members of the Church. By the time of his death in December 1931, he was one of Burnie's oldest and most respected residents. Woods said at the time that if he ever left the choosing of the hymns to Dowling, Dowling would confine himself almost entirely to hymns which spoke of Christ's atoning sacrifice. On Dowling's death, Woods said of him,

As I gazed on that rugged manly face in its last earthly sleep, I almost felt tempted to cry out, "There goes the last of the Puritans of Burnie!" For indeed there was in him a real strain of Puritan simplicity and sternness, yet there was no Puritanic sourness of disposition, nothing of a harsh critical spirit in his judgment of those who differed from him. His was a wonderful blend of Christian whole-heartedness and devotion, with an almost melting tenderness, which won for him the love and esteem of hundreds of children through the well-nigh one third of a century that he had been the Sunday School Superintendent.

In the fly-leaf of his well-worn Bible, Dowling told of how he in 1896, at the age of thirty-five years, accepted Christ at the Christian Mission Church in Launceston, then under the Rev Joseph Tanner Piercey. Prior to this, he acknowledged that he had been a rough, ungodly man. He always ended his prayers at the prayer meetings with the petition that, at the end of the days of those gathered there they might "see His (Jesus') face without regrets". On his death it was said,

> His massive figure, commanding presence, eloquent addresses, and racy humour, and his kindliness and sympathy combined to make him an ideal president (of the Baptist Churches), and he was always a welcome visitor to the churches throughout the state.[1149]

## Conclusion

Lectures and conferences on the Second Coming are a thing of the past in our Tasmanian Churches but not so in the late 19th and early 20th Centuries. Not long after his arrival in the colony the Rev Albert Bird delivered week day evening lectures on the subject at the new Launceston Tabernacle.[1150] The Revs. J. S. Harrison and Albert Bird and many others were all expecting the imminent return of the Lord. The Rev William Gillings was a lead organizer for annual Second Coming or Prophetic Conferences at the time in Victorian population centres.[1151] These conferences were pre-millennial and had their stress not just on an imminent Second Coming of Christ but also on the conversion of the Jews. Key scriptures were the Biblical books of Daniel and Revelation. It was not a good show if the pastors of the larger Churches did not participate. The Second Coming was seen as a fundamental doctrine of Christianity in the same sense as the Deity, atonement and resurrection of Jesus Christ. For many of the conference attenders the Second Advent of Christ was the only cure for all of society's ills.

Yet if the Second Advent was so imminent, what was the point of social reform? The churches then as now need to realize that they have a civilizing mission as well as an evangelistic responsibility. Further, the Pre-millennial view was pessimistic about the ability of the

*12-19 Henry T. Dowling*

---

[1149] LEx 17 December 1931 p5. Dowling was no relation to the Dowlings of the former York Street Chapel in Launceston.

[1150] LEx 23 August 1884 p2.

[1151] Bendigo Advertiser 16 September 1887 p2.

Gospel to improve the world before Christ's return.

Today, it is as if we Tasmanian Baptists have taken to heart the words of the Rev C. H. Spurgeon which he wrote of Gillings back in 1874. Not impressed on his over-emphasis on the Second Coming, Spurgeon wrote,

> There are good brethren in the world who are impractical. The grand doctrine of the Second Advent makes them stand with open mouths, peering into the skies, so that I am ready to say, "Ye men of Plymouth, why stand ye here gazing up into heaven?" The fact that Jesus Christ is to come is not a reason for stargazing, but for working in the power of the Holy Ghost. Be not so taken up with speculations as to prefer a Bible reading over a dark passage in the Revelation to teaching in a ragged-school or discoursing to the poor concerning Jesus. We must have done with day dreams, and get to work. I believe in eggs, but we must get chickens out of them. I do not mind how big your egg is; it may be an ostrich's egg if you like, but if there is nothing in it, pray clear away the shells. If something comes of it, God bless your speculations, and even if you should go a little further than I think it wise to venture, still, if you are more useful, God be praised for it. We want facts - deeds done, souls saved. It is all very well to write essays, but what souls have you saved from going down to hell?[1152]

---

[1152] S&T April 1874.

# Chapter 13 Ulverstone & Penguin Baptist Churches

## Introduction

At the 1901 Tasmanian Baptist Annual Assembly William Dubrelle Weston, the Union honorary legal adviser, proposed that the assisted churches and the home mission stations be grouped in a Home Mission Union, with a superintendent. "The paid superintendent would hold a small church and be paid jointly by that church, the Home Mission and the Sustentation Fund," he said. He continued, "The Churches are doing so little for the support of the Home Mission. There is zeal for foreign missions. 'This ought yet to have done, and not to have left the other undone.'" The Home Mission stations were enabling the State work to grow steadily.

At the same Assembly and in agreement was the Rev Thomas Vigis of Burnie who said that where there was true Home Mission enterprise, there was true Foreign Mission enterprise and *vice versa*.[1153]

At an Assembly six years later the Rev F. W. Boreham of Hobart, formerly of New Zealand, gave a very warm tribute to the excellence of the contributions of the Tasmanian Home Missionaries. He said,

> Everything that I saw of them, everything that I heard of them, convinced me that the Tasmanian Union is to be felicitated on such workers. They are the scouts and path-finders of the entire body. Men of intense spirituality and dogged determination are a strength to the whole denomination. I know that there were times in New Zealand when we would have eaten our hats for a handful of just such men.[1154]

A few years later again, the Rev William L. Heaven, a Home Missioner himself, claimed that home and foreign missions were "like the Siamese twins - inseparable."[1155] Time and time again Baptists at Assemblies were told that,

> strengthening of the home base was in a large measure the key to

*13-1 Penguin's 1864 Primitive Methodist Church*

---

[1153] SB 15 May 1901 p118.
[1154] SB 11 December 1906 p301.
[1155] SB 30 November 1909 p290.

success in world-wide evangelisation; that Home and Foreign Missions were inseparably linked as one great enterprise for the extension of the kingdom; that the Master's call to go into "all the world" carried with it the injunction to "begin at Jerusalem"; that the glory of sacrificial service was manifested in the homeland, as truly as amid the darkness of heathendom.[1156]

During November 1902, the Rev Samuel Harrison, the pastor of the Burnie Church, began a Home Mission work in Ulverstone with its population of about 1,150. The Burnie Church also commenced a new work at Penguin only twelve kms away from Ulverstone with its population of 540.

Yet in deciding to focus on Ulverstone and Penguin the Baptists were moving into an area already reasonably catered for with churches. Beginning in 1867, Anglican Sunday school and services were conducted in Ulverstone. Its first church was opened on 26 November 1868. This building was replaced in 1893 and the new building opened on 24 December 1893.[1157] St Stephens Penguin Anglican Church was built in 1874.

The Presbyterians began in Penguin in 1886 with services in a local hall. On 18 March 1888, they opened their own building.[1158] Penguin's first Primitive Methodists began in 1864 and their Chapel which was opened on 14 January 1866[1159] was taken over in 1872 by the "Independent Methodists", a group who seceded and called themselves the United Methodist Free Church. A second Primitive Methodist Church was formed in 1874 with the opening of their chapel on 26 January and continued until 1903. In 1887, there were only eighty persons living in the town catered for by just three churches. In 1903, the two Methodist congregations united and the new body, the United Methodist Church erected a new

*13-2 Penguin's 1874 Primitive Methodist Church*

---

[1156] AB 8 November 1927 p3. The speakers were the Rev Dr. Waldock and the Rev Hugh McDonald.
[1157] Cornwall Chronicle (Launceston), 16 November 1867 p5; LEx 5 December 1868 p5; Daily Telegraph (Launceston) 23 March 1894 p4.
[1158] Daily Telegraph (Launceston) 19 March 1888 p3.
[1159] The Cornwall Chronicle (Launceston) 10 January 1866 p6.

building on the outskirts of Ulverstone.[1160]

The Ulverstone Congregational church opened on 23 January 1878 in Alexander Road but by 1901 services ceased.[1161] Around 1910 the Presbyterians temporarily used the church while they were building their new church on Main Street.[1162]

In Penguin, the Baptists hired the Rechabite's Hall for the meetings. The Burnie Church was also conducting services at Wynyard and Stowport. But soon the Ulverstone-Penguin mission was transferred to the Devonport Church's care.

The extending of this work on the North West coast was agreed at the Annual Assembly of the Baptist Churches in 1903 and a steady stream of Tasmanian young men were employed in the task.

In Ulverstone Church services began at the Town Hall on 15 February 1903. The Rev George J. Mackay of the Devonport Baptist Church and Amos Sidwell of the Hobart Church conducted the first service. It was reported that the Town Hall "was crowded to the doors".

## George Edgar Harrison

On 7 June 1903, George Edgar Harrison, the eldest son of the Rev Samuel Harrison, was inducted into the Ulverstone work. Services were now held in the Odd Fellows Hall at 19 Main Street (the Hall was later known as the Gaiety Theatre.).[1163] Union Council had approached young Harrison and he agreed to head up the work for twelve months as well as study for ordination. He did his general rounds on a bicycle.

The Advocate and Emu Bay Times reported on an important event,

A baptismal ceremony was conducted in connection with the Baptist Church at Button's Creek, in the vicinity of the beach. There was a large concourse of people assembled to witness what in Ulverstone is an unusual spectacle. The Rev

*13-3 Ulverstone's Congregational Church*

---

[1160] Cornwall Chronicle (Launceston) 1 May 1874 p3; LEx 27 October 1904 p7. The Tasmanian Methodism, Stansall account differs somewhat with what is found in newspaper reports.

[1161] Devon Herald, 26 January 1878, p2; Daily Telegraph 5 November 1901 p3.

[1162] NWA&EBT 7 April 1910 p2.

[1163] NWA&EBT 5 September 1903 p2.

G. J. Mackay delivered an appropriate address upon the subject of believer's baptism, after which the ceremony was carried out. Pastor (G.E.) Harrison delivered an earnest address concluding the service. At 7 o'clock, Mackay preached in the Odd Fellows Hall taking his text from 2 Cor. 5.7. There was a very large congregation, and the rev. gentleman gave a most powerful exposition on his subject. At the close he intimated it was his intention to visit Ulverstone at regular intervals alternately with Pastor (Samuel) Harrison of Burnie.[1164]

Other baptisms connected with the Ulverstone work were sometimes conducted in the Devonport Baptist school room.[1165]

In November 1903, the Ulverstone work was removed from Devonport's care and placed under control of the Home Mission with George Edgar Harrison designated Home Missionary.

But in June 1905 he resigned; his health had deteriorated and "he has been recommended a long sea voyage". Present at his farewell was Jack Fisher who was formally installed in his place.[1166] Harrison stayed on in the district for many years retaining his church membership.

## Pastor John (Jack) William Fisher

John (Jack) William Fisher had been brought from Victoria to replace Harrison. The Baptist Union really wanted to place him at Wynyard but considered that the need was greater at Ulverstone-Penguin. He had been for a short time at the Launceston Tabernacle but now at Ulverstone he was placed under the supervision of Mackay and began his studies towards ordination.

At the transfer of the pastorate, Baptist Association Council member, William Dubrelle Weston, sent him a set of T.W. Robertson's sermons saying, "I am sure you will find these of the greatest use." Weston handed out advice to Mackay. He said, "Fisher is fluent but will require a good deal of coaching from you in the way of preparation of regular addresses. Recommend him to the Ulverstone people as a very fair speaker and a very good young man." To Harrison Weston said, "Fisher doesn't have the same eloquence in speaking as you have, but certainly has an exceeding nice

---

[1164] NWA&EBT 11 August 1903.
[1165] NWA&EBT 21 May 1904 p2.

[1166] LEx 28 June 1905 p3.

manner and will, I am sure, get on well with your people."

Fisher was to be paid a minimum £80 and no more than £100 per annum, according to what was in the collection. In August 1905, the Baptist Union Council agreed that the two churches would be called the "Ulverstone and Penguin Church".

The Ulverstone Mission was now meeting in the Odd Fellows Hall. It was in this hall on the evening of 24 September 1905 that the Church was constituted with five members, among them George Harrison. The Rev Joseph Tanner Piercey of Burnie, who had replaced the Rev Samuel Harrison, was also present. Both Mackay and Piercey preached.

The local newspapers recorded the event,

> The Rev. G. J. Mackay, vice president of the Baptist Union of Tasmania, conducted divine service in the Odd Fellows Hall, Main Street, on Sunday night. The attendance was large, all available seats being occupied. The rev. gentleman preached an eloquent sermon from the words, "I am the good shepherd," the audience listening in rapt attention. During the evening Mr Mackay contributed a vocal solo which was much appreciated. At the close the sacrament of the Lord's Supper was administered, after which members were enrolled, and the services which have hitherto been conducted as a mission, will be constituted as those of a regularly formed church.[1167]

*13-4 W. D. Weston*

The Penguin church was constituted four days later in the Rechabite Hall. In January 1906, Ulverstone agreed to open a building fund. Fisher only stayed for nine months, leaving for the Longford-Perth Baptist Church circuit on 31 March 1906 to work as Harry Wood's assistant. As a farewell gift, the Ulverstone-Penguin Church presented him with his own bicycle.

## The Rev John Robertson

The Rev John Robertson from Victoria replaced Fisher. He had recently returned from England. He was living in Launceston and had planned to live and work in Ulverstone before the pastorate was offered. He commenced in April 1906. It was understood that he would be there for just a short

---

[1167] NWA&EBT 26 September 1905.

term.[1168] George Harrison continued to be of assistance.

## Pastor Ernest Albert Salisbury

A Baptist Union Council meeting in August 1906 agreed that "the distinctive truths of the denomination should be taught in every town along the coast." Realising the importance of the Ulverstone work, Union Council sent them the best man they could secure and that man was Ernest Albert Salisbury to replace Robertson, who had been in charge and had completed his agreed term. In June 1906, Salisbury had been welcomed to the Bracknell district as an assistant to Pastor Robert Steel but his stay was brief.[1169]

In 1906, authority was given to find land for building a church. By July 1907, the Church purchased for the sum of £155 a centrally situated block of land in King Edward Street, close to the Post Office as the Church continued conducting services in the Odd Fellows Hall. Whether it had to do with the purchase of the land or not, the "Day Star" reported, "Several members and sympathisers have left our town."[1170] The church was experiencing "large congregations".

*13-5 Home Missioners 1913-1915: Back row: Fred J. Wood, J.W. Fisher, J.G. Duncan, Ern. C. Walsh, Albert Butler. Front row: Robert Steel, W. L. Heaven, Superintendent Rev F. J. Dunkley, H. E. Saunders, E.A. Salisbury*

For the Annual Assembly of the Baptist Association in April 1908, 200 gathered for an evening "tea meeting" at the Ulverstone Town Hall. A special feature was the decoration of the stage which was laid out as a drawing-room. In front was a table on which the golden offerings were to be laid. In the evening "with the hall packed to the doors", the golden offering took place. Pastor Salisbury then

laid the voluntary golden offerings of the people on the table amidst profound silence, the glistening heap of gold (some 170 sovereigns) making a fine sight. Mr Salisbury then read out the names of the different donors and collectors. The vast audience then rose and sang the doxology in thankfulness for so fully answering their prayers. The site for the (Ulverstone) church will be more than paid for, and it will

---

[1168] NWA&EBT 10 August 1906 p2; SB 10 April 1906 p90.

[1169] LEx 14 June 1906 p8.

[1170] "Day Star" August 1907.

not be long before the building is erected.[1171]

The Baptist paper, the Southern Baptist reported it thus,

> The great thank offering taken at the suggestion of Pastor Salisbury is an example and an inspiration to all the churches. Those who were privileged to be present speak with one voice of the beauty and solemnity of the great response. In a tiny country village, to see the people come forward with glowing faces and pour out their gold upon the "altar", is in these days "a sight for sore eyes."[1172]

But the now debt-free land was never used.

Meanwhile in 1907 in Upper Castra twenty kms inland from Ulverstone, William Kenner donated funds so that land near where he lived could be purchased for a church building. With the assistance of Martin Spellman of Launceston, who had been one of Kenner's converts in the early days, a little chapel was opened in July 1908.[1173] Prior to the erection of the chapel, the mission there under Kenner had rented out the State School and the Anglican schoolroom for services. In 1908 there were thirty-one Sunday school scholars. Local Walter Filleul was among those who contributed generously to the cause. The Education Department had appointed Kenner as teacher at Upper Castra in March 1908.[1174]

With the Upper Castra cause established, the incumbent at Ulverstone was required to make the forty-four kilometre return journey by any means possible, even if that meant a bike.[1175]

The Ulverstone Sunday school began on 1 December 1907[1176] and the work grew with Deacon Barker as its first Superintendent. He was also Treasurer for a number of years. Baptismal services continued to take place at the beach.

By June 1906, the Penguin Church had purchased land in South Street, Penguin. On 16 August 1908, they opened its new building and ten days later Salisbury baptised ten candidates in the new structure.[1177]

Early in 1909, a Christian Endeavour Society was formed at Ulverstone. Church meetings were now held in a room adjoining R. A. Whitlock's shop in Reiby Street. Even though he was well liked by the congregation, because of ill health, Salisbury concluded his work in January 1909.[1178] He was advised to live

---

[1171] Daily Telegraph (Launceston) 10 April 1908 p6.
[1172] SB 12 May 1908 p114.
[1173] LEx 14 July 1908 p3, opened on 12 July.
[1174] LEx 23 March 1908 p6.
[1175] A Methodist Church too had just been opened at Upper Castra. LEx 14 July 1908 p3.
[1176] LEx 7 December 1908 p 6.
[1177] LEx 26 August 1908 p7, 28 August 1908 p8.
[1178] LEx 8 Jan 1909 p5.

inland. He soon transferred back to Bracknell.

## The Rev Charles Henry James Warren

The Rev Charles Henry James Warren was moved from the Sheffield Church in December 1908 to the Ulverstone–Penguin District Church. But the placement of Warren was unsuccessful as he found the sea air far too trying for his constitution; he was suffering from an affliction of the throat so by the end of April 1909 he and his wife Amy moved to Victoria.[1179]

## Pastor William Llewellyn Heaven

In July 1909, New Zealander William Llewellyn Heaven came to Tasmania to enter the Home Mission work at Ulverstone and Penguin. A welcome was soon given to him, his wife Mary Florence, and four children.[1180]

In October 1909, fund raising for the new building at Spreyton commenced and the building was finally opened on 22 September 1909. By January 1910, the Upper Castra members wanted their work closed but the Union Council felt that their troubles would pass. The Ulverstone Church which never expected any financial assistance from the Upper Castra work, refused at this time to be responsible for the work.

Attention now turned to a new building in Ulverstone itself. At the Rechabite Lodge in Penguin in June 1910 Heaven spoke from personal and lengthy experience on "Temperance Legislation in New Zealand."[1181]

In December 1910, the Congregational Union offered to sell for £400 its "Leven" church property situated almost in the centre of the town and the Ulverstone Baptists unanimously decided to purchase it because the Odd Fellows Hall was "a cold, unconsecrated, and in some respects uncomfortable and an unsuitable place to hold Divine service".[1182] The Presbyterians who were using the Congregational Union Church vacated it near the end of 1910 having built their own church.[1183]

In 1910, the Home Mission reported that all work stations were proceeding satisfactorily except Ulverstone. Heaven, who was in his second year, was on £140 annually. In the next year all Home Missioners received rises except Heaven.[1184] In

---

[1179] NWA&EBT 4 December 1908 p2, 2 April 1909 p3; SB 13 July 1909 p165.
[1180] NWA&EBT 5 July 1909 p2, 12 August 1909 p4.
[1181] The Mercury (Hobart) 23 September 1909 p6; NWA&EBT 8 October 1909 p2, 16 October 1909 p4, 10 June 1910 p2.
[1182] Day-Star November 1909.
[1183] LEx 25 October 1910 p 3.
[1184] HM Minutes p4, p8.

February 1911, he transferred to Bracknell but not before the Ulverstone folk expressed their unhappiness about the change. A petition was circulated through the District asking that Heaven's services be retained but it failed to persuade the Home Mission Committee.[1185]

## Sterling George Clarke

Even though the Home Mission thought of bringing Jack Fisher back to Ulverstone in February 1911 they chose instead Sterling George Clarke from his home church of Longford. Early in Clarke's pastorate the purchase of the Congregational Church was finalized with the offer of just £210[1186] and this provided a new impetus to the work. In June 1911 the Church celebrated with a working bee declaring,

> We are in high glee because we are soon going to worship in our own Church. Our Pastor had called a working bee to clear up the ground and clean out the Church. The men rolled up with picks and shovels, spades and hoes, slashers and mattocks, and a wheelbarrow. Being Empire Day, some thought a revolution had broken out. They thought probably someone had been dishonoring the great Empire, or speaking lightly of our King and we were going to avenge that slur. But when our Pastor came along armed with buckets of boiling water they thought someone had started a bacon factory, and there was going to be a wild boar hunt; and when the ladies flourished their brooms folks did not know what to make of things; eyes scanned the heavens to see if there were any cobwebs in the skies. But the small boy is right every time: "It is the Baptists! It is the Baptists! They are alive at last; they are going to show Ulverstone they mean business." A good afternoon's work was put in. We all returned home tired out, but determined to have another go on Saturday.[1187]

Long term member of the Church, Stuart McDonald, well remembers the Congregational Church building. He recalls,

> The old weatherboard building beside the two Norfolk Pine trees became a substantial and meaningful part of my life in that period from the cradle to marriage. The old manse was behind the church, as were the two "dunnies". How times have changed! I remember a banana passion fruit vine hanging over the neighbour's fence. When they were ripe, they were most attractive.[1188]

---

[1185] Daily Telegraph (Launceston) 24 January 1911 p4.
[1186] LEx 7 March 1912 p 6.
[1187] Day Star June 1911.
[1188] Interview with Laurence Rowston in 2003.

The building was officially opened on 11 June 1911. Ulverstone Baptists worshipped in this building until it was demolished and sold off in 1957. In June 1911, a Band of Hope was formed.

Clarke only spent a year at Ulverstone. The Baptist Annual Assembly report on Ulverstone was not encouraging, "The work at Ulverstone had for some little time been giving us some concern, and it was thought advisable to make an alteration there. S. G. Clarke should go to Bracknell."[1189] At the time there were forty church members but 50% had not attended in the last twelve months. Following a roll revision, the membership stood at twenty. Only fifteen of the twenty were regular attendees.

Clarke preached his farewell sermon at Upper Castra in February 1912. The Home Mission Superintendent, the Rev Frederic Joseph Dunkley, was present. The next day Clarke baptised five people in the Wilmot River. The spot chosen was close to Spellman's Bridge and William Kenner participated. The service commenced with the singing of the hymn, "Down in the valley with my Saviour I would go," and the baptism service was considered by some a fitting testimony to the "successful" ministry of Clarke in the district.[1190]

## The Rev Albert Butler

The Rev Albert Butler transferred from Yolla and commenced in March 1912. On 8 April 1912, he married Miss Laura Martha Ball, the youngest daughter of Mr. and Mrs. H. S. Ball, at their residence, the Temperance Hall in Longford.

A Junior Christian Endeavour Society began in 1913 and it soon had forty-eight on the roll. As with former Ulverstone pastors, Butler served on the Committee of the local Hospital. He was also a most enthusiastic member of the Ulverstone Literary and Debating Society. The Church's monthly Band of Hope Society flourished.[1191] In 1914, the site that had been purchased in King Edward Street was sold and the money applied to debt reduction for the purchase of the empty Congregational church. At the beginning of 1914 Butler transferred to the Deloraine Baptist Church.

## The Rev Vincent George Britton

In January 1914 the Rev Vincent George Britton was appointed Pastor, transferring from the Sheffield Church. During his twenty-seven months, evening services saw forty to fifty people in attendance.

Two appointments and one world situation greatly overshadowed his

---

[1189] Footnote needed.
[1190] LEx 27 Feb 1912 p3.

[1191] The North West Post (Formby) 23 June 1913 p3, 18 July 1913 p3.

input to the Church. The first and most important to his appointment was as Home Mission Superintendent in succession to the Rev Frederic Joseph Dunkley. This new position involved extensive time away visiting the Home Mission churches and their outstations. The other was his appointment for a year as President of the Baptist Association, until March 1914.[1192] But after eighteen months or so in the Pastorate the war effort impacted greatly on his life and ministry. He became a Chaplain to the men at the Claremont Camp just outside Hobart and this meant being away for as many as eight days at a time. His son, Vincent Derwent enlisted. In 1916, Britton senior took a keen interest in the recruiting movement with his lecture titled, "Why I should vote Yes." He urged his listeners,

> Our men were fighting for freedom, honor, virtue and home; they had suffered and died for these principles, while we are content to look on, and like the men of Moron (Judges 5) wait to take a share of the benefits of victory. It was every man's duty to go, and there was no reason why, by means of vote, the shirker should not be made to do his duty.[1193]

The Ulverstone Church still had charge of the Church at Penguin and small works at Upper Castra and Wilmot. James Clemens Salter's assistance was vital, that is until Salter enlisted in the war himself.

Britton saw the young Home Missioners in his charge such as Salter as those "who can live on little, do a lot of work and come up smiling every time."

Britton continued giving Magic Lantern lectures both at home and away. Some of these Magic Lantern viewings were given to aid various causes such as the Red Cross in its work with the troops and for the Belgian Fund. Beginning with his second year at Ulverstone, the realization that the War was going to last much longer than initially thought, the majority of viewings dealt with the War effort with many of the venues well filled with appreciative audiences.[1194] There was no report of the Temperance Band of Hope meetings at Ulverstone after the end of Britton's first year.

Still Britton took on various other appointments. Among these were being on the Board of the local hospital, President of the Christian Endeavour Union, a member of the Agricultural Society and a Religious Education teacher at the local Primary School. Britton fitted into the role of being a "jack of all trades", the chairman of every committee

---

[1192] LEx 25 March 1914 p3.

[1193] NWA&EBT 21 October 1916 p4. Compare what recruiter Robert Steel said to encourage young men to recruit; see p.

[1194] NWA&EBT 1 September 1914 p2, 25 March 1915 p2, 26 August 1915 p2; Daily Telegraph (Launceston) 3 July 1915 p11.

Lessons from our first 20 years

and involved with the local school which was expected of every minister. He was also involved with the "Early Closing Crusade".[1195]

In 1915, the Devonport Baptist Church offered him its Pastorate and as he had been seventeen years with the Home Mission overall and a settled pastorate did have its attractions, but he turned the offer down.[1196]

Stables were erected at the rear of the Ulverstone church in 1914. In October 1915, Joshua T. Soundy of Hobart laid the foundation stone for a weatherboard manse at the rear of the property behind the Church.[1197]

With the extension of Christ's Kingdom in the "back blocks" as the Home Mission was called, in 1914 there were 530 Sunday school children, with sixty-three teachers, while the sum of £70 was raised by the children for foreign missions.[1198]

Improvement all round took place in the following years although there were far fewer baptisms in 1922.

The town gave Britton a Town Hall farewell in March 1917.[1199]

## The Rev F. J. (Jack) Fisher

The Rev F. J. (Jack) Fisher was welcomed back to the Ulverstone Church in April 1917. His wife, Sarah, became the church organist. Fisher joined the committee of the Ulverstone Hospital. In 1917 the Church participated in the United Churches Intercession Services for the War effort. Welcome home services for their returned soldiers increased in number.[1200] In February 1919, the Church unveiled an honour roll listing twenty-four of the young men who had volunteered from the district.

13-6 Jack Fisher with his mother, wife Jane and daughter

A fine woodworker, Fisher built the Church's communion table and trays with funds raised by the Sunday school children.[1201]

In 1919, the worldwide Spanish flu struck and interrupted church life for some months across the nation. Meetings within doors were

---

[1195] Daily Telegraph (Launceston) 14 January 1916 p2; NWA&EBT 4 August 1915 p3, 15 March 1916 p2, 28 July 1916 p2.
[1196] NWA&EBT 26 July 1915 p2.
[1197] NWA&EBT 29 October 1915 p2.
[1198] AB 14 April 1914, 9 Nov 1915.

[1199] AB April 1922 (check); NWA&EBT 28 March 1917 p2; AB 17 November 1925 p7.
[1200] NWA&EBT 9 May 1917 p3, 4 August 1917 p4, 5 December 1917 p3; 12 February 1919 p2.
[1201] Daily Telegraph (Launceston) 28 November 1922 p8.

forbidden and they were replaced by open-air services. One who succumbed was Herbert J. Walker, superintendent of the Baptist Sunday School at Spreyton.[1202]

In order that Fisher could more rapidly travel about his extensive district, he was given a motor cycle in July 1919.[1203]

The practice of bringing in evangelists to reap "the harvest of souls" was again seen in 1922 with the visit of the Rev Adam Clark of Victoria for a ten-day mission. That year the Home Mission purchased its own tent complete with organ for special evangelistic work at various centres. They possibly took a lead from the Queensland Baptist evangelist, Wilfred Jarvis, who had his own tent. Jarvis was the Tasmanian Baptist Association's evangelist for the year. The following year the church was involved in a United Mission in Upper Castra as the Baptist work was at low ebb due to removals from the district. For the year 1922, eight churches were under Home Mission control - Smithton, Yolla, Wynyard, Ulverstone, Latrobe, Deloraine, Bracknell and Longford - with about thirty outstations. There were 700 children in Sunday school, over seventy teachers, and nearly 300 church members, 13 local preachers, conducting seventy-six baptisms and having eighty professed conversions, nearly seventy of whom were baptised and added to the church rolls. For the year the Home Mission stations raised toward their own work about £800, and for Foreign Missions about £300. The cost of the work was now £1600 a year.

The previous year, even though manses had been acquired for three of the stations, Yolla, Wynyard, and Smithton – it was reported that the work was at a standstill and that a "marktime" policy was not in the best interests of the denomination! The membership of the Home Mission churches had reached a total of 370. No new work had been started for several years, the reason being that the Home Mission churches were not becoming self-supporting; hence a continual drain was made on denominational funds to maintain them.

The lull was not only in the Home Mission, but in the wider denomination in Tasmania as a whole. In the following year the situation was such that the Rev Edward B. Woods of Burnie gave a paper at a 1921 Assembly entitled, "Is the Baptist Witness in Tasmania Justified?"[1204] Fisher remained until May 1923 and remained Secretary of the Association up to this time.[1205] His next move would be to the Rainbow Baptist Church in Victoria.

---

[1202] LEx 14 November 1919 p3.
[1203] Advocate (Burnie) 25 July 1919 p4.

[1204] AB 7 April 1920, 10 January 1922 p10, 29 August 1922 p8.
[1205] LEx 27 October 1922 p6; Daily Telegraph (Launceston) 22 May 1923 p8.

# Appendices

## Appendix 1: George Edgar Harrison

Family connections greatly influenced George Edgar Harrison as he was the son of the influential Primitive Methodist, now Baptist Pastor, the Rev Samuel Harrison. In George's case his aspirations to join the ministerial ranks saw limited fulfillment.

George was Harrison's eldest son and knew well the Primitive Methodist Churches until 1896 as his father was one of their pastors. After a number of Baptist pastorates, Harrison Senior arrived in Burnie in 1903 from NSW.

For all his father's connections, early in 1884 George Edgar was working with the Rev Dan Hiddlestone at the Christian Mission Church in Launceston.[1206] He married Annie Hooper of Ulverstone, a devoted Church worker and the third daughter of William and Ann Hooper of Clare, SA.[1207]

George Edgar found employment in 1889, first with the Tasmanian Government Railways; he was stationed first at Railton and then at Lilydale. He then became a postmaster, money order and savings bank agent.[1208]

Following his time in the Ulverstone pastorate, he began a chain of delicatessen businesses.[1209] On 22 July 1912, George and Annie were involved in a serious motor car accident resulting in Annie's death. They had a six month old son. Just over a year later George married again. He and his new wife joined the Sheffield Baptist Church and George conducted the Bible class.[1210]

## Appendix 2: The Rev Ernest Albert Salisbury

The Rev Ernest Albert Salisbury had three placements with the Tasmanian Baptist Home Mission where his work was much to the satisfaction of both the congregations and the Mission Committee. But when Salisbury saw his future with the Anglican Church and made the move he never looked back. In Salisbury, and Annie his wife, the Tasmanian Baptists lost first class workers. In time he became for the Anglicans "a great church builder, by raising money for and building no less than fourteen churches."[1211]

Salisbury was born on 7 December 1881 at Launceston to Thomas Salisbury and his wife Jane (nee

---

[1206] LEx 12 February 1884 p3.
[1207] NWA&EBT 22 July 1912 p3.
[1208] The Tasmanian (Launceston) 31 August 1889 p20; LEx 3 July 1894 p5.
[1209] NWA&EBT 22 June 1905 p2.

[1210] LEx 1 February 1912 p1, 23 July 1912 p5, 19 November 1915 p7; Daily Telegraph (Launceston) 17 April 1913 p6.
[1211] LEx 4 Nov 1950; Mudgee Guardian and North-Western Representative (NSW) 15 August 1932 p7. Salisbury's family history by Barbara Coe.

Parker). In May 1904, he began work with the Baptist Home Mission and was attached to the Christian Mission Church in Launceston as an assistant first to the Rev Joseph Tanner Piercey and then to Rev Edward Isaac; at the time the church had a mission at Summerhill.[1212] In Victoria in 1908 Salisbury married Annie Gertrude Hardeman (1874–1929). Annie, who was born in Rhyl, Wales, came to Tasmania with her family in 1883.

Salisbury's story and that of Jack Fisher suggest that when young men arrived in the State to work with the Home Mission they were sometimes placed in a church to see if they were capable of the work before them. Salisbury's case also speaks of the close link that existed between the Christian Mission Church and the Baptist Churches, a link which has never been severed and was inextricably fastened in 1935.

## Appendix 3: The Rev Charles Henry James Warren

From Ulverstone the Rev Charles Henry James Warren and his wife, Amy, moved to Victoria for a brief time at the Barraport Boort Baptist Church located in the Wimmera District. Then they moved in October 1914 to Western Australian to the Wagin Circuit which included Ballaying, Lime Lake and Nallian.[1213] Warren served on the Wagin District Returned Soldiers' Association.[1214] At the conclusion of his fourth year, the Church asked him to stay another three years at a considerable increase of stipend which he did. In May 1919, he accepted the nearby pastorship of the Woodanilling and Cartmeticup District Baptist Churches.[1215]

A year later, Warren accepted a call to the Mount Gambier Baptist Church in South Australia. In his third year Warren moved on to the Glen Osmond Baptist Church situated in suburban Adelaide. After eighteen months, he moved to being a supply. His last pastorate, of four years, was at the Edwardstown Baptist Church also in Adelaide. The Rev Charles Henry James Warren, a man of "strong personality and genial disposition", died in Adelaide on 4 December 1946. He was chaplain of four branches of the Masonic Lodge in thirty-six years. He was survived by Amy and their two

---

[1212] Daily Telegraph (Launceston) 2 May 1904 p4, 24 September 1904 p4, 31 May 1906 p7; Mudgee Guardian and North-Western Representative (NSW) 15 August 1932 p7.

[1213] Wagin is in the Great Southern region of Western Australia, approximately 225 km south-east of Perth on the Great Southern Highway between Narrogin and Katanning.

[1214] NWA&EBT 2 April 1909 p3; The Herald (Melbourne) 17 June 1912 p3; The Southern Argus and Wagin-Arthur Express (Perth, WA) 15 September 1917 p3, 31 August 1918 p2.

[1215] Woodanilling is a small town in the Great Southern region of Western Australia about twenty km south of Wagin.

sons and a daughter.[1216] Amy died on 15 May 1949 in Adelaide.[1217]

## Appendix 4: Pastor William Llewellyn Heaven

William Llewellyn Heaven could be seen as a career Tasmanian Baptist Home Missionary of near thirty years service with just a short interstate break; he was always in charge of Home Mission causes. Although the Home Mission Council was never too happy with his work, the folk in the churches loved him greatly and regretted his forced transfers.

Heaven was born in Gloucester, England, in 1867 to Walter and Sophia Heaven. He came with his parents to New Zealand in 1874 on board the Merope SS. At first the family lived in Christchurch where his father worked as a bricklayer. In 1888, the family moved to Waimamaku, Hokianga, Northland, where Walter leased land in return for breaking in the land. They went as part of the Canterbury Settlement scheme. In Waimamaku, Willie worked as a blacksmith. Willie's sister Laura was one of the first white people in the Waimamaku settlement to get married. William came to a Christian commitment in March 1888 and was baptised and became a member of a Baptist Church. While in Kaipoi just north of Christchurch, on 22 September 1893 he married English born Mary Florence, the second daughter of Mr. and Mrs. W. Box originally of Oxford, England.

**13-7 William Heaven and his bride Mary Florence Box**

William began preaching in 1898. He entered the Baptist ministry in 1902 and served the Owaka Church as its pastor for two years. He associated with the Rev F. W. Boreham who was at Mosgiel just out of Dunedin. Owaka is South of Dunedin.

Then until July 1909 he had charge of Kaiapoi and Rangiora Baptist Churches, a combined charge in Canterbury.[1218] At his farewell it was said,

> Mr Heaven during his stay here has endeared himself to many, not only in his own congregation but among other denominations, and his departure is contemplated with sincere feelings of regret. At the same time it is felt that the Rev gentleman is

---

[1216] Tambellup Times (WA) 17 April 1920 p3; The Register (Adelaide) 9 December 1922 p5, 31 May 1924 p4; The Advertiser (Adelaide) 18 September 1936 p8; Barrier Miner (NSW) 7 December 1946 p5.

[1217] News (Adelaide) 16 May 1949 p10.

[1218] Evening Star, BUNZ 4 June 1903, January 1906, August 1909; Advocate (Burnie) 19 May 1938 p6.

fitted for better things than we can offer, for the congregation is small and the salary correspondingly so.[1219]

The family then migrated to Tasmania as he was to enter the Home Mission work.

**Following his time at Ulverstone**, Heaven was transferred to the Home Mission work at Bracknell. Yet after a year he was transferred again, this time to the Home Mission work at Wynyard.[1220]

## Appendix 5: Albert Butler

At the beginning of 1914, Albert Butler commenced at the Deloraine Baptist Church. For Harvest Festivals at Chestnut, one of its outstations, close to one hundred people gathered in a large tent erected at the Herbert Harris homestead. They had conducted church services in their home for seven years. Sunday school classes too had been conducted there. The use of the Herberts' homestead ceased when the new Chestnut chapel was opened on 13 December 1914. It was built on land donated by William and Elizabeth Warren.[1221]

The foundation stone for the new Deloraine manse was laid on 27 October 1915. On 10 May 1916 Butler was ordained to the Christian ministry in the Deloraine Tabernacle.[1222]

While at the time young men were farewelled to the War, Butler was farewelled too as part of the War effort. He commenced at the Moonah Baptist Church just out of Hobart so he would not be far from the Claremont Army Camp where he would serve as Chaplain.[1223]

For eight years Butler remained at the Moonah Church and with his oversight the work grew in a remarkable manner. In July 1918, he gave the principal address at the meeting of the Loyal Orange Institute in Hobart.[1224] Butler was now a member of the Council of the Baptist Union and was President of the Association in 1921/1922. On his Presidential visit to Yolla in January 1922, he expressed his

*13-8 Albert and Laura Butler*

---

[1219] Otago Witness (Owaka) 20 May 1905.

[1220] NWA&EBT 4 February 1911 p4, 13 March 1912 p2. I am indebted to Sue Heaven of Amberley, NZ for her family history details and Noelene Heaven of Howrah, Tasmania, for family photographs.

[1221] LEx 11 April 1914 p5; Daily Telegraph (Launceston) 12 January 1914 p2, 15 December 1914 p7.

[1222] NWA&EBT 29 October 1915 p2, 12 May 1916 p2.

[1223] NWA&EBT 14 August 1916 p2.

[1224] The Mercury (Hobart) 8 July 1918 p3.

optimism for the future but this proved wide of the mark,

> There is a great future in store for the Christian church. Evidences of a mighty spiritual awakening are to be seen on every side, and the Church is entering upon a new era, and there were great things in store for her. Her prospects are very bright. Evidences of revival are to be seen on every hand, and it would not be long before a mighty spiritual awakening will come throughout the whole world.[1225]

For nearly two years he was editor of the "Baptist Church Chronicle". He was also Secretary of the Hobart Council of Churches and Secretary of the Hobart Ministers' Fraternal. For the 13th anniversary of the Moonah Church in 1921, about 200 folk gathered.[1226]

In May 1924, Butler was welcomed to the large Concord Baptist Church in NSW. During his ministry a new church was erected at the cost of £5,000. In 1928, he visited the Australian Baptist Mission stations in India. In August 1930, he celebrated the 21st anniversary of his ministry. As President of the Baptist Union of New South Wales in 1934, he explored with the Church of Christ a possible union between the

*13-9 Albert Butler, Unknown, Robert Steel, Jack Fisher*

two denominations.

He was farewelled from Concord on 4 November 1935.[1227]

Butler's final pastorate was that of the Brisbane City Tabernacle from 1934.[1228] The family's arrival in the city, a first for Laura his wife, was noted by a society columnist bent on trivia,

> I wonder if the Baptist Tabernacle's new minister felt like a prima donna or a leading lady when he was presented on his arrival in Brisbane last Tuesday with a huge basket of artistically arranged flowers and mixed fruit? The basket was so big that it needed two boys to carry it, and when Mr. Butler had to attend to his luggage a couple

---

[1225] Advocate (Burnie) 4 February 1922 p11, 7 February 1922 p2, edited.

[1226] The Mercury (Hobart) 7 June 1921 p4; for sermons by Butler see The Mercury (Hobart) 18 July 1921 p6; 3 October 1921 p3; World (Hobart) 29 November 1921 p8; Advocate (Burnie) 3 February 1922 p5.

[1227] AB 19 July 1927 p13; Daily Pictorial (Sydney) 9 August 1930 p9; The Daily Telegraph (Sydney) 2 November 1934 p7; The Telegraph (Brisbane,) 30 October 1935 p7; The Recorder July 2007 p3.

[1228] The Courier-Mail (Brisbane, Qld) 10 August 1935 p13.

of men in the reception party undertook to look after the gift for him. I don't know whether the minister rewarded them with some of the fruit, but certainly one man was noticed shortly afterwards with an apple in his hand! The Butler daughters, Lorna and Roma, both possess glorious, dark brown wavy hair, and apparently favour the latest mode whenever possible, for their heads were bare last Thursday at midday when I saw them in a car in Queen Street with their parents.[1229]

The Church had chosen the right man and he fulfilled all expectations and became a leading minister in the city; the Baptist banner flew high during his pastorate. The prophecy made near twenty-five years earlier at an anniversary at Sheffield, Tasmania, if it wasn't fulfilled at Concord, it was certainly fulfilled in Brisbane, "All who had the privilege of hearing him were unanimous as to his capabilities and earnestness, and predict for him a successful ministerial future."[1230]

In the capital, his sermons were constantly reported in the newspapers. His literary gems were plucked from sermons and added to that of the gems of other preachers in the town. At first the column was under the heading, "Points from the Pulpit" and later, "Yesterday I went to Church". Typically his read:

BLAMING OTHERS. I HAVE never yet met a religious deceiver who when his sin has been found out has not tried to place the blame on someone else. No doubt men have inherited this weakness from their first parents. Adam blamed Eve for his transgression, and Eve blamed the Serpent. Many men even go as far as trying to blame God for their wrongdoing.[1231]

THE INFINITE LOSS. HERE is a loss which is infinitely greater than that of physical powers and sadder than mental decay: it is the loss of a man's spiritual power. That is the greatest loss in life, and there are many people like Samson who experience that disaster in the world today. They imagine that they can live just as they like and play false to God, while they still think that they have the same old power, which they had in earlier life. But the day will come sooner or later when they will discover that the power is departed from them, and Ichabod is written over their spiritual doorposts, unless they repent and seek restoration.[1232]

GLORY OF THE CROSS. YOU have something in Brisbane that is equally as demoralising to our

---

[1229] Sunday Mail (Brisbane) 10 November 1935 p20.
[1230] The North West Post (Tas.) 11 January 1911 p2.
[1231] The Telegraph (Brisbane) 9 December 1935 p14.
[1232] The Telegraph (Brisbane) 13 January 1936 p12.

people as the Golden Calf was to the people of Israel - it is the Golden Casket. This thing is making many people sin. It is not the Golden Calf or the Golden Casket that can meet the need of the people today, but the glory of the Cross.[1233]

PILATE'S VERDICT. Two thousand years ago Pilate said that he could find no fault with Jesus Christ, and it is impossible to reverse that verdict today. Whatever faults may be found within the Church, no fault can be found with its Lord.[1234]

THE HAND OF GOD. LIKE many people of to-day, Jacob came to the conclusion that life was against him. He had had the experience of attending the funerals of three of his nearest and dearest, he had had to face the disgrace of two of his sons, Reuben and Judah, and there was dissension in his own home. There was little cause for wonder in his lament in the midst of sorrows such as these, but the day came when Jacob saw that the hand of God had been guiding him all through his life.[1235]

At the end of his first year at the Brisbane Tabernacle, in November 1936, between thirty and forty new members had joined the Church and "all branches of the work were in an active and successful condition." By August 1939, the membership had reached 403.[1236]

Butler became President of the Queensland Council of Churches, President of the Queensland Auxiliary of the British and Foreign Bible Society, a prominent member of the Temperance League, President of the Christian Endeavour Union and was Chairman of the Queensland Baptist Union Foreign Mission and College Committees. Thus he filled the Presidential office in the three States. His voice was frequently heard over the national radio network in devotional services not

*13-10 Brisbane Tabernacle*

---

[1233] The Telegraph (Brisbane) 9 March 1936 p14.
[1234] The Telegraph (Brisbane) 2 November 1936 p14.
[1235] The Telegraph (Brisbane) 20 September 1937 p12.
[1236] The Telegraph (Brisbane) 7 November 1936 p6, 26 August 1939 p26.

only on Sundays, but also during the week.[1237]

Large congregations consistently gathered. In conjunction with the Rev H. M. Arrowsmith, he established a mid-week Intercessory Service in the Brisbane City Hall.[1238] Asked in 1938 what was his typical week he replied,

> MONDAY (Recognised Rest Day) - Morning. - Attend Ministers' Fraternal. Afternoon. - Address mothers' meeting. Night. - Christian Endeavour meeting. TUESDAY. - Morning. - Study. Afternoon. - Visits to sick, or meeting. Night. - Church officers' meeting, or denominational meeting. WEDNESDAY. - Morning.- At City Tabernacle. Afternoon. - 12.30: Intercessory service in basement of the City Hall. Night. - Mid-week service in the Tabernacle. THURSDAY. - Morning and afternoon. - Visits. Night. - Baptist Union council meeting, or address at a suburban church. FRIDAY. - All day. - Preparation of services for Sunday. SATURDAY. - Morning. - Varying duties. Afternoon. - Visit to country church. Night. - Church organisation meeting. SUNDAY. - Morning and night. - Church-services. In between there are wedding and funeral services. Of course, the work varies from week to week," he said "but there is scarcely ever a free night. We do not stop when the whistle blows at 5 o'clock."[1239]

The Rev Albert Butler died suddenly on 15 July 1947 at the age of sixty-seven years. He left behind his wife Laura and two daughters, Roma and Lorna, and two sons, Dudley and Graham. Laura Martha Butler, born 1888, died in May 1975. Albert and Laura were both buried at Brisbane General (Toowong) Cemetery.[1240]

## Appendix 6: Sterling George Clarke

Encouraged by his pastor, the Rev Frederick Joseph Dunkley, local Longford man Sterling G. Clarke developed aspirations for the pastoral ministry but after two Home Mission placements returned to his first love, poultry farming and made it his life's work.

Sterling Clarke's home church was the Longford Baptist Church. He was a poultry farmer who delighted in egg-laying competitions. In time he was appointed Superintendent of the Sunday school. In mid-1909, Dunkley commenced in the dual capacity as joint Home Mission Superintendent and Pastor of the Church. The following year Dunkley made Clarke his assistant and naturally Clarke was encouraged to preach at times. In 1910, he became

---

[1237] The Courier-Mail (Brisbane) 17 September 1938 p4.
[1238] Citation from BUQ Yearbook, 1940, From Witnessing for Christ throughout a Century 1855-1955 City Tabernacle Baptist Church.
[1239] Sunday Mail (Brisbane) 19 June 1938 p1.
[1240] BCC August 1947 p3; AB 22 July 1947 p4, 29 July 1947 p2..

honorary secretary to the Longford Empire Patriotic Demonstration Committee.[1241] Clarke Senior, a preacher himself, "an old identity in the District" would walk from Longford to Bracknell and then onto Blackwood Creek to fulfil preaching appointments "preaching the old, old story". Then on the same day he would return to Longford by foot.[1242] On his farewell from Longford in January 1911, young Sterling was given a copy of "Foster's Encyclopedia of Illustrations".[1243]

Following his leaving Ulverstone in February 1912, Sterling commenced at Bracknell in March 1912; he stayed for a year and then returned to his home church at Longford. Reports from Bracknell during his time indicated that nothing was amiss although by now the Rev Ernest Salisbury was busy "sheep-stealing" from the Bracknell Baptist congregation. All through his time with the Home Mission Sterling's interest in poultry farming never waned.

In 1918, he wrote to the Home Mission seeking a new position but was told that there were no openings for married men. In 1918, he moved to Invermay, a suburb of Launceston, to open a business and he accepted preaching opportunities when they arose, yet poultry farming remained the passion of his life; he became Chairman of the Penquite egg-laying Competition.[1244]

## Appendix 7: The Rev Vincent George Britton

While at Ulverstone in 1913, the Rev Vincent George Britton was appointed Home Mission Superintendent succeeding the Rev Frederic Joseph Dunkley. This appointment obliged his termination at Ulverstone and his removal to Latrobe. Britton was the right man for the job,

**13-11 Army Chaplain Vincent Britton**

He knew nearly every nook in the State, and could say authoritatively that there was a great need. Right through the North-East there did not exist a Home Mission representative of the denomination. A large proportion of the population of

---

[1241] SB 31 March 1910 p212; Daily Telegraph (Launceston) 4 April 1910 p7; in Longford Sterling had also had a happy association with the Longford Presbyterian Church, The North West Post (Formby, Tas) 22 February 1911 p2.
[1242] Daily Telegraph (Launceston) 1 December 1884 p3. Roughly fifty km for the day.

[1243] LEx 27 January 1911 p5.
[1244] HM Minutes p70; Daily Telegraph (Launceston) 5 April 1918, 15 March 1920 p2; LEx 27 January 1923 p7, 13 July 1946 p11.

the State was not merely outside the kingdom, but outside the pale of the Church. There had been great advances in home mission work. Twelve years ago he was the only home missionary in the denomination; now they had seven.[1245]

Britton was at Latrobe for nearly thirteen years and his duties as Home Mission Superintendent included looking after a large district incorporating Sassafras, South Spreyton, Moriarty and Virginstow. Thus he required assistance in his work. James Clemens Salter, H. Roy Tunks, William J. Bligh and Reg Wootton, all received their earliest training under his direction. Britton served as part-time chaplain in eighteen camps during World War 1 and Senior Chaplain of the United Board for twenty years.

Some of the Home Mission outstations closed. In 1920, Home Missionaries such as Jack Fisher were only getting salary and allowances of £169 annually. By 1921, this was raised to a maximum of £180 per annum. By 1926, this had dropped to £150. In 1921, there were fifty-seven baptisms in the Home Mission churches. This was seen as satisfactory. Four years later, at the end of July 1925, the total membership of all the Baptist churches including the Home Mission Churches was 1,449 up from 1305 in January 1921.[1246]

What advance was being experienced ceased with the coming of the Great Depression. Home Mission money was tight. There was an overdraft of £230, £130 over the limit that the bank allowed. All staff, including the Superintendent's salaries, were reduced by 10%. The bank soon pegged the overdraft to £200. While at Latrobe during the Depression, Britton opened a butcher's shop so his Baptist people could purchase meat at reasonable prices.

The total membership of all the Baptist churches including the Home Mission Churches at the end of July 1930 was 1,500 with 1,000 children in Sunday school.[1247]

For the year 1931 new members were added: seventy-four by baptism and fifty-seven by transfer. There had been a decrease for the year of forty-four. In the following year the statistics revealed that there was a total of 1910 scholars in the Home Mission Sunday Schools and over 500 Home Mission Christian Endeavour members.[1248]

In 1931, on account of shortness of funds, all new Home Mission work ceased. There were 400 members in the Home Mission churches, 600 children in their Sunday schools,

---

[1245] SB 11 April 1912 p232 - edited.
[1246] Total Tasmanian Baptist membership was only 1454 in 1933 with the Census indicating 4,666 Baptists in the State. AB 8 January 1935 p2.
[1247] AB July 1930 p123.
[1248] The Mercury (Hobart) 28 October 1925 p8; AB 16 November 1926 p1.

sixty-six teachers, eighty Christian Endeavour leaders and thirty-five local preachers. The financial shortfall for 1931-32 was £67 of an income of £1943.

New Home missionaries were badly needed. The call for help was sent interstate pleading, "We cannot offer princely salaries, nor feed ambition with great churches, but we can offer great and effective spheres of service for the Master." By now the Home Mission churches, halls and manses were generally in a bad state of repair.

During his ministry Britton sustained three severe accidents. The first occurred in 1922 near Wynyard when his motor cycle collided with a horse drawn vehicle. In December 1924, the second occurred through the breaking of the car steering-gear near Perth. Sarah, the wife of his son, Vincent Derwent, was killed. Vincent Derwent sustained injuries of a serious nature while Britton only suffered minor injuries. Vincent Derwent himself was killed in another car accident eighteen years later leaving a widow and a son. A returned soldier, he was fifty-six years of age.[1249] In 1933, Britton was involved in a level-crossing accident in which his car was totally destroyed.[1250]

Years later, in 1950, Leah Cubit was farewelled for missionary service with the Borneo Evangelical Mission.

*13-12 Vincent and his motor cycle*

"My introduction to missionary work," she explained, "was when the Rev V. G. Britton of Perth Baptist Church rode his bicycle out to our farm, now the Research Farm at Cressy. He was collecting money for 'the brown boys and girls'. I was six, and I believe he prayed for me that day."

During his forty-three years of unfailing energy and untiring service, Britton was pastor of only six churches. Apart from Latrobe (thirteen years), there was Bracknell (seven years), Deloraine twice (a total of six years), Sheffield (four years), Ulverstone (four years) and

*13-13 Deloraine's outstation of Montana built during Jack Fisher's time at the Church*

---

[1249] AB 4 August 1942 p3.
[1250] BCC April 1922 p1; AB 30 December 1924 p4; 22 March 1932 p11; another report said that the cause was a punctured tyre which caused the car to swerve.

then Perth/Longford (eight years). "VG" held the position of Home Mission Superintendent for over twenty years. In 1934, his Home Mission leadership came to an end. This pioneer preacher on whom the brunt of the Home Mission work had rested, had explored every part of the State. "Battle worn and battle scarred" he had earned his retirement. Ida died on 10 January 1944, seventy-eight years of age. The Rev Vincent George Britton died on 4 October 1950 eighty-four years of age.[1251] In Britton's honour, land behind the Perth Baptist Tabernacle on which Baptist youth camp took place in later years was named "Britton Park".

Interestingly, when the Rev Richard W. Dobbinson of the Launceston Tabernacle took over as Home Mission Superintendent in 1935 his assessment that year was sober in the least,

> We have (in the Home Mission) no men with any degree of evangelistic fire coupled with balance and the whole field shows our lack in this respect. I want to make a big change in the field. Everywhere it is beset by the traditions of the last century.

In January 1936 Dobbinson wrote again about the work,

> I want no cranks. Sane and energetic men are needed before any other qualifications. At the same time we must have College trained men. If I can only get hold of a few fellows as above who are not burdened with large families and can make do with a small salary, both they and the work will quickly advance.[1252]

*13-14 Vincent and Ida in later life*

Up to this time any young fellows in our churches who were busy in Sunday school and Christian Endeavour and who did some preaching, were accepted as a ministerial candidate and placed under a senior Pastor if they so wished. The trouble was the candidate only knew what he had heard from the pulpit and he usually set about regurgitating that. The new policy was in time to send the candidates to College.[1253]

---

[1251] AB 20 Apl 1920, January 1944, 18 January p2, 25 January 1944 p5; Advocate (Burnie) 5 October 1950 p19.

[1252] AB 1 January 1935 p4.

[1253] A lack of a decent theological education often leads to an emphasis on the wrong things, such as Creationism, an inerrant Bible and End Time prominence. The problem is still evident among lay people who show leadership in our churches.

## Appendix 8: The Rev John (Jack) F. Fisher

The Rev Jack Fisher was among a number who came from interstate to work in the Tasmanian Home Mission where they would fulfill their call and find their feet in ministry. From humble beginnings, he made his way from one Home Mission Church to another. After nearly twenty years in what could be considered to be a lengthy apprenticeship, he transferred to the mainland and served faithfully in Baptist churches there for the rest of his days.

Fisher was born in 1876 and grew up in the Port Melbourne area and would have attended the Albert Park Baptist Church and then the Port Melbourne Baptist Church, the latter the Chapman Memorial Church when it opened in 1892. At the age of twenty-three and at some danger to his own life, he saved an eleven year old who nearly drowned in the Yarra as the lad went down for the third time.[1254]

Fisher opened a dairy produce shop near his home in Albert Park.[1255] While Tasmanian Ernest E Watson was at the Baptist Theological College, he preached at Clark Street Mission which was an outreach of the Port Melbourne Church. Since Fisher was teaching Sunday school there maybe it was from Watson that the idea of working with the Tasmanian Home Mission arose.[1256] As he was leaving in 1902 for Tasmania, Fisher was farewelled from the School; he was its superintendent and at the Port Melbourne church itself, he was a foundation member and deacon. Oscar Linden was also being farewelled, to Queensland, on the same day.[1257] Accompanying Fisher to Tasmania was his invalid mother and largely dependent sister. In Tasmania he was placed at the Launceston Tabernacle and joined its Literary and Debating Society. He was appointed Superintendent of the Launceston Tabernacle's Percy Street Sabbath Mission School.[1258]

Fisher was soon moved to the Longford Baptist Church as assistant to Pastor Harry Wood and Miss Sarah Rawson from one of the leading families of the Launceston Tabernacle followed for good reason; they were to be married on 25 September 1907. They then transferred to the Wynyard Church.[1259]

After the joint pastorate of Wynyard and Yolla for one year, he was at Longford for five years, at Deloraine for five years (1909 to 1914) and remembered with the erection of a

---

[1254] Standard (Port Melbourne) 29 April 1899 p2.
[1255] Standard (Port Melbourne) 10 November 1900 p2.
[1256] Standard (Port Melbourne) 16 August 1902 p3.
[1257] Standard (Port Melbourne) 24 October 1903 p2.
[1258] LEx 23 March 1905 p4, 13 May 1905 p6; The Argus (Melbourne) 20 May 1947 p2.
[1259] Daily Telegraph (Launceston) 1 November 1906 p3, 27 September 1907 p6.

building at Montana. The Deloraine Church now had ten out-stations. He was then at Longford again for three years. Fisher subsequently served the Victorian Baptist Union of Churches at Rainbow. He then commenced at the Marshall Street and Belmont churches in Geelong in November 1924. The Rev D. S. Harvey, Baptist, previously of Elphin Road Baptist Church, Launceston, was also welcomed to the Geelong District at the same time.[1260]

In July 1929, Fisher was inducted into the pastorate of the Warrnambool Baptist Church where he served for six years.[1261]

The next pastorate was that of the Victoria Street Baptist Church Ballarat East from August 1935. He remained until April 1939 as he then transferred to the Regent Baptist Church in the Western suburbs of Melbourne replacing the Rev E. A. Blackwell.[1262] The Regent Church had a high pulpit and the story goes that one morning about the year 1942 while he was preaching the top plate of his teeth shot out and fell to the floor below and one of the deacons came forward and picked them up in a handkerchief and handed them back. Fisher put them back in and went on with the sermon as if nothing happened.[1263]

In April 1946, Fisher resigned from the list of ordained ministers of the Baptist Union of Victoria due to ill health. He died on 18 May 1947 aged seventy-one years and was survived by his wife Sarah and their daughter. The Memorial pulpit and platform rails at Regent Baptist Church were dedicated to his memory. Wesley J. Bligh wrote of him, "He was remembered as a man of gracious personality, generous mind and deep spiritual conviction. In all churches where he laboured, he left affectionate memory and solid work." It was said also of him, "He is a man of few words but of fine fidelity."[1264]

## Conclusion

120 years ago Sunday observance was a lively religious issue and ministers strenuously opposed Sunday trading, including commercial entertainment on the day. In October 1926, the Ulverstone Ministers' Fraternal, of which the Rev James C. Salter was President, objected to the Local Government Council proposal of a dance hall on the beach. They were successful as it was still accepted that the Christian churches were the authority on what was right or wrong.

The churches held the line partly on Sunday observance, gambling

---

[1260] The Age (Melbourne) 19 November 1924 p15.
[1261] The Argus (Melbourne,) 10 July 1929 p22.
[1262] The Argus (Melbourne,) 15 July 1935 p12, 13 April 1939 p9.

[1263] Related to me by the Rev Barry Wollmer who was in attendance as a child that morning.
[1264] The Age 18 May 1946 p4, 28 May 1949 p8; Bligh; BCC May 1921 p9; AB 27 May 1947 p4.

facilities and six o'clock closing. But by the end of the 1960s it was clear that their political influence had diminished. Sunday night films were introduced, Sunday sport began to take root, Sunday papers appeared.

By now their objections would not be placed on local Council agendas at all as society was now accommodating a pluralistic society that sought to equally accommodate all versions of faith and values. While there was a church boom in the 1950s, the 1960s brought an end to religious revival and comfortable social values. There was more change in this decade than in the preceding sixty years. Up to that time Christianity was the favoured view of those who rarely attended church practising grace at meals and being married in church. It was the start of post-Christian Australia. These years saw the introduction of TV which shaped our perception of the external world. Then there was the general use of the motor car which provided an enormous opportunity for families to move outside their towns. Further, there was the introduction of greater opportunities for higher education. Those who dropped off church attendance often were not really connected in the first place. People soon experienced how easy (or how difficult) it was to live without their church. Obligation and duty no longer made up for a lack of connectedness, devotion or faith itself. The result was that families began going elsewhere on weekends. Sunday sport was just one of the Sunday "amusements".

Further, women were beginning to enter the work force in greater numbers and they found out that they needed the Sunday morning to rest. Concessions followed allowing innocent amusements and recreation, but not as yet Sunday trading and work. Coupled with this was the willingness to challenge religious authorities especially by the young who, encouraged by their schooling, would not simply accept what their parents and teachers told them.

Thus the Sunday school and Christian Endeavour numbers dropped, Christian Endeavour being the link between the Sunday school and the Church itself, both being "feeders to the church". So instead of the village chapel being the social forum and the house of God it now became solely the house of God and as such simply one of the many Sunday "amusements". The Christian Church no longer dictated to the community how it should live on the basis of what the Bible decrees. Further, the church could no longer expect understanding from the world. All it could hope for was tolerance and equal treatment with all other groups in society.

This authority and honour are no longer ours to enjoy and this loss of authority invites us to think again. It invites us to be prophets instead of power players. It calls us to relearn the value of sacrifice instead of celebrity. We need to keep in mind the saying when thinking of Church today, "The past is a foreign country; they did things differently."

# Chapter 14 Wynyard Baptist Church

## Introduction

Throughout the North-West Coast in the years on either side of 1900 the country was gradually opened up, and there was in consequence an increase in population. This was accompanied with an increase in the erection of public buildings, particularly churches which entailed heavy financial responsibility but indicated that the outlook was very bright and that the folk were sincerely concerned about their religious welfare. In the district earlier church structures were now too small to accommodate the larger congregations so they were assigned to becoming Church halls or being replaced and the new church structures generally were of a substantial character which meant that they would last for many decades to come.

It was often considered desirable to have a church building where there was no sign of a township, that is, no hotels, stores nor blacksmith's shops "so that the outer settlers in the district, under God's blessing, would hear the Gospel regularly proclaimed."[1265] A new structure away from the township could also be used as a community hall taking no account of whether the rural folk were Baptist, Methodist or whatever. Another use for these outstation structures was that of being day-schools during the working week. In time, the Wynyard Baptist Church circuit would be known for such rural structures and they were found first at Upper Moore's Plain, Myalla, Deep Creek, Yolla's Camp Creek, Boat Harbour, Henrietta Plains and later Upper Calder and Upper Flowerdale.

Prior to the arrival of the Baptists the town was served by three denominations. In the mid-1850s, Wynyard was first served by the Anglicans with their small wooden structure which was replaced by a larger building in 1873.[1266] The United Free Methodists became active at Wynyard in the early 1870s and secured a building in 1881 while Wesleyan Methodists held services

*14-1 Wynyard Anglican Church of 1873*

---

[1265] Day-Dawn December 1906, edited.

[1266] Cornwall Chronicle (Launceston) 17 March 1871 p2, 2 January 1874 p3; Tasmanian 18 March 1871 p13, 3 January 1874 p4.

in the Town Hall before the erection of their building. In 1902, the Methodist Union took place.[1267] On 12 February 1922, a new brick Methodist church building was opened. The Congregationalists began in Wynyard about 1870 and opened their church on 3 November 1878.[1268]

## Baptist Beginnings[1269]

As early as 1891, Baptists in Wynyard wrote to the Baptist Association seeking help in commencing a Baptist work in the town,[1270] and this request was raised at the Assembly. But it was not for some years that action was finally taken and a mission opened in the town led by a delegation from the Launceston Tabernacle comprising its Pastor, the Rev Albert W. Bean, President of the Baptist Association for 1905/06, William Dubrelle Weston and George Darling Gould. Weston took a keen interest in the Wynyard work and visited a number of times. Initially the meetings were held in the home of Mr. J. Turnbull.[1271]

Later in the year the Rev Robert Williamson, the Vice-President of the Baptist Association, conducted a week-long mission in Wynyard to consolidate the work. The meetings were "fairly attended, and the prospects are encouraging."[1272] A Fellowship was formed. The Rev Joshua T. Piercey of the Burnie Church was given the task of overseeing matters and his successors, the Revs. Peter W. Cairns and Samuel Harrison, continued the oversight. Wynyard's first baptism took place in the Burnie Church but Wynyard's swift-flowing Inglis River soon sufficed.[1273]

## Pastor William Henry Short

In 1905, Pastor William Henry Short was secured as the first Home Missioner for Wynyard, moving from Deloraine. On another visit the Rev Robert Williamson, now President of the Association, oversaw the constitution of the church on 3 October 1906 with eighteen foundation members and a secretary, a treasurer and deacons. On 24 February 1907, the first Sunday school anniversary was celebrated in the Town Hall where

---

[1267] Advocate (Burnie) 8 July 1941 p4; Daily Telegraph (Launceston) 23 July 1895 p4.
[1268] Cornwall Chronicle (Launceston) 2 January 1874 p3, 11 November 1878 p2; Weekly Examiner (Launceston) 23 November 1878 p20.
[1269] For an account of the Wynyard Baptist Church's story told by those who year by year served faithfully across the pastorates see Max Austin's Centenary History, "To God be the Glory".

[1270] The Mercury (Hobart) 8 April 1891 p1.
[1271] Wynyard's History, Max Austin; Gould was made Lieut.-Colonel during the War, second in command of the 25th Infantry Regiment of the Australian Imperial Forces.
[1272] LEx Friday 17 November 1905 p3.
[1273] Day-Dawn March 1906, October 1906, March 1907.

services were being held until the erection of a Tabernacle in 1908.[1274]

In the Sunday school the missionary spirit was

> burning brightly in the hearts of both teachers and children ... Every penny or half penny given for mission work among the heathen is money invested in God's business, "little copper-coloured soldiers" to bear the "Message of the Cross" across the seas; and are not the threepenny bits, the sixpences, and shillings given to this work little tongued heralds going forth to tell of Him who died for the world?[1275]

The Church was greatly heartened that year when Stephen W. Margetts and Charlotte his wife from the Burnie Church came to live in the town and involved themselves in the Church. Margetts' "massive figure, commanding presence, eloquent addresses, and racy humour, and his kindliness and sympathy combined to make him always a welcome visitor to the churches throughout the state. He freely gave his services as a local preacher."[1276] A Christian Endeavour Society commenced in 1907.

In August 1906, meetings began in rural Myalla situated about twenty-four kms from Wynyard and arrived

*14-2 Myalla Baptist Chapel of 1922*

at "over very bad roads". Local Ambrose Walters with a group of men erected a Sunday school hall on land the Walters had given. It would serve as a public school during the week and as a Sunday school on Sundays. The building cost £9 10 shillings and was fitted with backless seats. Within six months twenty-five children were attending the Sunday school. Then an approach was made to the Education Department for a State School teacher and soon one was provided.[1277]

It was discovered that "the Walters not only had a healthy baby but a healthy baby organ" and Short and local Mr. King soon carried the second baby the few hundred metres to the schoolroom.[1278]

The Moore's Plain Road outstation began in 1906 with services and a Sunday school. On 3 March 1907, Gospel services were started at Boat Harbour in the local State school with about thirty adults in

---

[1274] LEx 12 September 1906 p7, 1 March 1907 p6.
[1275] Day-Dawn October 1906.
[1276] Day-Dawn August 1907; LEx 1 October 1930 p5.
[1277] LEx. Friday 17 November 1905 p3; Wynyard's History; Day-Dawn March 1907.
[1278] Day-Dawn September 1906.

attendance and soon the first Sunday school in the town commenced. Boat Harbour's first baptismal candidates were the Walters and "the day was cold and stormy, and the white surf beat on the sea shore."[1279] Boat Harbour's chapel opened on 15 October 1907.

Short's time at Wynyard lasted just under two years as in the second year he suffered ill-health and fortunately Jack Fisher was already there at times to assist. Finally, Short felt it desirable to look for a more congenial climate and a farewell social took place at the Town Hall on 30 October 1907. The family eventually moved back to Bendigo in Victoria but before doing so he filled in at the Sheffield Church and elsewhere. The family with four children sailed on 24 May 1909 concluding their Tasmanian odyssey.[1280]

## Pastor John W. (Jack) Fisher

In September 1907 Pastor John W. (Jack) Fisher moved from the Longford Church to the Wynyard-Yolla circuit. Evening services were particularly difficult to maintain as the milking and farm work had to be attended to before folk travelled the miles to their place of worship. By April 1908, good numbers had gathered at Wynyard.

In December 1907, the Rev Vincent G. Britton of Deloraine visited for three weeks for rest and a change and while with them,

> he travelled about 150 odd miles to and from the different out-stations, preached six times in Wynyard, three times at the out-stations; lectured three times, conducted three evening prayer meetings and raised about £50 for the new building.[1281]

On 12 August 1908, the foundation stone was laid for its church building and within less than a month, on 6 September 1908, the new church was opened with Britton officiating. In the morning he took as his text, "Upon this rock will I build my church." At 3 pm. he took Isaiah 42.4, "Thou shalt not fail," and closed the day in the evening with an earnest old-time Gospel address.[1282] Ashby White was the builder. The land was donated by James King Percy, a lay preacher. On 8 March 1908, the second Sunday school anniversary was held. On 24 October 1908, the first Church Anniversary was held.[1283]

On one Sunday Fisher did not arrive on time as his horse and trap had become stuck in the mud on one of the main dirt roads. When Lou

---

[1279] AB November 1906; Day-Dawn April 1907.
[1280] LEx 31 October 1907 p3; NWA&EBT 24 May 1909 p4; Day-Dawn October 1907.
[1281] Day-Dawn January 1908.
[1282] LEx 19 August 1908 p36, 9 September 1908 p7.
[1283] Day-Dawn October 1908.

Austin went to town two or three times a year, he took a bag of chaff for Fisher's horse.

The Wynyard district in these years was rapidly growing and the number of settler's homes was increasing. During the busy milking season the preaching stations were commencing their evening services at the rather late hour of 8 pm. Fisher only stayed for twelve months as he was transferred to the Deloraine Baptist Church, in December 1908. [1284]

## Pastor Robert Steel and Albert Butler

At the beginning of 1909, after three years ministry in the Bracknell circuit, Home Missioner Robert Steel was transferred to Wynyard. After two years at the Hobart University, twenty-two year old Albert Butler joined him as his assistant. Butler was the first to leave the Perth Church with a call to ministry and when he did he was presented with Burkett's complete full expository commentary on the New Testament. The Rev John D. Williams, who worked closely with Robert Steel in later years, was told by Steel that in his (Steel's) association with the youthful Butler, Butler always tried to outshine him. By April 1910,

Butler was transferred to Bracknell as Pastor in his own right.

Steel spoke at a welcome to a new Methodist pastor in Wynyard commenting that all churches were made up of "shirkers, jerkers and workers".[1285] This labelling was doing the rounds,

> shirkers were those who did nothing but talk, who complained that other people did not do more. The jerkers were the anniversary people - they showed up on anniversary occasions, when a big man came from the city. They were splendid on occasion. They were like a bottle of lemonade, very fizzy for a few minutes. The workers were those upon whose shoulders there rested the great burdens of the Kingdom of God. They had the aggressive work of God to do. They were faithful to the last. They were the calm, faithful, plodding, patient men and women who spent their lives in the service of God until the shadows faded away.[1286]

Steel was no shirker for soon at one of the Church working bees he, with many helpers, was erecting a new fence around the property. Again an appeal was made for a trap as Steel

---

[1284] NWA&EBT 12 December 1908 p5.
[1285] LEx 19 January 1909 p4, 8 April 1910 p3; NWA&EBT 6 August 1909 p2; From the Rev John Williams' memories of Steel in an interview with Laurence Rowston. In December 1937 Williams was appointed as assistant to Steel at Deloraine when he (Williams) was accepted as a candidate for the ministry; NWA&EBT 3 May 1909 p 4.
[1286] Bunyip (Gawler SA) 3 March 1905 p3; SB 10 October 1905 p242.

had left the Bracknell one behind.[1287]

Services opened at Upper Calder on 14 March 1909 with forty present. The roads were generally so bad that horses could get stuck requiring locals making tracks through the adjoining farms. So it was for Steel on one of his journeys: "On the journey out to a meeting being held at Upper Moore's Plain, Steel riding through one night got stuck three times and once right up to the horse's chest."[1288]

Steel had his mannerisms as John D. Williams related, "If he over stepped the line he became over excited, but he would not be blunt." Further, his collection of sermons was limited after twelve months; he just repeated them. For Steel life was a case of "Fighting the devil". John T. Robertson McCue, Victorian Baptist Home Missioner sent to Tasmania for experience, was Steel's assistant for a short time. Steel stayed for only a year in Wynyard moving then to Smithton. He was replaced again by Albert Edward Salisbury.[1289]

## Pastor Ernest Albert Salisbury

By February 1910, Pastor Ernest Albert Salisbury was moved from Bracknell to the Wynyard-Yolla circuit.[1290]

A serious issue for the churches in those years was how people were treating the Christian Sunday. Salisbury joined with the other Christian ministers in Wynyard signing a letter to the Table Cape Council "emphatically protest(ing) against the action of the council in letting the Town Hall for Sunday evenings' entertainments." They were successful in their protest and the hall was no longer let out on Sundays for such pastimes.[1291]

In December 1911, Salisbury, who stood high in the affection of the Wynyard congregation resigned from the Home Mission. He put it to the Home Mission Committee that he was considering "taking up work in one of the sister states" but the Home Mission Committee received reports that indicated otherwise. The Committee responded, "But in the event of the rumour concerning Salisbury's contemplated entrance into the Anglican Church proving correct, we shall send no representative (for his

---

[1287] Day-Dawn April 1909.

[1288] Day-Dawn April 1909, July 1909.

[1289] Day-Dawn March 1909, July 1909. Upper Moore's Plain was on the Oldina Rd; From the Rev John Williams' memories of Steel in an interview with the author; NWA&EBT 6 August 1909 p2.

[1290] Daily Telegraph (Launceston) 10 February 1910 p8.

[1291] NWA&EBT 13 February 1911 p2.

farewell)."[1292] Yet the Revs. Frederic Joseph Dunkley, Home Mission Super-intendent, and Charles Palmer did attend.

The rumour proved correct and in 1912, now as an Anglican, he was found at Bracknell. The Baptist Council recorded, "Anglican services have commenced (in Bracknell) and he is assiduously visiting the Bracknell District and is drawing away a number of Baptists; the number at the Baptist church has fallen." The incumbent at the Church at the time, Sterling G. Clarke, resigned from the Home Mission as his support base had collapsed. Even though Salisbury had brought about the disintegration of the work, the poignant thing is that in Salisbury and Annie his wife the Baptists lost first class workers.[1293] On the other hand Salisbury's work in Bracknell proved to be of no avail as an Anglican church was never established.

## The Rev William Llewellyn Heaven

The Rev William Llewellyn Heaven commenced in the Wynyard circuit on 10 March 1912. He began his ministry by touring the district and also Smithton, Forest, Irishtown and Stanley all the while giving lantern lectures on "God's Own Country - New Zealand".[1294]

Soon a corrugated tin bath baptistry was housed under the pulpit of the Wynyard Church building but one's baptism was not a forgettable event as cold water was the norm with only a small amount of warm water added. In the dead of winter this act of commitment certainly made the baptismal candidate gasp. By September 1914 ,Heaven was assisting in the War enlistment drive and was fund raising to alleviate the distress in London. On Sunday 20 December 1914, Heaven preached his farewell sermons at the Wynyard Church after which he proceeded to Sheffield.[1295]

## Ernest Charles Walsh

Ernest Charles Walsh commenced in the Wynyard-Yolla circuit on 30 March 1912. Prior to this posting he had assisted at Sheffield for a time and there he shared the manse with the Home Mission Superintendent, the Rev V. G. Britton. Walsh had previously been working under him.

On some Sundays he conducted three services and they entailed visiting Boat Harbour and Yolla and this meant cycling forty-five kms with a return on the Monday to Yolla from Boat Harbour. On other Sundays it was a case of the morning

---

[1292] HM minutes p10, p12; Tasmanian Baptist April 1912 p4. Day-Dawn March 1912.
[1293] HM Minutes p22, p32; SB June 1911.
[1294] NWA&EBT 13 March 1912 p2; Circular Head Chronicle (Stanley, Tas) 17 July 1912 p2.
[1295] Daily Telegraph (Launceston) 11 September 1914 p6, 23 December 1914 p7.

service at Wynyard, then on to Myalla for a 3 pm service; and after having supper with a family at Myalla, a sermon at Boat Harbour in the evening. A number of lay preachers was constantly required to fill the pulpits. Most of the Tasmanian Home Mission circuits in these years with their four or five outstations in scattered areas entailed considerable distances to be traversed for preaching and pastoral engagements and they depended on a bike or a horse as they were the only means of transport. Britton on his visit to Yolla in May 1913, was pleased with Walsh's work.

During Walsh's time in the Wynyard-Yolla circuit, on 1 February 1914 at Yolla, he conducted its first baptismal service in an artificial lake owned by one of the congregation with 150 spectators of all denominations. The day of the Yolla baptism was the last day of the Wynyard-Yolla circuit arrangement.[1296]

The Rev F. A. Marsh, General Secretary of the Australian Baptist Foreign Mission, visited in 1915 and described the town of Wynyard thus,

> this town is in a hobble-de-hoy stage. It is like a boy that has made his mind up very late to grow, and then is anxious to make up for lost time. Like a well-fed boy it is bound to grow. It has the feeding that comes from a big stretch of rich back country.[1297]

In January 1916, Walsh enlisted in the War effort with forty others in the district but he remained behind to serve as a chaplain; his ministerial training was not complete. Walsh was ordained on 10 August 1916.[1298]

He resigned his position at Wynyard in January 1917 and went to England as a Baptist Chaplain with the Australian Forces stationed at Salisbury Plain. Welcomed home in December 1917, he resumed the Wynyard pastorate. In the churches he now gave illustrated lectures on his recent experiences. On 2 October 1918, he married Alice Margaret Daisy Snare at Wynyard with Britton officiating.[1299] The work at Wynyard also included the conducting of services at Table Cape and for that reason on his leaving in May he mentioned that he had "found the long journeys in his work very trying, and that he was willing to accept the opportunity of a transfer to an easier district where he would have more time for study."[1300] That easier district was

---

[1296] Daily Telegraph (Launceston) 22 January 1915 p7.
[1297] AB 5 January 1915.
[1298] Daily Telegraph (Launceston) 2 February 1916 p7; NWA&EBT 12 August 1916 p2.

[1299] Daily Telegraph (Launceston) 8 October 1918 p7; Dorothy May Davis was born 15 October 1894.
[1300] LEx 26 January 1917 p6, 26 January 1917 p6; NWA&EBT 8 February 1917 p2, 6 December 1917 p2, 6 March 1918 p2; Advocate (Burnie) 23 May 1919 p2, 2 June 1920 p1; Daily Telegraph (Launceston) 8 October 1918 p7.

the Longford Baptist Church. At his farewell it was said of him,

> He had come as a young man and by his earnest, humble, and consistent godly life had won the respect and admiration of all. He had worked in perfect harmony with his people and deacons for nearly six years. Two strong features in his success had been saintly modesty, and saintly humility. Men and women all over the district not only esteemed him but said of him, "He is a good man." His life had spoken as loud as his preaching. There may be more brilliant speakers, but none had set a more consistent example of practising what he preached.

In his reply he said,

> I have received nothing but kindness since I came in fear and trembling to Wynyard and George Sargent, whom I have feared most when coming, has proved one of my greatest helpers.

George Newton Sargent from an old English Baptist family of literary talent was a builder and contractor, the church secretary for twenty-five years, the church organist for thirty years and lay preacher and he was one of the mainstays of the small church.[1301]

The Half-Yearly Assembly to be held in Wynyard in 1919 was abandoned on account of the Spanish influenza epidemic which interfered greatly with church attendances across the nation.[1302]

## The Revs Arthur Charles Jarvis and Wilfred Lemuel Jarvis

When the Rev Arthur Charles Jarvis and his wife, Harriett and family came from Queensland in June 1920, they were welcomed at both the Wynyard Baptist Church and at "Seaview", the home of the Smith family in Yolla. Jarvis took part in the Ulverstone Prohibition League which was seeking a State referendum on the "early closing question". The Baptist Association purchased a manse and a stable, a coach house and chaff room were erected. Jarvis formed a Christian Endeavour Society.[1303]

*14-3 Rev A. C. Jarvis*

But his coming was not just seeking a cooler climate for health reasons but for an extended evangelistic outreach. He was accompanied by

---

[1301] Advocate (Burnie) 9 June 1920 p1.
[1302] AB 14 October 1919.

[1303] Advocate (Burnie) 16 June 1920 p2, 18 June 1921 p4; Daily Telegraph (Launceston) 26 August 1920 p4; AB April 1922 p6.

his son, the Rev Wilfred Lemuel Jarvis, the Queensland itinerant evangelist working under the auspices of the Queensland Evangelisation Society. Wilfred had just concluded a successful united campaign in Brisbane. They had come at the invitation of the Tasmanian Baptist Association and Wilfred was to spend the next fifteen months as the Association's evangelist. Jarvis and son were recognized by the Association as part of this ministerial team for the time of their stay.[1304]

Wilfred commenced his missions at Wynyard on 8 July 1922 working with the Baptist and Methodist churches and making use of the Town Hall. A month earlier it was noted that among Baptists "there are many indications of coming Revival in the district." The mission commenced with afternoon week day services. He was accompanied by evangelist J. R. Hope-Morgan. The newspapers were unanimous in their opinion that Wynyard had seldom seen a more accomplished, arresting and convincing preacher than in Wilfred. In the meetings no attempt was made to work up emotionalism, but the Gospel was presented in a simple and convincing manner. The mission in Wynyard concluded on 5 August.[1305]

*14-4 The Wilfred Jarvis team, Baptist Church Archives of Qld (used with permission)*

At his meetings Wilfred would begin by referring to the shyness felt even by many Christian people of what are called "revival methods". He disclaimed entirely all intention of seeking to produce religious excitement by artificial means. He did not believe in working "sensational stunts" to get people to do, under the excitement of the moment, what they would not have done in moments of deliberation. "Nothing done in this mission will be unworthy of the Gospel of the Lord Jesus Christ. Nothing will be done to embarrass any who come. There will be no traps laid to catch people, or to force anybody to do things against their will. Christianity does not insult a man's intelligence. It appeals to the entire man, and claims the

---

[1304] BCC June 1922; AB 8 June 1920, 29 April 1924.

[1305] BCC June 1922; Advocate (Burnie) 10 July 1922 p5, 15 July 1922 p4, 19 July 1922 p4.

entire man for the service of Christ and the will of God.[1306]

His mission at Latrobe revealed the theology of this most acclaimed, fluent and brilliant speaker,

> No sensible man could deny the fact of God, and a man's conscience apart from the Scriptures proclaims His existence. The word of God appealed to reason, and it was because man did not think long enough and deep enough that he did not believe. Only a fool said in his heart that there was no God. The rise and fall of nations and kings were directed by the greatest King of all, who planned everything for a purpose. If man were able to explore God, then he would be greater than God. People were inclined to look upon the Supreme Being as a God of the past and not of the present. Others were wont to regard Him as an austere God, the great detective of the universe, demanding an eye for an eye and a tooth for a tooth. Such was the caricature of the devil! The true God was the one found in the Scriptures, and to know Him was to have Him revealed.[1307]

During his missions the story was told,

> A little girl went home from the Jarvis Mission held at Sassafras and said to her father, "Dad, why did you not hold up your hand, and then teach us to be good?" The words went home, and "dad" subsequently took a decision card, and is now rejoicing in a free salvation.[1308]

Over his time in Tasmania, Wilfred generally ran united missions working with the Methodist, Anglican, Congregational, Salvation Army and Presbyterian Churches. His mission at Sisters Creek Hall commenced in August 1922. Burnie followed in September 1922, Ulverstone in November 1922, Devonport in both November 1922 and September 1923, Stanley in February 1923, Longford in March 1923, Deloraine in May 1923, Smithton in June 1923, Sheffield in August 1923, Sassafras September 1923 and finally Stanley in October 1923.[1309]

The missions involved at times a united children's rally, women only meetings and open-air preaching, all where appropriate. Wilfred in all conducted fifteen missions in the Tasmanian Baptist churches with notable results which were measured in terms of converts who were won.

---

[1306] Advocate (Burnie) 18 September 1922 p2.
[1307] Advocate (Burnie) 22 October 1923 p4.
[1308] AB April 1923 p9.
[1309] Advocate (Burnie) 19 August 1922 p4, 18 September 1922 p2, 30 September 1922 p4, 31 October 1922 p4, 1 August 1923 p4, 10 September 1923 p4; Daily Telegraph (Launceston) 8 February 1923 p7; LEx 29 March 1923 p9, 8 May 1923 p6; Circular Head Chronicle (Stanley, Tas) 27 June 1923 p5; The Mercury (Hobart) 4 September 1923 p3; AB 30 October 1923 p11.

## The Rev Alan Paton Dawson

The Rev Alan Paton Dawson commenced at Yolla on 12 March 1922 and after ten months he was transferred to the Wynyard Church. There were now sixty members at Wynyard. One of the Wynyard diaconate, Stephen W. Margetts, was appointed President of the Baptist Union of Tasmania that year and became Church Secretary. There was a joint pastorate with Yolla at the time. When Dawson took over the work in the Myalla district it was nearly defunct but he concentrated on this centre and the work was re-established and a new building was erected at the cost of £240 with £200 of the amount previously raised. Mr. Williams had donated the land. The state of Myalla previously was also the state of the cause at Boat Harbour, "at bedrock", but attendances improved, the "majority being young people". After four years at Wynyard, Dawson and his wife Gwynne and their daughter were farewelled on 9 March 1926 to the South Melbourne Baptist Church.[1310] The Rev William Heaven, a former pastor of the Church, took over.

*14-5 Alan Paton Dawson*

## Appendices

### Appendix 1: William Henry Short

In 1908, William Henry Short who had come from Deloraine to Wynyard won the first prize at the Artists' Exhibition in Launceston. A number of his many paintings stayed behind in Tasmania after he settled back in Melbourne and were exhibited for sale. In Melbourne, he continued to paint and exhibit his works and to preach. He was subsequently engaged by the Sunday School Union as bush missionary, a work dear to his heart.[1311]

During the First World War he became one of the Bible Society's distributors of the New Testaments in the Broadmeadows Training Camp. He gave lectures on how a man moved from civilian to soldier, from training camp to Egypt. The Bible Society was ensuring that every soldier received a copy of the New Testament and more than 150,000 copies were distributed

---

[1310] BCC June 1922; Advocate (Burnie) 8 March 1926 p4; AB April 1926.
[1311] Daily Telegraph (Launceston) 19 March 1908 p7; 13 March 1909 p5; NWA&EBT 2 May 1908 p6, 3 April 1909 p5, 15 May 1909 p3; The Age (Melbourne) 31 October 1912 p15; Geelong Advertiser 28 December 1912 p5; Bligh.

among Victorian army men.[1312] He married again, this time to the daughter of John Petrie, staunch Presbyterian of Hobart, Tasmania. He died on 23 June 1917.[1313]

## Appendix 2: John W. (Jack) Fisher

At Deloraine in 1909, Sarah Fisher, now the minister's wife, entered fully into the work. There for a Sunday school event it was reported she was "untiring (in) effort as instructress and accompanist (on the organ). All credit was to her for the excellent manner in which the children acquitted themselves in their various pieces." In July 1913, at Deloraine the Fishers were all packed and ready to move to the Bracknell Baptist Church when the message arrived that someone from Victoria had been secured to fill that position. In less than six months they were again packed, this time to go back to the Longford Baptist Church where Fisher would replace as Pastor the retiring Home Mission Super-intendent, the Rev Frederic Joseph Dunkley.[1314]

Two months later he was appointed Secretary of the Baptist Association. Fisher involved himself in the community in Longford, whether it was the Empire Day celebrations, the local school, the Longford Tourist and Improvement Association, the local Municipal Council, the Literary and Debating Society or the Six O'clock Closing meetings. For the Empire Day celebrations, the teachers and scholars of the local state school marched from the school to the large Foresters' Hall, headed by a Drum and Fife Band; Fisher was one of the speakers. He was required to speak on Canada, one of the nations of the Empire. With the nation at War, monthly Intercessory Prayer meetings began in September 1915, the venues being the different churches. On 25 March 1917, Fisher preached farewell messages at Longford as he was transferring to the Ulverstone Church.[1315]

## Appendix 3: The Rev Albert Butler

The Rev Albert Butler, a local boy from the Perth Church who from church services at a farm house made his way to important pastorates until he took control of the Concord Baptist Church in NSW and then the Brisbane Tabernacle. Blessed with a University education, wherever he went he fulfilled all expectations as he set for himself a punishing schedule, never sparing himself, and paying the price of an early death.

Albert Butler, the son of Edmund Butler and his wife of Perth,

---

[1312] The Reporter 13 April 1917 p7.
[1313] The Argus (Melbourne) 24 November 1917 p22; The Herald (Melbourne) 25 June 1917 p1.
[1314] LEx 13 July 1909 p2, 18 March 1913 p4; Daily Telegraph (Launceston) 17 July 1913 p5;
The North West Post (Formby) 2 December 1913 p2.
[1315] LEx 25 March 1914 p3, 23 May 1914 p9, 9 September 1915 p6, 27 March 1917 p6.

Tasmania, was born in the town on 4 June 1880. His father was a deacon of the Perth Baptist Church for some years and worked for about ten years for William Gibson Junior of "Scone". About 1898, church services were commenced at "Creekton", one of William Gibson's Estates. They were held in the large kitchen at the home of the manager, Charles Walsh. A large bread trough was used as a pulpit and the congregation crowded into the room. At first Sunday evening Gospel meetings and monthly temperance meetings were held in a large wool shed and it was not an uncommon experience to have more than a hundred persons present. In time, all the services were held in the woolshed and new seats were supplied.[1316] Tribute to the enduring quality of this work is found in the fact that Albert made a Christian commitment through these gatherings and entered the Christian ministry.

At the Baptist Half Yearly Assembly in November 1910, Butler now at Bracknell, refrained from speaking of himself. He said that,

> he would not speak of his mud baths and thrilling experiences. He had to be the pastor, legal adviser and referee of his flock, which required knowledge of the Word, sound commonsense and an abundance of patience.[1317]

But he was on the move again in January 1911 after only twelve months, this time to Longford to fill in for the Rev Frederic Joseph Dunkley so Dunkley could take an extended visit to the Home Mission Churches. Butler was moved again in September 1911, this time back to Wynyard. The Home Mission Council was anxious to have him there to replace Salisbury. Wynyard at this time was a joint pastorate with Yolla.[1318]

During Butler's time at Wynyard and Yolla the work prospered with a good number of young men regularly attending the Yolla services. Further, in November 1911, a block of land on the Henrietta Plains, which was only five kms away from the Yolla Church, was cleared in preparation for the erection of a church hall. There church services were being held in Mrs. Graue's lounge room. Once completed the new hall was also made available for community use. For functions, the hot water was prepared over the road at Crisp's home. A pole was inserted through the kerosene container handle for two to carry it in. The hall lacked heating and there were no proper paths. Years later, Nancy Herbert who lived next door to the church, recalled witnessing a wedding. "It was a very wet day," she said, "and with no proper paths, a row of potato sacks was put on the ground

---

[1316] Bligh; BCC February 1902; Day-Dawn May 1900.
[1317] NWA&EBT 4 November 1910 p4.

[1318] LEx 27 January 1911 p5; Circular Head Chronicle (Stanley, Tas) 13 December 1911 p3.

to the church for the bride to walk on." At the time another Yolla outstation commenced in the local school room at Moore's Plains (now Oldina), sixteen kms further in from Henrietta.

It was further reported that "at Yolla it is a pleasure to speak to upwards of one hundred attentive listeners." While every Home Missionary was supporting a horse at the time, the animal was considered an expensive means of transport. Butler was remembered for his grey nag which died at the end of 1912. The Home Mission Committee sent Butler £12 to help him out.[1319] Butler remained at Wynyard only six months, departing for the joint Ulverstone-Penguin pastorate in March 1912.

## Appendix 4: The Rev Ernest Albert Salisbury

In resigning the Wynyard Baptist Church in 1912, the Rev Ernest Albert Salisbury also resigned from the Baptist ministry and entered the Anglican Church. In December that year he was welcomed as the new curate of the Exeter Anglican Church. In May 1913, he was admitted to the order of deacon in the ministry of the Church having passed "most creditably" the diocesan examinations. He had been in residence at St. Wilfred's College for five months; further studies followed. After three years he was appointed rector of the Ulverstone and Forth Parish.[1320] With the nation at war, on one Sunday evening in the Holy Trinity Church in Launceston, he began his sermon with this text, "He that is not with me is against me." He then went on to say,

> I make no apology for asking you to consider with me the subject of Conscription. In doing so, we are not obscuring or forgetting the great Christian principles in which the pulpit is a mighty power, but are showing an earnest desire to point out our country's need ... Let us be true to the old flag, to the glorious traditions of the past, and to the brave and faithful dead who have fallen in the cause; of freedom, truth, civilisation, and the righteous ideals of our Empire. So shall we give God His due. So shall we honor the heroism of the living, the sacrifice of the dead.[1321]

Salisbury, as an Anglican, was present in the Town Hall the night of the Rev V. G. Britton's farewell from the Ulverstone Baptist Church and was gracious with his words to his old boss.[1322]

Salisbury's next posting in July 1918 was to St. Stephen's Church in the Wynyard parish. During his time a new brick church was built at a cost

---

[1319] SB February 1911; HM Minutes 23 April and 10 July 1912.
[1320] LEx 18 December 1912 p5, 10 May 1913 p6; Daily Post (Hobart) 12 June 1916 p4.
[1321] The full sermon is given in NWA&EBT 18 October 1916 p4.
[1322] NWA&EBT 28 March 1917 p2.

of over £3000. Through Salisbury's effort and that of his people, it was not only built but well-furnished and consecrated and opened in November 1920 entirely free of debt. In March 1921, he was moved to Launceston to head up the newly formed St. George's parish in Invermay. In November 1923, he was installed as Vicar of St. Margaret's in Mildura, Victoria, the first rural dean appointed to the Mildura rural deanery.[1323]

In April 1926, he was appointed to St. Mark's Church in the parish of Islington, diocese of Newcastle in NSW. In January 1928, he was appointed to the Cure of Donald, in the new Victorian Diocese of St. Arnaud. The following year his wife was killed in a car accident when he was driving. Then he was appointed rector and Archdeacon of the Parish of Mudgee in NSW.[1324] The next posting after a vacation in England, was the Church in O'Connell, NSW.[1325]

In 1933, he went to England for his health taking ministerial work and resigning the Mudgee appointments. Then, in 1936, he was appointed chaplain of Christ Church Rio de Janeiro and Archdeacon of Brazil.[1326]

The Rev Albert Ernest Salisbury died on 1 October 1950 in Odiham, Harts, England; he was sixty-seven years old. He had been "a man of outstanding gifts and striking personality ... well known in many parts of Australia as a conductor of parochial missions." He had been also "a great church builder, having during his

*14-6 Ern Walsh with Mr. Ratcliffe of Sheffield*

---

[1323] NWA&EBT 20 August 1918 p2; LEx 13 April 1921 p6; Advocate (Burnie) 8 March 1921 p4; Sunraysia Daily (Mildura) 1 November 1923 p2.
[1324] The Sydney Morning Herald 3 April 1926 p5; Advocate (Burnie) 18 January 1928 p2; The Newcastle Sun (NSW) 24 June 1929 p6. The next posting after a vacation in England was the Church in O'Connell, NSW. News (Adelaide) 25 October 1930 p1; Lithgow Mercury (NSW) 16 February 1931 p4; Mudgee Guardian and North-Western Representative (NSW) 15 August 1932 p7.
[1325] News (Adelaide) 25 October 1930 p1; Lithgow Mercury (NSW) 16 February 1931 p4; Mudgee Guardian and North-Western Representative (NSW) 15 August 1932 p7.
[1326] Mudgee Guardian and North-Western Representative (NSW) 8 July 1935 p5; The Age (Melbourne) 7 November 1936 p30.

ministry raised money for and built no less than fourteen churches."[1327]

## Appendix 5: Ern Charles Walsh

The likeable Tasmanian, Ernest Charles Walsh, grew up in a godly family connected to one of the oldest Baptist churches in the State. After working with the Home Mission for some years he moved to Victoria for ministerial training and subsequently ministered in South Australia where he contributed greatly in the Baptist Churches in that State.

Walsh was born on 24 May 1886 at Longford, Tasmania, to Charles Walsh a well-known resident of Perth and his second wife, Elizabeth Ann (nee Thomas) of Perth. His parents were staunch members of the Perth Baptist Church. His father was overseer at Woodhall, Scone Farm, Creek Tor and Eskdale for William Gibson Junior. He was also a local preacher. Early in life Ernest was a chicken farmer whose hobby in his teen years was homing pigeons. He too participated in the church services which had commenced at "Creekton".[1328] Walsh was appointed to the Home Mission Wynyard-Yolla pastorate.[1329]

Following the Wynyard-Yolla position, Walsh commenced at the Longford Baptist Church in June 1920. He continued giving lectures on his War experience and in Longford kept up his interest in poultry farming and homing pigeons. A year later, on 15 May 1921, his wife Alice (Daisy) who had just given birth died, the baby boy, Bruce Charles, dying the day before, and they were buried in the Perth Baptist cemetery. He was left with his two-year old daughter, Dorothy.[1330]

In March 1923, this "old Perth boy" was farewelled for two years to continue his studies at the Baptist College and attend University in Melbourne; the initiative came from the Baptist Council. In Longford he had taken an interest in the Boy Scouts, the local Primary school, the Rifle Club, the Regatta Association and the Homing Society. He was made a life member of the Homing Society. Up to the time of his leaving for College, he had been involved with the Home Mission work in the

---

[1327] LEx 4 November 1950; Mudgee Guardian and North-Western Representative (NSW) 15 August 1932 p7.
[1328] The Mercury (Hobart) 12 April 1939 p9. See Appendix Three: Albert Butler.
[1329] Daily Telegraph (Launceston) 8 September 1905 p4, 22 November 1912 p2.

[1330] Advocate (Burnie) 25 July 1919 p2; The Mercury (Hobart) 29 September 1921 p7; LEx 18 May 1921 p7, 1 December 1921 p8, 30 March 1927 p2; Daily Telegraph (Launceston) 21 January 1922 p4; AB 31 May 1922 p4; At the age of ten young Dorothy was playing the organ in church.

north and north-western portions of the State for fourteen years.[1331]

## Appendix 6: The Revs Arthur Charles Jarvis and Wilfred L. Jarvis

It is through the ministry of Queenslanders the Rev Arthur Charles Jarvis and his son, the Rev Wilfred Lemuel Jarvis, for eighteen months in Tasmania we see great fellowship and cooperation among the various Tasmanian church denominations but limited to questions of evangelism, temperance advocacy, welfare of the needy and propagation of the scriptures. Wilfred, an outstanding evangelist, conducted evangelistic missions in many centres.

Arthur Charles Jarvis was born in Poplar, London, on 13 May 1866 to Charles and Emily Jarvis. At the age of eighteen years Jarvis married Harriet Ann Pratt on 10 June 1884 at Holy Trinity, Canning Town, Essex. Jarvis early showed signs of being a public speaker and became associated with the Liberal Party, having decided to enter upon a political career. In those days he was a member of a group of lecturers who travelled England in the interests of their particular school of politics. He was intimately acquainted with such men as Lloyd George, Henry Asquith (later Lord Oxford), Sir Henry Campbell Bannerman, and John Burns. At this time he was a member of the Church of England to which he was very strongly devoted, his father being a preacher in that denomination. Yet careful study of the New Testament convinced him of the need of being baptised, and on his decision to follow his Lord in this way; he was turned out from home by his father who was strongly opposed to such practices. At the age of twenty-seven years he felt that God had called him to the work of the ministry and so relinquished his political activities to study for the service of Christ. Jarvis was a diligent student having had the advantages of study in London and at Oxford. He now belonged to the "Old Baptist Union" in England, having been a minister of that organization for upwards of sixteen years, and having held pastorates in both the north and south of England. For five years he preached in the largest church in the northern district, and during that period over 300 adult persons professed conversion and ninety-seven were baptised. He had a strong logical faculty which, in combination with his rich store of general knowledge and remarkable acquaintance with the Scriptures, made him a doughty opponent for debaters. His memory was phenomenal and rarely could be faulted when asked to locate even little used passages of Scripture. As a member of the Christian Evidence Society, he did notable work in various parts of England, and as a strong Protestant who had made a

---

[1331] Daily Telegraph (Launceston) 7 March 1923 p2, 10 March 1923 p11; Advocate (Burnie) 20 December 1924 p2.

*14-7 Jireh Baptist Church, Brisbane*

special study of the. Reformation movements, he was much in demand for big demonstrations. He took every opportunity to hear outstanding preachers as Spurgeon, Parker, McLaren, Liddon and others. When Dwight Lyman Moody visited England, Jarvis took an active part in several campaigns. Even yet not affiliated with the Baptist Union of Great Britain, the family came to Australia from Brighton departing in January 1910. He commenced work in Brisbane at the historic "Jireh" Church, coupled with the overseeing of the Clayfield Church. Jarvis formed part of the executive committee for the Queensland campaign of the Chapman and Alexander Mission in 1912.[1332] In 1913 he became the instructor of the Lay Preachers' Society of the Baptist Association.

In 1914, his son, Wilfred L. Jarvis was appointed pastor at the Yandina Baptist church and four years later enrolled as a student at the Victorian Baptist College.

Jarvis Senior himself was a committed member of the Loyal Orange Institution and spoke often at their meetings. He was a keen student on Socialism.[1333]

Twice he was elected Vice-President of the Queensland Union, but had to decline the presidency the second time around through ill-health. From "Jireh" he went to Ipswich. He was elected President for two years of the Temperance Society and President of the Six O'clock Closing League. For the League he worked with the Rev Henry Ebenezer Saunders who was treasurer. Working together, they had a writ for slander served against them by hoteliers. Jarvis maintained a notable ministry for over eight years when he was farewelled to the Central Baptist Church, Ipswich, and was welcomed on 22 September 1918.[1334]

**After his time at Wynyard**, Jarvis began at Longford on 11 March 1923 with his wife Harriett and their daughter-in-law, Bessie Jarvis. Bessie would often sing publicly with her daughter Irvine. On one occasion she sang a setting of "Rock of Ages" which was composed by her

---

[1332] Queensland Times (Ipswich, Qld.) 21 September 1918 p5; The Brisbane Courier 14 May 1910 p15, 18 October 1913 p5; The Week (Brisbane) 16 September 1910 p27; The Telegraph (Brisbane) 4 July 1912 p8.
[1333] The Brisbane Courier 28 March 1914 p6, 3 August 1918 p4; Daily Standard (Brisbane) 13 July 1914 p6; AB 23 November 1920.
[1334] The Brisbane Courier 11 March 1916 p16, 27 May 1916 p15; The Beaudesert Times (Qld.) 25 August 1916 p5; The Telegraph (Brisbane) 8 September 1911 p3, 16 April 1917 p2; AB 6 March 1934 p9; Daily Standard (Brisbane) 28 August 1918 p4; Queensland Times (Ipswich, Qld) 23 September 1918 p7.

father. Within weeks Jarvis and Wilfred conducted a three week tent mission in Victoria Square in Longford drawing large attendances.

But by October Jarvis Senior was compelled to resign his pastorate of the Longford Church owing to ill-health; he had to seek warmer climes. Wilfred remained to November as Harriett was training the Sunday school scholars for their anniversary and their daughter, Irvine, was organist.[1335]

On his return to the mainland he ministered to the church at Islington, NSW, commencing 3 December 1923. But his health completely gave way and he was compelled to resign from active work within two years.[1336]

All his life Jarvis had a big battle against ill-health, brought on through overstrain during one of his earlier pastorates in the North of England. He and Harriett seemed to have had far more than their share of sorrow and suffering. Six children predeceased them, one by drowning and the several breakdowns he suffered brought them into very difficult circumstances. Harriett died on 27 August 1933 aged sixty-six years. The Rev Arthur Charles Jarvis died on 1 March 1934 aged sixty-seven years. They left three sons and two daughters to mourn their loss.[1337]

## Appendix 7: The Rev Alan Paton Dawson

Following his time at Wynyard, the Rev Alan Paton Dawson commenced at the South Melbourne Baptist Church in March 1926 replacing the Rev Horace H. Jeffs. During his time at Albert Park, the South Melbourne and Port Melbourne Circuit was formed, assisted by Baptist College students and lay preachers. At the commencement of 1927, for six months he made the evening services as attractive and interesting as a picture show or a theatre with a "big feature" programme. He borrowed the idea from his father, the Rev William Dawson, who was doing the same at his church in Albury. As it was advertised at South Melbourne (Emerald Hill), "Every popular method will be used to delight the imagination, comfort the heart, and uplift the soul." The evenings included orchestral music, instrumental and vocal items, still and moving pictures. He imported from America an extra powerful DeLuxe electric film lantern, the only one of its kind in Australia at the time. The audiences heard from the Southern Choral Society of sixty voices. One evening in February 1927, 300 attended. Said one who attended, "I didn't think that church

---

[1335] AB 23 November 1920; LEx 14 March 1923 p6, 29 March 1923 p9; The Newcastle Sun (NSW) 16 October 1923 p4.
[1336] Newcastle Morning Herald and Miners' Advocate (NSW) 4 December 1923 p6; The Maitland Weekly Mercury (NSW) 6 February 1926 p1.
[1337] The Brisbane Courier 18 December 1912 p4; AB 6 March 1934 p9.

could be so interesting." Another said, "I haven't been to church since I've lived in the South, but I'm going again next Sunday." Said another, "It's good to find a church with new ideas." Then another who frequently attended the central city churches, "He's on the right lines, he'll get the people. It was the most wonderful service I have ever attended."[1338] At an "Open Air" Baptist conference in 1932, Dawson endorsed the idea of a greater emphasis on open-air preaching. He stated,

> The church is only nibbling at open-air preaching. We should get out into the air again in the natural method of the Gospel, where the temple has no walls, and the ceiling is the blue sky.[1339]

In February 1933, after seven years at South Melbourne, Dawson accepted a call to the pastorate of the North Perth Baptist Church in W.A. commencing on 4 April 1933. There he shared the preaching equally with the young Merlyn Holly who was studying for the ministry. Holly was chairman and secretary of the Young People's Department of the Association and later would be at the Hobart Tabernacle. By 1938, Dawson was Secretary of the Home Mission Committee of W.A. The following year he was the President of the Association. In his address he said that England was not blameless in view of the coming conflict. "He saw this unrighteousness illustrated in that the beaches were crowded on Sundays but the churches were struggling, the picture palaces were full while the prayer places empty.[1340]

In July 1941, he accepted a call to the East Kew Baptist Church in Melbourne. During the War he accepted a position with the Y.M.C.A. as R.A.A.F. Chaplain.[1341]

In November 1945, he began an interim fourteen month pastorate at Greenslopes Baptist Church in Queensland, and then one for five months at the Fairfield Baptist Church in Melbourne. Following these, he accepted the position as senior house master at the Melbourne Orphanage, Brighton.[1342] He retired in 1955 and died in May 1957 in Warburton, Victoria. He had married again on 22 March 1953 following the death of his wife Gwynne.[1343]

---

[1338] The Herald (Melbourne) 25 March 1926 p22; Record (Emerald Hill, Melbourne) 2 December 1944 p4, 12 February 1927 p4, 19 February 1927 p7; Advocate (Burnie) 14 February 1935 p2.
[1339] The Herald (Melbourne) 17 October 1932 p1.
[1340] The Argus (Melbourne) 24 February 1933 p9; The West Australian (Perth) 7 April 1933 p6, 11 May 1935 p25, 30 September 1939 p4; The Albany Advertiser (WA) 18 May 1939 p5. Moore, Parish p88.
[1341] The Herald (Melbourne) 31 July 1941 p20; The Age (Melbourne) 10 December 1942 p2.
[1342] The Courier-Mail (Brisbane) 3 November 1945 p4; The Argus (Melbourne) 22 February 1947 p17; The Age (Melbourne) 12 July 1947 p11.
[1343] The Argus (Melbourne) 23 May 1953 p18. Gwynne was buried in the Melbourne General Cemetery.

## Conclusion

Revivalist activity among the churches across the Australian colonies took off after 1890 through imported preachers such as the men from the Pastors' College. Regular evangelistic effort was essential for colonial Baptists if they wished to grow and a number of Tasmanian Baptist preachers profiled in the book's time frame fit this revivalist mould; they were sometimes the means of revival in their churches but not always; in this regard the local pastor could easily be seen as the "prophet without honour in his own country". His directness was not easy in the pastoral situation hence an outsider was more fitted for the evangelistic task.

At the time there was consistency in society of language and culture and so the Biblical stories these evangelists used were familiar to their hearers. But on this saw-dust trail were a few dominating preachers with their guilt-ridden, judgment-infused messages offering "a creed without history, without scholarship, without depth and without context", using the fear of death and eternal punishment to coerce their listeners. In their cases, this technique may have brought about a response but not necessarily to faith in Christ. At this time individual judgment or knowledge was not sought and even discouraged. Many an evangelistic crusade was at its heart unsatisfactory.

Yet evangelistic missions had their good side even if they did not make a great difference to actual church attendances or church membership; they reawaken religious devotion in those who had gone cold as well as bringing the conversion of the church attending unbeliever.

But by the 1920s, questions were being asked as this evangelistic preaching meant the challenges of modern life could not be worked through using reason and allowing questions to be raised. The doctrinaire preaching firmly laid down all that need to be known and conclusions were not to be contested.[1344]

Yet for all its unhelpful qualities, revivalism among Tasmanian Baptists was one of the most distinctive elements in our religious life for decades. Most conversions occurred among the ten to twenty year olds. But conversion is a misnomer, better a heightened commitment to Christianity by those brought up in its beliefs and practice.

---

[1344] Wrote the AB after the Evan Robert's revival in Wales, "Every revival movement is beset with dangers. Like the vultures which came down upon Abraham's sacrifice, there came down upon the Church and the young converts teachers of every conceivable phase doctrine — Millennial Darwinists, Perfectionist Latter Day Saints, Christian Scientists, Seventh Day Adventists, the Gift of Tongues sect, Tramp Preachers, etc., all claiming the mind of Christ. Not a few were unsettled, and, alas! alas! as subsequent years have shown, made shipwreck of the convert's faith. This is an aspect of revival movements that is rarely touched upon." SB 28 March 1905 p74.

The value of the evangelist was to clinch the religious decision of the young. Further, the message did have the power to transform the moral, social and spiritual conditions of the generation.

In time, this unquestioned proclamation was replaced with teaching, caring and participation by those in congregational worship. What is more, a relaxed attitude to godly matters was coming in. The uniqueness of Wilbur Lemuel Jarvis is that he appreciated the need to accommodate the questioning mind and made many of his messages, apologies thus commending the Christian faith. Further, inter-denominational support was a fundamental principle of Jarvis' approach. Revivalism became a leading mechanism of church growth when it promoted allegiance to organized Christian community. Revivalism also provided a blueprint of what church life could be, with its music and sensation but its penetration into community was rarely as deep as desired.

In this day and age are we still enamoured by the revivalist or do we in our local churches follow the lead of Wesley knowing the value of life-long Christian discipleship for ourselves and for those who have indicated that they too are willing to follow Christ? Wesley raised up a growing company of lay witnesses for Christ who were in turn to extend the revival. Every believer was to be an evangelist and Wesley's societies became agents of mission.

# Chapter 15 Yolla Baptist Church

## Introduction

By 1904 the Baptist Home Mission stations of Longford, Bracknell, Deloraine, Ulverstone (1903) and Wynyard (1904) all embraced large areas. They were all in the North and along the North-West coast. Most of them had a number of outstations. They were being efficiently worked by the home missionaries and assisted by earnest local preachers.

The first church building in the Yolla District was not a Baptist chapel but a "small unpretentious" weatherboard and shingle roofed Methodist structure situated at Camp Creek on the road to Mount Hicks, less than a km from present day Yolla. The chapel opened on 24 May 1896. It was enlarged in 1905 and moved into the town in 1922 to meet the needs of the growing district and reopened on 7 and 8 October the same year.[1345]

## J. W. (Jack) Fisher

Under the supervision of the Wynyard church, the work at Yolla began in 1907 with one of the Wynyard local preachers, Peter Clingeleffer, conducting services in the local Yolla school room. The services were then conducted at "Sea View", the farm residence of Daniel Smith and his wife Isabella Maria.[1346] The first service at "Sea View" was conducted by both Pastor William Henry Short stationed at Wynyard and the Rev Joseph Tanner Piercey stationed at Burnie. When Pastor Jack Fisher took over in the Wynyard-Yolla circuit, he conducted evening services at Yolla every alternate Sunday and afternoon services on every other week. By April 1908, good numbers had gathered at Yolla. He only stayed for twelve months

*15-1 Camp Creek Methodist Church*

---

[1345] Originally Methodist services in Yolla were held in the home of James C. and Annie Diprose, the first settlers who arrived in 1888. As the congregation grew in numbers, the need for a church building became apparent, and so on 24 May 1896, this small chapel was opened. A new brick Methodist church was opened in Yolla on 17 September 1967, with the former chapel retained as a Sunday school. See Bessie Smith and Margaret Pegus, Yolla – The First Century, p17; Daily Telegraph (Launceston) 11 June 1896 p4; LEx 25 February 1909 p8; Advocate (Burnie) 26 October 1922 p4, 22 May 1946 p2.

[1346] This couple was involved with the early Baptist services in the Burnie Town Hall and were signatories with twenty-nine others in the establishment of a permanent Baptist church building in the town.

as he was then transferred to the Deloraine Church in December 1908.[1347]

The Baptist Church in Yolla was important because it was used as God's training field for the new recruits. The leading church in the South, Hobart Baptist Church, in its first 100 years had just ten pastors, Yolla had thirty-eight![1348]

## Albert Ernest Salisbury

Ernest Albert Salisbury followed Fisher at Yolla in 1910. He had been employed in the joint Ulverstone-Penguin pastorate. He was then transferred to assist the Rev Vincent G. Britton in the Bracknell District which was followed by the Wynyard-Yolla circuit.

It was during Salisbury's term in the circuit that a contract was awarded to Ashby White to erect the present Yolla building on land donated by Daniel Smith. Earlier in November 1909, the Yolla folk had informed their fellow Tasmanian Baptist sisters and brothers that the dining room at "Sea View" was too small. They pleaded with them, "... there is great need for a church being built – great need for help, great need for you to ask the Lord how much you have to give towards this worthy object."[1349] Eventually, two foundation stones were laid, one by Daniel Smith and the other by the Rev Frederic Joseph Dunkley, now Superintendent of Tasmanian Baptist Home Mission. Dunkley, a prominent Baptist leader in New South Wales, had arrived from Wellington, NSW, in 1909.[1350] The Tasmanian Home Mission Committee had been reformed the year before.[1351] In the seven years before Dunkley's arrival the Home Mission had been busy erecting seventeen buildings and opening twenty-five preaching stations.

During Dunkley's time a steady stream of young men began training for the ministry. Soon he had

*15-2 The Daniel Smith family with Seaview in the background, c1908*

---

[1347] NWA&EBT 12 December 1908 p5.
[1348] AB 26 November 1918.
[1349] SB November 1909.
[1350] Dunkley was born at Motherwell in Scotland and grew up in a Presbyterian home. At an early age he migrated to New Zealand and became a Salvation Army officer for seven years before entering the Baptist ministry of New South Wales.
[1351] AB 29 August 1922 p8; The Recorder February 2005 p3.

seven students and these home missionaries were supplemented by one or two ordained men. One of the students would be his assistant at Longford where he was based, while the others were generally under the care of senior ministers.[1352] The preaching work was assisted by local preachers.

The Yolla building, costing £160, was officially opened on 28 August 1910. It was the second church building in Yolla. At the first committee meeting of the Church, it was resolved to raise four shillings per week by collections for the first six months to reduce the debt. A typical Sunday church collection at the time was twelve shillings.

In 1910, struggling Baptist churches such as Wynyard, Deloraine, Bracknell and Longford came under the Home Mission control. Dependent as they were on the support of the Mission, they received financial aid but in return they submitted control to the Home Mission Committee.

At his first Tasmanian Baptist Assembly, that of April 1910, the Home Mission Superintendent, the Rev Frederick J. Dunkley, began his appeal to the delegates, by saying, "The foreign mission provided novelty and romance, in the form of strange expressions and incidents. Yellow men in rice fields, dark men in tea plantations, were vastly different from white men in potato fields."

Dunkley without saying it, implied that the Home Mission work was aimed at these "white men in potato fields" and he maintained,

> "we have a distinctive witness, and are called upon by God to preach the Gospel in that distinctive way. Before we can do anything, we must recognise the need which can only be satisfied, first, by prayer; second, by money; third, by men."

Tasmania's Home Mission staff numbers more than doubled that year.[1353] The census for the following year indicated that there were 4,898 Baptists in Tasmania.[1354]

The President for the 1911/12 year, the Rev Frank W. Boreham, at

*15-3 Opening day in August 1910 of the Yolla Baptist Church building*

---

[1352] SB 30 November 1909 p290.
[1353] SB 21 April 1910 p262 edited.
[1354] Our Yesterdays Vol.13 p7.

Assembly in November put it this way,

> The backblocks are calling us! There is a man of Macedonia in every little settlement calling us to go over and help, and we ought to go. Beyond the great bush tracks, between the wattle and the gum, we hear the call of the Churchless settlements. To respond by establishing a preaching station is to create a new centre of Christian activity, from which beneficent influences will radiate even as far as Serajgunge. But if, on the other hand, we steel our hearts against the appeal, the call will not long be heard. Bush settlements easily acquire habits of indifference, and settle down to animalism and godlessness.[1355]

At the same Assembly Salisbury told delegates of his work at Wynyard and Yolla and that he was glad to be a (Baptist) home missionary but his ardour for this denomination would dissipate in the next twelve months. At the end of his time in the Wynyard-Yolla circuit, Salisbury resigned from the Home Mission. He informed the Home Mission Committee that he was considering "taking up work in one of the sister states". This was not so; he was throwing his lot in with the Tasmanian Anglicans.

## Alfred Butler

The Home Mission was heartened by the man who replaced Salisbury in the Wynyard-Yolla circuit. Under Alfred Butler, who commenced there in September 1911, it was the work at Yolla that prospered. It was reported, "At Yolla it is a pleasure to speak to upwards of one hundred attentive listeners."

A good number of young men were now regularly attending the Yolla services. In the early years in the town a Sunday school was conducted by the Methodists. At the time another outstation commenced at Moore's Plains (now Oldina) in the local school room. Moore's Plains was sixteen kms further inland from Henrietta.[1356]

By 1912, a Methodist missionary had been placed at Yolla and was

*15-4 Any local church was both the social centre of the town, and the 'House of God'*

---

[1355] SB 5 January 1911 p21. Serajgunge was Tasmania's Foreign Mission in Thailand.

[1356] SB November 1911; Jennifer Hemsley, Around the Country Circuits, p158; SB November 1911.

conducting services. His arrival caused concern to the Baptists as the missioner was "deliberately" conducting them at the same time as the Baptists despite a mutual agreement that he would not do so. In 1912, the Yolla Baptist church was constituted with eleven members.[1357] Butler, now twenty-two, departed for two years study at University.

## Ernest Charles Walsh

Ernest Charles Walsh commenced as pastor in the Wynyard-Yolla circuit in March 1912. He had previously been working under Britton's direction at Boat Harbour, one of the circuit's outstations. His "assiduous visitation" in the Yolla district resulted in "splendid congregations".

Some Sundays he conducted three services including one at Wynyard's outstation at Boat Harbour; in all it required him to cycle sixty-five kms. He returned to Yolla by bicycle from Boat Harbour on the Monday. A Home Missioner's labours were strenuous and his task a big one.

The annual Sunday school Anniversary and prize giving was a highlight of the year. It was a large community affair. The children were prepared with special hymn singing. On the day, overflowing floral arrangements decorated the stage. There was usually a visiting speaker. This event was usually followed by a concert on the Monday night.

The yearly Sunday school picnics were also a highlight of the church calendar as well as a community fair. They were held on the Mondays following the church's Sunday school anniversaries at "Sea View". Being within walking distance of the town, transport was not a problem. The children played rounders, competed in races, enjoyed the swings and the lolly scramble, while the men played cricket and the women prepared a basket lunch. Hampers bulging with picnic fare were placed on tables under the trees. A treat vied for by most children was Elsie Smith's rainbow cake. Photographs of such picnics reveal the very formal dress of the time: men dressed in suits, tie and hat and the women equally formal in their attire.[1358] In later years the beach at Somerset became the venue.

On the Monday evening a concert of songs and elocution items given by the adults was held concluding with a "coffee supper". In 1912, 160 folk attended.[1359] In March 1912, there were thirty Sunday school scholars on the roll. Since the church building comprised only one room, classes were held in its four internal corners.

---

[1357] HM Minutes 28 May 1912.
[1358] Bessie Smith and Margaret Pegus, Yolla – The First Century p18.
[1359] SB March 1912.

Autumn saw Harvest Festival, a time to acknowledge and give thanks that again the harvest had been plentiful. Home-grown produce was displayed: shiny red apples, bread, sheaves of hay, vegetables and eggs. There was usually a concert held after the sale of goods on the following evening. Walsh's final Sunday at Yolla was 1 February 1914, the occasion of its first baptismal service at "Sea View". Two years study at the Baptist College in Melbourne followed. In January 1925, Walsh commenced at the Smithton Church.

## Walter Stanley Simpson

Walsh was replaced early in 1914 by Victorian, Walter Stanley Simpson. He was assisted in his pastoral duties by a foundation member of the church, carpenter James Robertson Rattray. Encouraging reports were sent to the Home Mission meetings about Simpson's work.[1360] Late in 1914 he made application for admission to the Baptist College in Melbourne, and, as a requirement for entry, he visited the mainland to preach. The Yolla church understood, after all, that it was to some extent ministering to these young men. The church wrote,

> We trust he may be successful in being accepted as a student. We shall be sorry to lose him, for we know that the desire of his life is an earnest endeavour to do the will of God, and to follow where He leads and a more genuine out and out disciple of Christ would be hard to find.[1361]

But Simpson never entered College. In July 1915, as soon as the call came for men to enlist in the draft of World War I, he responded. Once accepted into the AIF, he left immediately.

During the next twenty-eight years Yolla enjoyed the distinction of providing the training ground for young men whose ministries at Yolla seldom lasted for more than a year. The main reason for their short stay was that they were there to gain pastoral experience before College training.

Simpson was one of a couple of home missionaries who signed up and left the work. In the churches the able-bodied men were also absent. During those War years the Home Mission found it difficult to recruit men for its work and

*15-5 Walter Stanley Simpson*

---

[1360] HM Minutes 15 September 1914; South Australian Register (Adelaide) 25 April 1900 p7.

[1361] SB November 1914.

financial giving decreased. Further William Gibson Junior ceased his £60 pound annual subscription as did Joshua T. Soundy. Soundy's annual subscription was £250.[1362] The Home Mission work ceased at Stanley, Smithton, Forest and elsewhere. But the War had an even more marked effect. It was found that a considerable proportion of those who had gone from the churches to War did not return to them on their return. It was a time of mental and spiritual upheaval. The routine of their lives had been broken and the habit of church-going interfered with. The War introduced an age of doubt about everything. It has been said that until the War Australians were a nation of creedless puritans, a nation with a morality but without a faith. The War increased this lack of faith in a personal God and in the belief of the world to come. For many, their prayers had been unanswered.

## Alfred Harrald James

Mainlander Alfred Harrald James had aspirations of becoming a Baptist Pastor but after a time in one Tasmanian Baptist Mission church enrolled in war service and then returned home.

Twenty-three year old James of the Knightsbridge Baptist Church in South Australia began at Yolla in April 1915. Alfred was the son of G. James of Norwood. Young Alfred had been training for the foreign mission field but decided instead for the Home Mission and an opening was offered in Tasmania. But within months he enlisted in the War effort and trained at the Claremont Training Camp. He embarked with the troops on 17 June 1915 and was first employed at the 1st Australian General Hospital at Luna Park, Cairo, Egypt, and then in France with the 3rd Field Ambulance. He returned to Australia on 27 July 1919 and, the following year, married Miss Grace Evelyn Morphett.[1363] James was followed in quick succession by K. J. Campbell who commenced in February 1915 but only stayed until July. He was not considered suitable for ministerial duties. [1364]

*15-6 Lance Corporal Alfred Harrald James*

---

[1362] HM Minutes 15 September 1916.
[1363] Marie Lines supplied this information.
[1364] The Advertiser (Adelaide) 24 October 1913 p19, 28 May 1919 p9, 24 April 1920 p10; The North West Post (Formby) 30 January 1915 p2.

# Yolla Baptist Church

## The Rev Albert Edward Holloway

On his return from South Australia in December 1915, the Rev Albert Edward Holloway was put in charge of the Church at Yolla which proved for him a quiet two years.[1365] Then in January 1918, he was moved back to Bracknell and this proved to be his final Home Mission position in Tasmania. On 11 April 1918, he married the church organist, Ruth Cure of Leesville in the Smithton Church and the next day of all days officiated at a wedding at Blackwood Creek. While on tour in 1922, Britton found the properties at Bracknell in "splendid" condition and Holloway received a commendation. Holloway was farewelled to Deloraine on 5 March 1922 and ordained at the end of the year.[1366]

## Alan Paton Dawson

Holloway was succeeded in April 1918 by twenty-one year old Alan Paton Dawson. Dawson had a short pastorate of eight months, having married Gwynne Clark at the Latrobe Baptist Church on 11 December 1918. Gwynne was the daughter of John Clark and his wife. John was a deacon of the Latrobe Church, choir conductor and the Sunday school superintendent. During Dawson's time at Yolla seven members departed "from our small company" and he was moved to Deloraine Church.[1367]

## Henry Roy Tunks

Henry Roy Tunks came to Yolla from the Latrobe Baptist Church under protest as he was a town boy and therefore he didn't think he would mix well with country folk. Years later he related how he was accepted by the youth of the town.

*15-7 Alan Paton Dawson*

The young chaps in the district challenged me to ride a horse but they didn't know that I had been trained to ride by a jockey. To begin, I mounted the wrong side on purpose. The wager was a horse race. The boys were to attend the service if I won the race. I did win and the boys attended church but sang out of tune! This episode helped me to be accepted by the community.

As with all the young trainees, the folk who made up the congregation

---

[1365] NWA&EBT 14 December 1915 p3.
[1366] Daily Telegraph (Launceston) 10 March 1922 p8; BCC December 1922 p3.

[1367] NWA&EBT 13 December 1918 p3, 24 October 1918 p4; LEx 29 June 1944 p5.

looked after their pastors of the time.

> I boarded at Gran Neal's and I remember a trip that I made to Wynyard and Myalla on my bike as a relief for the Baptist Minister Rev E. C. Walsh. It was a very wet night and I arrived home at 2 a.m. drenched to the skin. Mrs. Neal told me to rub myself down and gave me a drink. I thought it was "black", straight whisky but others who knew Mrs Neal well, told me that it was one of her favourite remedies "O.T." which was a general 'pick me up' used in many households. Another of her cures was brandy, sugar and hot water.[1368]

Tunks was at Yolla during the time of the "Spanish Flu". He continued,

> During my ministry there was an epidemic of "Black Flu" and services had to be conducted in the open. Seats had to be apart and people were not to sit close together, just three to a pew. The epidemic went on for some weeks. Mrs. Neal organised visitations to light fires in the homes and help feed patients. Mrs. Richard Smith, a nursing sister, organised the nursing.

*15-8 Yolla streetscape*

He added recalling more of his early days,

> I remember the week night study group. After I had lit up the church, I would stand on the hill and watch people coming with their lanterns, the lights bobbing along in the dark. It was quite inspiring, like fairyland, like fireflies.

After Tunks left in February 1921, the church was without a resident pastor for some months.[1369]

Since it was reported at the end of the War in 1919 that there was a vacancy at the Yolla Baptist for Home Missioners, sixty-one year old George W. Ellis volunteered in 1920 for one year.

## Ernest Eric Watson

Ernest Eric (Wattie) Watson commenced his pastoral ministry at

---

[1368] "Gran" Neal was the wife of Mr. H. Neal. She died on 17 June 1950.

[1369] Advocate (Burnie) 23 February 1921 p3.

Yolla in March 1921 with a strong desire to serve his beloved island's Baptist people. A manse had been purchased for £500 so he saw the conclusion of Yolla as a single man's station.[1370] Wattie proved a great favourite with the local young people and by September 1921 he had gathered about twenty-five of them into the Endeavour Society. On one occasion he bussed them to Wynyard for a combined Christian Endeavour meeting where

> papers were read by the visiting members on "Prayer", "Consecration" and "Responsibility", each of which showed careful preparation, and were much appreciated. Musical items, congregational singing, and social interaction over refreshments made it a very enjoyable evening. A return visit is being arranged by the Wynyard Society at an early date.[1371]

Church attendances at Yolla increased and baptisms took place at Wynyard for as yet Yolla had no baptistry. During this time Wattie felt a call to the foreign field. He concluded on 5 March 1922.

## Return of Alan Paton Dawson

With Yolla now a married man's station, Alan Paton Dawson returned in March 1922. He was ordained there on 9 November 1922 having completed his "special studies". During his time services were commenced at Takone and a Sunday school commenced at Upper Mount Hicks and one recommenced at Henrietta. Dawson commenced preaching classes for some of the young men. After ten months, in June 1923, he was farewelled as he was considered a man to "do the work in the back country" hence his appointment at nearby Wynyard Church which was no longer a joint pastorate with Yolla. Gwynne his wife was "a great favourite" with all, and being a soloist, she was a great help at socials.[1372]

All Home Missioners were now being paid a salary of £180 a year and each Home Mission station was required to forward to the Home Mission a return the amount of up to 60% of the pastor's salary which was reimbursed.[1373]

## Arthur T Jessop

Arthur T Jessop and his wife Gladys and family were welcomed at Yolla in June 1923 and remained twelve months. Both Arthur and Gladys were long-standing teachers with the Education Department employed in the North-West of the island as far as Marrawah. Prior to the part-time Yolla Church

---

[1370] The Mercury (Hobart) 15 April 1921 p5, July 1921; AB April 1922; the manse later became the residence for the Yolla Post Office.
[1371] Advocate (Burnie) 16 September 1921 p5.
[1372] Advocate (Burnie) 21 March 1922 p4, 16 November 1922 p4, 7 June 1923 p4.
[1373] HM Minutes April 1923. At the end of 1937 it was as much as 115%.

appointment, he was at one time head teacher at the Sassafras school.[1374] They had come to Yolla from the Beulah Baptist preaching station which was part of the Sheffield Baptist circuit.

During their time at the Yolla Church, Arthur was in charge of the Mt. Hicks State school while Gladys was in charge of Henrietta State school.

At Yolla Gladys prepared the children in singing for the Sunday school anniversaries. During their time Sunday Services commenced at Upper Mount Hicks and Upper Henrietta. The debt on the Upper Henrietta building was cleared and an organ was purchased for it.[1375] The influenza which had been prevalent during Tunks' time continued, curtailing the attendance numbers. Through these years the church made good use of the gifted evangelist Wilfred Lemuel Jarvis of the Queensland Evangelisation Society. Eventually, the men Dawson had trained for preaching were participating in the services.

In July 1924, Arthur was moved to the Claude Road School and Gladys to the First Gowie Park School and these placements meant the conclusion of the Jessops' time at the Yolla Church. At their farewell at Yolla Arthur was given Papini's "Life of Christ" and Gladys was presented with Weymouth's "New Testament in Modern Speech".[47] The church also farewelled Hilton J. Preece, formerly of Bracknell, as he set off to engage in Home Mission work at Preolenna and Myalla.[48] Following his time at Preolenna, Preece spent a short time at Latrobe and then moved to Sydney to train at a Missionary College.

## Wesley J. Bligh

By April 1924, Pastor Wesley J. Bligh was placed at Yolla in his own right. By the end of the year the financial position of the church was so critical that non-attending members were written to asking for a donation.[1376]

In January 1925, Bligh made application to work with the Victorian Home Mission as "a result of my failure to qualify for entrance to College as a student for Tasmania this year" but there appears that there were no Victorian openings so by March he became an assistant to Britton at Latrobe. He left for Melbourne early in 1926 as he had now been accepted to study that year at the Melbourne Baptist College.[1377]

---

[1374] NWA&EBT 27 August 1917 p2; Advocate (Burnie) 20 August 1919 p2, 23 June 1924 p4, 5 July 1924 p4, 20 August 1926 p1. The newspapers at this time speak of three A. T. Jessops in Tasmania: the teacher, a Presbyterian minister Rev A. T. Jessop in the Scottsdale area and an A. T. Jessop a contractor.

[1375] The Home Mission did not assist financially with the erection of the 1913 Henrietta building; it was local effort. Home Mission Minutes 26 March 1913.

[1376] Yolla Church Minutes.

[1377] Letter of 29 January 1925 Baptist Union of Victoria archives; The Mercury (Hobart) 28

## Edwin Charles Mcintosh Brown

Edwin Charles Macintosh Brown, who entered the work of the Baptist Home Mission at Yolla in April 1925, followed Bligh. At his welcome Britton said that Brown "came to Yolla with the Baptist Union's fullest confidence." He carried a letter of recommendation from the Tasmanian Methodist Home Mission; he had been stationed at Waratah. The Rev Edward B. Woods of Burnie had introduced him to the Baptist ministry. Brown, with his military bearing and moustache was an outstanding preacher.[1378] He defined a home missionary thus,

> He must know his God, but he must also know his fellow man, and to know them he must go where they are, live amongst them, share their tasks and their burdens, and throughout it all point to Jesus Christ.

For himself, he felt that his work was among men. Brown could also handle a hammer and soldering iron. While he was at Yolla, he made a very fine baptistry thus saving the church much expense. Further, a vestry was added to the building in 1927.

The first candidates to use the baptistry walked five miles on very rough terrain in very wet weather for the occasion. Brown stayed for less than a year, departing in January 1926. He had accepted the invitation of the Tasmanian Council of Churches to take up evangelistic work at Adamsfield amongst the diggers for six months and he commenced there at the end of February 1926.[1379]

*15-9 Macintosh Brown & Family*

## E. D. Mackey

The next to come to Yolla was E. D. Mackey from the mainland who was welcomed in February 1926 but sadly he soon proved unsuitable for Home Ministry work. He resigned in August and returned immediately to the mainland "where he will continue his studies."[1380]

## Cecil M. Jobling

Between a Methodist Maria Island appointment in March 1925 and lasting until January 1927, Methodist Home Missioner Cecil W. Jobling had a change of thinking and became a Baptist. Subsequently he

---

October 1925 p8; Advocate (Burnie) 13 February 1926 p3.
[1378] The Mercury (Hobart) 28 October 1925 p8.

[1379] The Mercury (Hobart) 23 January 1926 p8.
[1380] Advocate (Burnie) 3 September 1926 p4.

applied to the Tasmanian Baptist Home Mission for a position and was appointed to the vacancy at Yolla.

He was inducted on 10 January 1927. Jobling and his wife were gifted singers, and his wife took part in musical competitions "with considerable success". But after a short pastorate he was farewelled to Smithton in March 1928. Following their leaving the Church was without a pastor for some months and the Burnie Church supplied preachers for most of the services.[1381]

## Appendices

### Appendix 1: Henry Roy Tunks

Tasmanian Henry Roy Samuel Tunks grew up in a godly family connected to the Longford Baptist church. He responded to a call to full-time pastoral ministry and trained under the Rev V.G. Britton before pastoring a church in his own right. Following ministerial training at the Victorian Baptist College he attended to a number of Victorian churches before becoming involved with a para-church ministry. He then transferred to the orders of the Anglican Church where he ministered for the rest of his days. The pageantry of this unofficial State Church attracted him.

Tunks was born in Launceston in 1900 to George Albert Tunks and his wife Christina Pinkard and the family attended the Longford Baptist Church where his father was the Sunday school Superintendent.[1382] From his application in 1924 to the Victorian Baptist Candidates Board for training he spoke of how he was raised in a godly home,

*15-10 Padre Tunks*

I had a Christian Mother whose teaching and influence made an early impression on my boyhood. Though I cannot quite explain; yet Jesus Christ has always been intensely real to me, and I know that my belief in Him came with understanding. It increased as I grew, and then in my teens, during a mission conducted by the late Rev (J. T.) Piercey, (of the Victorian Evangelisation Society) I definitely consecrated my life to the Lord Jesus Christ, and was baptized. My conversion was not a sudden change. After my consecration I took up Sunday school work, and was a teacher for some time.

---

[1381] Advocate (Burnie) 17 March 1928 p4; LEx 29 April 1930 p7.

[1382] Daily Telegraph (Launceston) 19 February 1914 p3.

At the age of fourteen he was participating in the Longford Debating Society. By the age of seventeen he was the scholars' choir master for the Sunday school anniversary.[1383]

By March 1918 he was for twelve months assistant to Britton and he was put in charge of the Church Sunday school.[1384] He was then given sole charge of the Yolla Baptist Church.

During his time at the Baptist College in Melbourne, he was pastor of the Churches at the Eaglehawk and White Hills for six months and then pastor of the Sunshine Church for eighteen months.[1385]

He was transferred in April 1923 to the Ballarat South Churches for eight months under guidance of the Rev S. A. McDonald. His next pastorate was that of the Melbourne suburb of North Carlton.[1386] Ministerial studies which he completed in 1927 would not have been easy for him as he had only received a State School Education to sixth grade.

Tunks then began at the Melbourne suburban Church of Coburg in January 1928 and was ordained. There he married Victorian Adie Agnes Robertson, youngest daughter of William Adie Robertson and his wife Jane (nee) Mathieson.[1387] Under his direction at Coburg services were begun at Merlynston, in 1932. He remained at Coburg for eight years.[1388]

Tunks became a padre for the Toc H movement, and as the Victorian representative for the organization he left for England for twelve months in part to attend the Coming-of-Age Festival of Toc H in London[1389] and he undertook an eight month preaching itinerary. Once back in

*15-11 Coburg Baptist Church opened 1910*

---

[1383] LEx 10 July 1914 p6, 22 February 1917 p7.
[1384] Advocate (Burnie) 17 February 1919 p2.
[1385] The Argus (Melbourne) 4 March 1922 p20; Sunshine Advocate (Vic) 12 April 1946 p2.
[1386] The Argus (Melbourne) 26 November 1923 p16; Advocate (Burnie) 24 February 1925 p4.
[1387] The Herald (Melbourne) 23 February 1940 p8, 26 February 1942 p12; The Argus (Melbourne) 26 April 1948 p3.
[1388] The Age (Melbourne) 14 March 1936 p31; Advocate (Burnie) 5 December 1929 p9; Wilkin p135, 178.
[1389] Toc H is an international Christian movement which came to the fore in WW2 as it formed clubs where all soldiers were welcome regardless of rank. The Rev Harold Hackworthy of the Hobart Church was also much involved at this time.

Victoria he travelled extensively to raise funds for the Baptist Centenary Appeal. The Toc H connection probably provides a clue to this next change in his life.[1390] At the time a number of Baptist pastors became involved with multi-denominational organizations such as the Mission for the Lepers and moved to a more prominent Church to gain greater acceptance in their deputation work. If this was the case with Tunks, that would explain his move in March 1939 when he became a preacher of the Church of England's St David's Church in Moorabbin, something he would have found difficult to explain to his father.[1391] On 22 February 1942, following training for Anglican ministry at Ridley College, he was ordained Anglican priest of the Anglican Diocese of Melbourne. He was initially ordained as a deacon, then curate. On 23 December 1943, he was given the upgraded designation and licence as "Minister of the Parochial District of Moorabbin". During his time at Moorabbin, until 1965, a new brick church was built. When he retired from Ministry of St David's, he engaged in locum and relief preaching in country Victoria, including Swan Hill and Red Hill, Geraldton in WA and parishes in Tasmania. He and his wife ran a milk bar in Dromana and then lived their remaining years in Blairgowrie on the Mornington Peninsula. Roy and his wife Adie had four children: Maurine, Cynthia, Spenser and Jocelyn. Adie died on 21 October 1964 and Roy died on 17 April 1987.[1392]

## Appendix 2: George W. Ellis

In 1908, George W. Ellis, a well known long time resident in Penguin and a Justice of the Peace, lived in his "little snug farm" opposite his brother's farm in Blythe Road. For years he had been a Sunday school teacher and preacher at the local Methodist Church.[1393] On the anniversary of fifty years of Methodism in Penguin it was said of him,

> He was a lad of six (fifty-one years ago) when he came to Penguin with his father. They sailed from Launceston, and after twenty-three days reached the Leven River remaining there ten days. He and his father walked to Sulphur Creek there being no roads, and he found it trying. In walking back in the evening he passed the church, where he heard the people singing very heartily for the first time. After settling down he walked 4 miles each way to a Sabbath school, conducted by the late Robert Smith.[1394]

---

[1390] The Mercury (Hobart) 10 July 1937 p9; The Herald (Melbourne) 17 November 1938 p35.
[1391] Tunk's father was now dead.
[1392] Family details were supplied by granddaughter Jennie Munro.
[1393] NWA&EBT 10 April 1908 p3, 22 August 1908 p4; Advocate (Burnie) 15 August 1944 p2.
[1394] NWA&EBT 19 January 1916 p2.

His mother was the daughter of Joseph Roberts. Joseph was a Baptist who attended Henry Dowling's York Street Baptist Chapel in Launceston.

Ellis in 1936 recalled his early days as a lay preacher in "the Wild North-West",

> One of the hardest things I ever had to face was the first time I stood up and preached the Gospel of Jesus Christ to many sturdy young fellows who, I believe, had been constantly in dread of me for some time. Now this was all ended forever, and they came in large numbers to hear me, and I hope were all the better for doing.

In the same article he added,

> And what about you, my fellow-travellers to eternity, whose day of life, like mine is drawing in? Take then the message here I give: "Inquire within, and be at peace with God, through our Lord Jesus Christ, whose precious blood cleanses from all sin. He that believeth is justified by Faith."[1395]

## Appendix 3: Ernest Eric (Wattie) Watson

Tasmanian Ernest Eric (Wattie) Watson grew up in a godly family connected to one of the oldest Baptist churches in the State. His missionary aspirations were fulfilled on the foreign field for some years after training. He returned to Victoria to administer the Mission and then returned to Tasmania to serve his beloved Baptist people for the remainder of his working days.

*15-12 Young Wattie*

Wattie Watson was born on 2 February 1900. When he was three his parents, Ernest and Esther Watson now with three children, moved from Grudgery, near Budgerbong, N.S.W, to Perth, Tasmania, the home of his father's people. Wattie was the first of a big family of ten children. He was never a stranger to firm parental discipline: work, prayer and love. The family was itinerant living in various Northern Tasmania areas as their father sought work as a farm labourer. At one stage Wattie and four of his siblings lived with their mother in the little cottage across the road from the Perth Baptist Church while his father at that stage rode off on his bicycle each Monday to work on a farm some

---

[1395] Advocate (Burnie) 31 August 1936 p5.

distance away only returning to the family on Friday evenings.

As for most farming families in the 1920s and 30s life was hard, money was tight and each person had to be resilient. At thirteen, Wattie went to a Launceston bakery to earn his own way. He was reported by a customer for "endlessly reading novels while delivering bread!"

Wattie became a member of the Perth church about 1915.

The Rev Horace H. Jeffs visited Perth on Sunday evening to conduct the Sunday school anniversary service. Reaching the church, he noticed a number of lads outside and urged them "to go in, to give their hearts to God, join the church and help in any way they could." A few months later he visited Longford for a Christian Endeavour rally and was met at the gate by a youth who asked him if he remembered him. Jeffs replied that he did not. The lad then told Jeffs that he was one of the lads to whom he spoke outside the door at Perth and that he had done as he suggested, been baptised, joined the church, and was now an Endeavourer. That was Jeffs' second acquaintance with Wattie.

15-13 Horace H. Jeffs

Later Wattie transferred to the Launceston Tabernacle. There the Jeffs took him in for two years and influenced him greatly. Wrote Jeffs of when Wattie first arrived,

Mrs. Jeffs and I decided to take him into the Manse. It was not long before I recognised in him preaching gifts and a diamond in the rough. The proposal to think of the ministry was received with amusement, then consternation, but later with anxious thought and prayer.[1396]

When he was eighteen years of age he enlisted in the War effort but time was on his side, he saw no action.[1397]

**Then in 1922, after a year at Yolla**, he entered the Melbourne Bible College. Wattie then went to the Baptist College of Victoria for the

15-14 Missionary Candidates: A. B. Rogers SA, A. E. Smith Qld, E. E. Watson, C. Baldwin Vic., W. G. Crofts WA.

---

[1396] AB 13 June 1933 p9.

[1397] World (Hobart) 28 October 1918 p3.

*15-15 Missionaries in Comilla in 1931. Front row centre is Elsie with Avril and Wattie*

four year course where he completed ordination studies. Then at the end of 1925 the Australian Baptist Foreign Mission called for five men to go to East Bengal. One of them, Wilf Crofts, a fellow-student and missionary enthusiast, had influenced Wattie to such an extent that he too decided for India. When the initial struggles were over Wattie was told, "Every tub shall sit on its own bottom". For him the call to go to the East Bengal field was like a call to "go to Ninevah". Apart from Crofts, Wattie joined three other ordained men - Cyril Baldwin, Austin Rogers and Ted Smith in responding. To gain support before he left, Wattie did a circuit of the Tasmanian Baptist Churches. In October 1925 Ted Smith and Wattie set sail.[1398]

In his 1923 correspondence to Crofts Wattie wrote,

> As regards India, Bill, I am quite happy about having offered and if I could but realize that I was really going to do something instead of being a dead weight or something else, I would be much happier. But as you say, the fight is going to be a stiff one and it's just grace that Christ gives us the privilege of engaging in it.

Wattie found language school in India to be a priceless experience since men and women from all parts of the world studied, argued and lived together, never afterwards to feel quite so isolated in their adopted land when they had scattered each to his own sphere of service. He spent up to fourteen hours a day in language study but it took him ten years to master Bengali.

In India Wattie sat in awe in Carey's chair. Then they set out via the Sunderbans of the Ganges Delta, for his first post of Orakandi. Having served briefly in Serajgunge with the Rev Thomas Churchward-Kelly and his wife Stella Mary Churchward-Kelly, and in Mymensingh and Birisiri, they finally settled in Comilla for about seventeen years.

Converts did not come easily, but contacts with the people of this college town, with its intelligentsia as well as market people, were many. In Bible classes, lectures in English on the Bible, and in the bazaar preaching there were endless opportunities to use the Indian

---

[1398] LEx 25 September 1925 p3; The Argus (Melbourne) 29 October 1925 p15.

mother tongue. He was one of the most competent linguists that the mission has ever had. When the Language School for Missionaries in Darjeeling reopened after the war, he was made its Principal for three years.

On 17 December 1927, he married Elsie May of Eaglehawk in William Carey's own Baptist Church in Bowbazar, Calcutta. With that marriage began a partnership of over fifty years. They met while Wattie was taking Victorian country pastorates. Elsie had been prepared for missionary service by the many visits to Eaglehawk of the Rev Hedley Sutton. Wattie returned on furlough in November 1932 bringing with him Elsie and their daughter Avril. The furlough comprised a tour of the principal Baptist Churches in Tasmania. Wattie spoke of the conditions in India, where the caste system, unemployment and other factors were causing wide-spread unrest. He also told of the magnificent achievements of Christian missionaries in India, and commended the workers in India to the support of those at home.[1399]

On their return to India in February 1934, he remained in charge of the Comilla station, East Bengal, soon to be East Pakistan.[1400] He was Field Secretary from 1937-1939 and from 1946-1947. Another furlough took place in 1940.

During 1947, just before partition, they returned home from an India seething with unrest and anticipation of a golden age to come, free from its overlords. He spent four years with the Rev Frank Marsh in the A.B.M.S. Melbourne office as Associate Secretary. To be effective as a writer of missionary themes for the Australian Baptist public, he went back to school to learn journalism. Then he turned "Our Indian Field" into "Vision". He also wrote a short history of Australian Baptist missions called "Our Heritage" and also two biographies of Bengalis who became Christians. He wrote "An exile Returns", the biography of Mozahar Munshi, a Muslim who turned to Christ. He also wrote "Son of Light", the story of Aksoy, the Bengali convert.

*15-16 Wattie street preaching in East Bengal*

---

[1399] Wattie was stationed with the Victorian Home Mission as a student pastor at Koondrook in 1923-1924. Advocate (Burnie) 22 November 1932 p5, 6 April 1933 p4.
[1400] The Argus (Melbourne) 5 January 1934 p5.

In 1951, Wattie finally served his beloved Baptists in Tasmania as General Secretary of the Baptist Association, Home Mission Superintendent and Book Room manager. At first the positions were part-time: he also served as pastor of the Launceston Central Baptist Church meeting in the Upper Room of Duncan House at 45 Brisbane Street commencing in November 1952.[1401] The Tabernacle had been sold to the Commonwealth Government P.M.G. Department in 1950.[1402]

But the load was too heavy for Wattie so the task of being Pastor at Central was relinquished. He had previously relinquished the position of Associate Secretary of the A.B.F.M. In March 1953, a new Baptist Sunday school work commenced at Kings Meadows and Wattie took charge.[1403]

In 1989, Wattie and Elsie retired to Geelong but they had been in retirement for only twelve months when he suffered a stroke and he died on 19 January 1991.[1404]

## Appendix 4: Walter Stanley Simpson

With a call to spend his life in pastoral ministry, Walter Stanley Simpson arrived from interstate to work with the Tasmanian Home Mission but was not long in the job when he responded to the call-up and was sent to the Front in France where he lost his life in the battle of Fromelles.

Simpson was born in Collingwood, Victoria, in January 1900, his, father being Robert Simpson. At first Walter was a salesman and then went into the Home Mission service with Tasmania Baptist Churches in 1914. Maybe he attended the George Street Baptist Church, Fitzroy, it being less than a mile from his home and at the time was in its heyday. From September 1905 to 1910 the Rev George J. Mackay from Devonport was George Street's Pastor.

**Following Simpson's time at Yolla** on 26 November 1915 his Unit, 23rd Battalion 7th Reinforcement, embarked from Melbourne on the troopship HMAT A73 Commonwealth. Whilst on board in midocean he wrote the newspaper article, "The Sailing of the Troopship".[1405] On 23 February 1916 he joined 58th Battalion in Egypt. Then he joined the British Expeditionary Force in Marseilles, France, on 29 June 1916. In the

---

[1401] AB 5 September 1951 p16. The hall below was renovated and services commenced in it on 3 October 1954. Most of the old Tabernacle fittings were renovated and re-used and the hall had a seating capacity for 300. AB 13 October 1954 p1.
[1402] AB 9 August 1949 p11, 3 January 1950 p14.
[1403] The Age (Melbourne) 27 September 1952 p16; LEx 23 March 1953 p3.
[1404] See Tasmanian Baptist Advance July 1991 for a full account of Watson's time in Bengal.
[1405] Heidelberg and Greensborough, Eltham and Diamond Creek Chronicle (Vic) 4 November 1916 p4.

battle of Fromelles on 19 July 1916 he was posted missing, pronounced "Killed in Action, Presumed Buried in No Man's Land". As the Australian War Memorial Encyclopedia records,

> The battle of Fromelles on 19 July 1916 was a bloody initiation for Australian soldiers to warfare on the Western Front. Soldiers of the newly arrived 5th Australian Division, together with the British 61st Division, were ordered to attack strongly fortified German front line positions near the Aubers Ridge in French Flanders. The attack was intended as a feint to hold German reserves from moving south to the Somme where a large Allied offensive had begun on 1 July. The feint was a disastrous failure. Australian and British soldiers assaulted over open ground in broad daylight and under direct observation and heavy fire from the German lines. Over 5,500 Australians became casualties. Almost 2,000 of them were killed in action or died of wounds and some 400 were captured. This is believed to be the greatest loss by a single division in 24 hours during the entire First World War. Some consider Fromelles the most tragic event in Australia's history.

For many who served in places of extreme danger, the Christian God was given a high place on the list of missing persons. Further what the churches claimed would be the result of the war – a national spiritual cleansing - did not occur hence a loss of further credibility.

## Appendix 5: The Rev Albert Edward. Holloway

The Rev Albert Edward Holloway with extended Baptist family connections worked with the Tasmanian Baptist Home Mission for more than a decade before moving to Western Australia where he contributed greatly to their Churches. He returned home to Tasmania to pastor another of the Tasmanian Baptist Churches before transferring to South Australia to see out his days.

Holloway was born in 1878 to John Alexander Holloway and Frances Amy (nee Elmore). In his youth Albert was one of Sheffield Baptist's "most prominent Endeavourers".[1406] His sister, Rhoda, married Ivy Opie Smith, the son of Daniel and Isabella Smith of "Sea View", Yolla. Holloway commenced with the Home Mission.

On his return from South Australia in December 1915, he was put in charge of the Home Mission Church at Yolla which proved for him two quiet years.[1407]

Then in January 1918, Holloway was moved back to Bracknell and this proved to be his final Home Mission position in Tasmania. While on tour in 1922, Britton found the properties

---

[1406] The Mercury (Hobart) 1 June 1889 p1.

[1407] NWA&EBT 14 December 1915 p3.

at Bracknell in "splendid" condition and Holloway received a commendation. Holloway was farewelled to Deloraine on 5 March 1922 and was soon ordained.[1408] His years at Deloraine were "a time of reaping" during which a number were added to the church. A church building was erected at Meander.[1409]

He was farewelled in December 1925 as he went to replace the Rev George Wainwright at the Sandy Bay Baptist Church. The Church had been told that he had always left a church numerically, financially and spiritually stronger than when he came to it. He commenced in early 1926.

In March 1928, the Sandy Bay Baptist Church was constituted with the transfer of thirty-six members from the Hobart Tabernacle.[1410]

**After three years at Sandy Bay** he moved again, this time to Wagin in West Australia commencing in the second half of 1929 to follow the Rev George Philp who had been at Smithton. Wagin is a farming town and shire in the Great Southern region of Western Australia, approximately 225 kms south-east of Perth on the Great Southern Highway between Narrogin and Katanning. His keen interest in Foreign Missionary work continued and he remained there until October 1935. The Holloways now had two daughters. In October 1934 there were community discussions on moving the Aborigines from a native camp overlooking the town to a new site. At a public meeting on behalf of the Parents' and Citizens' Association, Holloway said, "There was no objection to native children attending school with whites on the ground of color, but merely on health grounds." There was concern that "hordes of half-castes" near the town could obtain liquor.[1411]

Following Wagin, he went to Victoria Park and Mount Hawthorn Baptist Churches, both suburbs of Perth, in November 1935 and stayed for nearly two years. Then Holloway ministered at the South Perth Baptist Church for a year.

Another West Australian church followed: East Fremantle for nine years. During this time he was appointed President of the Western Australia Baptist Union in 1941/1942. In the West he was appointed State President of the Christian Endeavour Movement in which his wife, Ruth, was a representative.[1412]

---

[1408] Daily Telegraph (Launceston) 10 March 1922 p8; BCC December 1922 p3.
[1409] Deloraine Church history of 1934.
[1410] Laurence F Rowston, One Hundred Years of Witness: A History of the Hobart Baptist Church, 1884–1984 (Hobart Baptist Church 1984); S&T: G. D. Hooper, Bournemouth West.

[1411] BCC April 1929 p6; AB 1929 p132; The Daily News (Perth, WA) 22 October 1934 p4.
[1412] Advocate (Burnie) 27 April 1940 p8; The Wagin Argus and Arthur, Dumbleyung, Lake Grace Express (WA) 3 October 1935 p7; Presidential address, AB 18 November 1941 p1.

Holloway and family returned to Tasmania in 1946 to take the pastorate of the Ulverstone Baptist Church. It was acknowledged that he was one whom

> the West can ill-afford to lose ... so completely did he immerse himself in denominational activities here that he seemed to belong to us entirely. But he has felt the call so strongly to return from whence he came that go he must.[1413]

He was welcomed at Ulverstone on 17 February 1946. This was a time when attendances at Ulverstone were growing and a good number of young people were coming into membership. In 1949, he was elected President of the North West Ministers' Fraternal.[1414] Among the Christian Endeavourers in the church at the time was Stuart McDonald. In an interview he related his vivid memories of Holloway. He said,

> We used to have a laugh at Holloway's expense. Like the time when he was driving me and two others to Hobart for a Christian Endeavour convention. His car was a little Ford Prefect. When he came to the top of Spring Hill[1415] he slipped her out of gear and explained that he could get to the top of the next hill without engaging gear. So as we lost momentum near the bottom of Spring Hill, Gordon Gillam and I in the back seat began rocking backwards and forwards to help the car along. Did we succeed? No, because the "next hill" was a bit steeper than Bertie remembered.
>
> Bertie also couldn't keep his eyes closed when he was praying the offertory prayer and we used to watch him counting the collection. At least, that was the opinion of a few of us rebels.
>
> He hung on to his position for six years and vainly tried to stay longer so that he could get his name on the foundation stone of the new church building which was in the planning stage. He and his wife left in high dudgeon when the church failed to extend his term.
>
> He had one son named Wilfred who failed to attract friends. He was self-opinionated (in the minds of us locals) but a sucker for gags. When he began work in a local hardware shop he fell for

---

[1413] AB 8 January 1946 p7.

[1414] Advocate (Burnie) 16 February 1946 p6f, March 1949 p4; for a published sermon by Hollowell see Advocate (Burnie) 7 April 1949 p15.

[1415] *Spring Hill* Tier is at an elevation above sea level of 561 m above sea level, about 50 km from Hobart.

*15-17 The Rev William Dawson family*

the old striped paint trick, being sent by colleagues to another hardware shop to obtain some. Another message they sent him on was to obtain a rubber-faced stone hammer! His main asset was the ability to play the old pedal organ in church moderately well.[1416]

In May 1952, Holloway concluded at Ulverstone and returned to South Australia. In June 1952, the Clare circuit, which included the churches at Saddleworth, Tarlee and Leasingham, welcomed the family.[1417] The Clare Church membership rose in two years from twenty-nine to fifty-two. There were lesser numbers at the other churches in the Circuit. He was elected as Vice President of The Northern Districts Baptist Association. Holloway spent five years in the Clare circuit during which time the circuit became self-supporting, that is it no longer relied on the SA Baptist Union for financial support. Although Holloway experienced two very serious illnesses at the time, in early 1957 he moved to the Georgetown-Clover Hill-Laura Circuit. On 16 January 1959, he suddenly died in Crystal Brook in South Australia.

## Appendix 6: The Rev Alan Paton Dawson

Growing up in a Congregational church manse in Tasmania, Englishman Alan Paton Dawson eventually came to a Baptist understanding of baptism and joined the Baptist Home Mission in Tasmania. In time he transferred to the Baptist ministry interstate and served effectively in three mainland pastorates and contributed greatly to their Associations.

Dawson was born in 1897 at Stockport in Cheshire, England, the son of the Rev William Dawson and his wife Annie Royal. William was a Congregational minister born in Manchester in 1864 who held a pastorate in England for ten years but became a general carrier in 1911 before they migrated to Australia in 1914. Here he was Pastor of the Latrobe, Don and Forth Congregational Churches from 1914

---

[1416] Interview with Laurence Rowston.

[1417] The Baptist Record 20 August 1952; Clare is 135 km north of Adelaide.

to 1920.[1418] After his short pastorate of eight months at Yolla in 1918, Alan Paton Dawson and his wife Gwynne commenced at the Home Mission Deloraine Church in December. The Church's history of 1934 recorded,

> He faced an ominous task with undaunted faith and courage. During the three years of his ministry the church was restored to a healthy state and at the time of his leaving the prospects were better than they had been for some years.[1419]

He departed in March 1922 and turned to Yolla.

## Appendix 7: Arthur T Jessop

Ten years earlier than the Yolla appointment, Arthur T. Jessop and his wife Gladys (nee Rockliff) had been involved with the Anglican Church at Montagu which was fourteen kms from Smithton; sometimes Arthur preached there and Gladys was organist. Some years later they were associated with the Methodist Church at Sassafras which in time became a Community Church. In 1918 Arthur *was* a member of the Temperance Alliance.[1420]

Arthur's move to the Claude Road School in 1926 made possible the opportunity to preach at the Bracknell Church, and by May 1927 he was appointed its pastor; he remained there until December 1929.[1421] At the service at Blackwood Creek on 7 April 1929, he held up a copy of the "Mercury" newspaper and preached from its report on the Derby flood. Some days later the Mercury reported on what had taken place that morning in the small church,

> The congregation, many of whom had had to depend upon unconfirmed rumours for what they knew of the disaster, listened with the closest attention to the thrilling details, and also to the preacher's view of the catastrophe in relation to the character of God as revealed in the teaching of Jesus Christ there was suffering, in the universe, but the loving Father who felt it when even a sparrow fell, must have suffered as those 14 human beings at Derby were swept to their deaths. He still felt the sorrow of the bereaved and (sorrowing).[1422]

Gladys Jessop was the second teacher at the First Gowie Park

---

[1418] 1911 British Census. Advocate (Burnie) 14 February 1935 p2.

[1419] Another short history of the Church records, "Pastor A. P. Dawson came to the rescue of the church and began to build again but the work never seemed to regain the vigour and vitality it knew in those early years."

[1420] Circular Head Chronicle (Stanley, Tas.) 21 December 1910 p3, 11 April 1912 p2; NWA&EBT 27 August 1917 p2; LEx 23 August 1918 p6.

[1421] LEx 2 December 1926 p7; Daily Telegraph (Launceston) 11 May 1927 p6.

[1422] The Mercury (Hobart) 13 April 1929 p9.

School which opened in 1922. As Alan Dyer records,

> Each day Arthur brought wife Gladys to Gowrie School in the sidecar of his motorbike, then returned to Claude Road. Gowrie children had never seen a sidecar before, which perhaps explains why that year Gowrie was the only school in the State to achieve 100% attendance. However, in July 1925 Mrs Jessop was replaced somewhat under a cloud by **Miss Edith Wyatt**.[1423]

Following their Education Department's appointment to Sorell in the south, the Jessops then attended the Sorell Congregational Church.[1424]

## Appendix 8: Wesley J. Bligh

Tasmanian Wesley J. Bligh, diligent and scholarly, grew up in a godly family connected to one of the oldest Baptist churches in the State. In time he worked with the Tasmanian Baptist Home Mission before moving to Victoria where he contributed greatly in their Baptist Churches but much to his own dismay and that of others, unexpectedly he transferred to the Presbyterian ministry as there were no openings in his own Baptist churches.

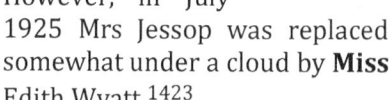

*15-18 Wesley Bligh delivering "The Church Hour" on 3XY radio in Melbourne*

Wesley was born in 1906 to William Joseph Bligh and his wife Margaret Elizabeth (nee Cumming) and he attended the Quamby Brook Baptist Sunday School. An earlier history of the Deloraine Church records,

> The memory of Mr. William Bligh (senior) is fragrant in the hearts and minds of hundreds still. Pastors in ministering to him left his home feeling they themselves had been remarkably refreshed and encouraged by the grand man of Quamby Brook.

In June 1911, at a mission with evangelist Sisters Miriam and Winnie at the Deloraine Town Hall, young five year old Wesley Bligh performed three selections on the accordion. That year Young Wesley was attending the Quamby Brook State School concert one evening and gave a melodeon solo but "the little fellow was almost hidden behind the instrument, and was the piece of the evening." Scripture lessons were part of the curriculum

---

[1423] See "Historic Gowrie Farm & First Gowrie School" by Alan Dyer.

[1424] HM Minutes p145.

and when he was thirteen years old Wesley gained 89%.[1425]

At the age of seventeen he was the Rev V. G. Britton's assistant at Latrobe which entailed weekly preaching opportunities at the Church's outstations.

From 1926 to the end of 1929, while studying for the ministry at the Baptist College, he pastored churches at Hawthorn West and Colac.

Wesley was among the eleven students Tasmania sent to the Victorian College between 1898 and 1938. Those who did not train in the Melbourne institution received help which was available through local ministers. Tasmania lacked the resources to establish its own college and over the years was helped by the Federal extra-mural course.

Once back in Tasmania in May 1930, Bligh was placed at Bracknell. He was ordained to the ministry on 8 September 1930. On 10 October 1931 he married Miss Ida Uren. Ida was a foundation member of the Altona Baptist Church. In October 1934, the 50th anniversary of the Bracknell Church was celebrated.[1426] Bligh was now Secretary of the Foreign Mission Committee of the Baptist Association.

The following year Bligh made an outstanding contribution to the understanding of Tasmanian Baptist denominational history by presenting to the Federal Baptist Education Board his post-graduate diploma titled, "The Altars of the Mountains" which contains biographies of the Rev Henry Dowling, the Gibsons, the Revs. Harry Wood and V.G. Britton, and Messrs Joshua T. Soundy and William Dubrelle Weston. Much of the material was gained from those who knew these people.

In 1936, he moved to the mainland to Pastor the Baptist Church in Rainbow followed by the Melbourne suburban Baptist Church at Darling for four years.[1427] Armadale Baptist Church and its associated Church of Malvern East, came next in February 1940.[1428]

With the outbreak of War, he wrote,

> The way of the Gospel is the way which seeks to establish the Universal Brotherhood — the Church; it is the way of good-will and mutual understanding between peoples and nations, it is the way of reasoned and peaceful settlement of differences, the way of forgiveness of enemies. It is the

---

[1425] Deloraine and Westbury Advertiser (Tas) 21 October 1911 p1; LEx 17 December 1919 p10.
[1426] AB 1 December 1931 p9; LEx 2 November 1934 p5.
[1427] The Herald (Melbourne) 22 October 1936 p21, 3 December 1936 p24, 9 November 1939 p36.
[1428] The Herald (Melbourne) 15 February 1940 p30.

way by which spiritual values may survive and increase.[1429]

During this time at Armadale he became secretary of the Baptist Immigration Committee and also secretary for the Federal Inter-Church Immigration Council. His sermons were published in the press. With the Rev Howard Crago, he wrote the book, "Champions of Liberty". In 1952/53 he was appointed President of the Baptist Union of Victoria. He also contributed to radio broadcasts in "The Church Hour" on 3XY.[1430]

From 1955, Bligh and his wife, Ida, managed "Weller Lodge", an old mansion property in Canterbury Road that the Baptist Union of Victoria had purchased for use as a hostel for overseas missionary trainees.[1431] In the six years they were there they ministered to 170 of whom fourteen joined a Baptist church and five entered the ministry. They resigned in 1960, hoping to return to pastoral work.

Bligh took an interim pastorate at the Canterbury Congregational Church until a Baptist position became available, but when this did not happen, in 1961 he resigned from the Baptist ministry and entered the Presbyterian ministry. When he resigned, the Secretary of the Union spoke of his "excellent record of devoted and capable service" which included being Secretary of the Baptist College. He was saved from explaining his move to his father who died seven years earlier.

In a letter dated 13 April 1961 and written to a Colleague he said,

> You know enough to understand that I would not take a step so important unless I was completely convinced that I was doing the right thing. Up to the moment of my decision to resign - not one single reproach of any kind had been made to me ... My sense of call to the Christian ministry burns within it. I could not conscientiously renounce it altogether and go into secular occupation. Needless to say my resignation has caused considerable distress to some of my closest friends who, I know, are in no way responsible for the situation which has forced me to resign, who, through the years, with yourself have done the very best they could to find a sphere of service, for me within the denomination ... It is my deepest wish to go out quietly without a fuss but if my going can prevent the same kind of situations occurring for other men, then I shall not feel that it is in vain.
>
> I want you to know that I have won the battle over any

---

[1429] AB 17 September 1940 p3.

[1430] The Argus (Melbourne) 29 September 1947 p2, 9 March 1953 p15; The Herald (Melbourne) 16 May 1953 p8.

[1431] The Argus (Melbourne) 6 March 1948 p20.

resentment or bitterness. I have no malice in my heart against anyone. I do not blame anyone in particular. It is just a particular situation that can occur within the Baptist set up over which, with all the good will in the world; those who think well of me and desire my well being have no control. I know that my close friends whose friendship I esteem and who value mine will not think any the less of me or blame to me. I know that I have tried to do my best for the denomination that I leave with a clean record throughout my 25 years of service with the Baptist Union of Victoria.

Bligh's first church in the new denomination was that of East Malvern Presbyterian. The Rev Wesley J. Bligh died at Hamilton, Victoria, on 17 June 1993, aged eighty-seven.[1432]

## Appendix 8: The Rev Edward Charles McIntosh Brown

The Rev Edward C. McIntosh Brown walked his own path through the different denominations of Congregational, Methodist, Baptist and finally Presbyterian Churches. A man's man, he took up evangelistic work where few would go and involved himself in political affiliations.

In 1907 McIntosh Brown, the son of E. T. Brown of Northcote in Melbourne was associated with the Congregational Church in the Esperance District of Tasmania which took in Dover. He was working with the Rev J. Ebery. The following year he was also on the Port Esperance Council acting as clerk pro tem. During his time the debt on the Congregational Church hall was cleared and the property upgraded so that it became a replacement in the community for the dilapidated Town Hall. Brown's time at Dover ceased at the end of 1913.[1433]

In 1916, Brown was now living in the Greensborough and Diamond Creek area on the outskirts of Melbourne and attending the Arthur's Creek Methodist Church. At the Loyal Diamond Creek Lodge he gave lectures on "Port Arthur" and "The Distillation of Eucalyptus" and was soon enrolled in the War effort. In March 1920, he was appointed to the Methodist Home Mission Church at Cann River in South Gippsland. The following year he arrived back in Tasmania and was posted to the Methodist Church in Waratah and ordained to the Christian ministry.

---

[1432] See also "The Second Exodus: Australian Baptist Ministers who joined the Presbyterian Church 1885 to 1970", by Michael Petras, The Recorder February 2005 pp27ff. I was visiting the Grampians in Western Victoria a year or two before his death and rang and spoke to him so I could arrange to see him and talk with him about some of the early Baptists profiled in "Altars of the Mountain" and show him my first major work, "Baptists in Van Diemen's Land", but sadly he didn't want to or could not see me. Author.

[1433] Tasmanian News (Hobart) 6 March 1907 p4; The Mercury (Hobart) 9 January 1908 p6, 17 June 1908 p8; LEx 6 November 1913 p7.

*15-19 **Adamsfield***

At Waratah he was on the committee of the Association Football Club.[1434]

**Following his nine months** at the Yolla Baptist Church, Brown spent six months on the Adams River Osmiridium Fields at Adamsfield as evangelist of the Council of Churches; the Baptist Home Mission released him for this work. Brown was no stranger to Osmiridium mining. During his residence at Waratah he received favourable reception with the diggers on the Savage River field, many of whom were now at Adamsfield. It was his intention to construct a large building at the main camp, where, in addition to provision being made for writing, reading, and services, accommodation would be provided for a few days for new arrivals on the field. At the Baptist Assembly in 1926 "he gave an account of his work amongst the diggers. His racy description of the work being done, coupled with his undoubted earnestness, touched all hearts."[1435]

His work among the miners ceased when he commenced at the Sheffield Baptist Church in September 1926. Sheffield at the time had five stations and it required a large amount of travelling and also some power of endurance during the winter months.[1436] It was the opinion of the Rev Edward Burchell Woods that Brown's work for the men on the Osmiridium fields had stamped him as a true Christian.

In 1930, Brown completed his sixth year's examination and was ordained. During his time at Sheffield the Tabernacle was destroyed by fire and soon tenders were called for a new brick building. But by February 1932 he requested a change and with the work at Latrobe "under very trying circumstances", he was immediately moved there.[1437]

With his political bent, he stood as a candidate in the Federal Parliament for the House of Representatives for Darwin but the retiring member was

---

[1434] Heidelberg News and Greensborough and Diamond Creek Chronicle (Vic) 22 April 1916 p2; The Argus (Melbourne) 16 March 1920 p7; Advocate (Burnie) 17 December 1921 p8; LEx 22 June 1923 p3.

[1435] HM Minutes January 1926 p119; BCC February 1930; The Mercury (Hobart) 8 March 1926 p3; AB 1 June 1926 p11.

[1436] AB 1932.

[1437] The Mercury (Hobart) 7 October 1930 p5, 8 April 1932 p2; HM Minutes p170, p188.

returned with a lead of 1,636 votes over Brown. While in Latrobe he was Toc H Secretary and also Chairman of the local hospital.[1438] Brown was farewelled from Latrobe in February 1939 as he took leadership of the Ulverstone Church. At the time it was said of him,

> Mr. Brown needs no commendation to our churches. For years now has he served us and we ought to be proud of the work that he has done among young people, particularly at Latrobe. As a preacher he has no superior in our work and as a man he is well beloved by all who know him. His political activities have made him known to the public in general but always he is first and last a minister of Jesus Christ.[1439]

For some reason, in June 1939, the Rev Harold Hackworthy wrote to the Home Mission of Brown in derogatory terms, "(Sid) Hawkes simply displays his usual methods; McBrown is an ass."

Brown became chairman of the Devon Hospital yet in January 1940, after only nine months, he resigned from the Ulverstone Church and from the Baptist denomination and moved to Melbourne.[1440]

On his leaving the Tasmanian Baptist denomination acknowledged him and his work,

> It is with a twinge of sadness in our hearts that we say farewell to Mr. Brown, who has, during his stay in Tasmania, entered the hearts of the ministers and people of the Baptist Churches; also of the people of the wider public, with an ease all his own. Mr. Brown is a man with a conviction born of experience, study of the word of God, and of history; and his preaching, based on theology has the same note. He wisely evaded emotional preaching, as such, in favour of sound, solid teaching. He makes the claim that his work is amongst men; a claim which is substantiated by his work on the mining fields, and by the remark of a young man from one of his churches, who, when asked if it is true, replied, "Well, he has proved it to be." Above all Mr. Brown is a man of God. His abhorrence of everything mean, shady or underhand - of all that is evil - and his love of truth, stamp him as such. If he were asked to give briefly, a definition of the theme in which he revelled most he would say, "The Grace of God".[1441]

In Victoria, Brown entered the Presbyterian Church ministry and

---

[1438] The Mercury (Hobart) 31 July 1934 p7, 25 October 1937 p7, 22 January 1938 p10; LEx 17 September 1934 p10; The Advertiser (Adelaide) 1 June 1937 p17.

[1439] BCC January 1939.

[1440] LEx 23 June 1939 p6; HM Minutes p239.

[1441] BCC March 1940 p5.

took charge of the Knox Memorial Church at Red Cliffs situated some sixteen kms south of Mildura. At the end of this pastorate in 1945 he returned to the Baptist fold and took charge of the stately South Yarra Baptist Tabernacle in Melbourne. The Rainbow Baptist Church followed in 1947.[1442]

In 1950 he reverted to the Presbyterian ministry and was Pastor of the Wedderburn Presbyterian Church just out of Bendigo where he gave enthusiastic support to a suggestion that a mining shaft be sunk in the grounds of the Church which stood just across the roadway from a claim which already had yielded some rich nuggets of gold! The Rev Edward C McIntosh Brown died in 1957.[1443]

### Appendix 9: Cecil M. Jobling

Cecil M. Jobling came from an extended Methodist family in the Ballarat district. He served in World War 1. In March 1923 he was appointed to Cowangie in the Sunraysia region of Victoria by the Methodist Home Mission.[1444]

On assignment he sailed for Tasmania early in 1924 and participated in the 70th anniversary of the Deloraine Methodist Church as he was now to be employed in its Circuit. The Circuit Committee purchased a motor cycle for his use. At the time he would have been acquainted with Wesley Bligh who was Pastor of the Deloraine Baptist Church. In March 1925 Jobling was appointed to Maria Island Methodist Mission which came under the St Helens Circuit.[1445]

## Conclusion

Most of Tasmanian Baptist Churches are small churches and as such they are wrongly defined as one in which the number of active members and the total annual budget are inadequate relative to organizational needs and expenses. It is a church struggling to pay its minister, heat its building, and find enough people to assume leadership responsibilities.

The majority of churches in Australia could be classified as small churches, those averaging fewer than fifty congregants per Sunday. It is important to emphasise at the beginning that small is not a synonym for inferior.

Small churches are not smaller editions of larger churches. Big churches have large capacity for innovation and setting trends, and they can create specialised ministries for special audiences. But

---

[1442] BCC February 1940 p2, March 1945, March 1947 p7.
[1443] The Mercury (Hobart) 14 April 1950 p24; VBW August 1957.
[1444] The Mercury (Hobart) 7 May 1925 p12; Cowangie is a locality situated on the section of the Mallee Highway between Ouyen and the South Australian border in the Sunraysia region of Victoria; The Ballarat Star (Vic) 15 March 1923 p7.
[1445] The Ballarat Star (Vic) 12 January 1924 p12; LEx 12 August 1924 p4, 6 March 1925 p5.

there is an advantage to smallness. Surprisingly, effectiveness of a large church has often depended on the success they have had in retaining some of the qualities of small church.

There is a quality of fellowship in the small church that is difficult to duplicate elsewhere. This supportive fellowship is made possible by the fact that church members truly know each other personally and are in a unique position to minister to the needs of one another. Beneath that surface however, there is a deep and genuine concern for one another. As they work through their differences and participate together in the ministries of the church, a sense of community can develop that gives them the strength to face the challenges in their personal lives as well as in the life and ministry of their congregation.

Many in today's world are longing for a sense of community that the small church can provide.

Persons in a body of fifty worshippers know that their presence and absence are significant to the congregation. Their singing and speaking make a difference. Their money in the offering plate adds up. Smaller churches are also well suited to grafting into the family new persons of faith.

It is difficult for members in a small church simply to drift into anonymity or inactivity without some intervention taking place on the part of caring members.

In the small church every church member can have input in every decision (large or small) that the church makes. This direct type of democracy carries with it a sense of ownership that in turn can translate into commitment.

A disadvantage of small churches is their lack of entry points. An entry point is a way new members can come into the church. Small churches do not have the personnel or money for many programs; therefore, their entry points are fewer. There is also possessive leadership and the lack of money.

Finally, many small churches develop a survival mentality. Rather than looking to expand God's kingdom, they focus on survival. Your small church can truly be an oasis in a desert of anonymity, superficiality and purposelessness. Your small congregation, however, must be very vigilant lest some of its very attractive qualities become barriers for those who are not-long-term members of your wonderful church family. Our needy world needs your small church.

This oft quoted statement is still true, "The genius of the Baptists is in small churches." The value of the ministry in such places is out of all proportion to the size of the sphere.

# Chapter 16 Smithton Baptist Church

## Introduction

It was always thought there were great possibilities for the extension of Church work in the Smithton district since it is the largest agricultural area in the State and also known for saw milling, but it was wrongly thought at the time that it was going to carry the largest population in the State. In the winter season, owing to the excessive rains and consequent bad roads, it was difficult to get about. The horses of the bush missionaries sometimes were up to the girths in slush. There were no metal roads except near the coastline. Smithton, at the time, was an insignificant village with few made roads. The bush missionaries went around preaching in houses and barns, disused blacksmiths' shops, or any place where they could get a few people together to listen to them.[1446]

With the establishment of the Smithton Home Mission station in 1910, the Baptist churches reached their limit in the North-west Coast for some decades to come. There was no Baptist work going on within forty to fifty miles of Smithton or Stanley. Other Home Mission stations at the time were Longford, Bracknell, Deloraine, Ulverstone (1903), Wynyard (1904) and Yolla (1908) thus embracing a very large area. These were all on the north and north-west coast, and each station had a number of outstations and all were being efficiently worked by Home missionaries and assisted by earnest local preachers.[1447]

The Christian Brethren had been the first there in the area to conduct regular services making use of a small hall at Scotchtown some six kms south of Smithton. A few years later they erected their hall. Then the Anglicans and Roman Catholics made use of the Smithton State School. From 1910, Malley's Hall, a comparatively newly erected building, became the venue for church services with the Roman Catholics in the morning, the Anglicans in the afternoon and the Baptists in the evening. Once the Baptists bought the Hall in 1910, the Anglicans purchased land and opened St. Stephen's on 4 December 1921.[1448] The Presbyterian Church followed and erected a building in Smith Street. The Methodists established a Sunday school in 1907 with services first held in a potato shed, then the State schoolroom, in the open-air and in private residences until April 1910 when the Presbyterian Church building

---

[1446] AB 2 September 1913, November 1921 p3.
[1447] AB 26 November 1918.
[1448] NWA&EBT 13 May 1910 p2, 2 August 1910 p4; Circular Head Chronicle (Stanley, Tas) 30 November 1921 p3; Advocate (Burnie) 6 December 1921 p4.

became available as Presbyterian services had ceased. In 1912, a resident Presbyterian minister arrived and immediately the Methodists, who had planned to buy the building, vacated it and built their own weatherboard church conducting their first service on 6 October that year, their building unfinished as the windows had yet to be installed.[1449]

The Presbyterian cause only lasted three or four years and the building was eventually demolished. The Salvation Army too started in the town about 1900.[1450]

## Robert Steel

In April 1910, Home Missioner Robert Steel moved to the town as its first Baptist pastor arriving at the same time as the Methodist, the Rev F. C. Bremer. Steel preached his first sermon in Malley's Hall. He had the privilege of breaking in a horse for Bremer after his first steed "was so devout that it continually went on its knees, several times shooting its rider over its head."[1451] Subsequently, the Baptists acquired the hall for themselves and, with Robert Steel's help, made improvements. Soon about sixty folk were in attendance at his services and this grew to eighty. Steel was making use of a Magic Lantern. Soon there were outstations at Leesville, Irishtown and Mengha, Mengha being the site of a slate quarry. Other outstations would follow at Forest and Stanley. At Stanley use was made of Shaw's Philharmonic Hall. On 27 November 1910, the Smithton Church was constituted. In his second year the Church had as it were "been busy ploughing and sowing the precious seed, (and) praying for the harvest of souls." From now on show and sale of gift days would be a regular feature of the church calendar. In Stanley, in 1913 as well as conducting Sunday services, Steel was running successful Temperance Band of Hope meetings and on Friday evenings gymnasium classes.[1452] One of Steel's proudest achievements was the church structure they built at Forest.

On Wednesday 16 April 1913, a proposal of Steel the "carpenter-cleric", and his assistants, to erect

*16-1 Young Robert Steel*

---

[1449] Circular Head Chronicle (Stanley, Tas) 9 October 1912, Supplement p1.
[1450] NWA&EBT 29 April 1910 p4; Circular Head Chronicle (Stanley, Tas) 27 May 1931 p3.
[1451] Circular Head Chronicle (Stanley, Tas) 23 September 1936 p2.
[1452] Day-Dawn November 1909, December 1909, July 1910, August 1910, September 1911, March 1912, June 1912; Circular Head Chronicle (Stanley, Tas) 4 December 1912 p2; North West Advocate (Burnie) 3 June 1913.

# Smithton Baptist Church

16-2 Digging the first sod for the Forest Church

At the end of 1912 it became necessary for Steel to move house to Stanley as he lost all his belongings in a fire, but there was another reason, the work had recently closed down through lack of workers. Then after over eight years' service with the Home Mission and settled at Stanley, he severed his connection with the Mission. Married men could not be kept at such places and there was no other Home Mission vacancy.[1454]

a chapel in a day "was although not actually realised, it was so well executed that by night-time the building was three parts completed. The porch and vestry were roofed, half the main roof was on, the flooring completed, half the lining, and the structure three-parts weather-boarded. The foundation had previously been put down, and the framework cut. A dozen willing workers started operations at 7.30 am. and the staff increased to twenty-six as the day advanced. A hot meal provided by the ladies at midday was relished by the hungry workmen ... The building was subsequently completed by hired labour. The opening services took place the following Sunday with the Home Mission Superintendent preaching and a concert followed the next day.[1453]

## Albert Edward Holloway

Albert Edward Holloway was moved as a trial Home Missionary from Bracknell to Smithton in January 1913 to replace Steel. Smithton now had another outstation, at Mowbray Swamp with its building opened in early 1915. In October 1913, the Rev Joshua T. Piercey of the Victorian Evangelistic Society spent a month in the area in a United Mission and twenty-five of those who responded decided to meet with the Baptists. Holloway proved popular with the folk and he stayed until February 1915 when he left to study for a year at Angas College, an interdenominational missionary and

---

[1453] Circular Head Chronicle (Stanley, Tas) 23 April 1913 p3; they finished the day's work at 9.30pm – Tasmanian Baptist Advance June 2002 p3.

[1454] Day-Dawn June 1912; The Mercury (Hobart) 23 November 1912 p6; AB 5 May 1914.

evangelism training school in South Australia.[1455]

## Edward Robert Bampton

Having sold off his motor car and machinery back in South Australia, Edward Robert Bampton and his wife, Mabel, were welcomed at Stanley in March 1915 when the Church was still making use of Shaw's Philharmonic Hall. Fittingly, Sunday services included intercessions for "our King and Empire, Our Army and Navy" and sermon subjects included "Heroes and Cowards".[1456] Bampton wrote a hymn set to the tune of the National Anthem for those at the front.

> **God** save our sons and friends
> Who in this war defend
> Their country's rights.
> Who fight for honor's sake,
> Never because of hate,
> But for the cause of right,
> And weaker friends.
> **May** Thine Almighty Power,
> Protect in this dark hour,
> And shield them all.
> If it should be Thy will,
> Keep them from death and ill,
> Whatever post they fill
> Guide Thou them all.
> **Save** them from cannon's blight,
> Midst storms of bitter strife,
> O strengthen them;
> When called to suffer pain,
> On beds of sickness lain,
> O, God in love sustain
> And comfort them.
> **Now** in this hour of need,
> We would Thy mercy plead,
> Thou God of all.
> May this great strife soon cease,
> Wilt Thou to men bring peace,
> May it our God now please
> To help us all.[1457]

As part of his ministry Bampton sent newspapers to the troops in Egypt, and later on in Europe, as the men were always eager for news of home. A sheet of writing paper and an envelope were included in each one. One week he dispatched 178 papers including envelopes and paper.[1458]

Bampton also produced a small booklet for distribution among the soldiers whether they were still in camp or on the field. It was widely advertised and it contained helpful texts and verses from the best sources. As the publicity said,

> It is published with the two-fold object of helping the Sick and Wounded Soldiers' Fund and conveying words of comfort to anxious, weak, and dying soldiers. The retail price is fixed at sixpence, and the wholesale at £1 15s per 100, but to all Red

---

[1455] Circular Head Chronicle (Stanley, Tas) 9 April 1913 p3; Day-Dawn November 1913; NWA&EBT 22 February 1915 p2; AB 27 April 1915.
[1456] North West Advocate (Formby) 3 June 1913; Circular Head Chronicle (Stanley, Tas) 17 March 1915 p5, 16 June 1915 p5.
[1457] Circular Head Chronicle (Stanley, Tas) 28 July 1915 p5.
[1458] Circular Head Chronicle (Stanley, Tas) 18 August 1915 p2, 25 August 1915 p5.

# Smithton Baptist Church

Cross and patriotic societies it will be supplied at a reduced rate, viz., 10/- per 100, or £4 10s per 1,000, to enable such societies to raise money for their local funds. Any Society wishing to do so may have a short message with the name of their Society printed on the back cover of the booklet for the payment of 10/- per 1,000 extra.

At the Patriotic Carnival held in Smithton in August 1915, they raised ten shillings by selling books. In February 1916, they sold up everything again as they had done in South Australia and moved to the Baptist Church in Nambour, Yandina, Queensland to work with the Y.M.C.A. which was working with the troops both in Australia and overseas.[1459]

## George Levison Dibden

George Levison Dibden arrived at Smithton for work in September 1915 and was accepted by the Baptists as one of its pastors. At the time the Home Mission was appealing nationwide for workers. In October 1916, he conducted a preaching tour along the coast journeying as far as Balfour, one of the westernmost localities in Tasmania and as far East as Detention River. It was reported that he had "remarkable energy and is worth hearing, having a surprising gift for telling humorous stories". His preaching stations included Marrawah where years later a Baptist Church would be formed. In 1916, George married Alice Winifred Smith.[1460] That year Pastor J. F. Hopkins from Western Australia was placed at Stanley but by 1917 he was moved to Longford where his tenure did not last. The Home Mission made it clear, "this place needs an energetic man and prosperity is earnestly prayed for."[1461]

*16-3 George Dibden*

## George Philp

Scottish born George Philp came from Victoria to the Bracknell Baptist Church in August 1913 to work with the Home Mission. He and his wife settled well into the work and maintained the congregation with his wife at times speaking at services. He involved himself with the local cricket club rising to President. After four years at Bracknell he began at Smithton in

---

[1459] The Narracoorte Herald (SA) 27 August 1915 p2; Circular Head Chronicle (Stanley, Tas) 25 August 1915 p2; AB 11 April 1916.

[1460] Alice was born on 17 March 1891 in Goodwood, South Australia.

[1461] Circular Head Chronicle (Stanley, Tas) 11 October 1916 p5; AB 9 May 1916.

February 1918 as "it was thought advisable to re-open the work at Smithton and surrounding districts under the charge of Pastor G. Philp." The size of the town now was indicated by the number of children attending Sunday School was nearly 200. Philp was ordained on 4 June 1919. By 1920, there was another outstation, this time at Broadmeadows. A year earlier the Smithton Church was running an annual fair. After only two years in this Home Mission Church Philp resigned and returned to Scotland to see his aged mother promising to return to Tasmania in nine months but that was not to be. In Scotland, he accepted a pastorate at Alloa Baptist Church but then returned to Australia and accepted pastorates in the Great Southern region of Western Australia, first at Wagin and then Gnowangerup (October 1922 – 1930) and then they departed Australia for good.[1462]

## The Rev James Clemens Salter

James Clemens Salter commenced at Smithton Baptist Church in June 1921. Salter undertook needed maintenance work on their building yet there was great need for a manse as housing was in short supply. This need was attended to with one erected in the second half of 1921. In the town, Salter soon became the President of the Art Club, committee member of Progress and Tourist League, secretary of the New Settlers' League, committee member and then President of the State School Parents' Association, committee member of the Circular Head Branch of the Returned Soldiers' League, chaplain of the Orange Lodge, member of the Choral Society and part of the Library movement. The Home Mission seemed blind to what he was endeavouring to achieve in the town through his many personal contacts, for within two years, in June 1923, he was transferred to the Ulverstone Baptist Church.[1463]

*16-4 James C. Salter*

---

[1462] LEx 19 August 1913 p3, 16 April 1914 p3, 28 February 1917 p3, 16 February 1918 p8, 2 March 1920 p3, 20 April 1920 p2; Daily Telegraph (Launceston) 15 June 1914 p7; AB 19 November 1918, 1 July 1919, 16 December 1919, 20 February 1920; Circular Head Chronicle (Stanley, Tas) 28 May 1919 p5. The Philps were farewelled from Smithton on 29 February 1920. All Western Australia is My Parish by R. K. Moore p286.

[1463] Advocate (Burnie) 14 February 1922 p5, 9 September 1922 p4, 29 November 1922 p6, 1

## The Rev Alfred Ernest Albury

The Rev Alfred Ernest Albury arrived in Smithton from Queensland in June 1923. It was reported in July that "the work was never more hopeful in the Smithton district." At the anniversary social at Myalla, now one of Smithton's outstations – it was as previously under Wynyard's care - a great crowd of enthusiastic people gathered and a new church building was in process of erection. It was reported, "The people had a mind to work, making the prospects bright." The Myalla Chapel was opened on 27 April 1924. In 1925, Albury was joined by "evangelist" Hilton J. Preece, a native of Tasmania and well known in Baptist circles. Preece worked in the Preolenna district which involved the Lapoinya Church. Preece remained in Tasmania until October 1927. He became the founder-director of the Australian Evangelical Mission which worked among isolated people in the remote parts of New South Wales.[1464]

*16-5 Alfred E. Albury*

At the Tasmanian Baptist Ministers' Fraternal meeting Albury delivered a paper on "The Minister in his study and the use of Books". At the time the Seventh Day Adventists were posing a threat in the district and the subject came up at the Fraternal with a paper, "The Best way to meet Seventh Day Adventists". Albury was farewelled to the Elphin Road Baptist Church, Launceston, in January 1925.[1465]

## The Rev Ernest Charles Walsh

Following his time in the Wynyard-Yolla pastorate, the Rev Ernest Charles Walsh commenced at Smithton in January 1925 with its outstations of Stanley, Montumana at Rocky Cape, Myalla, Irish Town and Boat Harbour. Every Sunday he took a service at Smithton and then visited an outstation during the afternoon. When unable to make arrangements for the evening service at Smithton itself, he had to return to Smithton, so taking four services in one day. Service times at outstations were arranged to suit the convenience of people living

---

February 1923 p2, 26 May 1923 p6; Circular Head Chronicle (Stanley, Tas) 22 February 1922 p2, 30 May 1923 p2; AB 25 May 1920, September 1921, April 1922.
[1464] AB 22 December 1954 p5.

[1465] *Advocate (Burnie)* **2 June 1923** p6, 3 May 1924 p6, 20 October 1927 p4; AB 23 July 1923; The Mercury (Hobart) 28 October 1925 p8 *Daily Telegraph (Launceston)* **12 July 1923** p6; LEx **14 June 1924** p3; *Circular Head Chronicle (Stanley, Tas)* **14 January 1925** p5.

there. Walsh took upon himself to be "the registrar of unattached Baptists" and collected the names of Baptists in the State who were unattached to Baptist churches so that the denomination's Church papers could be sent to them. In August 1926, electric light was installed in the Smithton building, the year the Christian Endeavour Society was formed. A portable "Deloc-Light" had been operating for four years. His interest in egg-laying competitions continued. He imported a White Leghorn Cockerel from Victoria and his egg-poultry pursuits won him first prize at the Penquite Winter Test, that is, one of his birds reached the score of ninety-nine eggs for the four months, that is, in 122 days.[1466]

In January 1928, Walsh accepted an invitation to the Port Lincoln Baptist Church in South Australia, thus concluding fifteen years with the Home Mission in Tasmania.

On leaving he took someone with him as did Elliot at Deloraine, a fitting wife. For Walsh she was Miss Dorothy M. Davis, an outstanding musician who played and taught the violin and mandolin. She had trained with the London Trinity College of Music. For some years she was connected with interdenominational religious work in the slum areas of Hobart. She also worked with the Hobart open-air mission. She arrived in Smithton in December 1925 and opened a studio in Allen's Buildings, and owing to the increase of numbers of violin and mandolin students, she formed a string orchestra in which Walsh's daughter, Dorothy, took part. The orchestra took part in church services at the Smithton Church. Ernest and Dorothy married on 11 February 1928.[1467]

*16-6 Ernest C. Walsh*

## Cecil M. Jobling

On the day of the Rev Ernest Charles Walsh's departure, 19 March 1928, Cecil M. Jobling and his wife, "both gifted singers", were welcomed. He was seen "as a young man of good

---

[1466] Circular Head Chronicle (Stanley, Tas) 25 February 1925 p2, 4 August 1926 p5; AB 24 May 1927 p4; Daily Telegraph (Launceston) 16 September 1926 p2; The Mercury (Hobart) 27 October 1926 p9; BCC September 1922; LEx 10 January 1925 p6.
[1467] LEx 14 February 1928 p7; The Advertiser (Adelaide) 7 January 1928 p8; The Sydney Morning Herald 10 December 1924 p9; Dorothy was the daughter of George Frederick Davis and his wife - The Times and Northern Advertiser, Peterborough (SA) 10 November 1950 p2; Port Lincoln Times (SA) 6 April 1928 p13; Advocate (Burnie) 13 August 1926 p4; Circular Head Chronicle (Stanley, Tas) 1 December 1926 p5.

character in whom the Baptist connection had every confidence." In September 1928, Salter returned for a week's mission. Yet within a year Jobling resigned and moved to live in nearby Irish Town.[1468]

## Charles Percy Gordon Nibbs

Pastor Charles Percy Gordon Nibbs commenced his ministry at Smithton in February 1929. He became secretary of the local Ministers' Fraternal. Norman Lumsden and Fred Levett conducted a mission in December 1929 in conjunction with the Methodists in the town. Unfortunately, Nibbs did not have a long ministry at Smithton because of his health, always rather fragile since his childhood bout with Polio. It made it impossible for him to continue and he concluded in December 1931.[1469]

Gordon and Corrie Sherriff were married in the Deloraine Tabernacle during his tenure at Smithton, on 7 September 1929 with the Rev V.G. Britton officiating. They became staunch members of the Smithton Church and Gordon became Sunday school Superintendent. He also became well-known in the district as a very acceptable preacher to most denominations. During this time their four sons were born: Edward (Ted), Charles, David and Sidney. Ted was born in the front room of the manse. It was reported,

> The advent of a little son, Edward Claude, has brought great joy into the hearts of his parents at the manse, and their earnest prayer is that, if spared, he may grow up to be a true servant of God.[1470]

Ted and Charles would sit in the church front row so their father could keep an eye on them.[1471]

# Appendices

## Appendix 1: The Rev Robert Steel

By 1917, after seven failed attempts, Robert Steel was accepted to go to the Front leaving behind for a period of two and one half years a wife and five children and they went to live with relatives. Prior to this he had engaged in the recruitment drives.[1472]

In one of his recruitment drives he exclaimed,

> I am here on behalf of the Empire to appeal for you to relieve those who had borne the heat and burden of the day, who, if not relieved, will have a smaller chance of returning to their loved ones. You have seen the empty sleeves and the injuries of those

---

[1468] Circular Head Chronicle (Stanley, Tas) 21 March 1928 p2; BCC November 1928.
[1469] BCC February 1930.
[1470] BCC September 1930.

[1471] Advocate (Burnie) 13 March 1931 p6; Circular Head Chronicle (Stanley, Tas) 30 November 1938 p4.
[1472] Daily Telegraph (Launceston) 29 September 1917 p8.

who had returned home after doing their bit, and if there is a voice which speaks to you this night it is the voice of those who had lost their lives or limbs in defence of the Empire. Their call comes to you again and again and they want you to show a practical sympathy with their comrades who were fighting for liberty and justice. To you who had been rejected, I say, "Try again" until you succeed in getting into khaki.[1473]

Steel served with the Australian 4th Light Horse in Egypt, Palestine and Syria rising to sergeant. On two occasions he was asked to become padre, but he preferred to remain with his comrades in the rank and file. On his return he became a keen worker in the interests of returned men, serving on their committees and also as a fund raiser. He often lectured with Magic Lantern slides, war souvenirs and photographs; the slides numbering over 200 which he had taken at the Front. He boasted, "The Australians were the best fighters in the war, and only for them the war would not have been won. Second to them come the Scotsmen." He would often be a speaker on Anzac Day parades.[1474]

Years later, as a member of the Launceston R.S.L. at a returned servicemen's church service held at the Newstead Baptist Church, he preached on the subject: "War, Digger, and Religion", He said,

> War under some circumstances (is) right, manly, noble and glorious. The apostle's word of command was fear God, not with timidity, but with loving, filial reverence. There was never a more splendid specimen of the human race than the truly God-fearing Digger wearing the King's uniform. The stronger the sense of religion the Digger possessed the better soldier he was. The Digger had a wonderful spirit of brotherhood, and the Christian and the churches could learn from him. The Diggers were all working for one common cause which they all knew, and shared the common danger; with religion the Digger did not make much show. He did his job, was faithful to duty, and his prayers were real. These were the men the world needs to-day: bold, fearless, and ever ready to risk and even sacrifice their lives; religion is judged by its fruits. A religion that lacks charity or love is not religion at all. This love to God by the Digger was shown in many ways, even to the enemy. We must not forget that the time shall come when the Lord of Hosts shall make wars to cease unto the ends of the earth. A bright and peaceful future is in store for this earth. The time is

---

[1473] The Mercury (Hobart) 24 October 1917 p8 edited.
[1474] LEx 26 April 1929 p5, 27 September 1930 p7, 2 November 1943 p4; Advocate (Burnie) 18 November 1931 p6, 25 July 1933 p4, 22 August 1933 p6.

not yet, but it shall be a time when there shall be no tyrants, no ambition, no hostile rivalry, no hatred, no revenge, no restless vigilance and alarm, and no alienations from the pursuits of industry to maintain mighty apparatus for the destruction of mankind. The future is hidden from view, but of the coming of that time we were sure, for the mouth of the Lord hath spoken it.[1475]

In 1921, he was petitioned to become a local councillor candidate in the Circular Head Municipal Council, Stanley Ward, but he proved unsuccessful. In 1928, he was endorsed Labor Candidate for Darwin for the Circular Head District in the general election but again he was not successful. He was a merchant at the time.[1476]

His political affiliations continued. In 1924, he chaired a meeting of the Stanley Branch of the Waterside Workers' Federation at its annual meeting. He sought an income where he could. For the Stanley Annual Show he looked after the car parking. He also bought into his father's trucking business which was based in Stanley. He belonged to the Independent Order of Odd Fellows (I.O.O.F.) Loyal Wellington Lodge No. 7.[1477]

*16-7 Robert Steel and wife Florence*

While no longer employed by the Home Mission and still living at Stanley, his Baptist Church affiliations continued. On one occasion for the Burnie Baptist Sunday School Anniversary he made use of a large magnet and so "kept the attention of the children in his demonstration of the drawing Power of Jesus," a favourite he used on other occasions.[1478]

In effect, Robert Steel's wilderness days ended in 1931 when he rejoined the Home Mission and was placed at Ulverstone for twelve months. He also had to look after the nearby Penguin Church with its Band of Hope and later an outstation at Upper Castra. By March 1932, the Ulverstone folk wanted him to stay for three years. The Home Mission Committee agreed and requested that he place himself in the hands of the Education Committee to begin studies under the Tasmanian Extra

---

[1475] LEx 15 November 1943 p4, edited.

[1476] Circular Head Chronicle (Stanley, Tas) 2 November 1921 p2; Advocate (Burnie) 30 March 1928 p4; The Mercury (Hobart) 3 March 1928 p9, 3 May 1928 p5.

[1477] Advocate (Burnie) 26 September 1924 p4; Circular Head Chronicle (Stanley, Tas) 3 November 1926 p2, 9 March 1927 p2; LEx 8 July 1927 p4.

[1478] LEx 4 December 1928 p4.

Mural scheme. In Ulverstone he successfully formed a Boy Scouts Troop, joined the Board of the Ulverstone Hospital, and took part in organizing the Ulverstone Singing Festival, himself being a singer. He was also busy with the Christian Endeavour movement and other annual Church events. He associated with Toc H. It was said of him, "His tolerance towards those whose views are somewhat different has made him many, many warm and sincere friends in the Ulverstone district." He presided over a meeting for the unemployed in the district. The Ulverstone Sunday school had ninety-seven scholars at the end of 1933.[1479]

Following the death of his wife, he married again in August 1932, this time to Miss Florence Gertrude Jowett, eldest daughter of the wealthy Mr. and Mrs. C. Jowett, of "Hydale", South Spreyton. Florence entered greatly into the life of the Church. During his time there Church member Miss Elvie Mary Braid left for Victoria to enter upon a course of study at the Bible Institute and became a missionary in the South Pacific. She married Cyril Radcliffe, a lay preacher for the Methodist church. On the Island she developed a virus which eventually caused her death.[1480]

At the beginning of 1936, after a most successful pastorate and as a Home Missioner, Steel was transferred back to Smithton commencing on 5 January. To begin with, the inside and the outside of the building were painted. Repairs were also made to the Irishtown building. It was a Community Church even though for many years the Baptists had regularly conducted services and an attempt to hand it to the Baptists did not eventuate. Under Steel's supervision a vestry was added to the Smithton building and a new organ installed. Steel concluded in early 1937.[1481]

Early that year he again became the endorsed Labor Candidate for Darwin for the Circular Head District in the general election but was not successful.[1482]

In March 1937, Steel accepted the placement at Deloraine remaining until April 1939. Latrobe followed for three years. At the Half-Yearly Assembly in April 1940, he was finally ordained. He had by this time reached normal retiring age. He then accepted the Newstead pastorate in August 1942, staying until May 1945. For the year 1943/1944 he

---

[1479] Advocate (Burnie) 11 August 1932 p4, 16 November 1932 p6, 23 November 1931 p4, 14 July 1932 p4, 20 August 1932 p2, 28 September 1932 p2, 10 October 1934 p2, Febuary 1936, 6 October 1933 p6, 2 November 1933 p6.
[1480] LEx 13 August 1932 p10; BCC July 1933; Advocate (Burnie) 21 January 1935 p4; information on Eva supplied by Les Braid.

[1481] Circular Head Chronicle (Stanley, Tas) 13 November 1935 p3; BCC February 1936, October 1936, January 1937.
[1482] Advocate (Burnie) 11 February 1937 p4.

was appointed President of the Baptist Union. As the war drew to a close he continued to plead the cause of the returned digger being often referred to as "Padre Steel" by the returned soldiers.[1483]

He then accepted the Victorian Altona Baptist Church for five years from 1945. His second wife, Florence died during this time and he married again.

He returned to Launceston to act as interim of the Christian Mission Baptist Church in March 1951 and stayed for two years. Not one to retire, in mid-1953 he offered to work in the mining towns of Rossarden and Storey's Creek. Working under the auspices of the Baptist Union, and assisted by Messrs. J. Cass, Eric Turnbull and S. Hurst, he erected the settlement's first church.[1484]

Then he worked at Newstead however it was far from being his last church. The Newstead people remember him as a happy and caring person who took a close interest in the children. At the State School he took Religious Instruction classes and, as well as teaching the children, he would play with them in the school ground during lesson breaks. In conjunction with his ministry at the Newstead Church, open-air evangelical meetings were conducted in the nearby shopping centre.[1485]

In 1955, he worked at Montello, an outstation of the Burnie Baptist Church, staying until May 1958. By now the Montello Church had its own building. He was one for going to where there was work to be done. His final pastorate was a pioneering work in George Town commencing in September 1958. He served there long enough to see the erection of a church hall towards which both he and his wife worked untiringly. He retired in April 1962 at eighty-seven years of age. A month earlier when asked what age one should retire, he answered, "As near ninety as you can get!" Robert Steel died 1 November 1969, at ninety-four. At the time he was described as "an enthusiast for physical fitness and a man of big heart and boundless energy."[1486]

## Appendix 2: The Rev Ernest Charles Walsh

As well as duties as pastor of the Port Lincoln Church in South Australia, the Rev Ernest Charles Walsh was appointed Superintendent of the Home Mission Churches on Eyre's Peninsula district commencing on 1 April 1928. The missions included Darke's Peak, Little Swamp, Charlton, Kirton Point, Mt. Dutton

---

[1483] HM Minutes p230; Advocate (Burnie) 31 July 1944 p5; LEx 19 May 1945 p6.
[1484] LEx 13 November 1952 p11, 22 August 1953 p8; BCC June 1952, May 1953.
[1485] On This Corner, History of the Newstead Baptist Church p19.

[1486] Family History research by Barbara Coe. Advocate (Burnie) 3 August 1957; Tasmanian Baptist Advance June 1962 p13, December 1969; For memories of Steel's time at Montello see the Rev Graeme Goninon's account in Tasmanian Baptist Advance June 2002.

Bay, Big Swamp, Poonindie and Mt. Cooper. He held open-air meetings often in the Port Lincoln Rotunda on Friday nights. Some years later he also conducted Sunday church services in the Rotunda.[1487] In 1929, a new Sunday school hall was erected at Port Lincoln and other new structures on Eyre's Peninsula district followed.[1488] In 1935/36, he was appointed President of the Baptist Union of SA. By now he exchanged egg-competitions for the game of tennis.

In January 1937, after nine years at Port Lincoln, he accepted a call from the Peterborough Baptist Church, Peterborough being a town in the mid-north of South Australia, in wheat country 560 kms north of Adelaide, just off the Barrier Highway. The circuit took in Hill View and Ucolta and was part of the Northern District Baptist Association.[1489] He often preached at the local Methodist Church. He was in constant demand as a speaker at Anzac Day services.

Walsh, Dorothy and the children were farewelled from the Peterborough Baptist Church in April 1942 as he took charge of the Gumeracha Baptist Church in the Adelaide Hills. The posting included looking after the churches at Salem, Kenton Valley, Forreston and Birdwood. He involved himself in the local Gumeracha school and hospital, the Kenton Valley Devotional and Literary Society and the Gumeracha Tennis Club. After eight years he transferred to the Churches of Broadview and Hampstead. This was his last posting. This gracious, capable and beloved pastor, a person who had early shown considerable promise and had fulfilled it and who had "special gifts in dealing with men", being held in high esteem by all who knew him, died at the age of sixty-four after a brief illness on 15 November 1950 in Adelaide. Following his death, Dorothy and their son Briar and two daughters, Dorothy and Jan still needed a house and one was purchased for them in 1951 by the South Australian Baptist Association but she was soon able to obtain one for herself.[1490] Dorothy died on 18 May 1983 in Geelong, but was buried with Ernest at Gumeracha in South Australia.[1491]

---

[1487] Port Lincoln Times (SA) 24 August 1928 p8, 7 September 1928 p13, 24 February 1933 p6, 4 October 1935 p12.

[1488] The Advertiser (Adelaide) 15 June 1929 p22, 23 October 1936 p11. For one of his sermons at this time, "Hope in Prayer for the Depressed Soul", see Port Lincoln Times (SA) 23 September 1932 p3.

[1489] Port Lincoln Times (SA) 15 January 1937 p1.

[1490] The Times and Northern Advertiser, Peterborough, (SA) 18 September 1942 p2; The Mount Barker Courier and Onkaparinga and Gumeracha Advertiser (SA) 12 January 1950 p8; The Times and Northern Advertiser, Peterborough (SA) 24 November 1950 p3; Hill, AC, "Still Thy Church Extend" (1963) p58; AB 28 November 1950 p6.

[1491] Family history research by Barbara Coe.

## Appendix 3: James Clemens Salter

James Clemens Salter remains an example of what today is known as missional living. From a Baptist family living in the sparse open Mallee Scrub of Northern Victoria, and from the hell of World War One, he lived a committed life seeing ministry opportunities all around and set a standard of ministry which would be hard to beat today. He spent his working life in the ministry of the Tasmanian Baptist circles and his contributions live on.

Salter was born on 4 December 1892 on a farm at Gannawarra in Northern Victoria where the Victorian Home Mission had a station. His family of eight was well occupied with the Baptist work: sister Lynette Salter served at Joyramkura Hospital, Bangladesh; his brother was the Rev William (Bill) J Salter.

James served in the First World War in the Middle East with the Light Horse Brigade and took part in the siege of Tobruk in the Second World War[1492]

In 1948 it was written of the brothers,

> Two brothers who are not twins have set a record which should be quite hard to beat. They are the Rev J. C. Salter, of Hobart, and the Rev W. J. Salter, of Melbourne. Not only are they both ministers of the Baptist Church, but they were Diggers together in the First World War and padres in the Second World War. They are both very keen painters each displaying a similar style and a fondness for the same subjects ... the only sphere in which these brothers may be outclassed is in appearance, they do not look alike.[1493]

James Salter returned from the war in 1919 and went to Tasmania to work with the Baptist Home Mission as men were badly needed in the work; the call for willing workers had been far and wide. James began as assistant to the Rev V. G. Britton at Latrobe from March 1919. Britton's duties as Home Mission Superintendent at Latrobe for nearly thirteen years included a large district incorporating Sassafras, South Spreyton, Moriarty and Virginstow.

In the circuit churches James gave his lecture, "With the A.I.F in Palestine and Syria". He was perfectly suited to welcome the men back from the Front. In Latrobe he wrote his own poems on war themes which included "The Home-Coming" and "Reconstruction". Then there was "Tobruk".[1494] But there is a poem written at an earlier time,

---

[1492] Dyer, Alan F, "God Was Their Rock: Set Against a Background of Local History" (Sheffield, 1975). p176; The Mercury (Hobart) 26 November 1932 p 8; The Mercury (Hobart) 5 March 1943 p5.

[1493] The Mercury (Hobart) 29 June 1948 p3.

[1494] Advocate (Burnie). Then there was "Tobruk". 15 July 1919 p2, 28 July 1919 p1, 16 August 1919 p8, 2 April 1945 p6.

written in Egypt and sent home after receiving a gum leaf,

> What is it that claims the attention
> Of this group of men that I see?
> What is it, they're handling so gently?
> What! merely the leaf of a tree?
>
> Can it be that those rough-looking soldiers
> Are anxious to look at a leaf?
> That amongst all the objects of interest
> That small, worthless thing should be chief?
>
> Yes! merely the leaf of a gum tree,
> That one in a letter received!
> And the way in which that small token
> Was cherished you'd scarce have believed.
>
> But to those boys out yonder in Egypt,
> Out there in the desert and sand,
> That leaf was a touch of Australia;
> A link with their own native land.
>
> It carried them back, that small token,
> To the land they had bidden good-bye:
> And from more than one of those soldiers
> I fancied I heard a faint sigh.
>
> And their eyes filled with infinite longing,
> Though never a word did they speak,
> But I noticed on some of their faces
> A tear course its way down their cheek.
> It recalled to their minds friends and loved ones
> In the land from whence they had come
> Out there in far distant Australia,
> The land of the wattle and gum.
>
> It was only the leaf of a gum tree,
> With a tender thought on it express'd,
> But in cottage or mansion or palace,
> Was never a more welcome guest?[1495]

Prior to his leaving Latrobe for the Smithton Church on 16 February 1920 he married Rosie Walker, the daughter of Mr. and Mrs. C. M. Walker at the Devonport Baptist Church. Musically gifted, she played the organ in church.[1496]

Salter transferred from the Smithton Church to the Ulverstone-Penguin circuit in June 1923. To begin with Salter visited his flock by bike. He soon graduated to a horse and jinker. Finally, he took possession of a car.

Salter was ordained on 20 March 1924. He continued to write poems and the newspapers published them. One of June 1924 was titled, "God Knows Best". He even entered into the Australian Nursery Rhyme Competition writing about a kookaburra.[1497] He wrote to Paramount Films,

---

[1495] Bendigo Advertiser 15 October 1917 p2.
[1496] Advocate (Burnie) 18 February 1920 p4.
[1497] Advocate (Burnie) 27 June 1924 p5, 17 July 1924 p3.

As one who looks upon a great deal of the modern picture film as being a menace to public morals, I have much pleasure in placing on record my appreciation of the very fine production, "The Ten Commandments". It is a picture with a message, and its message needs especially to be heard at the present time. It not only has a message to deliver, it delivers that message so powerfully that all who witness it must be impressed. Such pictures must make for the moral uplifting of the community. Let us have more of the same type.[1498]

Queensland evangelist, the Rev Wilbur L. Jarvis, returned to Ulverstone for another mission late in 1924. Up to 1926, hopes were high for the erection of a "modern" brick church at Ulverstone but it was a difficult year. The membership had dropped and money was tight, not only for this Home Mission church, but all Home Mission churches. In 1926, the Home Mission's yearly grant from the Sustentation Fund, which had been set up by William Gibson Senior, was £660. The Home Mission raised another £2000 that year. It had twenty-eight outstations connected to its seven churches.

The Ulverstone Church now had sixty members. The collections for February 1928 were the highest ever for a month, £11-0s-8d. By early 1927, there was an attempt at reviving the Sunday evening services which had been basically prayer meetings.

In October 1926, the Ulverstone Ministers' Fraternal, of which Salter was President, objected to the Local Government Council proposal of a dance hall on the beach,

> It would have a great tendency to undermine the morality of the town. They regarded the matter so seriously that they were prepared to fight it to the last ditch. It was pointed out that the only place where such a thing was tolerated was at St. Kilda, Victoria, where the conditions were entirely different, the surroundings being cleared and well lighted up.[1499]

The Fraternal was successful in that the development did not proceed.

On the matter of Sunday sport, the Fraternal also urged the council to take steps to discountenance any form of pastime being indulged in on the public reserves on the Lord's Day. The Fraternal's wish was not granted. Later that year Salter was elected to the Council.[1500] In 1927, he wrote a 1200 word essay titled "The Charms of Ulverstone" for the Advocate Newspaper's "Most Beautiful Town Essay Competition".[1501] It was said that he

---

[1498] Circular Head Chronicle (Stanley, Tas) 13 May 1925 p5.
[1499] LEx 18 October 1926 p4.
[1500] Daily Telegraph (Launceston) August 1927 p6.
[1501] The full text is in the Advocate (Burnie) 5 February 1927 p13.

could never sell his pictures. This was not true but an art critic wrote in 1947, "Landscapes by the Rev J. C. Salter appear to have colour washed out of them instead of into them." Salter, with his wavery voice, continued until February 1929 when he resigned. Ulverstone was losing a man who had greatly contributed to so many aspects of the community. Those who gathered for his farewell service spoke of his many commitments in his six and one half years in the town. He had been State President of the Christian Endeavour societies, President of the Ulverstone Arts and Crafts Society, President of the Ulverstone Tourist Council, first President of the Ulverstone Branch of the Australian Natives' Association which by the time of his leaving it now had 200 members, Secretary of the Ulverstone Ministers' Fraternal Association and interested himself in the Returned Soldiers' League and the local State School.[1502] His next posting was to Moonah in the South.

Salter commenced at the Moonah Baptist Church on 3 March 1929. He held office as President of the Baptist Association during his time at Moonah. His Presidential Address

*16-8 Moonah Baptist Church*

summed up his world view, the title being "A Paradoxical World needs a Practical Religion" which was printed in full in the North West Advocate and the Examiner.[1503] He was for seven years Secretary of the Union, until the end of 1939. Earlier at the Baptist Assembly in October 1930, with the Depression starting to bite, he initiated a discussion, "The Church in relation to unemployment." His apt sermon on "The Church and the Crisis" was published in full in the Examiner.[1504]

In 1932, during his time at Moonah, he was holding services fortnightly in the afternoon at the Constitution Hill chapel. He took leave of absence in February 1941 to serve with the war effort. He became a senior chaplain in the Brighton Camp for a time. But during his time in Chaplaincy, he visited the Middle

---

[1502] The Mercury (Hobart) 11 April 1927 p10, 16 April 1947 p7; Advocate (Burnie) 10 February 1928 p2, 23 February 1929 p2.
[1503] Advocate (Burnie) 22 October 1929 p 7; LEx 23 October 1929 p 3.
[1504] Advocate (Burnie) 22 October 1929 p7; The Mercury (Hobart) 11 September 1929 p9, 31 December 1940 p8, 12 June 1942 p3, 31 October 1930 p11; BCC February 1960 p3; LEx 23 October 1929 p3, 20 July 1931.

East returning in June 1942. In 1949, a Kindergarten hall was built at the Moonah Church.[1505] In 1946, he published, "A Padre with the Rats of Tobruk". In 1953, the Moonah Church made possible the erection of the Moonah Scouts' District Headquarters by providing the land behind the church. The hall also became the home for the 2nd Moonah Scout Troop. He continued his fight against Sunday trading and took up the fight against extended hotel trading hours. He was appointed President of the State Council of Churches. He was a lover of old pictures and souvenirs of Tasmanian aboriginal life. In respect to the aboriginal people, when the Australian Aborigines League decided to hold a day of mourning concurrently with the nation's day of rejoicing in 1938 to celebrate the 150th anniversary of the coming of the white man to Australia, Salter the chairman of the League wrote, "This pathetically significant gesture should be well calculated to set Australians thinking very seriously about the unhappy condition of these unfortunate people." He remained at Moonah until early 1954. Salter and his wife, Rosie, had two sons: Allenby and John.[1506]

James Clemens Salter died on 6 January 1960 at an Aged Care Home in Moonah. This Baptist Tasmanian minister, with a long record of service, had exercised the whole of his ministry in the Tasmanian churches. Rosie died on 20 September 1976.

## Appendix 4: The Rev A. E. Albury

Scotsman Alfred Ernest Albury followed the call and trained for Christian ministry and that call took him to Australia's north and south where he proved a diligent pastor and a help mate to all. At the end of his two decade pilgrimage, he and his wife returned to England.

Albury was born on 2 June 1873 at Basildon, Berkshire, UK, the son of John and Caroline (nee Pagson) Albury. John, a grocer, died when Alfred was seven years of age. Alfred gained employment as a grocer's assistant and then undertook ministerial training in Glasgow. He arrived in NSW from Liverpool in 1913[1507] and moved first to Cairns in Queensland before arriving in Brisbane where he spoke at a YMCA evangelistic meeting for men.[1508] In July 1915, he became Pastor at the Ryan Street Baptist Church in Charters Towers. He was present at the Queensland Baptist Association meetings in September 1915. He earned further income by being a supervisor at the University of

---

[1505] AB 28 June 1949 p5.
[1506] The Mercury (Hobart) 23 September 1937 p2, 17 January 1938 p3, 28 November 1938 p8, 23 July 1945 p7, 15 June 1953 p6, 3 September 1930 p10, 10 October 1931 p7.
[1507] Family History research by Barbara Coe.
[1508] The Brisbane Courier 14 June 1913 p6.

Queensland public examinations. At Charters Towers on 16 June 1920 Alfred married Edinburgh born Lily Bissett. By January 1923, they had returned to Brisbane. One of his speaking engagements in 1923 was at a special mission in relation to Christ's second coming held in a large tent in the town.[1509]

*16-9 Elphin Road Baptist Church*

**Albury arrived at Elphin Road Baptist Church from Smithton** in April 1925 and stayed until September 1932. He gave considerable time to visitation and while the numbers grew, the membership stayed small. Albury conducted weekly Religious Instruction at the East Launceston State School. Lily was active in the Woman's Guild. In these years, with voluntary labour, a Sunday school Kindergarten room and a vestry were added to the property. At the Tasmanian Baptist Ministers' Fraternal in July 1925, Albury gave a paper, on "The Holy Spirit in Relation to Jesus". In January 1927, Albury chaired a meeting of the Northern Tasmania Evangelistic Society and took part in its Launceston mission that September. Albury and his people ministered to those who were made homeless in the Launceston and districts flood of April 1929 which was the worst in its history. The suburb of Invermay was almost completely under water. 2,000 people were evacuated and taken to Albert Hall. Fifteen churches in the city, including his own, provided regular meals. The emergency lasted for a week and kept the women of the Elphin Road Church busy. But by May 1931, Albury's health was poor and in August 1932 he was farewelled. He and Lily envisaged a return to England.[1510]

But first they returned to Queensland. The now retired Albury gave interim pastorates at the Ann Street Presbyterian Church and the Cracknell Road Congregational Church. He also accepted an executive position with the newly

---

[1509] The Telegraph (Brisbane) 29 May 1913 p2, 15 September 1915 p7; The Northern Miner (Charters Towers) 24 July 1915 p1; The Evening Telegraph (Charters Towers, Qld.) 15 November 1917 p2; The Daily Mail (Brisbane) 6 January 1923 p18.

[1510] LEx 29 April 1929 p8; "A Church and Its People" by Olive Dowling; Advocate (Burnie) 22 August 1932 p2.

formed Australian Inland Mission.¹⁵¹¹

The Alburys were present in Launceston for the Jubilee Celebrations of the Christian Mission Church in June 1935. Also present for the occasion were many former Pastors of the Church. The Alburys returned to England in 1935 to live in Reading where they attended the Wycliffe Baptist Church. The Rev Alfred Ernest Albury died on 1 February 1940. Lily Albury died on 4 December 1953.¹⁵¹²

## Appendix 5: George Levison Dibden

With a proven record for church planting in Western Australian and pastoral ministry in Victoria, George Levison Dibden sought entry into the Tasmanian Baptist Home Mission and served faithfully at Smithton before moving with the family interstate to settle down.

Dibden, born on 22 July 1885 to Henry Owen Dibden and Rosey Jane Esther (nee George)¹⁵¹³, grew up attending the Perth Baptist church, WA, and engaged in preaching regularly. He was also part of the Baptist Union of Western Australia from its commencement in 1897 and was soon on the Council. He was a chemist in Perth and also for a time chairman of the Municipal Council of Sutton.

Dibden was the founding pastor of the Kalgoorlie Baptist Church which was constituted on 2 October 1898. It met in the Friendly Societies' Hall, Porter Street. The church began with seven members and the membership rose to twenty-seven in a year. By then the church had bought a well situated block of land and was anxious to build. The new building, "a neat little structure", opened free of debt on 28 March 1900.¹⁵¹⁴

Early in 1915, Dibden moved to Eaglehawk just outside Bendigo in Victoria to pastor its Baptist Church for six months. His next pastorate was that of the Smithton Baptist Church in Tasmania.

**Following his time at Smithton** Dibden and his wife Alice Winifred moved to South Australia and spent the rest of their days at Robe and nearby Kingston and reared a family of four children. George Levison Dibden died on 19 December 1948 in Kingston.¹⁵¹⁵

---

¹⁵¹¹ Telegraph (Brisbane) 15 April 1933 p12; The Brisbane Courier 7 January 1933 p11.
¹⁵¹² Reading Standard (UK) 18 October 1935 p12; LEx 29 June 1935 p4, 20 March 1940 p6; UK National Probate Calendar 1853 p48.
¹⁵¹³ Henry was born on 18 June 1857 in Brighton, Sussex, England, and Rosey was born on 26 October 1861 in Kensington, South Australia.
¹⁵¹⁴ The Daily News (Perth, WA) 30 May 1896 p4, 20 June 1986 p4; The West Australian (Perth) 28 January 1898 p3, 11 November 1899 p10, 2 December 1898 p10.
¹⁵¹⁵ The Bendigo Independent 25 June 1915 p7; The Advertiser (Adelaide) 28 December 1948 p8.

## Appendix 6: Edward Robert Bampton

In response to the inner promptings to serve their Lord more fully, layman Edward Robert Bampton and his wife Mabel moved interstate to enter fully into ministry with the Tasmanian Home Mission in its far outreach in the North West during the War years. Then they moved to the Sunshine State for further ministry no matter what the denomination and settled down to work with the Bible Society.

In 1910 and 1911, Bampton was in demand as a lay preacher at the Magill Baptist Church in Adelaide, South Australia, as the Pastor was indisposed. Mabel too, was a preacher. Later that year the Bamptons sold off cheaply an Avery weighing machine and a Wolseley motor car as they were moving to Tasmania where there was the offer of work for the Tasmanian Baptist Home Mission at the Smithton Church.[1516] They were living out Jesus' words in Luke 9.62: "No one having laid the hand upon the plow, and looking on the things behind, is fit for the kingdom of God."

**In February 1916, after their time at Smithton,** the Bamptons sold up everything again and moved to the Nambour Baptist Church Circuit in the Sunshine Coast Region, Queensland. Its preaching stations took in Yandina, Cooloolabin and Maroochy River. In December 1917, he joined the ministry of the Church of Christ and accepted the pastorate at the Toowomba Church in Queensland.[1517]

In July 1920, Bampton became Deputation Secretary of the British and Foreign Bible Society (BFBS) for NSW which gave him entry to churches of many denominations including the Anglican Church with which in 1932 he affiliated. This BFBS ministry continued in both NSW and Queensland until October 1935.[1518]

By October 1938, Bampton, now ordained to the Christian ministry with the Congregational Churches in NSW, was employed by the Scriptural Colportage Society of Australasia with its emphasis on Bibles for the Blind. The Rev Edward Robert Bampton died in June 1941 in Manly, Queensland.[1519]

## Appendix 7: Charles Percy Gordon Nibbs

With church the centre of his life, Charles Percy Gordon Nibbs was open to God's call and entered into ministry with the Tasmanian Home Mission but his fragile health made it

---

[1516] The Express and Telegraph (Adelaide) 30 June 1911 p5; The Advertiser (Adelaide) 20 May 1911 p21, 6 November 1911 p5.
[1517] Chronicle and North Coast Advertiser (Qld) 28 April 1916 p2; The Telegraph (Brisbane) 15 December 1917 p10; Newcastle Morning Herald and Miners' Advocate (NSW) 2 March 1918 p10.
[1518] The Evening Telegraph (Charters Towers, Qld.) 10 July 1920 p2; Northern Star (Lismore, NSW) 15 July 1932 p3, 27 October 1933 p3, 15 October 1935 p3.
[1519] Cairns Post (Qld) 25 October 1938 p6; The Courier-Mail (Brisbane) 12 June 1941 p16.

impossible to continue what was his heart's desire so he settled for many years of local church preaching and the demand was constant. Yet one of his sons followed in his footsteps and gave many good years in pastoral ministry to the Tasmanian churches.

Nibbs was the fifth child in a family of ten children. His parents, Job and Elizabeth Nibbs, were committed Christians. Gordon attended school at West Kentish where he was influenced by a godly teacher, Alex Dalziel.

The family moved to East Devonport. It was while they were at East Devonport that Gordon was literally struck down with Polio while walking home from school. He was completely paralysed for much of two years.

The family moved then to Parkers Ford near Port Sorell and his father took over the management of a nearby orchard and Gordon worked with him.

Several years later a travelling salesman asked Gordon to work in his store which he did and when the business was sold Gordon was asked to take on the role of travelling salesman and Gordon pioneered the Sheffield, Latrobe, Devonport (and possibly Wynyard) districts.

While in Sheffield, he was converted under the teaching of its Pastor, the Rev Henry Ebenezer Saunders, and in 1923 was baptised and came into membership. He was also greatly influenced by Pastor Alvin Higgs of the Bracknell Church who encouraged him to consider entering Bible College. In 1924/25, Gordon attended the Missionary and Bible College in Croydon, NSW.[1520] He returned home in 1926 and was appointed as an assistant to the Rev V. G. Britton stationed at the Latrobe Church. This meant weekly sermons in its outstations of South Spreyton, Sassafras, Moriarty and Virginstow until October 1927. While at Latrobe, studies were mandatory.[1521]

Gordon was then appointed to the Wynyard Circuit under the supervision of the Rev William Heaven which meant responsibility for the small fellowships of Lapoinya, Calder, Preolenna, Moorleah, Myalla, Sisters Creek, Boat Harbour and Montumana with his main concern for him being that of Preolenna. Gordon was stationed in Smithton from March 1929.

*16-10 Gordon and Corrie Nibbs*

---

[1520] His son Edward (Ted) attended the same College in 1953/54.

[1521] The Mercury (Hobart) 26 October 1927 p11.

After his time at Smithton, Nibbs had various areas of employment. Eventually, after an accident he was unable to work for a time and Corrie his wife, a splendid cook, supported the family.[1522]

During the war Nibbs worked for Clements and Marshall's Devonport Dehydration Factory producing rations for the Armed Forces. In 1944, the family moved to Devonport and became very involved in the Baptist Church. Gordon's father and mother had previously retired to Devonport and Gordon's father had been Sunday School Superintendent, Deacon and also Life Deacon before his death. Gordon was also Deacon and then Life Deacon. Gordon had now a deep interest in Christian work among Jews.[1523] Corrie influenced many young lives during her years as leader of the Christian Endeavour Society. Gordon still accepted preaching appointments.

Eventually, Gordon's health deteriorated and he died on 13 July 1961 of a massive heart attack. The doctors said his heart was so scarred from all his previous sickness that it was a miracle he had not died years before. Gordon left a legacy of devotion to God and preaching His word. His Bible was almost worn out from constant daily reading and his ministry is remembered by many.[1524]

## Appendix 8: Cecil M. Jobling

In June 1930, following his time at the Smithton Church, Cecil M. Jobling commenced a shoeing and general smith business in Irish Town all the while attending the Smithton Church. In July 1931, they moved back to Smithton and were also associated with the Methodist Church. His wife contributed to the Smithton Branch of the Australian Women's National League.[1525]

In June 1932, they moved to Launceston and Jobling preached at times at the Christian Mission Church's outstation of Summerhill. But by May 1934, Jobling had "been appointed blacksmith" in Smithton. Subsequently they moved back to Melbourne and in time his wife associated with the Collins Street Baptist Church's branch of the Baptist Women's Association. In 1945, with the idea of ministry still before him, Jobling approached the Home Mission of the Presbyterian Church of Victoria and he was appointed to one of its stations at Maldon.[1526]

---

[1522] Circular Head Chronicle (Stanley, Tas) 20 January 1932 p3, 5 August 1942 p3.
[1523] Advocate (Burnie) 19 July 1946 p4.
[1524] I'm indebted to the Rev Ted Nibbs for this account of his father.
[1525] The Australian Women's National League (AWNL) was a conservative women's organisation established in 1904 to support the monarchy and empire, to combat socialism, educate women in politics and safeguard the interests of the home, women and children.
[1526] Circular Head Chronicle (Stanley, Tas) 11 June 1930 p1, 6 May 1931 p2, 22 July 1931 p2, 14 October 1931 p3, 9 May 1934 p3; LEx 10 June 1933 p15; The Age (Melbourne) 4 May 1939 p3; The Argus (Melbourne) 3 January 1945 p2.

# Conclusion

Many of our churches are dying, there is no argument about that and they know it. Their age grouping destines them for extinction. Within them they don't have the persons capable of initiating outreach. For the rest, one possibility for growth could be in what is designated the creation of a liquid church, that is, to set up a separate age-group church, say at 5pm Sunday afternoons with a target audience of eighteen to thirty years targeting the culture of this age group. In doing so, we dispense with trying to change the morning traditional service to a more encompassing service through the introduction of a band, choruses and the like and leave these traditional services as they are and see the 5pm services as a missionary venture. It would be a regular and weekly commitment.

As an aside, don't expect those who run the 5pm service to be equally committed to the morning service. There would be no need for other venues or equipment, both the buildings and the power point systems are already in place. There would be no Sankey's hymn books or King James Bibles. More than four centuries have passed since the KJB was published. In that time our speech has so changed that the KJV, for all the glories of its language, has become less familiar. There is no doubt that the old Sankey hymns are impediments to reaching out.

These liquid churches will operate under the blessing of our existing congregations. These days there is no longer the guarantee that by building a church or chapel we will draw a congregation. That position belongs to one hundred years ago. Today, we should be rather seeking to facilitate the development of groups of people who will order their lives around the one called Jesus. The question is to gather together groups of people who see in Jesus a better way to live and are transformed as a result.

This will be one of the many new non-threatening, comfortable entry points we have in our churches. We spend too little time, energy and money on reaching out versus the amount we spend on reaching in.

Meaningful worship for the postmodern generation dialogues with the culture while seeking to avoid the twin perils of becoming either indistinguishable from the larger culture or divorced completely from it.

Christian leaders who want to reach out need to be serious students of contemporary culture and adapt worship to reach it. They also show us that churches that successfully reach the unchurched know what they're seeking. Despite perceptions, I feel that most our churches are not reaching the lost and it could be said that some of our growing churches aren't reaching non-believers. Many seemingly successful churches, Baptist and non-Baptist, create a climate attractive to people who already are believers, and thus they experience mainly "transfer growth". Am I right in saying that our primary problem is that we do church in a way that is culturally irrelevant to the unchurched?

# Table of Images

1-1 Extract from 'The Examiner' ............... 14
1-2 The 1862 Perth Baptist Chapel .......... 14
1-3 The Rev Alfred W Grant...................... 15
1-4 Charles Clark...................................... 17
1-5 Thomas Spurgeon............................... 18
1-6 Robert Williamson ............................. 19
1-7 Rides Cooper..................................... 20
1-8 Rev John Walton................................. 23
1-9 Perth Baptist Tabernacle: "a kind of Baptist Cathedral"................................ 24
1-10 Alfred Metters.................................. 25
1-11 Ballarat Baptist Tabernacle .............. 27
1-12 William Clark.................................... 28
1-13 George Gillings ................................ 30
1-14 Crimea St Baptist Church, St Kilda. 33
1-15 Robert Williamson later in life ........ 35
1-16 Henry and Ada Clark ....................... 39
1-17 The Rev Henry Clark (third from left in the front row) with the staff of Perth Baptist Sunday School........... 40
1-18 Stephen Howard................................ 42
1-19 Perth Baptist Church Sunday School Picnic................................................. 44
1-21 Kapunda Church, SA ....................... 45
1-20 Laura Baptist Church, SA................ 45
2-1 Blackwood Creek Baptist Chapel ...... 48
2-2 William Ross..................................... 49
2-3 Vincent G Britton............................... 52
2-4 Mountain Vale (Upper Liffey) Primitive Methodist Church ............................. 53
2-5 Memorial to William Ross which hangs in the Blackwood Creek Chapel...... 54
2-6 George Lake and the Gospel Van ...... 55
2-7 Band of Hope Member's Card ........... 60
2-8 Typical source for poems and short stories used at Band of Hope meetings and the Gospel Van .......... 61
3-1 Bracknell Primitive Methodist Chapel ........................................................... 63
3-2 Bracknell Baptist Tabernacle............ 64
3-3 Bracknell Church Manse at the corner of Elizabeth and Louise Streets ...... 66
3-4 Cluan Baptist Chapel with Rev Albert Butler and Mrs Dunkley .................... 67
3-5 Robert Steel with his mother & sisters ........................................................... 70
4-1 Christian Mission Church Launceston with the two storey Parr's Hotel on the left .............................................. 73
4-2 Evangelist Emilia Baeyertz ................ 74
4-3 Henry Reed........................................ 75
4-4 Dan Hiddlestone ................................ 76
4-5 Dr. H G Guinness.............................. 79
4-6 George Soltau ................................... 81
4-7 Charles Mortimer Cherbury ............... 88
4-8 Henry Lambert.................................. 89
4-9 Joseph T. Piercey .............................. 90
4-10 Mrs. Margaret Reed .........................91
4-12 John H. Shallberg in his army days. 94
4-11 Terowie Baptist Church SA............. 94
4-13 Christ Church Congregational Church, Launceston......................................... 95
4-14 Brunswick Baptist Church ............... 96
4-15 Cherbury's Collingwood Tabernacle ......................................................... 101
5-1 The Chapel at 73 West Barrack Street ......................................................... 116
5-2 Henry Varley.................................... 117
5-3 Launceston Examiner 30 March 1880 ......................................................... 118
5-4 Deloraine Tabernacle facing the Meander River................................. 119
5-5 Samuel Shorey's Flour Mill (now Harvey's Roller Flour Mill, Deloraine) ......................................................... 119
5-6 Edward Vaughan .............................. 122
5-7 William Gibson Senior ..................... 123
5-8 Alfred Hyde ..................................... 125
5-9 Sunday School at one of Deloraine's outstations: the Quamby Brook Chapel.............................................. 126
5-10 Howard Elliott................................. 128
5-11 Main Street of Deloraine ................ 129
5-12 S. J. Harrison.................................. 133
5-13 Aberdeen Street Baptist Church, Geelong............................................ 134
5-14 Auckland Tabernacle NZ ................ 134
5-15 Great Assembly Hall, Mile End Road, Aberdeen.......................................... 135
5-16 Harry Wood.................................... 136
5-17 Saddleworth Baptist Church, SA .. 137
5-18 Young Samuel Harris during his Baptist College years...................... 143
5-19 Maldon Baptist Church, Vic........... 144
5-20 Oxford Terrace Baptist Church, Christchurch................................... 145
6-1 Longford Assembly Rooms............. 148
6-3 Robert and Eva McCullough ........... 149

Lessons from our first 20 years

6-4 William Gibson Jnr and wife Elvina ................................................................ 150
6-5 "The Blue" Band of Hope medal ...... 151
6-6 Henry G. Blackie .................................. 153
6-7 The Longford Tabernacle .................. 154
6-8 John Macalister ..................................... 155
6-9 Cornish miner, Billy Bray .................. 156
6-10 The Longford Manse ......................... 157
6-11 Robert McCullough ............................ 160
6-12 Harry Wood "Locked indoors by Giant Ill-Health" .................................. 161
6-13 H G Blackie's advertisement of Nov 1902 ....................................................... 163
6-14 H G Blackie's gravestone .................. 164
7-1 The Congregational Church met in Milton Hall, on the right .................. 170
7-2 Alfred Bird ............................................. 172
7-3 Mary Clement Leavitt ......................... 173
7-4 Sketch of the Launceston Tabernacle ................................................................ 174
7-5 Alfred James Clark ............................... 176
7-6 Baptist Union Council of 1889: Front row: JT Soundy, W Gibson Jnr, R McCullough, HG Blackie. Middle Row: J Chamberlain, AJ Ratcliffe, unknown, A Hyde, SB Pitt, H Wood, WJ. Murphy, JE Walton. Back Row: AJ Stokes left end, WD Weston right end, of those unidentified – HD Archer and Dr Benafield ................................................ 177
7-7 Edward E Harris .................................... 179
7-8 Launceston Tabernacle Sunday School picnic in 1902 at Kilafaddy ............. 180
7-9 Walter Eddy ............................................ 181
7-10 Bloomsbury Baptist Church, London ................................................................ 182
7-11 West Melbourne Baptist Church .. 186
7-12 Sketch of the Burton Street Tabernacle, Sydney ............................. 189
7-14 Hargreaves Street Baptist Church, Bendigo .................................................. 190
7-13 Alfred Clark and his wife Jane Clark ................................................................ 191
7-15 Aberdeen Street Baptist Church 1853 ................................................................ 192
7-16 George Street Baptist Church, Fitzroy ................................................................ 194
7-17 George Wainwright ............................ 197
7-18 The original Fenwick Street Baptist Church, Geelong, on the left and the 1911 building on the right ............. 198

7-19 Daylesford Baptist Church, Victoria ................................................................ 199
7-20 South Yarra Baptist Tabernacle .... 201
7-21 Inside the Launceston Tabernacle ................................................................ 202
8-1 Construction of the Hobart Exhibition Buildings ................................................ 205
8-2 North Hobart area prior to the purchase of the Church land .......... 209
8-3 The School Room ................................. 210
8-4 Laying the foundation stone of the Hobart Tabernacle .............................. 212
8-5 The Stately Hobart Tabernacle ........ 213
8-6 Amy Sherwin ......................................... 216
8-7 Morison Cumming ............................... 219
8-8 Collins St Baptist Church, Melbourne ................................................................ 220
8-9 Constitution Hill Chapel .................... 222
8-12 Dr. Harry Benjafield ........................... 224
8-10 Lilly Soundy's Bible Study Class with George Craike sitting to her left ... 224
8-11 Dr Joshua Tovell Soundy .................. 225
8-13 Parkside Baptist Church SA ............ 227
8-14 Rev F W Boreham ............................... 228
8-15 North Adelaide Baptist Church ..... 229
8-16 Garland St Baptist Church, Bury, St Edmunds ................................................ 231
8-17 James Blaikie ........................................ 232
8-18 Castlemaine Baptist Church ........... 236
9-1 Thomas Hainsworth ........................... 239
9-2 Gilbert Street 1912 ............................... 241
9-3 Rev G. Moysey ....................................... 242
9-4 Sunday School at Devonport. John Chamberlain and Harry Wood standing in back row ...................... 244
9-5 John Chamberlain ................................ 245
9-6 Latrobe Tabernacle .............................. 246
9-7 Winding Track by William H. Short, 1891 ........................................................ 249
9-8 Samuel B Pitt ......................................... 250
9-9 Mary Ann Gibson ................................. 252
9-10 Charles and Phoebe Palmer ............ 253
9-11 Henry G. Blackie .................................. 255
9-12 John Chamberlain in old age .......... 257
9-13 Baptist Union Council of 1889: Front row: JT Soundy, W Gibson Jnr, R McCullough, HG Blackie. Middle Row: J Chamberlain, AJ Ratcliffe, unknown, A Hyde, SB Pitt, H Wood, WJ. Murphy, JE Walton. Back Row: AJ Stokes left end, WD Weston right end, of those

unidentified – HD Archer and Dr Benafield..................................258
9-14 The First Kerang Baptist Church ..259
10-1 Christian Brethren Sunday School ........................................................263
10-2 The original Sheffield Tabernacle: "Now what to do as Sunday school is over for the day?"...................264
10-3 Young Albert Blackwell......................268
10-4 Missionary Miss Allen Arnold .........269
10-5 William & Mary Heaven ....................272
10-6 Henry and Frances Saunders .........274
10-7 Rev A. E. Blackwell............................275
10-8 Rev E. McIntosh Brown, with dog-collar, standing in the ruins of the Tabernacle.................................276
10-9 Ethel Blackwell and her Newmarket Young Ladies' Bible .......................277
10-10 The Newmarket Baptist Church.278
10-11 Laying the foundation stone at Spreyton 4 Aug 1907......................282
11-1 Formby's original Anglican Church ........................................................290
11-2 Torquay's Wesleyan Methodist Church..............................................291
11-3 East Devonport: Torquay................292
11-4 George James Mackay .......................295
11-5 Rev John Walton ................................297
11-6 The laying of the Foundation Stone on 3 Sept 1903; Cowle's Hall to the left ........................................................299
11-7 The Devonport Tabernacle adjoining Cowle's Hall....................................300
11-8 Alfred Metters ....................................301
11-9 Hussey's Bible-Selling Book Store ........................................................303
11-10 Fairfield's Church Building-in a day ........................................................306
11-11 The completed Fairfield's Church ........................................................307
12-1 Burnie's Primitive Methodist Church ........................................................312
12-2 Harry and Emily Wood and family ........................................................313
12-3 The Original Burnie Baptist Church ........................................................314
12-4 Samuel Harrison ................................316
12-5 Joseph T. Piercey................................317
12-6 Peter Cairns .......................................319
12-7 Charles Palmer .................................321
12-8 Frederick Leeder ...............................322
12-9 Edward Woods ..................................323

12-10 Laying the foundation stone of the New Burnie Baptist Church in 1925 by J. T. Soundy ................................324
12-11 Thomas Vigis.....................................326
12-12 Peter W. Cairns .................................335
12-13 Port Melbourne Baptist Church.339
12-14 Oswald Linden..................................340
12-15 Ballarat East Baptist Church........346
12-16 Whyte's Causeway Church, Kirkcaldy, Fife................................347
12-17 Henrietta Woods ..............................348
12-18 Edward Albert Joyce ......................350
12-19 Henry T. Dowling.............................351
13-1 Penguin's 1864 Primitive Methodist Church..............................................353
13-2 Penguin's 1874 Primitive Methodist Church..............................................354
13-3 Ulverstone's Congregational Church ........................................................355
13-4 W. D. Weston......................................357
13-5 Home Missioners 1913-1915: Back row: Fred J. Wood, J.W. Fisher, J.G. Duncan, Ern. C. Walsh, Albert Butler. Front row: Robert Steel, W. L. Heaven, Superintendent Rev F. J. Dunkley, H. E. Saunders, E.A. Salisbury ..........................................358
13-6 Jack Fisher with his mother, wife Jane and daughter......................................364
13-7 William Heaven and his bride Mary Florence Box ...................................368
13-8 Albert and Laura Butler...................369
13-9 Albert Butler, Unknown, Robert Steel, Jack Fisher.......................................370
13-10 Brisbane Tabernacle .......................372
13-11 Army Chaplain Vincent Britton..374
13-12 Vincent and his motor cycle .........376
13-13 Deloraine's outstation of Montana built during Jack Fisher's time at the Church..............................................376
13-14 Vincent and Ida in later life..........377
14-1 Wynyard Anglican Church of 1873 ........................................................381
14-2 Myalla Baptist Chapel of 1922 ......383
14-3 Rev A. C. Jarvis..................................389
14-4 The Wilfred Jarvis team, Baptist Church Archives of Qld (used with permission) ....................................390
14-5 Alan Paton Dawson...........................392
14-6 Ern Walsh with Mr. Ratcliffe of Sheffield..........................................396
14-7 Jireh Baptist Church, Brisbane......399

Lessons from our first 20 years
15-1 Camp Creek Methodist Church ..... 404
15-2 The Daniel Smith family with Seaview in the background, c1908 ............... 405
15-3 Opening day in August 1910 of the Yolla Baptist Church building ....... 406
15-4 Any local church was both the social centre of the town, and the 'House of God' ........................................................... 407
15-5 Walter Stanley Simpson .................... 409
15-6 Lance Corporal Alfred Harrald James ................................................................ 410
15-7 Alan Paton Dawson ............................. 411
15-8 Yolla streetscape .................................. 412
15-9 Macintosh Brown & Family ............ 415
15-10 Padre Tunks ......................................... 416
15-11 Coburg Baptist Church opened 1910 ................................................................ 417
15-12 Young Wattie ....................................... 419
15-13 Horace H. Jeffs .................................... 420
15-14 Missionary Candidates: A. B. Rogers SA, A. E. Smith Qld, E. E. Watson, C. Baldwin Vic., W. G. Crofts WA. ....... 420
15-15 Missionaries in Comilla in 1931. Front row centre is Elsie with Avril and Wattie .............................................. 421
15-16 Wattie street preaching in East Bengal ....................................................... 422
15-17 The Rev William Dawson family 427
15-18 Wesley Bligh delivering "The Church Hour" on 3XY radio in Melbourne ................................................................ 429
15-19 Adamsfield ........................................... 433
16-1 Young Robert Steel ............................. 438
16-2 Digging the first sod for the Forest Church ..................................................... 439
16-3 George Dibden .................................... 441
16-4 James C. Salter ................................... 442
16-5 Alfred E. Albury ................................. 443
16-6 Ernest C. Walsh .................................. 444
16-7 Robert Steel and wife Florence ..... 447
16-8 Moonah Baptist Church ................... 454
16-9 Elphin Road Baptist Church ........... 456
16-10    Gordon and Corrie Nibbs ........ 459

# Biographies

## Newspapers and Periodicals

Adelaide Observer
Advocate (Burnie)
Alexandra and Yea Standard, Gobur, Thornton and Acheron Express (Vic)
Australian Baptist (1913-1986)
Australian Evangelist
Australian Town and Country Journal (Sydney)
Baptist Union of Tasmania Home Mission Minutes (in the Baptist Union of Tasmania holdings at the Tasmanian State Archives)
Barrier Miner (Broken Hill, NSW)
Bathurst Free Press and Mining Journal (NSW)
Baptist Church Chronicle (in the Baptist Union of Tasmania holdings at the Tasmanian State Archives)
Bendigo Advertiser (Vic)
Bendigonian (Bendigo)
Brisbane Courier
Bunyip (Gawler SA)
Cairns Post (Qld)
Camperdown Chronicle (Vic)
Chicago, Bible Institute of Colportage Assn. (c1901)
Christian Colonist (SA)
Chronicle (Adelaide)
Chronicle and North Coast Advertiser (Qld)
Chronicle, South Yarra Gazette, Toorak Times and Malvern Standard (Vic)
Circular Head Chronicle (Stanley, Tas)
Cootamundra Herald (NSW)
Cornwall Chronicle (Launceston)
Critic (Adelaide)
Daily Advertiser (Wagga Wagga, NSW)
Daily Examiner (Launceston)
Daily Herald (Adelaide)
Daily Mercury (Mackay, Qld)
Daily Pictorial (Sydney)
Daily Post (Hobart)
Daily Standard (Brisbane)
Daily Telegraph (Launceston)

Day-Star (1886-1894) (in the Baptist Union of Tasmania holdings at the Tasmanian State Archives)
Day Dawn and Baptist Church Messenger (1900-1917) (in the Baptist Union of Tasmania holdings at the Tasmanian State Archives)
Daylesford Advocate, Yandoit, Glenlyon and Eganstown Chronicle (Vic.)
Deloraine and Westbury Advertiser (Tas)
Devon Herald (Tas)
Evening Journal (Adelaide)
Evening News (Sydney)
Evening Star, BUNZ
Fitzroy City Press (Vic)
Frankston and Somerville Standard
Freeman's Journal (NZ)
Geelong Advertiser
Gippsland Times (Vic)
Goulburn Evening Penny Post (NSW)
Goulburn Herald (NSW) Newcastle Morning Herald and Miners' Advocate (NSW)
Gympie Times and Mary River Mining Gazette (Qld)
Hamilton Spectator (Vic)
Harper's New Monthly Magazine
Heidelberg and Greensborough, Eltham and Diamond Creek Chronicle (Vic)
Independent (Footscray, Vic)
Kapunda Herald (SA)
Kerang New Times (Vic)
Kyabram Union (Vic)
Launceston Advertiser
Leader (Vic)
Launceston Examiner and later Examiner
Lithgow Mercury (NSW)
Lucas, an Evangelical History Review
Macleay Argus (Kempsey, NSW)
Malvern Standard (Vic)
Maryborough Chronicle, Wide Bay and Burnett Advertiser (Qld)
Mataura Ensign (NZ),
Mercury (Fitzroy)
Mercury and Weekly Courier (Vic)
Morning Bulletin (Rockhampton, Qld)

# Lessons from our first 20 years

Mount Alexander Mail (Vic)
Mount Barker Courier (SA)
Mudgee Guardian and North-Western Representative (NSW)
Murray Pioneer and Australian River Record (SA)
National Advocate (Bathurst, NSW)
New Zealand Tablet
Newcastle Morning Herald and Miners' Advocate (NSW)
News (Adelaide)
Newsletter of the Victorian Baptist Historical Society
North African Mission Journal
North Coast Standard (Tas)
North Melbourne Advertiser
North Melbourne Courier and West Melbourne Advertiser
North Melbourne Gazette
North West Advocate (Burnie)
Northern Argus (Clare, SA)
Northern Star (Lismore, NSW)
The North West Post (Formby, Tas)
North-western Advocate and Emu Bay Times (Tas)
Observer (Adelaide)
Otago Witness (Owaka)
Our Yesterdays (Camberwell, Victorian Baptist Historical Society).
Ovens and Murray Advertiser (Vic)
Wood, Harry, Pioneer Work for the Lord in Tasmania (1892)
Port Adelaide News
Port Lincoln Times (SA)
Portland Guardian (Vic)
Prahran Chronicle (Vic)
Press (NZ)
Queensland Baptist
Queensland Times, Ipswich Herald and General Advertiser
Reading Standard (UK)
Record (Emerald Hill, Melbourne)
Renmark Pioneer (SA).
Sea Lake Times and Berriwillock Advertiser (Vic)
Seymour Express and Goulburn Valley, Avenel, Graytown, Nagambie, Tallarook and Yea Advertiser (Vic)
Shepparton Advertiser (Vic)
South Australian Advertiser
South Australian Chronicle and Weekly Mail
South Australian Register (Adelaide)
South Australian Weekly Chronicle (Adelaide)
Southern Baptist (1895-1912) (1895-1910 in the Baptist Union of Tasmania holdings at the Tasmanian State Archives; 1895-1912 in the Victorian Baptist Union archives).
Southern Cross (Tas)
Spectator and Methodist Chronicle
Sporting Globe,
Standard (Port Melbourne)
Sunday Mail (Brisbane)
Sunraysia Daily (Mildura, Vic)
Sunshine Advocate (Vic)
Sword and Trowel (Journal of Metropolitan Tabernacle, London)
Sydney Morning Herald
Table Talk (Melbourne)
Tambellup Times (WA)
Tasmanian Baptist (1910-1913) (in the Baptist Union of Tasmania holdings at the Tasmanian State Archives)
Tasmanian Baptist Advance (in the Baptist Union of Tasmania holdings at the Tasmanian State Archives)
Tasmanian Baptist Union Council Minutes (in the Baptist Union of Tasmania holdings at the Tasmanian State Archives)
Tasmanian Family History Society
Tasmanian News (Hobart)
The Adelaide Express
The Advertiser (Adelaide)
The Age (Vic)
The Albany Advertiser (WA)
The Areas' Express (SA)
The Argus (Melbourne)
The Australasian (Melbourne)
The Australian Star (NSW)
The Bacchus Marsh Express
The Ballarat Courier
The Ballarat Star
The Baptist Recorder (Baptist Historical Society of NSW)
The Beaudesert Times (Qld)
The Bendigo Independent
The Brisbane Courier
The Bundaberg Mail and Burnett Advertiser (Qld
The Burrowa News (NSW)
The Catholic Press

The Christian Witness
The Coburg Leader (Vic)
The Colac Herald (Vic)
The Colonist (Launceston)
The Cornwall Chronicle (Launceston)
The Courier (Hobart)
The Courier-Mail (Brisbane)
The Cumberland Argus and Fruitgrowers Advocate (Parramatta)
The Cumberland Free Press (Parramatta, NSW)
The Daily News (Perth, WA)
The Daily Telegraph (Sydney)
The Evening Echo (Ballarat)
The Evening Star (NZ)
The Evening Telegraph (Charters Towers, Qld.)
The Express and Telegraph (Adelaide)
The Gippsland Farmer
The Grafton Argus and Clarence River General Advertiser (NSW)
The Grenfell Record and Lachlan District Advertiser (NSW)
The Herald (Melbourne)
The Horsham Times
The Kadina and Wallaroo Times (SA)
The Kyneton Observer (Adelaide)
The Kyneton Observer (Vic)
The Laura Standard (SA)
The Mail (Adelaide)
The Maitland Mercury and Hunter River General Advertiser (NSW)
The Mercury (Hobart)
The Mount Barker Courier and Onkaparinga and Gumeracha Advertiser (SA)
The Narracoorte Herald (SA)
The Newcastle Sun (NSW)
The North Coast Standard (Latrobe, Tas)
The North Eastern Ensign (Benalla Vic)
The North Queensland Register (Townsville)
The North West Post (Formby, Tas)
The North Western Advocate and the Emu Bay Times (Tas)
The North Western Courier (Tas)
The Northern Miner (Charters Towers)
The Pioneer journal of the Christian Mission Church
The Port Augusta Dispatch, Newcastle and Flinders Chronicle

The Prahran Telegraph (Vic)
The Record and Emerald Hill and Sandridge Advertiser (Vic)
The Reformer (Perth, WA)
The Register (Adelaide)
The Reporter (Vic)
The Riverine Herald (Vic)
The South Australian Advertiser (Adelaide)
The Southern Argus and Wagin-Arthur Express (Perth, WA)
The St George Call (Kogarah, NSW )
The Sydney Mail and New South Wales Advertiser
The Sydney Morning Herald
The Tasmanian
The Tasmanian Democrat (Launceston)
The Telegraph (Brisbane)
The Telegraph, St Kilda, Prahran and South Yarra Guardian
The Times and Northern Advertiser, Peterborough, (SA)
The Victorian Freeman
The Wagin Argus and Arthur, Dumbleyung, Lake Grace Express (WA)
The Week (Brisbane)
The West Australian
The Daily Advertiser (Wagga Wagga, NSW)
The Tasmanian Historical Research Association Papers & Proceedings
Truth (NZ)
UK National Probate Calendar
Victorian Baptist Witness September 1939
Warracknabeal Herald (Vic)
Warrnambool Standard (Vic.)
Warwick Examiner and Times (Qld)
Watchman (Sydney)
Weekly Times (Melbourne)
Wellington Times (NSW)
Wellington Times and Agricultural and Mining Gazette (Tas)
Western Mail (WA)
Williamstown Chronicle (Vic)
World (Hobart)
Zeehan and Dundas Herald (Tas)

Lessons from our first 20 years
# Books, Pamphlets and Annual Reports

A Handful of Grain, The Centenary History of the BUNZ

A Short History of the Sheffield Baptist Church of 1918;

Alexander, A., A Turning Point in Women's History? The Foundation of the Woman's Christian Temperance Union in Australia, Tasmanian Historical Studies, Vol.7, No. 2 (2001).

Austin, Max: Centenary History Wynyard Baptist Church, To God be the Glory.

Australian Dictionary of Biography, (Melbourne University Press, Melbourne, 1966).

Bailey, Anne: Launceston Wesleyan Methodists 1832-1849: contributions, commerce, conscience, PhD thesis University of Tasmania, Hobart, 2008.

Baptist Union of Great Britain Handbook

Baptist Union of Tasmania Home Mission Minutes (in the Baptist Union of Tasmania holdings at the Tasmanian State Archives)

Barna, George, The Second Coming of the Church (Word Publishing 1998)

Bebbington, David, Spurgeon and British Evangelical Theological Education, Chapter 11 of Theological Education in the Evangelical Tradition, edited by D G Hart and R Albert Mohler, Jr (Grand Rapids, Michigan; Baker Books, 1996).

Bebbington, D W: Baptists and Fundamentalism.

Bligh William: Altars of the Mountains in which is told the story of the Baptist Church of Tasmania, Baptist Union of Tasmania, Launceston, 1935.

Bolton, Barbara: Booth's Drum: The Salvation Army in Australia 1880-1980 (Sydney, Hodder and Stoughton 1980)

Brown, Basil, Members One of Another; the Baptist Union of Victoria (Melbourne, Baptist Union of Victoria, 1962).

Cyclopedia of Tasmania (Hobart, Maitland and Krone, 1900).

Dallimore, A, Spurgeon (Chicago, Moody, 1984).

Dowling, Olive: A Church and Its People

Dugan, C C: A Century of Tasmanian Methodism. 1820-1920 (Hobart, Tasmanian Methodist Assembly, 1920),

Dyer, Alan F: God Was Their Rock: Set Against a Background of Local History" (Sheffield, 1975).

Dyer, Alan F: With the Pioneers

Dyer, Alan: Historic Gowrie Farm & First Gowrie School

Fullerton, WY: Thomas Spurgeon, a Biography (London, Hodder and Stoughton, 1919)

Garner, Mark and Sue: A Cause in their Neighbourhood, a history of the Newmarket Church.

Glover, Willis B: Evangelical Nonconformists and Higher Criticism in the Nineteenth Century (London, Independent Press, 1954).

Grubb, The Rev. George C: The Same Lord.

Hemsley, Jennifer: Around the Country Circuits.

Heyer, J: The Presbyterian pioneers of Van Diemen's Land (Launceston, Presbytery of Tasmania, 1935)

Hill, AC: Still Thy Church Extend (1963)

His Excellent Greatness – The Story of Sandown Baptist Church and its Ministers, 1882-1982.

Hoare, Laurie: Tasmanian Towns in Federation Times

Hovenden, Methodism in Launceston 1864-1890, BA Honours thesis, University of Tasmania, Hobart, 1968,

Hughes, H Escourt: Our First Hundred Years: The Baptist Church of South Australia, (Adelaide, Baptist Union of South Australia, 1937).

Hussey, Henry: Colonial Life and Christian Experience (Adelaide, Hussey & Gillingham, 1897)

Lockley, G Lindsay: Centenary of Congregationalism in Australia (Melbourne, Transactions of the Congregational Historical Society, 2001).

Long, Gwyneth: True to Life: A Story of the Rivett Family, typescript, 1992,

Manley, Ken R: From Woolloomooloo to 'Eternity': A History of Australian Baptists, 2 parts (Milton Keynes, Paternoster, 2006).

Manley, Prophecy and Passion: Essays in Honour of Athol Gill, edited by David Neville. Adelaide: Australian Theological Forum,

Manton, Jill: A History of the Kew Baptist Church 1856-1981

Moore, R. K: All Western Australia is My Parish

On This Corner, History of the Newstead Baptist Church.

Petras, Michael: Extension or Extinction, Baptist Growth in New South Wales 1900-1939 (Sydney, Baptist Historical Society of N SW, 1983)

Petras, Michael: The Second Exodus: Australian Baptist Ministers who joined the Presbyterian Church 1885 to 1970

Phillips, Walter, Defending 'a Christian Country': churchmen and society in New South Wales in the 1880 (Brisbane, University of Queensland Press 1981)

Pullen, Glenn Charlton: Jesse Pullen in Tasmania, 1822-1871, (Hobart, 1983), p12. Pullen file TSA.

Pullen, TL: From Little Acorns, being The Pullen Story in Tasmania, with occasional excursions into mainland Australia (1974).

Rawson, J: History of the Presbyterian Church of NZ 1840-1940

Evans, R: The Evangelisation Society of Australasia

Rowston, Laurence F: Baptists in Van Diemen's Land Part 1: The Story of Tasmania's First Baptist Church (Hobart, Baptist Union of Tasmania, (1985).

Rowston, Laurence F: Baptists in Van Diemen's Land Part 2: The Story of Launceston Particular Baptist Chapel, York Street (Baptist Union of Tasmania, (2021).

Rowston, Laurence F: Spurgeon's Men MA thesis.

Rowston, Laurence F: God's Training Ground, the History of the Yolla Baptist Church.

Rowston, Laurence F: One Hundred Years of Witness: A History of the Hobart Baptist Church, 1884–1984 (Hobart Baptist Church 1984);

Skinner, Craig: Lamplighter and Son (Nashville, Broadman Press, 1984)

Smith and Pegus, Bessie and Margaret: Yolla – The First Century

Stansall, M, Tasmanian Methodism 1820–1975 (Launceston, Methodist Church of Australasia, 1975).

Thompson, Arthur: Living Stones, A History of Vernon Baptist Church, King's Cross,

von Stieglitz, K R: A Short History of Sheffield: The Kentish Municipality and its Pioneers,

Vedder, HCA Short History of the Baptists (Philadelphia, The American Baptist Publication Society, 1892).

Walker, J: The Baptists in South Australia, cira 1900 to 1939, PhD thesis, Flinders University, South Australia, 2006.

Watkin-Smith, H: Baptists in the Cradle City. The Story of Parramatta Baptist Church 1838-1986 (Eastwood, Baptist Historical Society of NSW, 1986).

Wenger, Edward Steane: The Story of the Lall Bazar Baptist Church, Calcutta Being the History of Carey's Church from 24th April 1800 to the Present Day

White, CA: The Challenge of the Years, a History of the Presbyterian Church of Australia in the State of NSW.

White-Ribboners, Jordan, R: the Woman's Christian Temperance Union of Tasmania, 1885-1914, Unpublished BA Hons thesis, University of Tasmania, 2001

Wilkin, FJ, Baptists in Victoria: Our First Century, 1838–1938 (Melbourne, Baptist Union of Victoria, 1939).

Wilkin, FJ, A Romance of Home Missions – An Account of the Early Days of the Baptist Home Mission Work in Victoria (Melbourne, Baptist Home Mission and Church Extension Committee, 1927).

Witnessing for Christ throughout a Century 1855-1955 City Tabernacle Baptist Church.

York Street Baptist Chapel Minutes (in the Baptist Union of Tasmania holdings at the Tasmanian State Archives)

# ABBREVIATIONS:

AB - Australian Baptist (1913-1986).

BUT - Baptist Union of Tasmania Home Mission Minutes (in the Baptist holdings of the archives of the State Library of Tasmania).

Manley - Manley, Ken R, From Woolloomooloo to 'Eternity': A History of Australian Baptists, 2 parts (Milton Keynes, Paternoster, 2006).

Baptists in VDL Part 1 - Laurence F Rowston, Baptists in Van Diemen's Land: The Story of Tasmania's First Baptist Church (Hobart, Baptist Union of Tasmania, 1985).

Baptists in VDL Part 2 - Laurence F Rowston, Baptists in Van Diemen's Land: The Story of Launceston Particular Baptist Chapel, York Street, (Baptist Union of Tasmania, 1985).

BCC - Baptist Church Chronicle

Bligh - Wesley J Bligh, Altars of the Mountains in which is told the story of the Baptist Church of Tasmania, Baptist Union of Tasmania, Launceston, 1935.

HM – Home Mission

Hughes - Hughes, H Escourt, Our First Hundred Years: The Baptist Church of South Australia (Adelaide, Baptist Union of South Australia, 1937).

LEx - Launceston Examiner (1842-1899) and as Examiner (1900 on).

NW Post - The North West Post (Formby, Tas)

NWA&EBT - The North Western Advocate and the Emu Bay Times to Advocate (1899-continuing)

Our Yesterdays - Our Yesterdays (Camberwell, Victorian Baptist Historical Society, 1993 continuing).

Rowston, Baptists in Van Diemen's Land Part 1 - Rowston, Laurence F, Baptists in Van Diemen's Land, The Story of Tasmania's First Baptist Church (Hobart, Baptist Union of Tasmania, 1985).

# Lessons from our first 20 years

SB - Southern Baptist (1895-1912) (1895-1910 in the Baptist holdings of the archives of the State Library of Tasmania; 1895-1912 and in the Victorian Baptist Union archives).

Stansall - Stansall, M, Tasmanian Methodism 1820–1975 (Launceston, Methodist Church of Australasia, 1975).

Spurgeon's Men - MA thesis Rowston, Laurence F, Spurgeon's Men: The Resurgence of Baptist Belief and Practice in Tasmania 1869-1884, MA thesis.

Wilkin - Wilkin, F J, Baptists in Victoria: Our First Century, 1838–1938 (Melbourne, Baptist Union of Victoria, 1939).

# INDEX

a'Beckett, Ada M.Sc. 105
Abbotsham School 56
Aberdeen Street Baptist Church 133, 193,196
Aborigines in Western Australia 233
Adelaide West End Mission 328
Advent Testimony and Preparation Movement 186
Albury, Alfred Ernest 442, 454
Annual Boxing Day Regatta 28
Archer, Herbert Davies 125, 141, 154
Archer, William 141
Arnold, Miss Allen 268
Auckland Tabernacle 117, 128, 133, 163, 234
Australian China Inland Mission 185
Bacchus Marsh Baptist Church 195
Badger, David 43
Baeyertz, Emilia Louise 29, 74, 80, 171, 185, 194
Ballarat Baptist Tabernacle, Dawson Street 16, 28, 99, 184, 277
Ballarat East Baptist Church 344
Bampton, Edward Robert 439, 457
Band of Hope 60, 79, 150
Baptist Association, formation of174
Baptist churches statistics in 1930
Baptist contributions to Tasmania
Baptist Home Mission (Tasmania) 64, 65, 71, 236, 352, 364, 373f, 405, 408
Baptist Home Mission stations (Tasmania) in 1904 311
Baptist Mutual Improvement Society 16, 39, 175, 201, 215, 231, 251, 276, 327
Baptist Principles 277
Baptist Union Council of 1889 177
Baptist Union of Tasmania Sustentation Fund 71, 126, 157
Baptists in Tasmania, progress of 309
Benjafield, Dr. Harry 174, 205, 225
Bennett, John, Congregationalist 239
Bethel Sunday school at Fishermen's Bend 338
Bird, Alfred 172, 182
Black Forest Baptist Church 165, 304, 347
Black, Joseph 17
Blackie, Henry George 152, 163, 241, 254, 263

Blackwell, Albert Edward 267, 271, 273
Blaikie, James 109, 185, 221, 232
Bligh, Wesley J. 374, 413, 428
Bligh, William and Margaret 428
Bloomsbury Baptist Church, London 183, 199
Blue Ribbon Gospel Temperance Missions 20, 79, 125, 138, 150, 171, 188, 206, 243
Blue Ribbon Hall, Footscray 259
Boat Harbour 387
Booth, Richard T. and T. W. Glover 124, 173, 206
Boreham, Frank W. 228, 318, 352, 367, 405
Box Hill Baptist Church 196
Bracknell Annual Flower and Produce Show 67
Bracknell Good Templars' Hall
Bracknell Primitive Methodist Church 48
Bray, Billy 156, 181, 268
Brighton Baptist Church, Melbourne 43, 279
Brighton Baptist Church, SA 304
Brisbane City Tabernacle 369
Britton, Vincent George 52, 59, 64, 131, 159, 181, 202, 253, 269, 361, 373, 383, 394
Brown, Edwin Charles McIntosh 414, 431
Brunswick Baptist Church 96
Buck's billiard room and saloon, Devonport 291
Burnett, Matthew 207
Burnett, Thomas 151
Burnie in 1899 311
Burton Street Tabernacle, Woolloomooloo, NSW 189f
Burwood Baptist Mission NSW 190, 259
Bury St. Edmunds Church, UK 231
Butler, Albert 361, 368, 384, 392, 406
Cairns, Peter William 317, 334
Carey, Samuel Pearce 299
Casley, A. John 156, 167, 267, 278
Castlemaine Baptist Church 224, 235
Cater, Charles 16, 26
Chamberlain, John 113, 243, 253, 255, 263
Chapman and Alexander Mission 203, 332
Cherbury, Charles Mortimer 15, 87, 100

473

Christian Endeavour Societies 23, 87, 89, 180, 186, 223, 296, 374, 379, 412
Christian Endeavour Union London 296
Christian Mission Church Launceston 52
Christian Mission Church Sunday School, Ravenswood 77, 173
Church in a day, building a 305, 437
Church services as "big feature" programmes 400
Churchward-Kelly, Stella Mary 420
Churchward-Kelly, Thomas 420
Citizens' Six O'clock Closing League, Local Option movement 282, 343, 388, 398
Clark Henry 39
Clark Street Mission, Port Melbourne 377
Clark, William 3, 27
Clarke, Alfred James 139, 176, 187
Clarke, Charles, of Albert Street Baptist Church 17
Clarke, Rev. George 174
Clarke, Sterling George 360, 372, 386
Cluan Baptist Church 67
Collingwood Tabernacle 87, 101
Compton, William 21
Concord Baptist Church, NSW 369
Constitution Hill Chapel 59, 109, 222, 256
Conversion, what it means 276
Cooper, James Rider 20, 36
Cowle, Daniel George
Cowle's Hall 291, 294
Crabtree, Thomas 15
Craike, George 73, 90, 108, 316, 319
Creekton, a Gibson Estate 392, 396
Crofts, Wilf 420
Crymelon Baptist Church, Victoria 55
Cumming, Morison 219, 227, 230
Dale, Robert W. 217
Davis, Dorothy M. 443
Dawson, Alan Paton 391, 399, 410, 412, 426
Day Star publication 216
Daylesford Baptist church 56, 199
Deloraine Baptist chapel West Barrack St 116
Deloraine outstation at Quamby Brook 126
Derby flood of 1929 427
Derby, Lord Secretary of State for the Colonies 234
Devonport (Formby and Torquay) described
Devonport Church formation

Devonport Early Churches in
Devonport Tabernacle opening 299
Dibden, George Levison 440, 456
Dippers, the nick-name 160
Disputes within churches 204
Dobbinson, Richard W. 377
Dowie, John Alexander 102
Dowling, Henry T. of Burnie 117, 319, 349
Dowling, Rev. Henry 27, 69, 117
Driver, Harry H. 20
Duncan House 422
Duncan, Andrew 175
Dunkley, Frederick J. 71, 361, 372, 386, 405
Duthoit, Everard 119, 182, 250
Eddy, Walter J.
Eddy, Walter J. 181, 198, 312
Elliott, Howard Leslie 144, 128
Ellis, George W 411, 417
Elphin Road Baptist Church 311, 455
English Social Purity Alliance 80
Evandale "Evangelistic Hall"75
Evandale Baptist Church 20
Evangelisation Society of Victoria 55, 333
Evangelistic preaching questioned 218
Exhibition Building, Hobart 205
Fairfield Baptist Church 305
Farmilo, J. T. 247
Fenwick Street Baptist Church, Geelong 198, 203, 326
Fisher, John F 355, 363, 377, 383, 392, 403
Flinders Street Baptist Church, SA 103, 303, 346
Forest Baptist Church, a church in a day at 437
Formation of the Tasmanian Baptist Union 163
Free Education in Tasmania 129
Fundamentalism 169
Gawler Baptist Church, SA 43, 328
George Street Baptist Church, Fitzroy 101, 142, 194, 305
George, Muller 30
German Baptists 211
Gibson, Elvina Beaumont 22, 151, 265
Gibson, Mary Ann 14, 21, 48, 116, 149, 161, 251, 314
Gibson, William Junior 49, 55, 117, 174, 177, 181, 211, 245, 250, 264, 292, 409

Gibson, William Senior 14, 18, 21, 48f, 117, 126, 137, 139, 149, 174, 205, 211, 225, 292
Gillings, George William 17, 30, 117
Glennie, Henry, aka "Silverpen" 19, 75, 78, 118, 122, 123,
Goble, Joseph H. 339
Goulburn Mission, NSW 260
Grand Orange Lodge 260, 318, 441
Grand Orange Lodge, NZ 41, 145
Grand Orange Lodge, SA 191
Grant, Alfred 15, 59, 73, 84, 148
Guinness, Dr. Henry Grattan 73, 80, 160, 173, 188
Hainsworth, Thomas 56, 239
Hamilton Baptist Church, Vic. 302
Hampson, Margaret 29, 171, 207
Hargreaves Street Church, Bendigo 30, 95, 192, 275
Harris Street Baptist Church, Sydney 332
Harris, Edward Chapman 196
Harris, Edward E 111, 178, 193
Harris, Samuel Archer 128, 142
Harrison, George Edgar 354, 356, 365
Harrison, James Samuel 117, 133, 138, 160, 188
Harrison, John Pearson 110, 332
Harrison, Samuel 298, 315, 328, 355
Heaven, William Llewllyn 271, 286, 352, 359, 367, 386
Henrietta Plains Baptist hall
Henrietta Plains Baptist hall 412
Henry, Reed 73
Hiddlestone, Dan Walter 75, 97, 365
Hiddlestone, William Robson 79, 97
Higher Criticism 42, 120, 146, 169, 174, 222, 250
Hindmarsh Baptist Church, Adelaide 67, 95, 191, 308, 347
Hobart Baptist Church's "shedificc" 209
Holloway, Albert Edward 410, 423, 438
Home Missioner defined 352, 363
Homes of Hope for Destitute Children Melbourne 102
Hope-Morgan, J. R. 389
Howard, Stephen 42
Humby, A G. 206, 209
Hussey, Henry 15, 303
Hyde, Albert 124, 141, 151, 242, 302
Icely, Canon A. W. of Sheffield 265
Ironside, Samuel 148
James, Alfred Harrald 409

Jamestown, SA 43
Jarvis, Arthur Charles 388, 396
Jarvis, Wifred L 396
Jarvis, Wilfred Lemuel 322, 389
Jeffs, Horace H. 305, 419
Jessop, Arthur T 413, 427
Jobling, Cecil M. 414, 434, 443, 459
Johnston, W. Corrie 98
Joyce, Edward Albert 348
Kalgoorlie Baptist Church, WA 456
Kenner, William 51, 56, 358, 361
Kentish Christian Brethren 263
Kew Baptist Church, Melbourne 44, 233
Koroit Baptist Church, Vic. 155, 164
Lake, George 50, 55, 64, 152
Lall Bazar Baptist Church, Calcutta 255
Lamb, Susan 61, 67
Lambert, Henry James 88, 103
Language School for Missionaries Darjeeling 420
Latrobe Tabernacle 245
Latrobe, Early Churches in 239
Latrobe, township in 1896 238
Launceston and districts flood of 1929 455
Launceston earth-quake of 1892 84
Launceston Tabernacle Inveresk Mission 60
Launceston Tabernacle Percy Street Mission 181, 377
Launceston, City of 170
Laura Baptist Church Circuit, SA 327
Leavitt, Mary Greenleaf Clement 173
Leeder, Frederick Augustus 321, 341
Levett, Fred 444
Linden, Oswald Rupert 319, 338
Liquid church 460
London Evangelistic Society 141
Longford Assembly Rooms 148
Longford Primitive Methodist Church 148
Longford Tabernacle 149
Longford Temperance Demonstration 151
Longford Wesleyan Methodist 148
Lumsden, Norman 444
Macallister, John 153, 165
Mackay, George James 294, 297, 304
Mackey, E. D. 414
MacNeil, John 280
Magic Lantern lectures 23, 52, 65
Manton,-Smith J. 187
Marshall, Robert 60, 96, 174, 182
Mateer and Parker 82
McAllister, John Ferguson 165

McCullough, Robert 49, 117, 133, 148, 159, 174, 177, 205, 227, 320, 341
Methodists at Camp Creek, Yolla 403
Metters, Albert 25, 45, 249, 300, 307,
Meyer, Dr. Frederick B. 109, 186
Ministerial training 62
Mission for Lepers (Leprosy Mission) 203, 277
Mitcham-Coromandel Valley Baptist Church SA 230
Moody and Sankey 80, 95
Moonah Baptist Church 281, 312, 368, 453
Mount Bischoff Mine 106
Mountain Vale Primitive Methodist Church 53
Moysey, George Bickford 241
Muller, George 133
Newstead Baptist Church 447
Nibbs, Percy Gordon 444, 457
Noakes, Elizabeth 17, 148
Northcote Baptist Church, Melbourne 305
Northern Victorian Baptist Home Mission 259
Norwood Baptist Church, Adelaide103
Osmiridium Fields, Adams River 432
Oxford Movement in the Church of England 270
Palmer, Charles 252, 258, 319
Pappin, Miss Alice 215
Parkside Baptist Church, Adelaide 182, 200, 229
Pastors' College, Friday afternoons at the 142
Paterson Street Methodist Church, Launceston 73
Pearse, Mark Guy 215
Penguin Baptist Church 317, 354, 356
Penquite egg-laying Competitions 373, 443
Petersham Baptist Church, NSW 112
Philp, George 440
Photographic Club 65
Pickering, Charles 121, 140, 266, 307
Piercey, Joseph Tanner 89, 106, 315f, 333, 350, 356, 381, 403, 415
Pilgrim's Rest for Aged Destitute Gentlewomen, Melbourne 103
Pitt, Samuel B. 110, 206, 213, 249
Plymouth Brethren 255
Port Melbourne Baptist Church 280
Portland Baptist Church, Vic. 142, 194

Preece, Hilton J. 413, 442
Primitive Methodist Church, Hobart 108
Princes Square Congregational Church, Launceston 171
Prophetical Conferences 32
Protestant Defense Association 41, 110, 318
Pullen, Jesse 15, 116
Quincy 123
Ratcliff, Harry 67
Reed, Margaret 75, 79, 82, 90
Religious liberty, infringement of 57
Revivals 389, 401
Roberts, Joseph 418
Robertson, John 356
Roman Catholic Passionist Fathers 83
Ross, William 48
Ross, William 48, 54, 63, 127
Salisbury, Ernest Albert 253, 357, 365, 373, 385, 394, 404
Salter, James Clemens 374, 441
Salter, William (Bill) J 450
Salvation Army 171
Salvation Army 239
Sandringham Baptist Church, Melbourne 306
Sandy Bay Baptist Church 348, 424
Sargent, George Newton 388
Sassafras Baptist Church 245, 253
Saunders, Henry Ebenezer 271, 280, 398
Second Coming or Prophetic Conferences
Second Coming or Prophetic Conferences 32, 185, 350
Seventh Day Adventists 140, 153, 442
Shallberg, Johann Heinrich 74, 94
Sheffield Baptist Church outstations
Sheffield Baptist Church, outstations of 264, 268f
Sheffield Baptist Church, Pentecostal revival of 283
Sheffield, district of 262
Sheffield, early churches in 263
Sherwin, Amy, the "Tasmanian Nightingale" 216
Shorey, Samuel 120
Short, William Henry Alexander 130, 247, 381, 391
Short, William Howes Wackenbarth 257
Simpson, Salter Stanley 408, 422,
Skelbrook Baptist Chapel 245
Slade, George 259
Small churches, the genius of 435

Smith, Daniel and Isabella 403
Smithton, early churches in 436
Soltau, George 80, 98
Soltau, Grace 87
Somerville, Dr. Alexander Neill 29
Soundy, Joshua T. 66, 205, 213, 225, 249, 299, 324, 363, 409
South Melbourne Baptist Church 399
South Spreyton Baptist Church 253
South Yarra Baptist Church, Melbourne 34
Spreyton Baptist Church 253
Spurgeon, C.H. 142
Spurgeon, C.H., and Second Coming preaching 350
Spurgeon, C.H., secession of 217
Spurgeon, Thomas 18, 20, 37, 48, 117, 137, 154, 160, 172, 174, 187
St David's Church, Moorabbin, Melbourne 417
St Kilda, Crimea Street Baptist Church 29, 34
Stabb Brothers builders 212
Steel, Robert 66, 384, 437, 444
Stokes, W. L. 174
Sudan United Mission 204
Summer School of Theology 323
Sunday observance 260, 286, 378, 452
Sunday school prizes 153
Tasmanian Baptist Home Mission 72, 311, 364, 374, 405, 436
Tasmanian Baptist Home Mission Committee 65, 406
Tasmanian Baptist Home Mission work during the WW1 364, 409
Tasmanian Baptist statistics 72, 374, 405
Tasmanian Particular Baptists 146
Tasmanian Women's Christian Temperance Union 87, 173
Tattersall's Sweeps 202, 223, 266, 301
Teasdale and Co.'s coal mine, church services at
Temperance Movement 77, 125, 171, 189
Tinning, D.B. 15
Toc H movement 417, 433
Torrey, Dr. A. Reuben 90, 181, 285
Torrey-Alexander Simultaneous Missions 90, 181, 195
Trafalgar Day demonstrations 25
Trot, Tommy 83
Tunks, Henry Roy 410, 415
Ulverston Baptist Church 452
Ulverstone, early churches in 353

Upper Castra mission 358, 364
Upper Liffey Baptist Chapel 53
Urquhart, John 307
Varley, Henry 18, 22, 117, 171, 215
Vaughan, Edward 121, 139, 266
Victoria Hall, Perth, Tasmania 22
Victorian Baptist Home Mission 55, 140, 164, 194, 259, 280, 306, 450
Victorian Evangelistic Society 55, 188, 415
Victorian Home Mission work, Footscray 188
Victorian Protestant Defence Association 41
Vigis, Thomas 224, 229, 314, 325
Wainwright, George 180, 196, 324
Walker, Robert 66
Walsh, Ernest Charles 271, 386, 396, 407, 442, 448
Walton, John Edwin
Walton, John Edwin 21, 38, 61, 177, 251, 257, 295, 312
Warren, Henry James 269, 279, 359, 366
Warrnambool Baptist Church, Vic. 332
Watkins, William Edward 152
Watson, Ernest Eric 411, 418
West Melbourne Baptist Church 187, 195
West, Theodore and Charlotte 69
Weston, William Dubrelle 176, 178, 182, 352, 356, 381
White, William 170, 172
Wilkin, Frederick W. 194, 259
Williams, John D. 384f
Williamson, Robert
Williamson, Robert 18, 33, 75, 174, 249, 269, 279, 381
Wilson, S. 15
Women's Christian Temperance Union 173
Wood, Harry 20, 48, 63, 75, 120, 127, 135, 140, 150, 156, 158, 161, 174, 177, 246, 264, 312
Woods, Edward Burchell 322, 284, 345, 432
World War I, welcoming home 272
Wright, J. G. 252
Wright's Picture Company 271
WW1, Fromelles 422
WWI, effect on Australians 409, 423
Wynyard, early churches in 380
York Street Particular Baptist Chapel 14, 69, 117, 123, 170